THE JUDICIAL PROCESS

AN INTRODUCTORY ANALYSIS
OF THE COURTS
OF THE UNITED STATES,
ENGLAND, AND FRANCE

THE

JUDICIAL

PROCESS

SECOND EDITION
REVISED AND ENLARGED

HENRY J. ABRAHAM
University of Pennsylvania

NEW YORK
OXFORD UNIVERSITY PRESS
LONDON   TORONTO
1968

To Philip

PREFACE TO THE SECOND EDITION

The success of the first edition prompted the undertaking of this second revised and enlarged version. Its scope and approach are the same as that of the original work. Changes, however, will be found on almost every page; approximately one-third of the material is entirely new; and the book has been completely up-dated through January 1968. The procedural innovations are: three separate indexes, an informational chart of all Supreme Court justices appointed to date, and the categorized classification of bibliographies I and IV. The set of bibliographies, which has been expanded to include more than 3000 listings, represents the most extensive compilation of its kind extant as an appendix to any book.

I owe an enormous debt of gratitude to a host of colleagues whose thoughtful criticism and support of the earlier edition encouraged me to undertake the second. I should like to add a special expression of appreciation for my research assistant, Judy F. Lang, who helped so much.

Wynnewood, Pennsylvania   H. J. A.
February 1968

PREFACE TO THE FIRST EDITION

When my *Courts and Judges: An Introduction to the Judicial Process* appeared in 1959, I began its Preface by pointing to the general absence of even the most rudimentary knowledge of the judicial process on the part of the vast majority of students of Political Science entering elementary or even advanced courses, and observed that equally striking was the unavailability of accessible materials providing basic data in the field. The measure of success my small book has enjoyed encouraged the writing of the present volume, which is far more ambitious in scope than its predecessor.

This new book is a selective comparative introduction to the judicial process, and seeks to analyze and evaluate the main institutions and considerations affecting the administration of justice under law. The rather extensive coverage of certain significant features and elements of comparative judicial processes was prompted not only by several helpful suggestions by users of the earlier book, but by the continued neglect of these processes in basic textbooks.

An important segment of this work is thus devoted to the judicial process in England and Wales, and France, and—to a necessarily considerably lesser extent in this context—the Soviet Union. Other states are included whenever appropriate, especially in connection with the doctrine and practice of judicial review. Nonetheless, at least half of the material deals with the judicial process in the United States.

The detailed Table of Contents obviates capsule explanations of the substance of each chapter in this volume. I have compiled numerous graphs, figures, and charts, all designed to facilitate comprehension. There are two indexes, one general, one for cases. And there are four extensive bibliographies dealing with (1) works in general on American Constitutional Law; (2) biographies and autobiographies of and by justices of the United States Supreme Court; (3) Comparative Constitutional Law; and (4) Civil Liberties.

Although I have endeavored to be objective in analysis and presentation throughout, in some circumstances it is neither possible nor desirable to shun value judgments; I have thus stated frankly my own opinions where it seemed appropriate to do so.

Once again I express my profound appreciation to the many colleagues who stimulated and urged me on in the writing of this book and whose generous suggestions were so helpful. I am especially grateful to Professors William M. Beaney, David Fellman, Wallace Mendelson, Jewell Cass Phillips, and R. J. Tresolini. Above all, I owe a particular debt of gratitude to Mr. James Wellwood, M.A., of Gray's Inn, Barrister-at-Law, Lecturer in Law at King's College, University of London, for his unselfish counsel and essential criticism on the sections on England and Wales. As they have been throughout my pleasant association with the Oxford University Press, Mr. Byron S. Hollinshead, Jr., and Miss Leona Capeless have been delightful and invaluable co-workers. Mrs. Helen White performed the thankless but so essential task of typing the entire manuscript cheerfully and efficiently. Whatever errors remain are mine. My wife, Mildred, gave me the kind of constant encouragement and confidence that only a devoted partner can provide.

And the book is happily dedicated to one who also helped in his own way.

Wynnewood, Pennsylvania   H. J. A.
February 1962

CONTENTS

THE JUDICIAL PROCESS

I

INTRODUCTION:
THE LAW AND COURTS

Respect for the law is one of the select group of principles which we have come to regard as essential to the effective and equitable operation of popular government. As a democratic principle it is recognized as binding on both the governed and those who govern.

In fostering this principle the role of the judiciary is crucial, for, in the words of Mr. Justice Arthur T. Vanderbilt:

> . . . it is in the courts and not in the legislature that our citizens primarily feel the keen, cutting edge of the law. If they have respect for the work of the courts, their respect for law will survive the shortcomings of every other branch of government; but if they lose their respect for the work of the courts, their respect for law and order will vanish with it to the great detriment of society.[1]

This is true, whether the judicial branch be technically separated from the other two branches of government, as in the United States; partly fused with them, as in France; or largely fused, as in the United Kingdom of Great Britain and Northern Ireland. The law will be respected as long as it is interpreted and applied within the structures of justice as accepted by the majority of society—in the long run, if not always in the short run. It is, after all, the expressed will of those who rule society.

But the law, in its procedural as well as its substantive aspects, is essentially made and administered by men whose views and interpretations are buffeted by the winds of change through the years, so that it has become a "truism that the quality of justice

[1] *The Challenge of Law Reform* (Princeton: Princeton University Press, 1955), pp. 4–5.

4

depends more on the quality of the men who administer the law than on the content of the law they administer."[2] Judicial activity, observed Roscoe Pound in one of his lectures, is really the creative element in law. Accordingly, if man's great interest on earth is justice, as Daniel Webster put it, then perhaps a more immediate interest is the securing of the most highly qualified individuals to administer justice impartially with a minimum of chicanery and obfuscation. It follows logically that judges must be assured of an optimum degree of independence and relative freedom from pre-judicial pressures from forces both inside and outside of government. Moreover, they must be able to function in a hierarchical structure that is effectively conducive to the performance of the basic task at hand—the impartial administration of justice under law.

They pursue this task through the medium of a court, an institution. As Carl Brent Swisher noted concisely, along with such other characteristics as it may incidentally possess, a court,

> . . . determines the facts involved in particular controversies brought before it, relates the facts to the relevant law, settles the controversies in terms of the law, and more or less incidentally makes new law through the process of decision. Over the centuries of Anglo-American history our judiciary has been developed and geared to this process so that it has an integrity or integratedness peculiar to its own. In particular it has a mode of informing the minds of the responsible officers—in this instance the judges— which is unique and which must be kept in sharp focus in any attempt to estimate the capacity of a judiciary to perform competitively in the gray areas which lie between it and institutions which are primarily legislative or executive.[3]

THE NATURE OF LAW

For at least twenty-five centuries, and perhaps longer, men have discussed the nature of law. In one way or another, it touches every citizen of every nation. The contact may be pleasant or un-

[2] Evan Haynes, *The Selection and Tenure of Judges* (National Conference of Judicial Councils, 1944), p. 5, as quoted in Jewell Cass Phillips, *State and Local Government in America* (New York: American Book Co., 1954), p. 237.
[3] Presidential Address, delivered before the American Political Science Association, New York City, September 8, 1960. (Reprinted in 54 *American Political Science Review* 879–80, December 1960.)

pleasant, tangible or intangible, direct or indirect, but it is none-theless a constant force in the lives of people everywhere on the globe. It is essential that we have some understanding of its nature and of the human beings who interpret and administer it.

"What is Law?" has been asked by priests and poets, philosophers and kings, by masses no less than by prophets. A host of answers might be given, yet the answer to the question remains one of the most persistent and elusive problems in the whole range of thought. For one may well view the entire gamut of human life, both in thought and in action, as being comprised within the concept Law.[4]

It may seem strange that the true essence of such a ubiquitous phenomenon as law should be beyond the grasp of general human understanding. Since law deals with human conduct, in order to grasp its nature it would appear necessary merely to distinguish it from the other factors relating to that conduct: religion, science, morals, ethics, custom. Yet herein lies the difficulty, so ably stated by James Coolidge Carter more than half a century ago:

> Law, Custom, Conduct, Life—different names for almost the same thing—true names for different aspects of the same thing —are so inseparably blended together that one cannot even be thought of without the other. No improvement can be effected in one without improving the other, and no retrogression can take place in one without a corresponding decline in the other.[5]

There is but little doubt that law has much in common with all these other aspects of human conduct, yet it is true that it also possesses at least one unique characteristic lacking in all others: its sanction is applied exclusively by organized political government.

Three Historical Categories. Some kind of law has always existed[6]—however inadequate, or even entirely absent, both legal organization and enforcement machinery may have been. First came *primitive* law, based chiefly on primitive custom and lacking

4 William A. Robson, *Civilization and the Growth of Law* (New York: The Macmillan Co., 1935), p. 3.
5 *Law: Its Origin, Growth and Function* (New York and London: The Knicker-bocker Press, 1907), p. 320.
6 The earliest known system of written law was the Code of Hammurabi, so named in honor of its founder, a King of Babylonia. It was promulgated about 2050 B.C.—there is considerable disagreement among scholars on the precise decade or even century—and was the embodiment of the existing rules and customs of the land. It presented the idea that justice was man's inherent right, derived from supernatural forces rather than by royally bestowed favor.

even rudimentary machinery and organization. Prevailing among some of the early Indian, Oceanic, and Asiatic tribes, it was and is the law of those "preliterate" peoples who, although un- or under-developed, have nevertheless recognized social rules, and have discovered means of coping with social conflict.

Archaic law, featuring some manner of courts and officialdom—institutions that are basic to every legal system—and introducing certain codes of procedure and substance, arrived on the scene during the days of Rome and feudalism and among primitive Germanic and African tribes. However, Moses' *Pentateuch*, given in the fifteenth century B.C., may well lay an earlier claim. Certainly the *Great Sanhedrin*, the seventy-one-man supreme council of the Jewish nation in Greco-Roman days, headed by a chief justice, was a judicial body which enacted decrees of religious observance *and* interpreted the law of the Hebrews prior to the destruction of the Temple in Jerusalem by Roman forces in A.D. 70.

Mature law heralded the professionalization of the law. It fathered the law we know today. As Roman law it existed from the third century B.C. to the fall of Rome. As English law it appeared in the twelfth century.

POSITIVE AND NATURAL LAW

The three kinds of law cited above are prongs of *positive law*, the type of law with which we will be concerned throughout this book. It is held to derive from man for the purpose of ruling man; it is a command based upon the relationship between ruler and ruled; its primary nature is that it is *man-made*. It springs from no source higher than the human will. This is what John Chipman Gray alluded to when he defined a man's legal rights as

> . . . power which he has to make a person or persons do or refrain from doing a certain act or . . . acts, as far as the power arises from society.[7]

In other words, according to the tenets of positive law—as defined by John Austin, the English utilitarian jurist (1790–1859) who,

[7] *The Nature and Sources of Law* (New York: Columbia University Press, 1916), p. 19.

inspired by the French social theorist Auguste Comte, became the founder of the analytical school of jurisprudence—law consists of definite rules of human conduct with appropriate sanctions for their enforcement, both of these being prescribed by duly constituted human authority.

Natural Law. But in the eyes of many there is another category of law, *natural law*, known also as "higher law" or "the law of nature." It is law which would be binding upon human societies in the absence of, or as a supplement to, positive law. Witness, for example, its impact upon the American Declaration of Independence and the Constitution;[8] its citation by conscientious objectors to military conscription; and its invocation by the civil rights movements of the 1950's and 1960's, for example, by the Reverend Dr. Martin Luther King's exhortations to disobey "unjust" laws. The theory of natural law originated with the Stoics by whom it was regarded as embodying those rules of justice discernible by right reason. This view was sometimes taken by Roman jurists such as the statesman and theorist Cicero (106–43 B.C.), who, in defining law, was explicit in indicating his concept of its essence as follows:

> Law is the highest reason, implanted in Nature, which commands what ought to be done and forbids the opposite . . . the origin of justice is to be found in law, for law is its natural force; it is the mind and reason of the intelligent man, the standards by which justice and injustice are measured.
>
> I shall seek the root of justice in nature. . . .[9]

Justinian (483–565) adopted Ulpian's (170–228) definition of natural law as that law which "nature has taught all living beings," thus forecasting the modern bionomic view. The Scholastics generally regarded natural law as that part of the divine law which is not directly revealed but its discernible to reason; and the Rationalists of the eighteenth century derived from their analysis of human

8 Its classic exposition in that connection is Edward S. Corwin's superb *The Higher Law Background of American Constitutional Law* (Ithaca: Cornell University Press, 1929), known to every student of constitutional law and the judicial process.
9 Cicero, "The Laws," in Francis William Coker, *Readings in Political Philosophy*, rev. ed. (New York: The Macmillan Co., 1955), pp. 145–6.

societies certain *natural rights* as to life, liberty, and the pursuit of happiness—which they regarded as of prior validity to institutional law.[10] Thus it is the thread of rationality that holds the system together and gives a definite order to it:

> . . . the universe obeys God; seas and lands obey the universe, and human life is subject to the decree of supreme law.[11]

It would seem that natural law thus stands on two assumptions: first, the rationality and intelligence of man; second, the existence of a higher *rational* order of things. Since man is presumed to be intelligent, he can hence readily "find" the law, that is, understand the higher rational order.

Without endeavoring to prove or disprove this theory and estimate of man, man's history at least places the issue in doubt. At best, it appears that man is equally capable of capricious action based upon passion as of rational action based upon intelligence. If man's intelligence is placed in doubt, so is his ability to understand a higher rational order. Indeed, it is difficult for man to believe in a higher order or a universal law of justice because of what he sees in real life—as pointed out by Carneades so many years ago. Holmes, who rejected natural law with vehemence and sarcasm—for which was scathingly attacked in word and in print by prominent Jesuit law professors—regarded it as "mystic over-law" and the "product of wishful thinking."[12]

Nonetheless, today natural law is identifiable with the abiding sense of justice that pervades the community of man—regardless of its changing substance—a sense of justice based upon a body of rules and customs which the general development of mankind shows to be essential to human society. But it is the positive law that governs us as law-abiding members of the body politic of organized society. And, as we shall presently see, although natural law, like equity, has had marked influence on English common law, "it is not the same as common law and has never absorbed it."[13]

10 Webster's *New International Dictionary of the English Language*, 2d ed. Unabridged (Springfield, Mass.: G. & C. Merriam Co., 1958).
11 Cicero, op. cit. p. 151.
12 See Francis Biddle, *Justice Holmes, Natural Law, and the Supreme Court* (New York: The Macmillan Co., 1961), especially Ch. II, "The Attack on Justice Holmes."
13 Ibid. p. 31.

COMMON LAW AND STATUTORY LAW

For our purposes, then, law—broadly speaking—represents the rules of conduct that pertain to a given political order of society, rules that are backed by the organized force of the community. As it has evolved through the centuries, law has been made either by the political representatives of the people—sometimes rather inaccurately styled "bar-made" law—or it has been "bench-made" by judges and justices. The former type is generally known as *statutory law*, the latter as *common law*. Both will bear close examination, but, at the risk of some oversimplification, the crucial distinction between the two is that between codified written law and unwritten law based on custom and tradition. (The terms "bar-made" and "bench-made" are never used in England, where the two types are "statutory" and "judge-made.")

COMMON LAW

Utilized by most English-speaking states, *common law* is variously known also as *English, Anglo-Saxon*, or *Anglo-American* law. Despite its conceptualization by Lord Coke as "the perfection of reason," it is indeed a vast and complex instrument of justice. Although at first glance it may well seem chaotic and abstruse, on closer examination it is readily possible to discern a logic which binds the many diverse components that comprise it into a comprehensive and comprehensible entity.[14]

Common law is judge-made, bench-made, law rather than a fixed body of definite rules such as the modern civil law codes. In Roscoe Pound's words, it is a "mode of judicial and juristic thinking, a mode of treating legal problems."[15] He might have added "a mood." Often based on precedents, it embodies continuity in that it binds the present with the past. Since it thus necessarily grew, and still grows, by virtue of judicial decisions, it is best to explain and analyze it historically.

14For an excellent description see F. H. Lawson, *The Rational Strength of English Law* (Stevens, 1951).
15 Roscoe Pound, *The Spirit of the Common Law* (Boston: Little, Brown and Co., 1921), p. 1.

Historical Background. With the decline and fall of Rome came the growth of Christianity and Christian philosophy. The concept of the state as the highest form of society began to be questioned with the rise of the Christian Church. Concurrent with the Norman invasion of the British Isles "precise and orderly methods into the government and law of England" were introduced.[16] Thus began under the Norman and Angevin monarchs of the eleventh and twelfth centuries the gradual growth of a central administration and the development of the courts of law. The term "common law" was used for the law developed in the King's Courts and was generally employed in order to distinguish between it and that of the ecclesiastical courts. In effect, the concept "common law" was adopted from the *canon law* of the Christian Church, which was the common law of Christendom. The common law of the King's Courts was made by the royal justices from the mass of customary law of the realm and became the common law of England.

There were three great courts of common law: *King's Bench*, *Exchequer*, and *Common Pleas*. As the routine of these royal courts became firmly established, it was possible to forecast their decisions in terms of similar cases decided by them in the past. However, according to Theodore F. T. Plucknett,[17] the practice of basing decisions upon precedent did not come about because it was the best rule to follow in decision-making but because it enabled all existing courts to function with a minimum of trouble.

In many respects the common law reflects the feudal structure whence it was derived. Over a period of centuries the law defining the relationship between the Anglo-Norman monarchs and their tenants-in-chief became the law that was applicable to all Englishmen. At first this dealt solely with private law, but it was gradually extended to cover public law as well. The core of the feudal law was the concept of fealty which long prevailed after the passing of feudalism. Ruler as well as subject was bound—theirs were well-defined rights and obligations to be adhered to by all parties. Private rights of freemen were not subject to arbitrary change, and the primary task of the monarch was to preserve and protect the law.

---

[16] Theodore F. T. Plucknett, *A Concise History of the Common Law*, 5th ed. (Boston: Little, Brown and Co., 1956), p. 9.
[17] Ibid. p. 342.

But the groups whose rights the monarch had to acknowledge were limited to the nobility, the landed gentry, and some segments of the rising bourgeoisie. Hence it is hardly astonishing that the common law—which was essentially a law of property, in particular landed property—was "regarded by the politically influential class . . . as its shield."[18] Ordinary freemen had access to the King's Courts only in exceptional circumstances. However, during the twelfth and thirteenth centuries the practice of issuing *royal writs* was introduced, although these covered merely a few classes of civil cases. But early in the reign of Henry II (1154–89)—often termed the Father of the Common Law, although some would credit Henry I (1100–1135) with that title—an ordinance proclaiming that no man could be denied his freehold without a royal writ rendered centralization in a royal court inevitable. This was followed by several writs which continued the trend and culminated in the *Assize of Novel Disseisin of 1166*; it ordained that anyone who was denied his freehold could seek a remedy in the King's Court. (The Assize also provided for a jury of one's neighbors in questions of fact.) Thus, by 1166 the King was firmly established as the protector of the freehold.

By 1178 the work of the King's Court had become more than King and Council could handle, and five full-time judges were appointed, some of whom would travel about the countryside, settling disputes in each locality according to the prevailing mores. They attended to the bulk of the cases although the monarch and his Council still disposed of "novel and difficult" matters. This arrangement ultimately led to the schema of legal proceedings based on writs, which were promulgated in ever increasing numbers, and came to be sold to the litigants at a fixed price. Until the middle of the thirteenth century the King issued new writs to deal with a host of new problems. However, the barons became increasingly jealous of his power to make law, and in 1258 the King was forbidden to issue writs without the specific consent of his Council. In the absence of a new writ the thirty or forty writs then extant were often interpreted and stretched in order to deal with problems they were not designed to cope with.[19]

18 Sir Charles Ogilvie, *The King's Government and the Common Law: 1471–1641* (Oxford: Basil Blackwell, 1958), p. 6.
19 Ibid. p. 13.

With the founding of the Inns of Court unofficial reports of cases commenced to be published in annual *Year Books*. These books were records of court proceedings dealing mainly with procedural points for the benefit of practitioners rather than full reports of "casebook law" in the modern sense. Nevertheless, they did quite naturally come to serve as a gradually mounting source of precedents and were frequently referred to by those practitioners in the courts. *Stare decisis et non quieta movere*—stand by past decisions and do not disturb things at rest—began to have genuine meaning as a matter of judicial policy. According to Charles Ogilvie, the first inkling of the future English system of case law may be found in the *Dialogus de Scaccario*, written by Richard Fitz-Nigel between 1177 and 1179:

> "There are," he said, "cases where the courses of events, and the reasons for decisions are obscure; and in these it is enough to cite precedents."[20]

Thus were laid the bases on which the common law rests. As society became more complex, so did the law. At first it was made by the royal courts, but from the thirteenth century on it was always accepted as the supreme and fundamental law of the land. The Divine Right of Kings was a sixteenth-century idea, not a medieval one. Bracton (Henry of Bratton), a judge of the King's Bench under Henry III, writing in the thirteenth century in his *De Legibus*, stated that the King was "under God and the Law . . . for the Law made the King." And the great Sir Edward, later Lord, Coke—Attorney General, Member of Parliament, and Chief Justice of the Court of Common Pleas—when called before his King, James I, echoed Bracton in declaring that the monarch should also be bound by law. When the King told him that he could not be subject "to any man," Coke replied that, agreed, the King "is not subject to any man, but to God and the law." It was Lord Coke, who, more than any other individual of his time, compiled and analyzed precedents of common law and who was largely responsible for the then increasingly accepted practice of reporting cases fully. From these he drew a set of maxims and rules, later to be amplified and explained precisely by the famed Sir William Blackstone. The latter's monumental work, *Commentaries on the*

[20] Ibid. p. 17.

Law of England, ultimately became the bible of practically all legal training in both England and America.

Any notion that the judges are to serve the popular majority was and is utterly wrong. For under the tenets of the common law, while recognizing the authority of King and Parliament, all must bow to the law and act within its limits. England's judges have ever abided by their judicial oath to "administer the law without fear or favor." Various attempts were made to displace common law in England by civil law—to no avail.[21] Common law not only proved victorious, but over the years it was exported to countries such as Canada, Australia, New Zealand, India, Pakistan, and Israel, and taken to the United States by the colonists. Scotland, although itself a member of the United Kingdom of Great Britain and Northern Ireland, is an interesting exception. Its existing legal system was derived from Roman law, as were the Continental systems; but it has been greatly influenced by the common law.

Characteristics. As has already been pointed out, common law is predominantly *judge-made law.* Under it the judge is the creator, interpreter, and modifier of laws. Even when he merely "interprets" law, he may well be creating it. To that extent, statutory law, the law enacted by legislative bodies, is tentative. Discussing the benefits of judge-made law, Mr. Justice Cardozo pointed out that the judge can use "free scientific research" when analyzing a problem. By "free" he meant that the common law removes the judge to a very real extent from action by positive authority; by "scientific" he referred to the objective element in the judge's decision. Thus he may come closer to the just and the true, for law under the common law system develops by "judicial experience in the decision of cases."[22]

Another significant characteristic of common law is the doctrine of *precedent*, under which the judges refer to a previous decision or decisions in order to adjudicate the case at issue. The importance

21 Of course, a key problem concerning England's laws today (1967–68) is that they are now so entangled in some 45 volumes of Acts of Parliament going back to 1235 that finding the law on a simple point may require a search of 60 different Acts, 99 volumes of legislative orders, and some 350,000 reported court cases! In 1965, the Lord Chancellor, Lord Gardiner, was instrumental in having Parliament establish a permanent commission of distinguished jurists whose sole task would be to recommend changes in the laws systematically until a new framework is completed. But this promised to be a task of years.

22 Pound, loc. cit. p. 216.

14

of precedent varies with individual judges, for although common law has a rule demanding the recognition of precedent, the judges may distinguish between various precedents in evolving the new law. Moreover, times and conditions change with changing society, and, true to the thought that "every age should be mistress of its own law," an era should not be hampered by outdated law. "It is revolting," wrote Mr. Justice Holmes in characteristically forthright language, "to have no better reason for a rule of law than that it was so laid down in the time of Henry IV. It is still more revolting if the grounds upon which it was laid down have vanished long since, and the rule simply persists from blind imitation of the past."[23] It is the readiness of the common law judges to discard that which does not serve the public which has contributed to the survival and adoption of common law, wholly or partly, in so many lands. Nevertheless, although Mr. Justice Cardozo applauded this elasticity and timeliness, he cautioned that while a judge may discard the old and adopt the new, he must remember that the past is often a reflection of the present and he must know and understand it, "for the depths are the foundation of the heights."[24]

Because common law as such is uncodified, it is generally described as *unwritten law*. However, case precedents really are not unwritten; they are derived from the principles of law embodied in the judgments of cases which are decided and reported. Presumably most courts keep records, although they are not all required to do so. An example is the typical Justice of the Peace on the level of the constituent states in the United States of America, who, in contrast to his English counterpart, must follow the precedent of decided cases.

In summary, the common law appears to have three distinct characteristics that together have enabled the system to develop and expand. The first is its *vitality and capability to sustain change*. It does not impress its own peculiarities upon any other law; it only aids in the systematic development of a richer and presumably more just law. The second is its *practical quality*. It is unwilling to accept anything a priori and follows the notion that ideally all laws ought to be tested at the bar of courts. Thus, rules and

23 From an 1897 address, reprinted in his *Collected Legal Papers* (Boston: A. Harcourt, 1920), p. 187.
24 Margaret E. Hall (ed.), *Selected Writings of Benjamin Nathan Cardozo* (New York: Fallon Law Book Company, 1948), p. 78.

regulations are treated as working hypotheses, continually re-tested in what Mr. Justice Cardozo called "those great laboratories of the law, the courts of justice." Third is its *rendition of law as a moral obligation to be obeyed*. The results of the laboratory tests of the law are accepted as valid and everyone is obliged to obey them. After all, in the famous words of Mr. Justice Oliver Wendell Holmes, Jr.:

> The common law is not a brooding omnipresence in the sky, but the articulate voice of some sovereign or quasi-sovereign that can be identified.[25]

And as the great jurist put in both so well and hauntingly in his *The Common Law* in 1881:

> The life of the law has not been logic; it has been experience. The felt necessities of the time, the prevalent moral and political theories, intuitions of public policy, avowed or unconscious, even the prejudices which judges share with their fellow-men, have had a good deal more to do than syllogism in determining the rules by which men should be governed. The law embodies the story of a nation's development through many centuries, and it cannot be dealt with as if it contained only the axioms and corollaries of a book of mathematics. In order to know what it is, we must know what it has been, and what it tends to become. . . . The very considerations which judges most rarely mention, and always with an apology, are the secret root from which the law draws all the juices of life. I mean, of course, considerations of what is expedient for the community concerned.[26]

Some three decades later Holmes emphasized this ever recurring theme in his opinion for the Supreme Court of the United States in *Gompers v. United States*: "The provisions of the Constitution are not mathematical formulas having their essence in their form; they are organic living institutions transplanted from English soil. Their significance is vital not formal; it is to be gathered not simply by taking the words and a dictionary, but by considering their origin and the line of their growth."[27]

25 *Southern Pacific Co. v. Jensen*, 244 U. S. 205 (1916), at 222.
26 Oliver Wendell Holmes, Jr., *The Common Law* (Boston: Little, Brown and Co., 1881), pp. 1–2.
27 233 U. S. 604 (1914), at 610.

EQUITY

A branch of Anglo-American jurisprudence, born hundreds of
years ago and closely related to the common law, *equity* is actually
a supplement to the common law. Although the *Court of Chancery*
did not appear until the fifteenth century, equity courts arose in
England in the fourteenth century—apparently as early as 1340—
as a result of a practice that permitted a disappointed litigant at
common law to lay his plight before his sovereign. That is, he could
petition the King to "do right for the love of God and by way of
charity," the King being empowered to mold the law for the sake of
"justice," to grant the relief prayed for as an act of grace, when
the common law gave no remedy, or no adequate remedy.

Chancellor and Chancery. The monarch, on the other hand,
habitually referred these petitions to his Chancellor. This member
of his Council, who until the Reformation was always a cleric, became known as the "Keeper of the King's Conscience." He was
the Council's most important member and the Keeper of the Great
Seal, an office to which considerable powers were attached. It was
he who could, for example, issue a writ of *subpoena*, the well-
known writ commanding a person to appear before a duly constituted legal authority. From many points of view the Chancellor was
second in power only to his monarch. Ultimately, the volume of
these petitions brought about the establishment of a separate court,
known as the *Court of Chancery*. This was the early court of equity.
It maintained its separate existence until 1875, when it was merged
in the Supreme Court of Judicature by the Judicature Act of 1873.
Its jurisdiction is now mainly exercised by the Chancery Division
of the High Court of Justice, but all courts now administer both
common law and equity.

The United States of America never had *separate* courts of
equity on the federal level. But several states retain such separate
courts. others, the same jurist doubles as law judge and equity
judge, sitting one day as the former and one as the latter! In others
still, no separate equity courts exist at all—the same courts that
decide matters of common and statutory law also administer equity.

Defining Equity. But what is equity? We noted that it is a "supplement" to the common law, thus apparently the "conscience" of

the law. It is a supplement to the common law in the sense that the principles of equity—which are now part of the fabric of the common law—were developed by the Court of Chancery as an addition to the principles of the medieval common law. Equity began where the law ended, and it is in that role that we know it today. Thus, it created and continues to create precedents. It takes the form of a *judicial decree*, not of a judgment of "yes" or "no." Equity leaves the judge reasonably free to order *preventive* measures—and under some circumstances even *remedial* ones—usually in the form of a writ, such as an *injunction*, or restraining order, designed to afford a remedy not otherwise obtainable, and traditionally given upon a showing of peril. The judge in the original Court of Chancery exercised his decision, since remedies in equity were discretionary—and so they are today.

For instance, in equity an injunction may be issued by a judge to prevent members of a local of the United Steel Workers of America from going out on strike without having banked the furnaces of the Jones and Laughlin Steel Corporation, despite the inapplicability of the permissive injunctive provisions of the Norris-LaGuardia Act in this case, and despite the fact that the union had given due notice to strike in accordance with the requirements of the Taft-Hartley Act. True, the steel firm involved could probably recover monetary compensation for resultant damages from its insurance company, or from the U.S.W. if it should be found that a contractual provision had been violated by the action of the workers. However, the company here is not interested in such money; its sole aim is to prevent its furnaces from the certain destruction that would result from a failure to bank them. Hence the demand for an equity decree in the form of an injunction against the union.

Another illustration, although considerably less in the realm of immediate peril, might be Mr. John Miller's lovely old virgin copper beech on the edge of his private property, directly in the path of a future highway to be built by the Commonwealth of Pennsylvania. The latter has every right to chop down the tree under its power of *eminent domain*, provided only that it does so for a public purpose, which a state public highway certainly is, and that it grant just compensation, which it usually does quite liberally in these circumstances. But Mr. Miller is not interested in financial compensation, either; he wants to continue to enjoy the beauty and the shade of the magnificent tree and the sentimental attachments that go with it—he proposed to his wife under it; his children and grandchildren climbed it with relish for years. Thus, he, too, may appeal to the courts for equity. His chances for success are undoubtedly considerably less than were those of the steel firm mentioned above, but judges are human beings, not automatons.

STATUTORY LAW

Despite the fact that the concept of *statutory law*—variously known as *code* law, *written* law, *Neo-Roman* or *Roman* law, or *civil* law—comes to us from ancient Rome, the question of its broader application is essentially a modern one. Whereas the common law has dealt traditionally with matters of a private character, the relations between individuals, statutory law is concerned more frequently with society as a whole. It is law that originates with specifically designated, authoritative lawmaking bodies—presumably legislatures, but it also embraces executive-administrative decrees and ordinances, treaties and protocols, all of which are committed to paper.

Historical Background. Statutory law developed in and from the homogeneous city-state, exemplified by the Codes of Emperor Justinian I (527–65), the *Corpus Juris Civilis*, which was promulgated about A.D. 535. Hence it is frequently referred to as Roman law and, to confuse teachers and students alike, as *civil* law—which has nothing whatever to do with civil jurisdiction (see below). In contrast to diversified England with its manifold customs that veritably seemed to cry out for some sort of common law, Rome in its glory lent itself ideally to the development of a statutory system, one that could be readily written down, codified. Statutory law had—and has, of course—the advantages of preciseness, simplicity, and clear-cut applicability, although it still remains subject to interpretation by administrators as well as judges.

Enacted by legislative and/or executive-administrative bodies of government, codified and spelled out in writing by the legal profession, the Bar itself, clearly and readily available for all to see—statutory law has survived as the generally accepted law for most of the states of continental Europe, Russia, Latin America, and many of the newly emergent African nations. Justinian's Code had been initially introduced into western Europe in 544 when the Eastern Empire reconquered Italy. But it did not assume genuine significance for the West until the systematic study of Roman law was revived at the Italian universities in the twelfth century.[28] One of its most famous codifiers was Napoleon I, whose Civil Code was published in 1804, Code of Civil Procedure in 1807, and others subsequently. Indeed, the *Code Napoleon* has been far more enduring than most of the colorful Emperor's famed military triumphs. Its first major change did not take place until the Gaullist reforms of 1959 that gave France's married women increased property rights.

"MIXING" COMMON AND STATUTORY LAW

England and the United States today have legal systems based on the common law that readily and naturally found its way across the Atlantic Ocean from the Mother Country to the Colonies. But although it must be categorized as a common law system, the Anglo-American legal framework in effect now consists of a mixture of common *and* statutory law. A great deal of contemporary law is necessarily statutory; it is coded. However, this is a relatively recent development, for although statutes as a basis of Anglo-American law were not unknown, they played no really significant role until the second quarter of the nineteenth century.

The mixture came into its own largely, although certainly not exclusively, as a result of the perpetuating conservatism of the common law, particularly in the realm of the sanctity of private property, based on the overriding concept of economic *laisser faire*. With the advent of a rising spirit of common social consciousness and responsibility, and a gradual movement toward the service or welfare state on both sides of the ocean, legislative bodies everywhere—but considerably more slowly in the United States than in the United Kingdom—commenced to change or even displace the age-old concepts and practices of the common law in favor of what were viewed as primary considerations of necessary public interest.

Nonetheless, common law remained as an important basis of legislative motivations and actions, and often an enacted statute

[28] A. T. von Mehren, *The Civil Law System* (Englewood Cliffs, N. J.: Prentice-Hall, Inc., 1957).

would—as indeed it still does today—simply spell out the grand sweep of certain aspects of common law. Furthermore, no legislative body—and sometimes not even the executive—is consistently, or even largely, capable of pinpointing in writing all the aspects and ramifications of a statute or order, nor would that necessarily be desirable, even if it were possible. The result is interpretation, usually first by administrative units, then often by the courts, and —as we shall have ample opportunity to observe in Chapters V to IX—when courts interpret, they cause statutes to grow and/or contract. This interpretation becomes part of the statutes and orders, thus giving them meaning in the spirit and application of the common law. Truly, England and America resort to a framework of law that is a generally wholesome blend of common, statutory, and equity law.

Of course, there are certain areas of statutory law where little, if any, discretionary elements remain for the judge. The United States Criminal Code, for example, represents a compendium of laws that prescribe what shall constitute a crime and what the penalties therefor shall be. A judge may have a modicum of leeway regarding the former, but the sole substantive discretion left to him in the realm of the latter is one specifically written into the code. Thus, a particular law may conceivably permit him to exercise his considered judgment as to the severity of a sentence which he is called upon to impose for a given criminal infraction, but this discretion will be strictly limited by the minimum and maximum penalties as provided in it. Moreover, it may well be limited by the nature of the verdict of the jury. Indeed, *criminal law* is becoming more and more codified everywhere among the common law lands, and hence is becoming statutory. The same applies to *public law* generally, although the great bulk of *private* law is still common law. A few words of explanation about these two and some additional legal concepts are in order.

SOME ADDITIONAL
LEGAL DEFINITIONS AND CONCEPTS

Although they do not even half cover, let alone exhaust, the vast and sometimes exasperating ranges and spaces of legal terms and concepts, a few terms and concepts related to notions that play a part in these pages must be elaborated upon here, however briefly. A host of others will be treated throughout the book. (A standard legal dictionary, e.g. *Black's Law Dictionary*,[29] will readily supply answers to any others that may occur to the inquiring reader.) We begin with a distinction between the two types of law into which *municipal law*—the law that applies within a state—is normally divided, namely *private* and *public* law.

Private law governs the relationship between private citizens or persons; that is, it regulates the relations of individuals with each other. It is concerned with the definition, regulation, and enforcement of rights in cases where both the person[30] in whom the right inheres and the person upon whom the obligation devolves are private individuals. Obvious examples of private law are the law governing contracts between individuals or corporations and that pertaining to marriage and divorce. In the sense that infractions of the legal obligations inherent in these areas are subject to adjudication by courts, the state is involved, of course, but it is neither the subject of the right nor the object of the duty.

Public law, on the other hand, is a branch or department of law which is very much concerned with the state in its political or sovereign capacities—including the important two subheadings of administrative and constitutional law (to be described presently). Public law deals with the definition, regulation, and enforcement of rights in those cases where the state *is* viewed as the subject of the right or the object of the duty, including criminal law and criminal procedure. In other words, it is that portion of law that is concerned with political conditions and situations—with the powers, rights, duties, capacities, and incapacities that are characteristic of and peculiar to both supreme and subordinate political superiors.

Public law applies to and effects the entire people of a nation or state that adopts or enacts it—in contrast with private law, which affects and applies to only one or a few individuals—for it regulates both the relations between individuals and the state and the relations between the branches of the government. Thus, the vast majority of legislation enacted by Congress is in the category of Public law—and its statutes are codified, preceded by the term

---

[29] The definitions used in this section are based in part on its 4th ed. (St. Paul: West Publishing Co., 1957), pp. 1394, 1359, 385, and 67.

[30] In 1886 the Supreme Court declared corporations to be legal "persons" under the Constitution. (See p. 349, *infra*.)

"Public Law_____ [Number]." Social welfare, defense appropriations, subversive activities control, farm subsidies, all these areas of legislation represent illustrations of the vast and diversified content of public law.

Administrative law, which has quite naturally achieved ever increasing prominence over the past few decades, consists of those rules and regulations that are promulgated by the sundry administrative agencies of government that have been empowered to deal with the operation of government under the delegated rule-making authority of the legislative body. That branch of public law prescribes in detail the activities of the agencies involved—such as those concerned with the collection of revenue; regulation of competitive practices; coinage; public health, welfare, safety, and morals; sanitation; and regulation of the armed forces.

Constitutional law is the other great branch of public law. It determines the political organization of a state and its powers while also setting certain substantive and procedural limitations on the exercise of governing power. Because of its position and nature it stands legally above all other types of municipal law, public as well as private. In the United States, with its written Constitution, constitutional law consists of the application of fundamental principles of law based on that document, as finally interpreted by its highest judicial organ, the Supreme Court of the United States. A fairly recent example is the famous *Steel Seizure Case*.[31] Believing himself invested with the power to act in his capacity as Commander-in-Chief, coupled with what he and his advisers viewed as "inherent authority," President Truman seized the steel mills on April 8, 1952, in order to forestall a nation-wide strike in the midst of the Korean War. The owners filed a writ to enjoin him, charging the absence of both constitutional and legislative authority for his actions. After a series of dramatic skirmishes in the lower federal courts, the United States Supreme Court received the case for adjudication—clearly a matter in the realm of constitutional law. On June 2, 1952, the Court rendered its decision, featured by seven different opinions! But six of the nine justices did agree on *one* crucial point: that by *usurping legislative power* President Truman had violated the Constitution, and that the seizure of the steel mills was hence *ultra vires*—particularly so since Congress

31 *Youngstown Sheet and Tube Co. v. Sawyer*, 343 U. S. 579 (1952).

had expressly refused to enact a suggested amendment to the Taft-Hartley Act authorizing such governmental seizures in an emergency.[32]

In brief, constitutional law prescribes generally the plan and method under which the public business of the political organ, known as the state, is conducted. And it differs further from the other types of law we have seen in that it is both enacted and changed either in an extraordinary manner by ordinary legislative bodies or by extraordinary bodies, such as a constitutional convention, constituted especially for that purpose.

In the United States changes in the letter of the fundamental document are based on the special constitutional amendment provisions of its Article V, which combine extraordinary federal with extraordinary state action. In the United Kingdom, where no formal writen constitution and no power of judicial review exist, Parliament is supreme and may affect changes in the constitutional law of the land by ordinary legislation. But it is highly unlikely to tamper with the great cornerstones of its unwritten Constitution— that intriguing British concept consisting of the heritage of the common law, great statutes, important documents, decisions of the courts (other than judicial review), and customs and conventions, that combined constitute the very life blood of the realm. In France the written Constitution of the Fifth Republic may be altered only by extraordinary action of Parliament with the co-operation of the President of France, either with or without ratification by a popular referendum, depending upon the procedure invoked by the President in the course of the initiating stages. And in Switzerland, not only do constitutional alterations by the government call for mandatory ratification by popular referenda, but the Swiss citizens may take the initiative directly by drawing up a proposed constitutional amendment and submitting it for direct popular referendum approval.

---

[32] Quipped *The Economist* (May 10, 1952) in commenting on the case as it was about to reach the Supreme Court: "At the first sound of a new argument over the United States Constitution and its interpretation, the hearts of Americans leap with a fearful joy. The blood stirs powerfully in their veins and a new lustre brightens their eyes. Like King Harry's men before Harfleur, they stand like greyhounds in the slips, straining upon the start. Last week, the old bugle-note rang out, clear and thrilling, calling Americans to a fresh debate on the Constitution."

CIVIL AND CRIMINAL LAW

Another basic distinction of considerable importance which confronts the observer of the judicial and legal process is that between *civil law* and *criminal law* (the former not to be equated here with the concept of "civil law" when used as a synonym for statutory or Roman law, here the reference to it is in connection with the subject matter governing in a particular case). Whether a particular offense is of a civil or criminal nature determines not only the severity of the punishment that may be invoked, but frequently also the type of tribunal before which the case at issue will be heard. As we shall see in subsequent chapters, some courts are empowered to hear cases involving *both* types of law, as in all three major federal constitutional courts of the United States; but in many instances the judicial hierarchy provides for a separate set of criminal and civil courts, as is the case, to a greater or lesser extent, in both England and France—although some of the English judges are used interchangeably.

Civil Law. A case at *civil law* is normally one between private persons and/or private organizations, for civil law governs the relations between individuals and defines their legal rights. A party bringing suit under it seeks legal redress in a *personal* interest, such as for a breach of contract, a divorce action, a defamation of character, the use of a copyrighted story without permission. Yet while suits at civil law far more often than not are suits among private persons, as indicated, the government, too may conceivably be involved. For example, under the Sherman Anti-Trust Act of 1890, as amended, the federal government in the United States is empowered to bring either civil or criminal action against an alleged offender. It has much more frequently brought civil than criminal actions under that statute, probably because the former are not so difficult to win and cause less of an uproar in the interested community. Also, cases at civil law are often more difficult for courts to dispose of, for as a rule they neither lend themselves to ready "guity" or "not guilty" judgments, nor do they commonly involve the verdict of a trial jury—whatever the merits of that institution may be.

Criminal Law. A case at *criminal law* is invariably brought by and in the name of the legally constituted government, no matter at what level—national, state, or local—it may arise. Chiefly statutory in the United States, criminal law defines crimes against the public order and provides for appropriate punishment. Prosecution brought under it by the proper governmental authority involves an accusation that the defendant has violated a specific provision of a law, an infraction for which a penalty has normally been provided by statute. Criminal cases comprise such felonies or major crimes as homicidal, espionage, sabotage, rape, and perjury, to name but a few. The coverage is as extensive as the lawmakers choose to make it. Since the prosecuting authority in a criminal case is necessarily an agent of the sovereign, the latter's name appears in its title. Hence, assuming one Brown's indictment for murder in Pennsylvania, the case would be docketed for trial as either *The Commonwealth of Pennsylvania v. Brown* or as *People v. Brown*. Moving to the federal level, one of the cases brought under the membership clause of the Smith Act of 1940 read *United States v. Scales*.[33] However, by far the largest volume of criminal law is still enacted at the state level in the United States and, thus, is enforced by state officials under state law. Unitary countries, such as France and the United Kingdom, are not confronted with that jurisdictional problem.

But in all cases and at all levels it is the jurists who render the decisions. As Alexis de Tocqueville put it so well: "Hardly any question arises in the United States that is not resolved sooner or later into a judicial question." To the jurists, then, to their fascinating and significant tasks, and the hierarchical framework in which they perform their duties, we now turn.

[33] 367 U. S. 203 (1961).

II

STAFFING THE COURTS

SELECTION

What principles should govern the selection of the men—and women—who dispense justice? To raise this question brings us face to face with moral, as well as political, questions of the greatest importance. However awe-inspiring their functions may be or seem, our judges are still human beings. As such they make the ultimate decisions in the judicial process. In essence, there are just two basic methods of selection: *appointment* and *election*—no matter who does the actual appointing or electing—although, as we shall see below, a compromise between the two modes has been devised and is practised on certain levels of the judiciary in some jurisdictions. A collateral question is whether judges should be members of a career service as in France, chosen from a special group of lawyers as in England, or selected through appointments essentially political, without regard to their qualifications or professional endorsement, as in the United States. Practices of selection differ in large measure in acordance with the traditions and needs of the country concerned. A crucial consideration here is the very position of the judiciary in the framework of government that provides the rationale for the particular mode adopted and adhered to. Under the Roman law tradition of the Continent, the judiciary is a part of the over-all administrative hierarchy and, as such, represents a position and profession other than that of the ordinary lawyer. Under the common law system, on the other hand, the judges are drawn exclusively from the ranks of the legal profession. Nevertheless, the guiding principles for the selection and tenure of the judiciary in the three countries that concern us most here—the United Kingdom, France, and the United States—display a commonly held ideal: judges are expected to be impartial and hence must be given assurance of independence, security, and dignity of tenure. When these are present, the fact that different techniques govern selection in these lands is hardly of great significance. Nevertheless, these techniques must be studied and understood. The process of selection is assuredly more complicated than the otherwise trenchant observation of W. Curtis Bok's imaginary Judge Ulen who quipped: "A judge is a member of the bar who once knew a Governor."[1]

The Two Chief Methods

With the important exception of most of the roughly 9000 judges in state and local courts, the *appointive* method is employed predominantly in the United States. It is used *exclusively* at the *federal* level of the government, regardless of whether the tribunal concerned is a constitutional or legislative court (a distinction that will be described in detail in Chapter IV). Britain and France use appointment exclusively at all levels.

Appointment. In the *United States* all of the approximately 400 federal judges are appointed by the President, subject to confirmation by simple majority vote of the Senate, on a political basis more or less. Depending upon the Chief Executive involved, the President's heavy responsibility has been largely delegated to the Attorney General and, in practice, to the Deputy Attorney General. This was noticeably true during the later years of the Administration of President Eisenhower when the selection of members of the federal judiciary was left almost exclusively to Attorney General William P. Rogers and Deputy Attorney General Lawrence E. Walsh. But three other important factors enter here. One is the obvious need for consultation with the United States Senator(s) and/or other seats of political power in the home state of the candidate for judicial office—provided these political figures are of the same party as the appointing authority. Thus, care must be taken that the appointee is not "personally obnoxious" to a home-state Senator, on pain of having the latter invoke the age-old, almost invariably honored, custom of "senatorial courtesy"—a certain

1 *Backbone of the Herring* (New York: Alfred A. Knopf, 1941), p. 3.

death-knell to the candidacy at the bar of the Senate. The custom is based on the assumption that the President will, as a matter of political patronage, practice, and courtesy, engage in such consultation prior to the nominee's designation—provided that the Senator is a member of the President's party. If the President fails to adhere to the custom, the aggrieved Senator's colleagues will support him on his call for the nominee's defeat, as a matter of fraternal courtesy. Let it be said at once that as a practical matter it is not possible for the Chief Executive to designate a member of the federal bench and see him confirmed without at least the grudging approval of his Senators. And some powerful Senators of the President's political party will insist not only on the right of prior approval of the President's choice, but also on the right to have particular candidates of their own designated. At the very least, this pertains to the federal district bench.

The second factor that has played an increasingly significant role in the appointive process of the federal judiciary in the United States, especially since the latter months of the Truman Administration, is the American Bar Association's twelve-member Committee on the Federal Judiciary established in 1946.

That committee, which was widely utilized subsequently during President Eisenhower's terms of office—a practice continued under President Kennedy and President Johnson—has generally produced good results and is understandably popular with the legal profession, although there is no unanimity on any evaluation. There are those who believe deeply that the selection of the members of the judicial branch of the government must rest, in fact, as well as in name, with the executive branch, its head being specifically charged to do so under Article III, the judiciary article of the Constitution; and that the apparent delegation of important aspects of that authority to a private body, no matter how qualified and how representative—a crucial point—is at best questionable, and at worst a dereliction of duty. Nor is the bar free from political or personal biases. Had President Wilson, for one, heeded the advice of the A.B.A., Mr. Justice Brandeis would never had been nominated. Furthermore, as an intriguing book-length study of the committee's activities over a period of two decades demonstrated convincingly,[2] its membership is all but inevitably composed of the "legal establishment." Almost all were successful lawyers, older

[2] Joel B. Grossman, *Lawyers and Judges: The Politics of Judicial Selection* (New York: John Wiley & Sons, Inc., 1965).

men, partners in large, big-city firms, veterans of local bar association politics. Of the relatively few lawyers the committee asked to give an evaluation of judicial candidates, 70 per cent were officers of local bar associations and 80 per cent were senior partners in "respectable" law firms.[3]

Whatever the merit of demurrers, the committee has become a powerful and respected vehicle in the vital initial stages of the nominating process. After an investigation customarily lasting from six to eight weeks, it reports to the Justice Department on the qualifications of the prospective nominee and rates him in one of four ways: Exceptionally Well Qualified (EWQ), Well Qualified (WQ), Qualified (Q), or Not Qualified (NQ). In a number of cases the consideration of nominees for the federal bench was dropped after the A.B.A.'s committee found them less qualified than others; also its reports have enabled the Justice Department to rule out certain names recommended by the home-state Senator(s).

To illustrate, in September 1961 the Senate confirmed 60 lower court federal judges nominated by President Kennedy of whom 52 had been rated by the A.B.A. Nine had been rated Exceptionally Well Qualified, 27 Well Qualified, 14 Qualified, and 2 Not Qualified. Yet the two rated Not Qualified—James R. Browning, then the Clerk of the U. S. Supreme Court, and an Oklahoman, Luther Bohanan—had sufficiently powerful support to gain confirmation. However, a finding of Not Qualified is not necessarily a reflection on a nominee's character or ability. The A.B.A.'s committee will not approve anyone who has reached the age of sixty-four. President Kennedy's selection of Sarah T. Hughes of Texas[4] to be a federal district court judge was disapproved on that ground, but she was confirmed. Further, the committee is loath to recommend lawyers without trial experience—which was true of both Browning and Bohanan.

On occasion, it has even been proposed that various bar associations run their own candidates for judgeships if the political parties fail to choose "properly qualified candidates," as did Pre-

---

[3] Ibid. pp. 82–92. On the other hand, Professors Richard G. Watson, Rondal G. Downing, and Frederick G. Spiegel, in an article concerned with the members of Missouri's Bar, contend that the notion that the bar is inevitably conservative is *disproved* by the Missouri experience: "Bar Politics, Judicial Selection and the Representation of Social Interests," LXI, *American Political Science Review*, 54 (March 1967).

[4] Judge Hughes swore in Lyndon B. Johnson in the Presidential plane "Air Force 1" after President Kennedy's assassination on November 22, 1963.

siding Justice Bernard Botein of the Appellate Division for Manhattan and the Bronx in a speech to the New York State Bar Association in July 1961. Nor would an affirmative response to this appeal have constituted a novelty; in both 1906 and 1932, the bar sponsored independent nominees on the "Judiciary Nominators Republican" ticket, but both were defeated by Democrats slated by Tammany Hall, in the first instance by 190,000 to 113,000 votes, in the second by 585,000 to 293,000. The losers thus polled a respectable total, yet lost to the normal political process.

Considerably more will be said on the point later, but it should be re-emphasized here that in selecting his nominees no alert and prudent Chief Executive of the United States and his entourage would nowadays attempt to designate members of the judiciary *purely* on the basis of political considerations. Too much is at stake in matters of policy and public awareness, and the American Bar Association is a powerful factor in the selection process. Yet, granted the sundry and largely salutary needs and drives for appointments on the basis of over-all merit and excellence, the political pressures must nevertheless be reckoned with and are disregarded only at the appointing authority's peril. Moreover, a federal judgeship is viewed as such a "plum" by all concerned that it represents a potent patronage-whip in the hands of the executive vis-à-vis state politicians as well as Congress.

Both the problem and its flavor are suggested rather nicely and candidly by the following passage in Senator Joseph S. Clark's newsletter of August 11, 1961, to his constituents in Pennsylvania:

> I have forwarded to the Attorney General recommendations to fill additional Judgeships recently authorized by Congress in the United States District Courts in Pennsylvania, and one vacancy in the Court of Appeals for the Third Circuit. I regret that, by custom, Senators have the obligation of making these recommendations after appropriate consultation with their State political leaders. I believe the selection of judges should be entirely nonpartisan and should be made by the Attorney General and the President without Senatorial intervention. Nevertheless, I must live with the rules as they exist until they are changed. After consultations with Governor Lawrence, Democratic State Chairman Otis Morse II, Congressman William J. Green, Jr., and others, I

am satisfied that the recommendations made for existing vacancies are men of ability and integrity. The Attorney General and the President will make the final decisions on these Judgeships of course, and may disregard our recommendations if they wish.

There is a third factor: increasingly demonstrable evidence of the role that sitting members of the Court itself, especially the Chief Justice, may play in consulting with and being consulted by the President in the selection process of a new Supreme Court Justice. Chief Justices Taft, Hughes, Stone, and Warren—Taft quite openly—have all been thus involved.[5] It is entirely possible to make a good case for the practice—within limits.

In Britain—we are here again almost exclusively concerned with England and Wales, for convenience hereafter referred to as England, since Scotland and Northern Ireland, the two other members of the United Kingdom of Great Britain and Northern Ireland, operate separate court systems—judges are designated by the Crown with little or no surrender to politics. Practically speaking, they are the choices of the Lord Chancellor, the senior law member of the government, who is the Queen's chief adviser on the selection. Since the Lord Chancellor is chosen by the Prime Minister, the latter does have an indirect voice in the selection of judges, small and more or less inaudible that voice is, however, especially on the middle and higher levels. Among these are the Lords of Appeal in Ordinary (the Law Lords), the Lord Chief Justice, the Master of the Rolls, the President of the Probate, Divorce, and Admiralty Division of the High Court of Justice, and the Lord Justices of the Court of Appeal. In the cases of the Lord Chief Justice and the Master of the Rolls, the highest ranking judicial offices, the Prime Minister in effect designates the appointees but acts on the advice of the Lord Chancellor. But it must be clearly understood that it is the Queen who actually issues the commission of appointment.

The Lord Chancellor himself, however, is the politically designated head of the judicial hierarchy of the United Kingdom. In addition he advises on the appointment to judicial office from the

5 For a good description of Taft's role in Harding's designation of Pierce Butler, see David Danelski, *A Supreme Court Justice Is Appointed* (New York: Random House, 1964). See also Alpheus T. Mason, *William Howard Taft: Chief Justice* (New York: Simon and Schuster, 1965) and *Harlan Fiske Stone: Pillar of the Law* (New York: Viking Press, 1956).

rank of Justice of the Peace to the higher offices of the English Judiciary. He presides over the House of Lords as its Speaker from the Woolsack (a bright red padded bench, its name signifying the importance of wool trade to the British economy); is a member of the Cabinet; and as head of the Judiciary combines in his person the threefold function of executive, legislator, and jurist—a complete refutation of the principle of separation of powers so dear to the Baron de Montesquieu. His office—which pays the equivalent of $40,600 (1967), the highest British government salary—is older than that of Prime Minister. Since the group of barristers from whose ranks the Lord Chancellor[6] chooses judges is small and select, he knows a good many of them, and when members of the Opposition seem to give promise as competent judges, he will certainly not hesitate to cross party lines to make appointments. If he does not personally know, or know of, a candidate, he will consult with the head of the division to which the judge is to be appointed and obtain his views—but *not* his prior approval. Incidentally, barristers must resign from the bar when they go on the bench.

No letters of recommendation are accepted, and efforts to put political pressure on the Lord Chancellor are scouted strongly. R. M. Jackson, Reader in Public Law and Administration in the University of Cambridge, in his excellent study on the machinery of justice in England,[7] contends that political considerations have hardly entered the process of judicial selection since 1907—although they died a slower death in the case of the office of Lord Chief Justice; and he insists that, as a consequence, there has been no apparent connection between the "political antecedents" of the judges and their decisions in over a century. However, members of the House of Commons may be appointed to county-court judgeships and also to the High Court.[8] Yet, to this day, because

---

[6] The title was once held by two British saints, Thomas à Becket and Sir Thomas More.

[7] Richard M. Jackson, *The Machinery of Justice in England*, 4th ed. (Cambridge: Cambridge University Press, 1964), pp. 257, 263.

[8] For example, in 1962 two of the members of the High Court were from the House of Commons, and the then new President of its Probate, Divorce, and Admiralty Division was the former Solicitor-General, a member of the House. Indeed, there used to be a tradition that the Attorney General was entitled to claim the office of Lord Chief Justice—e.g., Sir Gordon Hewart became Lord Chief Justice as Lord Hewart (Viscount Hewart of Bury) and served from 1922 to 1940.

of the fear of executive interference with the administration of justice, no Ministry or Department of Justice exists in the United Kingdom.

In *France,* and in many other countries on the Continent, the trained judges are appointed to, rise in, and are promoted from a type of career service which is an adjunct of the general civil service. The de Gaulle Constitution of 1958 specifically makes a point of the time-honored concept that an ideal judge is an impartial judge. There is a Ministry of Justice, but the judges of France do not really feel its authority, although the Minister is part of the appointing process. Political patronage plays scarcely a role in their selections. They have all been either schooled as judges for four years at the Center of Judicial Studies (established in 1959) or have had experience as such, and they enter the judicial service on the basis of passing competitive examinations.

Theoretically, the President of the Republic, who is charged by the Constitution to be "the guarantor of the independence of judicial authority,"[9] selects the judges; actually, they are chosen either by the eleven-member *Conseil Superieur de la Magistrature* (High Council of the Judiciary) in the case of the *Cour d'Appel* and the *Cour de Cassation,* or by the Minister of Justice, who may consult with, or receive advice from, the High Council, in the case of the lower courts. The High Council consists of the President of the Republic (as *le président*), the Minister of Justice (as vice president), and nine persons with legal background chosen by the President for a once-renewable term of four years, partly on the recommendation of the *Cour de Cassation* and the *Conseil d'État,* as follows: one from the latter; three from the former; three from other courts; and two selected for their general legal knowledge and competence. In any event, the selecting authorities have but little choice—considerably less than in England and infinitely less, of course, than in the United States.

The assets and liabilities of the appointive versus the elective method are rather obvious. In general the main argument in favor of appointment hinges on the contention that a candidate for a judicial post who is obliged to run on a partisan ballot cannot possibly serve as an *impartial* judge, and that he is selected, as Al Smith once put it, "by an electorate who are not really in a position to pass upon the legal and other abilities of the individ-

[9] Title VIII, Article 64.

ual."[10] On the other hand, the champions of election on a partisan ballot argue that appointment by a political executive contains even worse features of political beholdenness than election. As is so often the case, neither side of the argument is *ipso facto* correct on all counts; both contain some merit, and it is easy to oversimplify. Someone, however, has to assume responsibility for staffing the courts; it might as well be the executive, who not only possesses the expertise and has access to all pertinent data, but also is fairly well known to the populace at large on almost all levels and, in fact, is usually the sole officer of government with an all-embracing constituency. At least in theory, the people are always in a position to hold him accountable in a free society. To make him responsible for unfortunate judicial appointments is more meaningful and more palatable to the electorate than an arrangement that requires the latter not only to submerge judges into the political arena, but also to become intimately familiar with their adjudicatory record. Whatever the ramifications of this balancing of scales, executive appointment of judges has proved to be the preferred method of selection in England, France, and the United States (with notable state-level exceptions). Although compromise arrangements of the type illustrated below may well move onto the scene here and there, there is no chance that election will supplant appointment for the selective process of judges in the vast majority of countries in the free Western world.

Election. Nevertheless, election of members of that branch of the government is not unknown, even at the national or federal level of governments. In Switzerland, a major exception to the *federal* appointment principle, judges are elected by the two federal chambers—the *Nationalrat* and the *Ständerat*—sitting jointly as the *Bundesversammlung* (National Assembly) to assure that German-, French-, and Italian-speaking members are appropriately distributed on the bench. However, re-election is so usual that to all intents and purposes permanent tenure of office is the logical result of the practice. In a drastically different category, the Soviet Union, too, practises the elective method exclusively, but (a) the victorious candidates serve for short terms only and (b) they have been approved by the political hierarchy of the state in advance of their candidacy.

[10] As quoted by Arthur T. Vanderbilt, "Brief for a Better Court System," *The New York Times Magazine*, May 5, 1957, p. 9.

Election of judges in the Western world is most widespread at the state level of most, but not all of the states in America—a result of the early nineteenth century trend to "democratize" government. There it may take place by either the electorate (e.g. Florida) or the legislature (e.g. the higher judges in South Carolina) for at least some of the members of the judicial hierarchy in all except a handful (e.g. Hawaii). True, judges *sometimes* appear on bipartisan tickets (e.g. Pennsylvania), even on a nonpartisan one (e.g. Minnesota) on occasion, but loyal service in partisan politics tends to be a prerequisite for nomination—in line with Jacksonian tradition. True also that while the elective term of office is on the average but six years, it extends to life for certain judgeships in some states (e.g. Supreme Court of Rhode Island) and to rather lengthy periods in others (e.g. twenty-one years, nonrenewable, for the post of Supreme Court Justice in Pennsylvania). In a few states the concept of supporting the sitting judge has been adopted when he is up for re-election,[11] but this theoretically laudatory practice has been honored almost as much in the breach as in the observance. Moreover, the mitigating factors that are inherent in the deviations from the straight, partisan, short-term ballot election are found in but a few states, and even in these they are usually confined to the upper echelons of the judiciary.

Other practices worthy of note in this general consideration of selection are those of gubernatorial appointment subject to some legislative consent (e.g. the Delaware Senate); direct selection of some by the legislature itself (e.g. the presiding justices of the Supreme Court and county courts of Vermont), some by courts (e.g. trial judges in county courts, and juvenile or domestic relations court judges by the judges of the circuit or corporation courts of Virginia). Massachusetts' gubernatorially appointed judges serve for life; those of New Jersey for seven years, and then for life.

A Compromise?

An intriguing attempt at a compromise between the elective and appointive methods of choosing state judges in America has been advanced and popularized, in somewhat different versions by states

---

11 Thus New York State Court of Appeals Associate Judge Stanley H. Fuld, who had demonstrated great talent in twenty years of service on that tribunal, was nominated for the post of Chief Justice on the November 8, 1966, ballot by all four political parties: Republican, Democratic, Liberal, and Conservative.

such as California, Missouri, Alaska, Kansas, Illinois, Iowa, and Nebraska at the Supreme Court and/or other appellate levels. It may also be found at certain low-level, often municipal or metropolitan courts, as in Utah, Tuba County (Oklahoma), Denver County (Colorado), Dade County (Florida), and Birmingham, Alabama. It is designed to minimize political influence and provide a degree of security of tenure, while retaining an element of popular control. Although repeatedly and even enthusiastically supported by leading spokesmen of the legal profession and by knowledgeable laymen alike, it has not been widely adopted by the states—chiefly owing to powerful political opposition, which views this compromise as a genuine threat to the patronage aspects of judicial selection, as well it might be. California and Missouri were the pioneers in the compromise movement.

The California Plan. The first well-known original attempt at a solution to the vexations problem of judicial selection was the *California Plan*, adopted by referendum vote of that state's electorate in 1934. A vigorous campaign for ratification of the plan had begun two years earlier by the California State Bar Association, encouraged by its national parent body, closely allied with the California Chamber of Commerce. The two powerful state groups had become convinced of the inadequacy of the system under which California then operated—judicial appointment by the Governor with subsequent popular approval, which in their eyes constituted little more than public rubber-stamping of the appointing authority's rank political designations.

Under the California Plan, which applies to the judges of the Supreme Court and District Courts of Appeals only, the Governor nominates *one* person to the Commission on Qualifications. This body is composed of the Chief Justice of the State Supreme Court, the Presiding Judge of the District Court of Appeals of the area concerned, and the Attorney General. If the commission approves the Governor's nominee, the latter is deemed appointed for the duration of *one year only*. At the end of that year he stands for popular election for a full twelve-year term of office—his name being the only one on the nonpartisan ballot. The sole question appearing on the ballot in connection with the nominee's candidacy is "Shall _____ be elected to the office for the term prescribed by law?" There are no limits on the number of terms to which a successful candidate may aspire. Should the electorate's response to the question on the ballot be in the negative, his successor will be designated by the Governor in the same manner, ultimately to go before the electorate as well. In any event, the burden of approval is on the people, who must familiarize themselves with his record—or at least they ought to do so.

The first test of the plan returned the sitting judges by a 2:1 affirmative vote, a margin of approval that has steadily widened since that time. Appraisals of the California Plan have been generally favorable, but some have criticized as inadequate what in their view is the essentially negative restriction placed on the Governor's power by the commission. To refuse to confirm a gubernatorial appointment takes a certain amount of courage—not inevitably demonstrated by the commission. There have also been doubts voiced concerning the wisdom of placing a measure of control over judicial appointments, however negative, into the hands of the chief law officer of the state, the Attorney General. Nonetheless, the plan has worked well and has been favorably received by the vast majority of those concerned.

The Missouri Plan. Desirous of adopting a modified version of the California Plan, and learning a tactical lession from its defeat in popular referenda in 1938 in both Ohio and Michigan, the supporters of the *Missouri Plan* waged a vigorous and enlightened campaign, headed by both professional and lay groups. The movement for its adoption was spearheaded by the Missouri Institute for the Administration of Justice, an educational corporation composed of one-third lawyers and two-thirds laymen, who successfully enlisted the active support of civic, labor, farm, and business organizations. They explained to the electorate the true purpose of the plan: to secure an intelligent and impartial selection of personnel for the bench, to eliminate as much as possible the haphazard results of the elective system, and to relieve the judges of the pressures of political campaigning. And the supporters of the plan pointed out prudently that neither the California nor the Missouri Plan was designed to supplant the elective method entirely—that this was clearly a compromise between appointment and election. Characterized by the American Bar Association as the "most acceptable substitute available for direct election of judges," the plan became law in the form of an amendment to Missouri's Constitution in 1940.

The Missouri Plan is mandatory for the judges of the Missouri

Supreme Court, all other state appellate courts, the circuit and probate courts in St. Louis and in Jackson County, and the St. Louis Court of Corrections. It is optional, subject to popular referenda, in the thirty-eight other circuits of the state. Thus, judges of a number of courts, especially those of the lower levels, may well remain outside the compromise plan, as do the judges in California. Under the Missouri version, nonpartisan nominating boards known as the Missouri Appellate Commissions, operating on different court levels, select *three* candidates for every vacant judgeship. For the Supreme Court and the appellate courts, the commission consists of the Chief Justice of the State Supreme Court, the chairman; three lawyers, elected by the state bar, one from each of the three courts of appeals; and three citizens *not* members of the bar, appointed by the Governor, again on the basis of one from each of the three appellate districts. The commissions for the circuit and other lower court judges comprise the presiding judge of the court of appeals district in which the circuit happens to be situated; two members of the bar elected by its own members residing in the circuit involved; and two similarly resident nonbar citizens appointed by the Governor. The members of all these nonsalaried commissions are designated for staggered six-year terms of office, with changes taking effect in alternate years. Since the Governor has a four-year term and cannot succeed himself, it is thus impossible for him to appoint all of the lay members. To ensure an additional degree of impartiality, commissioners are permitted to hold neither public office nor an official position in a political party.

The Governor of Missouri is obliged to choose *one* of the three individuals selected by the Appellate Commission and appoint him for *one year*, as under the California Plan. After this probationary period, the appointee must offer himself to the electorate for a full twelve-year term (in the appellate courts) or six-year term (in the trial courts), running unopposed on a separate, nonpartisan judicial ballot at the time of the general election. The question on the ballot, very similar to that of California, is "Shall Judge . . . of the . . . Court be retained in office? Yes ( ) No. ( ) (Scratch one)."

Generally deemed to be the most adult and most commendable system of judicial selection extant in the various states, the Missouri Plan embraces a number of commendable features. It combines the democratic notion of accountability to the electorate with an intelligent method of selecting qualified candidates for judicial office. The necessity of facing the electorate on his record provides the judge with an incentive of judiciousness, and the fact that he runs on his own record rather than against that of an opponent allied with a specific political party goes far toward taking the courts out of the more crass aspects of politics. On the other hand, a case could be made for the contention that the awareness of establishing a "good record" for the electorate's eyes and ears may lead to timid and/or "popular" judgments. The results of the Missouri Plan in action, however, do not generally support that theory.

An examination of the election returns for a number of years demonstrates the over-all acceptance of the plan by Missouri's electorate. In 1942 the state went Republican, but two judges of the Supreme Court, both Democrats, were retained by a favorable vote of 2:1; six circuit court judges in St. Louis were similarly returned for new full terms in that same election. In 1944 Missouri went Democratic, yet two judges of the Supreme Court, one a Republican and one a Democrat, received the same proportion of the popular vote. In 1946 St. Louis went Republican, but retained its ten circuit judges, all Democrats, seven of those rolling up 4:1 majorities. In 1948 the state went Democratic, yet of the two judges retained by Kansas City by an identical vote of 5:1, one was a Democrat and one a Republican. In St. Louis, in the same general election, five Democratic and one Republican circuit judge were returned for full terms of office, the Republican and two Democrats receiving 4:1 votes, the other three Democrats 3:1.[12]

From November 1940 through March 1960, some forty-four appointments were made by four governors of Missouri: *only one* of these was to replace a judge *rejected* by the vote of the people! The political parties have respected the plan and, by and large, have made no effort to influence elections under it. The plan has been strongly defended also by the judges, who find themselves in a position to attend to their court dockets free from worries and pressures about forthcoming political campaigns.

Since 1958 a number of states have adopted variations of the Missouri Plan. Kansas, which long elected all judges on a partisan ballot, now permits its Governor to appoint the judges of the Kan-

sas State Supreme Court from a list submitted to him by a nominating commission, with the judges subsequently either approved
or rejected at the next general election. When Alaska became a
state in 1958, its Constitution contained a provision allowing the
Governor to appoint the judges of the Supreme and Superior
Courts from a list of two or more nominees per vacancy submitted
by a judicial council. After three years the judges run for re-
election on their record for terms of ten and six years, respectively.
Iowa and Nebraska adopted the Missouri Plan in 1962, Illinois's
electorate approved a similar scheme by referendum in 1964, and
Colorado one in 1966. As indicated above, there has been scat-
tered acceptance on sundry local levels.[13] A good many other
states, including Oklahoma, Vermont, North Dakota, Minnesota,
New York, and Indiana have evinced considerable interest in the
California and Missouri schemes—as has Pennsylvania, whose
Pennsylvania Plan, a mixture of those of California and Missouri,
has been widely studied of late, but has not been adopted anywhere,
least of all in Pennsylvania.[14]

The two leading plans described represent what is probably a
happy compromise between the appointive and elective systems of
selection, and they have deservedly engendered considerable support among professionals and laymen. Yet most students of the
political scene are inclined to agree that in a representative democracy the appointive system is the more desirable one for the judiciary, provided it is backed up by long—preferably for life—tenure
and it possesses a genuine degree of independence.[15] Even when
one constructs a pattern based on party allegiance, it becomes evident that *appointed* judges are *much* more willing to "vote" against
"their" party on the bench than are elected judges.[16] The appoint-

13 See p. 36, *supra.*

14 But its Governor W. W. Scranton broke precedent in 1964 by becoming the
first state Governor to create a Judicial Nominating Commission by executive
order. He subsequently nominated five state judges from a list of fifteen names
submitted to him by the seven-member commission.

15 There are notable exceptions: Stuart Nagel, for example, argues in an interesting article, "Political Party Affiliation and Judges' Decisions," LV *American
Political Science Review* 850 (December 1961), that "if judges should have
value positions that are representative of the public at large, then it seems
arguable that judges (at least on the higher court levels) should be elected,
since presumably a judge elected at large will tend to have more representative
values than a judge chosen in another manner."

16 Ibid. pp. 848–9.

ing authority is not beyond accountability—and there is no meaningful substitute for effectively lodged governmental responsibility in a free society. As it has been well said elsewhere, "on balance our judicial system still represents primarily a compromise between representatives and neutral compromise."[17]

TENURE OF OFFICE

Essential to the independence of the judiciary is the security of tenure, particularly in the case of appointed judges—our main concern here. Without a lengthy term of office, preferably life, decent remuneration, and stringent constitutional and/or statutory safeguards against removal the concept of judicial independence becomes a mockery. The record of the three major Western democracies in this regard described in these pages has been laudatory generally, and their practices at the level of the national judicial hierarchies are relatively similar.

THE UNITED STATES

At the *federal* level of the United States of America all judges of the *constitutional* courts—those appointed under the provisions of Article III of the Constitution (the judicial article)—hold their positions during the aforementioned "good behavior," which in effect means for life or until they choose to retire. The other federal judges—those of the *legislative* courts, created under the provisions of Article I of the Constitution (the legislative article)—occupy their positions for whatever period Congress may have prescribed at the time of its establishment of the court or in subsequent legislation. In some instances this has meant "good behavior" tenure for them too, but also, and at least as frequently, terms of office ranging between four and fifteen years. The constitutional judges have the additional safeguard, required by the basic document in Article III, that their ". . . compensation . . . shall not be diminished during their continuance in office." Hence, while their salaries may be increased during their incumbency, they may not be lowered—short of a constitutional amendment of the section

[17] Herbert Kaufman, *Politics and Policies in State and Local Governments* (Englewood Cliffs, N. J.: Prentice-Hall, Inc., 1963), p. 60.

concerned. And were a judge of a constitutional court to be removed from office other than in the manner expressly permitted by the Constitution, his salary would indeed be rather drastically "diminished."

Although far from commensurate with the responsibilities and prestige of their office, and infinitely lower than comparable positions in private enterprise, judicial salaries are passably adequate. In 1967 the annual range on the federal level—as will be demonstrated in more detail in Chapters IV and V—was from $30,000 for judges of the United States Customs Court to $40,000 for the Chief Justice of the United States Supreme Court, his associates receiving $500 less. But it is hardly for financial gain that a person would aspire to high judicial office. (Compared with those of federal judges, the salaries of state judges are surprisingly good, ranging from an *average* of $22,500 for appellate courts down to $18,500 for all courts in 1967—with New York paying as much as $41,000.)

Partly to enable aging jurists to step down from the bench in dignity, and concurrently render their replacement with younger personnel more palatable, Congress enacted a vastly improved retirement statute in 1937. Under its provisions, federal judges may retire—a more accurate description is "enter inactive status," subject to temporary calls to duty at the discretion of the Chief Justice of the United States—on full pay at the age of seventy after having served ten years on the federal bench, or at sixty-five after having served fifteen years.[18] These requirements are waived in the presence of physical disability, in which case retirement pay is computed in accordance with length of service. Widows and dependents receive an annual purse equivalent to 37½ per cent of the judge's average salary.

[18] More than half of the justices served fifteen years or more on the highest bench. An official example of an assignment order directed to a "retired" member of the Court is the following, issued by Mr. Chief Justice Warren to retired Associate Justice Stanley Reed: "Assignment Order: An order of the Chief Justice designating and assigning Justice Reed (retired) to perform judicial duties in the United States Court of Claims beginning November 1, 1965, and ending June 30, 1965, and for such further time as may be required to complete unfinished business, pursuant to 28 U.S.C. Section 294 (A), is ordered entered on the minutes of this court, pursuant to 28 U.S.C. Section 295." (Quoted as it was published in *The New York Times*, October 19, 1965.) Late in 1965 *retired* Justice Charles E. Whittaker submitted his *resignation* in order to accept a legal position with the General Motors Corporation.

Despite the liberal provisions of the act, the average federal judges—in particular, the judge of the Supreme Court—are reluctant to leave active service. Far more vacancies occur as the result of death in harness, particularly at the higher levels. Of the eighty-nine Supreme Court vacancies between 1789 and 1967, death in office was responsible for forty-eight with forty-one representing voluntary retirement—although since the passage of the 1937 statute of twenty-two vacancies, the latter was responsible for fifteen. It is human to cling to power and influence, and particularly so to a role of such significance and general esteem.

Removal. Apparently, the removal of federal judges wishing to remain on the bench is to date possible by the process of impeachment and conviction only—although it is evidently legal for the Judicial Council of a United States Circuit to discipline one of its federal judges by stripping him of his duties and authority while permitting him to retain both his title and his salary.[19] In accordance with constitutional requirements, impeachment for "Treason, Bribery, or other High Crimes and Misdemeanors"[20] may be voted by a simple majority of the members of the House of Representatives, followed by conviction by a vote of two-thirds of the members of the Senate present and voting, there being a quorum on the floor. To date, the House of Representatives has initiated a total of twelve such impeachment proceedings, of which nine were directed against federal judges (eight others resigned before formal charges were lodged against them); one against United States Senator William Blount of Tennessee in 1789 (charges were dismissed in 1790 for want of jurisdiction, the Senate already having expelled him on grounds of conspiracy to seize Spanish Florida and Louisiana with British and Indian help); one against President Andrew Johnson in 1868 (who was acquitted by the margin of one courageous vote); and one against Secretary of War William Belknap in 1879 (who was subsequently acquitted).

Of the nine impeachment trials involving federal judges, five resulted in acquittals and four in actual removals. The former, briefly sketched below, are headed, both chronologically and in impor-

19 This was done by the Tenth Circuit's Judicial Council in the case of Oklahoma federal district court judge Stephen S. Chandler in January 1966. He unsuccessfully appealed to the U. S. Supreme Court for review. (*Chandler v. Judicial Council of the Tenth Circuit*, 382 U. S. 1003 (1966).)

20 Article II, Section 4.

tance, by the sole impeachment trial to date involving a justice of the Supreme Court, Associate Justice Samuel Chase.

(1) Samuel Chase. A staunch and partisan convert to the Federalist cause from Maryland, one of President Washington's last two appointments to the Supreme Court, Mr. Justice Chase was impeached by the House in November 1804. He had made himself obnoxious to the Jeffersonians and others by a long series of injudicious and partisan attacks against them, both on and off the bench; by his "tyranical trials [of opponents] under the Alien and Sedition Law [of 1798]," and by his obvious general favoritism toward Federalists. His was indeed not a happy judicial posture, but he had not committed any impeachable offense per se. Accordingly, he was justly acquitted by the Senate by a four-vote margin in March 1805, with Vice President Aaron Burr presiding and Mr. Chief Justice Marshall as an important defense witness. The result represented not only a signal victory for the narrow interpretation of the impeachment process but also for an independent judiciary. Chase remained on the highest bench until his death in 1811.[21]

(2) James H. Peck, a judge of the U.S. District Court for the District of Missouri, impeached in April 1830, acquitted in January 1831 by a vote of 22:21.

(3) Charles Swayne, a judge of the U.S. District Court for the Northern District of Florida, impeached in December 1904, acquitted in February 1905.

(4) George W. English, a judge of the U.S. District Court for the Eastern District of Illinois, impeached in November 1926, but proceedings in the Senate were dismissed when the accused resigned his office.

(5) Harold Louderback, a judge of the U.S. District Court for the Northern District of California, impeached and acquitted in May 1933.

Four impeachment trials, however, did result in conviction, with the first of these probably unjust, the second questionable, and the third and fourth justified:

(1) John Pickering, a judge of the U.S. District Court for the District of New Hampshire, was impeached for "insanity" by the

---

[21] For an authoritative commentary and interpretation see Richard Tillich, "The Chase Impeachment," 4 *American Journal of Legal History* 49 (1960).

House in March 1803 and removed from office by the Senate by a 19:7 vote in March 1804, although the language of the impeachment article of the Constitution, as noted above, does not provide for removal for such a reason. John Adams categorized the Pickering removal as "an infamous and certainly an illegal conviction." Indeed, the unfortunate Pickering had been hopelessly insane and an alcoholic for three years.

(2) *West H. Humphreys*, a judge of the U.S. District Court for the Middle, Eastern, and Western Districts of Tennessee, impeached for "support of secession" and removed by the unanimous vote of 38:0 in June 1862.

(3) *Robert W. Archbald*, an associate judge of the U.S. Commerce Court—which was abolished in 1915—impeached in July 1912 for "taking favors from litigants" and removed in January 1913. No final record roll call was taken by the Senate; the *viva voce* vote in favor of conviction satisfied the presiding officer that the "ayes" had it on seven of the thirteen counts. (An earlier, preliminary record roll call vote had found him guilty on six.)

(4) *Halsted L. Ritter* was the last jurist to be both impeached and convicted. A judge of the U.S. District Court for the Southern District of Florida, he was impeached by the House in April 1936 on seven counts of "bringing his court into scandal and disrepute." Shortly thereafter, the Senate acquitted him on six of the seven counts, but found him guilty as charged on the seventh by a vote of 56:28.

The undoubtedly fortunate paucity of success of the impeachment process is not, however, an indication of lack of verbal efforts by legislators who, partly sincerely and partly for constituent consumption, are eager to "get" federal judges—usually for decisions repugnant to them for a variety of reasons—in particular the justices of the Supreme Court. To cite but one modern example: In June 1953 a special subcommittee of five members was created by the House of Representatives to consider the impeachment of Mr. Justice William O. Douglas of the Supreme Court. Introduced by Congressman W. M. Wheeler (D.-Ga.), the resolution for impeachment charged the jurist with "high crimes and misdemeanors in office" for having granted a brief stay of the scheduled execution of the convicted atom spies, Julius and Ethel Rosenberg—a stay dissolved by the full Court almost at once. Nothing came of Mr.

Wheeler's efforts.[22] Nor are these efforts confined to the people's representatives. In February 1959 a group of some two dozen men and women filed with the Clerk of the House of Representatives a petition to impeach the entire membership of the Supreme Court; it consisted of foot-long pages, headed "Impeach Warren," a battle cry taken up with a vengeance by the John Birch Society in subsequent years. And in a colorful brochure decorated with its state flag, Georgia's[23] General Assembly distributed "A Resolution Requesting Impeachment of Six Members of the United States Supreme Court"—namely Justices Warren, Black, Reed, Frankfurter, Douglas, and Clark (Burton, Harlan, and Brennan escaping somehow). The main charge: "Unconstitutional . . . pro-Communist racial integration policies."[24]

The great majority of *states* follow the federal pattern regarding removal of their appointed judges who have lengthy or life tenure, with impeachment and conviction being the normal process available. Among the few states that have found it necessary to resort to it are Tennessee in the case of Criminal Court Judge Raulston Schoolfield for "corrupt and injudicious conduct" in 1958, and Oklahoma in the case of its Supreme Court Justice Napoleon Bonaparte Johnson in 1965. But a good many other modes of removal exist in various states. In Massachusetts and New Hampshire judges may be removed by address of the Governor to both houses of the legislature; in California, Utah, Washington, and Wisconsin by a joint resolution of the legislature; in Texas, Louisiana, Alabama, and Michigan removal power is vested, on varying terms, in the state supreme courts; in Oklahoma (since 1966), Michigan, Illinois and New York special courts are provided to hear removal charges. In New York the court is known as the *Court on the Judiciary*, created by constitutional amendment in 1947 (until then the state legislature held the removal power). After having heard its first case in 1960, in which it voted not to remove either of the

---

22 In July 1966 Rep. George W. Andrews (D.-Ala.) introduced another unsuccessful impeachment resolution against Douglas, this time on the grounds of his "character" in view of the then sixty-seven-year-old Justice's fourth marriage (to a twenty-three-year-old girl). He was joined by Reps. Paul Findley (R.-Ill.) and Thomas G. Abernathy (D.-Miss.).

23 A "Warren Impeachment Packet" was widely advertised by the Society. For $1.00 postpaid it could be purchased from "The Movement to Impeach Earl Warren," Belmont 78, Mass.

24 H.R. No. 174, "A Resolution," adopted on February 22, 1957, pp. 3–12.

two judges brought before it for removal action—Kings County Court jurists Nathan R. Sobel and Samuel S. Leibowitz—the Court did oust New York Supreme Court Justic Louis L. Friedman and New York Claims Court Judge Melvin H. Osterman in 1963 in two separate actions.[25] In several western states, sitting judges may be recalled from office by popular vote[26]—an intriguing and controversial manifestation of "direct democracy," of which the referendum and the initiative are both illustrations.

BRITAIN

Having come a long way since the days of and before James I (1603–25) and Charles I (1625–49), when the English judges held their office *durante bene placito nostro* ("according to our good pleasure"), English judges today, very much like their cousins in the United States, enjoy what to all intents and purposes is tenure for life. The custom of appointing judges for indefinite terms of office during their "good behaviour," dates back to the Act of Settlement of 1701, which provided that judge's "commissions" be made *quam diu se bene gesserint* ("as long as they will have performed well"). One significant recent change must be noted, however. As a result of the mandate of the Judicial Pensions Act of 1959, a seventy-five year retirement limit for judges of the superior courts has been adopted for all future appointments at that level, and a seventy-two-year limit, with possible three-year extension, for those of the county courts—who had already been recognized by the County Courts Act of 1934, as amended by that of 1959. Retirement pensions are paid on a graduated scale that rises from one-quarter of basic salary after five years of service to a maximum of half of the last annual salary after fifteen years.

25 Friedman was removed by a 4:2 vote for having engaged in "unethical judicial conduct and violation of the "concept, spirit, and letter" of the canons of judicial ethics. He unsuccessfully appealed for U. S. Supreme review (*Friedman v. Court on the Judiciary*, 375 U. S. 10 (1963), *certiorari* denied). Osterman was removed by unanimous vote for his refusal to sign a waiver of immunity and answer questions before a New York grand jury investigating the 1963 New York State liquor license scandals. His appeal to the U. S. Supreme Court also met with a denial of review (*Osterman v. Court on the Judiciary*, 376 U. S. 914 (1964), *certiorari* denied).
26 For details see the informative article by Sheldon D. Elliot, "Court-Curbing Proposals in Congress," 33 *Notre Dame Lawyer* 597 (August 1958).

48

For practical purposes, the English judges, notably those of the superior courts, are irremovable, the Judicature Act of 1925 providing that all judges, except the Lord Chancellor, hold office "during good behaviour subject to a power of removal by His [now Her] Majestry on an address presented to His [now Her] Majesty by both Houses of Parliament."[27] However, the judges of the county courts are deemed to be removable at the insistance of the Lord Chancellor for "inability" and "misbehavior" under various statutes, e.g. the County Courts Act of 1959. The justices of the peace are also removable for similar reasons of "misconduct" or "proved incapacity." In effect, the English judges are not protected in any way from a change by statute; Parliament retains, of course, its fundamental power to alter their tenure and emoluments of office. Suffice it to say that it is highly unlikely to do so in a detrimental sense! In any event, a dismissal of a judge for political reasons is impossible today for all practical purposes. Indeed, the *sole removal* of an English judge since the Act of Settlement of 1701 on any grounds took place in 1830 (although official complaints have been lodged against seventeen), when Sir Jonah Barrington, a superior judge—a judge in admiralty—was deprived of his office by petition of both houses of Parliament as a result of an inquiry into the Irish courts of justice carried out during that year.

The salaries of the judges, which range between £5300 (for judges of the County Court) and £14,500 (for the Lord Chancellor, who receives £9500 for being a judge and £5000 for being Speaker of the House of Lords), are set by Act of Parliament. The executive branch may not move to reduce these while the recipients hold office, and the legislature is similarly enjoined since judicial salaries do not even come up for parliamentary review. A further indication of effective judicial independence is the parliamentary custom that no questions at all may be asked about the conduct of courts in particular cases. Moreover, according to two court rulings now firmly regarded as *res judicata* in England,[28] a judge may not be held for civil or criminal proceeding because of anything he may have said or done in his judicial capacity, even if it is alleged to have been malicious or in bad faith. Given these

27 Jackson, loc. cit. p. 258.
28 *Anderson v. Gorrie*, 91 L.J.K.B. 897 (1922) and *Heddon v. Evans*, 35 T.L.R. 642 (1919).

cherished safeguards of judicial strength and independence, the English bench has reciprocated in full measure with a record of efficiency and impartiality not likely to be readily matched anywhere in the free world today. Well might Sir Ivor Jennings contend in 1954 that "no allegation" of partiality or corruption or political influence is ever made against judges of the United Kingdom.[29]

FRANCE

The career judges of the Fifth French Republic who, as we have seen, comprise a branch of the national civil service, also have life tenure. There is no doubt that they are at least as secure today as are their English and American counterparts. But it took a considerable while to attain that cherished goal. During the *ancien régime* judicial office went customarily to the favorites of the monarch and especially to those who could afford to pay for it. *La révolution* replaced that interesting system of patronage *cum* purchase with popular election of judges—which was not much of an improvement, if any. Napoleon Bonaparte grandly eliminated that method and announced the principle of "irremovability," which, in practice, meant rather complete dependency on him. A period of minor changes and ameliorations was affected by the institutions and individuals that succeeded the colorful Corsican until the days of the Third Republic barely a century ago, when the status of the French judges improved without, however reaching a truly separate status.

Irremovability as an avowed policy for the career judiciary was resuscitated by a proclamation of the Provisional Government a few days after V-E Day in 1945. It was made a part of the basic document of the de Gaulle Republic by the specific verbiage of the Constitution of 1958, which asserts that these judges are "irremovable." Actually, that is technically incorrect, for they *are* removable—but solely for "misconduct in office," and then only upon the recommendation of the High Council of the Judiciary, which acts as a disciplinary court for judges. When it sits as such, the President of the *Cour de Cassation* is its presiding officer.

29 *The Queen's Government* (London: Penguin Books, 1954), p. 147.

The judges of France are not so well paid as those across the English Channel,[30] but there is no evidence that they are in any sense more susceptible to corruption or injudiciousness than their English counterparts. Strengthened even more by the specific proviso of the de Gaulle Constitution making the President of the Republic the "guarantor of the independence of the judicial authority," and the genuine protective power of the High Council of the Judiciary, they enjoy an extensive degree of both professional freedom and authority.

QUALIFICATIONS
AND MOTIVATIONS: THE UNITED STATES

Although attitudes and practices regarding tenure of office do not differ significantly among the American, British, and French judiciaries, substantial, indeed crucial, distinctions become immediately apparent in any consideration of the qualifications—background, experience, and training—of the judges in these three countries. They represent distinctions that flow rather logically from different traditions and theories regarding the role of government in society, and they are attuned to what, for better or for worse, are deemed the needs and experiences of each land. With these thoughts in mind we turn to a consideration of the interesting problem of judicial qualifications in the United States.

BASIC PREREQUISITES?

In contrast to the specialized requirements that obtain in Britain and France, there is but one standardized prerequisite for qualification as a *federal* judge today—the LL.B. degree of the aspirant. The possession of that degree is neither a constitutional nor a statutory requirement for appointment, but custom would automatically veto anyone without it for judicial service at the federal level. Moreover, the legal profession, which, as we have noted, has

30 The average salaries of the French jurists in 1967 ranged from approximately NF 20,000 ($4000) for the lowest to NF 82,000 ($16,400) for the highest echelon, not counting certain allowances that might add up to 20 per cent. (Data provided by the Deputy Director of the *Ministère de la Justice, Directions des Services Judiciaires*, dated September 14, 1967.)

a very real voice in today's appointive process, would remonstrate so determinedly that the political powers of the government involved would assuredly acquiesce. Yet at the *state* and local level not even the LL.B. is necessary in many instances![31]

Theoretically, any graduate of an accredited bona fide school of law with his eye on a federal judgeship may thus look forward to an appointment to the coveted niche—provided that he is politically "available" *and* acceptable to the executive, legislative, and private forces that, in the order enumerated, constitute the powers-that-be which underlie the paths of selection, nomination, and appointment in the judicial process. In the final analysis, of course, it is the President and his immediate advisers concerned—here the Attorney General and his Deputy—who take the crucial step of submitting the nominee to the Senate. Thus, all of America's chief executives, except William Henry Harrison, Zachary Taylor, and Andrew Johnson, have had an opportunity to designate at least one nominee for membership in the highest court of the land—which will be our chief concern in these particular pages. Of the exceptions, the first two were removed too quickly from the scene by death, and Johnson was the victim of congressional machinations which successfully prevented him from filling several Supreme Court vacancies. Table I illustrates the number of justices each President appointed and who *actually served*, including those not ultimately confirmed by the Senate. An example of the latter is John Rutledge's designation as Chief Justice by President Washington in 1795. The Senate refused by a vote of 10:14 to confirm the President's recess appointment of the man whom it had approved as Associate Justice in 1789, but who had resigned that post two years later without ever sitting in order to accept the post of Chief Justice of the Supreme Court of South Carolina) and hence listed as only one Washington appointment). Counting Mr. Justice Rutledge once, and Justices E. D. White, Hughes, and Stone twice, since the latter three all actually served both as Associate Justice *and* Chief Justice and were appointed by a different President in each instance, the ninety-six individual justices who had served on the Court as of the beginning of the 1967–68 term provided thirty-two Presidents with ninety-nine successful appointments.

31 See Ch. IV, infra, pp. 139–42 and fns. 5 4–6.

JUDICIAL EXPERIENCE AND ITS ABSENCE

In view of the minimal, formal basic requirement, it is hardly astonishing that many a newly appointed United States jurist lacks practical judicial experience.[32] Among the appellate courts this has been especially true of United States Supreme Court designees—those of the court level immediately below, that is, the United States (Circuit) Court of Appeals, have often had some lower court experience on the United States District Court—the federal trial court. Among the ninety-six individual justices who had served on the Supreme Court between 1789 and the end of 1967, only twenty had had ten or more years of previous judicial experience on any lower level, federal or state, at the time of their appointment, and forty had no judicial experience whatsoever. Yet, as Table II demonstrates the totally inexperienced group contains many of the greatest and most illustrious names in America's judicial history. Among them are six of the fourteen Chief Justices (eight if one does not "count" Hughes's and Stone's years as Associate Justices) —Marshall, Taney, S. P. Chase, Waite, Fuller, and Warren—and Associate Justices such as Story, Miller, Bradley, Brandeis, and Frankfurter, to name a few.

In a learned essay, calling for selection of Supreme Court justices "wholly on the basis of functional fitness," Mr. Justice Frankfurter argued keenly that not judicial experience nor political affiliation nor geographic considerations ought to play a significant role in the appointment of these highest jurists, whose job he viewed as necessarily requiring the qualities of *philosopher*—"but not too philosophical," commented his student Paul A. Freund—*historian, and prophet.*[33] Thus he asserted:

> One is entitled to say without qualification that the *correlation between prior judicial experience and fitness for the Supreme Court is zero*. The significance of the greatest among the Justices who had such experience, Holmes and Cardozo, derived not from

---

[32] By way of contrast, in addition to other requirements, nominees to the intermediate appellate judiciary in Pakistan, for example, must have a minimum of ten years of judicial experience; and they need fifteen years for appointment to the Pakistan Supreme Court (including five years at the intermediate appellate level).

[33] To which, in a conversation with the author in May 1954, Mr. Justice Brennan added "inordinate patience."

TABLE 1

NUMBER OF PRESIDENTIAL APPOINTMENTS OF UNITED
STATES SUPREME COURT JUSTICES WHO ACTUALLY
SERVED ON THE COURT (arranged chronologically)

President	Number of Successful Appointments
Washington	10
J. Adams	3
Jefferson	3
Madison	2
Monroe	1
J. Q. Adams	1
Jackson	6
Van Buren	2
W. H. Harrison	0
Tyler	1
Polk	2
Taylor	0
Fillmore	1
Pierce	1
Buchanan	1
Lincoln	5
Johnson	0
Grant	4
Hayes	2
Garfield	1
Arthur	2
Cleveland	4
B. Harrison	4
McKinley	1
T. Roosevelt	3
Taft	6
Wilson	3
Harding	4
Coolidge	1
Hoover	3
F. D. Roosevelt	9
Truman	4
Eisenhower	5
Kennedy	2
Johnson	2
	99

TABLE II

PRICE JUDICIAL EXPERIENCE OF U. S. SUPREME
COURT JUSTICES AND THEIR SUBSEQUENT SERVICE

Justice	Year Appointed	Number of Years of Prior Judicial Experience			Years of Service on Supreme Court
		Federal	State	Total	
Jay*	1789	0	2	2	6
J. Rutledge*	1789 and 1795*	0	6	6	½
Cushing	1789	0	29	29	21
Wilson	1789	0	0	0	9
Blair	1789	0	11	11	7
Iredell	1790	0	½	½	9
T. Johnson	1791	0	1½	1½	2
Paterson	1793	0	0	0	13
S. Chase	1796	0	8	8	15
Ellsworth*	1796	0	5	5	4
Washington	1798	0	0	0	31
Moore	1799	0	1	1	5
Marshall*	1801	0	0	0	34
W. Johnson	1804	0	6	6	30
Livingston	1806	0	0	0	17
Todd	1807	0	6	6	19
Story	1811	0	0	0	34
Duval	1811	0	6	6	24
Thompson	1823	0	16	16	20
Trimble	1826	9	2	11	2
McLean	1829	0	6	6	32
Baldwin	1830	0	0	0	14
Wayne	1835	0	5	5	32
Taney*	1836	0	0	0	28
Barbour	1836	6	2	8	5
Catron	1837	0	10	10	28
McKinley	1837	0	0	0	15
Daniel	1841	4	0	0	19
Nelson	1845	0	22	22	27
Woodbury	1845	0	6	6	6
Grier	1846	0	13	13	24
Curtis	1851	0	0	0	6
Campbell	1853	0	0	0	8
Clifford	1858	0	0	0	23
Swayne	1862	0	0	0	19
Miller	1862	0	0	0	28

*Indicates Chief Justice and date of his appointment and/or promotion.

TABLE II (*Continued*)

Justice	Year Appointed	Number of Years of Prior Judicial Experience			Years of Service on Supreme Court
		Federal	State	Total	
Roberts	1930	0	0	0	15
Cardozo	1932	0	18	18	6
Black	1937	0	1½	1½	
Reed	1937	0	0	0	19
Frankfurter	1939	0	0	0	23
Douglas	1939	0	0	0	
Murphy	1940	0	7	7	9
Byrnes	1941	0	0	0	1
R. H. Jackson	1941	0	0	0	13
W. Rutledge	1943	4	0	4	6
Burton	1945	0	0	0	13
Vinson*	1946	5	0	5	7
Clark	1949	0	0	0	18
Minton	1949	8	0	8	7
Warren*	1953	0	0	0	
Harlan	1955	1	0	1	
Brennan	1956	0	7	7	
Whittaker	1957	3	0	3	5
Stewart	1958	4	0	4	
White	1962	0	0	0	
Goldberg	1962	0	0	0	3
Fortas	1965	0	0	0	
Marshall	1967	3½	0	3½	

* Indicates Chief Justice and date of his appointment.

that judicial experience but from the fact that they were Holmes and Cardozo. They were thinkers, and more particularly, legal philosophers.[34]

And on this point, Mr. Justice Frankfurter has been fond of quoting the distinguished Judge Learned Hand, who for so many years rendered outstanding service on the United States Court of Appeals for the Second Circuit (New York, Connecticut, and Vermont), but who never attained his richly merited promotion to the Supreme Court:

[34] Felix Frankfurter, "The Supreme Court in the Mirror of Justices," 105 *University of Pennsylvania Law Review* 781 (1957). (Italics supplied.)

I venture to believe that it is as important to a judge called upon to pass on a question of constitutional law, to have a bowing acquaintance with Acton and Maitland, with Thucydides, Gibbon and Carlyle, with Homer, Dante, Shakespeare and Milton, with Machiavelli, Montaigne, and Rabelais, with Plato, Bacon, Hume, and Kant as with books which have been specifically written on the subject.[35]

Attitudes Toward Experience. Yet the experience factor for Supreme Court justices, although more or less dormant during some Administrations, such as those of President Franklin D. Roosevelt, is sometimes revitalized by others, as it was by that of President Eisenhower. Roosevelt paid little, if any heed to it, whereas Eisenhower, after his intial appointment of Mr. Chief Justice Warren, insisted that his nominees have at least *some* judicial experience, no matter how slight. Of the nine men who sat on the Court as a result of President Roosevelt's appointments (or promotion to Chief Justice in the case of Stone), neither Mr. Chief Justice Stone nor Associate Justices Reed, Frankfurter, Douglas, Byrnes, and Jackson had any judicial experience whatsoever, while Mr. Justice Rutledge served on the Court of Appeals for the District of Columbia for four years, and Justice Black served one and a half years and Justice Murphy seven years on state tribunals. President Truman followed his predecessor's habit of ignoring judicial background: of his four appointees, Associate Justices Burton and Clark had none at all, Mr. Chief Justice Vinson had five years, and Associate Justice Minton had eight years of prior service on the lower federal bench. President Eisenhower's four appointees subsequent to that of the Chief Justice, Associate Justices Harlan, Brennan, Whitaker, and Stewart, all had seen some prior service although the total number of years for the four comprised but fifteen. Neither Associate Justices White and Goldberg, appointed by President Kennedy, nor Fortas appointed by President Lyndon B. Johnson, had any judicial experience.

Congress, too, is hardly of one mind on the matter of the necessity or even the desirability of judicial experience as a prerequisite for appointment to the highest court in the land. Bills are continually introduced that would require future nominees to the Supreme

[35] As quoted in *The New York Times Magazine*, November 28, 1954.

Court to have upwards of five years of experience on lower court benches. In the 89th Congress, for example, thirteen bills of this type were sponsored by members on both sides of the aisle in both houses of Congress. But all of these measures failed of enactment. Moreover, many legislators agree with what is clearly a majority of the closest observers of the Supreme Court as well as with the thesis of Mr. Justice Frankfurter just described, that judicial experience, because of the peculiar nature of that Court's work, is not essential. The Supreme Court is not a trial court in the sense of the federal district courts below, nor is it called upon to deal with a particular judicial constituency as are these courts of first instance and, to a considerably lesser extent, the federal courts of appeals that lie immediately above the district courts in the judicial hierarchy. Further, there is very little transition or connection between the experience in the lower and the highest federal constitutional court —the procedural and jurisdictional frameworks are quite different. The type of private litigation at common law, so prevalent below, is practically extinct at the bar of today's Supreme Court; the latter is almost exclusively occupied with questions of public law, led by cases at constitutional law or with constitutional overtones, review of administrative actions, and other related questions. Experience on the courts below may well be theoretically desirable —although there are some observers who would not even grant that much—but it should not become a *requirement* for qualification for the Supreme Court. Again returning to Mr. Justice Frankfurter and Judge Learned Hand, the business of the Supreme Court today is "with the application of rather fundamental aspirations," what Judge Hand called *moods*, that are embodied in constitutional provisions such as the due process of law clauses of the Fifth and Fourteenth Amendments—clauses and concepts that were quite evidently deliberately designed "not to be precise and positive directions for rules of action." In the well-chosen words of Mr. Justice Frankfurter:

> The judicial process in applying them involves a *judgment on the processes of government*. The Court sits in judgment, that is, on the views of the direct representatives of the people in meeting the needs of society, on the views of Presidents and Governors, and by their construction of the will of legislatures *the Court breathes*

life, feeble or strong, into the inert pages of the Constitution and the statute books.[36]

Small wonder that this function calls for a combination of philosopher, historian, and prophet.

A Case Study. A brief survey of the judicial experience factor in connection with the members of the 1967–68 Supreme Court may aid in demonstrating that even if that specific qualification is largely, or even wholly, absent in many instances, experience in other relevant areas of public service is often abundantly present. Of the members of that 1967–68 Court, which began its term on October 2, 1967, only five had past judicial experience, and in all but one of these cases it was rather negligible. Thus, Mr. Justice Black served eighteen months as a police judge in his native Alabama; Mr. Justice Harlan had one year on the U.S. Court of Appeals for the Second Circuit; Mr. Justice Stewart had four years of service on the U.S. Court of Appeals for the Sixth Circuit; and Mr. Justice Marshall had three and a half years on the Second Circuit Court of Appeals. Only Mr. Justice Brennan, a protégé of longtime New Jersey Chief Justice Arthur T. Vanderbilt, with a record of seven years on State of New Jersey benches, could lay claim to relatively extensive judicial background. Mr. Justice Black was appointed by President Franklin D. Roosevelt in 1937 at the age of fifty-one; the next three were elevated to the Supreme Court by President Eisenhower in 1955, 1959, and 1956, when they were fifty-six, forty-three, and fifty years old respectively; and Mr. Justice Marshall was appointed by President Johnson in 1967.

Yet *all* of the members of the 1967–68 Court had a record of considerable experience in public life, frequently of an administrative nature, in addition to or in place of whatever judicial experience they might have had. Thus, upon his designation as Chief Justice at the age of sixty-two by President Eisenhower in 1953, Earl Warren had practised law and then devoted thirty-four years of his full life to public office, eleven of these as Republican Governor of California—always with strong bipartisan support. Mr. Justice Hugo L. Black had practised law for seventeen years and had been a Democratic Senator from Alabama for ten when he was appointed to the Court. Mr. Justice William O. Douglas had prac-

36 Frankfurter, loc. cit., at 793. (Italics supplied.)

tised law, taught it for almost a decade, and had been both a member and chairman of the U.S. Securities and Exchange Commission for three years when President Roosevelt appointed him in 1939 at a youthful forty-one (only four justices were appointed at a younger age). Before he entered the federal judicial service in 1954, Mr. Justice John Marshall Harlan, the bearer of his grandfather's proud name, had practised private law and had served the State of New York in a host of capacities over a period of thirty years. Mr. Justice William J. Brennan, Jr., had practised law for fifteen years, was a decorated army officer during World War II, and had served the State of New Jersey when Governor Driscoll appointed him to the state bench in 1949. Mr. Justice Potter Stewart had practised law for more than a decade and had served on the City Council of Cincinnati for five years, when he first entered the federal judiciary in 1954. Byron R. White—that rare phenomenon of both Rhodes Scholar and professional athlete (known as "Whizzer White")—had practised law for fourteen years and was U.S. Deputy Attorney General when his wartime friend President Kennedy sent him to the highest bench in 1962 at the age of forty-five. Abe Fortas, sent to the Court as the first Johnson appointment, in 1965, to succeed Arthur J. Goldberg, brought with him years of experience in the Department of Interior and Agriculture and on the faculty of the Yale Law School, and had had an eighteen-year-long senior partnership in one of the foremost law firms of the nation, Arnold, Fortas, and Porter. And President Johnson's second appointment, Thurgood Marshall—the first Negro to reach the highest Court—had practised law for three decades, much of it constitutional law at the bar of the Court he was destined to join; had been a nationally known leader in the civil rights movement; had served on the Second Circuit Court of Appeals from 1962 to 1965; and was the U.S. Solicitor-General when the President thus honored him in 1967.

If—for the sake of argument—one were to grant the wisdom of judicial experience as a pertinent requirement for Supreme Court nominees, a background rich in nonjudicial experience, such as that just described, does not compensate in and of itself for the lack of actual experience on a lower bench. However it does indicate that the men—there have been no women on a federal court level *higher than* the Court of Appeals (the first was Judge Florence

Allen of the Sixth Circuit[37])—who come to the Supreme Court of the United States, and for that matter to the lower federal courts, have had lengthy *legal* experience. Moreover, *all* of the 96 individuals who have sat on the highest bench, except Mr. Justice George Shiras (1892–1903), had engaged in at least *some* public service at various level of government, often elective, or had actively participated in political activity. Nevertheless, unlike the jurists of France, for example, it remains true that a great many among the judges of the major courts in the United States have not been primarily trained as judges per se. England relies on still another system, to be discussed presently. Table III indicates the occupations of the individuals (using the full figure 99 here) as of the time of their appointment to the Supreme Court.

TABLE III
OCCUPATIONS* OF SUPREME COURT
DESIGNEES AT TIME OF APPOINTMENT†

Federal Officeholder in Executive Branch	21
Judge of State Court	21
Judge of Inferior Federal Court	19
Private Practice of Law	17
U. S. Senator	8
U. S. Representative	4
State Governor	3
Professor of Law	3
Associate Justice of U. S. Supreme Court§	2
Justice of the Permanent Court of International Justice	1

* Many of the appointees had held a variety of federal or state offices, or even both, prior to their selection.

† In general, the appointments from state office are clustered at the beginning of the Court's existence, those from federal office are more recent.

§ Justices White and Stone, who were *promoted* to the Chief Justiceship in 1910 and 1930, respectively.

37 As of the fall of 1967, of the 472 federal judgeships then extant, only five were held by women. (The first female federal judge was the Coolidge-appointed Genevieve R. Cline to the United States Customs Court in New York in 1928.) Judge Allen was appointed to the Sixth Circuit by President Roosevelt in 1934 from her position as the first woman on the Ohio State Supreme Court. She became Chief Judge of the Circuit in 1958—another "woman's first"—and retired from the bench at the age of seventy-five in 1959. She died in 1966. Her earliest trail-blazing feat as a woman was her service on the Cleveland (Ohio) Court of Common Pleas from 1920 to 1922, whence she was elected to the seven-member Ohio Supreme Court. She had served for two six-year terms when F.D.R.'s call to the federal bench came.

THE JUSTICES IN COMPOSITE

Whatever individual exceptions may be applicable, and keeping in mind the subjective attitude many an observer brings to bear on the members of the Supreme Court of the United States and their decisions, the caliber of that so select group has been universally high. Indeed, no other unit on the scene of American government could easily match its general record of competence and achievement. An over-all analysis of the background and characteristics of the 96 justices to date (1967–68 term) would produce the following "composite":

> White (the first Negro was appointed in 1967); generally Protestant (there have been six Catholic and five Jewish justices); fifty to fifty-five years of age at the time of appointment; Anglo-Saxon ethnic stock (all except six); high social status; reared in an urban environment; member of a civic-minded, politically active, economically comfortable family; B.A. and LL.B. degrees; some type of public office; generally well educated.[38]

MOTIVATIONS UNDERLYING APPOINTMENTS

Regardless of learned commentaries and "inside information" revelations, it is obvious that the only person who knows with certainty why he appointed an individual to the Supreme Court of the United States—and, for that matter, to the lower federal courts, although his involvement is likely to be far less direct there—is the President of the United States who signed the commission. All the student of constitutional law or the historian can do with honesty and conviction is to hazard a reasonable inference based upon the facts at his disposal. It is always possible that this "educated guess" may be utterly erroneous, but there is an excellent chance that it will contain a considerable amount of truth. If this were not the case, the discipline of history, for one, would be a *non sequitur*. These thoughts as to the uncertainty of a specific analysis govern even when the President may have stated orally

[38] For two studies corroborating this "composite," see John R. Schmidhauser, "The Justices of the Supreme Court: A Collective Portrait," 3 *Midwest Journal of Political Science* 1 (1959) and his *The Supreme Court: Its Politics, Personalities and Procedures* (New York: Holt, Rinehart and Winston, Inc., 1960), Ch. 3, *passim.*

or in writing that he nominated X for reason Y, for the assertion may be but an attempt to conceal the rationale for the appointment; in any event, Y may well contain only a portion of the truth.

Even more relevant for present purposes than these thoughts is the patent fact that there is normally more than simply one motive behind any human decision. Idealism, altruism, and selfishness are all constituent aspects of the human personality, and a particular action may result from the interplay of a myriad of motivations arising from each or all of these factors. In other words, the reasons for the appointment to the Supreme Court by a particular Chief Executive of a particular individual are usually multiple rather than single, although one motive may, of course, be predominant. Generally speaking, five factors have been taken into account, singly or severally, by the thirty-five presidents when making selections for the ninety-nine vacancies that existed during the history of the Court down to the end of 1967. They are the same factors that may be expected to govern lower appointments as well, but they stand out more, and are more "interesting" when applied to the level of the highest bench, where appointments naturally come infrequently. Other factors exist, of course; no claim to exclusiveness is made at all, but the five that follow—not necessarily in order of importance—represent unquestionably those of greatest moment: (1) objective merit; (2) political availability of the designee; (3) his ideological appropriateness; (4) personal factors; and (5) geographical, religious, and other socio-political considerations. Something should be said about each of these, and some examples given.

(1) Objective Merit. This factor simply poses the question of whether the candidate possesses the ability and the background essential to an understanding of the complicated questions that come before the Court—Mr. Justice Frankfurter would here require his trinity of philosopher-historial-prophet—and/or is blessed with the creative imagination that a Supreme Court justice ought to have. To determine whether or not the individual under consideration does possess these qualifications, the President could look to the nominee's basic intellectual capacity, his reputation for legal scholarship, his competence in a particular area of law, his experience as a judge, lawyer, or public official, his reputation in and out of his vocational sphere, his temperament. Age may well also be relevant here. If the potential nominee is too young, he

may be deemed to lack maturity of judgment and wisdom; if he is too old, he may retire or die before he has acquired the experience—one may call it the style—necessary to bring to the fore his full talent as a member of that tribunal. Judge Learned Hand, universally recognized as one of the jewels in America's judicial crown, was usually regarded as "too old" when he was deemed "politically available," which he was never deemed to be when there was no issue of age.

On the other hand, some critics of President Eisenhower's ultimately successful nomination of Mr. Justice Potter Stewart held him to be "too young"—he was barely forty-three. Yet practically all of the other factors loomed favorable: although a solid Eisenhower Republican, having campaigned vigorously for the President in both 1952 and 1956, he had actively supported the presidential aspirations of Ohio's Senator Robert A. Taft, "Mr. Republican" himself, in 1948 and 1952; he was a personal friend of Ohio's Senator John Bricker who sponsored him; he had established a fine record during his brief service on the Sixth Circuit Court of Appeals, and his opinions were regarded as examples of superior legal writing by the Department of Justice as well as by at least some of his future colleagues; his father was Chief Justice of the Supreme Court of Ohio; he had enjoyed public service; and he was viewed as acceptable to both the liberal and conservative groups who knew his record. His confirmation by the Senate by a vote of 70:17 in 1959 was delayed for four months and received such sizable opposition, all from Southern Democrats, solely in the light of the latter's general antipathy toward the Supreme Court at that time because of the segregation-integration controversy and the nominee's fairly obvious sympathy with the Court's position. The opposition was not directed against the nominee personally.

Probably the most illustrative example of the objective merit factor and its recognition by the bar, the public, and the political elements alike was that of Mr. Justice Cardozo, whose selection was all but forced upon President Hoover by the country, and who was confirmed unanimously by the Senate the instant the nomination reached the floor. This despite the fact—conceivably detrimental or even fatal in the case of other nominees, depending upon circumstances—that the nominee came from New York, already "represented" on the bench at that time by Mr. Chief Justice

Hughes and Mr. Justice Stone, and that he was Jewish, a religion already "represented" by Mr. Justice Brandeis. Hoover raised these points during a command-visit by Republican Senator Borah of Idaho, chairman of the Committee on Foreign Relations, who had been very vocal in urging the Cardozo appointment—along with many others, including Mr. Justice Stone. (The latter, who was to play a major role in persuading the President to designate the man whom he had introduced to him initially, even offered to resign his own seat on the Court if that was what it would take to see his fellow New Yorker nominated.) Hoover handed Senator Borah a list, indicating the names of several prominent individuals he was considering for the vacancy on the Court left by Mr. Justice Holmes's resignation. The last name on the list was that of the Chief Judge of the New York State Court of Appeals, Benjamin N. Cardozo. "Your list is all right," commented Senator Borah, "but you handed it to me upside down!"[39] When the President then strongly urged that his visitor consider the geographical situation involved, and mentioned "possible religious and sectarian repercussions," Senator Borah told him in no uncertain terms that "Cardozo belonged as much to Idaho as to New York" and that geography should no more bar him than the presence of two Virginians on the high bench—John Blair and Bushrod Washington—should have prevented President John Adams from naming John Marshall Chief Justice.[40] Furthermore, Borah told Hoover, ". . . anyone who raises the question of race [sic] is unfit to advise you concerning so important a matter."[41] When the President bowed to what was all but unanimous professional as well as popular clamor for the Cardozo appointment, he became the recipient of much praise, typical of which was Senator Clarence Dill of Washington's remark that ". . . when President Hoover appointed Judge Cardozo . . . he performed the finest act of his career as President."[42]

(2) and (3) Political Availability and Ideological Appropriateness. These two criteria often go hand in hand. They include considerations such as whether the choice of an individual will render the President popular, or more popular, among certain groups

39 Claudius O. Johnson, *Borah of Idaho* (New York: Longman's, Green and Co., 1936), p. 452.
40 *The New York Times*, January 30, 1932.
41 Johnson, loc. cit. p. 453.
42 *The New York Times*, March 2, 1932.

in the body politic; whether the President is indebted to the potential nominee for political services rendered; whether the nominee has been a loyal member of the President's political party; whether, as was so true of President Kennedy's selection of White in 1962,[43] he favors the President's policies and programs—his *Weltanschauung*—regardless of his party membership; and whether he is acceptable, or at least not "personally obnoxious," to the kindred home state politicos, notably those in the Senate. It is a rather firmly adhered to unwritten law of the judicial nominating process at the level of the Supreme Court, that as a rule, the President will not normally select a man from the political opposition. To assuage charges of "packing the courts" below, this rule is relaxed purposely now and then at the level of the federal district courts and even at that of the courts of appeals, but only within "political reason." Nevertheless, it has also happened twelve or thirteen times on the Supreme Court including two promotions to Chief Justice—a ready explanation being present in all instances: Whig President John Tyler appointed a Democrat, Samuel Nelson, and Republican Presidents Abraham Lincoln, Benjamin Harrison, William H. Taft, Warren G. Harding, Herbert Hoover, and Dwight D. Eisenhower appointed eight Democrats—Taft alone three! The eight justices and their nominators were Stephen J. Field (Lincoln); Howell E. Jackson (Harrison); Horace H. Lurton (Taft); Edward D. White, promotion to Chief Justice (Taft); Joseph R. Lamar (Taft); Pierce Butler (Harding); Benjamin N. Cardozo (Hoover); and William J. Brennan, Jr., (Eisenhower). And Democratic Presidents Woodrow Wilson, Franklin D. Roosevelt, and Harry S Truman appointed three Republicans: Louis D. Brandeis (Wilson); Harlan F. Stone, promotion to Chief Justice (Roosevelt); and Harold H.

---

43 As *Washington Star* reporter James E. Clayton reported the decision: "Thinking back on the process months later, the Attorney General [Robert F. Kennedy] tilted back in his chair and said: 'You wanted someone who generally agreed with you on what role government should play in American life, what role the individual in society should have. You didn't think about how he would vote in a reapportionment case or a criminal case. You wanted someone who, in the long run, you could believe would be doing what you thought was best. You wanted someone who agreed generally with your views of the country.' Both he and the President believed that White and Arthur J. Goldberg met that test. They could not be as sure of the others on the list [Paul A. Freund of Harvard University and Judge William H. Hastie of the U.S. Court of Appeals for the Third Circuit]." Quoted in Clayton's *The Making of Justice: The Supreme Court in Action* (New York: E. P. Dutton & Co., 1964), p. 52.

Burton (Truman). Some would add as a thirteenth case President Franklin D. Roosevelt's appointment of Mr. Justice Frankfurter, who labeled himself an Independent.

Crossing Party Lines. The naming of Nelson by President Tyler came after Tyler had been defeated by Democrat James K. Polk in the election of 1844. Eager to have history show at least one of his own nominees attain the Supreme Court, the "lame duck" Tyler after three of his four first Whig choices had to be withdrawn because of obviously decisive opposition and the fourth one, John Spencer of New York, was rejected by the Senate 26:21, then named Nelson, who had not been an active political figure.

In 1863 *Field*, who was to serve longer than anyone else to date on the Supreme Court, 34½ years, was chosen by Lincoln, largely for three reasons: First, Field came from California, a part of the country not then represented on the Court, and even though he was Buchanan Democrat, Lincoln felt his nominee would help to "fuse" the Northern cause by preserving the loyalty of California and strengthening political ties. Second, Field's many influential friends, including Leland Stanford, put considerable pressure on the President. Third, Field's brother, David Dudley Field, a bitter and vocal opponent of slavery, had played a considerable role both in the organization of the Republican party and in Lincoln's nomination as its standard-bearer in 1860.

Harrison's choice of *Jackson* was motivated by reasons similar to those that governed the Tyler-Nelson case. Cleveland had already defeated Harrison when the vacancy on the Court occurred, the Democratic Senate was in no mood to confirm the Republican lame duck President's partisan choice, and, happily, Harrison and Jackson, who had served in the Senate together, were close friends —as were their wives.

The Taft appointments of *Lurton* and *Lamar* and his promotion of *White*, all three Southern Democrats appointed by a good Republican, are attributable to a combination of personal friendship or esteem, ideological kinship, and politico-sectional expediency. Taft and Lurton had served together for eight years on the U. S. Circuit Court of Appeals for the Sixth Circuit, where they became fast friends. Taft, who was its Chief Judge, was very much impressed with the legal and judicial ability of the Tennessee Democrat who had succeeded him as Chief Judge when the future President went to the Philippine Islands. Conservative kinsmen, they were usually at one in their opinions from the bench and in their general philosophy of government. Taft called the nomination of his friend Lurton "the chief pleasure of my administration."[44] Although Joseph R. Lamar of Georgia was not as close to Taft personally as Lurton, he readily met the Taft standards of conservatism and his general ideological bent. For example, the two men saw eye to eye on the tariff—a matter of the utmost importance to the President. And Taft saw in the appointment of the Confederate Army veteran an additional opportunity for strengthening his position among Southern political leaders who, if they would not vote for him at election time, would at least help him with his legislative program. He promoted White—then in his seventeenth year on the Court—in part because he considered him the ablest administrator among the justices on the bench; in part because his fellow justices apparently had petitioned the President to designate him rather than Hughes,[45] who had seemed to have the proverbial inside track ("White, Not Hughes, for Chief Justice," was the front-page headline in *The New York Times*[46] when the announcement was made); and in large part because in Taft's eyes he had voted "right" on the bench—among his votes there was one to uphold a military tariff in the Philippine Islands at the time Taft was Governor there.[47]

Wilson's hotly contested nomination of *Brandeis*, a registered Massachusetts Republican, was confirmed by the Senate by a vote margin of 47 to 22, after a delay of more than four months. Of the 47 affirmative votes 44 were cast by the 45 Democratic Senators present and voting; the three Republican votes in favor came from Senators La Follette (Wisc.), Norris (Neb.), and Pointdexter (Wash.). Twenty-one of the 22 negative votes came from the Republican Senators then present and voting.[48] The lone Democratic

---

[44] Silas Bent, *Justice Oliver Wendell Holmes* (New York: Garden City Publishing Co., 1932), p. 248.

[45] George Shiras, 3d, *Justice George Shiras* (Pittsburgh: University of Pittsburgh Press, 1953), p. 130.

[46] December 12, 1910.

[47] Cf. William Howard Taft, *Our Chief Magistrate and His Power* (New York: Columbia University Press, 1916), pp. 99–102.

[48] Among these were illustrious and powerful men such as: Henry A. du Pont, Henry Cabot Lodge, George Sutherland (a future colleague of the nominee!), Warren S. Harding, and Albert B. Fall. Of the remaining twenty-seven Senators, twelve—all Republicans—were paired *against*; twelve—ten Democrats and two Republicans—*for*; and three Senators were absent.

negative vote was cast by Senator Francis G. Newlands of Nevada. Twenty-seven Senators including the influential Borah, did not vote at all.[49] Brandeis, the famed "People's Lawyer," as Wilson was fond of calling him, was a personal friend of the President and a close ideological ally—a political and social liberal who shared Wilson's philosophy of life and government and who had worked hard for him in the 1912 campaign. It was primarily these two factors and his great regard for Brandeis's character and ability that prompted Wilson to ignore the sectional factor (Massachusetts was then already "represented" by Holmes); possible repercussions because of the nominee's religion (he became the first person of Jewish persuasion to reach the Supreme Court); and the danger during the 1916 election year of designating a controversial personage such as Brandeis in the face of the violent opposition of the most influential segment of the bar and the business community, particularly of his New England home base. Ironically, despite his convictions regarding the "curse of bigness," Mr. Justice Brandeis never wrote an opinion in favor of the Government in an antitrust case!

Harding's choice of Butler points to three motives. First, the President liked his record of almost four decades of service in the law and in public life; second, and probably most important, Harding found Butler's ideological ultra-conservatism to be entirely sympathetic—he became one of the two leading avowed reactionaries on the bench; and third, the President deemed it politically advantageous to appoint a man who combined what would seem to be the desirable factor of being a "safe" Democrat—most Democrats refused to regard Butler as one of their number in roughly the same fashion as the Republicans did Brandeis—with that of being a member of a then "unrepresented" minority religion (Roman Catholic) and a native Minnesotan, only the second nominee born west of the Mississippi to reach the bench. Initially rejected by the Senate, Butler was renominated by Harding on the following day and ultimately won confirmation easily—though veritably scorched by large segments of the public press.

The *Cardozo* appointment by Hoover has already been discussed; he was literally forced upon the President, who eventually

---

[49] For a fascinating account of the Brandeis nomination and confirmation battle, see A. L. Todd's *Justice on Trial: The Case of Louis D. Brandeis* (New York: McGraw-Hill Book Co., 1964).

came to be proud, indeed, that he had named this model public servant to the "Holmes seat."

President Franklin D. Roosevelt promoted *Stone*—who had been one of his professors at Columbia University Law School—largely as a manifestation of unity in the face of the incipient war crisis. When Mr. Chief Justice Hughes announced his intention to retire, speculation as to his successor revolved around Stone and the then Attorney General Robert H. Jackson. Roosevelt's heart was on the side of Jackson, but he deemed it wiser and more appropriate at this juncture of history to name Stone. In fact, he discussed the matter with Jackson who agreed and later, having become an Associate Justice of the Court, wrote that the need for judicial leadership and the "desirability for a symbol of stability as well as of progress" were evidently the reasons for Stone's elevation "in the interest of the [fostering of the] judiciary as an institution."[50] Morevoer, the retiring Chief Justice himself had strongly urged Stone's elevation on the basis of his record, and suggested that Roosevelt consult Mr. Justice Frankfurter in the matter. Frankfurter told the President:

> . . . when war does come, the country should feel you are a national, the Nation's President, and not a partisan President . . . [to bolster this assessment] you [should] name a Republican, who has the profession's confidence, as Chief Justice.[51]

President Truman's nomination of *Burton*—the first of his four —is often far too readily dismissed merely as a reward to "an old Senate crony.[52] Unquestionably, Truman's personal fondness of the Republican Senator from Ohio and mayor of Cleveland, who had served so well and so closely with the then Senator Truman on the latter's Special Committee To Investigate the National Defense Program, the "Truman Committee," was a factor in the appointment. But there were assuredly others: the advice given to the President that he designate a Republican to replace the retiring Mr. Justice Roberts, a Republican; Mr. Chief Justice Stone's advance approval of the nominee because of his valuable legisla-

50 Alpheus T. Mason, *Harlan Fiske Stone: Pillar of the Law* (New York: The Viking Press, 1956), p. 573.
51 Ibid. p. 567.
52 For example, see Glendon A. Schubert, *Constitutional Politics* (New York: Holt, Rinehart and Winston, Inc., 1960), p. 38.

tive experience; Truman's belief in Burton's judicial temperament; the absence of anyone from Ohio on the bench; the fact that the nominee's Senate seat would be filled by a Democrat, as indeed it subsequently was by the incumbent Governor Lausche through a rather unpredictable Democrat); plus the faithful support Burton had given to the Democratic party on foreign policy, and even on some domestic policy, throughout his tenure in the Senate.

Last is the designation of *Brennan* by Eisenhower, who chose this New Jersey Democrat for a variety of reasons. The President's initial choice had been that state's able Chief Justice, Arthur T. Vanderbilt, who had achieved an outstanding national reputation as head of the then recently reorganized New Jersey court system. Because of his advanced age and his failing health, Vanderbilt declined (he died in 1957) but highly recommended the nomination of his colleague and protégé, Associate Justice Brennan of the State Supreme Court. This recommendation was strengthened by the support of Secretary of Labor James Mitchell, a New Jersey Republican, the two Republican Senators from New Jersey, Clifford P. Case and Alexander H. Smith, and of Democratic Governor Robert B. Meyner. Moreover, it was the very eve of the 1956 election, and the choice of a Roman Catholic from the metropolitan East would hardly hurt the President in the impending campaign. With only Republican Senator Joseph R. McCarthy of Wisconsin voting "no," the Brennan nomination was confirmed by the Senate in March 1957.

The emphasis placed above on the twelve or thirteen deviations from membership in the political party of the appointing President is not intended to convey the impression that there is a national trend in that direction. Far from it! There will presumably always be some crossing of party lines, particularly at the district court level, in order to maintain over-all harmony, to placate the opposition, and to establish a measure of bipartisanship, but the practice may be safely predicted to remain exceptional. After all, as many a President has been told by his political advisers, Republican or Democratic as the case may be, ". . . why should we give these plums to the other guys? . . . surely there are just as many good and deserving lawyers on *our side of the fence.*" More often than not this is probably true, and no doubt political patronage will continue to govern as an appointment-maxim in the judicial process. Thus, Wilson appointed 73 Democrats and 1 Republican to the federal courts; Harding, Coolidge, and Hoover selected 198 Republicans and 20 Democrats; F. D. Roosevelt 194 Democrats and 13 Republicans; Truman 128 Democrats and 13 Republicans; Eisenhower 178 Republicans and 11 Democrats; Kennedy 105 Democrats, 10 Republicans, and 1 member of the New York State Liberal party; and by October 1967 President Johnson had sent 130 Democrats and 10 Republicans to the federal bench. It is simply axiomatic that judicial appointments will go predominantly to members of the party in power. However, when it comes to nominees to the Supreme Court, of the greatest importance to the designating President is what Theodore Roosevelt referred to as the nominee's "real politics"—of which more below.

(4) Personal Factors. Although it is perhaps something of an oversimplification, the basic point here is the close personal regard the President may have for an individual—a factor that may well override all other considerations. Although this concept is understandably impossible to measure, there is no doubt that it has played, and will continue to play, a very real role in individual cases. As we have already seen, it figured prominently in President Taft's appointment of Mr. Justice Lurton and, somewhat less so, in those of Mr. Justice Burton by President Truman and Mr. Justice Brandeis by President Wilson. Some other obvious examples of the personal friendship factor's undoubted significance are the Truman nominations of Mr. Chief Justice Vinson and Associate Justices Clark and Minton—it was probably *the* crucial factor in the latter appointment, although Minton was, of course, a good Democrat and had seen eight years of service, however colorless, on the federal appellate bench—and the L. B. Johnson appointment of his long-time friend and adviser, Abe Fortas (who also conveniently happened to be Jewish), to the seat vacated by Mr. Justice Goldberg's transfer to the post of United States Ambassador to the United Nations.

(5) Geographical, Religious, and Other Socio-Political Considerations. We have already observed in the case of several nominees that a President is less likely to look favorably upon a candidate who comes from an area in which reside one or more justices already on the Court. But, again, if he is determined to appoint a certain individual—for example, President Wilson's choice of Mr. Justice Brandeis—geography will not be permitted to stand in the

way. And in the case of Mr. Justice Cardozo, the country would not *permit* President Hoover to allow it to do so. It might well be argued that the consideration of geography is relevant merely to the political propriety of the appointment and, thus, should be relegated to the second and third categories discussed above. However, the notion that all sections of the country should be "represented" on the Court—to date the justices have come from thirty of the fifty states—has the advantage of being equitable as well as having a political appeal, Mr. Justice Frankfurter's eloquent demurrer notwithstanding. Furthermore, in the earlier days of the Republic when the justices used to ride circuit, it was obviously desirable to appoint for a given circuit a jurist who would be familiar with its area. The last appointees to the Supreme Court literally to ride circuit were Associate Justices John Catron, John McKinley, and Peter V. Daniel, who came to the Court in 1837, 1837, and 1841, respectively, all Van Buren appointees. Geographical considerations, in other words, must not be regarded as the equivalent of political considerations, and should hence be viewed as related to equitable factors generally.

TABLE IV
THE 30 STATES FROM WHICH
THE 99 SUPREME COURT APPOINTMENTS WERE MADE

New York	13	Illinois	3
Ohio	10	North Carolina	2
Massachusetts	8	Iowa	2
Tennessee	7	Michigan	2
Pennsylvania	6	New Hampshire	1
Kentucky	5	Maine	1
Maryland	5	Mississippi	1
New Jersey	4	Kansas	1
Virginia	3	Wyoming	1
South Carolina	3	Utah	1
Connecticut	3	Minnesota	1
Georgia	3	Texas	1
Alabama	3	Indiana	1
California	3	Missouri	1
Louisiana	3	Colorado	1

The same considerations apply, both more and less, to the religious factor. It is at once closely related to the political factor and represents one of the equitable considerations that have entered the governmental sphere. It is undoubtedly here to stay, for better or for worse—and surely for worse in this instance. Hence there exists the notion of both a "Roman Catholic" seat and a "Jewish seat" on the Supreme Court. Not a healthy development, the religious-group representation concept has become one of *the* facts of American political life, and it was probably a foregone conclusion that it would one day reach the Court as well. Although less of a problem or consideration there than in the make-up of election slates where, in some instances, such as the City of New York, it has become a maxim of politics, religious affiliation is a definite factor regarding Supreme Court nominees. With the exception of the seven years between Mr. Justice Murphy's death in 1949 and Mr. Justice Brennan's nomination in 1956—when, perhaps oddly in view of the charges of "politics" so frequently voiced against him, President Truman evidently deliberately ignored the practice—members of *both* the Roman Catholic and the Jewish faith have been on the Court ever since Mr. Justice Brandeis's ascent in 1916. (Roman Catholic: Mr. Chief Justice Taney, Mr. Chief Justice White, Associate Justices McKenna, Butler, Murphy, and Brennan; Jewish: Associate Justices Brandeis, Cardozo, Frankfurter, Goldberg, and Fortas.) The first Roman Catholic to be appointed was Mr. Chief Justice Taney[52] in 1835, by President Andrew Jackson, and since Mr. Justice McKenna's appointment by President McKinley in 1898, a member of that faith has always

TABLE V

ACKNOWLEDGED RELIGION OF THE 96 INDIVIDUAL JUSTICES OF THE SUPREME COURT (at time of appointment)

Unspecified Protestant	25
Episcopalian	24
Presbyterian	16
Unitarian	6
Roman Catholic	6
Baptist	5
Jewish	5
Congregationalist	3
Methodist	3
Disciples of Christ	2
Quaker	1

[52] Taney married a Protestant, Anne Key of Frederick, Maryland. They had seven children, all of whom eventually joined Protestant churches.

been on the Court, save for the seven-year interval of the Truman Administration. Whatever the merit or demerit of the religious factor, it will very l'kely remain as one of the elements of the socio-political aspects of judicial appointments that the nominating authorities, rightly or wrongly, have decided to take into account. And a new factor, that of *race*, entered upon the scene when in June 1967, on the retirement of Mr. Justice Clark, President Johnson designated as his replacement the first Negro ever to be nominated to the Supreme Court—the then U.S. Solicitor-General, Thurgood Marshall. The President, leaving no doubt that the nominee's race was a major, if not *the* major, factor in his selection, told the country: "It is the right thing to do and it is the right time. He is the right man in the right place."

"Packing the Court" and the Nominees' "Real Politics"

Regardless of the significance and the role each or all of the five factors may play in the President's selection of justices of the Supreme Court and the lower courts, especially at the highest level, the most important consideration is the nominee's "real politics"— his future voting behavior on the bench. If an appointing President had the power of clairvoyance coupled with that of a check upon the judicial decision-making process, that consideration would present no problem; but in their absence it is entirely normal for him to endeavor to "pack" the bench to a greater or lesser extent.

The practice of "packing," or of filling vacancies with individuals presumably safely of the President's own views and persuasion, has been associated in the popular mind most prominently with President Franklin D. Roosevelt, who presided over the transition of the "Old" to the "New" Court from 1937 on. Deaths and resignations permitted him to fill nine vacancies—a total exceeded only by President Washington. Moreover, his attempt to have his way all at once by virtue of his "Court Packing Bill" of 1937—which was reported adversely by the Senate Judiciary Committee and was defeated on the floor by a vote of 70:20 to recommit to the Committee—designed to permit him to appoint an additional justice for each incumbent above seventy years of age up to a total Court membership of fifteen, has closely linked him with the packing concept. Yet it is an historical fact that Presidents Jefferson, Jackson, and Lincoln, facing similar problems of what they viewed as Court opposition, followed solutions that were basically analogous. And the first President, George Washington himself, who is somehow placed on a pedestal far removed from what the public usually views as "politics," insisted that his nominees to the Supreme Court—and he nominated ten, even eleven if John Rutledge is counted twice—meet the following five criteria: (1) advocacy of federalism; (2) a record of active support of the Revolution, preferably as a "fighting participant"; (3) "fitness"; (4) past judicial service; (5) proper geographical apportionment. Every President is necessarily guilty of some packing—it is merely a matter of degree. In short, similarities of view of nominator and nominee are understandably and customarily a controlling factor; membership in the same political party is one as well, and an important one, as are some of the other factors discussed earlier—but far less so than that of the nominee's "real politics." *That* uncertain quantity once caused President Truman to observe with considerable justice that ". . . packing the Supreme Court can't be done, because I've tried it and it won't work. . . . Whenever you put a man on the Supreme Court he ceases to be your friend. I'm sure of that."[53] Most appointing authorities have come to that general conclusion, which is to the credit of the hallowed institution of judicial independence. And they may well be advised to heed the admonition of Professor Chafee that in order to forecast the behavior of a future jurist it is wiser to consider the books in his library than the list of his clients in his law office.

The Nominee's "Real Politics." One of those who endeavored to probe hard for that crucial factor on sundry occasions was President Theodore Roosevelt—and not always successfully. In discussing a potential nominee with his good friend, Republican Senator Henry Cabot Lodge of Massachusetts, the "All-American Boy President" put the matter well:

> . . . the *nominal* politics of the man [Horace H. Lurton, a Democrat] has nothing to do with his actions on the bench. His *real* politics are all important. . . . He is right on the Negro question; he is right on the power of the federal government; he is right on the Insular business; he is right about corporations; and

[53] Lecture at Columbia University, April 28, 1959. (Reported in *The Philadelphia Bulletin*, April 29, 1959.)

he is right about labor. On every question that would come before
the bench, he has so far shown himself to be in much closer touch
with the policies in which you and I believe.[54]

Although concurring in substance, Lodge replied, however, that
he could not "see why Republicans cannot be found who hold
those opinions as well as Democrats,"[54] and he strongly supported
the candidacy of another possibility for the position, the Republican
Attorney General, William H. Moody of Massachusetts, whom
Roosevelt then nominated. (Lurton, as we have seen, was subsequently sent to the Court, anyway—as the first appointment of
another Republican, President Taft.)

Nevertheless, in the words of that eminent student of the Supreme Court, Charles Warren:

> . . . nothing is more striking in the history of the Court than the
> manner in which the hopes of those who expected a judge to
> follow the political views of the President appointing him have
> been disappointed.[55]

Few felt the immediate truth of that statement more keenly than
did "Teddy Roosevelt with his nomination of the great Oliver
Wendell Holmes, Jr., whose early "anti-Administration" opinions
in anti-trust cases, notably in the *Northern Securities* case,[56] were
entirely unexpected.[57] President Madison was similarly chagrined
with his appointment of Mr. Justice Story in the face of Jefferson's
warning that the nominee was a Tory, and as predicted by Madison's political mentor, Story not only became an immediate supporter of John Marshall, their political and judicial nemesis, but
he even "out-Marshalled" the Chief Justice in his nationalism. Yet
perhaps the clearest example of an appointee who proved to be the
veritable antithesis of everything his appointor believed in and stood
for was the Woodrow Wilson-selected Mr. Justice McReynolds.

54 Henry Cabot Lodge, *Selections from the Correspondence of Theodore Roosevelt and Henry Cabot Lodge, 1884–1918* (New York: Charles Scribner's Sons,
1925), Vol. II, p. 228, and pp. 230–31.
55 *The Supreme Court of the United States*, rev. ed. (Boston: Little, Brown and
Co., 1926), Vol. II, p. 22.
56 *Northern Securities v. United States*, 193 U. S. 197 (1904).
57 "T. R." was furious about Holmes's "anti-anti-trust" vote in that case and
reportedly stormed: "I could carve out of a banana a Judge with more backbone than that!"—hardly a very appropriate remark in the light of Mr. Justice
Holmes's lifelong reputation. (As quoted by Clayton, op. cit. p. 47.)

Surely, there is a very considerable element of unpredictability
in the judicial appointing process. To the oft-heard "Does a man
become any different when he puts on a gown?", Mr. Justice
Frankfurter's pungent reply was always: "If he is any good, he
does!" As for the Chief Executive, he is of necessity a politician
and the leader of his party as well as the leader of the nation. To
play the first two roles successfully, he must pay at least some
attention to "politics"—real and nominal—in his choice of judges.
But he will probably be a failure in the judge-naming role if he
employs only that criterion in making his selections.

TABLE VI
AVOWED POLITICAL AFFILIATION OF THE 99
APPOINTED SUPREME COURT JUSTICES (at time of selection)

Federalists	13
Whig	1
Democrats	48
Republicans	36
Independent	1

ON THE ROLE OF THE UNITED STATES SENATE

Enough has been said throughout these pages about the general
role of the Senate in the judicial appointive process to obviate an
extended discussion. But a few additional comments would seem
to be called for, especially regarding lengthy delays in confirmation
and rejection of presidential nominees to the highest bench.[58]
There is no question, of course, that the Senate possesses a veto
over a nomination to the Court—and to the lower federal courts.
Certainly in theory, it may exercise this veto for whatever reason
it chooses—and it has done so on occasion. "Senatorial courtesy,"
described earlier, looms large here, particularly at the level of the
federal district courts, where the patronage factor is more overt
and more prominent than higher up. Conversely, the Senate will
almost inevitably treat as a *cas d'honneur* the presidential designation of one of their own members to the Supreme Court—witness

[58] These points are discussed in considerable detail in Henry J. Abraham and
Edward M. Goldberg, "A Note on the Appointment of Justices of the Supreme
Court of the United States," 46 *American Bar Association Journal* 147 (Feb-
ruary 1960) and, more generally, in Robert B. McKay, "Selection of United
States Supreme Court Justices," 9 *Kansas Law Review* 109 (No. 2, 1960).

the cases of the then Senators Byrnes of South Carolina and Burton of Ohio. Byrnes was confirmed unanimously without even being scrutinized by the Committee on the Judiciary, that stern and powerful stumbling block of quite a few nominations. And the Burton appointment was confirmed unanimously on the same day it reached the Senate. A notable exception to this unwritten rule was the controversial appointment of Mr. Justice Black by President Franklin D. Roosevelt, which was referred to the Judiciary Committee for full hearings. The initial reason for that unusual action was Senator Black's strong support of the President's Court Packing bill, which was anathema to a majority of the Senate. But the controversy over the nomination was compounded by the subsequent revelation during the committee's hearings that Black had once been a member of the Ku Klux Klan in Alabama. Nevertheless, the committee ultimately voted 13:4 in his favor, Black explained his then-defunct membership in a candid broadcast to the nation, and the Senate confirmed the appointment by a vote of 66:15.

Two aspects of the Senate's role will be considered here: *unusual delays* and *rejections* encountered by appointees to the Supreme Court. Fifteen nominations were characterized by what were clearly "unusual delays." Nineteen failed to win approval—*not* counting the ultimately confirmed though once rejected Justices Paterson, Taney, Matthews, and Butler—of whom nine were rejected outright by an adverse vote on the motion to confirm, whereas in the instances of ten others the Senate either refused to act or "postponed" action, thus resulting in rejection in all but name.

Unusual Delays in Confirmation. For our purposes an "unusual delay" is one which is markedly longer than that which normally took place during the period in which the appointment was made. Thus, a delay of one month in 1826 was as "unusual" as a delay of six months would be today, when a month's delay would be viewed as a common occurrence. An examination of the fifteen nominations at issue indicates not only that the periods of delay have tended to lengthen, but more significantly, that there has been a definite pattern of causes for these unusual delays. In many cases more than one factor played a role in the delay involved, but three causes seemed to be singly or severally present in all.

First, *involvement with a political question or problem*, on which there is a strong feeling on the part of the public, some senators, or organized pressure groups. For example, Mr. Justice Robert Trimble's confirmation was delayed for one month in 1826. During his service on the United States Court of Appeals—he was the first justice of the Supreme Court with a background of prior *federal* judicial experience—he had tended to support national powers at the expense of the states. Hence he incurred the wrath of several prominent "states' rights" senators, including John Rowan from his own state of Kentucky. But despite the latent implications of this early attempt to invoke "senatorial courtesy," Trimble was confirmed, largely due to the stanch support given by Senator Thomas Hart Benton of Missouri and Secretary of State Henry Clay. Mr. Justice Benjamin Curtis's confirmation was delayed for three months in 1851 by senators who believed that he opposed the abolitionist cause and supported the Fugitive Slave Law. It was poetic justice that Curtis turned out to be one of only two members of the Court to oppose the *Dred Scott* decision;[59] in fact he felt so strongly about it and the entire slavery controversy that he resigned from the bench in 1861.

Others whose appointments were delayed because of the political factor were Justices Joseph P. Bradley, by "hard money" Easterners for what was—correctly—believed to be his "soft money" philosophy, for six weeks in 1870; Lucius Q. C. Lamar of Mississippi, by Northern Republicans who disliked and mistrusted the man who had followed his state out of the Union and fought for the Confederacy, for six weeks in 1887; Joseph McKenna by antitrust and anti-railroad interests (and some anti-Catholics) who feared his close friendship with railroad magnate Leland Stanford, for five weeks in 1897; Mahlon Pitney, by labor because of his record as a New Jersey legislator and jurist, for one month in 1912; Louis D. Brandeis, by a host of elements in the legal and business community (and some anti-Semites) because of his long, outspoken activities as a champion of the social and economic underdog, for over four months in 1916—still the longest battle in the history of the Court; John Marshall Harlan, the younger, by ultraconservative groups and a new breed, the professional "anti-Supreme Court" elements, allegedly because of his supposed sym-

59 *Dred Scott v. Sandford*, 19 Howard 393 (1857).

pathy for the cause of world government, for three months in 1955; Potter Stewart, who was made a whipping boy because of emotional reaction to the Court's decisions in the segregation-integration field, for four months in 1958–59; and, in 1967, Thurgood Marshall, by implacable racists: he was the first Negro to be nominated—the great-grandson of a Congo slave.

Second, *opposition to the appointing President*, manifesting itself in opposition to the nominee. Probably the best cases in point here are the appointments of Mr. Chief Justice Roger B. Taney and Associate Justice Philip P. Barbour, whose confirmation in each instance was delayed for two and a half months in 1835. The opposition against the two men was not so much directed against them as nominees as it was against the nominator, President Andrew Jackson. However, the powerful anti-Jackson faction in the Senate—led by the three great names of the time, Clay, Webster, and Calhoun—failed to prevail against Jackson's strong leadership and drive, which was backed by his immense popularity with the electorate.

Third, *personal senatorial vendettas*. Thus, Mr. Justice Robert H. Jackson's confirmation was delayed over a month in 1941, chiefly because of the vehement opposition of Democratic Senator Millard Tydings of Maryland, who had a long-standing personal feud with the nominee, based on the latter's failure as Attorney General to prosecute two Washington columnists for what Tydings alleged was a libelous radio broadcast. Mr. Chief Justice Earl Warren was delayed for almost two months in 1954, chiefly because of a fight against his confirmation by Republican Senator William Langer of North Dakota, a senior member of the Senate's Judiciary Committee. Langer and some Southern Democrats went so far as to impugn the nominee's loyalty because of his alleged "left wing" or "liberal" views. It was then and is now widely assumed that the main motivation for the Langer attack was his long-standing wish to secure the appointment for someone, almost anyone, from North Dakota, Mr. Chief Justice Melville W. Fuller's appointment was held up for two and a half months in 1888, chiefly because of a personal filibuster against the nomination by Senator Edmunds of Vermont, the Republican chairman of the Judiciary Committee, who insisted that President Cleveland had promised him that the position would go to a man from Edmunds's home state, one Edward Phelps. When Cleveland denied this allegation, Edmunds turned the Fuller nomination into a battle of Republicans against Democrats, with Fuller emerging triumphant solely because of the defection of a few Republicans on the vote to confirm. And while his youth (44) and alleged lack of sufficient public experience may have played a role in the six weeks of delay in the confirmation of John Marshall Harlan, the elder, the real reason was the activity of Senators Timothy Howe of Wisconsin and Isaac Christiancy of Michigan, both of whom had unsuccessfully attempted to gain President Hayes's appointment for themselves.

Rejections. Including under this heading so-called postponements, which in fact were never acted upon and/or were withdrawn, an examination of the reasons for these direct or indirect Senate vetoes points to five major factors. Again, more than one factor was often present, but the five to be discussed comprise the principal ones for the rejection on record:

First, *opposition to the nominating President*, manifesting itself in oposition to his nominee. Five chief executives were affected in this way. President John Quincy Adams's nomination of John J. Crittenden in 1828 was "postponed" by the Senate by a strictly partisan vote of 17:23 two months after the nomination. The Democrats in the Senate thus foiled a last-minute Whig appointment by the outgoing President and preserved the vacancy so that it could be filled by the incoming President-elect, Democrat Andrew Jackson. In the cases of President John Tyler's five nominees, John C. Spencer was rejected without a record vote, and action regarding Ruben H. Walworth, Edward King, and John M. Read was postponed by votes of 21:26, 20:27, 18:29, respectively, in 1844–45, chiefly because of the—mistaken—hope and expectation on the part of the Clay Whigs that their leader would win the election of 1844. (*Polk* did.) Action on one of the President Millard Fillmore's nominees, George E. Badger, was postponed indefinitely in 1852, and no action at all was taken on his two others, Edward A. Bradford and William E. Micou. The purpose of these maneuvers was to enable the incoming Democratic President, Franklin Pierce, to fill these three vacancies—yet he suceeded in filling but one of them, falling victim to related senatorial tactics. President James Buchanan's nomination of Jeremiah S. Black was rejected by a vote of 25:26 in 1861 for several reasons, but chiefly because the Republicans wanted to hold the vacancy so that the incoming President Abraham Lincoln could make the nomination. And the seat for which President Andrew Johnson named Henry Stanberry was abolished by Congress in 1866 because of its bitter opposition to the long-suffering President.

Assuredly, in many of these cases, the opposition to the nominee also had other important political connotations in that major policy issues were involved, and these issues were naturally connected with the opposition to the President concerned. Hence it was not, of course, simply blind opposition to, or dislike of, the President which resulted in the rejections.

Second, *involvement with a political question or problem*, on which there is a strong feeling on the part of the public, some senators, or organized pressure groups. Thus, John Rutledge's nomination as Chief Justice in 1795 was rejected by a vote of 10:14. Already serving on a recess appointment, and having been *confirmed* six years earlier as Associate Justice—a position he resigned, however, without ever sitting—Rutledge was rejected primarily because of a speech he had made in opposition to the Jay Treaty. Despite the fact that both he and his nominator, President George Washington, were Federalists, the Federalist Senators refused to confirm a man who had actively opposed the treaty which they supported so wholeheartedly. President James Madison's selection of Alexander Woolcott in 1811 fell 9:24 largely, although not solely, because the Federalists opposed his vigorous enforcement of the embargo and nonintercourse statutes as U. S. Collector of Customs and his extreme partisanship in office. Similarly, President John K. Polk's designation of George W. Woodward was rejected 20:29 in 1845 because of what was termed gross "nativist American Sentiments"; among those opposing him was Senator Simon Cameron from his home state of Pennsylvania.

The nomination of Ebenezer R. Hoar by President Ulysses S. Grant in 1869 was rejected by an adverse Senate vote of 24:33 after seven weeks. Several senators objected to the recommendations Hoar had made as Grant's Attorney General regarding the appointment of nine circuit judges. Others did not care for his support of civil service reform. Again others still smoldered because of his opposition to the impeachment of President Johnson;

few appreciated his forthright independence. The last nominee to be rejected, U. S. Circuit Court of Appeals Judge John J. Parker, designated by President Herbert Hoover in 1930, was the victim of the narrow adverse vote of 39:41. Parker—the 107th Supreme Court nominee as of then—was opposed by organized labor because, as a judge, he had handed down an opinion affirming the upholding of "yellow dog" contracts by a lower court;[60] by Negro groups because he had allegedly made anti-Negro remarks in his campaign for Governor of North Carolina ten years earlier; by Progressive Republicans who deemed his economic views too conservative. Ironically, it was to be Judge Parker who wrote some of the earliest "pro-Negro" opinions in the segregation-desegregation realm, including *Rice v. Elmore*,[61] which sustained United States District Court Judge J. Waties Waring's 1947 outlawing of South Carolina's primary machinations designed to bar Negroes from the polls.[62]

Third, *"senatorial courtesy."* This custom accounted for several rejections. It appears to have been the *sole* factor involved in the unsuccessful nominations of William B. Hornblower and Wheeler H. Peckham of New York by President Grover Cleveland in 1893–94, by adverse votes of 24:30 and 32:41, respectively. In both instances, the rejection was directly attributable to the outspoken opposition of Senator Hill of New York, who was instrumental initially in Hornblower's defeat on grounds of senatorial courtesy, and who successfully applied the same magic concept when Cleveland substituted another New Yorker, Peckham, four months later. The doctrine was also invoked, although on a secondary basis, in the already described cases of Walworth and Woodward.

Fourth, *the limited ability of the nominee*, considered entirely objectively, has played a definite part in some rejections. In the face of swelling protests by the legal profession and the public, President Grant withdrew his 1873 nomination of George H. Williams five weeks after he made it. Williams's talents as a lawyer were mediocre; he had lost several important cases; and the bar simply adjudged him unqualified for this high office. Woolcott's

---

60 *United Mine Workers v. Red Jacket Consolidated Coal and Coke Co.*, 18F.839 (1927), based on a U.S. Supreme Court precedent of 1917 (*Hitchman Coal and Coke Co. v. Mitchell*, 245 U.S. 229).

61 165 F.2d 387 (1947).

62 *Rice v. Elmore*, 72 F. Supp. 516 (1947).

rejection was also due, in part, to the lack of support of his fellow Republicans, who considered him to be a man of limited ability.

Fifth, *political unreliability of the nominee.* The best illustration of this factor in rejections of nominees to the highest bench is another among the several unsuccessful Grant nominations—that of Caleb Cushing. Nominated in 1874, after the furor of the Williams designation had subsided somewhat, Cushing's age—seventy-four at the time—was used against him repeatedly in the confirmation debate. But the outstanding reason for the opposition to him was his political instability. A veritable political chameleon, Cushing had been, in turn, a Whig, a Tyler Whig, a Democrat, a Johnson Constitutional Conservative, and a Republican. (Shades of the Vicar of Bray!) No one really knew what his political and ideological positions were, and, with opposition from almost all political factions mounting daily, Grant withdrew his name.

Some Concluding Thoughts. Only two individuals both nominated *and* confirmed as Justice of the Supreme Court of the United States have declined to accept that august office. William Smith in 1837 and Roscoe Conkling in 1882; both men wished to stay in the active political arena. To them, as well as to others who declined to serve during the first half-century of the Court's existence, e.g. John Rutledge (as Associate Justice), John Jay, Levi Lincoln, John Quincy Adams, offices such as Chief Justice of South Carolina (Rutledge), Governor of New York (Jay), or active political federal office (Adams), seemed infinitely more inviting and important than that of Supreme Court Justice. For the Court did not really come into its own until the long Chief Justiceship of John Marshall raised it to the level of power and esteem it enjoys today.

The appointment procedure was evidently more casual in the early days of the country, for today, if a nomination is made, the President knows that the man will accept if confirmed. This indicates that the office is held in higher esteem, as well as the fact that communications are vastly improved. Of course, we have no way of knowing how many men decline presidential offers of appointment to the Supreme Court or their reasons for doing so, but speculation would indicate that there are not many who would turn down the post if offered to them.

During the first seventy-five years of the country's independence, a substantial number of appointments to the Supreme Court were rejected or delayed on the basis of opposition to the President, rather than opposition to the candidate. Frequently, the Senate decided to wait until after an election or until the inauguration of a new President before it would act. It even went so far as to reject two of Tyler's appointments despite the fact that the Whigs, under Clay, had lost the election of 1844. That no man has been rejected because of opposition to the appointing President since Stanberry was rejected in 1866, might be construed as a sign of increasing political maturity.

Senatorial courtesy or personal senatorial vendettas or both have been major factors in the confirmation procedure. Although some candidates have been rejected on this basis, often the Senator can do no more than delay confirmation for a period of time. While certainly important, these factors are not as potent as is commonly supposed.

Generally speaking, opposition to nominees does not seem to be based on the qualifications or lack thereof of the men appointed. Perhaps the nominee's personal shortcomings play a bigger role in the decision not to confirm the appointee, but even here such a generalization is difficult to make because when opposition is personal or political or both, an attempt is made to place the opposition on more "respectable" grounds.

While the name of Charles Evans Hughes (on his appointment as Chief Justice) does not appear on the list of "unusual delays," the struggle in his case had great bitterness—although within a fairly brief period—and almost caused him to withdraw. The man most fiercely opposed for his personal qualities or the deficiencies which his opponents thought they perceived in him was Brandeis. Here too, however, the overt opposition emphasized more "respectable" reasons.

In general, opposition to the confirmation of a Supreme Court Justice seems to reflect the existence of deep-seated concern in the nation. In the early years of the Court's history, relatively little concern was shown about the potentially "unfortunate effects" of justices of uncertain, or certain, convictions. It became more frequent and noticeable as the influence of the Court became more apparent. At the present time, when there are so many issues in which large numbers of people are deeply concerned, almost every appointee is made to run the gauntlet; he may even feel slighted if his appointment is unopposed, since this could be interpreted as a sign that he is not regarded as a man who carries very much weight. The nomination and confirmation procedure has become one more battleground on which large issues are fought out before the public eye.

QUALIFICATIONS AND EXPERIENCE:
THE SPECIAL CASES OF ENGLAND AND FRANCE

In endeavoring to explain and analyze the staffing of the courts of England and France and in comparing their respective judiciaries, it is necessary to remain cognizant of the two different types of law that govern the systems concerned—the common or Anglo-Saxon or Anglo-Norman law in England and the civil or Roman law in France. There are fundamental differences between the laws of the two countries—and far greater ones become apparent, of course, in contrasting one or both with the prevalent norms and practices in the United States. But it is above all the very position of the judiciary that provides the key to these differences. Under the Roman law tradition of the Continent, the judiciary is a part of the administrative-executive hierarchy, as will be explained in considerable detail in Chapter VI, and it constitutes a *profession* distinctly separate from that of the practising lawyer. Where the common law tradition holds, however, the legal profession is practically an autonomous body, the judges being drawn from its ranks—notwithstanding the different mode and mood of selection that governs in England as compared with that of the United States, where the common law tradition also holds.

Nevertheless, we have already observed that a common ideal, that of impartiality of the appointees, is held by all three lands for both selection and tenure of their judiciaries, and that each is therefore willing, as it must be, to protect their independence and provide a large measure of immunity in order to achieve it. But the techniques of training and selecting judges and ensuring their impartiality differ widely.

ENGLAND

Unlike the United States, England divides its legal profession into two major groups: the *solicitors* and the *barristers*—and it is impossible to be both *concurrently*. The former deal mainly with the general public; they conduct about 95 per cent of the ordinary legal business of the country, leaving the remaining highly important work of advocacy in the courts to the barristers, who see the layman only when so instructed by a solicitor. The best analogy of the difference between the two groups is found in medicine: the difference between the general practitioner and the consultant. Barristers are consultants for the solicitors—the latter do all the ordinary work of the law and call in the barristers when they need their services, either for advice or for conducting a case in court.

The Solicitors. The "office lawyers" of the judicial structure, the solicitors are obviously its veritable workhorses. It is they who deal directly with the clients, who do the routine legal office work, and who prepare the spadework for cases to be argued at the bar of the higher courts by the barristers. But they also enjoy the right of audience in the magistrates and county courts, and they do a great deal of advocacy in these courts. They handle practically all of the drawing-up of legal documents, such as transfer of property. In short, the approximately 17,000 practising solicitors do the bulk of England's ordinary legal work. Having determined to become a solicitor on the conclusion of his educational career, and having undergone additional legal training, the aspirant then takes a number of special professional examinations. Passing these, he becomes a "Solicitor of the Supreme Court" and commences his career. He will also probably join the Law Society, a voluntary association of solicitors with certain statutory powers. Every practising solicitor is entitled to become a member of this society, and usually does. Incidentally, university training is not an absolute requirement—over half of the solicitors are not university products.

The Barristers. The approximately 2200 practising barristers, however, comprise England's best-known legal talent. Their chief function is to render legal advice to solicitors at all times, either generally or in preparation for trial, and, of course, to conduct cases. Thus, they argue all cases in the higher courts—cases which, by custom and tradition, are almost always given to them directly by the solicitors who have processed them in a preliminary manner, rather than by the clients themselves. The barristers are professionally specialized and usually—although not inevitably—highly experienced members of the legal profession. It is from their ranks that the Lord Chancellor normally selects the judges on behalf of the Crown. Indeed, with the exception of justices of the peace, the English and Welsh judges have always been appointed from the ranks of practising barristers.[63]

The barristers are divided into two groups or ranks: "Junior Barristers" and "Queen's Counsel." The latter are referred to colloquially as "Silks" from the fact that they are entitled to wear a silk gown instead of the "stuff" gown wore by the Junior Barristers. The two gowns are different in style also: those worn by the "Juniors" are like academic gowns with flowing sleeves, those of the "Silks" are along simpler lines. One becomes a "Silk" upon the recommendation of the Lord Chancellor, on reaching the very top status in the profession, seldom until the completion of ten years' successful practice. The "Silks" constitute the elite among the barristers and they receive higher fees than the junior barristers. Their main tasks include appearances in court, where they must be accompanied by a "Junior." It is from the ranks of Queen's Counsel that judges are mainly chosen. Yet sometimes a man may become a judge without being a "Q.C."—e.g. Lord Chief Justice Parker was made a judge as a "Junior." He had been Junior Counsel to the Treasury, the Government advocate for Crown business in the High Court. Normally those who have "taken silk" for at least seven years, and in the cases of the higher courts for at least ten years, may expect to be considered for a judgeship in the event of a vacancy. But the number of superior court judges is low, and when one of the promotions does come it is viewed with a certain awe and respect by the legal profession and the public at large. Judges of the High Court are *invited* to become such by the Lord Chancellor—i.e. without soliciting the post—whereas those of the County Court are appointed from the ranks of those who have *applied* to the Lord Chancellor for consideration of appointment.

All barristers are members of one of the four historic *Inns of Court* in London: Lincoln's Inn, Gray's Inn,[64] Inner Temple, and

---

[63] A county judge, for example, must have been a barrister for at least seven years, a Lord Chief Justice of Appeal for at least fifteen.

[64] Sir Francis Bacon, one of Gray's Inn's most famous members, planned and planted its lovely garden, where he walked and talked with such statesmen as Sir Walter Raleigh. Today, the public may sit there in solitude from noon until 2:00 p.m. and never hear a sound from noisy Fleet Street.

Middle Temple.[65] In effect, they constitute both a "law school" and a professional organization. Separate colleges, each with its own hall, chapel, and library, they arose as a result of the custom of lawyers to live together during terms. Self-governing, historic organizations—officially dating back roughly to the time of Edward I (1273–1307)—the Inns of Court, literally meaning "town houses," used to be residences of noblemen and bishops. There students as well as members of the bar would study, live, work, eat, and pray. But they are no longer residences in the full sense of the term—although quite a few barristers, usually bachelors, still do live there.

In the past, under the tutelage of barristers, England's future lawyers were trained in the Inns rather than in a university law school. Today, these students may attend the lectures of the Council of Legal Education, a joint committee for education from the four Inns of Court. They are tested by examiners of the council, and on passing the examination and having kept their "dining terms" for three years, they apply to the "Benchers," the governing body of the Inn, for admission as a barrister. This "dining term" rule is a relic of the days when students of the common law lived in the Inns of Court and had to frequent the hall of their Inn for dinner, for the exercises in "mooting," and for other forms of learning before becoming barristers. To this day they must dine in the hall on three nights in each dining term.

Once admitted to the bar, the young barrister remains under the general jurisdiction of his Inn of Court throughout his career, in fact his life, and it is his Inn which constitutes both his professional protector and his disciplinarian. A full measure of *esprit de corps* flows naturally from life and membership in the Inn. Disciplinary problems are further under the supervision of the General Council of the Bar, a special body elected by the members

[65] The Inner and Middle Temples derive their names from the round temple which was built by the Knights Templar in 1160, and stood, until they were almost entirely destroyed—as were the other two inns—in the London Blitz, between the Strand and the Thames. They were rebuilt and rededicated in the early 1960's. What is now known as the Inner Temple covers what used to be the consecrated portion of the grounds surrounding the Temple Church. The Middle Temple covers what used to be the unconsecrated part. Gray's Inn derives its name from Reginald de Grey, who lived there and was Justician of Chester in the thirteenth century. Lincoln's Inn owes its name to the Earl of Lincoln, who was a member of the King's Council, also in the thirteenth century.

of the Bar to act for it in a wide range of matters. Authority to expel a barrister for misconduct is given to the "Benchers" of the Inn of which he is a member.

The legal education provided by the Law Society for solicitors, who have numerous offices at the Inns but do no study there, differs from that given to the barristers. It is based on intensive courses, practical training, and a year's compulsory attendance at a recognized law school. The future barrister, on the other hand, must pass the bar examinations which involve a background in general legal principles, despite the fact that he may not have had specific training in these; that he often does not attend the elaborate series of lectures provided by the Council of Legal Education; and that he is not required to have practical training. However, recently a pledge has been exacted from candidates to spend six months as pupils in chambers. In part as a result of this distinction in preparation, there has been some criticism and clamor, notably in certain segments of the press, e.g. *The Economist*—to effect the following changes: (1) include common basic training for both branches to make possible an easy interchange between them; (2) allow barristers to form partnerships—they are not permitted to do so now, or to deal directly with clients (even the fees are settled between the solicitor's and the barrister's clerks); (3) alleviate the allegedly strained relationship between the General Council of the Bar and the governing bodies of the Inns of Court.[66] Considerable doubt is thrown on the latter point, however, by the fact that many of the members of the General Council of the Bar are "Benchers" of their respective Inns.

Moreover, the reason the future solicitor is given a thorough practical training in a solicitor's office by being apprenticed to the latter for three years, if a university product, and five years, if not, is because solicitors are entitled to practise from the moment they are admitted and can do legal work of practically any kind *at once* for the general public. But a barrister is never employed directly by a member of the public; he is employed, or instructed, by a solicitor—and in practice is a highly trained lawer before he gets work of any importance from a solicitor.

Even given the possibility of a judicial appointment, his at-

[66] See the analysis in "How To Rescue the Bar?," *The Economist*, January 9, 1960, pp. 86–7.

tractive social status, and the "psychic income" he may receive from his membership in the profession, the future of the barrister's branch of that profession is nevertheless undergoing some examination. One of the several significant considerations is his relatively low income, which has undoubtedly been a factor in the gradually declining number of practising barristers. As of January 1967, fewer than 2200 men—and only 80 women—were active members of the British bar, 75 per cent of these in London. In 1957–58 only 91 barristers began practice—the lowest new entry on record, not to mention the 112 members who *left* the bar during that period.[67]

Yet whatever the problems of the parent profession may be—and they have been exaggerated at times—the English judges are very likely the most highly esteemed, the most independent, and, relatively speaking, the most generously paid in the West. There is little doubt that these three factors account in considerable degree for the universally high quality of British justice, properly so often cited and envied by much of the rest of the world.

FRANCE

The Republic of France, together with several other states on the continent of Europe, goes considerably farther than Britain in distinguishing between judges, public prosecutors, and officials of the powerful Ministry of Justice on the one hand, and privately practising lawyers on the other. Although there is a clear-cut distinction between the British solicitor and the barrister, both are nonetheless members of the legal profession and may commence their advanced legal training together. In France, however, the bench is a separate career; it is not viewed as a reward for legal excellence or renown as it is in both Britain and the United States.

A future French student of the law must decide at the very outset of his schooling whether he wishes to become a private lawyer or a judge or prosecutor or go to the Justice Ministry. If the former, he attends law school and chooses among three specialties open to him: *avocat*, roughly akin to the British barrister; *avouet*, the approximate equivalent of the British solicitor; or a third category, *notaire*—a lawyer especially trained in drafting and

67 Ibid. p. 86.

registration of legal papers, related in name only to the American notary public who need not be a lawyer. These three groups comprise the French *legal*, not the *judicial*, profession. The French youth desirous of becoming a judge of the lower or appellate courts or one of the other two allied vocations, follows a totally separate path of training, for—as has been explained earlier—the judiciary of France is, in effect, a branch of the government, of the civil service.

Training for a Judgeship. Until the judicial reforms of 1958–59 took place, after finishing law school the prospective member of the judiciary would initially gather some experience, a sort of apprenticeship, in a law office. From there he usually moved on to a minor office in a local court, while awaiting his appointment. In the meantime, when he deemed himself sufficiently qualified, he would take an examination and, if successful, could then look forward to the anticipated placement in the judicial system. It was common practice to assign him first as a public prosecutor and then gradually move him into a jurist's position.

However, as a result of a governmental decree in 1959, designed to broaden and further professionalize their background, experience, and training, all potential applicants for judgeships must also attend the *Centre National d'Études Judiciaires* (National Center of Judicial Studies) for four years. To become students there, the hopeful are selected on the basis of competitive examinations, both in legal subjects and in the general liberal arts. The students, who are paid by the government for attending the C.N.E.J., must be law school graduates and under twenty–seven years of age. The first year consists of on–the–job training in public departments on all levels of government, the next three of legal studies per se. The successful graduate is now assigned to one of the courts of first instance, the *tribunaux d'instance,* in accordance with his class standing—assuming he wishes to become a judge. But he is also eligible for the enquête,[68] for the office of the public prosecutor, or for service in the Ministry of Justice. The National Center of Judiciary Studies was evidently designed to do for the judiciary what the National School of Administration (*École Nationale d'Administration*) has done so well for the upper echelons

[68] Explained in Ch. III, *infra*, especially pp. 101–3.

of the general civil service—the creation of a competent, reputable, and esteemed group of public servants.[69]

In the United States and, to a more modified extent, in Britain, the selection of a lawyer as a judge customarily represents the culmination of a long and quite frequently distinguished career in the law—subject to certain obvious political contingencies in the United States. But in France the judge is chosen from the *judicial profession*, for which he prepared by special schooling and examinations—a profession just as medicine, teaching, and the law are. Although he is not particularly well paid, he enjoys considerable prestige and a high social rating. We shall now see him and his *confrères* in action on the bench.

[69] Early in 1967 the American Bar Association endorsed a plan of President Johnson to establish a Federal Judicial Center in the Administrative Office of the U. S. Courts (see Ch. III, *infra*) to train federal court employees, *including federal judges*. A bill to enact the proposal into law was passed by Congress in December 1967. In the President's words, the center would do research as well as training "to reduce the backlog of cases pending in the courts and to meet the urgent law enforcement problems." (*The New York Times*, February 15, 1967).

III

COURTS,
COURTROOMS, AND JURIES

TYPES OF COURTS: TRIAL AND APPELLATE

Each of the countries discussed in this book has a system of courts in line with its own needs and choice. Some have similar features, but no two are truly alike. Speaking broadly, however, each of these sysetms—and in fact practically every known judicial system in the world—has endeavored to separate the jurisdiction of *trial* (first instance) and *appellate* (review) courts. Some courts do fulfill both functions, but in that event—if justice is to have any meaning at all—it will at the very least have separate dockets for each area. This applies, for example, to an English Court of Quarters Sessions and a French *Cour d'Assize*. In a rather limited sense, the Supreme Court of the United States is also constitutionally empowered to exercise jurisdiction in the trial as well as in the appellate area, termed *original* and *appellate* by Article III of the Constitution, where these designations are found. However, that high tribunal's original jurisdiction docket is usually empty; seldom, if ever, has it exceeded more than 1 per cent of the volume of cases handled by the Court. The overwhelming number of cases and controversies that reach the highest tribunal in the American judicial hierarchy do so under its appellate jurisdiction. In fact, as will be explained in more detail in Chapter V, the Supreme Court may, save in the instance of litigation involving two or more of the fifty states, share its original jurisdiction with courts below— i.e. its original jurisdiction is thus *concurrent* with them—which, in effect, means that seldom, if ever, will the Supreme Court decide such a case in its role of a trial court.

TRIAL COURTS

Trial courts perform the function their title clearly implies: they *try* cases in the first instance, as tribunals of original jurisdiction. Cases commence there because they are statutorily required to do so. More often than not they are also completed upon the pronouncement of the verdict of guilt or acquittal which may or may not, depending upon organizational requirements and choice, have come about as a result of a trial by jury. Rather obvious illustrations of trial courts of varied jurisdiction are a United States District Court; a Court of Common Pleas in the Commonwealth of Pennsylvania; a French *Tribunal de Grande Instance;* and the Queen's Bench Division of the High Court of Justice of England and Wales.

Again depending somewhat upon the law of the land and governmental subdivision concerned, both law and fact are taken into account at the bar of a trial court, and both parties to the litigation, plaintiff as well as defendant, are presumably accorded a full opportunity to present their respective sides of the case or controversy. In common law countries, such as most of the English-speaking lands, a single judge customarily—but by no means always—presides over a trial alone; in statutory law systems, such as those found in most continental European states, normally a trio or more judges sit *en banc.* When a jury sits in a case, the judge *charges* (instructs) it at the conclusion of the presentation of pertinent evidence in the law and in the procedures attendant upon the case. The jury then returns a verdict upon completion of its deliberations, which may last from a few hours to several days.

APPELLATE COURTS

The *raison d'être* of a court of appeals is to provide an appellate forum for decisions rendered in a trial court. Such appeals are presumably limited to questions of law at issue in the litigation below, but in some circumstances they may also deal with questions of fact, either collaterally or on their own merits. In any event, it is often extremely difficult to separate categorically matters of law and fact, and the final word on such a distinction, if it is crucial to the question of the grant of the petition for review, will necessarily lodge in the appellate tribunal itself. In large measure, this decision depends upon the tribunal's statutory authority and the extent and nature of the discretionary review powers given to it. Some appellate courts *must* accept all cases properly presented to them for review—such as the United States (Circuit) Court of Appeals, which has no effective discretionary power to decline to accept appellate petitions. Others, for example the United States Supreme Court, possess all but complete statutory *discretionary* authority as to whether or not to accept a case brought before them for review from below, although in theory there are *some* cases of mandatory review (as will be shown in Chapter V). Again other appellate tribunals, the British House of Lords for one, have more discretionary power to accept or reject criminal cases than civil cases—or vice versa. Courts of appeals are usually multiple-member bodies; as a rule, three or more judges sit *en banc* to hear the appeal without a jury.

A well-known appellate court, in addition to those already named above, is England and Wales' important Court of Appeal (for civil and criminal cases). That court is empowered to *retry* a case, a departure from the normal role of appellate tribunals. The *Cour de Cassation,* at the apex of the regular French judicial system, is a further example of a court of appeals. In the instance of some appellate courts, such as the criminal division of the English Court of Appeals, appeals may be instituted only by the defendant. In the United States, although the federal government may usually appeal an adverse decision of a trial court on a point of law, absent "double jeopardy," it is barred from appealing on a point of fact; this means that, in effect, it cannot appeal an adverse verdict in a criminal proceeding on the basis of the factual evidence presented in court on pain of violating the double jeopardy safeguards of the Fifth Amendment to the United States Constitution. However, since this Bill of Rights provision does not automatically apply to the states[1]—unless it is present in their

---

[1] However, the 1960's witnessed an increasing number of "applications," "absorptions," or "incorporations" of provisions of the Bill of Rights, and the Fifth Amendment's double jeopardy provision is not at all "safe" from a similar mandate by the Supreme Court of the United States. For a full discussion of this intriguing constitutional problem, see the author's *Freedom and the Court: Civil Rights and Liberties in the United States* (New York: Oxford University Press, 1967), Ch. III, "The Applicability of the Bill of Rights to the States."

own constitutions, as it is in many instances—state governments are not necessarily similarly inhibited from appealing a defeat in a court below. A few states expressly permit such appeals by the authorities in these circumstances, among them Connecticut, whose empowering statutory provision was specifically upheld by the U.S. Supreme Court in the famous case of *Palko v. Connecticut*,[2] against Palko's contention that it deprived him of "due process of law" under the Fourteenth Amendment to the Constitution, as comprehended by the double jeopardy safeguards of the Fifth.

COURTROOM PROCEDURE: GENERAL

There are essentially two methods in which society, through its judicial and legal organs, may approach a member of its body politic accused of an offense—either by presuming his innocence until it has effectively succeeded in proving him guilty under due process of law, or by presuming his guilt unless he successfully disproves that assumption under similar processes.

"INNOCENT-UNTIL-PROVED-GUILTY":
THE ACCUSATORIAL PROCEDURE

It is a cornerstone of Anglo-Saxon justice that an accused is innocent until proved guilty beyond a reasonable doubt. Few, if any, concepts are more deeply rooted in our traditions. Admittedly, there have been violations of that principle from time to time, especially during periods of war and other emergencies when an occasional departure from it has been justified on the grounds of necessary expediency, however distasteful. Thus, writing painfully for a divided (6:3) bench that ". . . hardships are part of war, and war is an aggregation of hardships. . . ." Mr. Justice Black, one of the outstanding civil libertarians of all time to sit on the Supreme Court of the United States, upheld the compulsory evacuation of 112,000 persons of Japanese ancestry from their homes on the West Coast—among them some 70,000 native-born American citizens, none of whom had been *specifically accused* of disloyalty.[3] On the whole, however, the record of the common

[2] 302 U. S. 319 (1937). See Mr. Justice Cardozo's opinion for details.
[3] *Korematsu v. United States*, 323 U. S. 214 (1944).

law countries, such as Britain and the United States, has been good in this regard. The layman may quite naturally be quick to adjudge a person guilty in his own mind, more often than not joined by the press, particularly in America, but the Anglo-Saxon legal profession on both sides of the Atlantic Ocean and throughout the English-speaking world has done its best to adhere to the time-honored principle that a person is innocent until he has been proved guilty beyond a reasonable doubt by due process of law. As Mr. Justice Brennan wrote for the Supreme Court in a decision highly unpopular with Congress and the public at large, in which the Court by a vote of 7:1 reversed the conviction of one Clinton Jencks, a suspected Communist perjurer, who had not been permitted to attempt to impeach testimony given to the Federal Bureau of Investigation, on the basis of which he had been convicted in the trial court: ". . . the interest of the United States in a criminal prosecution is not that it shall win a case, but that justice shall be done."[4] And, in the words of Mr. Justice Frankfurter's majority opinion in a coerced confession case in 1961, ". . . ours is an accusatorial and not an inquisitorial system—a system in which the State must establish guilt by evidence independently and freely secured and may not by coercion prove its charge against an accused out of his own mouth."[5] Of course, this jurisprudential posture applies equally to civil proceedings, whether or not the government is a party to it. In the summary words of one of Mr. Justice Jackson's opinions concerning one attorney's right to compel another to disclose certain papers involved in the litigation concerned, "A *common law* trial is and always should be an adversary proceeding."[6]

Thus, the presumption of the innocence of the accused, until proved otherwise, is transformed into courtroom procedure in the Anglo-Saxon countries. Essential to it are the ancient basic safeguards inherent in that philosophy of the law, safeguards which, to a greater or lesser degree, are fundamental to the notions of liberty and justice that pervade the political system of the liberal democratic West. Among these are the privilege against self-incrimination; the right to cross-examine witnesses; the writ of

---

4 *Jencks v. United States*, 353 U. S. 657 (1957).
5 *Rogers v. Richmond*, 365 U. S. 534, at 540–41.
6 *Hickman v. Taylor*, 329 U. S. 495, at 516 (1946). (*Italics supplied.*)

100

habeas corpus—perhaps the most basic right of all; and many others in the same general category, however their interpretation may vary from jurisdiction to jurisdiction (e.g. in the fifty states of the United States, seen as separate entities when dealing with purely state matters in contrast to the specifically enumerated Bill of Rights provisions strictly applicable to the United States as a federal entity).[7]

The Judge's Role. An important feature of the accusatorial type of procedure is that the judge does *not*—except as noted below and in rare instances in order to call forth certain types of evidence, usually of a technical nature—insert himself into the substantive questioning during the trial. Quite naturally, he does, indeed he must, hand down rulings on various motions, points of order, and other problems that may arise during the course of the trial. He is—or certainly he is expected to be—in complete charge of courtroom procedure, and as such possesses a considerable residue of what legal parlance terms *judicial discretion*. In this connection, that intriguing compound noun demands an application

> . . . enlightened by intelligence and learning, controlled by sound principles of law, of firm courage combined with the calmness of a cool mind, free from partiality, not swayed by sympathy nor warped by prejudice nor moved by any kind of influence save alone the overwhelming passion to do that which is just. . . .[8]

In that discretion, the judge will question a witness only to avert grave injustice, not to advance the case for either side. He is not in any sense an active elicitor of truth regarding the testimony presented. In essence, he is an independent arbiter between the state and the individual or between the litigating parties. This is a concept basic to the common law adversary proceeding mentioned by Mr. Justice Jackson, a system that "sets the parties fighting." According to Professor Max Radin, one of the giant interpreters of jurisprudential theory and practice, that system has been in vogue since its adoption in Rome in the fourth or fifth century B.C., when —for better or for worse, and quite conceivably the latter—the

[7] But note the reference to recent developments in this connection in fn. 1, p. 97, *supra*.

[8] *Davis v. Boston Elevated Railway*, 235. Mass. 482, at 496–7. Quoted by Felix Frankfurter, *The Case of Sacco and Vanzetti* (Boston: Little, Brown and Co., 1927), pp. 90–91.

judge's task changed from determining the truth to the umpiring of a competition.[9] There is little doubt that many, probably most, of today's lawyers would have great difficulty of conceiving of a trial as anything else.

"GUILTY-UNTIL-PROVED-INNOCENT":
THE INQUISITORIAL PROCEDURE

In France, to use the most obvious example, a different philosophy regarding the legal process in this area obtains. Not independent arbiters, the French judges are part of the machinery of the state, and courtroom procedure in criminal trials is characterized by the *inquisitorial* method, know as the *parquet.* Here, the presumption may be said to be implicitly one of guilt, although it may be doubted that any civilized land actually proceeds on such an assumption. Indeed, Max Radin refers to the notion of presumption of guilt as a "curiously persistent calumny," and views the presumption of innocence as "inherent in the French Declaration of the Rights of Man and the Citizen."[10] Still, so much painstakingly accumulated preliminary investigation by a professional judge—the *juge d'instruction* (examining magistrate)—has already preceded the courtroom trial that the judge or judges presiding at the trial may indeed presume the defendant to be guilty of the offense charged. Nonetheless, they actively, often vehemently and acidly, participate in the courtroom questioning of witnesses as well as of the accused—who, incidentally, may not invoke the Anglo-Saxon privilege of refusing to take the stand on grounds of possible self-incrimination. Yet had the investigating judge been unable to find any evidence of apparent guilt, the accused would very likely never have been brought to trial. In a sense, this preliminary "investigation," the *enquête*, is an advanced form of grand jury investigation and indictment—still so prevalent in the American courts—but with the significant distinction that whereas the *enquête* in France is conducted by professional magistrates the American grand jury is composed entirely of laymen.

The "Juge d'Instruction" and the "Enquête." The office of the *juge d'instruction*—which is not a uniquely French institution—

9 Max Radin, "The Permanent Problems of the Law," 15 *Cornell Law Quarterly* 10–11 (1929).

10 *The Law and You* (New York: Mentor M34, 1948), p. 99.

combines the powers of a prosecutor and a magistrate. His function is to determine the truth on behalf of the state, with the aid of the police. But he may commence an investigation only upon notification by the public prosecutor (*procureur*), who must have been advised of the crime by the police. The powers of the *juge d'instruction* are awesome, indeed. He may call witnesses and badger them. He may ask suspects to re-enact the alleged crime. He may open mail and tap telephone wires. He may even keep people in jail indefinitely, since the revered Anglo-Saxon institution of the writ of *habeas corpus* is unknown in France. He may commission experts to investigate and report on special aspects. But perhaps the most potent weapon in his considerable arsenal is the famous *confrontation de témoins* (confrontation of witnesses), which is unlike anything in Anglo-American legal procedure. When two or more witnesses tell contradictory stories, the *juge d'instruction* calls them into his office together for a *confrontation*. There, under his watchful and experienced eyes and ears, and in the presence of a court official who writes down every uttered syllable, each witness is quoted repeatedly, with the other(s) invited to point out "errors" or "discrepancies" in his testimony. As a result of this *confrontation,* perjured testimony in criminal cases has been almost eradicated.

When the evidence, including that of the police, has been procured in a case, and both the defense and prosecution lawyers— the latter headed by the *procureur*—have had access to the complete *dossier,* the *juge d'instruction,* who will usually consult the *procureur,* can now send the case to trial on his own authority. Since he is highly unlikely to do so unless he has become convinced of the presence of guilt, the resultant trial itself turns largely into a public verification of the accumulated record. In the event of a statutorily designated *serious* crime, the entire record of the investigation must be reviewed before it is admitted to trial by a *chambre d'accusation,* a judicial body at the appellate court level.

Although the broad powers accorded to the *juge d'instruction* are sometimes criticized even by French legal scholars as being akin to a "star chamber" proceeding, that charge is grossly exaggerated. The *juge d'instruction* operates in a system which refuses to concede to the contending parties control over the presentation of evidence—either its submission or its impeachment by cross-examination. During the trial such control becomes the duty of the presiding judge. In the absence of cross-examination, the data procured by the *enquête* are necessary to ensure the accuracy of testimony. However "tough" it may have been, the *enquête* is characterized by a patient, painstaking discovery procedure, one that has presumably solved mysteries and eliminated discrepancies in testimony. All the evidence is recorded in the *dossier,* enabling the *juge d'instruction* and the *procureur* to build the case against the accused. But it does more: it permits the presiding judge to conduct the trial meaningfully.

In its final impact, the French system of the *enquête* would appear to be at least as effective as the Anglo-American accusational method, in which all the evidence is brought out for the first time, almost in the manner of a game, by testimony and cross-examination in open court before trial judge and jury. A grand jury indictment, after all, requires only a *prima facie* case. One may well contend that a criminal trial in a French court is an investigation rather than a battle between two opposing platoons of learned counsel—a "sporting theory" battle that in America, according to one legal authority, "denotes a bitter duel rather than a disinterested inquiry"—in which the duelers indulge in trickery and fight with "make believe" evidence that often bears scant relation to the facts at issue.[11]

"VOX DEI" OR "VOX POPULI" IN ACTION: THE JURIES

There is no doubt that the institution of the jury is at once one of the most fascinating and one of the most exasperating aspects of the judicial process. Many a curse has been uttered against a jury and what it stands for even while the other party to the litigation at hand has voiced a prayer of gratitude in its behalf! Sundry types of juries exist; but essentially a jury is plainly a group of citizens of predetermined number whom a duly constituted public official has called together for the purpose of answering a question. Used in Athens as long ago as five or six centuries *before* the birth of Christ, they went to Rome some ten centuries later, and then to

11 James Marshall, *Law and Psychology in Conflict* (Indianapolis: Bobbs-Merrill Co., 1966).

France in the ninth century. The modern Western world traces their origin to the England of almost 800 years ago, where, in the early stages, they were regarded simply as a body of men to aid the monarch in dispensing justice by attesting to certain facts. Whatever their age, they have been praised and attacked ever since. Although many countries, not necessarily excluding dictatorships, still resort to juries—apart from English-speaking lands they exist today largely in Austria, Belgium, Denmark, Greece, Norway, and some Swiss cantons—the institution has clearly suffered a steady decline. This is more true of the *grand jury* than it is of the *trial* (*petit*) *jury*, but both types have experienced decreased usage, especially in England and Wales, where the grand jury was abolished by the Administration of Justice (Miscellaneous Provisions) Act of 1933, and where the use of the trial jury in civil cases was seriously curtailed by the same law. Today, the jury is used in less than 10 per cent of all cases in the British Isles. In France, of course, the grand jury is not at all employed in view of the role of the *juge d'instruction.* Juries are still widely used in the United States, particularly on the federal level;[12] in many of the fifty states, however, juries, notably grand juries, have fallen into at least partial disuse. Everywhere, more and more cases are decided by jurists sitting without a jury, sometimes as a result of statutory or constitutional provisions, sometimes by the agreed-upon choice of the parties to the suit. Now it seems almost unbelievable that the courts of Athens in the fifth century B.C. were composed of a jury only—there was no judge at all! Moreover, the more significant the nature of the case, the greater the number of the jurors. Thus Socrates was tried by a panel of 501 in the fourth century B.C., and Alcibiades's trial on charges of treason in the fifth featured 1501 jurors. These able Attics were drawn from all over the Athenian communities by a complicated but apparently popular lot system.[13]

The foundation of the English jury system is traceable to the French empire under the Carolingian kings. As part of their suc-

---

12 Still, even in the United States the vast majority of cases are disposed of without juries. According to recent statistics, fully 92 per cent of the cases adjudicated in court do *not* go to jury trials! (See Attorney General Nicholas deB. Katzenbach's address to the American Society of Newspaper Editors, April 16, 1965.)

13 See Charles P. Curtis, *It's Your Law* (Cambridge: Harvard University Press, 1954), p. 102.

cessful attempt to unite their empire, a procedure called the *inquisition* or *inquest* was devised. Carried out by representatives of the monarch, its purpose was to call together various bodies of neighbors in order to ask questions and explain the sovereign's "immemorial" rights. The Norman conquerors subsequently carried the concept of the inquest to England and used it first in the compilation of the 1086 *Domesday Book*. This book, which listed the ownership of all English land, was compiled from data obtained from royal administrators who gathered neighbors together in various parts of the country and used them as their source of information. This served to establish the right of the state to obtain data from its citizenry.

The first true juries were used to discover facts under the various writs of the *Possessory Assizes,* e.g. litigant neighbors decided who was dispossessed and who owned a certain piece of land under the writ of *Novel Disseisin* ("newly dispossessed"). Thus, trial by jury was closely linked with the protection of possessions; indeed, Norman dukes and English kings sometimes specifically granted to both private persons and churches the privilege of having their rights ascertained by this method. However, these juries merely filled a particular need at a particular moment in English history; they were permitted to die out and are hence not the bona fide predecessor of the modern English jury. The latter institution— initially for civil cases only—was founded under King Henry II in the second half of the twelfth century. Today, it would look strange, indeed, in its original form, for then it represented what in effect was a combination grand jury and trial jury that enabled the accusing body (the modern grand jury) also to pass judgment on the guilt of the accused (the modern trial jury). Ultimately these two functions were separated, heralding the now axiomatic difference between them.[14]

THE GRAND JURY

The chief distinction between a grand jury and a petit (trial) jury is that the former does not pass on a defendant's innocence or guilt. The grand jury merely determines whether, in its hopefully considered judgment, sufficient evidence exists or has been brought

[14] See Frederick G. Kempin, Jr., *Development of the Common Law* (Philadelphia: Lecture Note Fund, University of Pennsylvania, 1959), I-3-2 and I-3-7.

to its attention to justify a trial on criminal charges. Grand juries do not ordinarily sit in civil charges. A trial jury, on the other hand, determines whether to convict or acquit. Hence a grand jury does not return a verdict; it listens to a bill of evidence presented to it by the legal representative of the prosecuting authority, who must draw up the formal written accusation, and who almost invariably dominates its deliberations. The grand jury then decides whether or not the evidence warrants an *indictment,* also known as a *true bill,* which it does in approximately 95 out of 100 instances. In effect, an indictment charges one or more persons with having committed a felony or misdemeanor. The indicted party does not actually have an opportunity to give his side of the story to the grand jury; his day will come in the courtroom in the event of a trial. He is entitled to know the names of witnesses that have appeared before the grand jury, but little else—except, of course, the evidence presented at the preliminary hearing before the committing magistrate. There is no *right* to appear before the grand jury; one is invited or ordered to come before it. When it does not find sufficient evidence the grand jury issues what is known as an *ignoramus,* or a *no bill,* in which case the would-be defendant is not brought to trial.

By most accounts, the institution of the grand jury antedates the Magna Charta of 1215, but its origin is a source of considerable disagreement. Some have claimed to find its traces among the Athenians, but Athenian history, while mentioning the trial jury repeatedly, is quite silent on any body of citizens whose duty it was to accuse. The first grand jury, then called *presenting jury,* was apparently established by the Assize of Clarendon in 1166 under King Henry II. Here was enacted

> . . . that inquiry be made in each county and in each hundred, by twelve lawful men of the hundred and four lawful men of every township—who are sworn to say truly whether in their hundred or township there is a man accused of being or notorious as a robber, or a murderer or a thief, or anybody who is a harborer of robbers, or murderers, or thieves, since the king began to reign. And this let the justices and sheriffs inquire, each before himself.[15]

Interestingly enough, this provision was not intended to protect

[15] Ibid. p. 7.

the liberties of freemen, but rather to protect the monarch's interests. By 1352, in the reign of Edward III, the principle that a man's indictors were not to serve both as grand and trial jurors was firmly established. The modern concept of the grand jury dates from 1368, when Edward III impaneled twenty-four men to act as county inquisitorial boards. It was not until three centuries later that a grand jury, in two successive cases—*Colledge's Case* and *Earl of Shaftesbury's Case*[16]—for the first time refused to return an indictment, on the grounds of "ignoramus," that it "knew nothing." According to at least one historian, the immediate reason for the ignoramus in one of the cases was that the sheriff and many of the grand jurors were friends of the Earl of Shaftesbury![17]

Information. In England and Wales, where the grand jury was abolished as a result of the aforementioned statute of 1933, and in parts of the United States, the fast and easy method of *information* has been adopted in its place. It is a simple and efficacious device whereby the public prosecutor merely submits his charges in the form of an affidavit of evidence, supported by sworn statements, to a court of original jurisdiction. Usually a preliminary hearing has been held before a committing magistrate here, too, and after these brief procedures the accused is ready to stand trial. In France, the already described *enquête* by a professional judge takes the grand jury's place. Only in the United States is the common law heritage of that body still somewhat popular.

The documented history of the process of information is not nearly so complete as that of the grand jury and the trial jury. However, Blackstone noted in his *Commentaries* that "there can be no doubt that this mode of prosecutions by information filed on record by the King's Attorney General, or by his coroner or master of the crown office in the Court of the King's bench . . . is as ancient as the common law itself."[18] Although its usage lagged until the twentieth century, the process did figure prominently in the now famous case of Peter Zenger, commonly recalled as a milestone in the battle against press censorship. In 1735, an attempt was made to indict that courageous editor of the *New-York*

16 8 How St. Tr. 550 (1681) and 8 How St. Tr. 759 (1681).

17 George J. Edwards, Jr., *The Grand Jury* (Philadelphia: George T. Bisel Co., 1906), p. 29.

18 IV *Commentaries on the Laws of England* 309 (Ch. 23, "Of the several Modes of Prosecution").

Weekly Journal for libel against the conduct of the royal government, as personified by Governor William Cosby. When the grand jury ignored the bill of charges against him, Zenger was then held on the basis of an information filed by the attorney general of the province. After a celebrated trial, in which he was so ably defended by famed Philadelphia attorney Andrew Hamilton, he was acquitted. It was the English settlers who had brought the grand jury with them from their native land, together with all of the other civil rights they had enjoyed there. America's revolutionaries thought of it later as a means to prevent political prosecutions, but it was never tested for that purpose after the founding of the new nation.

Grand Jury Guarantees Today. The opening sentence of the Fifth Amendment to the Constitution of the United States in effect guarantees grand jury action on the *federal* level. Exempting members of the armed forces, it specifies that no person may be held for a "capital, or otherwise infamous crime," unless on a presentment or indictment of a grand jury. In 1968 there are six capital crimes under federal law (murder, rape, bank robbery, kidnapping with resultant harm, treason, and espionage) for which the ultimate penalty may be imposed—although this is done but rarely today.[19] Under the several state laws some thirty crimes are classified as capital, including aiding a suicide in Arkansas and burning a railroad bridge in Georgia. The grand jury provision of the Fifth Amendment is not applicable to the *states,* the Supreme Court of the United States having held repeatedly that its absence in these constituent parts of the nation does not in and of itself violate those "fundamental principles of liberty and justice which lie at the base of all our civil and political institutions."[20] Indeed, barely one-half of the fifty states still retain the grand jury system, and some of these utilize it solely to investigate crime and corruption among public officials in a limited number of cases, such as homicide and treason. Pennsylvania's Chief Justice John C. Bell, Jr., has repeatedly called for its utilization only to investigate

[19] A body of judicial opinion, including some members of the Supreme Court of the United States, contends that the imposition of the death penalty should be regarded as being a priori violative of the provisions against "cruel and unusual punishments" of the Eighth Amendment.

[20] *Palko v. Connecticut*, fn. 2, *supra.* See also *Hurtado v. California*, 110 U.S. 516 (1883).

crime and corruption in capital crimes. The balance have replaced it with the device of information which may be also employed by the federal government in *noncapital* cases at the district court level and generally in civil cases, a famous early example of the latter being the 1886 case of *Boyd v. United States*.[21]

The standard federal or grand jury today consists of a panel of between 12 and 16 to 23 members, who are presumably chosen at random from the local register of voters. The appropriate judge selects the foreman and his deputy. Unlike the trial jury it need not be unanimous even at the federal level, but a minimum of 12 jurors must agree on an indictment or an ignoramus, and 16 constitute a quorum. A grand jury is usually impaneled for a maximum period of 18 months at a time—unless discharged earlier by the judge to whom it reports—and it is called together during that time whenever need for its services arises. Its proceedings are secret and may not be released to the public. The latter *caveat* is an essential aspect of the grand jury principle and a traditional one—against which the electrical corporation executives, indicted for price-fixing in 1961, fought unsuccessfully in U.S. District Judge J. Cullen Gainey's court in May of that year.

Presentments. In a sense, however, grand juries do considerably more than merely determine the sufficiency or lack of evidence submitted to them; they conduct certain types of public investigations, enabling them to hand up a finding known as a *presentment*. Such an action represents a formal accusation against one or more individuals, made on the grand jury's own motion, calling attention to alleged illegal or improper activities—but not including an indictment. The first presentment on record came in England in 1683, charging certain Whigs, including the Earl of Macclesfield, with disloyal and seditious conduct. The accused brought an action for libel, but the court held for the grand jury, thus establishing the propriety of its report.[22]

Presentments have a habit of stirring up the public as well as the bar, quite frequently giving rise to general anguish. Thus, when a New York grand jury during the "quiz-show" scandals in 1959 on its own initiative handed up a presentment highly critical of the television and radio industry, General Sessions Court Judge

21 116 U.S. 616.
22 10 How St. Tr. 1330 (1684).

Mitchell D. Schweitzer impounded and permanently sealed it. He declared that no grand jury had a right to return a report dealing with the activities or morals of a *private* individual or corporation. A bill designed to embody Judge Schweitzer's position in a law subsequently failed to pass the New York State legislature.[23] However, the matter was reopened tangentially two years thereafter when the New York State Court of Appeals ruled 4:3 in the *Wood* case that a grand jury has the following choices: return an indictment, dismiss the charge, or remain silent.[24] Since this case involved *public* officials only, the ban seemed to have been extended to all elements of the citizenry. The action in the suit was brought by one James F. Wood, the foreman of a Schenectady county grand jury, to compel Judge Charles M. Hughes of the New York Supreme Court to make public a report the jury had filed on its own motion regarding the county highway department.

The narrowly decided *Wood* case, which overruled a prerogative in existence since 1688, serves to put the role of the grand jury and its problems into proper focus. The majority decision, written by Judge Stanley H. Fuld—and applauded by most of the lawyers' associations of the State of New York—declared that the jury involved made an inquiry which, by its own admission, failed to find that there was "willful and corrupt conduct" by a public official. The quoted phrase represented the verbiage of the statute under which the jury had been impaneled and charged, yet it had simply decided to chart a course of action on its own, one that was both unauthorized and publicly deprecatory of reputations. The dissenters, on the other hand, urged that such action by the grand jury was simply a reaffirmation of a basic American principle under common law and of considerations of ethics in government— namely, that an authorized body of citizens may, indeed must, take appropriate action to counter the suppression or burial of evidence of "tyranny and corruption in public office." In April 1961, Judge Schweitzer augmented his earlier action by expressly warning four grand juries he impaneled that "under no circumstances" were they to submit a presentment to his court. And the New Jersey State Supreme Court ruled that presentments must not be used to

---

23 A similar bill, but outlawing *all* presentments, had passed in 1946 but was vetoed by Governor Dewey.

24 *Wood v. Hughes*, 212 N.Y. S. 2d 33 (1961).

rebuke individuals in the absence of conclusive proof of wrong-doing. On the other hand, Philadelphia Common Pleas Court Judge Joseph E. Gold permitted a 1962 special grand jury charged to investigate municipal corruption in Philadelphia to hand up a stinging presentment in 1963, publicly naming individuals as well as organizations.[25] And when in 1964 the New York legislature finally agreed on a bill to deal with grand jury presentments, it turned out to be a compromise: under it a grand jury is empowered to criticize a public official or employee, but *only* if its main purpose is to recommend remedial administrative or legislative action.

Whatever one's judgment of the merits of the above developments may be, there is little doubt that while grand juries have traditionally been vested with broad powers to investigate crimes, such powers are not, and cannot be, either unlimited or unbridled. Grand juries are not powers unto themselves, but are essentially lay bodies whose actions are subject to judicial scrutiny and remedial relief. In that role grand juries have existed for such interesting and significant investigatory and stand-by purposes as juvenile delinquency, waterfront crime, narcotics traffic, subversive activities, quiz-show manipulation, corruption, and tax evasion, to name but a few of the myriad assignments given to a panel of these jurors who necessarily become fairly well-steeped in their particular area of jurisdiction. And they have often done a good job. The grand jury may well be cumbersome, amateurish, time-consuming, annoying, emotional, and a fifth wheel in the legal process, but on balance it does appear to serve as a potentially powerful arm of direct democracy. This is true if one is willing to accept the philosophy of the institution in the first place and if one has faith in the competence and intelligence of one's fellow citizens—a not inconsiderable set of assumptions.

THE TRIAL OR PETIT JURY

Normally, when the average person or the public press refers to a jury, he has the trial or petit jury in mind. In some areas, e.g. in parts of Pennsylvania, it is known as the *traverse* jury, a term de-

25 For details of the presentment, see *The Philadelphia Inquirer,* March 9, 1963, p. 1.

riving from medieval days when Norman French was beginning to displace Latin as the official language of the Court of England. As has been indicated, the trial jury has suffered a decline in many parts of the world, but it is still a popular institution. In England and Wales it is employed only sparingly and almost exclusively in criminal cases; the same is true of France, possibly more so. Its last important, and evidently secure, stronghold in the Western world is in the United States, where the concept of a trial by a jury of one's peers still thrives.

In England and Wales, where trial by jury, first for civil and later for criminal cases effectively commenced during the reign of King Henry II (1154–89), the accused is still entitled to such a trial for all serious crimes and for a very limited number of substantial civil infractions. With certain important qualifications, this jury may be demanded in all English and Welsh courts save in the highest and the lowest, but the privilege may be waived if the defendant so wishes. A jury is always impaneled in criminal cases if the accused pleads not guilty to an indictable offense. However, since 1933 the courts in England and Wales have been given considerable discretion as to whether or not to call a jury in a case; it is hence not astonishing that this discretion has been used widely to prevent a jury impaneling. If a trial jury is employed in a case, it is compiled from local townspeople and customarily consists of ten men and two women, whose verdict of guilt or acquittal must be unanimous. But the requirement of unanimity became a thing of the past in the fall of 1967 when Parliament enacted Home Secretary Roy Jenkins's legislation permitting English juries to convict by a 10:2 majority. In Scotland, a simple 8:7 majority is now sufficient to convict in a jury of fifteen. There are a number of reasons for the decline of the trial jury in England and Wales, among which the more important are first, the belief that a judge sitting alone can perform the jury's functions at least as well, and usually better; second, the desire for a speedy trial; and third, the fact that the litigants rather than Her Majesty's government pay the jurors' fees.

The French Republic resorts to jury trials solely at the level of the assizes, the courts of original jurisdiction for serious crimes. Trial by jury has no deep roots in France. Indeed, although it once did exist as part of customary procedure in some parts of the country, it disappeared under Charles VII in the fifteenth century, not to be reimported from England until the Revolution. Today, it consists of nine local *citoyens* (who sit with one or more judges); there is no unanimity requirements, and frequently the verdict is rendered by a simple majority vote. The French have no great fondness for the jury system, and their adherence to the inquisitorial mode in the judicial process leaves little or no genuine purpose for the existence of a trial jury per se. In any event, they generally view the jury as an instrument designed to becloud and confuse the issues in a case.

But the United States, where a total of approximately a million jurors serve in some 100,000 cases annually, has remained broadly faithful to the concept of a trial by jury. Indeed, 80 per cent of the world's criminal jury trials take place here. This is necessarily true at the level of the *federal* courts because of the express requirements of the Sixth and Seventh Amendments to the Constitution. The Sixth ascertains a trial by jury in *all* federal criminal cases; the Seventh does the same for all civil cases where the value of the controversy exceeds the sum of $20—which today to all intents and purposes means in practically every instance. Although all fifty states also provide for at least *some* type of trial by jury, the specific guarantees of the federal Bill of Rights here again do not automatically apply to them—the Supreme Court not yet having viewed this procedural right as "implicit in the concept of ordered liberty."[26] But the highest tribunal does insist that a defendant in a state proceeding be given a *fair trial*, on pain of a violation of the Fourteenth Amendment's due process of law and equal protection of the laws clauses. Among the several state practices affecting juries that have *inter alia* been held to constitute an *unfair* trial, are *systematic* exclusion of Negroes from juries[27] and the labeling of Negro jurors with brown, and white jurors with white, selection tickets.[28] Moreover, if a state law or the state constitution expressly calls for trial by jury, that state must grant it.

However, since each of the states may prescribe its own brand of jury system, a variety of practises exists—and many, if not all, of

26 *Palko v. Connecticut*, fns. 2, 20, *supra*. But it hinted reconsideration in 1968.
27 *Norris v. Alabama*, 294 U.S. 587 (1935); *Hill v. Texas*, 316 U.S. 400 (1942); *Patton v. Mississippi*, 332 U.S. 463 (1947); *Whitus v. Georgia*, 385 U.S. 545 (1967).
28 *Avery v. Georgia*, 345 U.S. 559 (1953).

these would be unconstitutional if practised by the federal authorities. Thus, some states grant a jury trial only in criminal cases, others in just a few civil cases, again others in a few of each. In 1966 the frequency of jury trials varied widely—from only 3 per 100,000 accused in Connecticut to 144 in Georgia.[29] At the federal level, it is generally possible to *waive* a trial by jury, *provided* common consent of the parties to the suit and of the judge assigned to the case is obtained,[30] but many states will not permit such a waiver, especially in capital cases. Another significant procedural difference between federal and state practices of judicial procedure is that the common-law mandated unanimity requirement for the 12 federal jurors—a practice in vogue as early as the time of the adoption of the Constitution—is not necessarily applied by state juries. Using the calendar year of 1967, exactly one-half of the states authorized a jury verdict by 75 per cent of the jurors in civil cases, with eight states extending this form of split verdict also to noncapital criminal cases. Some 20 states authorized civil trials with juries of less than 12 members,[31] usually merely 6—the Central District Court of Worcester, Massachusetts, for example. The governing question concerning these state practices at the bar of the United States Supreme Court is not a matter of comparison or method, but the essential one of whether or not the defendant received a fair trial under conditions of due process of law.

SELECTION AND IMPANELING OF JURIES

As a rule, juries in the United States are drawn from the voting lists of area or district citizens by the jury clerk who uses these names to form a jury panel or *venire*. But it should be noted here that most federal, and many state, jury lists are compiled by the so-called "key man" system, under which "upstanding" citizens are asked to submit names of people who *they* think would make good

---

29 *Time Magazine*, August 12, 1966, p. 26.

30 In 1965, in *Singer v. United States*, 380 U.S. 24, the Supreme Court ruled unanimously that a defendant in a federal trial does not have a constitutional right to insist on trial by a judge rather than by a jury if the Government insists on a jury.

31 Why the number 12 was initially selected for a jury's composition remains a mystery. However, that number has been mathematically significant ever since the days of the Sumerians, 5000 B.C. It has also scientific or religious significance: 12 signs of the Zodiac; 12 tribes of Israel; 12 Christian apostles.

jurors; jury panels are then selected from these lists. However, the validity of the "key-man" system has come under increasing attack both inside and outside of government on the ground that it discriminates against the poor and against Negroes especially. Important elements of all three branches of the government—the Judicial Conference of the United States, the Department of Justice, and Senator Joseph D. Tydings (D.-Md.)—advocated its abolition in 1967; and a federal court had held one year earlier that a particular defendant's right had been violated because the jury had not been selected from a cross-section of the community.[32]

In England and Wales juries are selected by the sheriff from a list of householders complied by local authorities and in France from departmental lists of male citizens of thirty years of age and over who possess all civic and political rights. In Switzerland, juries sitting with the Criminal Chamber of the Federal Tribunal to try certain criminal cases are *elected* by the people for six-year terms on the basis of one juror for each 3000 inhabitants. Happily, in more and more jurisdictions, notably in the United States, automation has entered, with electronic data-processing systems increasingly taking over the task of clerks and mahogany drums in choosing the jurors to be called for service. In two tests in New York and New Jersey, these electronic jury pickers put on a fine show by selecting eight jury panels of 275 names, each in 20 minutes—a process that formerly took two days! Theoretically, every adult of voting age is eligible for jury duty and may expect a call, unless he has served for more than a year in prison on a criminal charge and has not been pardoned for that offense.[33] This limiting proviso is statutorily applicable only to the federal government, but most of the fifty states now have the same, or at least a similar, requirement. While everyone else of voting age may thus expect to get a jury call at one time or another, it is not only relatively easy to avoid jury duty—incidentally one of the chief criticisms leveled against the jury system—but entire segments of the body

---

[32] *Scott v. Walker*, 358 F.2d 561 (1966). The Senate so resolved late in 1967.

[33] The official qualifications for *federal* jurors—which are rather similar in the several states—are: (1) U.S. citizenship; (2) attainment of at least twenty-one years of age; (3) at least one year's residence in the district; (4) no prior conviction punishable for more than one year unless pardoned or amnestied; (5) ability to read, write, and understand English; and (6) no mental or physical disabilities that would hamper efficient jury service.

politic are exempt either by law or by custom. Among the occupational groups exempt almost automatically in the vast majority
of jurisdictions, especially in the United States, are professionals
such as lawyers (a jury composed of arguing and battling lawyers
would, indeed, be an interesting experience!); physicians (too
busy to serve); pharmacists (likewise more or less indispensable
professionally); clergymen (a jury must deliberate, not pray);
teachers (essential occupation); and others in similar capacities.
Other busy employed people can normally avoid jury service by
submitting affidavits of indispensability from employers. Again
others, such as nursing mothers and those with a large family of
young children, will normally have to do little more than to write
a letter to the court concerned in order to be excused by the judge.
But a failure to do at least that much may conceivably result in a
citation for contempt of court, which occurred in the case of one
young Waterloo, Iowa, mother who repeatedly and willingly flouted
requests for an explanation by the court and finally found herself
sentenced to be incarcerated for six months in the Rockwell City
Women's Reformatory for criminal contempt. Generally, however,
in most states women need not serve at all, if they so choose, and
in a good many others they are automatically exempt.

If none of the reasons cited is acceptable to the court as a bona
fide excuse, an irresponsible citizen can, of course still evade his
presumed civic duty by confessing to one of the many otherwise
validly disqualifying factors present in jury impaneling. Among
these are: confession of prejudice for or against one of the litigants;
acquaintance with either party to the suit, however slight; predis-
position against capital punishment in a crime for which it may
be imposed; allegation of sympathy with, or opposition to, certain
pertinent philosophies of life involved in the case, no matter how
tangentially; and so forth. In fine, only those who are really willing
and able to serve will normally do so in the long run.

Challenges. On the other hand, jurors may naturally be removed
from a panel for any of the above or a myriad of other reasons by
the procedure of appropriate *challenges* granted both to the defense and the prosecution as a matter of regular courtroom procedure in Britain and France as well as in the United States, although they seem to be moribund in the first two.[34] In the United

34 Challenges were first given credence by Roman tribunals during the Empire's heyday, when one was allowed to object to a jury to try any particular
case.

States, challenges are essentially of two types, *peremptory* and *for cause*. They play a major role in the adversary process. A peremptory challenge entitles either side of the parties to the suit to request the removal of a would-be juror by *fiat*—no reason need be given; the mere request, whatever the motivation, will be honored. As the Supreme Court held in a 6:3 decision in 1965, written by Mr. Justice White, ". . . the essential nature of the peremptory challenge is that it is one exercised without a reason stated, without inquiry, and without being subject to the court's control."[35] What *is* subject to court control, however, is the limited *number* of these challenges granted—although that is often determined by statute. It is customary to permit the defense more peremptory challenges, than the prosecution, but this is not inevitably the case. In federal trial courts normally three such challenges are permitted each side per juror, depending on the nature of the offense. On occasion a flat ten have been authorized. In Pennsylvania the usual rule for murder cases is twenty for both defense and prosecution. In the sensational trial of Richard Speck, ultimately convicted of the murder of eight student nurses in Chicago in 1966, Illinois Judge Herbert C. Paschen, endeavoring to be scrupulously fair and, guarding against reversals on appeal, permitted the unprecedented total of 320 peremptory challenges! Each side was permitted twenty for *each* of the eight murder charges—and a grand total of 2500 jurors was questioned![36] But when a panelist is challenged for *cause*, the challenger must be in a position to advance a bona fide reason for his demand for the disqualification, and it will have to be one sufficiently related to the substantive or procedural aspects of the litigation involved in order to be acceptable in the eyes of the court.

These challenges, their procedures regulated by the court concerned, not infrequently delay the impaneling of the trial jury for days, occasionally even for weeks. For instance, the arduous and delicate task of selecting a jury to sit in the trial of the eleven top-echelon members of the Communist Party-U.S.A. in Judge Harold Medina's U.S. District Court for the Southern District of New York in 1949, consumed a total of six weeks. In view of the nature of the charges of the case, which ultimately resulted in the conviction of all eleven (although with varying sentences),[37] both

[35] *Swain v. Alabama*, 380 U.S. 202, at 220.
[36] See the accounts in *Time Magazine*, March 24 and April 7, 1967.
[37] *United States v. Dennis*, 72 F. Supp. 417 (1949).

118

defense and prosecution were painstaking in their questioning of each prospective juror, many of whom managed to extricate themselves from serving by simply acknowledging that they could not possibly have an open mind regarding the guilt of the accused. In a completely different vein, it has proved so difficult at times to impanel a jury that clerks of courts literally have had to stoop to "grabbing" people off the streets in search of a trial panel—as happened to a strolling unemployed near City Hall in Philadelphia in 1965 and 1966 and to a U.N. delegate taking a walk in Paterson, New Jersey, in 1958. A judge in Kentucky sent state troopers in an unsuccessful attempt to impanel jurors for a case involving the murder of two deputy sheriffs in 1962, and New Jersey sheriffs collared seventeen Morristown residents for service in 1967.[38]

"Blue Ribbon" Juries. Among the charges voiced frequently against juries, both grand and petit, are that they merely give vent to the established community prejudices; that they are utterly unqualified to render judgment; and that, worse still, they are composed quite consistently of people who not only are uninformed in civic affairs but are actually not interested. In Illinois, at least for a while, the names of those persons who consistently failed to vote were placed at the top of prospective jury lists. This intriguing practice was apparently based on the assumption that nonvoters make excellent jurymen! In large part to meet the general criticism of unsatisfactory juries, some states in America have statutorily adopted either a special jury-test or, more commonly, the *blue ribbon jury.* This device is used in various jurisdictions of California and Utah, for example, with judges of certain courts giving potential veniremen a series of test questions involving legal terminology that the jurors would almost certainly encounter. If an otherwise eligible juror misses more than one or two of these chiefly multiple-choice and matching questions, his chances of disqualification in these courts are excellent.

Blue ribbon juries made their first appearance in England in 1730 (then called *struck juries*) and were employed solely at the level of the King's Bench and only for "trials of great consequence" or when the subject matter of the case was beyond "discussion of the ordinary freeholder." Court officials would choose 48 men "competent, intelligent, and less prejudiced than the ordinary

38 *The New York Times,* April 15, 1962 and ibid. October 26, 1967.

juror." Somewhat later, the privilege to impanel such a blue ribbon jury was extended to all courts, who could authorize it for either of the above two reasons or, generally, when an ordinary jury "could not be impaneled."

In New York County (Manhattan), where the controversial device of the blue ribbon jury was adopted at the turn of the current century, some 3000 among the regular jury panel of 60,000 veniremen are designated for that special jury duty. According to the New York State statute, which permits resort to the blue ribbon jury in all counties of more than one million population in those cases in which the court of jurisdiction believes "the public interest would be served," it may "in its sound discretion" order a trial by a panel of these blue ribbon jurors on application by either party in a civil action and by either the prosecution or the defense in criminal cases. However, as the law specifies, the motion may be granted only on a showing that "by reason of the importance or intricacy of the case, a special jury is required"; or "the issue to be tried has been so widely commented upon . . . that an ordinary jury cannot without delay or difficulty be obtained"; or that for any other reason "the due, efficient and impartial administration" of justice in the particular case would be advanced by the trial of such an issue by a blue ribbon jury. On the whole, the veniremen on these juries are professional people and white collar workers—but expressly exempted are clergymen, physicians, dentists, pharmacists, embalmers, optometrists, attorneys, as well as servicemen, firemen, ship's officers, pilots, editors, reporters, and copy readers. Women are equally qualified with men, but since they also are granted exemption, a woman may serve or not at her discretion; in general, this has meant that blue ribbon juries are practically always all male panels.

New York County blue ribbon jurors—or *special jurors*, as the law refers to them—are selected from those accepted for the general panel of 60,000 by the county clerk, but only after each has been *subpoenaed* for a personal appearance and has testified under oath as to his qualifications and fitness. The statute carefully prescribes standards for selection by declaring ineligible and directing elimination of sundry categories which necessarily go far beyond the ordinary panel disqualification tests. The special jury panel is not one brought into existence for any particular case under New

York State's practice or for any special class of offenses or type of accused. It it part of the regular machinery of trial in those counties that meet the above-mentioned required minimum population figure, which New York County, with its approximately two million inhabitants, does more than amply.

It is hardly surprising that the institution of the blue ribbon jury, which today is in general use in approximately one-quarter of the states,[39] would ultimately face a test at the bar of the highest court of the land. It came in 1947, not surprisingly involving the New York County special jury, and it was closely followed by a similar test barely one year later.[40] By the narrowest of margins, 5:4 the Supreme Court of the United States upheld the statute and the practice against the dual challenge that it violated both the due process of law and the equal protection of the law clauses of the Fourteenth Amendment to the Constitution. The majority of the Court contended that the professionals and white collar workers on the jury could well come from widely varying salary groups, and that neither clause cited requires that a jury must represent all components of society. As Mr. Justice Jackson wrote for the majority in the first case: "Society also has a right to a fair trial. The defendant's right is a neutral jury. He has no constitutional right to friends on a jury."[41] Furthermore, the majority felt that a state might reasonably use blue ribbon juries as a means of rendering the administration of justice more efficient. But four justices dissented vigorously, led by Mr. Justice Murphy, who insisted that an accused person was entitled to be tried by a jury fairly drawn from a true cross section of the population, and that a blue ribbon jury simply could not be representative of that basic concept. "One is constitutionally entitled to be judged by a fair sampling of all one's neighbors," wrote President Franklin D. Roosevelt's ex-Attorney General in his dissenting opinion, joined by Justices Black, Douglas, and Rutledge

> . . . not merely those with superior intelligence or learning . . .
> The vice lies in the very concept of "blue ribbon" panels—the
> systematic exclusion of all but the "best" or most learned or

39 E.g. Ala., Del., Ind., Mich., N.J., N.Y., Tenn., Vt., Va., W.Va.
40 *Fay v. New York,* 332 U. S. 261 (1947) and *Moore v. New York,* 333 U. S. 565 (1948).
41 *Fay v. New York,* loc. cit., at 288.

most intelligent of the general jurors. Such panels are completely at war with the democratic theory of our jury system, a theory formulated out of the experience of generations.[42]

However, the majority decision has never been overruled and thus stands as *res judicata*. A blue ribbon jury may be both unfair and undemocratic, but these qualifications do not render it *ipso facto* unconstitutional. Furthermore, it may be well to reiterate that the notion that juries should be composed of men and women from all walks of life is a relatively recent one. At its English origins, the jury was composed of favorites of the Crown, men of position, or men who were indebted to the Crown. In the early history of the jury in the United States, it comprised a handful of propertied men. Several decades passed before being male and owning property, to name but the two more obvious qualifications, were no longer prerequisites to participation in jury duty.

THE TRIAL JURY AT WORK

The typical trial jury of twelve men and/or women, augmented by one or more alternates to guard against a case of sudden indisposition of a juror, sits *en banc* throughout the course of the trial. It does so no matter how long the trial may take, generally compensated inadequately on a daily fee basis. Each of its members is presumed to listen impartially and with an open mind to both sides of the case; may not discuss the trial with anyone, no matter how near or dear; and, at least in theory, is not permitted to read, view, or head any media of communication whatsoever during the trial. The latter requirement may well be an illusory one: there is every reason to believe that, regardless of a juror's conscientiousness and dedication, few public-spirited individuals would in fact literally deny themselves the news of the day. However, if either side in the litigation succeeds in presenting incontrovertible proof of such an aberation, it may move for a mistrial or even a directed verdict of acquittal. The jurors are not permitted to take notes; they are to "register the evidence as it is given, on the tablets of [their] memory and not otherwise."[43] When the presiding judge

[42] *Moore v. New York*, loc. cit., at 570.
[43] Indiana Supreme Court, as quoted by L. L. Bromberger, "Jurors Should Be Allowed to Take Notes," 32 *Journal of the American Judicature Society* 57–8 (1948).

has delivered his charge (see below) to the jury at the end of the trial, the jury retires for its deliberation until it reaches a verdict. If this proceeding stretches into the night, the jury is "locked up" in a nearby hotel and subsequently continues its work on the following day or days. If, after a reasonable period of time and repeatedly unsuccessful balloting, a trial jury is unable to arrive at a verdict of guilt or acquittal, the judge will declare it to be a *hung jury*, dismiss it, and remit the case to the docket for a trial *de novo* before an entirely different judge and jury. *But* the average judge will battle hard to avoid a deadlock. U.S. District Judge Edward Weinfeld of New York declined to accept the request of a long-deadlocked jury in 1962; sent it back to a midtown hotel with orders to return to his court at 9 a.m. It did, re-deliberated, and later that day returned a verdict of "guilty."[44]

"Hung" Juries. A famous example of a hung jury was that of the first Alger Hiss case,[45] when the jury deadlocked 8:4 for conviction after countless ballots, and Federal District Judge Samuel Kauffman declared it hung. Not long thereafter, Hiss was convicted of perjury in a new trial and with a new jury before Federal Judge Henry W. Goddard.[46] A sensationalized illustration of not just one but two hung juries in succession was the highly publicized Finch-Tregoff murder-conspiracy case in California. The first trial ended in a hung jury in March 1960, after 13 weeks of courtroom action, with the jury hopelessly deadlocked upon 37 hours of deliberation. At that time it stood 10:2 for convicting Dr. R. Bernard Finch, but 8:4 for his mistress Carole Tregoff's acquittal. The retrial was completed in November 1960, and again ended in a hung jury, this time having lasted 17 weeks, with the jury taking 59 ballots during 70 full hours of active deliberation. Mr. Edwin Fry, foreman and the only male on the standard size jury, reported that the 12 jurors had unanimously found Dr. Finch guilty of the murder of his wife, but were divided 9:3 on the degree of murder to be charged—three jurors stubbornly insisting on a second-degree finding. On Miss Tregoff the jury had split 9:3 on the degree as well as the guilt—and that same count held against both regarding the conspiracy charge! Another seemingly interminable trial finally

44 *The Philadelphia Inquirer*, June 16, 1962.
45 *United States v. Hiss.* Jury hung in August 1949.
46 *United States v. Hiss*, 88 F. Supp. 559 (1950). See also *United States v. Hiss*, 107 F. Supp. 128 (1952).

resulted, ending the fiasco in March 1961 in a clear-cut verdict against the two defendants: both were found guilty of conspiracy, Dr. Finch being convicted of first-degree murder, Miss Tregoff of second degree. (Reference is sometimes made to a *hanging jury*, which is a *grand jury* that has earned a reputation for almost certain indictments.)

INSTRUCTING THE JURY: THE JUDGE'S CHARGE

One of the highlights of a trial in the pertinent federal and state courts of the United States, and a crucial point in its evolvement, is the presiding judge's *charge* to the trial jury upon completion of testimony, arguments, and motions by all concerned. It comes after the summations by the prosecution and the defense, the latter customarily speaking last. Much thought goes—or should go—into this charge, which is intended as an exposition of the law, and is rarely, if ever, given in writing. The judge must take great care to ascertain that its contents are clear, to the point, comprehensive and illuminating, and that they pose readily discernible alternatives to the jury panelists, who *now* may take notes and sometimes ask for further instructions on details. But the jury may not take copies of the charge to the jury deliberation room, nor may they tape-record it. It is a highly complicated business for them. Thus, in the words of an appellate tribunal:

> The trial judge should not as a rule limit himself to stating good set terms of law culled from the codes and the reports. Jurors need not legal definitions merely. They require proper instructions as to the method of applying such definitions after reaching their conclusions on the facts.[47]

Moreover, the judge must see to it that his charge is scrupulously fair to both sides in the dispute. But it is of overriding importance to the accused. It should be "the safeguard of fairness and impartiality and the guarantee of judicial indifference to individuals."[48] Many a charge has ultimately ended in a mistrial; many another has been found to be defective on points of law by appellate courts. In brief, the judge's charge to the jurors, which is almost always necessarily complicated, sums up the case, pinpoints the

[47] *People v. Odell*, 230 N.Y. 481 (1921), at 487–8.
[48] Ibid., at 488.

chief issues involved, and concludes with the admonition that the jury must bring in a verdict of "guilty" or "not guilty"—addressing itself to each of the charges and/or counts at issue and, if a choice is permissible under law in homicide cases, determining the degree of punishment. Any verdict of "guilty" must have taken into account the absence of *reasonable doubt*, often a very difficult problem. There are no in-between stages of a verdict, although in some cases in some of the fifty American states, juries are empowered to mitigate their judgment of guilt in homicide cases by a recommendation for mercy, which is normally binding upon the judge. It was just such a binding recommendation by the third jury in the Finch-Tregoff murder case that saved Finch from the electric chair.

Under certain limited circumstances, a judge may express a value judgment on the evidence in charging his jury, but this is valid only in isolated instances. Superior Judge Leroy Dawson in the second Finch-Tregoff case startled courtroom observers by telling the deadlocked jury that the evidence showed "a willful and deliberate taking of human life." When one of the defense attorneys repeatedly attempted to stop the judge from reading his comments, he found himself twice cited for contempt. Judge Dawson cited a 1934 amendment to the California Constitution as his authority and a San Diego case in 1958 as his precedent.[49] Since his own case resulted in a hung jury, Dawson's action was not challenged further. On the other hand, judges everywhere are free to comment upon a jury's verdict once that has been announced, although many jurists believe that practice, too, to be at least unwise if not unethical; but it is not illegal unless expressly interdicted by statutory or constitutional mandate.

Setting a Verdict Aside. In *civil* cases, but generally not in *criminal* cases save for a few states that permit it, a judge may *reverse* the jury's verdict. This frequently occurs in so-called *negligence* cases, in which jury lawlessness, in the form of excessive verdict, is not uncommon. A federal case of this nature, which was widely featured in the public press in 1959 because of an open clash between Justices Whitaker and Douglas, was *Inman v. Baltimore and Ohio Railroad*.[50] A District of Columbia jury had held the railroad negligent in stationing a man where he could be knocked down by a drunken driver, and it awarded the former $25,000. However,

49 *The Sunday Bulletin* (Philadelphia), November 6, 1960.
50 361 U. S. 138.

the judge who presided over the trial in his United States District Court set the verdict aside as being "irrational."[51]When the United States Court of Appeals upheld the district judge, Inman appealed to the United States Supreme Court which. in a 5:4 opinion, affirmed the judgment below. What provoked the headlined outburst by Mr. Justice Douglas, and his insistence that the Supreme Court has a duty to enforce the guarantee of a jury trial and to prevent the lower courts from setting too strict a standard, was Mr. Justice Whitaker's concurring opinion. In it, the latter had scoffed at the idea that the railroad had been negligent and suggested that the only way that it could have prevented the accident was to have the employee encased in an army tank. This, in the full glare of an "Opinion Monday" (to be described in detail in Chapter V) Mr. Justice Douglas denounced, in person and from the bench, as "smart-alecky." Barely one year later, however, with Justices Black and Douglas dissenting vehemently, the Supreme Court itself, for the first time in twenty-four years, reversed a jury's verdict awarding damages to an injured railroad worker.[52] Judge Charles E. Wyzanski, Jr., of the federal trial court below had upheld the jury's verdict, but denounced it in no uncertain terms, asserting the case was devoid of "any evidence of negligence"— and had refrained from setting it aside solely because he felt bound by what until then had been Supreme Court doctrine in these cases.[53] Of course, courts may also reverse and remand an award as being "too low," although this occurs far less frequently. Thus, the U.S. Court of Appeals for the Second Circuit held a $32,000 jury-awarded payment to a widow for the death of her husband killed in an automobile accident "as grossly inadequate," based on what Judge Irving R. Kaufman noted as the unfair influence of the trial judge's charge to the jury.[54]

The judges may also set aside a jury verdict if it is clearly based upon an obviously mistaken notion of the law involved in a case. Yet all these practices in American courts are a far cry from the

---

51 An example of a state court reversal of a verdict is the action by Philadelphia Court of Common Pleas, Judge Theodore L. Reimel in setting aside a $25,000 verdict by a jury for a local attorney's claim for fees due as being "excessive and perverse." (*The Evening Bulletin,* January 16, 1962.)

52 *New York, New Haven, and Hartford v. Hennagan,* 364 U. S. 441 (1960).

53 Ibid. As reported in 272 F. 2d 153, at 155–6 (1959), and in *The New York Times,* November 22, 1960.

54 *Caskey v. The Village of Wayland,* 362 F. 2d 1789 (1967).

English and Continental systems, where the trial judge is permitted, if not expected, to comment upon the weight of the evidence and the credibility of witnesses throughout the course of the trial, and to allow the jury to know his opinion on the merits of the case. On the other hand, the average judge in the United States, too, has the power in all cases to order a verdict of *directed acquittal* before a case goes to the jury—a motion made often by defense counsel almost as a routine matter, but granted rarely. If granted, however, it is not subject to reversal by any higher court on the *federal* level. Moreover, the judge may take a case out of the jury's hands if it becomes evident that there are only questions of law involved, no facts being in dispute at all. And among the myriad of reasons why a judge may order a *retrial* is, a clear case of basic confusion among the jurors—one that obviously affected the verdict in such a fashion that there is grave doubt in the mind of the presiding judge that the jury has fulfilled its part in seeing that justice is done. Thus, in a New Jersey automobile accident case the jury had returned from its deliberations, and its foreman upon being asked by the judge, "Have you agreed upon a verdict, Mr. Foreman?", answered, "My name isn't Foreman. My name is Admerman." When the trial judge refused to recognize this interesting reply as a sufficient reason to declare a mistrial, defendant Naomi Haberli appealed to the Appellate Division of the New Jersey State Superior Court, which unanimously ordered a retrial, citing Mr. Admerman's response, as well as the grossly excessive award granted by his fellow jurors, as a *prima facie* example of the type of "basic confusion" necessitating a new trial.[55] But it should be understood that no trial or appellate judge will readily tamper with a jury's verdict, no matter what his private opinion may be.

"General" and "Special Verdicts." On the basis of the somewhat questionable assumption that the jury fully comprehends the judge's instructions concerning the applicable substantive legal rules, it is usually required to return a *general* or *over-all* verdict in favor of one party or another. Theoretically, as already indicated, this jury verdict is based on the *facts* of the case, the judge himself having determined the rules of *law*—although it is not always possible to separate facts and law, and the U.S. Supreme Court has repeatedly

[55] *The New York Times*, December 15, 1960.

dismissed challenges to provisions that make juries the sole judges of the law as well as the facts in criminal trials.[56] In practice, however, the general verdict permits the jury to do what it pleases: it gives no details, simply reports its decision, and no one either really knows or may safely predict just what facts a jury found from the evidence. Judge Jerome Frank, a life-long and severe critic of the jury system as a fact-finding institution, viewed the judge's charge as little more than an elaborate ceremonial routine, and he argued that of all the possible ways that could be devised to arrive at the falsity or truth of testimony, ". . . . none could be conceived that would be more ineffective than trial by jury."[57] He and many other legal authorities have long contended that *special* or *fact* verdicts—employed in England centuries ago—in which the jury is asked to answer a *specific* question of fact, are a far preferable method of arriving at a verdict that is just to all concerned. In a special verdict procedure, which is now used in several of the fifty states, and was authorized for federal *civil* suits in 1938 (but is very rarely used), the trial judge charges the jury to report its findings—presumably even if these are simply beliefs —about certain particular issues of fact raised during the course of the trial, facts which, at least in theory, a jury should be able to weigh and determine with a modicum of accuracy and reliability. To those facts thus "found" the judge then applies the appropriate legal rule. Whatever the type of jury verdict advocated, the degree of perfection one may expect from the human institutions that comprise the judicial process is necessarily a limited one.

The British judges employ a charge rather similar to that found in the tribunals of the United States, but they provide more guidance to the jury during the trial. No charge is used in the courts of France. Instead, the French presiding judge, who actively directs the proceedings in the courtroom by interrogating the accused and witnesses, submits to the jury—in the infrequent instances of its presence in a case—a list of questions which the nine panelists are required to answer with a simple "yes" or "no." Standard examples of these queries would be, "Did the accused prove his alibi?"; "Was the accused present at the scene

---

[56] See, for example, *Giles v. Maryland*, 372 U. S. 767 (1962).

[57] Jerome Frank, *Courts on Trial* (Princeton: Princeton University Press, 1949), p. 20. (Italics supplied.) This is one of *the* great books on the judicial process.

of the crime when it was committed?"; "Was the act of homicide one of self-defense?"; and always, "If you find the defendant guilty, were there any extenuating circumstances?" Clearly, by his interrogation the judge tries to give to the jury the most lucid picture possible as a matter of guidance. The jury, its members voting individually and in secret, answers these questions specifically and thereby reaches its verdict—if necessary by a *majority* vote, in contrast to the *unanimity* requirements of the American federal judicial system. However, should the divisions among the jurors prove to be uncomfortably close, such as 7:5 or even 6:6, the presiding judge may assume the power of determining the verdict with the aid of the two associate judges (there are always three judges at the assize-trial level). But in that event the verdict is almost certain to be one of acquittal.

In West Germany today the entire courtroom examination in criminal trials is conducted by the judges, while the prosecuting attorney and counsel for the defense sit mute and take notes. Counsel is privileged to put a question only when the judges have completed an examination calculated to bring out fully and fairly all that a witness might tell. Jurors are taken from a local list of "outstanding" citizens and impaneled for a term of one year. Judge and jury sit on the bench together and participate jointly and equally in deliberation on a case—a procedure known as a *fused* jury.

JURIES: BLESSING OR EVIL?

It is not easy to be objective about juries—and few observers are. Certainly there is but little doubt that juries throughout the Western world have declined considerably both in significance and esteem during the past century. Often, when they are not held in utter contempt by their professional critics, they are merely tolerated as a necessary, and at times admittedly convenient, evil. In large measure, the juries have brought this opprobrium on themselves—no matter how innocent and perhaps even understandable their response to the demands of the legal process may be. But it is difficult, indeed, to defend the institution in the face of some of the seemingly inexhaustible fiascos in which they seem perpetually to find themselves. Examples are legion, and a few will suffice as illustrative of the patent fact that it is not easy to be a defender of the system.

Thus, we again turn to the aforementioned Finch-Tregoff case, this time the first 1960 trial, to find the jury at its worst. According to an interview (!) granted to United Press International by one of the members of the panel of five men and seven women that had just been declared a hung jury:

> . . . at one point a near fight broke out. At the height of one heated debate, a male juror threatened to throw another [a female] out of a window and turned over the jury table—he used to be a boxer—before she ran to the door. She was hysterical and pounded on the door for the bailiff.[58]

A different woman juror also readily and beamingly gave an interview to U.P.I., reporting that at least three "propositioning" notes had been passed to one of the women on the panel. An extra bailiff was then brought in to stand guard at another woman's hotel room door after those notes came to light.[59] A further illustration is the young mother from Bedford, Indiana, who confessed that as a member of a jury panel in the 1950's she voted to convict the accused of rape—despite the fact that she believed him to be innocent. She did so against her own judgment, she readily admitted, because "I knew I had those children at home and we would never get out of there if we tried to argue it out with the others."[60] Similar "interviews" were granted by jurors in the Wallace Butts-Curtis Publishing Co. 1963 libel suit. And to conclude the unfortunately almost inexhaustible instances of the kind of antics that have served to bring opprobrium to the institution: In March 1961, under the guise of registering a *coup* in what it called "public service," the Hearst Corporation-owned station WBAL-TV in Baltimore induced, evidently without any difficulty, nine of twelve jurors to appear before the studio camera and re-enact their deliberations that resulted in the conviction of one Melvin Davis Rees, Jr., for murder and kidnapping. This intriguing performance, which featured in great detail the thoughts and reasoning that culminated in the verdict, came on the evening *prior* to the scheduled sentencing of the convicted man! As a result, defense counsel succeeded in obtaining at least a temporary postponement of sentencing and raised a series of legal questions based

[58] *The New York Times,* March 13, 1960.
[59] Ibid. But judges may enjoin interviews (e.g. *U.S. v. Driscoll,* 1 Nov. 67).
[60] As quoted by John F. X. Irving, "The Jury May Be Out Permanently," 6 *National Review* 177 (September 1958).

upon this jury TV debut—which the *Baltimore News Post,* also a Hearst-owned medium, termed "a reportorial breakthrough of the traditional silence of the jury room."[61] Considerations of law, ethics, morals, and taste were evidently deemed insignificant.

Evil? Continuing naturally at this juncture of the analysis with the indictment of the institution of the jury—which Balzac once defined as "twelve men to decide who has the better lawyer," and Herbert Spencer as "a group of twelve people of average ignorance"—there is considerable, indeed fairly conclusive, evidence that the average jury reaches its verdict in most instances by a kind of "happy" compromise. Not being able to agree on a financial award in a civil case, for example, the various panelists will write down separate figures, add the total, divide it by the number of jurors, and thus attain peace of mind! In homicide cases a host of revelations again and again points to jury compromises. Thus, unless they are expressly forbidden to do so by statute or by the judge's charge, jurors will frequently decide a case of murder by "compromising" between first degree murder and acquittal by settling for a second degree conviction—usually totally unjustified by the facts in the case. For example, the 1967 Naples, Florida, jury that convicted Dr. Carl Coppolino of the poison-murder of his first wife, Carmela, brought in a verdict of murder in the *second* degree—when, obviously, the very use of poison carries with it premeditation, which calls for a *first*-degree murder conviction. Evidently, the jury had "compromised." Or the flip-of-the-coin or lot method is employed in order to get the nasty business over with. Or, as was demonstrated in a Hancock County, Kentucky, case, the jury became so confused as a result of its own deliberations that it formally "retracted" an already rendered verdict![62] Our legal periodicals and other literature are replete with data corroborating what has been said above.[63]

Moreover, it is almost impossible for the wandering mind of the ordinary juror to overcome conclusively the histrionics that so often characterize presentation by counsel. Both prosecution and defense generally conduct what is to all intents and purposes a legal sporting combat, with each side following evidence by

[61] See Jack Gould's article in *The New York Times,* March 25, 1961.
[62] *The New York Times,* April 15, 1962.
[63] See Frank, op. cit. p. 122, and the University of Chicago jury studies, conducted by Prof. Harry Kalven.

counter-evidence, examination by cross-examination, witness by counter-witnesses, each one sworn to tell the truth and nothing but the truth. Not infrequently, this touching search for the truth results in statements in open court that are clearly out of order. But even if the judge so holds, as he often does, and asks the jury to disregard the statement at issue, it has been uttered, of course, and it is conjectural at best whether it can be wiped from the jurors' minds. To arrive at the veritable truth behind what one long-time observer of juries styled "the curtain of flimflam and obfuscation,"[64] may well boil down to a jury verdict on the basis of which side, in its judgment, seemed to tell fewer lies. Hence, in the words of Judge Frank, based on his many years of active experience in the legal and judicial processes:

> . . . the jury is the worst possible enemy of the "supremacy of the law." For "jury-made law" is, par excellence, capricious and arbitrary, yielding the maximum in the way of lack of uniformity, of unknowability.[65]

Accordingly, he and others would prefer the trial judges to hear and decide cases alone, the assumption being that judges are presumabably trained in the law, which jurors are not, and that they function in a setting which is open to considerably more scrutiny than juries.

Blessing? A natural and main source of endorsement of the jury system in the trial lawyer, who has a vested interest in influencing it—even if this is done by persuading the generally bewildered jurors that black is really white. Few, if any, defense lawyers in a criminal case would argue against it! But the venerable institution's defense does not need to rest its case on such pragmatic grounds. Many a legal scholar, far from decrying the factors of emotion, prejudice, and sympathy that are undeniably major determinants in jury verdicts, holds that these very factors advance the cause of justice because they represent the "socially adapted intuitive law" of the various communities to which we belong. Thus, Charles P. Curtis and Harold J. Berman have contended repeatedly that the jury reflects "the intuitive part of us," which they view as a necessary counterbalance to the equally

64 David A. Dressler, "Trial by Combat in American Courts," 222 *Harper's Magazine* 32 (April 1960).
65 Frank, op. cit. p. 132.

essential "intellectual part of us" in the judge.[66] This is particularly appropriate if one keeps in mind that, in the final analysis, the first and foremost function of a jury is to choose between conflicting testimony, testimony so frequently beclouded by histrionics and legalistics as to render an "intuitive" judgment all but inevitable—at least up to a point. Something can certainly be said for the time-honored principle of being judged by a group of one's peers. Moreover, much of the adverse criticism would appear to depend on which side of the case one's interests lie, and whether the jury sits in a civil or criminal case.

One of the most articulate and influential champions of the jury system was the distinguished John Henry Wigmore, who advanced four main arguments in favor of the principle: First, that it prevents popular distrust of official justice since it gives the average member of the body politic a share in the political process. Second, that it provides for some necessary flexibility in legal rules and regulations in that it enables an adjustment of the "general rule of law to the justice of a particular case," whereas the judge is rightly expected to be consistent and consequential in his rulings for all. Third, that the jury system educates the ordinary citizen in the administration of justice by cultivating the judicial habit in him and by creating in him a respect for law and order, thus making him conscious of his duty to society and his share in the governmental process. Fourth, that the jury system ameliorates the verdict because it is based on the amalgam of a host of temperaments and viewpoints.[67] In essence, this is a plea on behalf of the institution based on the recognition of the role of common sense in the judicial process. It is a plea echoed by Law Professors Harry Kalven, Jr., and Hans Zeisel of the University of Chicago after a monumental study of the jury system, involving the questioning of 550 judges who presided over 3,576 jury trials across the country. Their conclusion was that the freedom of a jury to inject its own sense of justice is one of the greatest strengths of the system.[68]

Unquestionably, the Wigmore roster of exhortation is subject to serious exception—especially since it is based, at least in part,

[66] See Curtis, op. cit. pp. 101–4.
[67] As discussed and quoted by William Wirt Blume, "The Place of Trial in Criminal Cases," 43 *Michigan Law Review* 64–5.
[68] The study, Ford Foundation-financed, and known as the "Chicago Jury Project," was published under the title of *The American Jury* (Boston: Little, Brown and Co., 1966).

on a rather optimistic, happy, and sanguine view of human nature and the willingness as well as the ability of the average citizen to accept and adapt himself to these laudatory notions of participation in the responsibilities of society and state. Some of the illustrations presented in connection with the adverse criticism of the institution would appear to raise some crucial doubts regarding Professor Wigmore's analysis. Be that as it may, despite its shortcomings the jury system has been generally regarded by the public at large as a laudable instrument in the quest for justice. "It is so justly regarded," once applauded Joseph H. Choate,

> as the best and perhaps the only known means of admitting the people to a share in maintaining their wholesome interest in the administration of justice. . . ."[69]

The ultimate questions remains, however: is it and does it? It is difficult to discount the haunting doubts.

FROM OFFENSE
TO TRIAL: A PROCEDURAL NOTE

The practices and customs that characterize the legal process differ widely in the various jurisdictions discussed herein; this also applies to the procedures followed in the lengthy and often difficult path that leads from the commission of the offense to its ultimate adjudication in or out of the courtroom—for the vast majority of cases are in fact settled by mutual agreement before they reach the trial stage. Indeed, on the whole it is only the so-called trouble cases that actually traverse the tedious process through the entire courtroom sequence. The purpose of this procedural note is to illustrate in necessarily brief and generalized fashion the various stages that confront participants in a full-length legal proceeding. The model employed, which will distinguish between civil and criminal cases, is an average jurisdiction in the United States of America. And it should be noted that the very nature of an American court case requires the presence of the following four conditions: (1) an adversary process; (2) an actual disposition; (3) ripeness for judicial determination; and (4) an actual disposition.[70]

---

[69] As quoted by Justice Bernard Botein, *Trial Judge* (New York: Simon and Schuster, 1952), p. 195.

[70] See Ch. IX, *infra*, in this connection.

134

Procedure in Civil Cases

Step 1 is the *commencement of the action* by the *plaintiff*, the party bringing the suit, against the *respondent* or *defendant*. If it is a matter of an *appeal* rather than the bringing of an intitial suit, the party who appeals is known as the *appellant*, the other side as the *respondent* or *appellee*. The plaintiff or appellant may also be termed *petitioner*. A word of caution: while it is easily possible to determine who the two sides to a respective suit are at the initial stage of a new suit, once that proceeding has reached the various appellate stages it is considerably more difficult to do so, and the only safe manner is to read the first few paragraphs of the case. In order to bring his suit, a plaintiff will have to do at least three things: (1) select the correct and proper tribunal; (2) have the defendant or his possessions brought before it; and (3) present his charges and ask for appropriate remedies.

In order to achieve the second requirement, the plaintiff must ask the proper authorities to serve a *summons*, which is issued after the petitioner has "sworn it out". Presumably it will be obeyed. Failure to respond to the summons will normally result either in a judgment against the respondent by default or in contempt proceedings. An even more compellling order to appear is a *subpoena*, a writ that, unlike the summons, must always be served on the respondent or witness in person; it directs his appearance on pain of being held in contempt of court (or of whatever other judicial or quasi-judicial authority may be empowered to issue the writ). A subpoena *duces tecum*, a related writ, requires the respondent to *bring something* along, a specific document, for example. If the respondent resides outside of the court's jurisdiction, but owns property therein, the latter may be *attached*, in order to commence a suit, but only if the property attached is itself the subject matter of the suit. If it is not, the respondent cannot be brought into court by attachment of business property, even if he resides within the jurisdiction.

Closely related to the three tasks the plaintiff performs in order to commence the action, is an attempt by the two parties to the suit to narrow the factual and legal issues involved by virtue of an exchange of one or a series of formal written statements stating the claim at issue, known as *pleadings*. These follow logically as a result of the plaintiff's initiation of his *complaint*. *Step 2* is designed solely to formulate the issues in the case and consists of the formal pleadings, now presumably involving the legal battery for both sides. This stage of the pleadings features the formal exchange of documents between the two sides, with the respondent required to file an *answer*. Often the lawyers are able to settle matters at this stage, but since we are here concerned with a sketch of the entire procedure, we assume that instead of there being acquiescence or agreement, the future defendant will file a *motion to dismiss* the complaint, sometimes also known as a *demurrer*. If the plaintiff rejects these formal counterclaims, the stage will now have been set for the docketing of the case on the calendars of the court of proper jurisdiction. A *pretrial conference with the judge* may conceivably settle matters at this juncture and avoid an actual trial—it will very likely serve to narrow further some of the problems involved. The next formal stage is the trial itself.

The nature and character of *step 3*, the *trial*, depend largely on whether the issue between the litigants is one of law or of fact. If the issue is solely one of *law*, the court receives the case via a legal *argument* presented by the attorneys for both sides. Since there are no facts to be determined, jury and witnesses are not called; the judge decides the dispute strictly on the basis of the law, as he sees it. But if the dispute is either "mixed" or strictly of *facts* the case will be tried before judge and jury, depending somewhat upon its nature and, as has been described earlier in the chapter, whether or not a jury trial is waived by mutual consent where that is possible and desirable. The next four steps, *verdict, judgment, appellate review* (if any), and *enforcement*, if not self-explanatory, have already been delineated above or will be discussed in subsequent chapters.

PROCEDURE IN CRIMINAL CASES

Because of the very nature of the offense, the procedure in a criminal case is *ipso facto* both more formal and more elaborate, and it involves the machinery of the state to a much more important degree. Above all, the state, as was demonstrated in Chapter I, necessarily is a party to the suit—at least in the sense that it is responsible for the prosecution of the offense. *Step 1*, therefore, is very simply the *apprehension* of the prospective defendant within the territorial limitations of the governmental jurisdiction concerned—i.e. unless he voluntarily surrenders to the authorities, he is literally caught and arrested, either in the act of commission, while fleeing, or as a result of an arrest warrant, which the arresting officer must obtain in advance from properly constituted authority. *Step 2*, closely related to the first, sees the arrested person brought before a magistrate—a Commissioner on the federal level—[71] for the *preliminary* examination in order to determine whether he shall be released or shall be *held to answer*. If the latter, the accused will be held either in *custody* or released on *bail* to await the decision of the public prosecutor or the grand jury on the question of whether or not an *information* or an *indictment* shall be filed against him. The preliminary examination is a crucial and highly significant stage in criminal procedure: At the state level more than 50 per cent of the individuals are freed as a result of it, which, in effect, customarily closes the books on the matter. On the federal level, however, the percentage seems to be less than ten.

Step 3 represents the formal *accusation* by the grand jury or by the process of "information", depending upon the statutory requirements or practices in the several jurisdictions concerned. This is logically followed by the *arraignment* and *pleading*, constituting *step 4*. An arraignment consists simply of the official, formal reading of the terms of the indictment or the information to the accused by the court of jurisdiction. The arraignment concludes with the significant question, "How do you plead?"—giving the accused the choice of *"guilty"* or *"not guilty."*[72]

---

[71] See p. 163, *infra*, for a brief explanation of this office. See also Charles A. Lindquist, "The United States Commissioner's Role in the Judicial Process with Specific Reference to the Eastern District of Pennsylvania," Unpublished Dissertation, University of Pennsylvania, p. 21. See also John Hanna, "The Forgotten Man in the Federal Judicial System," 32 *Journal of the American Bar Association* (June 1946).

[72] Under some circumstances, but rarely in criminal proceedings, the accused may also plead *nolo contendere* or "no contest,"—specifically, "I do not wish to contend"—by which he throws himself upon the mercy of the court without admitting guilt per se. The penalties are potentially the same as for the plea of guilty, but the judge more often than not displays leniency in such cases—some say if for no other reason than that that plea saves time, effort, and money.

Step 5 is the *trial* itself, if there is one at all—if not, the judge's verdict takes its place as is true in many, but not all pleadings of guilty. A host of proceedings, with which we need not concern ourselves here, antedates the trial—including various motions for dismissal of the case, change of pleadings, placing of dispositions, request for change of *venue*, possible dismissal or change of charges. The trial is conducted by the judge, either with or without the jury as, the case and jurisdiction may mandate, and the process terminates with the next four steps: *verdict, judgment and sentencing, appellate review* (if any, and *execution of the sentence imposed* if any). Of course, no bare procedural sketch such as this can take into account the sundry aspects and ramifications of the manifold practices, procedures, and safeguards that surround this fascinating aspect of the judicial process; it should be regarded merely as the outline of its essential framework.

Despite the relatively drastic distinctions in judicial theory and practice between the common law lands and the statutory law lands of the free West, the justice meted out under both legal systems is similar in its ultimate degree of fairness, if not in its efficiency. Each system is characterized by obvious advantages and disadvantages, and each features methods that are peculiar to the needs or predispositions of the particular governmental jurisdiction concerned. As is so pre-eminently true of most practices in the realm of free government, they, too, are specifically adapted to the needs of the people directly involved. They are steeped in their own culture and tradition, and it is sheer folly for outsiders to endeavor to impose their own systems—even in theory. Sir Stafford Cripps once remarked wisely that methods and institutions of government are not simply commodities of international commerce, thus echoing the statement by Alexis de Tocqueville in his *Democracy in America* in 1831:

> The more I see of this country [the United States] the more I admit myself penetrated with this truth: that there is nothing absolute in the theoretical value of institutions, and that their efficiency depends almost always on the original circumstances and the social conditions of the people to whom they are applied.

IV

COURTS AT HOME:

I THE LESSER TRIBUNALS

A DUAL SYSTEM OF COURTS

As a result of the federal system that prevails in the United States, the national government and fifty state governments all make and enforce law. In effect, this means that there exist side by side, two major court systems—one could even say fifty-one—that are wholly distinct bodies in the sense that they are created under different basic authorities: the respective national and state constitutions. The jurisdiction of these two systems may, and in some highly significant instances does, regularly "merge" at the bar of the final interpretative authority of the Supreme Court of the United States. However, such a "merger" can come about only if a *substantial* federal question has been validly raised in the proper state court below and, all remedies at the state level having been duly exhausted, that question has been successfully brought to what is in all but a handful of cases the *discretionary* attention of the Supreme Court. It is axiomatic that the path to the highest court in the land is long, expensive, arduous, and difficult, and thus it is not traveled frequently. Other than in this appellate process, and possibly in the vexatious and procedurally intricate realm of injunctive relief, the national and state courts in the United States are separate entities. Nonetheless, it should be noted that through its constitutional power to establish *"inferior* courts,"[1] Congress possesses the power to draw a rigid line between the *jurisdiction* of these federal and state courts. But it has not seen fit to do so except in certain civil rights areas, notably some types of racial discrimination,[2] and in a number of fields of relatively narrow juris-

[1] U. S. Constitution, Art, III, Sec. 1, Par. 1. (Italics supplied.)
[2] For example, see certain provisions of the Civil Rights Acts of 1957, 1960, and 1964 and the Voting Rights Act of 1965.

diction, such as matters involving admiralty, bankruptcy, copyright, and patent.

THE STATE COURTS

It would require a book, or certainly a lengthy monograph, in order to describe adequately the courts in the fifty states, where the great majority of the legal business of the American public begins and ends. The character, jurisdiction, quality, and complexity of these courts vary considerably from state to state in accordance with the myriad considerations of public policy, need, size, and constitutional practice that characterize the heterogeneous component parts of the nation. Every state constitution either establishes a judicial branch for its invariably tripartite government or, either in whole or in part—as is true for the national level under Article III of the Constitution of the United States—authorizes the legislature to provide for a judicial system. Although the terminology and structure among the state courts differ significantly, a discernible structural pattern does exist. The base consists of a system of justices of the peace and trial courts, with the pyramid gradually winding its way upward through a more or less elaborate appellate system, culminating in a supreme court (not invariably termed "Supreme Court," however).

The Justice of the Peace

With rare exception, the lowest court at the state level—and there are those who would put the noun "court" into quotation marks in this particular connection—is the *Justice of the Peace*, that fourteenth-century Anglo-Saxon office, often, and sometimes irreverently, referred to as the "J. P." (standing for "Justice for the Plaintiff," in some eyes). He is also occasionally styled *squire* and, in many cities, e.g. New York, *magistrate*. By no means necessarily a lawyer, this official is usually elected for a two- to six-year term in counties, townships, and towns, but sometimes he is appointed for a term of similar length by the executive in the cities. The office he fills boasts of an honorable and indeed ancient tradition that came to the colonies from England, initially designed to aid in the administration of justice in minor matters at the local level. Today, the Justice of the Peace, who is usually also a notary public, still performs a modicum of court work, but most of his duties are quasi-legislative, quasi-judicial, and quasi-administrative, including the characteristic performance of civil marriages. Most of these tasks are performed on a fee basis—probably a regrettable practice in view of its close link to meeting out justice. He does, however, retain at least the appearance of a court of first instance in minor civil and criminal matters. In the former, his jurisdiction normally extends only to cases involving less than $200; in the latter, it is limited almost exclusively to misdemeanors.

With some notable exceptions, again usually confined to some urban areas—e.g. New York City, where the magistrates have legal background, are appointed for ten-year terms of office, and receive about $20,000 annually—the Justice of the Peace's lack of training and qualifications is exceeded only by his sure-fire penchant for convictions, which have averaged 96 per cent in civil cases and 80 per cent in criminal cases.[3] A study made in 1956 of the minor judiciary of North Carolina, for one, pointed out that not a single J. P. in that state then had a law degree; that 75 per cent had never gone to college; and that 40 per cent had never even attended high school![4] A similar study for Virginia a decade later showed that of 411 past and present members of the Association of Justices of the Peace of Virginia, a mere four were lawyers; that 71 per cent had never gone to college; that a mere five of the 29 per cent who did were graduated; and that 18 per cent were not even high school graduates.[5] In Oregon only nine of seventy J. P.'s had law degrees in 1966.[6] Even in a cosmopolitan city such as Philadelphia, and despite the salary of $12,500 ($15,000 for the Chief Magistrate), only one of its twenty-eight elected

[3] In 1962 in Pennsylvania, of 63,040 criminal cases handled by the then 4305 J. P.'s, 51,997, or about 83 per cent, resulted in conviction; another 6375, or 10 per cent, were bound over for court trial; and 4668, or about 7 per cent, were dismissed (XI *Horizons for Modern Governments* 5, May 1963, p. 4). For examples of conviction rates from 95 to 99.2 per cent in Michigan, Mississippi, and Tennessee counties, see Mitchell Dawson, "The Justice of the Peace Racket," in Robert Morlan, *Capitol, Courthouse, and City Hall*, rev. ed. (Boston: Houghton Mifflin Co., 1966), pp. 144–5.

[4] Isham Newton, "The Minor Judiciary in North Carolina" (Unpublished Ph.D. Thesis, University of Pennsylvania, 1956).

[5] "Justice of the Peace in Virginia: A Neglected Aspect of the Judiciary," 52 *Virginia Law Review* 151 (January 1966), describing a survey conducted by Weldon Cooper of the Institute of Government Studies of the University of Virginia.

[6] *The Christian Science Monitor*, May 9, 1967, p. 5.

magistrates held a law degree in 1967. All this represents an unfortunate state of affairs, for, given suitable attributes of integrity and proper qualification, the Justice of the Peace might well still provide able and inexpensive adjudication and settlement of minor legal problems in the judicial process. On the other hand, Philadelphia's then Chief Magistrate, Joseph J. Hersch, insisted in an interview in December 1961, seconded as recently as 1967 by his successor, John Patrick Walsh, that the job of a magistrate is "more social than legal"; he decried the need for a law degree, stating:

> A law degree doesn't make a magistrate more qualified. Living with people is more essential than going to a law library to find out what it's all about. . . If you take Purdon's law books away from them [the lawyers], they're out of business.

But, like many of their colleagues in other states, Philadelphia's magistrates have come under increasing attack, such as the scathing indictment by District Attorney Arlen Specter, long a foe of the entire magistrate system, who declared that ". . . the only difference between Chief Magistrate Walsh and his 27 cohorts and Ali Baba and the 40 Thieves is that one group is somewhat larger."[7]

THE MUNICIPAL COURT

Again because of varying needs, different nomenclature attends the *Municipal Court,* the next higher level of court ordinarily found in the several states. Some of the more common designations are *Traffic Court, City Court, Night Court,* and *Police Court.* The Municipal Court, whatever it may be called, is almost always a court of original jurisdiction and normally also the first court of record[8] in the judicial hierarchy of the state. Its jurisdiction is

---

[7] Public Statement, December 1, 1966.

[8] Although all courts are presumably required to keep records today, the expression "court of record" is still used to distinguish between courts presided over by members of the minor judiciary (magistrates or justices of the peace) and other courts of original jurisdiction presided over by judges. In 1964, the Municipal Court of the City of Boulder, Colorado, then presided over by Municipal Judge Rex H. Stout, was designated by the American Bar Association as "the best in the nation" for cities with populations from 25,000 to 50,000. It had won similar awards for 1958-59 and 1960-61. (The author had occasion to come before Judge Stout for a minor traffic violation on July 1, 1964, and can testify to a superbly conducted court!)

customarily limited to circa $500 to $1000 in civil cases, and to misdemeanors where it does have criminial jurisdiction. The municipal-level courts provide the parties before them with a fast and inexpensive procedure, and they are generally staffed by judges who possess legal training.[9]

THE COUNTY COURT

Next in line is what is by all odds the work-horse court of the average state judiciary, the *County Court*. It is a court of general civil and criminal jurisdiction, as a rule covering three major types of cases and controversies: ordinary civil beyond the limit of the court of jurisdiction just below; criminal other than routine misdemeanors; plus probate and inheritance. As its name implies, the County Court's geographical jurisdiction is limited to the level of that subdivision of the state. If juries are used by a state judiciary at all—and, of course, they usually are, althought there is still no *state* obligation to provide juries under the verbiage and interpretation of the Bill of Rights in the *federal* Constitution—they will be found here. Although Philadelphia, for one, has a separate tribunal called County Court (with jurisdiction over juveniles, domestic relations cases, certain crimes, and some civil matters) a whole coterie of allied or subsidiary courts is either present at this level or takes the place of the County Court. Among these may well be all or some of the following, often self-explanatory, judicial county helpmates: *Common Pleas* (a court to hear and determine civil cases, usually where the amount in controversy is in excess of $5000); *Oyer and Terminer* (a criminal court with jurisdiction

9 Frequently found at the Municipal Court level, but usually not regarded as a court of record, is the *Court of Small Claims*. Its jurisdiction is usually limited to claims of $200.00 or less; there are low fees, no juries, often no appeals (except for a trial *de novo*), sometimes not even counsel. An unusual, but highly promising, "non-court" system of case-disposition in the judicial process is Philadelphia's (and Pittsburgh's) fascinating system of "compulsory arbitration" of civil cases involving claims of up to $2000. Actually found administratively at the level of the County Court in Philadelphia since its statutory adoption by the state in 1958, it consists of teams of three-member lawyer panels who hear and decide a vast number of cases that would otherwise linger on the court dockets. The lawyers are appointed by the Arbitration Commissioners from an alphabetical list of volunteers: No matter how long

over capital crimes and other felonies—e.g. murder, manslaughter, treason, robbery, rape, kidnapping); *Quarter Sessions* (a predominantly criminal court with jurisdiction over a few technical civil cases and over crimes not tried by Oyer and Terminer, that usually meets four times annually, and sometimes consists of the same personnel as Oyer and Terminer); *Orphans; Probate* (for wills, estates, and deeds); *Juvenile* (for youthful offenders); *Domestic Relations; Surrogate* (similar to Probate in some counties); *Chancery* (specializing in equity matters); and *Equity*.

THE INTERMEDIATE COURT OF APPEALS

Beyond the County Court lies the intermediate court, or courts, of appeals, usually termed *Appellate Division, State Appellate Court, Superior Court, or Intermediate Court of Appeals*. The jurisdiction of this tribunal is almost wholly appellate—certain writs being the exception in some states. It receives and adjudges appeals from decisions of the County Court and the Municipal Court, in rare cases from others. More often than not its decisions are final, although it is, of course, possible to go up from here to the final level since it is an *intermediate* appellate court. Not all states resort to such an intermediate stage, but all of the larger ones do. Some of these have an elaborate appellate structure; The State of New York has an intricate system of more than 150 appellate courts at this level; and the appellate structure of the State of California enabled Caryl Whittier Chessman to file fourteen appeals in its system (which he augmented with twenty-eight appeals to the federal courts between 1948 and 1960 in an ultimately un-

a hearing takes, the lawyers are each paid a nominal fee of $20.00 per case, the chairman $30.00. The average cost per "trial" to date has been but $62.50! Not only their time and expertise, but also their quarters and any necessary secretarial help are provided by these volunteer members of the bar. The atmosphere of the proceedings is judicial and judicious, but rules of evidence are given liberal construction. Any appeals taken from a panel's decision is heard by a County Court judge *de novo* with or without a jury. But very few cases are in fact appealed, and the successful processing of an average of 8000 cases annually by these arbitration panels is proof positive of the system's success, and sensibility. (For details see the *Annual Reports* of the Commissioner of the Compulsory Arbitration Division of the County Court of Philadelphia, 1958ff.)

successful battle[10] to escape San Quentin's gas chamber. However, it should be noted that considerable strides have been taken in recent years by several states, in large measure owing to the fine example set by New Jersey under its Chief Justice, Arthur T. Vanderbilt, in the 1950's, to adopt more integrated hierarchical judicial pyramids.

THE FINAL COURT OF APPEALS

At the apex of any state system lies its *Final Court of Appeals*, which receives and adjudicates appeals on major questions emanating from the courts below, normally from the intermediate appellate level. It will not lightly accept cases that are merely concerned with questions of fact; its main purpose is to find the law. Usually this highest state court is known as the Supreme Court, but in New York, for instance, where the Supreme Court is a trial court at the lower rung of the state judiciary—its lowest court of record—it is called the *Court of Appeals*; in Maine it is termed the *Supreme Judicial Court*. It has the last word in the state on all constitutional questions. Its decisions are final and authoritative as to state and, by virtue of the unitary structure involved, local law. The United States Supreme Court insists that "all remedies below" must have been exhausted before it will consider a request for review from a party that "lost" in the final court of appeals of a state. Nevertheless, if a federal question of a substantial nature is allegedly involved, and if that question has been properly raised below, a chance, however slim, does exist that the highest court in the land will accept the case for review. In rare instances, the Supreme Court of the United States theoretically *must* accept a case appealed from the highest court—but, as will be described in the next chapter, this presumed duty is not without significant loopholes.

10 No longer a record, although still one in terms of its outcome: After more than thirteen years on death row—the longest such period in United States history—two Negroes convicted of rape and sentenced to death in 1953, were ordered freed in August 1966 by the United States Court of Appeals for the Fifth Circuit (because they had been denied a fair trial by the all-white jury system of Orleans Parish, then 32 per cent Negro, which had never allowed a single Negro to serve on a criminal jury). (*Labat v. Bennett*, 365 F.2d 698.)

THE FEDERAL COURTS

When we look at the other prong of the "dual system of courts" at issue, we are confronted with the federal system, which is in many ways considerably less varied and confusing than the understandably heterogeneous state system(s). Certainly the federal courts are infinitely less numerous and, indeed, the hierarchical and jurisdictional arrangements of the three major constitutional courts—as demonstrated in Chart A below—are readily comprehensible and clear-cut. Nevertheless, there is more to the structure and organization of the federal system of courts than is immediately apparent. Above all, there are two major *types* of federal courts from the point of view of their creation and functions: the *constitutional* courts and the *legislative* courts. Briefly, the former are created under Article III, the judiciary article of the Constitution, whereas the latter are created under Article I, its legislative article. Consequently, the safeguards of tenure, salary, and independence that accrue to judges of the constitutional courts by virtue of the explicit and inherent safeguards of Article III, are not necessarily present for the judges of the legislative courts. However, since they are created by Congress, nothing prevents that body from clothing the judges of the legislative courts by statute with the same or similar prerogatives as are constitutionally guaranteed to those of the constitutional courts. Indeed, even before Congress changed the status of three erstwhile legislative courts—the United States Court of Claims,[11] the United States Customs Court, and the United States Court of Customs and Patent Appeals[12]—to that of constitutional courts in 1953, 1956, and 1958, respectively, it had already granted them the same "good behavior" tenure provisions enjoyed by the judges of the constitutional courts. A more signifi-

---

[11] The constitutionality of the change was challenged, but it was upheld by the Supreme Court in a 5:2 decision in 1962. (*Glidden Co. v. Zdanok*, 370 U. S. 530). It held that the Court of Claims *is* a court created under Article III of the federal Constitution, and that therefore its judges may sit on all federal district and appellate courts.

[12] The same verdict as that accorded to the constitutionality of the Court of Claims was applied in a challenge to the United States Court of Customs and Patent Appeals and for the same reasons. (*Lurk v. United States*, 370 U. S. 530.)

cant difference between the two types of courts is that the legislative courts are endowed with functions that are nonjudicial, i.e. legislative and administrative, as well as judicial. Moreover, while they are tied into the constitutional appellate structure for certain purposes, they are primarily created to aid in the administration of specified congressional statutes. Nonetheless, their judgments are as much *res judicata*, authoritative settled law, as are those of the constitutional courts.

THE FEDERAL LEGISLATIVE COURTS

As its basic power for the establishment of *legislative* courts, Congress utilizes Article I, Section 8, Clause 9, which extends to it "the power to create tribunals inferior to the Supreme Court." The lawmakers (or their aids in the Legislative Reference Service) then expressly or impliedly join that fundamental power via the "necessary and proper" clause—the famous "implied powers" clause (I-8-18) of the Constitution—with that congressional authority in the particular field in which the court is to perform its main functions. For example, the taxing power (I-8-1) for the United States Customs Court (now a constitutional court) or the power to "make rules for the government and regulation of the land and naval forces" (I-8-14) for the United States Court of Military Appeals. Other legislative courts have existed in the past, of which the defunct (as of 1915)*United States Commerce Court* created under congressional power over interstate and foreign commerce (I-8-3) is an example. But today, if we exempt the now officially transformed United States Court of Claims, United States Court of Customs, and United States Court of Customs and Patent Appeals, there are merely two bona fide legislative courts: the United States Court of Military Appeals and the several Territorial Courts. Some observers would contend that the United States Tax Court, known as the *United States Board of Tax Appeals* until 1954, ought to be classified as a legislative court. Its sixteen members, who are appointed by the President with the advice and consent of the Senate for twelve-year terms at $15,000 annually, and who are removable in the same manner as members of the independent regulatory commissions, do have the official designation of judges. Yet in a very real sense the United States Tax Court is an adjunct of the executive branch, a quasi-administrative agency independent of the Internal Revenue Service, rather than a court per se. The Tax Court and its subdivisions have jurisdiction to review governmentally-proposed deficiency assessments of income, gift, self-employment, and prior excess profits taxes that have been challenged by the tax-payer concerned. The United States Commissioner of Internal Revenue is necessarily always the defendant party. This court, which may hold hearings anywhere in the United States, is a busy agency. Its removal from the executive branch was strongly recommended by the Hoover Commission, but no action to that effect has been taken to date despite considerable congressional interest.

The United States Court of Military Appeals. This "G.I.'s Supreme Court" was created in 1950 as part of the revised Uniform Code of Military Justice, which, in turn, had largely resulted from the severe criticism heaped upon the military's concepts and practice of justice before, and especially during and after, World War II. That system of justice, steeped in the court-martial tradition, had been predominantly concerned with notions of military efficiency and chain of command, and had lodged all but dictatorial powers in the persons of the various commanding officers. Other than the unlikely "court of last resort" in the person of the President of the United States, all appeals—if indeed they could be accorded that judicial terminology—went to higher military commanders. The new code altered this arrangement drastically and dramatically by granting accused military personnel new rights before a court-martial and by creating the civilian *Court of Military Appeals*, which Mr. Chief Justice Warren dubbed the "civilian supreme court of the military." *De minimis* this would mean that service personnel now had a genuine appellate tribunal to apply and interpret military law. In effect, the door was opened for civilian observance and at least a modicum of civilian control. But as the 1950's ripened into the 1960's it became clear that the service man had gained considerably more: the application of most of the Bill of Rights. Thus, in 1965 military personnel was assured that the Sixth Amendment's right to counsel entitled him not only to a lawyer in a military case, but to a *trained* lawyer. And in April 1967 the "G.I.'s Supreme Court" ruled 2:1 that the limitations on police interrogation and confessions announced in 1966 by the Supreme Court of the United States in its historic

Miranda v. Arizona decision[13] must also be applied in military law, because in the words of the majority opinion written by Judge Homer Ferguson, it announced standards for the enforcement of the Fifth Amendment, which is binding on *all* federal courts— including the C.M.A. (*United States v. Tempia.*[14])

The United States Court of Military Appeals is staffed by three judges who receive $33,000 annually; they must be appointed from civilian life, but may hold a reserve commission in "any armed force." They are nominated for staggered fifteen-year terms of office by the President, subject to confirmation by the Senate—and are eligible for reappointment. The President, who has the power to designate the Chief Judge, may remove a member of the court only for neglect of duty or because of a mental or physical disability. No more than two of the judges may be from the same political party. Those who had been appointed through 1967 had all had judicial and/or other public service, not necessarily excluding past military duty. For example, as of the time of his appointment in 1956 by President Eisenhower, Judge Homer Ferguson had been an attorney-at-law, a judge, a United States Senator, and Ambassador to the Philippine Islands; he had seen no military service.

This court, which determines its own rules of procedure, is authorized to review *at its discretion* decisions of courts-martial involving bad-conduct discharges and prison sentences of more than one year, on being petitioned by the accused serviceman, provided that the petition had already been passed upon by a Board of Review appointed by the Judge Advocate General. The court *must* review all courts-martial decisions, as affirmed by a Board of Review, involving general or flag officers—i.e. generals and admirals; all those cases in which the death penalty was decreed below, regardless of the rank of the accused; and all cases certified for its review by the Judge Advocate General after initial review by a Board of Review. (Such a board is a group of officers who are attorneys in civilian life and who, during their term of service, are stationed in the office of each service's Judge Advocate General.) However, the court's powers of review extend solely to matters of law, not of fact—although that line, as we shall have occasion to note repeatedly, is sometimes a very fine one.

13 384 U. S. 436.
14 16 USCMA 629 (1967), at 635.

An illustration of one type of decision the Court of Military Appeals may render is the case of one Russo, a member of the Air Force, whom a duly convened court-martial had found guilty of premeditated murder and sentenced to death. On reviewing the record of the case, the staff judge advocate recommended approval of the sentence by the convening authority, but concurrently recommended that it be commuted to a dishonorable discharge from the Air Force, coupled with life imprisonment. When the Board of Review received the case, it indicated its belief that the suggested commutation was appropriate. However, it held that it was ". . . powerless to effect the change in penalty . . . [because] Congress had not granted that power to Boards of Review." Hence, it affirmed both the findings of guilt and the originally imposed sentence. Since this judgment involved a death penalty, and had been approved by the Board of Review below, review by the Court of Military Appeals was mandatory. In a decision written again by Judge Ferguson, the court denied various other points of appeal advanced by Russo, but held that both a court-martial convening authority and a Board of Review have the authority to lessen the severity of a death penalty. The court then reversed the judgments below and returned the record of the Russo trial to the Judge Advocate General of the Air Force for action consistent with its decision.[15] More than half of all cases to date heard there have won reversals in the Court of Military Appeals.

There is no direct appeal from the final judgments of the Court of Military Appeals. However, the United States Supreme Court, as well as the other federal constitutional courts, could quite conceivably exercise jurisdiction to review or "pick up" a case in an *habeas corpus* proceeding—such as claims of illegal detention, illegal procedure, or deprivation of fundamental constitutional rights. In 1953, the Supreme Court did indicate that it had that power in a much-discussed case—that featured four separate opinions—but a majority of the justices went on to point out that under the law federal constitutional court review would probably be limited to determinations of military court jurisdiction and considerations of "fair claims of justice."[16] Justices Black and Douglas dissented vigorously, contending that all of the rights under the Fifth and Sixth Amendments of the United States Constitution should

---

15 *United States v. Russo*, 11 USCMA 252, 29 CMR 168 (1960).
16 *Burns v. Wilson*, 346 U. S. 137, at 144, 147.

be held to apply to military, as well as civilian, trials. Regardless of the merits of the dissent, or of speculation how the highest tribunal would "go" today (some fifteen years later), the Fifth Amendment issue has become moot in the face of the Court of Military Appeals' aforementioned 1967 confession and interrogation case,[17] in which Judge Ferguson wrote:

> The time is long since past when this court will lend an attentive ear to the argument that members of the armed forces are, by reason of their status, *ipso facto* deprived of all protections of the Bill of Rights.

Without necessarily guaranteeing the application of *all* aspects of the Bill of Rights in *all* circumstances to service personnel, the Ferguson opinion, coupled with reforms readily undertaken by the armed forces themselves (led by the Air Force), and the broad sweep of the Supreme Court's decisions in matters affecting Amendments Four, Five, Six, Seven, and Eight in the 1960's, it seems safe to say that the service man's constitutional protection now comes very close to that of the American in mufti. Indeed, July of 1967 saw the introduction by Senator Sam J. Ervin (D.-N.C.) of the proposed *Military Justice Act of 1967* (S.2009) which, if enacted, will in effect provide the necessary statutory framework toward that end. (It was still pending early in 1968.)

The Territorial Courts. Perhaps the several Territorial Courts are in a slightly different category than the standard legislative courts, but they are established by Congress under its power to "make all needful rules and regulations respecting the territory or other property belonging to the United States. . . ." (IV-3-2). Created for, and located in, such diverse areas as the Canal Zone (1912), Guam (1900), Puerto Rico (1900), and the Virgin Islands (1917), these courts have jurisdiction that is necessarily extremely varied.[18] Generally—but specifically excluding Puerto Rico where they have federal jurisdiction only, Puerto Rico having a set of separate local courts—it includes matters analogous to those in the jurisdiction of state and local courts *as well as* the federal District Courts. The judges of the Territorial Courts are

---

17 *United States v. Tempia,* op. cit., at 635, fn. 14.

18 For statistical purposes *only,* these courts and their judges have been counted throughout this work as "U. S. District Courts."

appointed in the usual manner by the President and confirmed by the Senate; but their term of office, which varies from four to eight years, represents an uncommonly brief period for members of the federal judiciary. In creating the various Territorial Courts, Congress has generally followed the wise policy of tailoring them to specific local needs, while retaining the *fundamental*, as distinguished from the *formal*, safeguards of the Constitution of the United States.

Ex-Legislative "Special" Constitutional Courts

Until their conversion by Congress from their status as legislative to that of constitutional courts in the 1950's, the three most important and best known of these federal legislative courts were the Court of Claims, the Court of Customs, and the Court of Customs and Patent Appeals. Although they are now constitutional courts, they nevertheless still occupy a special niche in the federal court system; they may be regarded as special constitutional courts with quasi-legislative court duties. Despite their new station, they still perform certain quasi-legislative and quasi-administrative functions—or at the least they may be viewed as performing them. However, there is no doubt that public laws by Congress specifically changed their erstwhile status, and it must be assumed theoretically that Congress will henceforth not bestow upon these three the kind of nonjudicial powers that have always been considered inappropriate for members of the bench of the constitutional courts.

The United States Court of Claims. Created in 1855, after four earlier bills seeking to establish it had failed, the Court of Claims consists of five judges, who receive $33,000 annually, and of eleven "commissioners" who report on their findings in citizens' suits for damages against the Government of the United States. Most, but certainly not all, of these suits represent claims arising out of public contracts. Others involve just compensation for the taking of private property for public use. Some represent suits for injuries caused by negligent or wrongful behavior of a government employee. The court is, in fact, an institutionally arranged denial of the age-old theory that the sovereign cannot be sued. Through the Court of Claims, sometimes referred to as "the keeper of the nation's conscience," the federal government does in fact permit itself to be sued by affected persons—and thus becomes the only proper defendant—but only within rather narrow limits, such as the already mentioned contractual disputes. Because of the volume of these complaints and the time consumed in their adjudication, the existence of the Court of Claims, with its jurisdiction extending to territories and possessions as well as the United States proper, represents a genuine blessing to the general courts, whose dockets might otherwise be clogged considerably more than they already are. Moreover, the Court of Claims as well as the other specialty-area courts are a welcome time-and-trouble-saving device for Congress itself; for there is no question that a good many of the matters now handled and adjudicated by these courts would otherwise have come to the halls of the federal legislature in the form of requests for special or local bills, or of amendments to general statutes.[19]

Essentially, the jurisdiction of the Court of Claims is thus limited to *original* jurisdiction in all contractual, tax, injury, and other *non-tort* claims against the Government of the United States. (A tort is any wrongful act, *other than* a breach of contract, for which an injured party may bring a civil action against the alleged wrongdoer.) It does, however, possess a very limited power of *concurrent appellate review* with the United States Circuit Courts of Appeals in certain tort actions against the federal government decided in the United States District Courts. Decisions of the Court of Claims are subject to Supreme Court review in appropriate instances, and some of the latter's more famous cases did in fact "come up" from the Court of Claims, among them *Humphrey's Executor* (*Rathbun*) *v. United States*,[20] which arose out of a suit in the Court of Claims against the United States to recover a sum of money allegedly due the deceased Humphrey. In 1933, President Franklin D. Roosevelt had removed him from his job as a member of the Federal Trade Commission to which he had been reappointed by President Hoover for a second seven-year term in 1931. Contending that he had been illegally removed, Humphrey—and upon his death his executor, one Rathbun—sued

---

[19] James Willard Hurst, *The Growth of American Law: The Law Makers* (Boston: Little, Brown and Co., 1950), p. 67.
[20] 295 U. S. 602 (1935).

to recover his salary. The Court of Claims, evidently somewhat uncertain of its grounds, certified (see Chart B, p. 182, *infra*) some questions regarding the President's removal power to the Supreme Court. That tribunal subsequently held unanimously that the Chief Executive had no authority to remove summarily members of independent regulatory commissions clothed with quasi-legislative, quasi-judicial, quasi-executive powers, thereby decisively restricting his power of removal. This decision stands today, reaffirmed and reinforced in a case in 1958, involving President Eisenhower's dismissal of War Claims Commissioner Wiener.[21]

The United States Court of Customs and Patent Appeals. Utilizing the severally delegated powers to regulate commerce with foreign nations and among the states (I-8-3), to levy taxes (I-8-1), and "to promote the progress of science and useful arts" (I-8-8), Congress established the Court of Customs and Patent Appeals in 1910. Its five members, appointed in the customary manner, receive $33,000 per annum, and now serve "during good behavior." The functions of the court are primarily threefold: (1) to review decisions of the *Customs Court* regarding duties levied on goods imported into the United States and the classification of such goods; (2) those of the *Patent Office* regarding decisions on patents and trademarks; and (3), on a more legally restricted scale, those of the *Tariff Commission* relating to import practices.

For example, in one case on record the Tariff Commission, on reviewing an appeal by an importer, held that the attempted importation and sale of certain synthetic sapphires and rubies described in an established United States patent represented not only "unfair methods of competition," but also "unfair acts in importation," which tended substantially to injure the industry of the patent's owner. The commission consequently recommended proceedings aginst the importer involved, and the latter appealed to the Court of Customs and Patent Appeals. The court held that the evidence at hand amply supported the findings below that the patent owner's industry was operated efficiently and economically within the United States; that the imported stones fell within the description of the patented articles; that the patent had been properly secured; that the importer's actions had a tendency substantially to injure the aforesaid owner within the meaning of the

[21] *Wiener v. United States,* 357 U. S. 349 (1958).

statute; and that where no holding of invalidity of patent was alleged, it would be regarded as valid.[22]

A rather different instance of the work of the court concerned an action in August 1955 by President Eisenhower, who, pursuant to a recommendation of the Tariff Commission, set certain new import duty rates on bicycles manufactured abroad. However, in so doing he had neither acted within the time limit prescribed by law nor really followed the Tariff Commission's advice—instead his announced rates represented a *compromise* with it. The importers filed a suit in the Customs Court which held against the United States Government. The latter appealed on the legal issue involved to the Court of Customs and Patent Appeals. The court ruled that, by following the course of action described, the President had violated the basic statute, which provides that Tariff Commission recommendations must either be accepted or rejected outright.[23] All parties concerned acquiesced in that 1960 decision. It was not until the late winter of 1961 that President Kennedy, acting on a new Tariff Commission advisory, restored the level set by his predecessor. The Court of Customs and Patent Appeals, unlike the Court of Claims, possesses only *appellate* jurisdiction and it is confined to matters of law. Appeals from its decisions may go to the Supreme Court.

The United States Customs Court. The largest of the three courts at issue, the Customs Court has nine members—of whom no more than five may be members of the same political party—who receive a somewhat lower salary than the other two courts, $30,000 annually. A successor of the United States Board of General Appraisers, and with roots extending back to pre-independence colonial days, the modern version of the court was created by Congress in 1926 under its commerce and taxing powers. Sitting in three sections or divisions of three judges each, this special court, which meets in its New York headquarters and all other ports of entry in both the continental United States and the territories and insular possessions, has jurisdiction to review the rulings and appraisals on imported goods by the ubiquitous collectors of customs. As we have seen, appeals from its decisions go to the Court of Customs and Patent Appeals, although, in rare instances, it is possible to go directly to the Supreme Court.

22 *re Von Clemm*, 229 F. 2d 441 (1955).
23 *United States v. Schmidt Pritchard & Co.*, 47 CCPA 152, C.A.D. 750 (1960).

An illustration of the work of the Customs Court is a case involving International Packers, Ltd., in 1959. Involved was the firm's contention that it should be permitted to deduct from the appraised value of goods imported from Argentina a certain percentage of the purchase price it had to pay to the Argentine authorities on their export. The United States Government's customs officials rejected this claim. On bringing action for ajudication in the Customs Court, the plaintiff convinced that body that the 15 per cent levy exacted by the Argentine Government was a "necessary expense from the place of shipment to the place of delivery." Accordingly, the court ruled that the percentage involved was properly allowable as a deduction in computing the United States value of the merchandise under the Tariff Act."[24]

Review of tariff controversies by the Court of Customs is not limited to the statutory provisions of the various congressional enactments. The right to sue before it, applies to practically every legal controversy between an importer-taxpayer and the federal government. The fact that the Secretary of the Treasury or some other public official might have handed down an administrative ruling does not preclude an appeal to this interesting watchdog-court.

THE FEDERAL CONSTITUTIONAL COURTS

We now turn to the three chief *constitutional* courts, the United States District Courts, the United States (Circuit) Courts of Appeals, and the United States Supreme Court—but the most important of these, the Supreme Court, will deservedly be the sole subject of the next chapter. All three were created under Article III of the United States Constitution. In its key Section 1, that article mentions only "one supreme court," but it goes on to point to "such inferior Courts as the Congress may from time to time ordain and establish." The two lower of these three constitutional courts hence owe their origin to one of the very first acts passed by the First United States Congress, the Judiciary Act of 1789,[25] of which Senator Oliver Ellsworth, who had been a delegate from Connecticut to the Constitutional Convention, and who was soon to be the second Chief Justice of the United States, was chief author.

[24] *International Packers, Ltd. v. United States,* 171 F. Supp. 854.
[25] Act of September 24, 1789, 1 Sta. 73.

The act established and fairly well spelled out the national system of constitutional courts, which, as has been demonstrated, received no hierarchical additions until the Court of Claims was designated a constitutional court in 1953, followed by the Customs Court in 1956 and the Court of Customs and Patent Appeals in 1958. These six courts and their judges are clothed with the significant and essential benefits of life (literally "good behavior") tenure, irreducible salary, prestige, and independence. In the opinion of many an observer of the American scene, including the author of this book, there are no positions of greater desirability and prestige in the entire structure of American government than those occupied by the members of the three leading constitutional courts.

General Jurisdiction. Omitting the already discussed jurisdiction of the several "special" federal courts, constitutional as well as legislative, the general jurisdiction of these three chief federal constitutional courts is amazingly well spelled out by the verbiage of Article III, Section 2, of the Constitution. In what is surely one of the most succinctly worded paragraphs of the entire basic document, the first sentence of the first paragraph of that section makes clear at once that the judicial power of the United States "shall extend to all Cases, in Law and Equity, arising under this Constitution, the Laws of the United States, and Treaties made, or which shall be made under their Authority. . . ." Thus, in addition to announcing the sweeping realm of over-all jurisdiction, that verbiage comes to grips with one of the crucial aspects of the jurisdictional process, namely that it is limited to "Cases" (and "controversies," by implication). This signifies the necessity of the presence of a bona fide case or controversy involving litigants of opposing points of view who bring to the federal courts a genuine conflict of interest. In the absence of these basic elements, the three constitutional courts have no jurisdiction—which pinpoints the important truth that they neither can nor will accept manufactured or trumped-up cases or controversies devoid of the essential elements described, nor can or will they render *advisory* opinions per se.[26] This collective ban is as applicable to official as it is to private personages, and even extends to the influential government official who might feel the urge of convenience

[26] For a detailed analysis of the "case or controversy" and other "maxims" of the judicial process, see Ch. IX, *infra*, pp. 355ff.

to run to the chambers of the Supreme Court with a fervent plea
for an opinion on the legality of an issue, be it pending or dormant.
Thus, as early as 1792, the Supreme Court declined to advise the
government because it deemed the advisory function to be one more
properly belonging to the Cabinet—a precedent that has not been
violated.[27]

After having disposed of that crucial aspect, the constitutional
paragraph at issue goes on to outline the particular types of jurisdiction available to these courts. Generally speaking, these fall into
two groups or classifications: (a) because of the character or nature
of the *subject matter* of the *case;* and (b) because of the character
or nature of the *parties* to the suit. Under group (a) the courts may
hear and dispose of cases and controversies in law and equity
arising under:

(1) the Constitution, a federal law, or a treaty;

(2) admiralty and maritime laws.

Under the necessarily larger and more complex group (b) the
courts may hear and dispose of cases and controversies in law
and equity if:

(1) the United States is a party to the suit;

(2) one of the fifty states is a party to the suit (*but*, in accordance with the provisions of the Eleventh Amendment, *not* if the
suit was commenced or prosecuted *against* a state by either an
individual—*any* individual—or by a *foreign* country);

(3) they are between citizens of different states;

(4) they affect ambassadors and other bona fide representatives, duly *appointed*, of a accredited *foreign* country;

(5) they arise between citizens of the *same* state because of a
dispute involving land grants claimed under titles of two or more
states.

However, despite this very specific and extensive jurisdiction it
does not necessarily follow that the federal courts will inevitably
exercise it. There is no barrier in the language of the Constitution
against congressional assignment of certain aspects of it (theoretically probably even all!) to the fifty states, either on a concurrent
or even exclusive basis—for example, the requirement that the
value of a controversy in civil suits between citizens of different
states must exceed $10,000 in order to qualify for original federal

jurisdiction. Moreover, Congress may distribute the seven areas of federal jurisdiction among the various federal courts. It has done so and continues to do so in accordance with felt need, more often than not as a result of suggestions by the members of the judicial branch itself.

Overlapping Federal and State Jurisdiction. Whether or not Congress assigns concurrent or even exclusive jurisdiction in *federal* matters to *state* courts, it is axiomatic, of course, that in some areas the *state* courts have *exclusive* jurisdiction. It may be possible to raise a *federal issue* in a matter arising under state law or the state constitution, but the *original* jurisdiction of state courts over their own affairs is exclusive, as is that of the federal courts in their own sphere. But there also some areas in which *both* court systems have jurisdiction, as in the case of bank embezzlement involving a federally insured bank or in that of the theft of an automobile that subsequently crosses state lines. In the two instances cited both systems have jurisdiction, depending somewhat upon the specific circumstances involved, and the guilty party or parties are subject to prosecution and punishment by *both*. The United States Supreme Court has held repeatedly that such dual prosecution and even dual punishment violates neither the Bill-of-Rights ban against double jeopardy nor the "due process of law" clause under the Fourteenth Amendment.[28]

As indicated above, Congress has purposely granted *exclusive* jurisdiction over certain federal matters to the states. More often than not it has done this to reduce the federal work load in otherwise routine areas, such as the vast realm of diversity of citizenship disputes—suits between citizens of different states. There it enacted the requirement of a minimum value of $10,000 as the admission ticket to the federal courts in these cases—here the United States District Courts. Going beyond that proviso, however, Congress has seen fit to grant *concurrent* jurisdiction in diversity of citizenship cases to the states even when the value meets or exceeds $10,000— provided the parties to the suit are willing to go there. As a further aid to the over-docketed federal courts, especially the work-horse District Courts, Congress in the late 1950's enacted a long overdue statute dealing with the citizenship status of corporations for purposes of legal actions. As a result, corporations are now viewed as "citizens" not only of the states in which they have been incorpo-

[28] See *Bartkus v. Illinois*, 359 U. S. 121 (1959) and *Abbate v. United States*, 359 U. S. 187 (1959).

rated—which had been the case heretofore—but also as "citizens" of those states in which they have their principal place of business, regardless of their status of incorporation in the latter.

On the other hand, Congress has seen fit to vest *exclusive* original jurisdiction in the federal courts in a number of areas: suits between two or more of the fifty states (Supreme Court only); cases involving *foreign* ambassadors and other accredited *foreign* representatives; all bankruptcy proceedings; and all prosecutions for violations of federal criminal laws. Chart A demonstrates the over-all jurisdiction of the three major federal constitutional courts.

CHART A
THE JURISDICTION OF THE THREE MAJOR FEDERAL
CONSTITUTIONAL COURTS OF THE UNITED STATES

COURTS CREATED UNDER ARTICLE III
OF THE FEDERAL CONSTITUTION†

1 *Supreme Court of the United States,* 9 judges, has:

Original jurisdiction in actions or controversies:

 *1. Between the United States and a state.
  2. Between two or more states.
 *3. Involving *foreign* ambassadors, other *foreign* public ministers, and *foreign* consuls or their "domestics or domestic servants, not inconsistent with the law of nations."
 *4. *Commenced by a state against* citizens of another state or aliens, or *against* a foreign country. (N.B.: if these actions are *commenced by the citizen or alien against a state,* or by a foreign country *against* a state, the suit must *begin in state court,* according to the provisions of Amendment XI.)

Appellate jurisdiction from:

  1. All lower federal *constitutional* courts, most, but not all, federal *legislative* courts, and the *territorial* courts.
  2. The highest state courts having jurisdiction, when a "substantial federal question" is involved.

† For the purposes of this chart, the three "special" courts (U. S. Court of Claims, U. S. Court of Customs, and U. S. Court of Customs and Patent Appeals) are omitted.

* *Jurisdiction not exclusive*—i.e. while, according to Article III of the Constitution, cases are to originate here, legal arrangements may be made to have them handled by a different level court. For example, Congress has the power to give the federal District Courts *concurrent original jurisdiction* over cases affecting foreign ambassadors and *some* cases in which a state is a party to the suit. See *United States v. Ravara,* 2 Dallas 297 (1793); *Bors v. Preston,* 111 U. S. 252 (1884); and *Ames v. Kansas,* 111 U. S. 449 (1884). And in late 1964 the Supreme Court declined to review a Ninth Circuit Court decision that United States District Courts have jurisdiction over suits *by the United States against a state.* (*California v. United States,* 379 U. S. 817.)

11 *United States (Circuit) Courts of Appeals,* 88 judges, have:

Appellate jurisdiction *only* from:

1. U. S. District Courts.
2. U. S. Territorial Courts, the U. S. Tax Court, and some District of Columbia Courts.
3. The U. S. Independent Regulatory Commissions.
4. Certain federal administrative agencies and departments (for review, but also for *enforcement* of certain of their actions and orders).

93 *United States District Courts,* approximately 346 judges, have:

Original jurisdiction *only*** over:

1. All crimes against the United States.
2. All civil actions arising under the Constitution, laws, or treaties of the United States, wherein the matter in controversy exceeds $10,000 (unless the U. S. Supreme Court has jurisdiction as outlined above).
*3. Cases involving citizens of different states or citizens and aliens provided the value of the controversy is in excess of $10,000.
4. Admiralty, maritime, and prize cases.
*5. Review and *enforcement* of orders and actions of certain federal administrative agencies and departments.
6. All such other cases as Congress may validly prescribe by law.

** A case can be made for the contention that it also has a measure of *appellate* jurisdiction, involving certain actions tried before specially designated U.S. Commissioners.

The United States District Courts. By all odds the work horses of the federal judiciary, the 93 District Courts, with their some 346 judges—perpetually an insufficient total—comprise the trial courts of the federal system. Established under the Judiciary Act of 1789, their jurisdiction extends to the initial trial of almost all civil and criminal cases arising under the vast realm of federal jurisdiction. It is here that the United States Government commences, and usually ends, its prosecutions—e.g. the government's victorious anti-trust suit against the electrical appliance concerns, which began and terminated in the United States District Court for Eastern Pennsylvania in Philadelphia in February 1961, Judge J. Cullen Ganey rendering the famous decision.[29] It is here also that most suits arising under the federal statutes begin and end—viz., one Abrikossoff's action to recover certain property that had been disposed of by the Alien Property Custodian under the Trading with

[29] Case not reported in F. Supp. See Reporter's Transcript in Office of the Clerk, U. S. District Court, Eastern District of Pennsylvania. Also see Clerk Gilbert W. Ludwig's letter to author, dated June 8, 1961.

the Enemy Act.[30] And it is here that the trial (petit) juries sit in the federal system; they do so in roughly half of all cases commenced at that level. The District Courts have *original* jurisdiction only. However, when necessary, they do have the obligation to *enforce* as well as review actions and orders of certain federal administration agencies and departments; certain actions tried before United States Commissioners (see below) may be reviewed by them; and certain other classes of cases may be *removed* to them from the state courts under certain specific statutory authorization. Hence, in the vast majority of instances, the decisions of the District Courts are, in effect, final. And there is a veritable flood of business: they now decide upwards of 275,000 cases annually. In 1966, to cite one busy year, a total of 301,980 proceedings were *commenced* in the District Courts.[31] No wonder that delays are common here—as well as elsewhere in the undermanned, overly litigous American judicial system. At the level of the *federal* courts the time interval between the point when a case was "at issue" and the trial itself ranged in 1959 from 4.1 months to 39.1 months, from 3.9 48.7 months in 1965–66; in the *state* courts, it varied from 1.0 months to 52.9 months in 1959; from 4.3 to 69.5 months in 1965–66.[32] Nor had matters improved by 1966–67.[33] A poignantly pertinent illustration is the case of a ten-year-old girl, Nancy Verona, who was hit by a car while riding her bike. When her case at last came to trial, she was a young mother, aged nineteen, who brought her baby to the court with her![34]

Each of the fifty states of the Union, the District of Columbia, Puerto Rico, Guam, the Canal Zone, and the Virgin Islands contains at least one federal district with a District Court and a District

30 *Abrikossoff v. Brownell,* 145 F. Supp. 18 (1956).

31 To be precise: 79,906 civil; 29,729 criminal; and 192,345 bankruptcy cases —representing an over-all increase of circa 30 per cent in five years, (*Annual Reports* of the U.S. District Courts).

32 See the symposium, "Lagging Justice," 328 *The Annals of the American Academy of Political and Social Science* (March 1960), and the series by Howard James in *The Christian Science Monitor,* "Crisis in the Courts," April-July 1967.

33 See statistics cited by Victor G. Rosenblum in James W. Fesler (ed.), *The 50 States and their Local Governments* (New York: Alfred A. Knopf, 1967), pp. 434–5. See also *The Christian Science Monitor's* table, April 19, 1967), p. 12.

34 Cited by Louis Banks, "The Crisis in the Courts," 64 *Fortune Magazine* 86 (December 1961), at 88.

Judge. There is no cutting across state lines, but in many instances the large number of cases to be adjudicated compels a subdivision of labor within a particular district. Thus, while many of the districts have only one judge, others have two or more. Indeed, one—the Southern District of New York (Manhattan, the Bronx, and the adjacent suburban counties to the north)[35] with its high proportion of complex commercial litigation—had the 1966–67 maximum of twenty-four. Almost half of all litigation occurs in the twelve District Courts that are located in the larger metropolitan areas.[36] The Chief Justice of the United States (who is the same individual as the Chief Justice of the Supreme Court of the United States) has the authority to transfer district judges temporarily from their home circuit to a more congested one, but only with the former's consent. These judges are then known as "visiting judges." It was as Visiting Judge for the Eastern District of Arkansas that United States District Judge Ronald N. Davies, whose home district was North Dakota, issued the now famous injunction[37] against Governor Orval E. Faubus and other state officials of Arkansas in September 1957, after they had actively interfered with an earlier court order upholding the Little Rock School Board's desegregation plan.[38] Judge Davies had been temporarily transferred to help deal with a mounting backlog of cases. To cite one other procedural example: in order to remedy a staggering congestion on the civil calendars of the District Court for the Eastern District of New York (Kings, Queens, Nassau, Suffolk, and Richmond counties), Mr. Chief Justice Warren—probably the finest student of judicial administration since Mr. Chief Justice Taft—acting on the invitation of Chief Judge M. W. Byers of that court in 1959–60, assigned fifteen district judges from other circuits to help in clearing the accumulation. The team, headed by Chief Judge William F. Smith of the United States District Court for New Jersey, did just that—and in short order!

But no matter how many judges may be permanently or temporarily assigned to a federal district, it is customary for a lone District Court judge, sitting with a jury—unless that institution has

35 Columbia, Dutchess, Greene, Orange, Putnam, Rockland, Sullivan, Ulster, and Westchester.
36 See the *Annual Reports* of the U.S. District Courts.
37 *United States v. Faubus,* 156 F. Supp. 220 (1957).
38 *Aaron v. Cooper,* 143 F. Supp. 855 (1956).

been validly waived—to preside over a trial in the roughly 350 localities where they now are held in the United States. However, in some instances of particular importance, Congress has statutorily provided for adjudication by *Three-Judge District Courts*. They customarily consist of two district judges and one circuit judge; in any event, the Judicial Code provides that at least one judge must be from the circuit—the next higher echelon in the judicial system. As a matter of practice, the Chief Judge of the Circuit Court involved rarely, if ever, assigns more than that absolute minimum. Suits required to be heard by these Three-Judge District Courts are usually those seeking to restrain *by an injunction* the enforcement, operation, or execution of both federal and state statutes and orders of state administrative agencies on grounds of *unconstitutionality,* or orders issued by the Interstate Commerce Commission. A few other instances are also provided by statute, some of these with injunctions to cover certain violations of the federal anti-trust laws.

The busy judges of the District Courts are provided with relatively ample assistants to carry on their tasks, all of whom are appointed by the judges themselves (some were mentioned in an earlier chapter). Among them are the *United States Commissioners, Law Clerks, Bailiffs, Court Reporters, Stenographers, Clerks,* and *Probation Officers*. These positions are more or less self-explanatory, except for that of the important *United States Commissioner,* who, as has been pointed out, is in charge of some of the preliminary steps involved in the pre-trial process. He may issue arrest warrants; hear evidence in order to determine whether to hold an accused person for grand jury action—in which case he may set the bail; and most of them can try petty cases and mete out sentences up to six months. Yet of the 700 Commissioners—only the Federal District Court in eastern Michigan does not have any—in 1966 one-third were not lawyers! They are appointed by the District Court judges for four-year terms of office, and are paid only by court fees (the annual maximum being $10,500).[39] The fee system as well as the office itself came under close scrutiny by Congress in 1966–67, led by Senator Joseph P. Tydings (D.-

[39] For an excellent article on this little-known office, see Charles A. Lindquist, "The United States Commissioner: An Evaluation of the Commissioner's Role in the Judicial Process," 39 *Temple Law Quarterly* 138 (Winter 1966).

164

Md.), and a modernization of this potentially useful office loomed at least as a possibility. In fact, in late June of 1967, the Senate passed—without debate—a bill to provide for full-time and part-time magistrates with fixed tenures and a sliding scale of salaries, based on expected work loads. They would have to be lawyers, except if no qualified lawyer was available, and would have to meet other minimum qualifications. As of this writing (early 1968) the House had not acted on this matter.

The two most significant officers at the district level, are the *United States Marshal* and the *United States Attorney*, who are not appointed by the judge directly. The latter, appointed for each of the districts by the President with the advice and consent of the Senate, functions under the authority of the Attorney General rather than that of his District Judge. He, in turn, appoints a number of Assistant United States Attorneys, often in conjunction with the patronage wishes of influential members of his political party. The U.S. Marshal,[40] appointed in the same manner as the U.S. Attorney, makes arrests; disburses federal judicial funds; serves court orders;[41] guards and transports all federal court documents, from jury notices to Supreme Court orders; and generally maintains the decorum of the courtroom of the District Court of the United States. In 1967 there were 92 such marshals and 729 deputy and chief deputy marshals.[42]

The United States (Circuit) Courts of Appeals. Standing immediately above the United States District Courts in the federal constitutional court hierarchy, the eleven United States (Circuit) Courts of Appeals—sometimes, simply called "Circuit Courts" or "Courts of Appeals"—are essentially what their name implies: *appellate* courts only. They do, however, have a statutory obligation to *enforce,* when necessary, as well as review, actions of a host of federal executive agencies that are clothed with quasi-judicial functions. Among these, to cite but a few, are certain

[40] The origin of the office traces back to medieval England, where the Old French noun *mareshal* (groom) came to mean a sort of royal sheriff in charge of procuring witnesses for the monarch.

[41] This is a task that frequently takes considerable ingenuity. For example, to serve a desegregation injunction on the evasive and defiant Alabama Governor George Wallace in 1963, one deputy marshal stowed away in the men's room aboard the Governor's plane!

[42] See *Annual Report* of the United States District Courts.

rulings of the National Labor Relations Board; wage orders of the Administration of Wage and Hour Division of the Department of Labor; and orders under anti-trust or unfair practice laws of the Interstate Commerce Commission, the Federal Communications Commission, the Civil Aeronautics Board, and the Board of Governors of the Federal Reserve System. But even if we are to classify aspects of the review and enforcement of the activities of these quasi-judicial units of the federal government as original jurisdiction—and they are that only by stretching the concept considerably—the vast majority of the work of the United States Courts of Appeals is clearly appellate. In effect, it is at once the first and last stop for appeals from below in all instances save those that go on up to the United States Supreme Court and those few that are permitted to bypass it from below en route to the Supreme Court. Other than the appeals from the highest state courts of record, which go directly to the Supreme Court without touching the other federal courts, the Circuit Courts of Appeals may be validly bypassed only if: (1) it is so decided by the Three-Judge District Courts, as explained above; (2) there is a direct appeal statutorily authorized to the Supreme Court from a limited number of ordinary District Court cases, such as a case where a federal statute has been held unconstitutional by a District Court and the United States is a party to the suit; and (3) it is shown that a case is "of such imperative public importance . . . as to require immediate settlement."

But in all other instances, both civil and criminal, the Circuit Court of Appeals is the natural appellate tribunal for the approximately 5500 cases that now come up to it annually from the United States District Courts in the fifty states, the District of Columbia, and the territories, and from the many independent regulatory commissions, agencies, and cabinet departments that are endowed with quasi-judicial powers and functions. In effect, it *finally* decides approximately 90 per cent of all federal cases. For example, the Court of Appeals for the District of Columbia, sometimes referred to as the Eleventh Circuit, thus held, on reviewing the denial of one Schachtman's passport application by the Department of State, that the latter had violated the due process of law clause of the Fifth Amendment in the circumstances at issue.[43] The Department

13 *Shachtman v. Dulles*, 225 F. 2d 938, (1955).

of State subsequently complied with the court's mandate. An illustration of a case arising from a decision of a District Court rather than that of an administrative agency or department is the (unsuccessful) appeal to the United States Court of Appeals for the Second Circuit by Alger Hiss for reversal of his conviction on perjury charges in connection with the theft of United States Government documents.[44]

Although officially stripped of the term "circuit" in 1948, the courts on this important level in the federal judicial process are still generally referred to as "Circuit Courts." There are ten such numbered circuits in the United States plus the unnumbered eleventh one, known as the *Court of Appeals for the District of Columbia*:[45]

First Circuit: Maine, Massachusetts, New Hampshire, Rhode Island, Puerto Rico.

Second Circuit: Connecticut, New York, Vermont.

Third Circuit: Delaware, New Jersey, Pennsylvania, Virgin Islands.

Fourth Circuit: Maryland, North Carolina, South Carolina, Virginia, West Virginia.

Fifth Circuit: Alabama, Florida, Georgia, Louisiana, Mississippi, Texas, Canal Zone.

Sixth Circuit: Kentucky, Michigan, Ohio, Tennessee.

Seventh Circuit: Illinois, Indiana, Wisconsin.

Eighth Circuit: Arkansas, Iowa, Minnesota, Missouri, Nebraska, North Dakota, South Dakota.

Ninth Circuit: Arizona, California, Idaho, Montana, Nevada, Oregon, Washington, Hawaii, Alaska, Guam.

Tenth Circuit: Colorado, Kansas, New Mexico, Utah, Oklahoma, Wyoming.

[44] *United States v. Hiss*, 185 F. 2d 822 (1950).

[45] In 1933 the United States Supreme Court ruled that both the United States District Court for the District of Columbia *and* the United States Court of Appeals for the District of Columbia are at the same time "constitutional" *and* "legislative" courts. (*O'Donoghue v. United States*, 289 U.S. 516.) But in 1930 it had held that "it is recognized that the courts of the District of Columbia are not created under the judiciary article of the Constitution but are legislative courts. . . ." (*Federal Radio Commission v. General Electric Company*, 281 U.S. 464, at 468.) Of course, *O'Donoghue* governs today.

Each of these circuits is theoretically headed by one of the nine justices of the United States Supreme Court who are historically said to be "riding circuit"—the junior justices usually, but not necessarily,[46] being assigned the two "extra" circuits. Indeed, this is what they used to do, more or less literally, at the beginning of America's nationhood, but the practice fell into disuse approximately a century later. Today, lack of time prevents them from more than nominal participation, although they continue to be faithfully and formally "assigned" at the beginning of each term. And, of course, they do retain the power to act on certain pleas that arise from court actions, particularly dispositive orders, in "their" circuits. A typical illustration is Mr. Justice White's refusal to set aside an Oklahoma District Court decision that had nullified the May 1964 primary, and had ordered a new primary for that September on a "one-man, one-vote" basis. White, as the justice in administrative charge of the Tenth Circuit, of which Oklahoma is a part, simply wrote "stay denied"—and "that," in Mr. Justice Holmes's language "was that!" (*Williams v. Mass.* 378 U.S. 558).

The eleven Circuit Courts of Appeals comprise a total of eighty-eight judges who, except for the judges of the District of Columbia, must be residents of the assigned circuit during the time they serve and even thereafter—because, though they may have retired, they are still subject to assignments by the Chief Justice of the United States. There is a Chief Judge for each of the Circuit Courts who, upon reaching the voluntary retirement age of seventy, retains his powers as a full-fledged member of his court—assuming he neither chooses to retire nor has accumulated sufficient time to do so on full salary—but ceases to be head of the court involved. This arrangement also applies in the District Courts, but not in the Supreme Court. From three to nine judges may sit *en banc* to hear cases, although there are usually only three in view of the work load; a quorum is two. Proceedings before the Courts of Appeals are conducted on the basis of the record made below—i.e. before the United States District Courts or one of the administrative agencies. New evidence may thus not be presented at the bar of this appellate tribunal, just as it may not be introduced in the appellate cases reaching the highest ranking

[46] In the 1965–66 terms of Court, for example, it was the Chief Justice and Mr. Justice White who took the two extra circuits.

court in the American judicial hierarchy, the Supreme Court of the United States.

ADMINISTERING THE FEDERAL JUDICIARY

Before turning to the latter tribunal in the following chapter, something should be said about the administration of the federal judicial system. Considerable thought may well have been given for many years to the establishment of a centralized administrative structure for these courts, but it was actually not until shortly prior to the second quarter of this century that the judicial and legislative branches, particularly the former, had recognized the urgency of the problem to the extent of doing something about it other than to declaim and exhort on what had become an increasingly deplorable state of administrative anarchy. Fortunately, Congress yielded to mounting pressure by bar, bench, and interested laymen, and the establishment of the Judicial Conference of the United States and the Administrative Office of the United States Courts in 1922 and 1939, respectively, effected considerable improvement.

The Judicial Conference of the United States. The 1922 statute requires "the Chief Justice . . . to submit to Congress an annual report of the proceedings of the Judicial Conference and its recommendation for legislation." This is done faithfully and to considerable advantage by the "Chief" in his position as head of that body, which, in addition to him, consists of the chief judge of each of the eleven federal judicial circuits, a district court judge from each of these circuits—chosen for a term of three years by the judges of the Circuit at its annual Judicial Conference—the Chief Judge of the United States Court of Claims, and the Chief Judge of the Court of Customs and Patent Appeals. The Judicial Conference meets at least once a year for the legislatively established purpose of making a "comprehensive survey of the conditions of business in the courts of the United States and [of preparing] plans for assignment of judges to or from circuits or districts where necessary." It is also required to submit suggestions to the various courts "in the interest of uniformity and expedition of business." This vital body of prestigious and influential experts has done an excellent job in keeping abreast of the needs of an efficient judiciary and has done its utmost—in conjunction with the Administrative Office of the United States Courts, for which it establishes policy—to realize these needs. In that capacity, to cite an example of its administrative and personnel role, it sent out the following admonition to all federal judges: "No justice or judge of the United States shall serve in the capacity of officer or director or employe of any corporation organized for profit."[47]

Although not all of the Judicial Conference's policy recommendations have either been adopted by Congress or adopted speedily —this applies especially to those involving the creation of new judgeships—the legislative branch has displayed considerable regard for the wisdom of the Judicial Conference at its committees. Thus, in 1958 Congress passed a Conference-recommended law authorizing the Judicial Conference to set up committees of judges, lawyers, and law professors to study the rules of procedure in the federal courts. On receiving the committees' recommendations, the Judicial Conference passses judgment on them and then sends them on to the Supreme Court for its action. Adopted changes become effective in ninety days unless they are specifically disapproved by Congress during that time. Another illustration is Congress's acquiescence in the Conference's request for federally appropriated funds for the defense of the indigents in federal courts, which resulted in the Criminal Justice Act of 1964.[48]

The Administrative Office of the United States Courts. This judicial housekeeping agency and veritable gold mine of statistics is the executive arm of the Judicial Conference. It is headed by the director, who is appointed by the Chief Justice of the Supreme Court.[49] The former possesses no administrative jurisdiction vis-à-vis the Supreme Court, but he and his subordinates are crucially involved in the administrative business of the subordinate federal courts. (Indeed, an increasing number among the fifty states have begun to establish similar bodies—e.g. California, Iowa, New York, and Pennsylvania.) Among these tasks are the compilation of the suggested budgets; determination of personnel needs; examination of the dockets; auditing of accounts; procurement and allo-

47 As quoted in *The Philadelphia Evening Bulletin,* September 22, 1963.
48 See the article on the subject and related issues by Anthony Lewis, *The New York Times,* October 14, 1964.
49 The director will also serve on the board in charge of the new Federal Judicial Center (mentioned in Ch. II, *supra*).

170

cation of supplies; preparation of all vital statistics in connection with the business of the courts (its *Annual Report* has become essential for all those interested in the judicial process); and all such other duties as may be assigned to the director and his staff by either the Supreme Court or the Judicial Conference—both headed by the Chief Justice of the United States. The Administrative Office of the United States Court has become an essential arm of the judicial system; it has been widely and just acclaimed; it has, in effect, become indispensable to the orderly and successful operation of the courts. The distinguished federal purist, who characterized its creation in 1939 as "probably the greatest piece of legislation affecting the judiciary since the Judiciary Act of 1789,"[50] was eminently correct in his analysis. Nonetheless, constant vigilance to bring about further improvement in the operation and function of the courts, high as well as low, is essential throughout the United States in the interest of justice.

[50] As quoted by Hurst, op. cit. p. 114.

V

COURTS AT HOME:

II THE SUPREME COURT

AT THE ZENITH:
THE UNITED STATES SUPREME COURT

The most dazzling jewel in the judicial crown of the United States is the revered and often controversial United States Supreme Court. It is the sole court mentioned specifically in Article III or in any other part of the Constitution, all other federal courts having been created by statute. The Supreme Court, the national symbol of justice, stands at the very pinnacle of the judiciary: there is no higher court, and all others bow before it—or, at least, are expected to do so. At times having had as few as five, and as many as ten, justices in the first eighty years of its venerable history, the Court has stood at nine ever since the first term of President Grant in 1869. Prior thereto, as dictated by various policy considerations, its congressionally fixed membership comprised: six in 1789; five in 1801; six in 1802; nine in 1807; eight in 1808; seven in 1811; nine in 1837; ten in 1863; and eight in 1866.

The Supreme Court consists of the Chief Justice and eight Associate Justices, the former being rewarded since 1965 with an annual salary of $40,000, the latter with $39,500 each—this is less than judges of some states, e.g. New York, receive.[1] But the nonsalary compensations, frequently called "psychic income" by college professors, are undoubtedly considerable. (The retirement prerogatives were discussed in Chapter II.)

---

[1] An illustration of petty congressional pique vis-à-vis the Supreme Court, motivated chiefly by its momentous and trail-blazing civil rights and liberty decisions of the 1950's and 1960's, was the refusal of Congress in 1964 and again in 1965 to give the Chief Justice and his associates on the Court the same $7500 pay increase granted all lower federal court judges. Instead the members of the highest tribunal had to settle for a $4500 raise.

172

ORIGINAL JURISDICTION

The United States Supreme Court has both *original* and *appellate* jurisdiction, but it exercises the former in only rare instances. Moreover, the Eleventh Amendment to the Constitution, ratified in 1798, has seriously abridged that phase of its work by removing from its jurisdiction, as had been spelled out in the original body of the Constitution, all those cases in which one of its own citizens or one of another state or of a foreign country, or even a sovereign foreign country itself, wishes to sue one of the states of the United States. In effect, the Eleventh Amendment enacted the necessity of obtaining *a state's permission to sue it* in all litigation involving the above-mentioned categories.

The Eleventh Amendment was adopted as a direct result of a Supreme Court decision in 1793 in the case of *Chisholm v. Georgia*.[2] There the Court, in a broad decision, but in accordance with the terminology of Article III of the Constitution, held 4:1 that one Chisholm, a citizen of one state (South Carolina), could sue another state (Georgia) in the federal courts—an outrageous and shocking pronouncement in the eyes of citizens with confirmed "states-rights" views. It was especially galling since the matter involved concerned debts owed to British creditors for whom Chisholm acted as an executor. The Supreme Court's judgment triggered instantaneous and profound opposition. For example, the lower house of the legislature of the State of Georgia passed a bill to punish by hanging "without benefit of clergy" any person endeavoring to aid in the enforcement of the decision! Merely two days had passed after the announcement in *Chisholm v. Georgia* when the future Eleventh Amendment was introduced into both houses of Congress.

Thus, the *original* jurisdiction docket of the Supreme Court has become a very minor factor in its work. Not counting *memorandum orders*, to be explained later, at the outset of its 1967–68 term the Court had rendered decisions under the original jurisdiction clause of the Constitution—Article III, Section 2, Paragraph 2, as amended—in only 129 cases since its first term in 1789.[3]

[2] 2 Dallas 419.

[3] For a detailed analysis, including a list of 123 of these cases, see "The Original Jurisdiction of the United States Supreme Court," 11 *Stanford Law Review* 665–719 (July 1959).

The cases that now still commence under it do so as a *matter of right* under its provisions. Theoretically, these comprise the following four categories of cases or controversies: (1) between the United States and one of the fifty states; (2) between two or more states; (3) those involving *foreign* ambassadors, other *foreign* public ministers, and *foreign* consuls, or their "domestics or domestic servants not inconsistent with the law of nations"; and (4) those *commenced by a state* against citizens of another state or aliens, or *against* a foreign country. (But note that if these actions are *commenced by the citizen or alien or even the foreign county*[4] against a state, that litigation *must begin in state court,* in accordance with the provisions of the Eleventh Amendment.)

However, the Supreme Court does not exercise *exclusive* original jurisdiction even in the four categories cited, with the sole exception of cases or controversies involving two or more of the several states. There it, and it alone, exercises original jurisdiction. But, accompanied by the Court's plaudits, Congress has extended *concurrent original* jurisdiction to the federal District Courts in litigation affecting category (3) and in *some,* but not all, cases in categories (1) and (4) in which a state is party to the suit at issue. Hence, most of the cases the Supreme Court has heard on its original jurisdiction docket have indeed involved two or more states. For example, the nine successive actions the State of Virginia filed against West Virginia in the lengthy and trying history of their debt controversy were all heard at the bar of the Supreme Court.[5] More recent controversies have involved Michigan and Ohio in a possession-dispute over a triangular piece of land in mineral-rich Lake Erie;[6] California and Arizona in their evidently equally persistent water squabbles;[7] a river boundary dispute between Louisiana and Mississippi;[8] and Delaware's unsuccessful attempt to have the Court declare unconstitutional the electoral college vote count in Presidential elections.[9] All of these cases must, and do, commence in the Supreme Court. Yet if a determination of *facts* is required, the Court here often utilizes the device

---

4 See *Monaco v. Mississippi,* 292 U. S. 313 (1934).

5 For example, see *Virginia v. West Virginia,* 246 U. S. 565 (1918).

6 *Michigan v. Ohio,* 386 U. S. 1009 (1967).

7 *Arizona v. California,* 370 U. S. 906 (1961); ibid. 373 U. S. 546 (1963); ibid., rehearing denied, 375 U. S. 892 (1963).

8 *Louisiana v. Mississippi,* 384 U. S. 24 (1966).

9 *Delaware et al v. New York et al,* 385 U. S. 895 (1966).

of referring these disputes to a special *master*—frequently an ex-jurist—for a hearing and report to it, as it did in the Western water litigation and in a 1966 suit by Ohio against Kentucky in a dispute over their boundary.

APPELLATE JURISDICTION

The primary task of the Court is *appellate*. In that capacity it serves as the final arbiter in the construction of the Constitution of the United States, *and* it thus provides a uniform interpretation of the law—although its very power to do so presumably also enables it to change its mind from case to case. However, at least to a considerable degree, it attempts to adhere to precedent, the afore-mentioned doctrine known as *stare decisis,* i.e. let the decision stand—giving to precedents the authority of established law. (We shall examine this philosophy of law and the extent of its success in Chapter VIII.)

Appellate cases come to the Supreme Court from the subordinate federal courts and the state courts of last resort (which are usually, but not always, the state supreme courts). Actually, there are five different sources of the appellate cases that reach the Court: (1) the state court of last resort having jurisdiction in a particular action, provided that a federal question has been raised validly and further provided that all remedies have been duly exhausted below; (2) the United States Circuit Courts of Appeals; (3) the United States District Courts; (4) the United States Court of Claims and the United States Court of Customs and Patent Appeals in *judicial* rather than *administrative* matters; and (5) one of the legislative or territorial courts, if permissible under the laws that establish it.[10]

WRITS OF REVIEW GENERALLY

Cases or controversies normally reach the Supreme Court for purposes of review under its appellate jurisdiction in one of three principal ways—with each member of the Court considering every application for review: (1) on a writ of appeal, as a matter of right (usually simply called *appeal*); (2) on a writ of *certiorari,* as a

[10] Ch. 81, Title 28, U. S. Code.

matter of Court discretion (usually simply called *certiorari* or *cert.*); and (3) by certification. The old writ of *error,* a common law process roughly akin to today's writ of appeal, was statutorily discontinued in the federal courts in 1928. It brought the entire record of a proceeding in a lower court before the Supreme Court for its consideration of "errors of law," allegedly committed below. We may also quickly dispose of *certification.* Rarely employed, it presents the Court with even less cases than those on its original jurisdiction docket. It covers "any question of law in any civil or criminal case in which instructions are desired" by the lower court, usually a Court of Appeals or the Court of Claims.

Appeal. In the instance of a writ of *appeal,* the aggrieved party —known as the *appellant,* the answering party as the *appellee* or *respondent*— has an absolute, *statutorily granted right* to carry a case to the United States Supreme Court, which in theory must review it. However, the high tribunal retains the very considerable discretionary power to reject such an appeal on the grounds that the federal question, otherwise validly raised, is "insubstantial." Moreover, the federal question must have been validly raised early in the state court, and even then the Supreme Court may not take the case if the state court's judgment can be sustained on an independent ground of state law. This highly significant multiple discretionary element in the area of the Court's so-called compulsory appellate jurisdiction caused it to dismiss seventy appeals in the 1965–66 term, for example. Of these, forty were rejected "for want of a substantial federal question," the balance on other jurisdictional grounds. In the 1959–60 term, sixty-three of a total of 113 appeals had been dismissed on the insubstantiality ground! An average of 50 to 60 per cent of the writs of appeal are thus dismissed or the judgment below affirmed without printing the record or oral argument—and Mr. Justice Douglas contended in an important statistical article that, as a rule, the Court actually grants no more tthan 15 per cent.[11]

In effect, the appeal is hence used but sparingly, to date in approximately only 9 per cent of all cases or controversies *presented* to the Court—but Douglas claims that these 9 per cent constitute 90 per cent of all "meritorious" cases.[12] Yet whatever

11 William O. Douglas, "The Supreme Court and its Case Load," 45 *Cornell Law Quarterly* 401 (Spring 1960), at 410.
12 Ibid., at 409.

the practice, there are a total of five instances in which an aggrieved party may resort to it: (1) if a state court of last resort has declared a federal law or treaty, or parts thereof, unconstitutional;[13] or, (2) if a state court *upholds a state law* or a provision of a state constitution *against a substantial challenge that it conflicts* with a provision of a federal law or treaty, or the United States Constitution;[14] (3) if any federal court declares a federal law or treaty, or parts thereof, unconstitutional, provided the United States is a party to the suit;[15] (4) if a federal Court of Appeals *strikes down a state law as being contrary* to a federal law, treaty, or the Constitution;[16] and (5) in certain statutorily specified cases from the federal District Courts and all other "courts of the United States" (e.g. if a case, required to be heard by any three-judge federal District Court, has resulted in an order granting or denying an injunction.[17] By far the largest number of cases on appeal come to the Supreme Court either from a state court of last resort —usually its highest court—or from one of the special three-judge courts at the federal District Court level (which must include at least one federal Circuit Court of Appeals judge). Many of the segregation-integration cases have reached the Supreme Court via the latter route.[18]

Certiorari. In all other cases involving a "federal question of substance" the disappointed litigant in a suit has *no right* to appeal to the Supreme Court the adverse decision he sustained, but he does have the *privilege* of petitioning the highest bench in the land to grant him a writ of *certiorari.* Generally, each such petition, a copy of which goes to each Justice, comprises the two sides' arguments both for and against its grant—the party bringing the action known as the *plaintiff* or *petitioner,* the other as the *respondent*— plus a record of the proceedings below. Ninety per cent of the cases decided by the Supreme Court reach it by that method, and practically all of these come to it from the Circuit Court of Appeal. (Neither in *certiorari* nor in *appeal* proceedings is a formal

13 E.g. *Reynolds v. Katzenbach,* 248 F. Supp. 593 (1965), consolidated with *South Carolina v. Katzenbach,* 383 U.S. 301 (1966).
14 E.g. *Torcaso v. Watkins,* 367 U.S. 488 (1961).
15 E.g. *Missouri v. Holland,* 252 U.S. 416 (1920).
16 E.g. *Reynolds v. Sims,* 377 U.S. 533 (1964).
17 E.g. *Wickard v. Filburn,* 317 U.S. 111 (1942).
18 E.g. *Brown v. Board of Education,* 347 U.S. 483 (1954).

printed record necessary until such time as the writ of *certiorari* is granted or the appeal noted.)

The grant of *certiorari*—a Latin term meaning "made more certain" or "better informed"—signifies the willingness of the Supreme Court to review a case, based upon a written petition initiated by the plaintiff together with a reply from the other side. A grant of the petition directs the lower court to send up the record in the case for review so that the decision "may be made more certain." Needless to say that Court is quite chary with its writs of *certiorari,* and unless it detects an issue of substantial significance in the case or controversy, or it happens to be especially interested in it, chances are that the application for the writ and will be denied with a terse "*certiorari* denied"—evident from the published listing of a large number of petitions thus disposed of. The Court's own Rule 19 states that *certiorari* will be granted only "where there are special and important reasons therefor." Among these, according to the language of Rule 19, are the following: where two federal Circuit Courts of Appeals or two three-judge federal District Courts have rendered conflicting decisions (e.g. two diametrically opposed judgments involving the constitutionality of the so-called Blue Laws by two three-judge federal District Courts sitting in Boston and Philadelphia, striking down and upholding such Massachusetts and Pennsylvania laws, respectively,[19] and, intriguingly, equally opposite judgments on the constitutionality of the Public Accommodations Title of the Civil Rights Act of 1964, where two three-judge courts in the *same* circuit (the Fifth), sitting in Atlanta and Birmingham, respectively upheld and struck down that title of the Act![20]; where a state court or a federal appellate court has passed on an important question of federal law on which the Supreme Court has never passed, or if these lower courts have made a decision that conflicted with applicable precedent established by the United States Supreme Court;[21] or where a federal court has so far departed from the accepted canons of judicial proceedings as to call for exercise

19 *Crown Kosher Super Market v. Gallagher,* 176 F. Supp. 466 (1959) and *Two Guys from Harrison-Allentown v. McGinley,* 179 F. Supp. 944 (1959).

20 *Heart of Atlantic Motel v. United States,* 231 F. Supp. 393 (1964) and *McClung v. Katzenbach,* 233 F. Supp. 815 (1964).

21 E.g. *Biddle v. Perovich,* 274 U.S. 480 (1927).

of the Supreme Court's power of supervision.[22] In any case, as Mr. Justice Frankfurter would view the Court's power to control its docket, ". . . [it] carries with it the responsibility of granting review only in cases that demand adjudication on the basis of importance to the operation of our federal system; importance of the outcome merely to the parties is not enough."[23] In an address to a group of Illinois lawyers he illustrated what the Chief Justice, who plays an important role in certiorari grants, might say:

> This is a very interesting and important question . . ., but we can't do any better than Judge Julian Mack [late judge of the United States Court of Appeal] did with it below. He really knows more about this field of law than the rest of us. I suggest we deny this petition for certiorari.[24]

This posture is symptomatic of what Mr. Justice Frankfurter used to term the need for "alert deference" to lower court opinions in general.

Still, a case of substance is not necessarily a "big" or "major" case. In its 1959–60 term, for example, the Supreme Court reached down to the Police Court of Louisville, Kentucky, to set aside, as a violation of the due process of law clause of the Fourteenth Amendment to the Constitution, two $10 fines for loitering and disorderly conduct.[25] The case symbolizes the willingness of the highest court in the land to look at the smallest matters if necessary to ensure justice. Here, in a criminal conviction, one Sam Thompson—who had been convicted of disorderly public conduct for "shuffling" in a cafe—took his claim of lack of evidence successfully to the Supreme Court on *certiorari* because, under Kentucky law, the fines involved were too small to be reviewed by any state appellate court. Speaking for the unanimous Court, Mr. Justice Black noted that "Our examination of the record presented in the petition for *certiorari* convinced us that *although the fines here are small, the due process questions presented are substantial and we* therefore granted *certiorari* to review the police court's judg-

---

22 E.g. *United States v. District Court* (*United States v. Haley*), 371 U.S. 18 (1962).

23 *Wilkerson v. McCarthy*, 336 N.J., 53 (1949).

24 As quoted by Anthony Lewis, "How the Supreme Court Reaches Decisions," *The New York Times Magazine*, December 1, 1957, pp. 51–4.

25 *Thompson v. City of Louisville et. al.*, 362 U.S. 199 (1960).

ment."[26] A few short years later Black was moved to restate this fundamental philosophy when, in dissenting from the Court's majority opinion in the 1964 Maryland "state-action-sit-in" cases, he observed that "the Constitution does not confer upon any group the right to substitute rule by force for rule by law."[27]

Since the Court has complete discretionary power over grants of *certiorari*—a power bestowed upon it in the necessary and desirable "Judges Bill" of 1925, which was largely the creation of Mr. Chief Justice Taft and Mr. Justice Van Devanter—it denies between 85 and 90 per cent of all *certiorari* applications, and does not usually explain its reason for the denial. Prior to the 1925 statute, the Court's appellate jurisdiction was obligatory to the extent of some 80 per cent of its appellate business. Gone are the days when the Court was expected to devote an all-too-large portion of its valuable time and energy merely to correct errors of lower courts which primarily affected the rights of parties to a particular case or controversy. In the words of Mr. Chief Justice Vinson:

> To remain effective, the Supreme Court must continue to decide only those cases which present questions whose resolution will have immediate importance far beyond the particular facts and parties involved.[28]

On the other hand, the Court has never forgotten the oft-quoted admonition by Mr. Chief Justice Marshall in *Cohens v. Virginia* back in 1821:

> It is most true that this Court will not take jurisdiction if it should not: but it is equally true that it must take jurisdiction if it should. The judiciary cannot, as the legislature may, avoid a measure because it approaches the confines of the Constitution. We cannot pass it by because it is doubtful. With whatever doubts, with whatever difficulties, a case may be attended, we must decide it if it be brought before us. We have no more right to decline the exercise of jurisdiction which is given than to usurp that which is not given. The one or the other would be treason to the Constitution.[29]

26 Ibid., at 203. (Italics supplied.)
27 *Bell v. Maryland,* 378 U.S. 226, at 346.
28 From an address to the Assembly of the *American Bar Association* in St. Louis, September 9, 1944, entitled "Work of the Federal Courts."
29 6 Wheaton 264, at 404.

In order to grant *certiorari,* at least *four* of the justices must vote to do so. At this stage each justice, without any consultation with the others, reaches his own conclusion as to whether the application should be granted or denied. A working rule devised by the Court itself, this Rule of Four also applies to noting probable jurisdiction on writs of appeal—an interesting development in view of the important distinction presumably governing the two writs. Of course, the Court can also change its mind on a grant for review; there is nothing to prevent it, on thinking the matter over, from ultimately dismissing a writ as having been "improvidently granted."[30] According to a statute of 1863, however, *six* justices constitute a quorum to hand down a decision. This means that a plurality of four justices can *decide* a case. In the event of a tie vote, the decision of the lower court stands as the final word in the controversy at issue. But a single justice may—unless, or until, overruled by action of his brothers on the bench—grant a stay of execution or a writ of *habeas corpus.* Pertinent illustrations of this significant prerogative are the grants of requests for stays of execution, although denying requests for writs of *habeas corpus,* by Mr. Justice Douglas, in the sensational case of the convicted atom spies, Ethel and Julius Rosenberg, in June 1953. Although vacating the stays of execution just twenty-four hours after they had been granted, Mr. Chief Justice Vinson took note inferentially of the intemperate reaction in the public press, and especially in Congress (where bills of impeachment were at once introduced in the House of Representatives), by writing that "Mr. Justice Douglas had power to issue the stay. No one has disputed this, and we think the proposition is indisputable."[31]

Considerable disagreement exists among not only the many observers of the Court but among the justices themselves as to the true meaning of a denial of an application for a writ of *certiorari.* Mr. Justice Jackson viewed "sincere worthiness" as a tacit agreement by a quorum of the justices that the decision below is good enough to stand. "The fatal sentence," wrote he in his beautiful prose, "that in real life writes finis to many causes cannot in legal

30 E.g. *Cichos v. Indiana,* 385 U.S. 76 (1966), a state double jeopardy case which it had originally accepted for review.
31 *Rosenberg v. United States,* 346 U.S. 273 (1953), at 285.

181

theory be a complete blank."[32] Mr. Justice Frankfurter, however, always insisted that no significance attaches to the denial of *certiorari,* that it "in no wise" implies Court approval of the decision below. All it means, he would point out, is that for reasons seldom, if ever, disclosed, four justices evidently do not think that a case ought to be adjudicated on its merits. On occasion he spelled his reasoning out thus:

> . . . [it] seemed . . . to at least six members [of the Court] . . . that the issue was either not ripe enough or too moribund for adjudication; that the question had better wait for the perspective of time or that time would bury the question or, for one reason or another, it was desirable to wait and see; or that the constitutional issue was entangled with nonconstitutional issues that raised doubt whether the constitutional issue could be effectively isolated; or for various other reasons not related to the merits.[33]

No matter which of these two contrasting views may be "correct," the effect in the eyes of the disappointed petitioner is necessarily the same—at least for the present he has lost.

Work Load

All cases to be disposed of are placed on one of the Court's three dockets: the *Original,* the *Appellate,* and the *Miscellaneous.* In the 1965–66 term the Court had more cases (3274) on these dockets and *disposed* of more (2683) with finality than ever before. It granted *certiorari* in 178, a considerable number, but falling well short of the record number of 208 established in the 1957–58 term. But of those many cases the Court disposed, it decided only 342 *on the merits,* with *full written opinions* handed down in just 107 cases—an average number—the remainder being disposed of by *memorandum orders*—e.g. "affirmed," "reversed," or "dismissed." Yet it must be recognized that the Court does *act* on each and every case of which it disposes, whatever the nature of that disposition. The large number of cases docketed and disposed of, representing a major increase in the work load over previous years, came almost entirely in the so-called *miscellaneous* cases,

---

[32] Concurring opinion in *Brown v. Allen,* 344 U.S. 443 (1953), at 543.
[33] Dissenting opinion in *Darr v. Burford,* 339 U.S. 200 (1950), at 227. See also *Maryland v. Baltimore Radio Show,* 338 U.S. 912 (1950), at 917.

CHART B
UNITED STATES SUPREME COURT REVIEW

CASES NORMALLY REACH THE U. S. SUPREME COURT FOR PUR-
POSES OF *REVIEW* (as distinct from original jurisdiction) IN ONE OF
TWO PRINCIPAL WAYS:

    (1) on APPEAL, i.e. as a matter of right;
    (2) on a writ of CERTIORARI, as a matter of Court discretion.

(A third way, by CERTIFICATION, will be omitted for present purposes.
It is rarely used—presenting the Court with even less cases than those on
its original docket. It covers "any question of law in any civil or criminal
case as to which instructions are desired" by the lower court, usually a
Court of Appeals or the Court of Claims.* The old writ of ERROR, a
common law process strongly akin to (1) above, was statutorily discontinued in the federal courts in 1928. It brought the entire record of a case
proceeding in a lower court before the Supreme Court for its consideration
for alleged "errors of law" committed below.)

N.B. Title 28 of the United States Code, formulated as a result of congressional legislation, governs the types of review available to an appellant.
(See Secs. 1257 and 1254.)

  I. *Cases reaching the U. S. Supreme Court on APPEAL* (i.e. the Court
    reviews because it *must*).

    A. *From the State Court of Last Resort* having statutory jurisdiction in
      any particular case (usually, but not always, the *Highest State Court,*
      which normally, but not always, is the State Supreme Court).

      1. When a state court has declared a federal law or a federal treaty,
        or provisions thereof, unconstitutional.

      2. When a state court has *upheld* a state law or a provision of the
        state constitution *against* the challenge that it *conflicts* with the
        federal constitution, a federal law, a federal treaty, or any provi-
        sion thereof.

    B. *From the U. S. (Circuit) Courts of Appeals:*

      1. When a state law or a provision of a state constitution has been
        invalidated because of a conflict with a federal law, a federal
        treaty, or a provision of the federal constitution.

---

* One of the very infrequent illustrations of its use is that by the Fifth United
States Circuit Court of Appeals in 1963, which certified the question of whether
its criminal contempt citation of Governor Ross R. Barnett and Lieutenant-
Governor Paul B. Johnson, Jr., of Mississippi necessitated a trial by jury.
The intermediate appellate tribunal was evenly divided (4:4) when it turned
to the Supreme Court in this ticklish case arising out of the admission of
Negro James H. Meredith to the University of Mississippi at Oxford. (*United
States v. Barnett,* 375 U.S. 805.) The highest tribunal ruled 5:4 against Barnett
and Johnson (ibid. 376 U.S. 681) in 1964. But one year later the Circuit Court
cleared the two because of "changed circumstances and conditions." (Ibid.
346 F. 2d 99.)

    2. When a federal law has been held *unconstitutional, provided* the United States, or one of its agencies, officers, or employees is a party to the suit.

C. *From the U. S. District Courts:*

    1. When a federal statute has been held *unconstitutional, provided* the United States, or one of its agencies, officers, or employees is a party to the suit.

    2. When the United States is a party to a *civil* suit under the federal interstate-commerce, communication, or anti-trust laws.

    3. When a *special three-judge District Court* (which must include at least one circuit judge) has granted or denied an interlocutory or permanent injunction in any proceeding required to be heard by such a court. (These three-judge courts usually sit in suits brought to *restrain enforcement, operation, or execution of federal or of state statutes or orders of state administrative agencies* on the grounds of unconstitutionality; *or* because of an order of the Interstate Commerce Commission.)

D. *From "Any Court of the United States"* (comprising the *constitutional, legislative,* and *territorial* courts)—and specifically including, a.o., the *Court of Claims,* the *Court of Customs and Patent Appeals,* etc.:

    1. When a federal statute has been held *unconstitutional* in any *civil* action, suit, or proceeding, *provided* the United States, or one of its agencies, officers, or employees is a party to it.

II. *Cases reaching the U. S. Supreme Court on a writ of CERTIORARI* (i.e. because a minimum of four Supreme Court Justices has agreed to a review.) Writs of *certiorari* are granted or denied at the *discretion* of the Court—subject always to the latent power of Congress to define and limit the *appellate* power of the Court.

A. *From the State Court of the Last Resort having statutory jurisdiction* in any particular case (usually, but not always, the *Highest State Court,* which normally, but not always, is the State Supreme Court).

    1. In all cases, *other than* those for which the remedy is APPEAL (see I, A, 1 & 2 above), in which a *"substantial federal question"* has been properly raised. (The Court itself determines just what constitutes such a question.)

B. *From U. S. (Circuit) Courts of Appeals* (and, in all pertinent cases, from the *U. S. Court of Claims,* and the *Court of Customs and Patent Appeals*):

    1. When a decision involves the *application or interpretation* of a federal law, a federal treaty, the federal Constitution, or provisions thereof.

    2. Where the U. S. Court of Appeals has *upheld* a state law or a provision of a state constitution *against* the chellenge that it conflicts with a federal law, a federal treaty, the federal Constitution, or provisions thereof.

which are largely handwritten or typewritten papers filed by indigent persons, often prison inmates. This category of cases rose sharply to a record of 1831. Indigents obtain authority to file from the federal *in forma pauperis* statute, which gives to a citizen of the United States the right to enter proceedings in any federal court, provided he executes such an oath. Of course, this does not guarantee a Supreme Court review—although in its 1965–66 term the Court did agree to hear 128 of these cases, an unusually generous number. Moreover, it summarily vacated or reversed a fair number of other lower court decisions challenged by indigent persons. The purpose of this interesting statute clearly was to protect indigent persons—a large proportion of whom, according to a bitter remark by Mr. Justice Jackson, represent "our convict population." And Mr. Justice Douglas, certainly a sympathetic friend of the underdog, commented that the claims made in these pauper cases "are most fantastic, surpassing credulity . . . [and] are for the most part frivolous."[34] Nevertheless, many vital criminal cases have reached the Court via this path, among them the momentous *Gideon v. Wainwright*[35] in 1963, which resulted in the overruling of the *Betts v. Brady*[36] precedent of two decades. Clarence Earl Gideon had petitioned the Supreme Court for a writ of *habeas corpus* in form of a hand-pencilled letter from his Florida prison cell.[37] Of the total number of 3274 cases filed during the 1965–66 term. 591 were not disposed of and, thus, went over to the 1966–67 docket. That residue represented the largest number of cases carried forward to a new term since the Clerk of the Supreme Court began to keep these statistics in 1930.

Although there is some disagreement among the justices themselves on the point, most observers of the work of the Court believe firmly that it is overburdened with cases. In large measure, this is due to the flood of petitions that reach it; but to some degree it may also be due to the fact that the Court has persisted in taking cases which are at best trivial, sometimes dealing simply

---

34 Address to the Cornell University Law School, April 18, 1960. (Published as "The Supreme Court and its Case Load," op. cit.)

35 372 U.S. 335.

36 316 U.S. 455 (1942).

37 See the superb book on the *Gideon* case by Anthony Lewis, *Gideon's Trumpet* (New York: Random House, 1964) which, in addition to its basic story, is highly instructive in the judicial process.

with matters of fact, without presenting any truly imperative constitutional questions. This, of course, is a matter of judgment. Yet
it would seem that at least in the tax cases or in railroad and maritime injury-negligence cases, particularly the latter which usually
involves a question of fact as to who was at fault in the accident,
the Court has at times unnecessarily overextended itself in granting petitions for review. That a good many of the justices feel
quite strongly about the matter is indicated by a veritable stream
of comments by Mr. Justice Frankfurter, who, in case after case
in this field, would pen a comment to the extent that "the case
. . . is so trivial that the Court should dismiss its grant of review as
improvident." And in a dispute, early in the 1960–61 term, involving the question whether a jury should hear the case of a
wrench falling on a seaman's "left great toe," Mr. Justice Harlan,
speaking for a minority of four justices, delivered a three-page
dissent that began with the comment:

> At the opening of a term which finds the court's docket crowded
> with more important and difficult litigation than in many years,
> it is not without irony that we should be witnessing among the
> first matters to be heard a routine negligence . . . case involving
> only issues of facts. I continue to believe that such cases, distress-
> ing and important as they are for unsuccessful plaintiffs, do not
> belong in this court.[38]

Mr. Justice Frankfurter went even further here and opined that
the Court should not even have agreed to consider such a case in
the first place, and he once again voiced his long-standing lament
against consideration of minor negligence cases.

An intriguing and possibly highly significant decision by the
Court, during the 1960–61 term, gave Mr. Justice Frankfurter
additional reasons for expounding on the theme of unwise, non-
jurisdictional, unnecessary case work. Over his lone fifty-eight-page
dissenting opinion, the eight-man majority held that policemen
and other local officials who violated a citizen's constitutional
rights under the Civil Rights Act of 1871 could be sued for damage in *federal* courts *even if these officials acted without state
authority*. The Frankfurter dissent not only charged the majority
with violating federal-state relationships, relying heavily on the

[38] *Michalic v. Cleveland Tankers, Inc.*, 364 U. S. 325 (1960), at 332–3.

legislative history of the act as he saw it to prove his point, but he also decried what he viewed as rank court interference. Envisaging a veritable flood of petitions, he insisted that the broad construction adopted here by the Supreme Court made the federal Constitution

> a law to regulate the quotidian business of every traffic policeman, every registrar of elections, every city inspector or investigator, every clerk in every municipal license bureau in this country.[39]

Whatever the number of cases docketed, it ought to be fairly obvious that the lawyer who grandiosely and proudly informs both his client and the public press that "we'll fight this case all the way to the Supreme Court," really means that *if* the funds are present he will attempt to do so—unless a pauper's oath is involved the standard case will consume a solid outlay of $10,000—and *if* the Court will grant review he will *endeavor* to convince it of the righteousness of his client's case. The average case takes from two to five years to reach the highest bench. The preparation and printing of the record and the writing of briefs alone normally consumes five months. Seldom does the Court actually *hear oral arguments* on more than 100 to 150 of the cases it disposes of annually: the balance is dismissed on procedural or some other jurisdictional ground. Of those actually heard, formal *written opinions* by the Court are usually handed down in 75 to 85 per cent of the cases, the others being decided *per curiam*—an anonymous opinion expressing the summary judgment of the Court as a whole and not the opinion of a single justice with whom the others concur. In other words, a *per curiam* is an *unsigned,* normally very brief, opinion for the Court, its authorship unknown to the outside world, applying *res judicata* (settled law). For example, it was employed in the initial disposition of the much-litigated *Girard College Case*[40] in Philadelphia in 1958. Usually *per curiam* opinions are written for a unanimous Court but there are exceptions. For example, in 1966, Mr. Justice Clark wrote a formal dissenting opinion to the Court's *per curiam* in *Riggan v. Virginia.*[41] in which he was specifically joined by his colleagues Black, Harlan, and Stewart. There, the thus now readily identifiable majority of five (Warren, Douglas, Brennan, White, and Fortas) reversed *without briefs or*

[39] *Monroe v. Pape,* 365 U. S. 167 (1961).

[40] *Pennsylvania v. Board of Directors of City Trusts of the City of Philadelphia,* 357 U.S. 570 (1958).

[41] 384 U.S. 152.

arguments a lower court decision upholding the validity of a search warrant issued by a Virginia tribunal. There has ensued considerable criticism about the increasing resort to *per curiam* decisions. However, it may very well be that this simply represents an attempt by the Court to resolve the conflict between rendering fully reasoned opinions and affording the finality of Supreme Court ajudication to as large a number of litigants as possible. Or it may represent a "stop gap" expedient—such as the Court's *per curiam* decision in a group of obscenity cases in 1967, an area that has evidently defied a firmly, universally applicable rule of law.[42]

Reconsideration. A petitioner whose request for review has been *denied* by the Court for one or more of the reasons discussed above is not, of course, barred from trying again. Accordingly, some sanguine souls are rather persistent in these efforts—although they rarely, if ever, succeed unless their new petition serves to convince four justices of the merits of the renewed appeal. Among well-known illustrations of such unsuccesssful attempts are the cases of Morton Sobell, convicted of complicity in the atomic espionage case of Ethel and Julius Rosenberg and the doomed-to-die-in-the-gas-chamber Caryl Chessman. Sobell filed nine petitions for review of his conviction between 1953 and 1958; all were denied by the Court without comment. Chessman filed fully sixteen petitions for review with the Court between his conviction in 1948 for seventeen crimes (including kidnapping, attempted rape, sex perversion, robbery, and car theft) and his execution in 1960, prompting even Mr. Justice Douglas to comment ". . . the conclusion is inevitable that Chessman is playing a game with the courts."[43] The latter's battle ended in failure only after having filed a total of forty-two appeals with various federal and state courts. This procedure covered twelve years, caused extensive debates on the merit of capital punishment, and made Chessman's name a household word throughout the world.[44] A rare occur-

---

[42] *Redrup v. New York, Austin v. Kentucky,* and *Gent v. Arkansas,* 386 U.S. 767 (decided together).

[43] *Chessman v. Dickson,* 361 U.S. 955 (1960), and *Chessman v. Teets,* 362 U.S. 966 (1960).

[44] Chessman's record years on "death row" were exceeded in 1966 by the thirteen years spent by both Edgar Labat and Clifton Alton Poret, two Negroes who had been convicted of raping a white young woman in 1950. However, not only were they released from "death row," but they were ordered freed from jail by the Fifth United States Circuit Court of Appeals because they had been convicted by juries from which Negroes were *systematically* excluded.

rence in this realm of the judicial process is a Court-solicited or encouraged reconsideration, such as that specifically requested by the 1961–62 bench when, in granting review to prison inmate Gideon,[45] it set down for argument against the specific *quaere*[46] whether it should now reconsider its 1942 ruling in *Betts v. Brady*.[47]

Rehearing. On the other hand, it is also possible for a *defeated* litigant to ask the Supreme Court for a *rehearing* after the announcement of the unfavorable decision, in the dim hope that the Court in the person of one or more of the justices, may undergo a change of mind on rehearing the case; this is especially true when the former decision was a very close one and featured a sharply divided Court. But under the rules of the Supreme Court a rehearing may not be granted unless a member of the *majority* in the original decision votes for one—and the court in effect granted only six rehearings between 1940 and 1965, to cite an otherwise especially active quarter of a century. Nevertheless, the rules clearly give every litigant the right to seek a rehearing of his case.

A notable illustration of one of the infrequent successes gained by a petitioner on rehearing—one of but three such victories in the twenty-five year period indicated—was the group of "military justice" cases, involving Mesdames Clarice Covert and Dorothy Smith-Krueger, both civilians, who killed their unfaithful Master-Sergeant and Colonel spouses with axe and knife, respectively, while with them at overseas bases. The cases were argued together at the bar of the Supreme Court initially in 1956, the constitutional issue being the validity of the section of the United States Uniform Military Code of Justice that authorized the military trial of civilians accompanying the armed forces abroad.[48]

[45] *Gideon v. Cochran*, 370 U.S. 908 (1962).

[46] "Should this Court's holding in *Betts v. Brady*, 316 U.S. 455, be overruled?" In *Betts* the Court had held 6:3 that indigent state criminal defendants are automatically entitled to state-furnished counsel only in *capital* criminal cases —unless certain "special circumstances" attended the case (and they did not in *Betts* in the Court's judgment).

[47] 316 U.S. 455 (1942). When the *Gideon* decision came down in 1963, *Betts v. Brady* stood unanimously overruled—in an opinion for the Court by Mr. Justice Black, one of the three dissenters in *Betts* (*Gideon v. Wainwright*, 372 U.S. 335).

[48] *Kinsella v. Krueger*, 351 U. S. 470 and *Reid v. Covert*, 351 U. S. 487 (June 11, 1956).

The Court upheld the disputed section in a 5:3 decision, delivered by Mr. Justice Clark, while the three dissenters—Warren, Black, and Douglas—protested they were being rushed at term's end; and Mr. Justice Frankfurter refused to participate other than to file a "reservation," because of "lack of adequate time to consider" the issues involved and "their complexity." Clearly, this was the type of decision in which able counsel for defendants might well see a distinct ray of hope for a rehearing. A motion for a rehearing was duly filed; it was accepted by a 5:3 vote, the three original dissenters and Mr. Justice Frankfurter being joined in approving the petition for rehearing by Mr. Justice Harlan, a member of the original majority.[49] Matters certainly seemed to look up for the grieving widows!

The case was duly reargued early in 1957, and during the waning days of that term the Court handed down its decision, reversing itself by declaring the section in question to be unconstitutional by a 6:2 vote.[50] Only Justices Clark and Burton remained of the erstwhile majority, Justices Minton and Reed having retired from the Court, Mr. Justice Harlan having changed his mind, and a new member, Mr. Justice Brennan, joining the majority. The ninth member, Mr. Justice Whittaker, just appointed to replace Mr. Justice Reed, did not participate in the decision. It should be re-emphasized, however, that a grant of a petition for rehearing is the exception to the rule. A promising indication of a possible chance for one is, of course, an officially announced change of mind from the bench. An illustration might yet turn out to be Mr. Justice Douglas's announcement in the *New York Prayer Case*[51] that he *now* believed the *New Jersey Bus Case* of 1947, in which he had provided the crucial fifth vote,[52] to have been wrongly decided!

Reargument. A related, but distinct, practice is an order for *reargument,* in which the Court—for reasons best known to itself —orders a case back on the docket for reargument rather than hand down a decision. At the end of 1956–57 term it did this in ten cases that had already been briefed and argued before it. The

49 *Reid v. Covert* and *Kinsella v. Krueger,* 352 U. S. 901 (November 5, 1956). On petition for rehearing.
50 *Reid v. Covert* and *Kinsella v. Krueger,* 354 U. S. 1 (June 10, 1957). On rehearing.
51 *Engel v. Vitale,* 370 U.S. 421 (1962), at 443.
52 *Everson v. Board of Education of Ewing Township,* 330 U.S. 1.

famed *Segregation Cases*[53] represent a pertinent earlier example. Initially argued in December 1952, they were ordered reargued in December 1953, and were decided in May 1954. A more recent illustration is the aforementioned, controversial water dispute case between Arizona and California, which the Supreme Court ordered re-argued in 1962—as an original jurisdiction case—despite the fact that it had spent a week hearing arguments in that complex litigation during the preceding January. A crucial reason for this order was the Chief Justice's (Warren's) voluntary disqualification —he had been Governor of California—coupled with Mr. Justice Frankfurter's illness and Mr. Justice Whittaker's retirement, the latter's successor—Mr. Justice White—not having heard the initial arguments. A decision was ultimately handed down in June of 1963, with the Chief Justice not participating, but with both Justice Goldberg—who had replaced the now retired Mr. Justice Frankfurter—and Justice White taking part and siding with the 7:1 Black majority opinion.[54] A later petition for a rehearing by the "loser," California, was denied.[55]

THE UNITED STATES SUPREME COURT AT WORK

The concluding sections above illustrated a marginal function of the Court. But how does this most impressive and most dignified of all governmental bodies in the United States generally conduct its work? Annually, since 1873, it has sat for thirty-six weeks customarily, from the first or second Monday in October until the end of June, sometimes longer. On rare occasions, such as in the case involving the Little Rock, Arkansas, school desegregation crisis in August-September 1958,[56] and the case of the seven German saboteurs in 1942,[57] a Special Session may be convoked. But there have been only four such sessions in this century. Yet, be it stated at once that the business of judging, at least at the level of the federal government, is a year-round occupation, regardless of formal sessions.

[53] *Brown v. Board of Education of Topeka,* 347 U.S. 483 (1954) and *Bolling v. Sharpe,* 347 U.S. 497 (1954).
[54] *Arizona v. California,* 373 U.S. 546 (1963).
[55] 375 U.S. 892 (1963).
[56] *Cooper v. Aaron,* 358 U.S. 1.
[57] *Ex parte Quirin,* 317 U.S. 1.

All of the Court's sessions are now held in its building of
magnificent Greek style architecture, Corinthian-order white marble
structure, at 1 First Street, N.E., near Capitol Hill in Washington,
D.C.,[58] guarded by a special thirty-three man Supreme Court police
force. The Court's present home was constructed in 1935, pat-
terned after the Temple of Diana at Ephesus—one of the seven

FIGURE 1
THE 1967–68 COURT

1. Mr. Chief Justice Warren

2. Mr. Justice Black	3. Mr. Justice Douglas
4. Mr. Justice Harlan	5. Mr. Justice Brennan
6. Mr. Justice Stewart	7. Mr. Justice White
8. Mr. Justice Fortas	9. Mr. Justice Marshall
10. The Clerk's Desk	11. The Marshal's Desk

12. Counsel's Desk

wonders of the ancient world. The noble words "Equal Justice
Under Law" are carved above the majestic entrance, which is
enhanced by great bronze doors. Here in its large and resplendent
forty-four foot high courtroom seating three hundred people—
amidst twenty-four Ionic columns of light Siena Old Convent marble and carved walls depicting both real and symbolic judicial
figures—convenes the Supreme Court of the United States. Its
nine justices are clad in black robes—those judicial vestments
Judge Jerome Frank always wanted to banish[59]—and they are
seated behind the raised bench in high-backed swivel chairs of
varying size against a background of full red draperies. At the appointed hour, the drapes part and from behind them appears the
Chief Justice, followed *seriatim* in order of seniority by the eight
associate justices. They—all assembled—remain standing until the
Marshal has completed his time-honored introduction: "Oyez,

58 The first term of the Supreme Court was the February Term 1790, held in
New York City, which then was the seat of the federal government. In February 1791 it moved to the (now restored) Supreme Court Building on Fifth
and Chestnut streets in Philadelphia, where it met until it moved in 1801 to
the office of the Clerk of the Senate (on the main floor of the East Wing
of the then still unfinished Capitol building). It remained there until its own
chamber in that edifice was readied in 1808.
59 See his amusing "The Cult of the Robe" in his classic *Courts on Trial: Myth
and Reality in American Justice* (Princeton: Princeton University Press, 1949).

Oyez, Oyez! All persons having business before the Honorable, the Supreme Court of the United States, are admonished to draw near and give their attention, for the Court is now sitting. God save the United States and this Honorable Court" (a remark that has been the butt of a number of tasteless jokes). The justices' seats are arranged according to length of continuous service on the bench; the Chief Justice sits in the center, flanked by the Senior Associate Justice on his immediate right, the second-ranking on his immediate left, then alternating in that manner in declining order of seniority.

ORAL ARGUMENT

In this impressive setting guarded by its special police detail on round-the-clock security and attended by four high-school-age pages (since 1963 mercifully no longer in knickers, long black stockings, and double-breasted jackets), the Court listens to oral arguments—in the cases it has agreed to hear—for the first four days in two weeks out of each month. Its justices spend the other two weeks behind closed doors in consideration of cases and writing of opinions. Forty copies of the printed briefs of the oral arguments—one set going to each justice[60]—had to be filed with the Clerk of the Court well in advance; to be exact, forty-five days after the case was placed on the docket by the party bringing suit, and the answering brief had to be filed thirty days hence. The briefs, which are filed in accordance with prescribed format and are preferably no longer than twenty-five pages, generally state the facts, issues, questions to be presented, decisions of lower courts, and all relevant legal arguments, together with the statutes and citations of cases to which they apply. As already explained, those bona fide paupers whose cases are treated on the special miscellaneous docket may, however, file handwritten or typewritten briefs. Oral argument, now heard on designated days from 10:00 a.m. to noon and from 12:30 p.m. until 2:30 p.m.,[61] is at once the most significant and the most fascinating aspect of the *public*

[60] All printed documents filed in the Court must be 6⅛" by 9¼" in size, with type no smaller than 11-point, "adequately leaded," and the paper "opaque and unglazed."

[61] From 1873 until 1961 the Court met and broke up two hours later.

portion of the Court's work. (Of the 300 seats available, 112 are allotted to the press, the justices' families, and members of the bar, the remaining 188 being available to the general public strictly on a "first come, first serve" basis. Usually there are two public queues for the 188: one a three-minute-stay line, the other a "stay as long as you wish" one.) There is at least a chance that skillful oral arguments, in supplementing the printed brief by oral emphasis,[62] may sway members on the spot, although this is far less likely in the great than in the small cases. Still, first impressions count—and Mr. Justice Douglas, for one, has insisted that ". . . oral arguments win or lose the case."[63] The pressure on the arguing lawyers, who must speak from the floor level, is naturally enormous. They are frequently questioned sharply by the justices who often have a bench memorandum prepared before the argument —questions that may conceivably forecast the ultimate decision of the Court, although in few, if any, instances is it possible to give an accurate prognosis. Some justices (e.g. Mr. Justice Douglas) customarily ask very few questions; others (Mr. Justice Frankfurter was a prime example) have a habit of asking a great many. John P. Frank reported that in one particular case he witnessed—perhaps a somewhat extreme illustration—the justices interrupted counsel 84 times during 120 minutes of oral argument, with 93 questions and interpolations chargeable to Mr. Justice Frankfurter alone![64] Woe unto counsel who is ill-prepared or uncertain of himself—and the justices frown on reading from the prepared text. In fact, Rule 44 of the Court states that it looks "with disfavor" on such a practice. But the justices may also well prove to be helpful to counsel. Thus, during one oral argument heard in the 1960–61 term, Mr. Justice Frankfurter sharply questioned an obviously flustered arguing lawyer several times, only to see Mr. Justice Douglas intervene each time with a helpful answer! "I thought *you* were arguing this case," shot Mr. Justice Frankfurter to grateful counsel, who responded, "I am, but I can use all the help I can get."[65] It should be clear that the Court, as

[62] See John M. Harlan, "What Role Does Oral Argument Play in the Conduct of an Appeal?" 41 *Cornell Law Quarterly* 6 (1955).
[63] *The Philadelphia Inquirer,* April 9, 1963.
[64] *The Marble Palace* (New York: Alfred A. Knopf, 1958), pp. 104–5.
[65] As reported by Anthony Lewis in "The Justices' Supreme Job," *The New York Times Magazine,* June 11, 1961. (Italics supplied.)

Frankfurter once put it, does not see itself as "a dozing audience for the reading of soliloquies, but as a questioning body, utilizing oral argument as a means for exposing the difficulties of a case with a view to meeting them."[66]

Unlike the days of old, especially during Mr. Chief Justice John Marshall's reign when a Daniel Webster would sometimes address the Court with mounting eloquence for days, the present-day lawyers are severely limited in the time granted to them for argument. Normally, the limit is one hour for each side, sometimes merely a half-hour. One of the rare suspensions of the time limit rule took place in the case of *United Steel Workers of America v. United States*,[67] involving the legality of the injunctive provisions of the Taft-Hartley Act. In the average term only circa 250 hours of argument are allotted to the counsels severally.[68] They use a lectern to which two lights are attached; five minutes before time is up a white light flashes; when the second light, appropriately a red one, flashes, the lawyer must stop instantly—unless he is granted permission by the Chief Justice to continue. According to one of Mr. Chief Justice Hughes's law clerks, that "Chief" was so strict on the score of time that he once stopped a leader of the New York Bar in the middle of the word "if"; and that, on another occasion, upon being asked by the same attorney how much time remained, Hughes replied icily, "Fourteen seconds, Mr. Counsel."[69]

To argue cases at the bar of the Supreme Court a lawyer must be admitted to practise before it. This is a relatively routine matter, although not without its ceremonial by-products. It is customary for the Solicitor-General of the United States to "introduce" to the Court all bona fide applicants at its first session in October; this being done, their admission is automatic. Thereafter, admission to the bar of the court is an almost daily routine occurrence during the term, available to all lawyers who have been

[66] From "Memorial for Stanley M. Silverberg," in Philip Elman (ed.), *Of Law and Men* (New York: Harcourt, Brace & Co., 1956), pp. 320–21.

[67] 361 U. S. 49 (1959). Another was *Arizona v. California*, sixteen hours (!), in January 1962. A third was *Brown v. Board # 2* in 1955 for which fourteen hours were allotted.

[68] In the 1958–59 term, for example, 220 hours.

[69] Edwin McElwain, "The Business of the Supreme Court as Conducted by Chief Justice Hughes," 63 *Harvard Law Review* 6 (1949).

members of the bar of their state's highest court for three years. There is a $25 "admission fee," which the Supreme Court uses to cover travel and printing expenses of Court-assigned lawyers who represent indigent parties that come before it. Admission may, however, be revoked, as occurred, for example, in the case of attorney Wilmer D. Rekeweg of Paulding, Ohio, in June 1967. Because of certain professional aberrations resulting in his disbarment from the practice of law in all courts of Ohio by order of the Supreme Court of Ohio, the Supreme Court of the United States, after a "show cause" procedure, suspended and then disbarred him in a special Order (1346 Misc.) which read: ". . . it is ordered that the said Wilmer D. Rekeweg be, and he is hereby disbarred, and that his name be stricken from the roll of attorneys admitted to practice before the bar of this court."[70]

The Solicitor-General. The *Solicitor-General* is the third-ranking official in the U.S. Department of Justice, following the Attorney General and the Deputy Attorney General. Because of its special relationship to the Supreme Court, the post of Solicitor-General has always enjoyed a high reputation in legal circles, has been eagerly sought by members of the legal profession, and has not infrequently been filled by legal scholars—viz., President Kennedy's appointment of Professor Archibald Cox of the law school of Harvard University as his first Solicitor-General and that by President Johnson of Cox's Dean, Erwin N. Griswold in 1967 (succeeding Thurgood Marshall).

The Solicitor-General is in charge of all of the government's litigation in the Supreme Court, which comprises in excess of 50 per cent of the Court's total work load. He and his staff argue all of the government's cases before it. His office supervises all government briefs filed in the Court, and he must personally approve, or disapprove, any case before the government takes it to the Court. Moreover, the Solicitor-General—whose post pays $28,500 (1968)—has supervisory authority over other government appeals. Only if he gives his approval may the government appeal from an adverse decision in a trial court. (In a federal criminal case, if either a judge or a jury has heard *evidence* and has found the defendant innocent on that evidence, the govern-

[70] "Actions in United States Supreme Court," June 5, 1967 (as reported in *The New York Times,* June 6, 1967).

196

ment cannot appeal at all. However, the Supreme Court has *upheld* appeals by some *states,* where state law—as in Connecticut —permits government appeals even in criminal cases.) Sometimes much to the chagrin of certain member of both the executive and legislative branches, the Solicitor-General's office has developed a commendable tradition of alertness toward any unfairness in government cases. When he detects such unfairness, the Solicitor-General will usually file a "Confession of Error" in the Supreme Court, in which he asks that it set aside a victory won by the government in the lower court. Although this practice is of the very essence of justice—which, after all, should be the aim of all litigation—it may be doubted that a large number of private counsel would be similarly willing to forego a victory. All too frequently litigation is viewed as a courtroom battle between two opposing teams of high-powered trial lawyers bent upon "victory" rather than upon the triumph of justice.

BEHIND CLOSED DOORS

Each Friday during the Court's term is *Conference Day.* (Until changed by Mr. Chief Justice Warren, Saturday used to be that important day.) On Conference Day, summoned by a buzzer five minutes before the hour, the justices meet in secret, usually from 10:00 a.m. until 5:30 or 6:00 p.m. with less than one hour for lunch, in the beautiful, oak-paneled from floor to ceiling, book-case-lined on one side, never-to-date photographed conference chamber, which is under the chairmanship of the Chief Justice, whose office is adjacent to it. The role of the "Chief" is that of *primus inter pares,* although some have tended to be more *pares* than *primus,* as we shall presently see. Here the justices discuss the cases they have heard, as well as all pending motions and applications for *certiorari.* They are expected to be ready to indicate their tentative stand, which they will have normally noted on their copies of the agenda, having been previously advised which cases would be up for discussion—generally those just heard by them on the four "argument days" during that week or those recently heard in the course of conferences meeting during the two recess weeks in which no oral arguments are presented. The conference "list" may run from 25 to 150 items; 75

is about normal. The importance of this traditional conference, for that matter any conference of appellate judges at which they review law cases and controversies, was well stated by Mr. Justice Jesse W. Carter of the California Supreme Court:

> . . . [The conference] is not a prayer meeting where everyone is expected to nod "amen"; it is more like a battleground where opposing philosophies meet in hand-to-hand combat.[71]

The justices are seated around a large rectangular conference table, each chair bearing a nameplate. In accordance with a tradition established by Mr. Chief Justice Fuller in 1888, all will have shaken hands with one another on entering the room. The Chief Justice sits at the south end and the Senior Associate Justice on the north end. On the sides, in the usual order of seniority, sit the remaining seven Associate Justices. Looking down on this scene is the sole portrait in the room—that of Mr. Chief Justice John Marshall. The incumbent Chief Justice, whose personality and administrative talent loom large in these meetings, customarily gives his own view first in the case up for discussion, followed by that of the other justices in order of seniority. Each justice must be prepared to recite and do so persuasively—if he feels strongly about an issue involved. Upon completion of this phase of their deliberations, the nine members of the Court take a tentative vote on the particular case, the justice with the lowest seniority voting first this time, presumably so that he will not be influenced by the votes of his more experienced brothers—a somewhat debatable rationale. Each justice has a hinged, lockable docket book, in which all votes are duly recorded.

The Role of the Chief Justice. Although he is theoretically merely *primus intra pares,* the "Chief," as already indicated, has a potential influence that may well outweigh that of the ordinary presiding officer. Two of his functions—probably the only two— lend themselves ideally to the exercise of that influence: One is the aforementioned chairmanship of the Court's own conference, including his highly important role in the sifting of writs of *certiorari,* the other his assignment of opinions (to be more fully described later in this section). When the "Chief" opens discussion of a case by giving his own views first, he has an excellent opportunity to

[71] As quoted in *The New York Times,* March 16, 1959.

state the case as he sees it, to indicate the questions to be decided, and to give his opinions on the issue or issues involved. This is a far from inconsiderable power, for there is a good chance that his initial analysis of a problem will have at least some influence on that of others in the room. It is, of course, by no means inevitable that the man who selects the issues to be discussed will dominate or determine the ultimate results—to which the lasting and profound differences in reading the meaning of the Constitution among justices on a host of issues bear witness. Still, there is a chance, and often a good chance, that he may do so.

But there are other tasks, implied or actual, that confront a Chief Justice and play a role in history's regard of him as an effective or ineffective leader. Among them is his ability to keep peace among the several justices, who are often deeply divided along intellectual as well as personal lines. Justices Jackson and Black, for example, became increasingly hostile during the waning days of Mr. Chief Justice Stone's tenure, resulting, or so it is believed, in President Truman's compromise "peacemaker appointment" of Fred Vinson as Stone's successor on the latter's death in 1946. Vinson, a person of far less judicial and intellectual stature than Stone, had a reputation as a conciliator and, apparently, succeeded at least in keeping the feud among the two justices *en famille*. Mr. Justice McReynolds, a confirmed anti-semite, refused even to speak to his newly appointed colleague, Mr. Justice Brandeis, from 1916 to 1919. Mr. Chief Justice White was unable to alter the situation, but the amiable and popular Mr. Chief Justice Taft apparently succeeded in mitigating it somewhat. Still, McReynolds caused Taft constant difficulties, too. For instance, he refused to sit for the Court's annual photograph in 1924 because he would have found himself seated next to Brandeis in seniority—and no photo was taken! And two years earlier he had refused to accompany the Court to a Philadelphia ceremony, writing to Taft: "As you know, I am not always to be found when there is a Hebrew abroad."[72] Other McReynolds quirks were almost constant carping at almost every opinion authored by Stone whom he disliked for philosophical reasons, and his overt hostility toward Mr. Justice John H. Clarke who,

[72] As quoted by Alpheus T. Mason in his *William Howard Taft: Chief Justice* (New York: Simon and Schuster, 1965), pp. 216–17.

he felt, had "betrayed" him by failing to vote on the Court as McReynolds, who as Wilson's Attorney General had played a role in Clarke's appointment to the bench, thought he should and would. While he was by no means able to stop entirely the public barbs exchanged on the bench on occasion between, for example, Justices Frankfurter and Whittaker, on the one hand, and Justices Black and Douglas, on the other, Mr. Chief Justice Warren apparently smoothed over many a ruffled feeling, despite his personal involvement in an outburst or two, as some of the illustrations to follow will indicate.

Another significant facet of the "Chief's" work is to keep an eye on the clock during the conference, with a view of getting its tasks accomplished. Although there has been some disagreement as to the extent of the Court's burden—Mr. Justice Douglas, evidently a minority of one on that issue, does not view the Court as overworked[73]—there is little doubt that the pressure of case work is enormous. Unless a firm hand rules the conference, time will flee—especially as the justices are quite naturally given to extensive speaking, Mr. Justice Oliver Wendell Holmes, Jr., interestingly enough, being a notable exception. No Chief Justice controlled his flock so firmly as did Hughes, whom most students and observers of the Court, as well as those who served with him, have generally regarded as the most effective—even if on occasion somewhat arbitrary—organizer, leader, and disciplinarian along these lines since Mr. Chief Justice Marshall's regime.

For example, Hughes would accord an average of three and one-half minutes of conference time and no more to a petition for *certiorari,* having himself gone through and thoroughly analyzed all of them *before* the conference and being fully prepared to make recommendations on each to his colleagues. And he would often force the end of a discussion that he viewed as unprofitable or dilatory by intoning: "Brethren, the only way to settle this is vote. So let us do just that—now." Mr. Justice Stone, whose philosophy of his role as "Chief" was drastically different, declined to put any time limit on either *certiorari* discussions or on a particular series of cases. Stone simply refused to engage in what he viewed as "high pressure tactics." Thus, where Hughes finished a conference docket in four hours, Stone would require four days

[73] See his address to the Cornell University Law School, fn. 15, loc. cit.

for a similar docket. This did not make Stone a less qualified jurist, but it probably made him a far less effective "Chief" than Hughes or another effective and popular Chief Justice, Taft—whose calibre, however, was certainly considerably below that of Stone as a *justice*. Some observers, although distinctly in a small minority, believe that the virtues of Hughes as Chief Justice were overstated and those of Stone underrated. One of these, John P. Frank, a law clerk for Mr. Justice Black, complained that Hughes's tactics of "business efficiency" meant that ". . . discussion in conference was perforce a statement of conclusions more than an exchange of mutually stimulating ideas . . ." and he charged the Chief Justice with "intellectual flexibility for the sake of the appearance of unanimity."[74] Be that as it may, Mr. Chief Justice Hughes was immensely popular as a leader of his bench, and he was the only member of the Court to whom Mr. Justice McReynolds would defer. We have Mr. Justice Frankfurter's word that ". . . if he made others feel his moral superiority, they merely felt a fact . . . all who served with him recognized [his] extraordinary qualities. . . . To see him preside was like Toscanini leading an orchestra."[75] Mr. Justice Black attested to his own "more than impersonal and detached admiration [for Hughes's] extraordinary intellectual gifts."[76] And Mr. Justice Roberts wrote that "Men whose views were as sharply opposed as those of Van Devanter and Brandeis, or those of Sutherland and Cardozo, were at one in their admiration and affectionate regard for their presiding officer."[77] There is little, if any, doubt that Charles Evans Hughes was the epitome of a great Chief Justice. And history may well place Earl Warren into a similar bracket.

ASSIGNING AND WRITING OPINIONS

As Eugene V. Rostow wrote when he was Dean of the Yale School of Law, "Judges must write down their reasons for a decision because they are partners with us, the citizenry, in an

---

[74] John P. Frank, "Harlan Fiske Stone: An Estimate," 9 *Stanford Law Review* 629n (1957).

[75] *Of Law and Men,* op. cit. pp. 133, 148.

[76] Black to Hughes, June 3, 1941. Hughes Papers.

[77] Address to the Association of the Bar of the City of New York and the New York County Lawyers' Association, December 12, 1948.

agreed procedure for reaching responsible decisions."[78] The practice of writing the Opinion of the Court[79] stems from the days of Mr. Chief Justice John Marshall, prior to whose adoption of this time-saving procedure the justices usually, but not always, delivered their opinions *seriatim*[80]—a practice still prevalent with the Law Lords of the British House of Lords, and one that Jefferson, as President, wanted to institutionalize in the face of Marshall's powerful influence. Today, following Marshall, who believed that the Court's power and prestige would be enhanced if it were to speak with a single voice, full opinions are written for the Court —some of these *per curiam,* as we have seen—in all cases heard by it on the merits, other than those decided by memorandum order. However, no opinion is written in the event of a tie vote, nor does the Court announce on which side of the tie the justices stood. The effect of a tie vote is the sustaining of the decision below; e.g. the Court's 4:4 vote in the case of *Bailey v. Richardson*[81] thereby affirmed the 2:1 upholding of the loyalty dismissal of Dorothy Bailey by the federal government in the Court of Appeals for the District of Columbia. The even division of the Court in this instance came about as a result of Mr. Justice Tom Clark's failure to participate in the case; since he had been the U.S. Attorney General at the time of Miss Bailey's travail and dismissal, he deemed it unethical to be involved in the disposition of her appeal. The members of today's Supreme Court, unlike most members of Congress, are extremely cautious about even the faintest of taints of conflict of interest, be this of a social, economic, personal, or political nature. "When in doubt, do not sit" is a firmly established custom among the justices, partially reinforced by two federal statutes and a canon of the American Bar Association.[82] This was not always so in the early days of

[78] *The Sovereign Prerogative: The Supreme Court and the Quest for Law* (New Haven: Yale University Press, 1962), p. 89.

[79] John P. Frank, a careful observer and student of the Court, once divided the writing styles of the justices into four categories: "legal lumpy," legal massive," "rock-bottom contemporary," and "legal lucid." (*The Marble Palace.* New York: Alfred A. Knopf, 1958, pp. 295ff.)

[80] A well-known illustration is the group of seriatim opinions by Associate Justices Chase, Paterson, and Iredell in the 1796 case of *Hylton v. United States,* 3 Dallas 171.

[81] 341 U.S. 918 (1951).

[82] For their exact verbiage, see Title 28, Sec. 454, U.S.C.A., Title 28, Sec. 455, U.S.C.A., and the Fourth Canon of the American Bar Association's Canons of Judicial Ethics.

the Court—as Mr. Chief Justice Marshall's refusal to disqualify himself in *Marbury v. Madison*,[83] in which he was clearly and directly involved, clearly demonstrated.

The work load of preparing opinions of the Court is usually very well distributed. If the Court is unanimous or if the Chief Justice is in the majority, he may, and often does, write the opinion of the Court himself. In the latter instance, provided he speaks for at least four other justices, it would be know as the *majority opinion*.

But, of course, nothing prevents him from asking another member of the Court, when it is unanimous, or of the majority, when he himself is on that side, to write the opinion. The only exception to this practice is the long-standing tradition of permitting every newcomer to the Court to select the first opinion he will write. Gone long ago are the days of Mr. Chief Justice Marshall who, especially during his early years on the bench, would himself write practically every opinion—no doubt at least partly because his fellow justices were rather lethargic, some would say browbeaten. In fact, during his first four full years (1801–5) he personally authored all save two of the opinions of the Court! But when the Chief Justice is on the minority side of a decision, the Senior Associate Justice on the side of the majority either writes the opinion of the Court himself or assigns it to one of the other members among the majority. All assignments are made by sending a formal note to the prospective author. For an illustration of an equitable distribution of the work load of preparing *opinions of the Court,* the 1965–66 term may be cited: Mr. Justice Harlan wrote eight opinions; Mr. Justice Warren, nine; Mr. Justice Fortas, ten; Justices Black, Clark, and White, eleven each; and Mr. Justice Stewart, twelve. (Ten opinions were *per curiam*.) In the realm of the thirty-seven concurring opinions filed, Mr. Justice Harlan led his brothers with eleven, Mr. Justice Douglas was next with eight. Harlan again headed the Court in the seventy-four *dissenting opinions* filed with twenty-three; followed by Justices Black (twelve), Douglas (ten), Stewart (eight), White and Fortas (seven each), the Chief Justice and Justice Clark (three each) and Mr. Justice Brennan filed only one. In all cases disposed of, whether by full opinion or memorandum order, the

[83] 1 Cranch 137 (1803).

justices cast one hundred and sixty-eight dissenting *votes,* led by Mr. Justice Harlan's thirty-nine. Although as a rule *unanimous opinions* are rendered in a minority of full opinion cases—they have averaged 25 to 30 per cent through the years—the Court was unanimous in fully 44 per cent of its full opinions in its 1965–66 term. Memorandum orders, which, quite naturally, enjoy a far higher degree of unanimity, were up to 83 per cent during that term of "sweet agreeability."[84]

Dissenting Opinions. As these statistics demonstrate, dissenting and concurring opinions as well as simple dissents and concurrences are quite common.[85] Yet only when the former method of registering disagreement with the decision and/or the opinion of the majority is employed does the practice become meaningful for the governmental process. A simple *dissent,* without explanation, for example, such as "Mr. Justice Butler dissents" in *Palko v. Connecticut,*[86] ranks as a vote on the other side; but it says little to the expert and layman alike save that a justice, for reasons known only to himself, chose to dissent—no matter how understandable and even predictable that dissent might have been to the close student of the Court and its personnel. Be that aspect of disagreement as it may, it is entirely possible, of course, for honest, competent men to arrive at sharply divided opinions in a case; hence, *dissenting opinions,* both short and long, are quite common. In fact, the first *reported* decision of the Supreme Court was rendered by a divided Court, Justices William Cushing and Thomas Johnson dissenting from the Court majority's grant of an injunction to Georgia.[87] As one of the best-known dissenters, Mr. Justice Holmes, said, "General propositions do not decide particular cases." One of the classic statements on the subject was made by the then ex-Associate Justice and future Chief Justice Hughes:

[84] Several good sources for these statistics exist; among others, the *Annual Report of the Director of the Administrative Office of the U.S. Courts,* and the law reviews, especially the November issue of the *Harvard Law Review.*

[85] Apparently there exists a tradition—albeit not an unbroken one—that precludes *any* qualifying opinion in a decision involving a new justice's first opinion for the Court. See Wallace Mendelson's "Neo-Behavioralism—A Rebuttal," 57 *American Political Science Review* 952 (December 1963), fn. 7.

[86] 302 U. S. 319 (1937).

[87] *Georgia v. Braisford,* 2 Dallas 402 (1792).

A dissent in a court of last resort is an appeal to the brooding spirit of the law, to the intelligence of a future day, when a later decision may possibly correct the error into which the dissenting judge believes the court to have been betrayed.[88]

And this from the pen of a jurist who rarely wrote dissenting opinions himself, who rarely dissented, and who exerted a greater dominance over the Court than any other Chief Justice save Marshall! Hughes often expressed the point of view that there is no reason to expect more unanimity on difficult problems of law than in the "higher reaches" of physics, theology, or philosophy. Mr. Justice Carter, the colorful state of California jurist mentioned earlier in these pages, was fond of observing: "I welcome dissents, for they test the soundness of my own opinions."[89] (Both men meant dissenting *opinions*, of course.) Or, as Roscoe Pound once remarked, ". . . dissenting opinions may be the symptom of life in the law of time."[90] To Thomas Reed Powell they were ". . . most valuable equilibrators in the undulating course of the law."[91]

Many among the most memorable opinions of the Court initially on the dissenting side, have eventually become majority opinions —especially some by eloquent spokesmen of the then minority viewpoints such as Justices William Johnson, Harlan, Sr., Holmes, Brandeis, Stone, and Black. One obvious example is the lone Harlan dissenting opinion in 1896, his eloquent remonstrance against the "separate but equal" doctrine in *Plessy v. Ferguson*[92] which became the unanimous opinion of the Court in 1954 in *Brown v. Board of Education of Topeka*.[93] Another is the lone dissenting opinion of Stone in 1940 in the *Gobitis* case;[94] Stone argued forcefully, but unsuccessfully, against the compulsory flag salute required by the Minersville, Pennsylvania, school district even from those who found it to be religiously objectionable.

[88] C. Evans Hughes, *The Supreme Court of the United States* (New York: Columbia University Press, 1928), p. 68.
[89] See fn. 71, *supra*.
[90] "Preface," in *Justice Musmanno Dissents* (Indianapolis: Bobbs-Merrill, 1956).
[91] "The Logic and Rhetoric of Constitutional Law," 15 *Journal of Philosophy, Psychology, and Scientific Method* 654 (1918).
[92] 163 U.S. 537. Harlan's memorable words: "Our Constitution is color-blind, and neither knows nor tolerates classes among citizens" (at 559).
[93] 347 U.S. 483.
[94] *Minersville School District v. Gobitis*, 310 U.S. 586.

Scarcely three years later this became the opinion of the Court when a majority of six held a similar West Virginia Board of Education requirement to be an unconstitutional attachment of freedom of religion in the *Barnette* case.[95] Mr. Justice Cardozo, also a not infrequent dissenter, viewed the dissenting opinion as an entirely proper place for recording "the best inspiration of the time," for instruction in moral values still battling for general acceptance in the political process.[96] "It's grand to fight," once remarked Mr. Justice Black. "The Supreme Court does disagree. I hope it always will. It does have men who express their differences. I hope it always will have. Because I subscribe to the theory that there is no progress when differences are stifled."[97] It was Black who was given the honor of writing the opinion for the unanimous Court in the 1963 *Gideon* case, which extended to indigents the right to be furnished counsel in non-capital as well as capital criminal cases—a decision that overruled the *Betts* case of 1942 in which Black had vigorously dissented (joined by his brothers Douglas and Murphy).

There is thus little doubt that a dissenting opinion is preeminently the result of a profoundly held conviction; consequently, it may well be regarded as strengthening rather than weakening the authority of a particular case. However, it may also serve to muddy the waters, to force extremist positions, and to confuse the public. For example, there are those students of the *Dred Scott* case—and not necessarily only the apologists for Mr. Chief Justice Taney—who contend that Taney's extremist position for the majority was a reaction to the extremist position of the politically ambitious Mr. Justice McLean's dissenting opinion.[98] (It should be noted here that dissent is *much* less common in the

[95] *West Virginia State Board of Education v. Barnette,* 319 U.S. 624.
[96] Benjamin M. Cardozo, *Selected Writings* (New York: Fallon Publishers, 1947), p. 274. (Edited by Margaret E. Hall.)
[97] Quoted in *The New York Times,* June 5, 1961.
[98] In his essay on "politically minded" justices, Alexander M. Bickel calls McLean the "most notoriously so." See his *Politics and the Warren Court* (New York: Harper & Row, 1965), p. 135. Indeed, McLean was a Presidential candidate of sorts five times: in 1832 as an Anti-Mason; in 1836 as an Independent; in 1842 as *both* a Whig and a Free Soiler; in 1852 he refused the Native American party's nomination; in 1856 came his most serious candidacy, as a Republican. No doctrinaire he! See Francis P. Weisenburger, *The Life of John McLean: A Politician on the United States Supreme Court* (Columbus: Ohio State University Press, 1937).

fifty state courts, where the average rate of dissent at the highest appellate level is but one case in ten.)[99]

Concurring Opinions. At times the reasoning of the justice assigned to write the opinion of the Court may not be palatable to all of the component members of the majority side. In that event, one or more *concurring opinions* may be written—an increasingly frequent practice during the past few decades. Broadly speaking, it usually signifies the concurrence of its author in the *decision,* but not in the reasoning of the Court. One illustration would be the two separate concurring opinions of Justices Black and Douglas in the 8:0 decision of the Supreme Court in *Rochin v. California.*[100] While agreeing with the Court that the State of California had engaged in grossly brutal, and hence obviously illegal, conduct in its apprehension and conviction of Rochin, a narcotics peddler, the two justices strongly disagreed with the grounds on which the Court based its reversal of Rochin's conviction: violation of the due process of law clause of the Fourteenth Amendment of the U.S. Constitution. But in the firmly held judgment of Black and Douglas, the State of California had actually violated individual liberty safeguards specifically enumerated in the Bill of Rights—in fact thus contending, as they had done ever since their appointment to the Court in 1937 and 1939, respectively, that the specific provisions are per se applicable to the states (via the Fourteenth Amendment) as well as to the federal government. Another example of the use of the concurring opinion is that by Mr. Justice Frankfurter—a frequent "concurrer"—in *Cooper v. Aaron (The Little Rock Case),*[101] which was decided in the Special Session in the summer of 1958. There, not only in order to show its continuous unanimity in cases basically following *Brown v. Board of Education,*[102] but also to make clear that those justices (Harlan, Brennan, and Whittaker) who had not participated in *Brown* were at one with the remaining six members of that historic opinion, the Supreme Court issued its opinion in the form of a joint authorship, with the names of each of its nine unanimous members specifically listed *seriatim* at the

[99] See the interesting article by Robert J. Sickles, "The Illusion of Judicial Consensus," 59 *American Political Science Review* 100 (March 1965).

[100] 342 U. S. 165 (1952).

[101] 358 U. S. 1 (1958).

[102] 347 U. S. 483 (1954).

head of the "Opinion of the Court." However, obviously deeply grieved and disturbed by the clear flouting of the law and the crass defiance of the federal judiciary by the officials of the State of Arkansas, led by Governor Orval E. Faubus, Mr. Justice Frankfurter was moved to write a separate concurring opinion, which was issued and published some weeks thereafter. In it, he gave what in effect was a profound and moving lecture to the country in general, and the South in particular, on the meaning of "the supreme Law of the Land" and the federal system. Written with scholarship and feeling, this independent statement nevertheless probably diminished somewhat the effect of the joint opinion of the Court. There are many legal scholars who hold to the firm conviction that whereas *dissenting* opinions are both eminently justifiable and necessary, *concurring* opinions are neither—that they are frequently nothing more than ego-manifestations and/or "quibbling," which would more profitably be confined to footnotes in the body of the majority opinion. Yet there is no doubt that the concurring opinion is a significant tool in the judicial process.

Techniques of Assignment. The preceding discussion raises the interesting problem of the selection of the opinion writers by the Chief Justice, or by the Senior Associate Justice when the duty of designation devolves upon him. Giving due attention to the need of distributing the work load relatively evenly (and, as explained earlier, permitting a Court newcomer to select his own first opinion to write), the average Chief Justice's assignments—approximately 85 to 90 per cent of the cases—may well be said to follow a fairly common pattern. It is a pattern, based upon the considerable influence that governs the actions of the "Chief" in making his selections, that will take account of all of the following considerations: First, the so-called "great," "big," or "important constitutional" cases—although these are necessarily somewhat subjective concepts—should be authored by the "Chief" himself, e.g. Mr. Chief Justice Warren speaking for the unanimous Court in *Brown v. Board of Education.*[103] Or Mr. Chief Justice Hughes's majority opinion for the narrowly divided Court (5:4) in the immensely significant case of *West Coast Hotel Co. v. Parrish*,[104]

[103] Ibid.
[104] 300 U. S. 379 (1937).

upholding the State of Washington minimum wage law for women —sometimes, perhaps flippantly but probably not altogether unjustly, called "the-switch-in-time-that-saved-nine" case. Here, the Court departed from its erstwhile stubborn adherence to the narrow construction of the concept of "freedom of contract" under the Fifth and Fourteenth Amendments to the Constitution by overruling the specific precedent of *Adkins v. Children's Hospital*[105] (where it had struck down [5:3] a similar, though federal, law for the District of Columbia). That departure clearly indicated a change of position by the Chief Justice *and* Mr. Justice Roberts. The latter's switch was especially significant because before that he normally represented the swing vote between the so-called pro- and anti-New Deal factions on the Court. His new stance heralded more or less clear sailing, at least on constitutional grounds, for the legislative programs enacted by the then still high-riding New Deal Roosevelt Administration.

Second, no matter what the importance of a case, the selection of a justice to write the opinion must take into account the possible importance of the decision as a precedent. Justices may well differ in their views on whether the decision should be lodged on a broad, or a narrow, construction of the issue and on the ground on which the decision is to be based. For instance, the movie, *Lady Chatterley's Lover,* had been banned by the New York State Board of Regents on grounds of a statutory provision that forbade showing of films that present "acts of sexual immorality, perversion or lewdness" as being "desirable, acceptable, or proper patterns of behavior," and the Court agreed *unanimously* that the movie did not fall under that ban. But a majority of only five justices (Warren, Black, Douglas, Brennan, and Stewart) would join in the latter's opinion for the Court, holding that particular provision of the New York licensing statute to be unconstitutional as a violation of the Fourteenth and First Amendments. There were five *concurring* opinions of which the principal opinion by Harlan (joined by Frankfurter and Whittaker), while agreeing that the New York statute could not be validly applied in this case, argued that the Court should have reversed New York on *statutory construction* grounds without reaching the *constitutional* issues. Frankfurter also penned an individual concurrence, and Clark noted that he concurred "in the result." Black and

105 261 U. S. 525 (1923).

Douglas, although members of the majority of five, joined one another in the two remaining concurring opinions, in which they contended that this statute, like all other prior censorship of movies, should be thrown out as being "unconstitutional on its face" as a prior restraint on freedom of speech and press.[106] Obviously, here the Chief Justice's assignment had to take into account that prospective authorship which would be sufficiently acceptable, or least offensive, to five justices—evidently Stewart's.

Third, although some observers would disagree, there is considerable evidence that the "Chief" is conscious of an element of "public relations" in designating his opinion writer. This is particularly true in cases undoubtedly unpopular to a sizable segment of the population. In other words, he is not unmindful of the importance of making a decision acceptable to the public, or, when applicable, of coating the bitter pill about to be swallowed. A fascinating illustration of this point was brought to light by Professor Alpheus T. Mason in his fine and very frank biography, *Harlan Fiske Stone: Pillar of the Law*.[107] In 1944, the Court conference on the Texas "White Primary" case, *Smith v. Allwright*,[108] had clearly evidenced that all of the justices save Roberts were agreed that this constitutionally challenged Texas statute was unconstitutional as a violation of the Fifteenth Amendment. The South was bound to react with great vehemence. Mr. Chief Justice Stone assigned the opinion to Mr. Justice Frankfurter, an eloquent stylist and profoundly serious and scholarly jurist, not given to pamphleteering. One day after the conference, having discussed his misgivings with some of the justices, Mr. Justice Jackson, a good friend of the principals involved, wrote a highly unusual and probably quite unprecedented letter to the Chief Justice, candidly and fervently suggesting that the nature and the importance of the issue in the case were so far-reaching and made of such emotional matter that the Frankfurter selection was bound to "grate on Southern sensibilities." He continued:

> Mr. Justice Frankfurter unites in a rare degree factors which unhappily excite prejudice. In the first place, he is a Jew. In the second place, he is from New England, the seat of the abolition

---

[106] *Kingsley International Pictures Corporation v. Regents*, 360 U. S. 684 (1959) —featuring a total of six opinions.
[107] (New York: The Viking Press, 1956), pp. 614–15.
[108] 321 U. S. 649 (1944).

210

movement. In the third place, he has not been thought of as a person particularly sympathetic with the Democratic party in the past.[109]

Jackson went on to point out that he realized that a consideration of every one of the listed factors was utterly distasteful, and that he mentioned them only with the greatest reluctance and "frank fear of being misunderstood." He had discussed the matter with Frankfurter and had advised him of his intention to write to the Chief Justice. Evidently persuaded by the Jackson argument, Stone, with Frankfurter's knowledge and agreement, substituted Mr. Justice Stanley Reed, who was: (a) an old-line Kentuckian; (b) a Protestant; (c) a native-born, in contrast to Mr. Justice Frankfurter who was born in Vienna; and (d) a Democrat of long standing. This did not render the wounds of the South any less severe, but at least they were administered, in a manner of speaking, by a one-time kinsman.

In the same general vein, the Chief Justice will normally make it a practice to assign so-called "liberal" opinions of the Court to "conservative" justices and so-called "conservative" opinions to "liberal" justices—again in the hope of making them more palatable. Thus, Mr. Chief Justice Stone assigned to one of the Court's leading liberals, Mr. Justice Black, the majority opinion in what has been widely labeled as the worst racist decision in the recent history of the tribunal, *Korematsu v. United States*.[110] There, the Court upheld 6:3 the forcible removal of 112,000 persons of Japanese ancestry, including 77,000 native-born American citizens, from their West Coast homes to inland war relocation centers. Although none of these evacuees had been specifically accused of disloyalty, the Black opinion upheld the removal as an emergency measure necessitated by the facts-of-life of wartime, as an "exercise of power of the government to take steps necessary to prevent espionage and sabotage in an area threatened by Japanese attack." When the Court, in a 7:1 opinion in 1957, severely limited the application of the Smith Act in the prosecution of Communist party leaders and members, Mr. Chief Justice Warren assigned the case to a member usually found on the "conservative"

[109] Mason, loc. cit. p. 615. Mr. Justice Frankfurter was not exactly pleased about the publicity given this event.
[110] 323 U. S. 214 (1944).

side, Mr. Justice Harlan.[111] And when the Court, in the emotion-charged field of religion, decided 8:1 in 1963 that no state or locality may either require or sanction the recitation of the Lord's Prayer or the reading of verses from the Holy Bible in the public schools, the Chief Justice assigned that delicate case to Mr. Justice Clark, a Presbyterian active in the affairs of his church (who was joined in separate concurring opinions by the Court's only Catholic and its only Jew, Mr. Justice Brennan and Mr. Justice Goldberg, respectively).[112] Such strategy, if that it be, is not always employed, but it is resorted to with sufficient regularity to make a distinct pattern detectable, mild and unpredictable though it may be.

Fourth, when the conference has indicated a split decision, no matter how many may be in the latent minority, the Chief Justice will endeavor to assign the opinion to a justice whose views come closest to the would-be dissenters without, however, being one of them. The theory here is that the justice would, in this case—and probably in others—be a "center justice," whose "middle" approach would be acceptable, more or less, to both majority and minority.[113] For example, in *United States v. Butler*,[114] a majority of six declared the Agricultural Adjustment Act of 1933 unconstitutional as an illegal use by Congress of its powers over taxation and commerce at the expense of the principle of "dual federalism." This was one of thirteen New Deal laws or provisions thereof that the Court would invalidate on constitutional grounds in little more than one year's time during 1935–36. Reasoning that an opinion by one of the four "ultra-conservative" justices—Butler, McReynolds, Van Devanter, and Sutherland—would only serve to increase the fury of both the executive and legislative branches, Mr. Chief Justice Hughes assigned Mr. Justice Roberts to speak for the Court. The latter wrote an opinion that adopted the broad Hamilton-Story interpretation of the "general welfare" clause of

111 *Yates v. United States,* 354 U. S. 298.

112 *Abington School District v. Schempp and Murray v. Curlett,* 374 U.S. 203 (1963).

113 For an able and extensive discussion of this, and related points, see the interesting paper by David J. Danelski, "The Influence of the Chief Justice in the Decisional Process of the Supreme Court," presented at the 1960 American Political Science Association Meeting, New York City, September 9, 1960.

114 297 U. S. 1 (1936).

the Constitution (I-8-1), but struck down the particular tax at issue as substantially an illegal regulation of local affairs. There is evidence that the Chief Justice went along with the majority only because Roberts wrote the opinion—and there was enough in that opinion to permit the minority of three, and their allies on both ends of Pennsylvania Avenue, to nourish hopes for a better day! It came scarcely a year later.

The critical role of the Chief Justice in assigning opinions is thus axiomatic. Much depends on his skill, diplomacy, tact, and sheer powers of persuasion. No other "Chief," in the opinion of Mr. Justice Frankfurter, a long-time member of the bench who served under four Chief Justices and knew three others, "equaled Chief Justice Hughes in the skill and wisdom and disinterestedness with which he made his assignments." Pointing out that Hughes's governing consideration was always "what was best for the Court as to the particular situation," he closed his observations with this wise admonition:

> The grounds for the assignment may not always be obvious to the outsider. Indeed, they are not always so to the members of the Court; the reasons normally remain within the breast of the chief justice. But these involve, if the duty is wisely discharged, perhaps the most delicate judgment demanded of the chief justice.[115]

Yet no matter how hard he may try, or how skillful he may be, a Chief cannot compel unanimity. As we have already seen, separate opinions are the rule rather than the exception. It is thus not at all uncommon to find five, six, seven, eight, or even nine opinions in a single case. The *Dread Scott Case*[116] and the *License Cases*[117] each featured nine such opinions! *The Steel Seizure Case*[118] had seven; the *Connecticut Birth Control Case*[119] and *Baker v. Carr*,[120] each six; *Dennis*,[121] the *Bible Reading Cases*,[122]

115 *Of Law and Men* op. cit. pp. 137, 142. Frankfurter regarded Marshall, Taney, and Hughes as the greatest Chief Justices.
116 19 Howard 393 (1857): Taney (Opinion of the Court); Wayne, Nelson, Grier, Daniel, Campbell, and Catron (Concurring Opinions); and McLean and Curtis (Dissenting Opinions).
117 7 Howard 283 (1849).
118 *Youngstown Sheet & Tube Co. v. Sawyer,* 343 U.S. 579 (1952).
119 *Griswold v. Connecticut,* 381 U.S. 479 (1965).
120 369 U.S. 186 (1962).
121 *Dennis v. United States,* 341 U.S. 494 (1951).
122 *Abington School District v. Schempp* and *Murray v. Curlett,* 374 U.S. 203 (1963).

and *Ginzberg v. United States*[123] each five opinions. The practice of writing separate opinions may be valuable and intriguing, yet it hardly lends itself to certainty in the judicial process. However, certainty is not inevitably an end in itself; indeed, certainty and unanimity in the law are generally possessed only under a dictatorial system of government—to which, in fact, they are indispensable.

Drafting and Circulating Opinions. Following the assignment of opinions—which does not take place at the Conference itself but formally in writing a few days thereafter—the laborious task of drafting commences. Here the power of persuasion by an author, presumably actively supported by the Chief Justice, whenever feasible, looms large in this phase of the judicial decision-making process. An opinion, as Mr. Justice Holmes once commented, must not only be informative and persuasive, it must show that the ". . . judge can dance the sword dance; that is he can justify an obvious result without stepping on either blade of opposing fallacies."[124] Again, we know but little of what takes place during these backstage activities, but from those few sources that are available—papers, biographies, law clerks, various memoirs and, lately, the research of persistent political scientists[125]— we do acquire an outline of this terminal phase of the preparation of a Supreme Court opinion, collective as an end product but with the distinct imprint of the minds and labor of nine individuals. As opinions are drafted, and on whatever side of the tentative decision they may be, printed "proof" copies are circulated by their authors among the members of the Court. These copies, indeed all of the Court's publications, are composed by a special unit of printers who labor in secrecy to the extent of locking themselves in during working hours and utilize the basement of the Court building for their work rather than the Government Printing Office. A private Supreme Court library, with a staff of fourteen and all conceivable facilities, is at the disposal of the justices and their law clerks at all times.

Depending upon comments by his brothers, an author of an opinion may draw additional drafts in an attempt to gain adher-

[123] 383 U.S. 463 (1966).

[124] Alpheus T. Mason, reviewing *The Holmes-Einstein Letters* (New York: St. Martin's Press, 1965), in *The New York Times Book Review*, November 22, 1964.

[125] See, for example, some of the important work concerning the innards of the Conference by lawyer-political scientist David J. Danelski of Yale University.

214

ence, or a concurrence rather than a dissent; or he may use any one of the other devices that may soften disagreement where disagreement exists, or make more forceful an opinion where unanimity seems attainable. Mr. Justice Brennan reported that once he circulated ten printed drafts before one was accepted as the Opinion of the Court.[126] This labor of persuasion is undertaken irrespective of how the several justices may have voted in conference, the theory being that there is always hope for their views to win out in future years. The process of opinion writing is frequently a difficult and laborious task, sometimes running into months, occasionally even years. The opinion for *Brown v. Board of Education* was in various stages of writing from 1952 to 1954, probably largely owing to Mr. Chief Justice Warren's herculean efforts to obtain not only a unanimous Court, but also a single opinion, undoubtedly a delicate and difficult matter on the subject at issue—the declaration of unconstitutionality of compulsory racial segregation in the public schools.[127] Although still very much a case of conjecture, apparently the last holdout on the Court was Mr. Justice Reed. It is certain that this decision was the collective product of painstaking labor.[128]

We do know of some specific cases of persuasion—"bargaining" would not at all be an inappropriate term here— thanks to the papers left by the justices. In one instance, Mr. Justice Butler, who had voted in conference to reverse the decision of the lower court, evidently succumbed to the persuasive powers of his colleague Stone. Sending a copy of his "surrender" to Mr. Chief Justice Taft, who ever tried to turn a dissenting opinion into silent acquiescence, he wrote to case-author Stone as follows:

> I voted to reverse. While this sustains your conclusion to affirm, I still think reversal would be better. But I shall in silence acquiesce. Dissents seldom aid in the right development or state-

[126] "Inside View of the High Court," *The New York Times Magazine*, October 6, 1963.
[127] For a surprising view that strongly *disapproves* of this obviously so deliberately planned and achieved unanimity, see Charles S. Hyneman, *The Supreme Court on Trial* (New York: Atherton Press, 1963), pp. 211–14.
[128] According to Yale Law Professor Fred Rodell, three justices—unnamed—came close to dissenting, and the bare minimum of four had voted to grant *certiorari* in the case. See his "It is the Earl Warren Court," *The New York Times Magazine*, March 13, 1966, p. 93.

ment of the law. They often do harm. For myself I say: "lead us not into temptation."[129]

In another and later Stone opinion, Mr. Chief Justice Hughes wrote to him: "I choke a little at swallowing your analysis, still I do not think it would serve any useful purpose to expose my views."[130] Although as Chief Justice, Stone exercised far less persuasive pressure than Hughes, he did work for unanimity whenever possible. At times, this would involve—as it does quite frequently—a switch from a decisional ground initially agreed upon to another. For example, in one of the cases brought during Stone's tenure, *Edwards v. California*,[131] he successfully persuaded Mr. Justice Byrnes to change his conference vote. Now delivering the opinion of the Court, Byrnes's switch resulted in adopting a *ground* for the decision on which five members of the Court could agree—the interstate commerce, rather than the "privileges and immunities" clause of the Constitution. Four justices concurred in the decision, thus rendering it unanimous, but indicated their preference for the latter ground. An extreme example of the drive for agreement was provided in a difficult double jeopardy case in 1959, when Mr. Justice Brennan wrote the opinion of the Court *and a separate opinion* in which he expressed views he had evidently been unable to persuade his colleagues to accept, stating that ". . . it cannot be suggested that in cases where the author is the mere instrument of the Court he must forego expression of his own convictions."[132]

Much of what has been said of the backstage give-and-take is corroborated by what to date is probably the only full-scale study of that phase of the Court's work, an excellent book by Professor Alexander M. Bickel of Yale University Law School, who was one of Mr. Justice Frankfurter's law clerks, *The Unpublished*

---

[129] As quoted by Danelski in "The Influence of the Chief Justice in the Decisional Process of the Supreme Court," pp. 19–20. See fn. 113, *supra*.

[130] Ibid, at p. 2.

[131] 314 U. S. 160 (1941).

[132] *Abbate v. United States,* 359 U. S. 187 (1959), at 196, fn. 1. Other similar illustrations which are cited by Brennan, are the actions of Mr. Justice Jackson in *Wheeling Steel Corporation v. Glander,* 337 U.S. 562 (1949), at 576, and those of Mr. Justice Cardozo in *Helvering v. Davis,* 301 U.S. 619 (1937), at 639–41.

Opinions of Mr. Justice Brandeis.[133] Based on the private papers
of Louis Dembitz Brandeis, as they relate to his career as Justice
of the Supreme Court of the United States from 1916 to 1939,
the book is rich in illustrations of the persuasive processes that
accompany the drafting of opinions for ultimate delivery. One or
two examples will suffice to illustrate the point further: A photograph of a note from Holmes to Brandeis indicates that Holmes
had revised his opinion in *Bullock v. Florida*[134] by adopting the
result Brandeis had urged upon him. Having been persuaded by
Brandeis's point of view, Holmes did so willingly enough, but his
note showed much concern lest his changed opinion cause dissat-
isfaction among the former majority and perhaps result in a re-
assignment of the case to someone else—which did not happen,
however.[135]

In another instance, it was Brandeis's turn to give in. He had
felt quite strongly about the construction of a statute at issue in
a 1924 railroad case opinion, which had been assigned to Mr.
Justice McReynolds.[136] In discussing the case some years later
with the then Professor of Law Felix Frankfurter, he said that he
had told the Chief Justice (Taft) that "he couldn't stand for"
McReynolds's opinion, that it contained too much that would
"bother us in the future." Mr. Justice Van Devanter, continued
Brandeis,

> worked with McReynolds and made changes, and the Chief asked
> me whether that will remove my sting. The corrections weren't
> adequate, and finally the Chief took over the opinion and put
> out what is now the Court's opinion and I suppressed my dis-
> sent, because, after all, it's merely a question of statutory con-
> struction and the worst things were removed by the Chief.[137]

On the other hand, the persuasion *cum* bargaining may well be
blunt and direct, as evidenced by a memorandum sent by the
usually gentle Mr. Justice Stone to Mr. Justice Frankfurter: "If
you wish to write [the opinion] placing the case on the ground

133 (Cambridge, Harvard University Press, 1957.) Subtitled, *The Supreme Court
at Work.*
134 254 U. S. 513 (1921).
135 Bickel, loc cit. insert between pp. 118–19, last photographic plate.
136 *Railroad Commission of California v. Southern Pacific Railway Co.,* 264
U. S. 331.
137 As quoted and described by Bickel, loc. cit. pp. 209–10.

which I think tenable and desirable, I shall cheerfully join you. If not, I will add a few observations for myself."[138]

But by far the most important fact revealed by this glimpse into the Supreme Court's inner sanctum is that many, if not all, of the Court's opinions, though ostensibly the work of one man, are really the product of many minds in the sense that the justice who writes the opinion often has to add to, delete, or modify his original draft in order to be able to retain the support of his colleagues, many of whom are far from agreeing with him or with each other. Indeed, it is essential to recognize that each member of the Court participates in each and every stage of the consideration of a case. Once we grasp this crucial notion, we can readily understand why a considerable number of the Court's decisions are vague or contain several apparently contradictory statements. Since the views reflected in a given opinion are rarely identical, that opinion may well turn out to be either ambiguous or maintain several varying postures, in order that each man who supports it will be able to reconcile it with his own particular position. A pertinent example is the laborious forging of Mr. Chief Justice Stone's majority opinion in *In Re Yamashita*,[139] in which the Court upheld the conviction by a United States military commission of the Japanese general who was accused of violating the laws of war in failing to prevent his troops from committing atrocities against American and Philippine citizens. This case is quite unclear on the question of whether the due process clause of the Fifth Amendment is binding on such a military commission. The opinion, on the whole, tends to give the impression that the answer to this question is in the negative, but some slight support can be found for the contrary view. According to Professor Mason, Stone's biographer, the latter's original draft contained the assertion that Yamashita's trial would have to adhere to the requirement of this clause. However, to meet at least in part the objections of Justices Black and Reed, who apparently were of the opinion that these commissions were not bound by the provisions of the due process clause, Stone deleted the assertion and made some confusing additions which Black and Reed could

[138] Quoted by Mason in *Harlan Fiske Stone,* op. cit. p. 501. (Stone's letter was dated January 20, 1941.)
[139] 327 U. S. 1 (1946).

more or less reconcile with their own views on this matter.[140]
The end product, though it did not entirely satisfy either its
readers or the bench as a whole, at least had the virtue—if that
it be—of receiving the support of the majority of the Court.

Secrecy of Deliberations. Even though these various data undoubtedly are intriguing and are important to an understanding
of the Supreme Court, the absolute secrecy that attends the
backstage work and deliberations of the Supreme Court—the
"Purple Curtain," as Professor Fowler Harper once called it—is
essential. Until 1910 it was customary for two page boys to be
present, but since that time (the justices suspected a "leak" by
one or more of the boys in a decision) no one save the nine
justices is present in the conference; no record of the discussions
is kept. When clerks bring messages, the justice who is junior in
seniority—no matter what his chronological age—goes to the
door to get them. There simply are no leaks. This is not to say,
however, that no leaks have ever occurred. The most serious of
these on record came in connection with the *Dred Scott* case.[141]
Not only did the pro-slavery Mr. Justice John Catron evidently
there, tell President-elect James Buchanan the "line-up" of the
justices in the pending momentous decision one month prior to
its announcement, but segments of the Northern press published
the dissenting opinion of Mr. Justice Curtis! The incoming President, troubled and weak, used the Catron information in his
inaugural address on March 4, 1857, and told the country that
the Court would soon settle the much disputed territorial question.
Two days later Mr. Chief Justice Taney delivered the 7:2 opinion
of the Court—which, as history proved all too soon, did anything
but settle the problem, and, indeed, acted as a catalyst in bringing
on the Civil War.

However, that instance was a rare and crass exception. Complete secrecy does, and must, exist. The Court can neither open
its backstage deliberations to the public nor hold news conferences. To do either would fatally affect its position as well as its
effectiveness. For a description of what goes on behind the doors
we depend almost entirely on the kind of papers and biographies
of the justices discussed above, duly analyzed by scholars, and,

140 Mason, loc. cit. pp. 667–9.
141 *Dred Scott v. Sandford*, 19 Howard 393 (1857).

on occasion, on revelations, usually appearing after the death of the justice involved, by their law clerks. Yet even these revelations are more often than not confined to matters of procedure. This is emphatically as it should be. We know enough of the operation and functions of the highest court in the land to enable us to appreciate, study, and, hopefully, understand them in the context of the Court's significant role in the process of free government. To repeat, the secrecy of the Court's proceedings behind that "Purple Curtain" is a necessary by-product of its work. In a widely read article endeavoring to explain Mr. Justice Roberts's famous so-called "switch-in-time" to the side of the "liberals" on the Court in 1937, Mr. Justice Frankfurter viewed it in these terms:

> Disclosure of Court happenings not made public by the Court itself, in its opinions and orders, presents a ticklish problem. The *secrecy that envelops the Court's work is not due to love of secrecy or want of responsible regard for the claims of a democratic society to know how it is governed.* That the Supreme Court should not be amenable to the forces of publicity to which the Executive and the Congress are subjected is essential to the effective functioning of the Court. But the passage of time may enervate the reasons for this restriction, particularly if disclosure rests not on tittle-tattle or self-serving declarations. . . .[142]

OPINION DAY

The final stage in the Supreme Court's decision-making process occurs on Opinion Day. On that important occasion, usually, but not always[143] on three Mondays of each month during the term, the entire Court meets in solemn public session and announces, or "hands down," the decisions it has reached. Other than those disposed of *per curiam* or decided by memorandum order, the cases now thus made public cover the full reasoning of the Court and set forth all viewpoints expressed by the justices. The

---

[142] "Mr. Justice Roberts" 104 *University of Pennsylvania Law Review* 313 (1955). (Italics supplied.) For further insights "behind the scenes," see Walter F. Murphy, *Elements of Judicial Strategy* (Chicago: University of Chicago Press, 1964).

[143] Until April 11, 1965, when Mr. Chief Justice Warren announced that he and the Court saw no reason why decisions should be announced only on Mondays, that day of the week was indeed "reserved" for that purpose.

various opinions are either read verbatim, or are paraphrased or summarized by their authors, as the spirit and the occasion may dictate; sometimes simply the decision is given. The reading of the opinions may run from fifteen minutes to several hours—although the Chief Justice would almost certainly try to discourage the latter. Nevertheless, a visitor to the Supreme Court Chamber on an Opinion Day ought to be prepared for an average session of two hours' duration. This interesting practice of announcing opinions orally is not generally followed in the lower courts, where a case is "announced" simply by filing its disposition with the clerk. Prior to the Chief Justiceship of Charles Evans Hughes, the Court's announcements were even lengthier, for the justices generally persisted in reading opinions word for word, not infrequently in an unrelieved monotone. Hughes, however, sensing a golden opportunity to make, in the words of Edwin McElwain, who was one of his law clerks, "a public demonstration of the dignity and responsibility of the Court to the bar and to the thousands of visitors who came to the new Supreme Court Building during his regime,"[144] not only encouraged paraphrasing and summarizing of opinions, but also impressed upon his brothers of the bench the need to deliver them forcefully and convincingly. The Chief Justice himself was such an impressive figure—with his magnificent head, white beard, and sonorous voice, that more than once, visitors to an Opinion Day, hearing him deliver one of his opinions with dramatic impact, likened him to a latter-day Moses—a concept not entirely displeasing to Hughes, not so much for himself but for Court and Law.

Even after the justices have assembled for the announcement of their opinions, should any one of their number have some last-minute qualms regarding one about to be handed down, all he has to do is to ask the Chief Justice to "let it go over"— such is the concern with each justice's sensibilities. It cannot be emphasized too strongly that *each and every justice* passes on all aspects of a case, at *each* of its stages; the Court most emphatically does not function by committee, panel, or section. The now published opinions presumably confine themselves to the issue involved in the various cases, but the voicing of profoundly held beliefs, and at times even a swipe at a colleague, is quite common.

[144] "The Business of the Supreme Court as Conducted by Chief Justice Hughes," 63 *Harvard Law Review* 20 (1949).

Thus cleavages among the justices of an intellectual, policy, and at times even personal nature, become apparent in the written opinions—no matter how skilled an arbiter the Chief Justice may be. Fortunately, less frequent are *ad hoc* outbursts from the bench on Opinion Day; these are not found in the written record, but they do occur. Perhaps the most famous one is Mr. Justice Mc-Reynolds's explosion in 1935, while reading his dissent in the *Gold Clause Cases*,[145] when he veritably screamed from the bench: "This is Nero at his worst. The Constitution is gone."

Judicial Tempers. But, to give brief recent illustrations of this aspect of Opinion Day, in November 1960, Mr. Justice Douglas, having just heard Mr. Justice Whittaker read the 6:3 opinion for the Court in a tax case, commented acidly from the bench that the issue decided this day was "narrow and technical"; that he would not have filed a dissent had not the "majority's error been so egregious"; and he closed with the observation: "But six make the law, and sometimes very bad law." Earlier that year, Mr. Justice Frankfurter had characterized as a "judicial somersault" an opinion for the Court by Mr. Justice Stewart in a criminal law case.[146] On Opinion Monday, March 30, 1959, Mr. Justice Frankfurter, while reading the majority opinion upholding the successive federal and state trials of one Bartkus for the same criminal act, against the charge of double jeopardy, made a passing reference to "the so-called Bill of Rights." When Mr. Justice Black's turn came to read his dissent in the case, he declared passionately: "This case concerns the Bill of Rights, not the 'so-called Bill of Rights!' "[147] And within little more than a month, during the waning days of the 1960–61 term, the public and the Court were treated to two serious *ad hoc* outbursts from the bench on two Opinion Days, involving Mr. Chief Justice Warren and, again, Mr. Justice Frankfurter. In the first instance, a sharp dissent by the latter provoked on oral rebuttal by the former, which was even more unusual because the Chief Justice, on the side of the 5:4 majority, had written no opinion in the case. But in stating his dissent, Mr. Justice Frankfurter—in an extemporaneous summary, as were all of his opinions—took nearly fifteen minutes to sharpen the written lan-

145 *Norman v. Baltimore & Ohio Railroad Co.* 294 U. S. 240.

146 *Elkins and Clark v. United States,* 364 U. S. 206 (1960).

147 As reported by Anthony Lewis, "Justice Black at 75: Still the Dissenter," *The New York Times Magazine,* February 26, 1961, p. 74.

guage and heighten his criticism of the majority position in the criminal case at issue. Evidently hurt and annoyed by Frankfurter's tone of voice and the contents of his summation, the Chief Justice told the courtroom that "since so much has been said here that was not in any written opinion," he wanted to add a word as to why he joined the majority.[148]

Yet an even more serious manifestation of judicial temper-flaring occurred several Opinion Days later, again featuring the same two justices. The Court, once again by a 5:4 vote, as is so frequently the case in criminal cases involving Bill-of-Rights interpretations, had reversed the murder conviction of one Stewart in the District of Columbia. In a ringing dissent, Mr. Justice Frankfurter, going far beyond anything he had written, accused the majority of "plucking out" of the lengthy trial record an isolated episode, and suggested that judges find in the record "what the mind is looking for." He went on to categorize the majority opinion as an "indefensible example of finicky appellate review of criminal cases," and warned against "turning a criminal appeal into a quest for error." When he had finished, Mr. Chief Justice Warren leaned forward, his face deeply flushed, turned on the senior justice, and with evident emotion stated that the dissent just heard was not a proper statement of an opinion, but rather a

> lecture . . . a closing argument by a prosecutor to a jury. It is properly made, perhaps, in the conference room [of the Court], but not in the court room . . . The purpose of reporting an opinion [there] is to inform the public and is not for the purpose of degrading this Court.[149]

But at the end of the session the two adversaries were engaged in friendly and cordial conversation! Even Supreme Court justices are human. . . .[150]

[148] As reported in *The New York Times*, March 21, 1961.

[149] As reported in *The (Philadelphia) Evening Bulletin* and *The New York Times*, April 25, 1961.

[150] Since the above-cited examples, other memorable judicial "outbursts" have involved: an unusually sharp attack by Mr. Justice Douglas on his brother Black in *Arizona v. California*, 373 U.S. 546 (1963); an acid exchange between Black and Mr. Justice Harlan in the congressional redistricting case of *Wesberry v. Sanders*, 376 U.S. 1 (1964); Harlan's scathing attack on the entire Court in the key state reapportionment cases of 1964, headed by *Reynolds v. Sims*, 377 U.S. 533; and Mr. Justice White's sarcastic references to his colleague Goldberg's reasoning in the now famous case of *Escobedo v. Illinois*, 378 U.S. 478 (1964)). There are, and presumably will always be, others.

Ratio Decidendi and Obiter Dictum. It is important to distinguish—although this is sometimes far more easily said than
done—between the *ratio decidendi* of an opinion and the frequently present *obiter dictum* or *obiter dicta*. *Ratio decidendi* refers to the essence, the vitals, the necessary core of the decision;
obiter dictum is a more or less extraneous, presumably unneces-
sary-to-the-decision, point made by the author of an opinion. In
other words, the former constitutes the legal rule to be followed
and adhered to below; the latter is an expression of a brief, viewpoint, or sentiment, which, at least in theory, has no binding effect.
It is not surprising, however, that, on occasion, an *obiter dictum*
lives long after the *ratio decidendi* has been forgotten! Moreover,
as U. S. District Court Judge P. M. Hall of California once put the
matter. "I am not unmindful of the fact that in the last analysis
the Judges of the Supreme Court are the final arbiters as to what is
or is not dicta in a previous opinion."[151] Nonetheless, it is the
ratio decidendi that makes the decided case one of record and
renders the matter at issue *res judicata*, i.e. a matter upon which
a competent court of law has passed judgment and which it will
therefore not examine (all other things remaining equal, which of
course is not always the case).

One of the most famous expounders of the *obiter dictum* was
Mr. Chief Justice John Marshall, who delighted in employing that
technique as a medium for the constitutional education of the
people of his time. His celebrated opinions in *Marbury v. Madison,*[152] *McCulloch v. Maryland,*[153] and *Gibbons v. Ogden,*[154] for
example, are full of *dicta* which history has so merged with the
ratio decidendi in these cases as to make the two concepts almost
indistinguishable. Nor has that approach become extinct in our
own days, to which illustrations on two levels of the judiciary bear
witness: In the case of *Shachtman v. Dulles,*[155] three judges of the
U. S. Circuit Court of Appeals for the District of Columbia held
unanimously that the grounds for the Secretary of State's denial of
a passport to the petitioner constituted an arbitrary, and hence
unconstitutional, denial of due process of law under the Fifth
Amendment. That was the *ratio decidendi* of the case, but the
author of the opinion of the tribunal, Circuit Judge Fahy, in an

[151] *Odikubo v. Bonesteel,* 60 F. Supp. 916 (1945) at 930, fn. 28.
[152] 1 Cranch 137 (1803).
[153] 4 Wheaton 316 (1819).
[154] 9 Wheaton 1 (1824).
[155] 225 F. 2d 938 (1955).

interesting *obiter dictum*, based the privilege of a passport upon the "natural right" to travel, "to go from place to place as the means of transportation permit." At the level of the Supreme Court, *Watkins v. United States*[156] dealt with the refusal of a former labor organizer, John T. Watkins, to answer certain questions put to him by a subcommittee of the House Committee on Un-American Activities, which was investigating "Communist activities in the Chicago area." In a 6:1 decision, speaking through Mr. Chief Justice Warren, the Court set aside Watkins's conviction for contempt of Congress in the District Court below because neither Congress nor the Committee had ever satisfactorily apprised him whether the questions he had refused to answer were "pertinent to the subject under inquiry." This failure on the part of the legislature was thus held to render the conviction void on the grounds of vagueness under the due process of law clause of the Fifth Amendment. Here we have the *ratio decidendi* of the *Watkins* case. But, resorting to the device of the *obiter dictum*, Mr. Chief Justice Warren also discussed matters, however related, which had not really been specifically raised by the petitioner Watkins in his allegations. Warren's long and fervant *dictum* clearly represented a lecture to Congress—and, hopefully, the public at large—on the rights of individuals and Congress's abuse of its power to investigate, featured by the admonition: "We have no doubt that there is no congressional power to expose for the sake of exposure."[157] Another important illustrative example is the Court's footnote dictum in *United States v. Barnett*[158] which indicated that anyone convicted of criminal contempt by a judge could not be given a sentence more severe than might be imposed for a "petty offense."

After the anouncement and reading of an opinion the case is presumably finished insofar as the members of the Court are concerned, and no further public comment thereon will normally emanate from the justices. On rare occasion, however, the public reception of a decision may move a justice to further comment. This occurred, for example, as a result of the *New York Prayer Case*,[159] when Mr. Justice Clark seized upon the occasion of a

[156] 354 U. S. 178 (1957).
[157] Ibid., at 200.
[158] 376 U.S. 681 (1964), at 695 fn. 12.
[159] *Engel v. Vitale*, 370 U.S. 421 (1962).

public speech to take note of the decision's critical reception by "explaining" his vote as a member of the majority. Referring to the Court's 8:1 judgment that New York's state-composed twenty-two-word non-denominational prayer for use in the state's public schools constituted a violation of the principle of separation of church and state as imbedded in Amendments I and XIV, he stated simply: "No to me means no. That is all the court decided, not that there should be no recognition of a supreme being."

COMPLIANCE

When officialy annnounced as decided, the case becomes binding on all lower federal courts and on all state courts where applicable. It is now *the* controlling opinion, *res judicata*, the law of the land, as enunciated and/or interpreted by its highest tribunal. Then it is duly recorded and published by the federal government in an invaluable, precise series of volumes known as the *United States Reports* which, duly compiled and edited by the Supreme Court's Reporter of Decisions, constitutes the sole *official* record of the actions of the Court—there are also several unofficial publications available.[160] (The *Reports* and their forerunners are on file back to 1790.) However, although compliance with the Court's decisions may be expected to be a foregone conclusion insofar as the lower *federal* courts are concerned—Chapter VIII will discuss some of the problems of compliance, and of enforcement by *nonjudicial* governmental bodies generally—it is not always necessarily simple and automatic.

By Federal Courts. For example, in September 1960, Judge Ashton Williams of the U.S. District Court for South Carolina disqualified himself from a desegregation suit on the ground that *he* considered the Supreme Court's decision and subsequent order in *Brown v. Board of Education*[161] to be unconstitutional. He announced that another judge would have to hear the case, brought by four Charleston Negroes, which involved compulsory segregation of the Charleston municipal golf course. Contending that the Supreme Court's decision barring separate facilities for Whites an

---

160 For example, the *Supreme Court Reporter* and the *Lawyers' Edition of the Opinions of the United States Supreme Court.*
161 347 U.S. 483 (1954) and 349 U.S. 294 (1955).

Negroes in such public recreational facilities was based "on constitutional grounds," he nonetheless stepped aside rather than disobey, and declared: "Since as a Federal judge I have to follow that decision I will disqualify myself because I have taken an oath to sustain the Constitution."[162]

Another U. S. District Court jurist, the then eighty-seven-year-old Judge William H. Atwell of Texas, went considerably further in 1956; he simply *refused* to carry out the desegregation ruling of the Court, and resorted to every conceivable judicial roadblock to prevent it. Although his ruling had been reversed by the Fifth U. S. Circuit Court of Appeals,[163] after his initial rejection of the plaintiffs' petition,[164] he again refused to set a date of desegregation of the Dallas school district because such a step would cause "civil wrongs." In order to make quite clear where he stood on the issue, Atwell announced:

> I believe that it will be seen that the [Supreme] Court based its decision on no law but rather on what the Court regarded as more authoritative, more psychological knowledge. . . . It will be recalled that in 1952, Mr. Justice Frankfurter said it [the Supreme Court] was not competent to take judicial notice of "claims of social scientists."[165]

The Court of Appeals naturally again reversed the second Atwell decision in short order.[166] But far from acquiescing, Judge Atwell now embarked upon a course of action in the opposite extreme by ordering all Dallas schools integrated in the middle of the academic year![167] This decision was also reversed by the higher court.[168] Three or four years later, Atwell retired permanently— he had been recalled for temporary duty—and another federal District Court judge, ultimately ordered a "mild" form of desegregation. This was broadened and amended by the Fifth Circuit Court of Appeals in accordance with the Supreme Court's 1954 and 1955 mandates,[169] with desegregation scheduled to begin on a

162 As reported in *The New York Times*, September 8, 1960.
163 *Brown v. Rippy*, 233 F. 2d 796 (1956).
164 *Bell v. Rippy*, 133 F. Supp. 811 (1955).
165 *Bell v. Rippy*, 146 F. Supp. 485 (1956), at 486.
166 *Borders v. Rippy*, 247 F. 2d 268 (1957).
167 2 *Race Relations Law Reporter* 985 (1957).
168 *Rippy v. Borders*, 250 F. 2d 690 (1957).
169 *Brown v. Board of Education*, 347 U. S. 483 (1954) and ibid. 349 U. S. 294 (1955).

one-grade-a-year basis in September of 1961[170]—which indeed it did without incident. It should be pointed out, however, that the nature of the implementation order, as handed down by the Court in the second Brown case,[171] was tailor-made for dilatory tactics by federal District Court judges. It vested in them inherent authority to use their discretion in ordering desegregation by suggesting that they take notice of the peculiarities of the local situation. In effect, they were guided solely by the Court's mandate that the judges require a "prompt and reasonable start toward full compliance" and that they take such action as may be necessary to bring about the end of racial segregation in the public schools "with all deliberate speed."[172]

But lest the impression arise that all defiance and deviation from the law as stated by the Court are confined to the segregation-integration controversy, we have another, and quite different example, involving an eminent jurist, Chief Judge John J. Parker of the Fourth U. S. Circuit Court of Appeals. In 1940 the Supreme Court had held 8:1 in the first of the *Flag Salute Cases*[173] that Pennsylvania could validly require children of Jehovah's Witnesses attending public schools to salute the flag, despite claims of violation of their constitutionally guaranteed freedom of religion. Only Mr. Justice Stone had dissented. But no Supreme Court reversal having taken place two years later, Judge Parker held an *identical* West Virginia statute unconstitutional.[174] He went to some length to point out that this really was not defiance, since three members of the 1940 majority had publicly confessed error on the occasion of a different case involving another constitutional claim by Jehovah's Witnesses,[175] and that two[176] others had retired from the bench in the two-year interim, thus leaving the supporters of the compulsory flag salute in a minority of three.[177] His analysis and

---

170 *Boston v. Rippy,* 275 F. 2d 850 (1960).

171 Loc. cit. 349 U. S. 294 (1955).

172 Ibid.

173 *Minersville School District v. Gobitis,* 310 U. S. 586 (1940).

174 *Barnette v. West Virginia,* 47 F. Supp. 251 (1942), at 253.

175 *Jones v. Opelika,* 316 U. S. 584 (1942), at 623–4. The three were Justices Black, Douglas and Murphy.

176 Mr. Chief Justice Hughes and Mr. Justice Byrnes.

177 Justices Roberts, Reed, and Frankfurter. The six constituting the new majority were the new Chief Justice (Stone); the three "confessors-of-error" (Black, Douglas, and Murphy), and the two newcomers to the bench, Justices Jackson and Rutledge.

228

implied prediction proved to be correct, because the Court did specifically overrule itself 6:3 when that very same West Virginia case[178] reached it—but, of course, Judge Parker could neither safely predict that event nor did it lessen the fact of his deviation.[179]

As a final example of defiance or deviation on the lower federal court level, we have the astonishing one of the then eighty-six-year-old U. S. District Court Judge T. Whitfield Davidson of Dallas. In 1962, fully four years after he had been ordered to do so by the Supreme Court of the United States, Judge Davidson refused resolutely to impose a $506.11 penalty on a Texas farmer who had wilfully and illegally exceeded his planting allotment of wheat under federal regulations by forty-three acres. The venerable judge simply insisted upon his own conclusions that the statute involved was unconstitutional—despite several Supreme Court holdings to the precise contrary[180]—and he further ruled that the highest court had no jurisdiction in the case at bar! When the federal authorities ultimately appealed Judge Davidson's obstructions to the Supreme Court, the latter made clear—in a curt and unsigned opinion—that it did indeed have jurisdiction and that it wanted its orders carried out forthwith "without delay."[181] They were! Had they not been, the Court could have issued a writ of *mandamus* to him.

However, these illustrations of deviations by lower court *federal* judges are exceptions to the general rule of compliance with the orders emanating from the highest tribunal above. There may be disagreement with such an order, but one must, and may, expect that it be followed. The comments below by U. S. District Court Judge Charles E. Wyzanski, Jr., of Boston are in the best tradition of compliance, no matter how extensive the substantive disagreement. At issue was one of the ever time-consuming negligence cases, involving a trial jury's grant of $30,000 in damages to an injured New Haven Railroad worker, one Mrs. Henagan. The New Haven, upon receiving the jury's verdict in Judge Wyzanski's court,

178 *West Virginia State Board of Education v. Barnette,* 319 U. S. 624 (1943).
179 For an enlightening article on compliance generally, see: Walter Murphy "Lower Court Checks on Supreme Court Power," 53 *American Political Science Review* 1017–31 (December 1959).
180 The leading—and unanimous—decision was *Wickard v. Filburn* 317 U.S. 111 (1942), which upheld the constitutionality of the Agricultural Adjustment Act of 1938.
181 *United States v. District Court (United States v. Haley),* 371 U.S. 18.

asked him to set it aside. He replied that he would if he could, but that he was not free to do so because the Supreme Court had consistently held in favor of railroad employees in similar cases, and that the Court's precedent commanded his obedience. But he went on to indicate his feelings in no uncertain terms:

> I cannot read the record as a whole in a way to find any evidence of negligence [by the New Haven]. But I know that my method of reading the record is different from that of a majority of the Supreme Court of the United States as exhibited in past cases, and I hope *I am a lawful judge,* and I recognize the limits of my authority whether appellate judges do or not.[182]

Ironically, as matters developed, the Supreme Court, for the first time in a quarter of a century in a Federal Employers' Liability Act case, a short time thereafter reversed a jury verdict by a 6:2 majority because it found insufficient negligence on the part of the railroad—and the case was that of Mrs. Henagan![183]

It should also be noted that the Court, by special order, may bypass proceedings in the lower federal courts—although this is not commonly done, as Congressman Adam Clayton Powell (D.-N.Y.) found out in 1967 when he unsuccessfully sought a Supreme Court order to bypass the U. S. Court of Appeals, where his appeal from an adverse decision from a U. S. District Court on his exclusion from the U. S. House of Representatives then lodged. However, an example of a successful plea is a 1964 antitrust action under the Clayton Act commenced by the federal government against the El Paso Natural Gas Co. There, Mr. Justice Douglas directed that El Paso divest itself of a firm it had acquired "without delay"—and without "further proceedings in the lower courts," an order from which only Mr. Justice Harlan dissented.[184]

By State Courts. When it comes to compliance with Supreme Court decisions by *state* courts an entirely different element enters. In effect, the Supreme Court has no power to make a *final determination* of any case in which it reviews *state* court judgments.

[182] *New York, New Haven, & Hartford v. Henagan,* as reported in 272 F. 2d 153 (1959), at 155–6. See *The New York Times,* November 22, 1960. (Italics supplied.)
[183] *New York, New Haven, & Hartford v. Henagan,* 364 U.S. 441 (1960).
[184] *United States v. El Paso Natural Gas Co.,* 376 U.S. 251.

All it can do in these instances is to *decide the federal issue and remand* it to the state court below for final judgment "not inconsistent with this opinion." Because the state courts possess the power to raise new issues after they receive the case back from above, they are provided with an opportunity to evade the substantive effects of the reversal by the Supreme Court in a number of ways. And once a new issue is raised, the ultimate disposition of the case may, of course, go either way. A notorious illustration is the case of Virgil Hawkins, a Florida Negro, who was denied admission to the University of Florida Law School. After lengthy legal strategems, delays, and assorted maneuvers on all levels of the judiciary over a period of nine years, Hawkins was finally ordered by the United States Supreme Court after the Florida Supreme Court continued to stall—yet Hawkins was in fact never allowed to go to the University, and he gave up.[185] That this whole matter of spotty and often unpredictable state court compliance is not an illusory conclusion is well demonstrated by, for instance, certain statistics gathered and published by the *Harvard Law Review* some years ago.[186] For example, from 1941 to 1951, the Supreme Court remanded 175 cases to the various state courts for further proceedings "not inconsistent with this judgment." In forty-six of these (almost 27 per cent of the total), further litigation ensued, with twenty-two of the parties who *won* in the Supreme Court now *losing* in the state courts as a result of the final judgment below. In the decade immediately preceding, the Court had reviewed 187 state court cases and remanded them. In 34 of these (somewhat above 18 per cent), new issues were raised below, and in a mere nine of these did the ultimate state court decision favor the party who had "won" in the Supreme Court of the United States.[187]

---

[185] Among the seven Hawkins cases were: *Florida ex rel Hawkins v. Board of Control*, 347 U.S. 971 (1954); ibid. 350 U.S. 413 (1956); and ibid. 355 U.S. 839 (1957). See the account of the Hawkins dilemma in Walter F. Murphy and C. Herman Pritchett, *Courts, Judges, and Politics* (New York: Random House, 1961), pp. 606–18.

[186] See the two *Notes*, "Final Disposition of State Court Decisions Reversed and Remanded by the Supreme Court, October Term 1931 to October Term 1940," 55 *Harvard Law Review* 1357 (1942), and "Evasion of Supreme Court Mandates in Cases Remanded to State Courts since 1941," 67 *Harvard Law Review* 1251 (1954).

[187] Ibid.

Whatever the difference in the degree of compliance with the decisions of the highest court in the land, it is fair to conclude that their nationwide impact is often uneven. The many diverse local conditions that characterize the federal system are all but tailor-made for considerable latitude in compliance. This fact of constitutional life clearly accounts for the spotty, often utterly absent compliance in the 1954 and 1955 decisions concerning desegregation, yet, conversely, for the amazingly speedy, if diverse, acceptance and at least over-all compliance, however varied, with the reapportionment-redistricting decision of the 1960's, following the historic Supreme Court ruling in *Baker v. Carr.*[188] On the other hand, some public school districts, egged on by local and state authorities, openly defied, and others circumvented by "interpretations" that seemed to ignore, the language of the Supreme Court's ruling in the *Prayer and Bible Reading Cases* of 1962 and 1963.[189] And until the Court issued its contentious, but specific and plainly understood rules in its historic criminal justice decision in *Miranda v. Arizona,*[190] different state courts—even so sophisticated a court as the Supreme Court of New Jersey—interpreted the decision in *Miranda's* antecedent, *Escobedo v. Illinois*[191] in a host of diverse, frequently clearly defiant, ways. If properly supported by responsible public and private sources of power and influence, the Court will of course ultimately generally have its way, more or less—unless it is reversed by legislative action or constitutional amendment, it overrules or modifies its own decisions (of which much more will be said in Chapters VII and VIII). But it must be accorded appropriate executive support—e.g. Little Rock, Arkansas—for, as will be emphasized and re-emphasized in these pages, the Court's only effective power is the power to persuade: purse and sword are in other hands.

[188] 369 U.S. 186 (1962). Some commentators were far from pleased with this excellent compliance record, however. Sneered the *National Review*: "Perhaps the most fascinating question raised once again by these decisions is this: Why does the nation accept this usurpation so passively, so supinely? The Court, after all, has even fewer divisions than the Pope. It is not written on high, and certainly not in our history, that every American citizen and institution must dance to the Court's whip." (June 30, 1964, p. 521.)

[189] See, for example, "The Supreme Court and the Bible Belt: Tennessee Reaction to the 'Schempp' Decision," by Robert H. Birkby, X *Midwest Journal of Political Science* 3 (August 1966).

[190] 384 U.S. 436 (1966).

[191] 378 U.S. 478 (1964).

OUTSIDE INFLUENCES ON COURT PERSONNEL

Much has been written and pronounced on various outside sources that allegedly prey upon and lobby with the Court and endeavor to influence its decision-making process. A good deal of this commentary has been exaggerated; much has been spurious; some has been made with nothing less than evil intent and ill will; and some has been sheer nonsense. Of course, the justices are subject to "influence." Any governmental body with the power to make significant discretionary choices—which the Court assuredly possesses —may be expected to be a target of interest groups and interest seekers. But it is an entirely different type of "influence" than that normally associated with "lobbying." Let it be stated at once and unequivocally, that the sort of lobbying and the button-holing and back-slapping approaches utilized by one and sundry to influence (a) legislators and (b) executives, not only would not work with the members of the federal judiciary, in general, and the justices of the Supreme Court, in particular, but would meet with withering disdain. As the British would say, "this simply is not cricket!" Moreover, the so welcome and necessary independence of the federal judiciary, and the almost Olympian position of regard and esteem the justices rightfully enjoy by and large in the popular mind, would militate against any of the myriad approaches, ingenuous or ingenious, to which the average official or unofficial lobbyist resorts in Washington and the various other seats of federal and state power in the United States of America. If, however, we mean by "influence" a well-reasoned and ably written brief, be it by one of the litigants or a brief *amicus curiae* (see below); a persuasive oral argument on behalf of an issue at bar; a timely, thoughtful, and convincing book, monograph, speech, or law review article on the general or specific issue; a strategically timed use of a bona fide test case—*that* type of influence, as well as the intriguing concept of the "climate of public opinion" (to be discussed in Chapter VII), falls into a different category. In the final analysis, here the justices remain the complete masters of their own house.

In elaborating somewhat on the several sources of outside influence that may bear upon the Court, we may omit the more obvious and self-explanatory, such as the well-written brief, the persuasive oral argument, and most literature. Some others do deserve separate treatment, including the alleged gray eminences behind the justices, the law clerks.

LEGAL PERIODICALS

Articles that appear in law reviews and other legal periodicals undoubtedly have exerted a formative influence on the law for some time. This is only natural since the best legal thinking finds expression in these periodicals (only the top law students "work on" law reviews while in law school). The jurists are part of the legal process and are quite naturally generally familiar with the thinking that presents itself in their pages; indeed, they must be familiar with it if they wish to keep their finger on the pulse of the profession and, as Mr. Justice Holmes put it so cogently, "the felt necessities of the times." In an interesting article, based on work leading to his doctorate, Chester A. Newland presented the results of a close study of the use made by the Supreme Court of legal periodicals during the period between 1924 and 1956.[192] In most cases the law review and other articles cited by the justices constituted minor references in the opinions concerned although a few seemed to be close to the *ratio decidendi*. An avowed and indeed acknowledged illustration of the latter is Mr. Justice Brandeis's significant opinion in the landmark case of *Erie v. Tompkins* of 1938[193] which overruled the century-old precedent on the judicial application of common law laid down in *Swift v. Tyson*.[194] Brandeis made a point of crediting "the research of a competent scholar"—Charles Warren's article, "New Light on the History of the Federal Judiciary Act of 1789," 37 *Harvard Law Review* 49 (1923).[195] In any event, there were numerous references in each term after 1937, with an average of twenty-five opinions (or about one-quarter of the number handed down by the Court in a typical term) citing a total of between forty and seventy periodicals. Not surprisingly, the justices varied in the frequency of use they made of these

[192] "Legal Periodicals and the United States Supreme Court," 3 *Midwest Journal of Political Science* 58–74 (February 1959).
[193] 304 U.S. 64.
[194] 16 Peters 1 (1842).
[195] 304 U.S. 64, at 72–3.

references, evidently depending, more or less, on their scholarly bent and interest. Of the justices appointed after 1937 who cited legal periodicals in at least twenty opinions thereafter, the most frequent citer of such periodicals was Mr. Justice Rutledge, whose per-term average was 7.4 opinions; next came Mr. Justice Frankfurter with 5.5; third was Mr. Justice Jackson with 4.1; low man was Mr. Justice Burton with a per-term average of 2.0. For whatever significance it may have, the statistics indicate also that the four most frequently cited journals during the thirty-two year period covered by Professor Newland's study, and the number of times they were referred to were the: *Harvard Law Review* (399); *Yale Law Journal* (194); *Columbia Law Review* (176); and *Michigan Law Review* (165).

There is little doubt that reliance on the legal peridoicals by both bar and courts during the past generation or so has increased. Although difficult to determine objectively, this particular genre of the written word exerts a formative influence, and it does, of course, represent an outside influence. Yet it may well be asked how much "outside" this particular type of influence is. Moreover, commentators as well as students of the legal process are hardly agreed upon its extent. To cite one of the more extreme points of view on the matter, in a speech in the House of Representatives, Congressman Wright Patman (D.-Tex.) viewed any reliance upon legal periodicals as all but evil and sinister, and contended that it was subversive of traditional judicial processes:

> In adopting and relying upon such pseudo-legalistic papers disseminated by the lobbyist-authors thereof the result is that the theories advanced by these pretended authorities were presented and received by the Court in an ex parte fashion.[196]

Replying to Patman in his article, Professor Newland, on the other hand, charged the veteran Congressman with "some measure of naïveté," and pointed out that if law reviews and other legal journals were not to limit their interests solely to the past, they were bound to be vehicles for the expression of views on current policy issues.[197] He concluded his observations by putting the problem into its proper focus:

[196] *Congressional Record*, 85th Congress. 1st Session, Vol. 103, Part 12, p. 16160.
[197] Newland, loc. cit. pp. 73–4.

Critics may properly object that some views expressed in legal periodicals and adopted by the courts are contrary to policies which they deem desirable. But no greater unanimity of opinion usually exists among law faculties and reviews than exists on the Supreme Court. Legal periodicals appear to be "political" in somewhat the same way that the Courts are.[198]

TEST CASES

Since the American federal judicial system is based on the concept of litigation by virtue of an actual case or controversy brought before the courts by parties directly concerned, who must have standing to sue either as individuals or as personally and directly involved members of a class (see Chapter IX), the solution of an issue in the judicial process depends upon the decision handed down by the tribunal having jurisdiction. Consequently, neither the United States Supreme Court nor any of the lower constitutional courts can decide an issue unless it is before it. Here the employment of "test cases" becomes a *fortiorari* crucial, and both the timing and the presentation of the case are of the utmost importance. So long as the plaintiff or petitioner is a bona fide litigant it does not matter whether or not he pays for the almost always considerable expenses involved; nor does it matter to the outcome whether he personally is vitally interested in the decision. Provided that he is directly involved and is willing to go to court, it is of no legal significance that, in effect, he may thus well act as a front or a foil. Some states do have laws against "barratry," a form of induced litigation, but it is extremely difficult to prove that barratry has been practised, unless the litigant so acknowledges. This is particularly unlikely in those "class action" cases personified by the segregation-integration controversy. The first really important case in that area came before the Supreme Court through the auspices of a Missouri Negro, Lloyd Gaines, to whom that state had statutorily denied admission to its public law school,[199] but who mysteriously disappeared just a few days prior to his significant 7:2 victory in the Court. Ever since that time, test cases have been brought with increasing frequency by dis-

198 Ibid. p. 74.
199 *Missouri ex rel Gaines v. Canada,* 305 U. S. 337 (1938).

criminated-against Negroes, avowedly with the active encouragement, backing, and financing of the interest groups such as the National Association for the Advancement of Colored People (NAACP). It is neither surprising nor subject to doubt that the latter organization, dedicated to the aim inherent in its title, has acted, and will assuredly continue to act, very much like a strategy board of a field command, with due regard to the manifold tactical and strategic problems that beset such a command. In that sense, it resorts to the device of the test case to get its day in court, as do a host of other organizations for their own purposes.

Another illustration of the practice is the concerted drive by the Jehovah's Witnesses to obtain a maximum of religious freedom, as the Witnesses conceive of it, through the device of testing in the courts alleged restrictions and attacks upon their members. During the second quarter of this century, individual members of that sect, actively supported by the parent body, brought in excess of fifty bona fide test cases to the Supreme Court. Of these they won all but five! Nor is this practice confined to so-called minority groups. Almost every segment of the body politic has resorted to the device of the test case to gain—or lose—a point. The question arises just how much pressure or influence-peddling on the Court is involved here? Those who suspect a burglar under every judicial bed would quite naturally view test cases as an all but subversive scheme. Yet test case or regular case, a case is a case, provided it meets the jurisdictional requirements of the Court. And the line between a "plotted" or "instigated" case and a "real" or "natural" one is so thin that it almost defies detection except in the most obvious cases. Moreover, the Court is the master of its own calendar and will not accept frivolous litigation, much less hand down a decision on it. Finally, if an issue of constitutional magnitude is duly and properly brought before the Court, all legal remedies below having been exhausted, all the requirements of the judicial process having been met, and the Court has agreed to review it, does it *really matter* whether the issue was instigated or just happened in the natural course of events?

THE BRIEF AMICUS CURIAE

Closely related, indeed often essential, to the technique of test cases encouraged and supported by interest groups is the resort

237

to the brief *amicus curiae*. It is a brief filed by an outside individual or group—it is almost always a formal organization in the latter category—who is not a litigant in the suit but who is vitally interested in a decision favorable to the side it espouses. The device of the brief *amicus curiae,* i.e. "friend of the court"—which may well be a misnomer in a given situation—enables the interested party filing these briefs to enter the case, however tangentially, either by way of a written statement, or by participating in oral argument—or both. But there are obstacles as well as limitations to the filing of an *amicus curiae*. If all parties consent to the filing of such a brief, the Supreme Court's rules require its own acquiescence thereto. However, such mutual consent by the litigants is by no means always readily forthcoming. In that event, a party may petition the Court itself for permission to file an *amicus curiae,* a request which may or may not be granted, depending entirely on the judgment of the justices. Moreover, in cases in which the United States Government is a party to a suit, which is true of approximately one-half of the total number of all cases before the Supreme Court, consent for leave to file briefs *amici curiae* must be given by the Solicitor-General ere the Court will admit them. In general, that high government official has been quite liberal in this connection, but on some occasions the Court has granted organizational requests for briefs *amici curiae* over the former's refusal to consent. The same general approach is true of cases involving *state* government—as was demonstrated by the Supreme Court's acceptance of briefs *amici curiae* in the 1965 case testing Connecticut's birth control statute over that state's objections.[200]

Who files these briefs? Theoretically any interested party may do so; in practice, however, most briefs *amici curiae* have come from active civic organizations and other pressure groups and, not surprisingly, from the federal government itself via the Solicitor-General. According to an authoritative study of applicants for leave to file during relatively recent times,[201] most requests have been filed—often, but by no means always, granted—by the following organizations: the American Civil Liberties Union (a tireless and effective battler for civil liberties); the NAACP (persistent

200 *Griswold v. Connecticut,* 381 U.S. 479. See the illuminating article in *Time Magazine,* February 26, 1965, pp. 50–51.
201 Clement E. Vose, "Litigation as a Form of Pressure Group Activity," 319 *Annals of the American Academy of Political and Social Science* 20–31 (September 1958).

and broadly successful spokesman for the Negro); the American Jewish Congress (in roughly the same category as the ACLU, but with emphasis on cases concerning matters involving its own particular interests); and the chief interest group for the vast labor movement, the AFL-CIO. Also very active have been the American Bar Association and the National Lawyers Guild (the splinter lawyer's group); various veterans pressure groups, led by the American Legion; and quite often of late in matters involving the segregation-integration field, the United States government.

To cite a specific case example of the successful use of an *amicus curiae* by the latter, the government filed such a brief in the 1960 case of *Boynton v. Virginia*[202] through the auspices of Solicitor-General J. Lee Rankin. Here a bus terminal restaurant in Richmond, Virginia, segregated passengers according to color, regardless of their destination. The plaintiff rested his brief on the equal protection of the laws clause of the Fourteenth Amendment, under which so many cases in the area of racial segregation had been won by Negro petitioners. However, the Solicitor-General's brief *amicus curiae* used an entirely different approach and contended that since the restaurant involved was an "integral part" of a bus line's interstate passenger service, the Interstate Commerce Act of 1887—a federal statute—forbade such segregation. More or less ignoring the litigants' arguments and briefs, the Supreme Court fastened upon the contents of Mr. Rankin's *amicus curiae* and decided 7:2 in the plaintiff's favor. In a dissenting opinion joined by Mr. Justice Clark, Mr. Justice Whittaker, however, chided the Court majority for deciding the case on the commerce clause which had been raised *solely* by the Government as *amicus curiae*.

Unless the evidence is as clear-cut as in the aforementioned instance, it is very difficult to determine how far, if at all, the Court's decision and/or opinion make use of briefs *amici curiae*. What some commentators in this field report as the gospel's truth is not infrequently laced with conjecture and sheer guesswork, some of it with prejudiced motivation. On the other hand, it would be fair to state that the flood of briefs *amici curiae* filed by the NAACP in the area of its own special interest had at least

202 364 U. S. 454 (1960).

some persuasive influence in the outcome of the many cases handed down by the Court in the fifteen years between the end of World War II and 1960, for example—in which the cause espoused by the NAACP gained fifty victories! A specific illustration of one of these is the momentous decision by the Court in *Shelley v. Kraemer*,[203] the most important of the *Restrictive Covenant Cases.*[204] That case held the record for the number of main briefs and briefs *amici curiae* filed and accepted until 1963: nineteen by the NAACP and others favorably disposed to its point of view here; five by opposing groups, chiefly real-estate interests; and one by Solicitor-General Philip B. Perlman on behalf of the U. S. Department of Justice, siding with the Negro plaintiff.[205] Speaking for the unanimous six-man Court—Justices Reed, Jackson, and Rutledge having disqualified themselves from participation—Mr. Chief Justice Vinson ruled that although racially restrictive *private* covenants did not in themselves violate the Fourteenth Amendment of the Constitution, *court enforcement* of such contracts would constitute state action and thereby violate the equal protection of the laws clause of that amendment—a signal victory for the cause of the NAACP.

Another illustration of the use of briefs *amici curiae* on *both* sides of a case is *Gideon v. Wainwright,* the influential 1963 decision that extended the right of indigents to be assigned counsel to *non*capital as well as capital cases. There a record number of such briefs was filed, 24 on behalf of Clarence Earl Gideon, two on behalf of Warden Wainwright of Florida.[206]

Surely, briefs *amici curiae* may, and sometimes do, influence members of the Court. To acknowledge that entirely plausible, and in many cases quite conceivably salutary, phenomenon is one thing; to lower it to the level of a sinister or subversive cops-and-robbers plot is quite another. In this realm of alleged outside influence, as well as in those discussed earlier, the fact remains

---

203 334 U. S. 1 (1948).

204 Ibid. plus *Hurd v. Hodge*, 334 U. S. 24 (1948) and *Barrows v. Jackson*, 346 U. S. 249 (1953).

205 Clement E. Vose, *Caucasians Only: The Supreme Court, the NAACP, and the Restrictive Covenant Cases* (Berkeley and Los Angeles, University of California Press, 1959), Ch. 8.

206 372 U.S. 335.

that the justices, when all is said and done, have the final word on whether or how far, if at all, they permit themselves to be influenced within the accepted framework of the judicial process.

The Law Clerks

In a somewhat different category among the "outside pressures" on the Court are its law clerks. Depending upon the point of view advanced, these able and intelligent young aides to the justices, all recent law-school graduates, are either in the category of a private secretary aide-de-camp to their justices or in that of a gray eminence, a sort of judicial Rasputin, indeed the veritable power behind the throne! Thus, in an angry speech on the floor of the United States Senate, Senator John Stennis (D.-Miss.), a vigorous critic of the Court's attitude on segregation and subversion cases, called for an investigation of the activities of the clerks; the establishment of statutory minimum qualifications for them; and their confirmation by the Senate just like the justices themselves— all this because of what the Senator termed "their ever-increasing importance and influence." The law clerks, he said, might be occupying roles in government far more important than those occupied by undersecretaries and assistant secretaries of the executive branch, and that:

> To the extent that they participate in shaping the work of the court, they are deciding vital questions of national effect. Within the Judicial branch, these are equivalent to policy-level decisions in the executive branch.[207]

Yet we have the word of ex-law clerk after ex-law clerk that their influence on the justices to whom they were assigned was nil in so far as the judicial decision-making process is concerned. Thus, John P. Frank, once clerk to Mr. Justice Black, wrote that in his years with the latter, "my Justice made approximately one thousand decisions, and I had precisely no influence on any of them."[208] Dean Acheson, one of several of Mr. Justice Brandeis's law clerks who later rose to national prominence, reported that his Justice would sometimes let him work on a draft opinion, largely for the sake of criticism, but:

[207] As reported in *The New York Times*, May 7, 1958.
[208] *The Marble Palace* (New York: Alfred A. Knopf, 1958), p. 119.

When I finished my work on a draft which had been assigned to me or got as far as I could, I gave it to him. [As is evident from the Brandeis files] he tore it to pieces, sometimes using a little, sometimes none.[209]

"Judging is not delegated!" snapped Mr. Justice Brennan once in response to a taunt by a reporter.[210] And all of the law clerks who have written or otherwise reported on their experiences behind the "Purple Curtain," only one, William H. Rehnquist, suggested the possibility of some "*unconscious* slanting of material by clerks."[211] But even he readily admitted of his experiences as Mr. Justice Jackson's clerk in the 1952-53 term that the notion of the law clerk "exerting an important influence on the cases actually decided by the Court, may be discarded at once . . . . I certainly learned of none."[212]

Just who are these law clerks—who, almost without exception, have gone on to notable careers in law and government[213]—and how are they selected? As indicated above, they are recent law-school graduates of the highest caliber. As of the start of 1968 all except two had been male, the two ladies being Lucille Loman and Margaret Corcoran, appointed by Justices Douglas and Black, respectively, in 1944 and 1966. Each is chosen by an individual justice to work for him for a year, sometimes for two. The practice was initiated by Mr. Justice Horace Gray in 1882. He paid them out of his own pocket until 1886 when Congress provided $1600 a year for a "stenographic clerk" for each justice. That figure had risen to $9614 by 1967. Today, each associate justice selects two, the Chief Justice three, although Mr. Justice Douglas usually contented himself with just one clerk.[214] Some justices do their own selecting, either as a result of a personal interview or

---

[209] As quoted by Bickel, op. cit. p. 92.

[210] *Time Magazine,* June 5, 1964, p. 67.

[211] "Who Writes Decisions of the Supreme Court?" *U.S. News and World Report,* December 13, 1957.

[212] Ibid.

[213] E.g. Dean Acheson (U.S. Secretary of State), Francis Biddle (U.S. Attorney General), Irving Olds (President of U.S. Steel), David Riesman (famed Professor of Sociology), Byron White (Associate Justice of the Supreme Court of the United States).

[214] The "left over" or nineteenth clerk was then customarily appointed as "Chief Clerk" for the Chief Justice at a 1967 salary of $10,836. (Letter to author from Clerk of the Supreme Court John F. Davis, July 31, 1967.)

written data, almost always the former; others rely chiefly on experts' recommendations—viz., Mr. Justice Frankfurter, whose clerks were chosen for him by Professors Sachs and Freund at the Harvard Law School—as are now Mr. Justice Brennan's. From there Professor of Law Felix Frankfurter sent a number of his own outstanding students, sometimes referred to as "Felix's Happy Hot Dogs," to the Court as clerks (and to government service with the New Deal). In short, the clerks are really the purely personal patronage of the justices, who are free to base their selections on whatever criteria they desire. John P. Frank avowed that his Justice, Mr. Justice Black, "tries to get Southern boys—and tennis-players where possible."[215] Mr. Justice Stewart preferred Yale Law School graduates; Mr. Chief Justice Warren Californians; Mr. Justice Clark graduates of lesser known law schools. Mr. Justice Harlan usually chose one boy from Harvard and one from a New York City law school. And Mr. Justice Douglas always turned to a West Coast law school for his choice. To use one year as an example, the 1965-66 term of the Court saw nineteen law clerks chosen by the nine members of the court, Mr. Chief Justice Warren selecting three, Mr. Justice Douglas one, all others two, plus one assigned jointly to retired Justices Reed and Burton—still "on call" for lower federal court spot tasks, as assigned by the Chief Justice. The young men came from ten different law schools; six from Harvard University; three each from Yale University and the University of Pennsylvania; two each from the University of Virginia and Stanford University; and one each from Columbia University, the University of Texas, and the University of North Carolina.

Exactly what work a justice assigns or delegates to his clerk depends upon the former's inclination—or, as Mr. Justice Jackson once stated, "on the justice's temperament and experience." Apparently, most of the justices—Mr. Justice Frankfurter evidently was an exception to the practice—use their clerks to wade through the manifold petitions for *certiorari* that are filed annually. Typically, a law clerk may read such a petition and the opposing party's response, and then type or pen a brief memorandum to his justice stating the issues involved and setting forth arguments for and against a grant of the desired writ. Suffice it to note that the justice

215 *The Marble Palace,* loc. cit. pp. 115–16.

concerned will, of course, make up his own mind. Some of the justices may go somewhat further in employing their clerks by asking for a so-called bench memorandum on a particular case now and then; such a memorandum may propound certain approaches and point to precedents and thereby suggest questions to be asked by the justices of counsel during oral argument. The most intensive task performed by the law clerks is probably that of the necessary drudgery of research once an opinion has been assigned to a particular justice. Here commences the time-consuming chore of investigating, of sorting and checking precedents, citations, historical data, congressional records—the host of materials so vital to the decision-making process. Beyond that, the chief role of the law clerk is to serve as a type of foil, friend, critic, sounding board. In the final analysis, however, quoting one former clerk:

> In the course of my year, we never changed the justice's mind on the result of any case. Our influence was close to nil. There was the fullest discussion, but he made the decisions. . . . The judge will listen if you say that some statement in his draft opinion is too broad or that a case is cited incorrectly. But if you tell him that such-and-such a constitutional amendment doesn't mean what he believes, you might as well stay in bed.[216]

The clerks are important tools for the justices in the judicial process, perhaps indispensable ones, yet they are hardly classifiable as powers behind the throne. Essentially, they are law *clerks*—able, intelligent, and undoubtedly often, if not always, of considerable procedural aid to their justices. But they are not members of the Court in any sense of the term. And, as has been contended repeatedly in connection with the entire matter of influence upon it, in fine the Supreme Court of the United States is master of its own house—which does not, however, mean that it is not aware of the existence of other houses both in and out of the governmental compound.

As we conclude this extensive consideration of the Supreme Court of the United States at work, it is both easy and natural to assent eagerly to a perceptive statement made by *The New York Times'* Supreme Court reporter Anthony Lewis as he left his seven-year coverage of the Court for a new assignment in London in

216 As quoted anonymously in *The New York Times,* October 14, 1957, p. 29.

1965: "The wonderful thing about the Supreme Court is that it does its work. It decides, as it has to decide. There has never been a Rules Committee to save the Justices on tough problems. . . . [T]he Supreme Court . . . is the last stronghold of personal responsibility for decisions."[217]

217 *The New York Times Magazine*, January 17, 1965, pp. 56–8.

VI

COURTS ABROAD

Constant reference has been made, especially in the early chapters, to the practices and theories of jurists and judicial systems of sundry lands, wherever appropriate, since the comparative element is one of the essential characteristics of this work. Newly emergent states of the world adapt their needs to the legal and social patterns of others. The United States has both profited from and contributed to other systems. Basically English in origin and design, features of its judicial system and process nevertheless both resemble, and differ drastically from, that of others. The legal systems of England and Wales, France, and the Soviet Union are most useful in an analysis in this connection. In the following pages a relatively brief view of the courts of these three countries will be presented, with a diagram for each system.

THE COURTS OF ENGLAND AND WALES

It is in fact incorrect to think of the courts of "Great Britain" or of the "United Kingdom" as a unified judicial system. For there exist actually *three different systems* in the United Kingdom of Great Britain and Northern Ireland: one for England and Wales; one for Scotland; and one for Northern Ireland. Only at the ultimate appellate level of the House of Lords is it possible to speak with accuracy of a unified system for the United Kingdom; because that body in its judicial role represents the final court of appeals —in those very few cases that manage to reach it—from the judgments of the highest courts of Scotland and Northern Ireland as well as from those of England and Wales. The following description is of the judicial system of England and Wales—for convenience hereafter referred to as "England"—unless specified otherwise.[1]

In the United States the *same* tribunals ordinarily have *both* civil and criminal jurisdiction, with some minor exceptions for certain low level state courts, such as the Court of Small Claims in Pennsylvania. But in the England of today justice is meted out in two separated judicial hierarchies, one for civil cases and one for criminal cases—although the judges are often the same. This separation is based upon the Supreme Court of Judicature (Consolidation) Act of 1925, as amended, the progeny of a series of Judicature Acts commencing with that of 1873. The latter statute brought order into what was a truly bewildering array of distinct tribunals—e.g. some seven or eight leading courts had original jurisdiction in civil cases! However, unlike France, neither England nor the United States has a bona fide system of administrative courts—although some of the English administrative courts, e.g. Railway Rate Tribunals, existed long before World War II and others have begun to make their appearance since the war; also some of the special and/or legislative tribunals in the United States are at least quasi-administrative.[2]

THE CRIMINAL COURTS' HIERARCHY

It is perhaps somewhat unorthodox to discuss the criminal courts hierarchy before that of the civil courts, but the English structure lends itself peculiarly well to such a procedure—in part because of a considerable amount of interchange of judges between the two hierarchies, despite the rigid structural segregation inherent in the system. Jurisdiction over criminal offenses has been exercised as a separate entity for some 700 years.

The Justice of the Peace and the Stipendiary Magistrate. At the base of the criminal courts hierarchy in England is the unpaid, volunteer lay magistrate, the *Justice of the Peace,* who must live within 15 miles of the judicial area of jurisdiction. His is an office established by law in 1326 or 1327 during the reign of Edward II.

---

[1] These courts are presided over by judges who wear wigs and robes of office, with the color of their robes depending upon the law they administer. The common law judges as well as those who administer to the criminal law wear scarlet robes; the others wear black.

[2] See Chapter IV, *supra,* for details.

Approximately 4000 "J.P.s" are at work today. In the larger cities there is instead the *Stipendiary Magistrate*—London alone, where he is called Metropolitan Magistrate, has roughly 35 of these officials—who, unlike his cousin, the Justice of the Peace, must be a full-time professional lawyer, usually a barrister, and is paid. With the exception of the Duchy of Lancaster, where they are designated by its own Chancellor, the magistrates at this lowest level of the criminal hierarchy are appointed on behalf of the Crown by the Lord Chancellor after careful screening and recommendation by local advisory committees in each county. That politically designated officer, who was discussed earlier,[3] is not only the highest judicial officer in the British system, but he is also a member of the Cabinet, its foremost legal adviser, and a member as well as *ex officio* the presiding officer of the House of Lords.

Sitting *en banc* without a jury, the Justice of the Peace or Stipendiary Magistrate, in his role as a tribunal of first instance, is exclusively a court of summary jurisdiction for criminal offenses. But he may also double as a committing judicial officer by holding an accused for action by a higher court in the event of "indictable" offenses. These would normally require grand jury action at the federal level in the United States; but in England, since the statutory abolition of the grand jury in 1933, the process of "information" has replaced it. Except for minor matters, trials at this lowest level of original jurisdiction are conducted by one, two, or three justices of the peace but by only one stipendiary magistrate —a vital distinction between the two types of similar officials. The chief function of these officials is to try relatively minor criminal offenses, although they do have jurisdiction in certain domestic relations—matrimonial, bastardy, and rate cases, and a few administrative functions—and, as indicated, determine whether there is sufficient evidence to commit the offender for trial before a jury in a higher court.[4]

Many of the offenses handled by the J.P. or the Stipendiary Magistrate concern traffic violators, and the maximum fine he may

[3] See Chapter II, *supra*.

[4] According to 1964 statistics provided by the Dower Marchioness of Reading— a member of the House of Lords—"97 per cent of the crime in England" is tried at this level of the criminal judicial hierarchy! (*The New York Times*, August 13, 1954.)

impose here is £5. Generally speaking, his jurisdiction is restricted to cases involving a maximum fine of £100 or a six months' jail sentence or both. In many instances the accused is permitted the option of a trial before the Justice of the Peace or the Stipendiary Magistrate or before a higher judge (and jury, when appropriate). Experience has demonstrated that the accused will almost invariably choose the former because of considerations of expeditiousness.

Still at the same level of the judiciary, when two or more justices of the peace, or one stipendiary magistrate. sit, a *Court of Petty Sessions* is said to exist. As will be explained subsequently, appeals from this level are possible either to the Court of Quarter Sessions or to a three-judge Divisional Court of the Queen's Bench Division of the High Court of Justice, depending upon the nature of the appeal, and provided that the defendant did not plead guilty—although in London he is free to appeal even in the latter event if the sentence is more than one month in prison or a fine of more than £3. Appeals in matrimonial cases go to the Divisional Court of the Probate, Divorce, and Admiralty Division of the High Court of Justice.

The Court of Quarter Sessions. Immediately above the J.P. level is the *Court of Quarter Sessions,* still called by that ancient name because it meets four times annually in its proper area of jurisdiction. Clothed with appellate as well as original jurisdiction, it is the first court in which an accused, given the proper circumstances, is entitled to a trial by jury. The Court of Quarter Sessions consists of all the justices of the peace in a given county, presided over by a legally qualified chairman. But since the enactment of the Justices of the Peace Act of 1949, no more than nine members of the Court may sit *en banc* in any given case. In some boroughs it consists merely of the paid *Recorder,* selected from barristers of at least five years' experience. He sits only occasionally as such, however, and continues in practice as a barrister.

In theory, the Court of Quarter Sessions may try any cases other than those permitting the death penalty or a sentence of life imprisonment on first offense; in practice, however, it rarely handles those cases that call for more than five years' imprisonment. The Court has an Appeal Committee, numbering from three to twelve justices, which constitutes an appellate tribunal for the defendant—without a jury, of course—for convictions and sentences by justices of the peace and stipendiary magistrates below, both on points of law and fact. But normally it is the court of last resort on questions of fact. The number of appeals coming to it is relatively small. In 1961, to cite a typical year, of 1,000,423 persons convicted below, only 3241 filed appeals.[5]

Appeals from the Court of Quarter Sessions do not go to the Court of Assize immediately above, but to the next higher level, the Court of Appeal. On a point of law any convicted defendant may appeal to the latter, and he may do so on a point of fact with leave of the trial judge or the Court of Appeal. The latter's permission is necessary for an appeal against the sentence itself.

The Assize Court. At the next level above lies the most important tribunal in the criminal hierarchy of England, the *Assize Court.* Its jurisdiction covers all major felonies, such as homicide, robbery, larceny, and rape. Justices commit cases either to it or to the Court of Quarter Sessions below, depending on the nature of the offense. The Assize Court meets three times annually in an important town in each county of the seven judicial circuits into which England is divided, but assizes sit throughout the year in most big cities. An Assize Court is ordinarily presided over either by a professional judge "on circuit" from the Queen's Bench Division of the High Court of Justice (a civil court) in London or by a *Commissioner*—an experienced Queen's Counsel, who is thus tried out for future judicial office. It was Lord Parker, the Lord Chief Justice, who, in his capacity as a judge of the Queen's Bench Division, presided over the important spy trial that took place in the spring of 1961 in England's capital. (The Lord Chief Justice, who is England's highest judicial officer, is the head of the Queen's Bench Division.)

Because of the nature of the offenses tried before them, the assizes always sit with a jury. Much traditional pageantry and fanfare attend their sessions, the proper judicial manner being very much in evidence. The Assize Court for Metropolitan London is the *Central Criminal Court,* widely known as the "Old Bailey" be-

---

[5] Richard M. Jackson, *The Machinery of Justice in England,* 4th ed. (Cambridge: Cambridge University Press, 1964), p. 114. This is an excellent book, and one of the very few relatively up-to-date ones available on the British judiciary. It presents a superb explanation and analysis of its subject matter.

cause of the name of the interesting building where it meets for its twelve sessions annually, one each month.[6]

Appeals from judgments of the Assize Court are possible to the next higher level court, the Court of Appeal, broadly in accordance with the terms and qualifications of appeals from the Court of Quarter Sessions to that tribunal, just described above. Again, an acquittal is not appealable.

The Court of Appeal. Appeals from the two lower levels in the hierarchy, to which only the defendant—not the prosecution—is entitled, were formerly taken directly to the *Court of Criminal Appeal,* created in 1907. Recently, however, the separate Court of *Criminal* Appeal was abolished, and its functions taken over by a *criminal division* of the *Court of Appeal*—an arrangement of chiefly administrative importance. Appeals come to the criminal division in the same way they used to go to the Court of Criminal Appeal, assuming the necessary jurisdiction is present and leave to file has been obtained. It is the most important tribunal of appellate jurisdiction in the criminal hierarchy of England. Sitting without a jury, it hears appeals on the transcripts of the evidence taken at the trial. But the hearing is not a retrial in the sense that the witnesses are heard over again by the Court of Appeal. The latter is composed of the legally qualified and salaried judges of the Queen's Bench Division of the High Court of Justice. Usually there are three members—the quorum—but whatever the number, it must be uneven.

Because of the stipulated assumption that any appeal involves a retrial, the Court of Appeal has the power to revise—i.e. alter or vary—the erstwhile sentence in three situations: (1) if it is not legally justified; (2) if it was based on improper evidence; and (3) if the length or severity of the sentence points to an error in "some matter of principle" by the trial court. The Court of Appeal may even substitute conviction of another offense for the initial one if it appears that the defendant should have been convicted for it rather than for the one for which he was convicted below. But it has no power to order a trial *de novo* unless there has been a mistrial in the lower court.

6 "Bailley" was the tenth-century English word for "enclosure," and the Old Bailey stands on the site of an enclosure which was originally part of Newgate Prison where public executions took place until 1868.

The House of Lords. In rare instances, the accused—never the prosecutor—has one last and very much restricted path of appeal from the Court of Appeal to the *House of Lords* (an institution to be more fully described in connection with the civil hierarchy). Yet such an appeal is possible only when a point of law of "general public importance" is involved, and leave to file for appeal to that august body must be given by the Court of Appeal or the Divisional Court of the Queen's Bench Division of the High Court of Justice—or by the House of Lords itself if refused by the aforementioned tribunals. Such appeals have averaged but one a year.[7] Moreover, since the House of Lords habitually confines its rulings on the specific, often narrow, point of law involved —here very much like the Supreme Court of the United States— broad legal pronouncements are unlikely indeed.

Until a statutory change was effected in 1960, permission to appeal to the House of Lords was even more circumscribed than the present procedure. Leave to appeal could be granted only by the Attorney General, the senior law officer of the Crown, and then only if the point of law involved was deemed of *"exceptional* public importance." Thus, in the famous Guenther Padola loss-of-memory murder case of 1959, the Attorney General, Sir Reginald Manningham-Buller, refused to grant such permission. All other channels of appeal had previously been exhausted, and the Old Bailey jury had decided in the trial court that the alleged amnesia was faked. The accused consequently paid the ultimate penalty.

THE CIVIL COURTS' HIERARCHY

Although some of the terminology will be similar and some of the judicial personnel, in fact, the same, the existing hierarchical distinctions between the criminal and civil courts are highly pertinent to a proper understanding of the judicial process in England. Again, we commence at the lowest level of the courts.

The County Court. The court of first instance in civil matters is the *County Court*—so called by virtue of the adoption of the ancient name of the local courts of the county in early Anglo-Norman times, despite the fact that the jurisdiction of these tribunals today does not necessarily coincide with county boun-

[7] Jackson, op. cit. p. 118.

daries. Indeed, it has nothing to do with them. The districts they serve are arranged so that a County Court is within ready reach everywhere; they are subject to geographic alteration by the Lord Chancellor. The between 400 and 450 county courts are presided over by some 80 judges who have been appointed by the Crown on the advice of the Lord Chancellor—again with the exception of the Duchy of Lancaster, as in the case of the justices of the peace. To qualify, they must be barristers in good standing with at least seven years of experience. They retire at seventy-two or exceptionally at seventy-five.

County court judges—who are well paid, as is generally true of Britain's jurists—live in their districts and hold court once or twice a month in appropriate towns, referred to as their circuit, depending upon the work load docketed. Each County Court is assigned a *Registrar,* a solicitor appointed by, and subject to removal by, the Lord Chancellor, who is not only in charge of the court's office staff, but who may also act as a lesser judge. By leave of his county court judge and in the absence of objections by any of the parties, the Registrar deals mainly with matters not involving more than £30, but he may exercise wider jurisdiction with the consent of the litigants.

The jurisdiction of the County Court, although strictly limited statutorily, is extensive, and the number of cases commenced at this level is vast. In 1965, for instance, a total of 1,536,621 proceedings were entered here,[8] and this astonishing total has not declined over the years since that time. Broadly speaking, the large majority of cases fall into the area of actions based on contract and many, but not all, types of tort claims up to a maximum of £400 (under certain conditions increasable by high authority to £500). Yet more than 95 per cent of these cases do not exceed £100 in value. Other areas of County Court jurisdiction include equity matters up to £500; real-estate actions up to £100; a limited range of admiralty and bankruptcy matters. And a highly significant field of its jurisdiction arises under so-called "social" or "collectivist" statutes, a by-product of today's welfare state. Since 1934, appeals from the county courts must be taken directly to the Court of Appeal, thus by-passing the next higher court level.

[8] *Whitaker's Almanak* (London: J. Whitaker & Sons, Ltd., 1967), p. 456.

The High Court of Justice. Immediately above the County Court in the hierarchy of the civil courts stands the *High Court of Justice*—an ancient institution deriving from the Norman *curia regis,* which was the monarch's personal instrument for the dispensing of justice. It has chiefly original but also some—divisionally restricted—appellate jurisdiction. The famous tribunal, established in 1873, is now staffed by three presiding officers and sixty-one distinguished *puisne* judges[9] who have had a minimum of ten years of experience as barristers—many have had twenty and twenty-five. The three divisions of the "High Court," as it is commonly called, thus comprise: the thirty-six-member *Queen's Bench Division,* plus its presiding officer, the Lord Chief Justice, who ranks immediately after the Lord Chancellor in the judicial hierarchy; the eight-member *Chancery Division,* plus its nonsitting presiding officer, the Lord Chancellor; and the President and seventeen judges of the *Probate, Divorce, and Admiralty Division.*

Of the three, the Queen's Bench Division is by far the largest and busiest, partly because its judges must—as was explained above—participate also in the work of the higher criminal courts as a matter of exercising original jurisdiction, and partly because with three or five of its judges sitting as the *Divisional Court* of the Queen's Bench Division, it hears certain appeals in criminal cases from the courts of summary jurisdiction, i.e. the Justice of the Peace and Stipendiary Magistrate Court and the Court of Quarter Sessions. Coupled with its jurisdiction over the general field of the common law, its work range thus extends to: (1) ordinary civil actions; (2) its appellate and supervisory jurisdiction *en banc* in its mantle of Divisional Court of the Queen's Bench Division; (3) appellate functions exercised by a single judge; and (4) its extensive, original criminal jurisdiction.

[9] The first woman to be appointed to the High Court of Justice was County Court Judge Elizabeth Lane, who reached her country's No. 3 tribunal in August 1965. At her appointment she was one of only four female barristers to hold the elite title of Queen's Counsel (Q.C.). A minor crisis arose over what to call the first woman judge? Would it be "Mr. Justice" or "Your Lordship"? Not at all, decreed the Lord Chancellor, Lord Gardiner: Upon her confirmation by Queen Elizabeth, it was announced that "henceforth and hereafter" Dame Elizabeth Lane would be addressed as "The Honorable Mrs. Justice Lane" and, inside the court room, as "My Lady" and "Your Ladyship." (*The Christian Science Monitor,* September 19, 1965.)

As the presiding officer of the Queen's Bench Division, the Lord Chief Justice enjoys a considerable degree of authority and prestige. In his capacity he is the directing figure of the criminal courts of England. Members of the British legal circles are fond of stating that the Lord Chief Justice is in somewhat the same position as the Pope in that what he says on any given occasion may influence not only the other judges but also the lawyers, the magistrates, and even the police.[10] He is indeed a towering figure on the scene of government, and he is regarded with much awe, confidence, and respect.

The Chancery Division has exclusive jurisdiction in some cases, and concurrent jurisdiction with the Queen's Bench Division in others. In the extensive former category are equity matters of bankruptcy, companies, execution of trusts, wardships, foreclosures of mortgages, etc. Its *Divisional Court* hears appeals on bankruptcy matters from the County Court.

The Probate, Divorce, and Admiralty Division has jurisdiction in the areas indicated by its name: giving valid title to the estate of deceased persons; matrimonial decrees as to divorce, nullity, restitution of conjugal rights, judicial separation, presumption of death and dissolution of marriage, and declaration of legitimacy; various matters affecting ships under maritime law. Its *Divisional Court* hears appeals from the Magistrates' Courts level in matrimonial cases. In popular lingo, the Probate, Divorce, and Admiralty Division is often referred to as the "Wrecks" Division because it is said to deal with "wills, wives, and wrecks." Lord Goddard, who was Lord Chief Justice for twelve years, amended this ancient jest recently as dealing with "wrecks of wills . . . marriages . . . and ships."[11]

In addition to its specialized jurisdiction just explained, the High Court of Justice has over-all jurisdiction in all cases that are eligible for hearings in the County Court as well as those that lie outside that tribunal's jurisdiction. But it will not normally entertain cases under its original jurisdiction if these can be handled by the County Court—e.g. routine controversies with a value of less

---

10 See *The New York Times,* March 23, 1961.
11 Lord Goddard, "Organization and Jurisdiction of the Courts of England," 44 *Journal of the American Judicature Society* 62 (August 1960). (See his entire article for a fine description, pp. 60–65.)

than £500. Together with the Court of Appeal, the High Court of Justice forms the *Supreme Court of Judicature*—a body that is actually neither supreme nor a court, but serves as a type of cover-all for these two entirely separate branches of the civil courts system.

The Court of Appeal. Appeals from any of the Divisions of the High Court of Justice go to the *Court of Appeal,* consisting of the Lord Chancellor; former Lord Chancellors; the Lords of Appeal in Ordinary; the Lord Chief Justice; the Master of the Rolls, England's second highest judicial officer; and the President of the Probate, Divorce, and Admiralty Division of the High Court as members *ex officio;* plus eight Lords Justices of Appeal, the regular sitting members, who must have had fifteen years of experience as barristers or been High Court judges. But of the *ex officio* members only the Master of the Rolls actually sits with three of the regular sitting judges of the Court of Appeal. Its appellate jurisdiction extends to points of law arising out of civil cases from the County Court or the High Court of Justice.

Appeals on points of law coming from the County Court reach the Court of Appeal as a matter of right if the amount of the claim involved exceeds £20 or when the remedy is an injunction. In other appeals the judge below must give permission. In the cases coming from the High Court, appeal is automatic on points of law but not on points of fact. If the Court of Appeal grants an appeal, retrial of the case will normally take place below; however, it may also reconsider the evidence itself, but without taking new testimony from witnesses.

The House of Lords. From the Court of Appeal, if the matter of law involved is deemed to be of sufficient importance, there remains the final path of appeal to the *House of Lords*—an expensive (£1000 for printing costs alone is an average expenditure) and uncommon one—provided that the appeal has been certified by the Court of Appeal[12] or granted by the House of Lords itself, a his-

---

[12] A famous illustration of a refusal by the Court of Appeal so to certify an appeal was the case of Dr. Robert A. Soblen in 1962. The sixty-one-year-old psychiatrist had fled the United States while under a life sentence for wartime espionage for the Soviet Union, and asked Britain to grant him asylum. The British Home Office refused, and Soblen commenced a lengthy, ultimately unsuccessful series of legal maneuvers to escape deportation. He later committed suicide to avert being sent back to the States.

toric right dating back to the practices of the Norman institution of the *magnum concilium*, the Great Council. The Lords do not, of course, sit in a mass body for that purpose—there are over 850 members! Instead, the legal section of the House of Lords comprises a small, highly skilled, distinguished group of judicial experts, the nine *Law Lords*, known as the *Lords of Appeal in Ordinary*, plus the Lord Chancellor, the presiding officer of the House of Lords. The ten officials are augmented by any other peer who may have held, or now holds, high judicial office under the Crown.

This small group of appellate experts was created originally by the Appellate Jurisdiction Act of 1876 to supplement the judicial strength of the House of Lords. It remains the sole United Kingdom-wide judicial body, and as such always has some members from Scotland and, on occasion, one from Northern Ireland. These few dignitaries with a background of at least fifteen years as barristers or of two years in high judicial office, who are all professional, paid judges with life peerages, and who ordinarily take no part, whatever, in the political business of the Lords, thus constitute the Supreme Court of the United Kingdom of Great Britain and Northern Ireland. But unlike the Supreme Court of the United States and the other United States federal and state courts, neither the House of Lords nor any other English or Welsh court, no matter how high, possesses the power of judicial review (which will be fully described in the following chapter).

The Judicial Committee of the Privy Council. One other major appellate tribunal, sitting somewhat astride the regular court system just described, exists in the British Isles. It is the important *Judicial Committee of the Privy Council*, which constitutes the final court of appeal for cases from the ecclesiastical courts of the Church of England, colonies, protectorates, trust territories, the Isle of Man, and the Channel Islands. It is also available as the ultimate appellate body for all those members of the Commonwealth that might wish to avail themselves of its services. But in recent years, with the rare exception of isloated cases from Ceylon, New Zealand, Australia, Ghana, Jamaica, and Malaya, Commonwealth members have normally preferred to adjudicate their problems in their own judicial structure. This is conclusively the case with India and Pakistan, for example. However, The Judicial Committee of the Privy Council did constitute the final court of

appeal from Canada on constitutional matters until 1949, when the right to appeal to it was abolished there by statute.

Only privy councillors are eligible for membership on the Judicial Committee. In practice, most of the work has been done by the Law Lords of the House of Lords, but other high judicial officers from the United Kingdom, as well as from the Commonwealth and other jurisdictions the Judicial Committee serves, have participated in its functions.

FIGURE 2
THE CRIMINAL AND CIVIL COURTS OF ENGLAND AND WALES

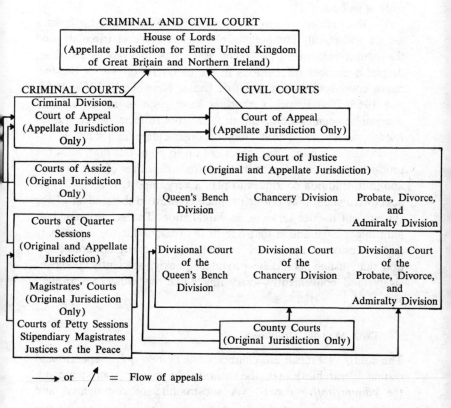

THE COURTS OF FRANCE

If imitation may be regarded as indication of approval, the popularity and acceptance of the French judicial system among the older as well as the newer states of the world represent such approval in the highest degree. Far more than the Anglo-American has the French administration of justice become a model abroad. To a large extent this is attributable to its base—those marvelous civil, criminal, penal, commercial, and procedural codes, drafted under the often personal direction of Napoleon Bonaparte at the end of the eighteenth and especially at the beginning of the nineteenth century, culminating in the famous, and still very much alive, *Code Napoleon*. With full justice have the French codes been called "well-balanced pieces of jurisprudential art, utterly systematic and conveniently accessible."[13] Here French logic was truly at its best.

Yet the judicial structure which applies the codes is far from a simple and readily comprehensible one. A maze of tribunals stud the countryside—as true today as it was in Napoleon's time, despite a number of revisions in the hierarchy of one of the two major court systems under the de Gaulle Republic in 1959, 1963, and 1965. The French authorities have gone so far as to take due public cognizance of the problem in an official governmental release, which noted that "judicial organization in France is exceptionally complex," but they went on to point out that "it is the product of successive contributions from centuries of our history, and in it, tradition continues to play a very important role."[14] This acknowledgment may not be of much comfort to the student of the system, but it does serve as an explanation. The government bulletin might have added that one of the reasons for the complexity and profusion of the French courts is the generally admirable notion that justice should be provided quickly, efficiently, inexpensively, and conveniently—very much like any other government service!

Two Major Divisions

The courts of France are characterized by two quite separate and distant hierarchies: first, the *ordinary* or *regular* courts; second, the *administrative courts*. (A substructure of commercial and

13 Robert G. Neumann, *European and Comparative Government*, 3d ed. (New York: McGraw-Hill Book Co., 1960), p. 289.

14 As quoted in Taylor Cole (ed.), *European Political Systems*, 3d ed. (New York: Alfred A. Knopf, 1959), p. 234.

certain other special courts need not concern us at this juncture; they may be viewed as falling generally under the ordinary courts.) In case of doubt as to proper jurisdiction, the eight-member *Tribunal des Conflits* (Tribunal of Conflicts), created especially for that umpire-role, and headed by the Minister of Justice, determines to which of the two major court systems a case goes.

Again, the chief reason for this interesting division of responsibility between the hierarchies is an historic one. Fearful that the ordinary courts might interfere with the administrative or executive branch of the government, the legislative bodies of France, dating all the way back to the days of the Revolution, wrote into laws and constitutions specific provisions that expressly forbade judicial bodies to intervene. For example, the Law of December 22, 1789, provided: ". . . . Judicial power should not trouble local administrative agencies in the exercise of their functions." And that of August 16–24, 1790, spelled the matter out more clearly:

> The judicial functions are and will remain forever separate from the administrative functions. The judges will not be allowed, under penalty of forfeiture, to disturb in any manner whatsoever, the activities of the administrative corps, nor to summon before them the administrators, concerning their functions.[15]

This was all very well in theory, but it soon became clear that someone or something would be needed to check certain administrative excesses of power. Hence the adoption of the system of administrative courts, designed to check administrative abuses and at the same time retain the cherished principle of separation of powers insofar as the judicial and executive-administrative functions are concerned. The separated hierarchies have flourished, and they survive essentially unchanged in design and principle, although not in certain organizational details and nomenclature.

THE ORDINARY OR REGULAR COURTS' HIERARCHY

On March 1, 1959, the de Gaulle government effected the first group of several judicial reforms, chiefly designed to give the courts a corps of more specialized judges and to distribute these more equitably geographically in a rearranged system of ordinary

[15] Stephan Riesengeld, "The French System of Administrative Justice: A Model for American Law," 18 *Boston University Law Review* 48 (1938).

courts, geared more closely to modern demands and realistic population distribution. The effect of these changes, as augmented in 1963 and 1965, is reflected in the following description.

The Court of Instance (TRIBUNAL D'INSTANCE). The first de Gaulle Reorganization Bill abolished the time-honored, but outdated, lowest of the ordinary courts, the local *Juge de Paix*—again our friend, the Justice of the Peace—and replaced that popular institution with a new local court of first instance, the *Tribunal d'Instance.* Heretofore 740 *juges de paix*—with law diplomas, unlike most of their Brtish and American counterparts—had brought justice, more or less, to the 3040 *cantons* of France by way of a completely informal, inexpensive, and often inconsequential procedure in the usual type of petty, chiefly civil, infractions, which obliged them to "ride circuit." Since 1959, 455 of the new *tribunaux d'instance* exist in the capitals of the various *arrondissements*—the administrative geographical level above the *canton*. Each of the new courts may have several judges—who are required to live in the area of jurisdiction of the tribunal—but decisions are rendered by a single judge. The *tribunaux d'instance* and their judges have been given considerably more effective adjudicatory power in civil and criminal cases than that possessed by the old *juges de paix.* Indeed, they are fully intended to become the most important unit in the revised judicial system.

The Court of Major Instance (TRIBUNAL DE GRANDE INSTANCE). The old civil *Court of First Instance* (*Tribunal de Première Instance*), of which one was located in every *arrondissement*, gave way to the newly created *Tribunal de Grande Instance.* The old criminal section of this level, the *Correctional Court* (Tribunal *Correctionnel*), has been retained, however. In place of the erstwhile 359 courts, the new 172 *tribunaux de grande instance* have jurisdiction throughout the *département*—the highest administrative subdivision in France—not merely in a single *arrondissement.* According to the number of inhabitants and the "degree of economic activity,"[16] the larger *départements* are entitled to two or more of the tribunals. Each case is tried by several judges sitting *en banc*, usually three, but always comprising an uneven number, with the decision reached by majority vote.

In civil cases the *tribunaux de grande instance* have unlimited original jurisdiction; they also have appellate jurisdiction from the *tribunaux d'instance.* In criminal cases the correctional courts sit

16 *Ambassade de France*, French Affairs Bulletin—No. 84 (May 1959), p. 32.

in the less severe felony cases and in misdemeanors such as assault, embezzlement, and theft. They are also empowered to hear certain limited appeals, primarily those dealing with infractions of police regulations.

The Court of Appeal (COUR D'APPEL). The 1959 and subsequent reforms did not make any substantial changes in the structure of the *Court of Appeal* (*Cour d' Appel*), the appellate tribunal for *civil* cases from below, and none at all in the number of the twenty-seven judicial districts (*Chambres*), each including several *départements*, in which one of these tribunals operates. However, the jurisdiction of the *Cour d'Appel* has been extended materially to include some of the special courts, alluded to earlier, particularly in the field of social and economic legislation. Thus, appeals to a *Cour d'Appel* may come from any one of the following, in addition to the considerable number of appeals that come up from the *tribunaux de grande instance* in the regular hierarchy below: the *Labor Conciliation Board* (*Conseil de Prud'hommes*), composed of an equal number of employers and employees who, chosen by their own groups for six years (one-half retiring every three years), hear disputes arising out of industrial contracts and arbitrate these; the *Commercial Court* (*Tribunal de Commerce*), consisting of businessmen elected by their local peers for two years to act in certain statutorily designated commercial cases; the *Juvenile Court* (*Tribunal pour Enfants*) one judge sitting for three years, chosen from a *tribunal de grande instance*; the *Farm Lease Court*, found at the seat of each *tribunal d'instance*; and the *Social Security Commission*, consisting of one judge from the *tribunal d'instance* plus two representatives of "interested parties." All of these special courts have several court units throughout the country. Each of the twenty-seven courts of appeal, with from five to seven judges sitting—always seven in the Parisian tribunal—hears a case before it entirely *de novo;* their decisions on points of fact are final.

The Assize Court (COUR D'ASSISE). Whereas the Court of Appeal hears appeals in civil cases, the appellate tribunal for *criminal* cases, functioning on the same level and collateral with the latter, is the *Assize Court* (*Cour d'Assise*). But in addition to being the appellate body for the Correctional Tribunal—the criminal section of the Court of Major Instance below—the *Cour d'Assise* has original jurisdiction in all major criminal cases, such as homicide. It does not sit with a jury when acting as an appellate tribunal, but a lot-chosen jury of nine plus three judges sits in cases of original jurisdiction. (A verdict of guilty requires a majority of eight votes.) There are ninety-five assizes, one in each *département*, each being usually staffed with three judges from the twenty-seven units of the courts of appeal. However, depending upon the work load and the availability of personnel, two of the three judges may be drafted from the local *tribunal de grande instance*, but the presiding judge is invariably a member of the *Cour d'Appel*.

In 1963, Parliament created a special tribunal to combat "subversive activity," the *Permanent Court of State Security*, largely as a direct result of terrorist activity by both civil and military elements involved in the Government's attempts to settle the difficult problem of Algeria. The tribunal consists of civilian judges and senior military officers; there is no jury. The sole appeal from its decisions is to the *Cour de Cassation*.

The Court of Cassation (COUR DE CASSATION). At the pinnacle of the regular courts of France stands its *Court of Cassation* (*Cour de Cassation*). Largely unaffected by the Judicial Reorganization Acts of 1959, 1963, and 1965, it may be regarded as the Supreme Court of Appeal of the Republic. Appropriately sitting in Paris—as ever the heart and pulse of *la patrie*—the 112-member body consists of 85 judges or, more precisely, 77 counselors (*conseillers*), the Chief Justice (*Premier Président*), 5 presidents of sections and 2 other senior judges, plus the Chief Prosecutor (*Procureur-Général*) who, together with 9 clerks of court and his staff of 17, is attached to it. Its jurisdiction extends throughout the French Republic, and it enjoys great prestige and respect.

The *Cour de Cassation* is divided into five sections (*chambres*) of fifteen judges, each headed by a président—a favorite French title—with the entire tribunal presided over by the First President or Chief Justice. Seven judges constitute a quorum to hear a case. Two sections deal with civil matters; one of these, known as the Screening Section, receives and evaluates all petitions and requests for review, conducts a preliminary inquiry into their merits, dockets those it deems to be worthy of review by the court, and rejects all others. The other three *chambres* handle commercial, social, and criminal matters, respectively. Like the House of Lords, but unlike the Supreme Court of the United States, the *Cour de Cassation* has no original jurisdiction; all cases that come to it in the hierarchy of the ordinary courts do so by way of appeal from the assizes and the courts of appeals immediately below.

Casser, the French for the verb "break" or "smash," indicates the actual role of this respected and dignified tribunal. It is distinctly a limited role, for the *Cour de Cassation* rules only on the legal appropriateness of the decision rendered—i.e. it merely passes judgment on *the point of law involved in the decision,* emphatically not on the substance of the case. It neither "decides" nor "retries" a case. It possesses simply the power to quash, *elle casse,* the legal point of a case, and *then to remand it below for retrial* by a court of the same rank as the one from which it came, but not the same court. Still, its legal interpretations are binding on all lower courts.

In no sense of the term does the *Cour de Cassation* have the power of judicial review. Indeed, it ruled itself in the case of the newspaper *Le National* that a law which had been "deliberately promulgated according to constitutional forms" was beyond attacks on grounds of unconstitutionality under the French system of separation of powers.[17] The absence of judicial review is a deficiency of power that the French courts have shared with their

FIGURE 3
THE REGULAR (ORDINARY)
COURTS OF THE FIFTH FRENCH REPUBLIC

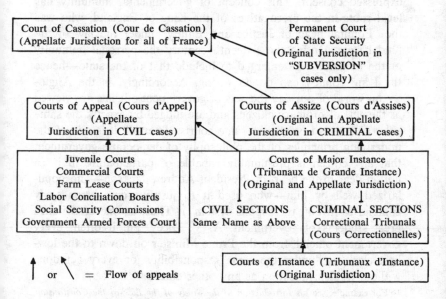

[17] See VII *Political Studies* 51–3 and 60–61 (February 1959).

264

friends across the British Channel. However, a system of what might be called quasi-judicial review, lodged in an extra-judicial body lying outside the judicial hierarchy, the *Constitutional Council* (*Conseil Constitutionnel*)—to be described in the following chapter—was adopted by the Constitution of the Fifth Republic as a successor to its rather anemic relative of the Fourth Republic, the *Constitutional Committee* (*Comité Constitutionnel*). But, as will be readily perceived, the French system of quasi-judicial review is a far cry from the bona fide power and authority vested in the United States judiciary.

Administrative Tribunals Generally

We now turn to what is unquestionably the more intriguing, because more novel, second judicial hierarchy in France, the popular and entirely separate *administrative courts* that are more or less foreign to the Anglo-Saxon world. Despite some modifications initiated in 1947 and 1946, respectively, the United Kingdom and the United States still hold, by and large, to the ancient Anglo-Saxon principle that "the King can do no wrong"—which, in effect, signifies that the sovereign, the state, cannot be used without its expressed consent. This concept of governmental immunity has legal roots in the prerogatives of the King of England, who was the "Fountainhead of Justice and Equity" under the law of the feudal state. During the sixteenth century the personal immunity of the monarch was enlarged to include that of the state—hence the King (State) can do no wrong. Accordingly, in the Anglo-Saxon world of our day the acts of government officials are viewed as the acts of ordinary citizens and are judged by exactly the same rules of law and before the same courts. After all, it is one of the underlying principles of the philosophy of democratic government that any citizen is presumably capable of participating in it (a notion dear to the heart of President Andrew Jackson—and popularized well by him—who used it to justify, some erroneously contend to invent, the "spoils system"). Thus, as one of Britain's great students of government, A. V. Dicey, put it often, every government official, from the Prime Minister on down to the lowliest clerk, is "under the same responsibility for every act done without legal justification as any other citizen."[18]

[18] For example, see his *Introduction to the Study of the Law of the Constitution*, 10th ed. (New York: The Macmillan Co., 1961).

This has meant that a British or American citizen who believes himself to have been aggrieved or injured by a government official in either of the two lands and wants to take action would *have to sue that official* who, in turn, would have to justify his actions at the bar of the regular courts. Thus, if Citizen John Smith believes that he has been wronged or maltreated by Sheriff James Doe, in the latter's capacity as an officer of the law, he may bring suit. But such a suit must be brought against Sheriff James Doe in a regular court of jurisdiction, *not* against Doe's state of Virginia, whose laws he was presumably enforcing (or against the United States, if the arresting officer had been a federal official), and the suit will read *Smith v. Doe*. Moreover, to collect damages, which would presumably come out of Doe's pocket, Citizen Smith must demonstrate successfully that Sheriff Doe has exceeded his discretionary authority under the law—an extremely difficult task in most instances.

Whatever the underlying philosophical justifications for personal liability of governmental officials, its practical implications are often unsatisfactory, to say the least, and may well be fraught with danger both to the individuals involved and the system which they serve and under which they live. Among these implications and the lessons of experience are: the possibility that an official may perform his duties timidly or haphazardly; that he may not perform them in accordance with his most considered judgment but according to expediency; the difficulty, already alluded to, of collecting from an individual government servant; the question why, in performing a duty for his government, he should be personally responsible in the first place. Moreover, there are the inevitable delays in getting a case docketed in the courts; the slowly grinding judicial process, especially in as large a country as the United States; the inconvenience and expense of bringing a case to court. All these represent factors that may well, and often do, outweigh any monetary recompense that might eventually accrue to the plaintiff.

In recognition of these very real problems, Britain and the United States have gradually begun to provide tribunals in which the state may be sued directly. No abandonment of the old philosophy of a single, unified judiciary has taken place, nor is it likely to take place in the near future. However, both countries have shown considerable interest in the institution of the Danish *ombudsman,* a sort of "people's watchdog" over administrative abuses, who commands a good deal of influence and esteem, though little direct power, and who disposes of some thousand cases annually with dispatch and expertise. Indeed, in 1967 Britain adopted a limited, highly restricted version of it—but it is so watered down that it is hardly a recognizable copy of the Danish model.[19]

Moreover, both Britain and the United States have taken some tangible steps in the direction of rendering matters a bit more palatable to government employees and citizens alike. Thus, Britain adopted the Crown Proceedings Act of 1947 which, under certain circumstances, makes the government responsible for the actions of its servants. Purposely provided with many loopholes and exceptions, the act nevertheless now enables ordinary citizens to sue the government in the same manner and before the same tribunals "as if the Crown were a fellow-citizen." Hence, the injured or aggrieved party sues the state as a matter of right. Furthermore, the act makes government departments responsible for common law as well as statutory duties. However, it should be noted that the act confines itself, more or less, to the *non-law-enforcing* agencies of government, thus leaving unchanged the path of claims that might arise under the law-enforcing units, such as police, military services, foreign affairs. Nevertheless, the statute does represent a wholesome and welcome change.[20]

What the above statute did for Britain, the Tort Claims Act of 1946 had done, broadly speaking, for the United States one year earlier insofar as the federal government is concerned. Under it, a citizen allegedly injured or aggrieved by an employee of the federal government, or the government itself, may bring suit in any civil action, other than a breach of contract—which is not a tort—against the United States for negligence or wrongful acts, no maximum monetary ceiling existing on the claim. It is also possible to

19 See the compendium on the *ombudsman,* edited by D. C. Rowat, *The Ombudsman: Citizen's Defender* (London: Allen & Unwin, 1965), containing chapters on Britain and the United States; the chapter on the United States is my "The Need for Ombudsmen in the United States." See also my "Denmark's *Folketingets Ombudsmand*: A People's Watchdog," 20 *Public Administration Review* 152 (Summer 1960).

20 For a brief evaluation of the Act, see Harry Street, *Government Liability: A Comparative Study* (Cambridge: Cambridge University Press, 1953).

make claims of less than $1000 directly to the head of any federal agency allegedly responsible for a loss caused by "negligent or wrongful act of omission of an employee," but the agency is *not required* to sanction such claims. Appeals under the provisions of the Tort Claims Act may be taken to the Court of Claims and, under certain conditions, to the regular consitutional court hierarchy.

The Court of Claims, established in 1855, as was demonstrated in some detail in Chapter IV, is itself a vehicle for citizens to sue the federal government for damages, and as such represents a modification of the "sovereign-can-do-no-wrong" principle. But its limited jurisdiction is confined to contractual, tax, and other non-tort claims against the Government of the United States. The Tort Claims Act contains, as does its British counterpart, many deliberate exceptions and ambiguities. For example, it excludes

> . . . any claim based upon an act or omission of an employee of the Government exercising due care, in the exercise of a statute or regulation, whether or not such statute or regulation be valid, or based upon the exercise or performance or the failure to exercise or perform a discretionary function or duty on the part of a federal agency or an employee of the Government, whether or not the discretion involved be abused. . . [21]

but, hopefully, it personifies a salutary trend in adjudication.[22]

[21] It should not be forgotten, of course, that in both countries exist numerous *quasi-judicial* agencies and/or tribunals that, among other duties, *adjudicate administratively* claims upon the government. These are, for example, the independent regulatory commissions and agencies in the United States, and the thirty-five odd, ministerially appointed "special administrative tribunals" in the United Kingdom, established to deal with cases arising out of the application of social policy, e.g. the Licensing Authority for Public Service Vehicles. An important development in connection with these British tribunals was the creation of the Council on Tribunals, established under the Tribunals and Inquiries Act of 1958, following the Franks Committee Report; it is charged with general supervision over all British administrative tribunals. For a perceptive explanation and analysis, see H. W. N. Wade, "The Council on Tribunals," *Public Law* 351 (1960).

[22] For an article that is still informative on the status of the doctrine of tort liability in the several states of the United States, see Robert A. Leflar and Benjamin E. Kantrowitz, 29 *New York University Law Journal* 1363 (1954), especially the "Five Major Groupings," pp. 1407–8.

THE FRENCH ADMINISTRATIVE COURTS

The hierarchy of courts that administers the *droit administratif* in France is very much part and parcel of the governmental system, however separated it is from the ordinary courts. To the French— and to many careful observers in the Anglo-Saxon world as well— theirs is the only logical system of supervising the administrative branch of the government, not only because of its rapid, convenient, and efficient adjudicatory process, but also because of the expertise inherent in the judicial personnel that staff its administrative courts. This is even more remarkable because these administrative courts are actually more closely linked to the executive, than to the judicial, branch. Evolving gradually since revolutionary days, the predominantly "judge-made" *droit administratif* has a long and honorable history, beginning with the creation of the first *Council of State* (*Conseil d'État*) under Napoleon Bonaparte.

The structure of the French administrative court system is infinitely less complicated than the regular court system. It consists of but two levels: first, the old *Interdepartmental Prefectural Councils* (*Conseils de Préfecture Interdepartmentaux*), now known simply as *Regional Councils* or *Administrative Tribunals* (*Tribunaux Administratifs*), since they are arranged no longer in *départements*, but in twenty-three national regions plus Paris; second, the famous multi-purpose, and powerful, *Council of State* (*Conseil d'État*) at the apex. (There is also a number of special collateral administrative tribunals, sometimes known as "inferior councils"—such as the *Council of Public Instruction* (*Conseil d'Instruction Publique*) and the *Draft Review Board* (*Conseil Militaire de Revision*), which may be omitted for present purposes.)

The Regional Councils (TRIBUNAUX ADMINISTRATIFS). It is to the *Tribunal Administratif* of his region that a French citizen with a complaint against the administrative branch of *La République* turns initially. In almost all instances involving the *droit administratif,* the *Tribunal Administratif* thus acts as the administrative court of first instance. It has power either to annul an illegal decision or action or to cause payment of damages. It is staffed with able, experienced civil servants who have been recruited either from the administrative branch itself, provided they have law degrees, or they are merit appointees who have passed competitive examinations. The caliber of the five members of each *tribunal administratif*—one *président*, of course, and four *conseillers*—is thus almost always outstanding even at this first instance level.

In line with the simplicity and inexpensiveness that so fortunately characterize the administrative court system of France, all a plaintiff at the bar of his *Tribunal Administratif* has to do is to execute and file the official complaint form which costs practically nothing. Normally, the tribunal will conduct the investigation of the complaint by way of written statements to both sides of the complaint. Sometimes an oral hearing is held, at which the litigants may either present arguments personally or through legal counsel. When the tribunal is ready to render a decision it will do so publicly; usually that settles the matter. Far more often than not, the complaining *citoyen* win his suit, and can then look forward to speedy compensation from the public treasury for any damages. So prevalent have been these citizen victories that considerable criticism has ensued among both legal scholars and practitioners, who believe that the administrative court system has caused the French Government to be "too tough on itself," that there exists what might be viewed as a distinct bias *against* it.

The Council of State (LE CONSEIL D'ÉTAT). With its appellate jurisdiction from the *tribunaux administratifs* as well as original jurisdiction in certain stipulated "important" and/or "delicate" cases, the *Conseil d'État* justly enjoys enormous prestige. Actually, it is far more than a merely administrative tribunal; only one of its five sections—a most renowned and most important one, the *Litigation Section (Section du Contentieux)*—deals with the *droit administratif*. The other four are concerned with drafting of legislation for the cabinet; advisory opinions on legislative and executive matters; supervision over rules of public administration; and other significant functions in the governmental process. Roughly one-half of the council's membership of 179, headed nominally by the Minister of Justice but actually by its vice president, works in the administrative court section, and its personnel is uniquely trained and qualified.

The 80-plus members of that Litigation Section are recruited in two ways, as are those of the other branches of the council: The "second class auditors"—those who enter the council at the bottom of the ladder—are drawn from graduates of the three-year course at the justly celebrated *École Nationale d'Administration*, which provides expert personnel destined for the highest levels of the corps of civil servants in France. Admission to the *École* is by stiff competitive examination, most of the applicants having had some training in the law or in political science. The school graduates fewer than 150 students annually—a figure that represents at most 5 per cent of the initial applicants—and those who do obtain their diplomas are indeed highly trained and qualified. The personel of the higher echelons of the council come from either the upper levels of the ministries, the ranks of the prefects or the legal profession, or they are promoted from lower echelons. France is justly proud of her distinguished corps of *conseillers* in the Council of State; it is truly an elite body and richly merits its great prestige and acclaim.

Eleven subsections, numbered chronologically, constitute the section of the council which handles the *droit administratif*. Each of these subsections consists of a *président* and a number of *conseillers*. Although roughly half of the subsections operate independently in readying cases for decision, two must meet jointly to render final judgment. Important cases are considered by the full "judicial section," consisting of the presiding officers of the eleven subsections plus two members of the subsection(s) where the report of the case was prepared. The highest organ of the *Conseil d'État* is its Plenary Assembly, for which are reserved cases of "extreme importance." It is composed of the seventeen highest officers of the council, in this instance including four *conseillers* from its administrative sections. Decisions by all of these organs are of equal weight, and they are final and binding.

Review Procedure. As already illustrated briefly, the procedure for obtaining review in the French administrative court hierarchy is as simple as it is inexpensive. In large measure, it is inexpensive because the French state assumes responsibility for investigating both the facts and the law involved in a plaintiff's petition. Moreover, since under the French inquisitorial procedure the judiciary plays an active role throughout the judicial process, the role of the petitioner is reduced to a summary statement as to the alleged facts and the relief prayed. He may request either of two types of review actions: (1) proceedings for the annulment of an *ultra vires*—beyond powers—administrative act (*recours pour excès de pouvoir*); or (2) proceedings to order some type of affirmative administrative action, such as payment of monetary damages (*recours de pleine jurisdiction*). Most petitions for review fall into the first category. Having received the petition, the administrative tribunal takes over; petitioner need not even retain legal counsel in the first type of case unless he chooses to do so. In any event, he need not worry, his interests will be amply guarded by the mills of the *droit administratif*. Moreover, the Council of State, *on its own cognizance*, has added a third ground for review going beyond the concept inherent in *ultra vires*—i.e. an official action beyond the scope of legal authority—namely, the famous French administrative law concept of *détournement de pouvoir*, most equitably translated as rank *abuse* of power. In its eyes, *abuse* of power is a concept different from that of an illegal *application* of power, which is governed by the first review category under *ultra vires*. Even President de Gaulle had to bow to a Council ruling in 1962: He had set up a special military tribunal to try terrorists who aided European extremists in Algeria. But when the lawyer for one of the leaders of the terrorist secret army charged de Gaulle with "an illegal administrative act" in setting up the tribunal, and took the matter to the Council of State, the latter agreed and ruled it illegal indeed! (One year later Parliament created the Court of State Security described earlier.)

Once the Council of State has granted the availability of review, it must define the extent or scope of its reviewing power on the merits. This is especially true in the first category cases, under which the legality of an administrative action may be challenged on three grounds, all of which fall under the *ultra vires* concept: (1) lack of jurisdiction; (2) failure to observe procedures defined by law; (3) errror of law. To these three the special category of abuse of power is then added.

Evaluation. It is hardly surprising that the Council of State is literally swamped with petitions for action and review! The same applies to the lower rung of the administrative court system. The French people look up to it as a reliable and virile guardian of individual rights against administrative encroachment. Moreover, as well they might, they have great faith in the ability of these high-class civil servants to dispose of the thousands upon thousands of cases that reach them year by year. Small wonder, as has been indicated, that Anglo-Saxon states have given considerable thought to the adoption of a similar system. The Task Force of the Second Hoover Commission in the United States, for one, urgently suggested some form of administrative court system for its federal government.

Not only does the French system provide for fuller review of administrative action than the average Anglo-Saxon one, but the cost of litigation is smaller; accessibility to the courts is greater; review is more easily available; scope of review is larger; state liability for damages is less circumscribed; and settlement is far more prompt and efficient. The French state, whatever the wisdom of its philosophy of government here may be, simply considers itself totally liable for service-connected faults of public officers and state agencies. That liability has even been extended to cover most cases in which the damage is caused by personal fault of public officials, for the administrative courts have held that such faults are often inseparably connected with the administrative service of which the official is an agent. In such cases, the state indemnifies the damages to the injured citizen, and the officer at fault becomes personally liable to the state.

Yet not only does the French state accept liability for fault under the *droit administratif*, but as outlined earlier, also for risk. In other words, if proper administrative action results in an unequal burden on, or a social injustice to, a citizen, the state bears the cost of equalizing the burden—without the need to introduce a private bill in the legislature. In effect, the *droit administratif* is developing in the direction of absolute liability to ensure equitable sharing among all citizens of the burden of government action. This may well be far from an unmixed blessing; but the French administrative court system, with the *Conseil d'État* standing at its apex,[23] has operated so successfully and has proved to be such a bulwark against arbitrary actions by the centralized state, that it richly merits the careful attention that has been extended to it increasingly by students and practitioners of government alike.

[23] For a superb, complete study of the *Conseil d'État*, see Charles E. Freedman, *The Conseil d'État in Modern France* (New York: Columbia University Press, 1961), and Karl Loewenstein's review of it in the *Annals of the American Academy of Political and Social Science* 166 (September 1961).

A NOTE ON
THE JUDICIARY OF THE SOVIET UNION

Because of the oligarchical nature of the effective instrumentalities of government in the Union of Soviet Socialist Republics, law and judiciary—the entire judicial process—are in a category of their own. Despite the series of mild reforms that were adopted in the mid- and late 1930's and the far more significant ones of the post-Stalin era, especially those of 1957–59 and 1961–63, law in Russia of today is still employed principally as a tool of the state; it is utilized for purposes of conformity; it is an organ of state power *par excellence*. The rights of the citizens under such a system are often illusory. Moreover, certain rights specifically enumerated under the Constitution of the USSR, are qualified by such tellingly realistic phrases as ". . . unless otherwise provided by law . . .," such as Article III of the Constitution of the 1936, as amended, dealing with the right to public trial.[24] However, the post-1953 Soviet law reforms have rendered this and a host of other substantive and procedural concepts more meaningful—if in a limited manner.[25]

Although theoretically all law is inherently coercive and conformist, the fundamentally arbitrary characteristic of Soviet law is a logical by-product of the traditional concept of Marxism, where law is viewed as an instrument of domination, as a coercive tool of the state in its transition from socialism to communism, where the *duties* of a citizen prevail over his *rights*. This characteristically coercive interpretation has been embraced quite naturally by the Soviet jurists, who follow Lenin's dictum that law is "nothing if there is no apparatus adapted to coerce people into observing its provisions."[26] Hence the absence of meaningful guarantees to freedom under Soviet rule. It should be noted, however, that the legal system and machinery of justice in the Soviet Union—which in its

---

24 *Constitution (Fundamental Law) of the Union of Soviet Socialist Republics* (Moscow: Foreign Languages Publishing House, 1962), p. 91.

25 For an informative analysis see Harold J. Berman, "Legality vs. Terror: The Post-Stalin Law Reforms," in Gwendolyn M. Carter and Alan F. Westin (eds.), *Politics in Europe: 5 Cases in European Government* (New York: Harcourt, Brace & World, Inc., 1965), pp. 179–205.

26 From V. I. Lenin, *Sochineniia*, as quoted by George C. Guins, *Soviet Law and Soviet Society* (The Hague: Martinus Nijhoff, 1954), p. 45.

outward structure and functioning was derived largely from the French system—grinds in an entirely different manner when it deals with an ordinary transgression, that is, one not involving the state as a politico-economic institution per se. In the former case, adjudication will be effected by the tribunals involved in roughly the same manner known throughout the world; but in the latter, law becomes the political organ of state power, the instrument of the class that constitutes the regime of the land, a mere adjunct of state power in pursuit of conformity within Soviet society.

THE ABSENCE OF AN INDEPENDENT JUDICIARY

There is not, indeed there cannot be, a truly independent judiciary under Soviet Rule. Any meaningful power to check and balance the other branches of the government—assuming there are purposeful distinctions at all—is necessarily illusory. On the contrary, the judiciary of the Soviet Union is effectively subjugated to the legislative bodies or to those governmental bodies that provide legislative functions—even if these are really nothing or little more than decrees sanctioned by the Communist party.

The judiciary does not, of course, possess the power of effective judicial review. If that power exists anywhere at all in the USSR— really an academic question—its resides in the Presidium of the Supreme Soviet, which is specifically charged under the Constitution with the "interpretation of the laws."

Moreover, throughout the judicial hierarchy, both the professional and the lay judges, known as *assessors,* are *elected* for short terms of office—not exceeding five years—by legislative bodies, soviets, or residents of the districts in which they serve, *and* they are all subject to recall at any time. Either faithful party members or acceptable "non-party Bolsheviks," these judges—aged twenty-five and over—represent the political power of the state, and the eyes of the dominant elements of Soviet society are constantly fixed upon them.

THE COURT HIERARCHY

One of the most salient features of the judicial hierarchy of the USSR is its high degree of centralization, despite the federal structure of the government and despite the myriad courts in the various and manifold geographic subdivisions below. The sole truly "federal" court is the Supreme Court of the USSR, which enjoys corrective power over the lower courts. But more important is the overriding supervisory power of the "boss" of the entire judicial system, the Procurator-General, the "supreme overseer of Soviet legality," who will be described more fully below.

The Comradely Court. At the lowest level of the Soviet judiciary is the *Comradely Court,* a rather unique institution that acually falls outside the regular hierarchy. More appropriately, these units, which may be found at local levels everywhere in the land, have been called "social" or "honour courts."[27] Staffed by local citizens for the adjudication of disputes between individuals, comradely courts are organized as *ad hoc* bodies in villages, farm co-operatives, apartment houses, factories, or any other place of work or dwelling where they might be needed to deal with the sundry petty offenses that invariably take place among people everywhere, whatever their political philosophy may be. The "judges" of the Comradely Court in a particular unit or locality are normally elected for each case that arises by the membership of the geographical or occupational unit concerned, or they may comprise all those present at a meeting of that unit. Their jurisdiction materially extended with the 1963 court reforms, they can now deal with petty hooliganism, petty thefts in the case of first-time offenders, petty speculation, plus a host of other minor infractions. They may also levy reprimands and small fines; order an offender to apologize; administer "public censure"; propose that an offender be evicted from his dwelling; propose that he be transferred to a job paying less; or require the payment of damages to the victim of up to $55.00. Probably the most important cases tried by these courts—which since 1963 may also operate in factories and other places of work to make non-obligatory recommendations to management for "corrective action"—are those involving breaches of "labor discipline" and "standards of behavior in communal apartments." In the words of a leading authority on Soviet courts, the basic aim is "reform" of the "anti-social offender" and "the entire procedure is conceived as a lesson in communist morality."[28]

27 Robert G. Neumann, op. cit. p. 616.
28 Harold J. Berman. *Justice in the U.S.S.R.*, rev. ed., enl. (New York: Vintage Books, 1963), pp. 289–90.

But since these comradely courts are really not recognized as courts per se, their decisions are subject to annulment by the level immediately above, the People's Court. This is true for all judgments *except* a new classification, devised in 1959, and confirmed and expanded in 1963, concerning decisions of special comradely courts in connection with "speculators, hooligans, unemployed elements, etc. and generally "unsocialist behavior." Those found guilty of one of these offenses at a meeting of "friends and neighbors" constituted as the Comradely Court of jurisdiction, may be punished by as much as five years' banishment from their place of residence.[29] The People's Court above may not review that type of decision, although the local *soviets* (legislatures) do have that power.

The People's Court. If we omit the level of the quasi-tribunal just discussed, the base of the Soviet judiciary is actually occupied by the *People's Court.* Organized on a district basis throughout the Soviet Union, the people's courts are strictly courts of original jurisdiction in both criminal and civil cases—except for their tangential supervisory power over the comradely courts. As the workhorse courts of the entire system, they handle the bulk of the minor criminal and civil cases in the USSR. The Council of Ministers of the pertinent Union or Autonomous Republic concerned determines the number of people's courts to be established in each district (*raion*). They are locally staffed by one judge, as chairman, and two assessors; the former is elected by the inhabitants of the district for five years and the latter for two. The judge is not statutorily required to be a professional, although he usually is; the assessors, being "lay judges," have no formal judicial or legal background.

Assessors, who come from all walks of life and who usually serve only for a brief period—perhaps up to two weeks annually—are emphatically not to be regarded as jurors in the typical Western sense. No juries as the West knows them exist in the Soviet Union. When the assessors hear and decide a case, they act as judges and have a full voice and vote on the various aspects of the facts and law of a case as well as in the decision itself. Although the experience of the professional judge on the People's Court normally carries more weight and more often than not prevails, it would be

[29]Neumann, loc. cit. p. 616.

erroneous to view the assessors as mere adjuncts or a fifth wheel. They are part and parcel of the judicial process here.[30]

The Courts of the Region, Autonomous Region, and Autonomous Republic. Now matters become somewhat more complicated. At the next level, or really at the next three levels, lie the intermediate courts, arranged according to territorial divisions that bridge the hierarchical gap between the level of the People's Court and that of the *Supreme Court of the Union Republic.* Not *all* multiple rungs of these intermediate courts will inevitably be present in *all* union republics, certainly not in the smaller ones—although sometimes there will even be a fourth (the Area)—but they are sufficiently standardized to represent a definite pattern. Their jurisdiction is both original and appellate. In the exercise of the appellate function, they review decisions coming to them from the sundry people's courts of their respective territories, and when an appeal has been decided by a minimum of three regular judges sitting *en banc* it is final.

The courts of the regions, autonomous regions, and autonomous republics have original jurisdiction in the more serious criminal and civil cases. Among the former, according to the criminal code, are "counterrevolutionary activities, crimes against administrative order when they involve particular danger to the state, the pillaging of socialist property, and other important economic crimes." In the realm of civil jurisdiction lie cases involving the state and social institutions, public enterprises, and organizations. The work of these courts is usually performed by panels of five professional judges and assessors, holding the titles of chairman, deputy chairman, members, and people's assessors, all of whom are elected for five-year terms by the soviets (legislative bodies) of the areas or regions concerned.

The Supreme Court of the Union Republic. In each Union Republic—the largest constituent part of the federal structure of the Soviet Union—lies a *Supreme Court of the Union Republic,* constituting the highest judicial body of that division. Its members,

---

[30] In the United States, Vermont's Constitution provides for an intriguing system of laymen or "side judges" in the county courts of that state. They are elected in each county to serve with a judge. It should also be noted that the institution of "assessors" is present, whatever its particular nomenclature, in several countries of Continental Europe and in European-based legal systems elsewhere.

headed by five professional judges—but also comprising the ubiquitous assessors—are elected for five-year terms by the Supreme Soviet of the Union Republic. These high courts have both original and appellate jurisdiction. In the latter sphere of their work, they are empowered to set aside the decisions of any inferior court in the Republic; and appellate decision rendered here becomes final and binding. Related to that jurisdiction is their power to supervise all inferior courts by receiving and acting on "protests" against verdicts rendered below, coming to them from the Procurator-General or the Chairman of the Supreme Court of the USSR or by the corresponding officials of the lower echelons—one of the more intriguing practices in the Soviet Union, which, in effect, institutionalizes double jeopardy at the discretion of the state! The Supreme Court of the Union Republic has original jurisdiction in the more serious criminal and civil cases, including those involving infractions committed in office by the higher officials of government in the Republic. Its decisions are final.

The Supreme Court of the USSR. At the pinnacle of the judicial hierarchy in the Soviet Union stands the *Supreme Court of the USSR,* classified by Article 104 of the Constitution of 1936 as its "highest judicial organ." Elected by the Supreme Soviet of the USSR for five-year terms of office, its membership consists of a chairman, two vice chairmen, nine professional judges, and twenty people's assessors. Moreover, attached to it as members *ex officio* are the fifteen chairmen of the supreme courts of the union republics, but these do not necessarily sit on a steady basis. The regular members of the Supreme Court are divided into three specialized *collegia* (panels), one each for civil, criminal, and military matters, but the entire Court is charged to meet at least once every three months in plenary session (the *plenum*). The chairman may preside over any case before the Court and he has the power to relieve or discharge any inferior court in the Soviet Union of a case in order to "protest" it in plenary session—sessions that are invariably attended by the Procurator-General.

Despite the implications of the Supreme Court's division of labor and jurisdiction, it is basically a court of review and appeals, a supervisory court. As such it even has the authority to initiate legislation dealing with the judicial system, although that power is not very meaningful. Yet, as already explained, it emphatically

lacks the power of judicial review; nor does it possess the authority to interpret laws, a function theoretically reserved, as is the
former, to the Presidium of the Supreme Soviet of the USSR. But
it may give advice to the Presidium in cases of interpretation.
Nevertheless, the civil and criminal *collegia* do serve as tribunals
of original jurisdiction in cases of exceptional nation-wide significance. When it exercises original jurisdiction, a *collegium* consists
of one professional judge as chairman and two assessors; in its
appellate or review jurisdiction all its members are regular judges.
The remaining *collegium,* the military, has jurisdiction in a small
number of particularly significant cases of treason, espionage, and
other high crimes against the state. It may also review appeals
from, and protests against, the judgments of lower military tribunals. Except in the sense that there is always the possibility of
an appeal to the Presidium of the Supreme Soviet, decisions of the
Supreme Court of the USSR are final and binding. But far more
significant on the scales of power and authority in the judicial
system of the Soviet Union than any court is the Procurator-
General and his own extensive hierarchy of procurators throughout
the land.

THE PROCURATOR-GENERAL

The best indication of the subordination, centralization, and lack
of independence of the judicial hierarchy in the Soviet Union is
the existence of the *Procurator-General,* sometimes known as
Public Prosecutor or Public Procurator. No official associated with
the legal or judicial process of comparable authority exists anywhere today—certainly not in the free world. An institution conceived by Tsar Peter the Great in 1722 and revived by Lenin after
a five-year lapse in 1922, he combines his position atop the entire
judiciary with that of watchdog of the application and interpretation of criminal law on all levels of government, either directly or
indirectly, as well as all civil law. Chosen by the Supreme Soviet
of the USSR for a term of seven years, the Procurator-General,
in turn, appoints, or causes to be appointed, the various procurators for five year terms on the lower levels throughout the USSR
(see chart below). His is truly a centralized and centralizing
posture, and although he is technically responsible for his actions

to the Supreme Soviet, in effect he is responsible solely to the Communist party's top echelon, the Presidium and the Secretariat. His subordinate procurators, too, are independent of all local organs of government; as guardians of local conformity they are responsible solely to their chief, the Procurator-General in Moscow.

Powers and Functions. Always held by a high-ranking, trusted member of the Communist party, the position of Procurator-General is eagerly sought and influential. Andrei Vyshinsky, who occupied the office during the famous purge trial years in the late 1930's, whence he steadily advanced, ultimately to become Foreign Minister and Russia's Representative to the United Nations, described the Procurator-General as the "watchman of socialist legality, the leader of the policy of the Communist party and of Soviet authority, the champion of socialism."[31] Even if this appraisal be somewhat embellished, it comes close to the verities of a system of law in which the Procurator-General personifies an omnipotent force. In Nikita Khrushchev's words, he "must stand guard over the laws of the Soviet Union."[32]

In addition to his basic authority—outlined in Article 113 of the Constitution—namely to ensure the strict observance of the law by all ministries and institutions as well as by all officials and citizens of the Soviet Union at large and, under a 1955 statute, to exercise the function of "general superviser" over the legality of acts of all state organs," he possesses the following prerogatives: He may conduct a *juge d'instruction* type of pre-trial preliminary investigation (as may also the KGB—the secret police—and the regular police); he may act in the nature of a Scandinavian *ombudsman* (see pp. 266 ff., *supra*), which the Soviet Union claims to have invented; he has the right to appear in any civil case on behalf of either party at any point during a trial; he may re-open a completed or closed trial by means of the now familiar "protest"—although the period of time during which this can be done seems to have been shortened from five years to two by the reforms of 1957; and he may review the judgment of any court,

31 *The Law of the Soviet State* (New York: The Macmillan Co., 1948), p. 537.
32 Quoted in Glenn G. Morgan, *Soviet Administrative Legality: The Role of the Attorney General's Office* (Stanford: Stanford University Press, 1962), citing *Izvestia* of January 25, 1958. Professor Morgan's fine book is exclusively devoted to the Soviet procuracy.

FIGURE 4
THE JUDICIARY AND PROCURACY OF THE USSR

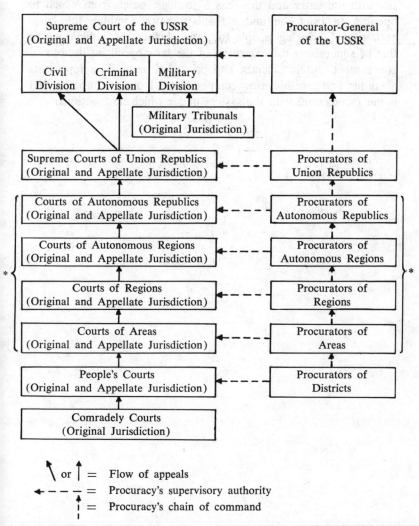

* These provincial or territorial subdivisions and levels are not necessarily present everywhere in the USSR, nor do they necessarily carry identical nomenclature in the various jurisdictions marked. This fact pertains to the procuracy as well as the courts.

regardless of whether the case was adjudicated in a lower court or the *plenum* of the Supreme Court of the USSR. Moreover, he sits with the latter and thus has a strategic perch from which to operate. In brief, he and his subordinates combine the basic authority of bringing people to justice before the judiciary with that of supervising the execution of the laws by all institutions of government, public officials, and private citizens. This represents a unique and awe-inspiring compendium of power, but one that is not inconsistent with the system under which he functions.

VII

JUDICIAL REVIEW:

I THE SUPREME POWER

DEFINING JUDICIAL REVIEW

Certainly the most controversial and at the same time the most fascinating role of the courts of the United States in general, and of the Supreme Court in particular, is the exercise of the power of *judicial review*. It is commonly viewed with almost equal amounts of reverence and suspicion. Edward S. Corwin regarded it as "democracy's way of covering its bet."[1] In its full majesty and range it is a power that the *ordinary* courts—i.e. those that are part of the formal judicial hierarchy—of merely a handful of other countries in the world possess with varying degree of effectiveness; among these are Australia, Brazil, Burma, Canada, India, Pakistan, and Japan, of whom most have federal systems of government.[2] It is all but axiomatic that the practice would be found more readily in federal than in unitary states. Briefly stated, judicial review is the power of any court to *hold unconstitutional and hence unenforceable any law, any official action based upon a law, and any other action by a public official that it deems*—upon careful, normally painstaking, reflection and in line with the canons of the taught tradition of the law as well as judicial self-restraint—*to be in conflict with the Basic Law, in the United States its Constitution.* In other words, in invoking the power of judicial review, a court applies the *superior* of two laws, which at the level of the federal judiciary of the United States signifies the Constitution instead of the legislative statute or some action by a public official allegedly or actually based upon it.

1 Review of Benjamin F. Wright's article, "Growth of American Constitutional Law," 56 *Harvard Law Review* 487 (1942).
2 For an informative summary discussion, see K. C. Wheare, *Federal Government*, 4th ed. (New York: Oxford University Press, 1964), Ch. IV, "The Constitution, the Courts, and the Law." Judicial review in *Switzerland* is confined to cantonal legislation.

284

In the United States, which will serve as the chief subject in
this treatment of judicial review, this highly significant instrument
of power—"the principled process of enunciating and applying
certain enduring values of our society"—is possessed theoretically
by *every* court, no matter[3] how high or low on the judicial ladder.
Although it is admittedly rare, it is not at all impossible for a
judge in a low-level court of one of the fifty states to declare a
federal law unconstitutional! Such a decision would quite naturally
at once be appealed to higher echelons for review and almost
certain reversal, but the possibility does exist. Conscious of the
nature and purpose of federalism and the need to permit legislative
bodies to act in accordance with their best judgment, no matter
how unwise that may well be at times, courts are understandably
loathe to invoke the judicial veto. Yet their power to do so, and
especially that of the Supreme Court of the United States, serves
as an omnipresent and potentially omnipotent check upon the
legislative branches of government. While that highest tribunal, in
a total of 94 or 95 cases (depending upon the count), has to date
(March 1968) declared but 102 provisions of *federal* laws unconstitutional out of a total of over 70,000 public and private
laws passed, some 750 *state* laws[4] and provisions of *state* constitutions have run wholly or partly afoul of that judicial checkmate
since 1789—some 650 of these coming after 1870. An example
of the latter action is the Court's unanimous ruling in *Torcaso v.
Watkins*:[5] in it it struck down a provision of the Maryland Constitution on the ground that to compel officeholders to declare
belief in God constituted a "religious test for public office" that
invaded the individual's right to religious freedom. In many ways,
the Court's power over state actions is of more significance to the
federal system than the much more publicized and more well-
known power over federal actions.

Tables VII and VIII illustrate in some detail the power of
judicial review over legislative enactments as exercised by the
Supreme Court at the *federal level only*. But it is interesting to
note that more statutes of the State of Louisiana have been de-

3 Alexander M. Bickel, *The Least Dangerous Branch* (Indianapolis. The Bobbs-
Merrill Co., 1962), p. 58.
4 E.g. three basic New York State "anti-subversive" laws and several related
regulations in one decision in 1967 (*Keyishian v. Board of Regents*, 385
U. S. 589).
5 367 U. S. 488 (1961).

clared unconstitutional than those of any other state—Louisiana being the only one of the 50 to employ *civil law* as its judicial system. Regarding the sparse number of federal statutes held unconstitutional by the post-"anti New Deal" Supreme Court in recent times, the eighteen provisions of congressional enactments that as of this writing (March 1968) have fallen since 1937—actually since 1943—all did so because they infringed certain personal liberties safeguarded under the Constitution. The sixteen Court decisions were as follows:

(1) *Tot v. United States* (1943).[6] A statutory presumption that a known criminal in possession of firearms or ammunition must have carried them in violation of the Federal Firearms Act of 1938, Section 2(f), was invalidated 8:0 as a violation of the due process of law clause of the Fifth Amendment.

(2) *United States v. Lovett* (1946).[7] Section 304 of the Urgent Defense Appropriation Act of 1943, which barred the salaries of certain specifically named federal employees, was struck down 8:0 as violative of the constitutional prohibition against a Bill of Attainder.

(3) *United States v. Cardiff* (1952).[8] Section 704 of the Food, Drug, and Cosmetic Act, which deals with factory inspection, fell 8:1 as unconstitutionally vague under the due process clause of the Fifth Amendment.

(4) *Bolling v. Sharpe* (1954).[9] The federal companion case to the *Public School Segregation Cases*,[10] unanimously held unconstitutional as a violation of the due process of law clause of the Fifth Amendment an 1862 federal statute that, insofar as pertinent here, provided for separate schools for white and Negro children.

(5) *United States ex rel Toth v. Quarles* (1955).[11] The Court held unconstitutional 6:3 Article 3A of the Uniform Code of Military Justice when applied to a *former* member of the United States Air Force, as violative of the guarantees of the civilian judicial process inherent in Article III of the Constitution.

(6) *Reid v. Covert* (1957) coupled with *Kinsella v. Singleton, et al.* (1960).[12] These two cases concerned a series of related

6 319 U.S. 463.
7 328 U.S. 303.
8 344 U.S. 174.
9 347 U.S. 497.
10 *Brown v. Board of Education of Topeka, Kansas, et al*, 347 U.S. 483 (1954).
11 350 U.S. 11.
12 354 U.S. 1 and 361 U.S. 234.

decisions in which the Court dealt with several aspects of Article 2(11) of the Uniform Code of Military Justice, and by votes ranging from a high of 7:2 to a low of 5:4, found some of these unconstitutional as applied to various civilians accompanying the armed forces. The pertinent sections of the Code in the five cases here fell as violative of the individuals' rights under Article III and Amendments V and VI of the Constitution, including the right to a trial by jury, indictment by grand jury, and public trial in a civilian court before an impartial jury of one's peers.

(7) *Trop v. Dulles* (1958).[13] Here the narrowly divided Court struck down section 401(G) of the Nationality Act of 1940, holding that Congress had exceeded its military and expatriation powers in making desertion in time of war punishable by expatriation. The Court ruled 5:4 that to expatriate for such a reason constituted "cruel and unusual punishment," forbidden by Amendment VIII.

(8) and (9) *Kennedy v. Mendoza-Martinez* and *Rusk v. Cort* (1963).[14] Although these two cases were decided together (and under the same citation), the Court's 5:4 decision in effect held two sections of different congressional statutes unconstitutional as violative of procedural safeguards found in Amendments V and VI. Thus affected was Section 349 (a) (10) of the Immigration and Nationality Act of 1952 and Section 401 (j) of the Nationality Act of 1940, which had provided for automatic expatriation of United States citizens who, in order to evade military service, either fled the country or refused to return upon draft-board notification.

(10) *Schneider v. Rusk* (1964).[15] In another citizenship decision the Supreme Court here invalidated 5:3 Section 352 (a) (1) of the 1940 Nationality Act, chiefly on due process of law grounds under the Fifth Amendment. Section 352 had deprived *naturalized* American citizens of their citizenship if they returned to the territory of their birth and then resided there for more than three years.

(11) *Aptheker v. Secretary of State* (1964).[16] Here a 6:3 majority of the Court declared unconstitutional on its face Section 6 of Title I of the Subversive Activities Control Act of 1950,

13 356 U.S. 86.
14 372 U.S. 144.
15 377 U.S. 163.
16 378 U.S. 500.

which proscribed the application or the use of a United States passport by any member of an organization required to register under the Act's provisions. The Court held Section 6 ". . . too broadly and indiscriminately restricts the right of travel and thereby abridges the liberty guaranteed by the Fifth Amendment."

(12) *Lamont v. Postmaster-General* and *Fixa v. Heilberg* (1965).[17] In its *first* decision voiding an Act of Congress on the ground that it violated the freedom of speech guarantee of the First Amendment, the Court unanimously declared unconstitutional a section of the Postal Services and Federal Employees Salary Act of 1962, which provided that all mail matter originating abroad, except first class mail, which the Secretary of the Treasury held to be "communist political propaganda," was to be detained and that the addressee was to be notified that it could be delivered to him only if he sent a card stating that desire.

(13) *United States v. Brown* (1965).[18] The Court, in one of its rare applications of the Bill of Attainder rule, held 5:4 that Section 504 of the Labor-Management Reporting and Disclosures (Landrum-Griffin) Act of 1959, making it a crime for a member of the Communist party to serve as an officer or employee of a labor union, was in fact such an unconstitutional piece of legislation.

(14) *United States v. Romano* (1965).[19] Unanimously, the Court reversed a conviction under a federal statute providing that the presence of a defendant at the site of an illegal still was sufficient to authorize a conviction for possession and control of that still, unless the defendant satisfactorily explained his presence to the jury. It held such a statutory presumption of guilt to be an unconstitutional violation of substantive due process of law under the Fifth Amendmment.

(15) *Afroyim v. Rusk* (1967).[20] Here, in an enormously significant decision, the Court ruled 5:4 that Congress lacks the constitutional authority to pass *any* laws that strip American citizens of their nationality *without their express consent.* Specifically, it declared unconstitutional that section of the already tattered Nationality Act of 1940 that deprived United States citizens of their nationality if they voted in a foreign election—and thereby

17 381 U.S. 301.
18 381 U.S. 437.
19 382 U.S. 136.
20 387 U.S. 253.

288

overruled a 1958 decision that had held 5:4 to the contrary![21]

(16) *United States v. Robel* (decided December 11, 1967). On its last Opinion Day of 1967, the Court 6:2 struck down as an unconstitutional infringement of the freedom of association guarantees of the First Amendment a section of the much-battered Subversive Activities Control Act of 1950 that made it a crime for Communist party members to work in defense plants.

(17) and (18) *Marchetti v. United States* and *Haynes v. United States* (both decided January 29, 1968). And in two 7:1 decisions the Court declared unconstitutional as a violation of the Fifth Amendment's privilege against compulsory self-incrimination pertinent sections of the Gambling Tax Act of 1951 and the Firearms Act of 1934.

State legislation, too has thus—with generally minor excep-

TABLE VII
U. S. SUPREME COURT DECLARATIONS
OF UNCONSTITUTIONALITY OF FEDERAL LAWS, I (Arranged chronologically in accordance with tenure of the Chief Justices.)

Time Span	Chief Justice(s)	Number of Declarations of Unconstitutionality	Commentary
1789–1801	Jay J. Rutledge Ellsworth	0	Weak, placid Court
1801–1835	Marshall	1	1803: *Marbury v. Madison*
1836–1857	Taney	0	
1857–1864	Taney	1	1857: *Dred Scott v. Sanford*
1864–1873	Chase	10	1870: *Legal Tender Cases*
1874–1888	Waite Fuller	8	1883: *Civil Rights Cases*
1888–1910	Fuller	14 (15)	1895: *Income Tax Cases*
1910–1921	White Taft	13	1918: *Child Labor Case*
1921–1930	Taft	13	1923: *Minimum Wage Case*
1930–1936	Hughes	16	Of these 13 came in 1934–36!
1936–1943	Hughes Stone	0	
1943–Present*	Stone Vinson Warren	2 1 15	See pp. 285ff., *supra*.
		94 (95)	

* As of March 1968.

[21] *Perez v. Brownell*, 356 U.S. 44.

tions[22]—been held unconstitutional largely because of infringement of civil rights and liberties, although a number of instances
involved cases of state interference with national interests, especially in the realm of interstate commerce.

After the famous decision in *Marbury v. Madison*[23] in 1803
in which Mr. Chief Justice Marshall enunciated the doctrine of
judicial review—although it was not really the first instance of its
application[24]—no other federal legislation was declared unconstitutional by his Court during the remaining thirty-two years of his
long tenure of thirty-four years.[25] Nevertheless, the Marshall Court
wielded immense power and, guided by the dominant figure of the
great Chief Justice, probably did more than either of the other two
branches of the national government to make the young United
States a strong, vigorous, powerful nation, and its Constitution a
living, effective, elastic Basic Law. Not until Mr. Chief Justice
Taney's crucial decision in *Dred Scott v. Sandford*[26] in 1857 was
another federal statute struck down by the Court; and the greatest
crisis evoked by that power of the Supreme Court did not arrive
until, dominated by the doctrinaire conservatives among the so-
called Nine Old Men, the Court declared unconstitutional no less
than thirteen New Deal laws in 1934–36.

TABLE VIII
U. S. SUPREME COURT DECLARATIONS
OF UNCONSTITUTIONALITY OF FEDERAL LAWS, II*

Under Chief Justice	Recorded Declaration Number	Citation of Case and Year Decided	Vote
Marshall	1	*Marbury v. Madison,* 1 Cranch 137 (1803)	6:0
Taney	2	*Dred Scott v. Sandford,* 19 Howard 393 (1857)	7:2
Chase	3	*Gordon v. United States,* 2 Wallace 561 (1865)	8:2

* As of Winter 1967–68.

[22] E.g. *Wood v. Lovett,* 313 U.S. 362 (1941) and *Morey v. Doud,* 354 U.S. 451 (1957).
[23] 1 Cranch 137.
[24] See this chapter, pp. 308–9 and fns. 58–65.
[25] The Circuit Court of Appeals for the District of Columbia did strike down by a vote of 2:1 a congressional statute in *U. S. v. Benjamin More* only six months after *Marbury v. Madison.*
[26] 19 Howard 393.

Under Chief Justice	Recorded Declaration Number	Citation of Case and Year Decided	Vote
Chase	4	*Ex parte Garland,* 4 Wallace 33 (1867)	5:4
Chase	5	*Reichert v. Felps,* 6 Wallace 160 (1868)	8:0
Chase	6	*The Alicia,* 7 Wallace 571 (1869)	8:0
Chase	7	*Hepburn v. Griswold,* 8 Wallace 603 (1870)	4:3
Chase	8	*United States v. DeWitt,* 9 Wallace 41 (1870)	9:0
Chase	9	*The Justices v. Murray,* 9 Wallace 274 (1870)	9:0
Chase	10	*The Collector v. Day,* 11 Wallace 113 (1871)	8:1
Chase	11	*United States v. Klein,* 13 Wallace 128 (1872)	7:2
Chase	12	*United States v. Baltimore & Ohio Railway,* 17 Wallace 322 (1873)	7:2
Waite	13	*United States v. Reese,* 92 U. S. 214 (1876)	7:2
Waite	14	*United States v. Fox,* 95 U. S. 670 (1878)	9:0
Waite	15	*Trade Mark Cases,* 100 U. S. 82 (1879)	9:0
Waite	16	*United States v. Harris,* 106 U. S. 629 (1883)	8:1
Waite	17	*Civil Rights Cases,* 109 U. S. 3 (1883)	8:1
Waite	18	*Boyd v. United States,* 116 U. S. 616 (1886)	7:2
Waite	19	*Baldwin v. Franks,* 120 U. S. 678 (1887)	7:1
None*	20	*Callan v. Wilson,* 127 U. S. 540 (1888)	8:0
Fuller	21	*Monongahela Nav. Co. v. U. S.,* 148 U. S. 312 (1893)	8:0
Fuller	22	*Pollock v. Farmers' L. & T. Co.,* 157 U. S. 429 (1895)	6:2
Fuller	22A	*Pollock v. Farmers' L. & T. Co.,* 158 U. S. 601 (1895)	5:4
Fuller	23	*Wong Wing v. United States,* 163 U. S. 228 (1896)	8:0

* Mr. Chief Justice Waite died before the case was heard and was not replaced by Mr. Chief Justice Fuller until after it had been decided.

Fuller	24	*Kirby v. United States,*	
		174 U. S. 47 (1899)	6:2
Fuller	25	*Jones v. Meehan,*	
		175 U. S. 1 (1899)	9:0
Fuller	26	*Fairbank v. United States,*	
		181 U. S. 283 (1901)	5:4
Fuller	27	*James v. Bowman,*	
		190 U. S. 127 (1903)	6:2
Fuller	28	*Matter of Heff,*	
		197 U. S. 488 (1905)	8:1
Fuller	29	*Rassmussen v. United States,*	
		197 U. S. 516 (1905)	9:0
Fuller	30	*Hodges v. United States,*	
		203 U. S. 1 (1906)	7:2
Fuller	31	*Employers' Liability Cases,*	
		207 U. S. 463 (1908)	5:4
Fuller	32	*Adair v. United States,*	
		208 U. S. 161 (1908)	6:2
Fuller	33	*Keller v. United States,*	
		213 U. S. 138 (1909)	6:3
Fuller	34	*United States v. Evans,*	
		213 U. S. 297 (1909)	9:0
White	35	*Muskrat v. United States,*	
		219 U. S. 346 (1911)	9:0
White	36	*Coyle v. Oklahoma,*	
		221 U. S. 559 (1911)	7:2
White	37	*Choate v. Trapp,*	
		224 U. S. 665 (1912)	9:0
White	38	*Butts v. Mer. & Miners' Co.,*	
		230 U. S. 126 (1913)	9:0
White	39	*United States v. Hvoslef,*	
		237 U. S. 1 (1915)	8:0
White	40	*Thames & Mersey Mar. Ins. Co.*	
		v. U. S., 237 U. S. 19 (1915)	8:0
White	41	*Hammer v. Dagenhart,*	
		247 U. S. 251 (1918)	5:4
White	42	*Knickerbocker Ice Co. v. Stewart,*	
		253 U. S. 149 (1920)	5:4
White	43	*Eisner v. Macomber,*	
		252 U. S. 189 (1920)	5:4
White	44	*Evans v. Gore,*	
		253 U. S. 245 (1920)	7:2
White	45	*United States v. Cohen Grocery Co.,*	
		255 U. S. 81 (1921)	6:2
White	46	*Weeds, Inc. v. United States,*	
		255 U. S. 109 (1921)	6:2

Under Chief Justice	Recorded Declaration Number	Citation of Case and Year Decided	Vote
White	47	Newberry v. United States, 256 U. S. 232 (1921)	5:4
Taft	48	United States v. Moreland, 258 U. S. 433 (1922)	5:3
Taft	49	Child Labor Tax Case, 259 U. S. 20 (1922)	8:1
Taft	50	Hill v. Wallace, 259 U. S. 44 (1922)	9:0
Taft	51	Keller v. Potomac Electric Co., 261 U. S. 428 (1923)	9:0
Taft	52	Adkins v. Children's Hospital, 261 U. S. 525 (1923)	5:3
Taft	53	Spalding & Bros. v. Edwards, 262 U. S. 66 (1923)	9:0
Taft	54	Washington v. Dawson, 264 U. S. 219 (1924)	7:2
Taft	55	Miles v. Graham, 268 U. S. 501 (1925)	8:1
Taft	56	Trusler v. Crooks, 269 U. S. 475 (1926)	9:0
Taft	57	Myers v. United States, 272 U. S. 52 (1926)	6:3
Taft	58	Nichols v. Coolidge, 274 U. S. 531 (1927)	9:0
Taft	59	Untermyer v. Anderson, 276 U. S. 440 (1928)	6:3
Taft	60	National Life Insurance Co. v. United States, 277 U. S. 508 (1928)	6:3
Hughes	61	Indian Motorcycle Co. v. United States, 283 U. S. 570 (1931)	7:2
Hughes	62	Heiner v. Donnan, 285 U. S. 312 (1932)	6:2
Hughes	63	Burnet v. Coronado Oil and Gas Co., 285 U. S. 393 (1932)	5:4
Hughes	64	Booth v. United States, 291 U. S. 339 (1934)	9:0
Hughes	65	Lynch v. United States, 292 U. S. 571 (1934)	9:0
Hughes	66	Panama Refining Co. v. Ryan et al., 293 U. S. 388 (1935)	8:1
Hughes	67	Perry v. United States, 294 U. S. 330 (1935)	5:4

293

Hughes	68	*Railroad Retirement Bd. v. Alton R. R.,* 295 U. S. 330 (1935)	5:4
Hughes	69	*Schechter Poultry Corp. v. United States,* 295 U. S. 495 (1935)	9:0
Hughes	70	*Louisville Joint Stock Land Bank v. Radford,* 295 U. S. 555 (1935)	9:0
Hughes	71	*United States v. Constantine,* 296 U. S. 287 (1935)	6:3
Hughes	72	*Hopkins Federal Savings and Loan Association v. Cleary,* 296 U. S. 315 (1935)	9:0
Hughes	73	*United States v. Butler,* 297 U. S. 1 (1936)	6:3
Hughes	74	*Rickert Rice Mills v. Fontenot,* 297 U. S. 110 (1936)	9:0
Hughes	75	*Carter v. Carter Coal Co.,* 298 U. S. 238 (1936)	5:4
Hughes	76	*Ashton v. Cameron County Water Improvement District,* 298 U. S. 513 (1936)	5:4
Stone	77	*Tot v. United States,* 319 U. S. 463 (1943)	8:0
None**	78	*United States v. Lovett,* 328 U. S. 303 (1946)	8:0
Vinson	79	*United States v. Cardiff,* 344 U. S. 174 (1952)	8:1
Warren	80	*Bolling v. Sharpe,* 347 U. S. 497 (1954)	9:0
Warren	81	*United States ex rel Toth v. Quarles,* 350 U. S. 11 (1955)	6:3
Warren	82	*Reid v. Covert,* plus *Kinsella v. Singleton, et al.,*** 354 U. S. 1 (1957) and 361 U. S. 234 (1960)	6:2
Warren	83	*Trop v. Dulles,* 356 U. S. 86 (1958)	5:4
Warren	84	*Kennedy v. Mendoza-Martinez****	
Warren	85	plus *Rusk v. Cort,**** 372 U. S. 144 (1963)	5:4

** Mr. Chief Justice Stone had died before the case was heard and Mr. Chief Justice Vinson did not take his place on the bench until after it had been decided.

***See p. 286, *supra,* for elaboration. Also see pp. 188–9 Ch. V, *supra.*

**** The two cases were reported under the same citation, but there were two declarations of unconstitutionality involving segments of two separate statutes, (See p. 286, *supra.*)

Under Chief Justice	Recorded Declaration Number	Citation of Case and Year Decided	Vote
Warren	86	*Schneider v. Rusk,* 377 U. S. 163 (1964)	5:3
Warren	87	*Aptheker v. Secretary of State,* 378 U. S. 500 (1964)	6:3
Warren	88	*Lamont v. Postmaster-General* plus *Fixa v. Heilberg,* 381 U. S. 301 (1965)	8:0
Warren	89	*United States v. Brown,* 381 U. S. 437 (1965)	5:4
Warren	90	*United States v. Romano,* 382 U. S. 136 (1965)	9:0
Warren	91	*Afroyim v. Rusk,****** 387 U. S. 253 (1967)	5:4
Warren	92	*United States v. Robel,* (decided December 11, 1967)	6:2
Warren	93	*Marchetti v. United States,* (decided January 29, 1968)	7:1
Warren	94	*Haynes v. United States,* (decided January 29, 1968)	7:1

***** Although the holding refers specifically only to one aspect of the statute, its breadth may be interpreted as reaching several more.

JUDICIAL REVIEW ABROAD

As already indicated, the practice of judicial review is not likely to be found in nonfederal states. Hence the other two major subject-lands of this study either do not, as in the case of Britain, or did not, until the adoption of the Constitution of 1958, in the case of France, clothe their courts with the power of judicial review —and in the instance of the French Fifth Republic it is judicial review only in a very limited and tangential sense.

BRITAIN

In Britain, Parliament is supreme in the sense that *any* law that has been enacted by it and has received the routine approval of the Crown becomes the law of the land and is *ipso facto* beyond overturning by the British courts. By virtue of the ancient writ of *quo warranto,* the courts do, of course, possess the authority to *interpret* legislation, and particularly administrative action based upon it—for all government officials are potentially accountable to the courts for their actions—*but they may not strike down the law itself.* In the immortal words of Walter Bagehot, the famous British economist and journalist, "there is nothing the British Parliament cannot do except transform a man into a woman and a woman into a man." Although he expressed this fact of *governmental* life a century ago, it is still as true today as it was then. The more or less homogeneous people of Britain, deeply steeped in the common experience of centuries, tradition, custom, and a firm, if not uncritical, faith in Westminster and Whitehall, continue to be quite content to entrust their treasured freedoms to the good judgment of their representatives assembled in Parliament—duly checked—"controlled" is a more appropriate term—by the powerful executive arm, the political parties, and public opinion itself. The British courts are revered and esteemed as necessary concomitants of the democratic process, but *not* in the role of ultimate guardians of the Constitution.

FRANCE

The French, too, insisting that a law is the expression of the sovereign will, had not endowed their courts with authority to declare laws unconstitutional even in a limited manner until the proclamation of the Constitution of the Fifth Republic in 1958. However, prior to it they did devise a rather interesting safeguard in order to ascertain that suggested legislation of dubious constitutionality did not become law per se short of an amendment to the Constitution. That safeguard was established by the framers of the Constitution of the Fourth Republic in the form of a special thirteen-member committee known as the *Constitutional Committee (Comité Constitutionnel).*

Chaired by the President of the Republic, the Constitutional Committee consisted, in addition to the President of the National Assembly and the President of the Council of the Republic, of three members selected by the latter and seven by the former branch of the legislature. In each instance these ten were chosen from personnel outside the membership of the respective chambers, usually professors of law in general concord with the several political parties represented in Parliament. Whenever it was requested to do so by the President of the Council of the Republic and an absolute majority of its members—and only then!—the committee was empowered to examine a law prior to its final promulgation to determine whether or not it was of such a nature as to require its recasting as a *constitutional amendment* rather than simply pass as a *law*. If the committee concurred that a law did in fact imply an amendment to the Constitution, it was referred back to the National Assembly for appropriate action. Not surprisingly, the Constitutional Committee was hardly a very busy institution; it was called upon in merely a few cases, and only one or two of these gave it an opportunity to perform a significant role. Whatever its performance, the institution was a far cry from bona fide judicial review.

The Constitutional Council. However, France moved a bit closer to bona fide judicial review—without actually attaining it—with the adoption of a provision in the de Gaulle Constitution of 1958 calling for a *Constitutional Council* (*Conseil Constitutionnel*).[27] Not a court at all, it actually lies outside the judicial system of the government; neither individual citizens nor groups nor courts of law can appeal to it. The council is composed of all the ex-Presidents of France—regardless of which Republic they may have headed—plus nine other distinguished personages, of whom three each are selected by the President of the Republic, the President of the Senate, and the President of the National Assembly. *M. le président* of the council is chosen from among its membership by the incumbent President of the Republic. The members may hold no public office of any kind, other than already held civil service appointments, for it was the intention of the authors of the institution that its membership be wholly independent, exercising no outside remunerative public activity whatsoever.

The nine appointive members of the Constitutional Council—usually lawyers who have been active in politics (five of the original nine had been active Gaullists)—serve for one nonrenewable, staggered nine-year term of office, whereas all ex-Presidents of France serve for life. In theory, the latter may not resign, but one, the venerable Vincent Auriol, first President of the Fourth Republic, announced on July 2, 1960, that, in protest of three allegedly

[27] Title VII, Articles 56–63.

unconstitutional actions taken by President de Gaulle, he would no longer participate in the Council's work. The disputed actions were first, a measure to increase vastly state aid to denominational schools; second, de Gaulle's refusal, in March 1960, to convene Parliament in special session despite a request by a majority of the deputies (who were duly backed by a constitutional provision); and third, the short-cut procedure employed to revise the Constitution on the structure of the French Community. The then seventy-five-year-old popular Socialist, who had done much to bring de Gaulle to power in the dark days of May 1958, concluded his letter of resignation to Council President Léon Noel as follows:

> This lack of deference for the national sovereignty and our fundamental charter orients the constitutional regime of 1958 toward a system of personal and arbitrary power in opposition to the essential rules and principles of democracy. . . . [T]hus, not wanting to remain powerless and mute before attacks on the national sovereignty, I regret to inform you that I will no longer sit with the Constitutional Council.[28]

The Council has the power to declare unconstitutional all *organic laws* (e.g. appointment and removal of high officials; finance bills) and *standing orders* (rules of procedure) of the houses of Parliament; both these categories *must* be submitted to the council prior to their promulgation. It is also empowered to strike down those *ordinary laws, treaties,* and *protocols* which *may* be voluntarily referred to it by the President of the Republic, the Premier, or the Presidents of the two houses of Parliament. Normally, it is expected to hand down a decision within one month, but if the government categorizes a referred measure as "urgent," it must rule on the matter within eight days. Among the other main functions of the Council are: supervision of the "regularity" of the elections of the President of the Republic, the members of Parliament—the Constitutional Council, not Parliament, establishes the credentials of the deputies[29] and senators—and of all popular referenda; it may decide disputes between the government (the Ministry) and Parliament regarding the "delimitation of executive

[28] As reported by Robert C. Doty in *The New York Times* (International Edition), July 2, 1960.

[29] Thus, after the November 1962 elections to the National Assembly, the Council invalidated the results in four assembly districts.

and legislative competence"; and it *must* be consulted by the President of the Republic when he is contemplating the assumption of emergency powers under Article 16 of the Constitution, as de Gaulle did in April 1961, as to both the existence of the emergency and the measures he proposes to take under it.

The Council cannot itself initiate action in constitutional cases, but it is autonomous regarding the other delimited areas of its power just outlined. A quorum for a valid decision is seven members, yet an absolute majority is required to certify Presidential disability—another of its responsibilities. One opinion only is delivered in behalf of the entire body, but all decisions of the Council must be written. Its decisions are final and binding and are not appealable to "any jurisdiction whatsoever." Yet it has no power to enforce its decisions, other than the power to persuade.

Given this distinctly limited range of power and authority, it would be highly misleading to characterize the functions of the Constitutional Council as judicial review. There are three debilitating weaknesses: First, the inability of private individuals and groups to challenge the constitutionality of a law—only the high public officers indicated above possess that right as an adjunct of their official station. Second, a challenge to the constitutionality of a law even by one of the latter—an admittedly unlikely event in and of itself—is possible solely as to the substance of the law and not as to its procedural application (one of the most frequent causes of court review in the United States, for example). Third, the extremely short period of time permitted to the Council for its deliberation on a validly challenged measure makes all but a mockery of the concept of an appeal. On the other hand, its record as of the date of this comment (winter 1967–68) indicates a definite inclination to assert itself in the constitutional evaluation of the writing of parliamentary rules. It remains to be seen whether this inclination is a harbinger of more assertion in other areas of its presumed competence—but this is unlikely, certainly as long as de Gaulle is President. In the opinion of one of the most astute commentators on the French scene, *le conseil constitutionnel* is best thought of as an adjunct to the President of the Republic in his endeavors to ensure respect for the 1958 Constitution.[30] This

30 William Pickles, *The French Constitution, October 4, 1958* (London: Stevens & Co., Ltd., 1960), pp. 33.

appraisal was assuredly vindicated when President de Gaulle in
October 1962 called for a national referendum on direct election
of the President—despite the Council's objections to such a referendum call on the obvious ground that the Constitution of 1958
did not provide for such direct action and that, indeed, the President's call represented a patent violation of the letter and the
spirit of the basic document. But when, predictably, de Gaulle
refused to be stopped; held the referendum; won it (albeit by a
narrow margin) and then saw his action and the attendant results
challenged at the bar of the Council, the Council promptly declared
itself "incompetent" to rule on the "subject matter approved" by
and in the referendum. The French Constitutional Council is no
Supreme Court of the United States!

SOME OTHER SPECIAL CONSTITUTIONAL TRIBUNALS

Several countries have created judicial bodies that approach or
even feature some of the manifestations of the power of judicial
review, yet they are usually found *outside* or astride the ordinary
court structure. Among the most active of these bodies are the
constitutional courts of West Germany, Italy, and Austria, all of
which practice at least some measure of judicial review. There are
other instances, but a brief treatment of these three will suffice to
illustrate the point. In each case, these post-World War II states
have empowered their special constitutional courts to guard against
infringement of their constitutions by simple legislation and other
governmental action—e.g. any action that would violate the constitutional guarantee, present in almost identical form in all three
lands, that "all persons shall be equal before the law." There has
been fairly general acceptance of their purpose and functions.[31]

The most active and most successful among the three is
West Germany's *Federal Constitutional Court* (*Bundesverfassungs-
gericht*), created in 1951 at United States insistence under the
Basic Law of 1949, and seated in Karlsruhe. (The framers of the
Weimar Republic had rejected judicial review because of what
they regarded as the "stultifying actions" of the United States
Supreme Court!) It consists of sixteen judges of at least forty years

31 See the informative article by Taylor Cole, "The Constitutional Courts: A
Comparison," in 53 *American Political Science Review* 963–84 (December
1959).

of age; all have considerable past judicial, legal, professional, or other high public experience and are eligible for judicial office as well as for election to the *Bundestag* (though they cannot be members of it). They are elected half by the lower house (*Bundestag*) by a special committee of twelve electors set up by it on the basis of proportional representation in the *Bundestag*, with nine of the twelve votes necessary for selection, and half by the upper house (*Bundesrat*) of Parliament by a two-thirds majority. The selections by the two houses are made from a list provided by the Ministry of Justice. It comprises *all* federal judges eligible for elevation to the *Bundesverfassungsgericht* as well as any other legally trained candidates who are nominated by the federal government, by the *Länder* (states) and by the political parties. Only six of those selected come from the ranks of professionally trained judges; they *must* be chosen from jurists then serving on the supreme courts of the several *Länder*. These six then serve for life; the balance for renewable eight-year terms of office; evidently, continuity seems to be considered in order, for of the jurists on the bench in 1965 all but three had served continuously for well over a decade.

The Federal Constitutional Court posseses the extensive power to decide all disputes involving the meaning and effectiveness of the Basic Law (*Grundgesetz*); it decides the constitutional validity of any federal or state (*Land*) statute, whether or not a case involving it has already come before one of the regular courts; and it adjudicates disputes between organs of government at the national level. Out of these powers arise the Court's two most significant functions: jurisdiction over disputes between the Federal Republic and the *Länder* regarding the latter's administration of the former's statutes, and guardianship over the fundamental rights and privileges of citizens as determined by the Basic Law both on substantive and procedural grounds—like judicial review in the United States and unlike its restricted practice in France.

The *Bundesverfassungsgericht* consists of two chambers or "senates" of eight judges each, one for all cases dealing with civil and constitutional rights, the other for the rest of the cases. The high tribunal's opinions are unsigned and no votes are recorded—a somewhat questionable policy. But the *Bundesverfassungsgericht* has been a busy and assertive court, and to the surprise of many a skeptic it has acted with considerable courage and vigor. For example, it braved the wrath and power of Chancellor Konrad

Adenauer when, in a momentous decision early in 1961, it declared unconstitutional as a violation of principles of federalism guaranteed in Article 30 of the Basic Law his executive action setting up a federally controlled, second television network that was to be financed largely through commercials[32]—a plan that had been expressly rejected by Parliament earlier! The decision was particularly remarkable since it resulted from a suit filed some months earlier by four *Länder* dominated by the Chancellor's opposition, the Social Democrats. Two other significant decisions served to declare both the Communist party in 1956 and in 1952 the socialist *Reich* party, a neo-Nazi organization, as unconstitutional as being detrimental to the constitutional and democratic order of the state.[33] And as another illustration of the Court's virility and assertiveness, it did not hesitate to strike down an executive decree based on what the Court viewed as unconstitutional delegation of legislative power by the *Bundestag* to the Executive.[34] The reasoning employed here was quite similar to that used by the United States Supreme Court in 1935, in the "Hot Oil" cases,[35] when it declared unconstitutional, as an illegal delegation of legislative power to the Chief Executive, an important section of the National Industrial Recovery Act which was soon to fall in its entirety. And as a final example of the Court's versatile jurisdictional determination, in 1966 it declared unconstitutional the federal statutes under which the three major political parties had been subsidized from public funds to the tune of DMK 38,000,000 ($9,500,000) annually. The Court held that such funds could be authorized only for legitimate election campaign expenses, not for general propaganda, and would have to be made available to splinter parties as well. "In a free society," said the tribunal, "the process of forming public opinion should be free of the state, and should move from the people themselves to the state institutions rather than from the state down to the people."[36] It is fair to say that the *Bundesverfassungsgericht* has assumed an importance hardly predictable, and that it has thus become a significant element in the *modus operandi* of the new German federalism.

[32] 12 BVerf GE 60 (1961).
[33] 5 BVerf GE 85 (1956) and 2 BVerf GE 1 (1952).
[34] 1 BVerf GE 14 (1951).
[35] *Panama Refining Co. v. Ryan*, 293 U.S. 388 (1935).
[36] 20 BVerf GE 56–59, 119, 134 (1966).

Another modern special constitutional tribunal is *Italy's Constitutional Court (Corte Costituzionale)*, established under the Italian Constitution of 1948—although it did not begin to function until January 1, 1956. This fifteen-member body is staffed with distinguished personages who have had at least twenty years of experience as practising lawyers, or who are experienced judges or professors of law. (Once more we note the high esteem in which the professor is held in Europe.) The members of the Court are appointed for staggered twelve-year terms, five each selected by the President of the Republic of Italy with the Premier's countersignature; five by a three-fifths vote of Parliament in joint session; and five by the "ordinary and administrative judiciary," i.e. three by the *Corte di Cassazione*, one by the *Consiglio di Stato*, and one by the *Corte dei Conti*. The Court is the final interpreter of the Constitution; it has the power to declare both national and regional laws unconstitutional—as it did in the case of a 1934 law that denied Sunday rest to shepherds[37]—between organs of government at the national level. Access of individuals to it is considerably less readily available than in West Germany and that fact, plus a general tendency to tread much more gingerly, largely because of the open hostility to its ultimate power by Italy's Attorney General, at first rendered the *Corte Costituzionale* less of a peacemaker in matters of constitutional checks than its counterpart north of the Alps. Nevertheless, it has asserted itself, and particularly so when dealing with the now familiar illegal delegation of legislative power to the executive branch. Indeed, two knowledgeable commentators found in 1964 that the Court had not only "insisted upon its prerogatives and successfully defended its position," but that it has "become a bulwark for freedom in Italian society."[38]

Austria, too, has its Constitutional Court, the *Verfassungsgericht*. This fourteen-member tribunal was re-instituted in 1945, based upon the Austrian Constitution of 1920, as amended in 1925 and 1929. Its members are appointed for life—unlike a majority of

---

[37] Decision of July 22, 1962. A few months earlier the *Corte Constituzionale* upheld the constitutionality of articles 559 and 560 of Italy's penal code which provides far sterner punishment for adulterous wives than for unfaithful husbands. (Decision of November 28, 1961.)

[38] Guglielmo Negri and Joseph La Palombara, "Principles of Italian Constitutional Law and the Structure of Central Government," in Negri, *Three Essays on Comparative Politics* (Milano: D.A. Ciuffre, 1964), pp. 33–7 and p. 8, respectively.

the German justices and all of the Italian justices—by the President of the Republic of Austria from nominees of the federal government, partly on the recommendations of the lower house (National Council) and the upper house (Federal Council) of Parliament. The tribunal has the power to review the constitutionality of legislation and to decide jurisdiction disputes between the courts and administrative authorities. Individuals have less ready access to the *Verfassungsgericht* than they do to its German counterpart yet somewhat more than to that of Italy. This center position of the Austrian tribunal applies also to its range of power and conception of functions. But it, too, has asserted itself and has not been loathe to examine legislation, even legislation extending to the social realm; i.e. it held unconstitutional a section of the Income Tax Law of 1953 that differentiated between the sexes for tax purposes.[39]

Yet of all the issues that have confronted these three constitutional courts of Europe, by far the greatest number has concerned the interpretation and application of respective constitutional provisions in the vexatious areas of delegation of legislative authority, federalism, and equality before the law. The first of these is really no longer a live issue at the bar of the Supreme Court of the United States, but the second and third, the latter particularly since the end of World War II, are very much in the constitutional weather eye.

An Historical Note

The notion that courts, or some other body should exercise judicial review as the guardian of a basic law or constitution[40] stems primarily from the early European rejection of the idea of the inviolability of an enacted law. One of the first statements clamoring for a type of judicial review in that connection was made in England—oddly enough in view of the subsequent rejection of the concept. It arose out of the famous *Dr. Bonham's Case* in 1610.

39 Decision of March 29, 1958.

40 An intriguing development on that front, albeit a completely unpredictable one in terms of its genuine role and meaning, is the establishment in 1964 of Yugoslavia's eleven-man Constitutional Court, elected by the Federal Assembly for a once renewable eight-year term of office. See Winston M. Fisk and Alvin Z. Rubinstein, "Yugoslavia's Constitutional Court," 15 *East Europe* 7 (July 1966).

The King, pursuant to an Act of Parliament, had granted to members of the London College of Physicians the exclusive right to issue licenses to practise medicine in that city. Dr. Bonham was charged with practising medicine illegally, for he was not a member of that College—the latter having refused to license him. The College then fined him, confiscating half of the fine for itself! When the case came before Sir Edward Coke, the Lord Chief Justice, he declared the charter void as a violation of the common law. Holding the latter to be supreme, Sir Edward simply stated that the courts could declare acts of Parliament null and void; therefore, he held in the now so famous dictum: "When an act of Parliament is against common right and reason, or repugnant, or impossible to be performed, the common law will control it and adjudge such act to be void."[41] Parliament then simply re-enacted the statute! If Sir Edward's view of judicial review was ever seriously adopted at all anywhere in England, it was promptly superseded when the Glorious Revolution of 1688 clearly established the supremacy of Parliament. In fact, already in 1653 Lord Coke's peers had held in *Captain Streater's Case*[42] that ". . . we must submit to the legislative power else things would run around."[43]

Nevertheless, the concept of judicial review subsequently found its way across the Atlantic Ocean to the British Colonies, there to be nurtured by several colonial courts. In eight or nine separate early judgments these courts refused to enforce legislative enactments that they deemed to be against "the laws of nature" (shades of Locke and future events) or "the laws of natural equity"—in a sense against the latent, unwritten Constitution.

JUDICIAL REVIEW AT HOME

Yet if the principle of judicial review was imbedded in the minds of the American Founding Fathers, they assuredly failed to spell it out—although the records of the Constitutional Convention in Philadelphia in 1787 prove conclusively that the idea of judicial

[41] 8 Co. 188a.

[42] 5 How St. Trs. 365.

[43] However, there are those who argue—a bit tortuously—that, in effect, by their common law power of *interpreting* legislation, the courts of England *do* practise judicial review. See, for example, A. Wilson, in "The Doctrine and Practice of Judicial Review of Legislation," 4 *Me Judice* 20 (January 1962).

review was widely recognized and accepted; that the matter was very much on the minds of the delegates, who after all distrusted unrestrained popular government; and that it was widely debated. In any event, the massed evidence is quite persuasive that a vast majority of the delegates, anti-Federalists as well as Federalists, favored it—although for quite different reasons. Between 25 and 32 of the 40 delegates are generally considered to have called for it. Leading constitutional authorities such as Professors Beard, Corwin, and Mason are fully agreed on that interpretation of the wishes of the delegates[44] who, with less than a handful of dissenters, in effect concurred in the pronouncement by Gouverneur Morris of Pennsylvania that the courts should decline to give the weight of law to "a direct violation of the Constitution." Morris admitted that such control over the legislature might have "its inconveniences, "but that it was nonetheless necessary because even the "most virtuous citizens will often as members of a legislative body concur in measures which afterwards in their private capacity they will be ashamed of."[45]

So prominent a framer as Alexander Hamilton declared in his famous *Federalist Paper* #78 that judicial review was definitely meant to be incorporated into the prerogatives of the judiciary. And the "Father of the Constitution" himself, James Madison, wrote:

> Judiciary is truly the only defensive armor of the Federal Government, or rather for the Constitution and laws of the United States. Strip it of that armor and the door is wide open for nullification, anarchy and convulsion.[46]

Despite this solid evidence it is still a matter of considerable academic dispute whether or not the framers intended the power of

[44] See Charles Beard, "The Supreme Court—Usurper or Grantee?," 27 *Political Science Quarterly* 1 (1912); Max Farrand, *The Framing of the Constitution of the United States* (New Haven: Yale University Press, 1913); and John Schmidhauser, *The Supreme Court as Final Arbiter in Federal-State Relations, 1789–1957* (Chapel Hill: University of North Carolina Press, 1958), especially Chs. I and XI. See also Beard's classic, *The Supreme Court and the Constitution* rev. ed., with an introduction by Alan F. Westin (Englewood Cliffs, N.J.: Prentice-Hall, Inc., 1962).

[45] As quoted by Alpheus T. Mason and Richard H. Leach, *In Quest of Freedom* (Englewood Cliffs, N.J.: Prentice-Hall, Inc., 1959), p. 124.

[46] As quoted by Charles Warren in *The Supreme Court in United States History* (Boston: Little Brown, 1937), Vol. I, p. 740.

judicial review to be given to the courts. But there are sundry additional grounds for the conclusion that such doubts as still remain ought to be laid at rest—that the debate over the legitimacy of judicial review is settled by history.

Further Historical Roots

The Constitution itself, while admittedly not providing for the power of judicial review in so many words, assuredly alludes to it by implication. The supremacy clause of Article VI, relating to the duty of state judges, may well be viewed as implying judicial review by federal tribunals over *state actions*. Moreover, that same provision of the Constitution requires acts of Congress to be made "in pursuance thereof," which would seem to call for someone to act as arbiter. It may be well to quote the entire supremacy clause:

> This Constitution, and the laws of the United States which shall be made in pursuance thereof, and all treaties made or which shall be made under the authority of the United States, shall be the supreme law of the land; and the judges in every state shall be bound thereby, anything in the Constitution or laws of any state to the contrary notwithstanding.[47]

Another relevant provision of the basic document is to be found in Article II which states:

> The judicial power shall extend to all cases, in law and equity, arising under this Constitution, the laws of the United States and treaties made or which shall be made, under the authority. . . .[48]

If nothing else, this section clearly indicated the authority of the judiciary over cases in a vast area of constitutional interpretation and thus implied its finite power as to the legality of those cases.

Moreover, as has already been briefly indicated, it is noteworthy that in the colonial period the British Privy Council had *established* judicial review over acts passed by the colonial legislatures. At least eight states ratifying conventions expressly discussed and accepted the power to pronounce legislative acts null and void.[49] Furthermore, between 1789 and 1803 the courts in ten of the states had *exercised* that power by declaring state laws to be in

[47] Constitution of the United States, Article VI, Sec. 2.
[48] Ibid. Article III, Sec. 2.
[49] Va., R.I., N.Y., Conn., Mass., N.J., N.C., S.C.

conflict with state constitutions,[50] and prior to 1789 eight instances of state court judicial review deciding against their state legislature took place. And Section 25 of the Judiciary Act 1789, the law under which the First Congress created the national judiciary, *conferred* on the federal government specific authority to *reverse* provisions of state laws and state constitutions that conflicted with the "Constitution, treaty, statute, or commission of the United States."[51] Still, since neither the Constitution for any level of government, nor the Judiciary Act of 1789 for the national level, specifically provided for judicial review, it remained for the Supreme Court of the United States to do so. This it did in 1803, in *Marbury v. Madison*[52]—though, as Thomas Reed Powell noted in his *Vagaries and Varieties in Constitutional Interpretation*, no one "had any premonition that the point of judicial review would be relevant to the disposition of the controversy."[53]

SPELLING IT OUT: MARBURY V. MADISON

With the possible exception of *McCulloch v. Maryland*[54]—of which James Bradley Thayer and Felix Frankfurter thought "that the conception of the nation which Marshall derived from the Constitution and set forth [in it] is his greatest single judicial performance"[55]—and, perhaps, *Gibbons v. Ogden*[56](but for different reasons), no more important case at constitutional law exists than the hallowed and revered *Marbury v. Madison*—which has been called "the rib of the Constitution."[57] All three were written by that great national constitutionalist, Mr. Chief Justice John Marshall, who had himself been a delegate to the Ratifying Convention of Virginia and a one-term Congressman from that state. The background of the *Marbury* decision is so colorful, and the decision itself so important, that no treatment of the judicial process would be complete

50 E.g. *Holmes v. Walton* (New Jersey, 1780) and *Trevett v. Wheeden* (Rhode Island, 1786).
51 Act of September 24, 1789, c.20, 25, 1 Statutes at Large 73, 87.
52 1 Cranch 137.
53 New York: Columbia University Press, p. 11.
54 4 Wheaton 316 (1819).
55 "John Marshall and the Judicial Function," in *Government Under Law* (Cambridge: Harvard University Press, 1956), p. 8.
56 9 Wheaton 1 (1824).
57 Glendon A. Schubert, *Constitutional Politics* (New York: Holt, Rinehart and Winston, 1960), p. 178.

without at least a brief analysis of the case, which is one that is not only still frequently cited by courts in the United States, but also, and again recently, in other countries—for example, Italy and India!

Prompt enactment of the Judiciary Act of 1789 enabled the national judiciary to begin to function at once in the fledgling United States, and questions of the existence of the power of judicial review and any possible challenge of it did not arise immediately. However, the issue was simmering. For example, in *Hayburn's Case* two Supreme Court justices riding circuit in Pennsylvania in 1792 had refused to carry out a congressional statute that they deemed contrary to the Constitution. Backed by the full Court, Associate Justices Blair and Wilson ruled that they could not perform certain duties imposed upon them by the law because they were not "judicial in nature."[58] Together with District Judge Peters they were to pass on disputed pension claims of invalid war veterans, with their determination subject to review by the Secretary of War and by Congress! If nothing else, this judicial refusal to carry out a legislative act called attention to the constitutional problem. Three years later, in *Van Horne's Lessie v. Dorrance*[59] Mr. Justice William Paterson—a delegate from the Constitutional Convention in New Jersey—held for the Court: "Whatever may be the case in other countries, yet in this *there can be no doubt that every act of the Legislature repugnant to the Constitution, is absolutely void.*"[60] A similar judgment was expressed by Mr. Justice Samuel Chase on another occasion soon thereafter.[61]

Moreover, the Supreme Court had struck down at least two relatively minor *state* enactments[62]—although the second of these decisions was of considerable importance since it held state laws subject to treaties by ruling that the Anglo-American Peace Treaty overrode a Virginia law on the delicate and potentially explosive issue of debts owed to British subjects by Americans.[63] Furthermore, depending upon the historical source, the Supreme Court even held an insignificant *federal* pension claim law unconstitu-

[58] 2 Dallas 409 (1792).
[59] 2 Dallas 304 (1795).
[60] Ibid., at 308. (Italics supplied.)
[61] *Cooper v. Telfair*, 2 Dallas 14 (1800), at 19.
[62] *Clerke v. Harwood*, 3 Dallas 342 (1797) and *Ware v. Hylton*, 3 Dallas 199 (1796).
[63] *Ware v. Hylton*, loc. cit.

tional in the case of *U.S. v. Yale Todd*, which was decided in 1794 but not reported until it became a footnote almost sixty years later in *U.S. v. Ferreira*.[64] Nevertheless, this was evidently the first instance of the declaration of unconstitutionality of a federal statute. Finally, two years after *Yale Todd* the Court—with three of its six justices not participating—expressly upheld a congressional statute imposing a duty on carriages as not being a "direct tax" and therefore not unconstitutional.[65] (Exactly ninety-nine years later the Supreme Court in effect overruled this decision in the *Second Income Tax Case*[66] thus precipitating the Sixteenth Amendment.) Yet regardless of these aforegone instances of incipient concern with judicial review, it was not until 1803 and *Marbury v. Madison* that matters actually came to a climax.

The Factual Setting. The second President of the United States, John Adams, had been defeated in his bid for re-election in 1800 by his arch political arch-rival, Thomas Jefferson. Laboring desperately to salvage something for his prostrate Federalist party, Adams was determined to pack the federal judiciary with as many judgeships as humanly and statutorily possible. With the aid of a more than obliging lame-duck Federalist Congress, which passed both the Circuit Court Act[67] and the District of Columbia Organic Law Act early in 1801, Adams, before leaving office on March 3, 1801, was able to nominate, have approved by the Senate, and commission the following into office: sixteen new circuit judges (under the Circuit Court Act); forty-two new justices of the peace (under the District of Columbia Act); and one Chief Justice of the United States Supreme Court—his own Secretary of State, the forty-five-year-old staunch Federalist John Marshall (who in 1798 had refused Washington's designation of him as Associate Justice). These nominees have often been called "Adams' Midnight Judges" because the President devoted his waning hours in office to signing their commissions of appointment.

It fell to the outgoing premier of the cabinet—Marshall,

64 13 Howard 40 (1851).
65 *Hylton v. United States*, 3 Dallas 171 (1796).
66 *Pollock v. Farmers Loan & Trust Co.*, 158 U.S. 601 (1895).
67 The Act—which was repealed in March 1802 at Jefferson's insistence—also provided that the next vacancy on the Supreme Court should *not* be filled, thus reducing the Court's membership from six to five and thereby rendering impossible any automatic vacancy-filling appointment by the incoming Jefferson, a "Democratic-Republican" rather than a Federalist. Barely one year later the new President succeeded in having Congress re-enact the membership as six.

whose appointment Adams came to regard as the single most important act of his Administration (just as Hoover would ultimately regard his of Cardozo more than 125 years later)—to affix to them the Great Seal of the United States and then to deliver the new judgeship commissions to the various appointees. But Marshall, at once fatigued and exhilarated on Inauguration Eve, failed to deliver seventeen of the forty-two justices-of-the-peace commissions, although, aided by his brother James, he worked until late into the evening, and indeed had taken care of all the important new circuit judgeships plus most of the other appointments. However, he would begin his first full day as Chief Justice in the morning, a post to which he had been appointed almost two months earlier upon the resignation of the elderly and feeble Oliver Ellsworth in favor of a diplomatic position, and upon John Jay's summary refusal to accept Adam's proffered second appointment as Chief Justice. As Chief Justice he would have the somewhat less than delightful duty of administering the oath of the Presidency to his avowed political enemy (and distant cousin) Thomas Jefferson. He left the undelivered commissions to the incoming Secretary of State, James Madison.[68] The stage was thus set for a towering battle of three veritable titans of the early days of Constitution and Nation.

Preliminaries. Angry because of the sustained packing of the judiciary with Federalist appointees, Jefferson upon taking office was delighted to find the seventeen undelivered justice-of-the-peace commissions on the desk of the Secretary of State—Madison arrived somewhat later. The new President, subsequently seconded enthusiastically by his new Secretary of State, determined not to deliver them, declaring that the ". . . nominations crowded in by Mr. Adams after he knew he was not appointing for himself I treat as mere nullities."[69] And, according to one account, the commissions at issue were "disposed of with the other waste paper

---

[68] For an unusually penetrating analysis of the more technical aspects of *Marbury v. Madison,* see Mr. Justice Harold H. Burton's article, "The Cornerstone of Constitutional Law: The Extraordinary Case of *Marbury v. Madison,*" 36 *American Bar Association Journal* 805 (October 1950). See also the more historical piece by John A. Garraty, "The Case of the Missing Commissions," in his *Quarrels that Have Shaped the Constitution* (New York: Harper & Row, 1964).

[69] Warren, op. cit. Vol. I, p. 201.

and rubbish of the office."[70] Neither subsequent pleas nor threats by such disappointed office-seekers as William Marbury were to sway them. Marbury, a forty-one-year-old Washingtonian and three other staunch Federalists—Denis Ramsay, William Harper, and Robert Townshend Hooe—subsequently sought aid of counsel and hired Charles Lee, Attorney General under George Washington and Samuel Adams.

Lee turned to the law and to the courts. He found what he believed to be the law in a provision of the Judiciary Act of 1789: Section 13 of that important law extended to the Supreme Court of the United States the power to issue a *writ of mandamus*—*mandamus* being the Latin for "we command"—an old Anglo-Saxon writ used as early as the reign of Henry II, commanding a public official to perform his official, ministerial, nondiscretionary duty. Invoking that provisions, Lee petitioned the Court for appropriate action—and, at the next term of the court in 1803, *Marbury v. Madison,* thus reached the original docket of the highest court of the land. It could readily have dismissed the petition for want of jurisdiction, leaving Marbury to seek remedy in the lower courts—but, as will become apparent, this would hardly have suited the purposes of the Chief Justice. For presiding over the Supreme Court now, of course, was Jefferson's mortal political enemy and Adams's loyal supporter, John Marshall, who had issued an order to Madison—who promptly ignored it—to show cause why the requested writ of mandamus should not be issued against him. Surely Marshall's decision would be in favor of Marbury, especially in view of the clear language of Section 13!

Marshall, C. J., for the Court. But both the Federalists and the Jeffersonian Republicans had underestimated the boldness and judiciousness, the craftsmanship and shrewd political acumen, the farsightedness and statesmanship, and, above all, the powerful dedication to the Constitution—*as he saw it and wanted to see it*—of the fourth Chief Justice of the United States Supreme Court. And it was John Marshall who spoke for the unanimous Court in a twenty-seven-page opinion, despite the fact that he had a direct interest in the case at bar—which today would almost certainly result in self-disqualification from the case. Whatever one may

[70] Charles S. Hyneman, *The Supreme Court on Trial* (New York: Atherton Press, 1963), p. 75.

think of his failure to abstain, it is not difficult to agree with Professor Corwin that "his compact presentation of the case marches to its conclusion with all the precision of a demonstration of Euclid."[71] The Chief Justice was confronted with a Hobson's choice: If he were to grant the writ in the face of almost certain disobedience by Madison, the Court would be powerless, and if he were to refuse to grant it, Jefferson would triumph.

Marshall's heart of course, was on the side of Marbury's cause —which happened to be that of his fellow Federalists—and he did not hesitate to chide Jefferson and Madison from the bench, to castigate them for their "rascality." Moreover, he distinctly concurred with the plaintiff's contention that (1) he had a legal right to the commission, and (2) the laws of the land afforded him a remedy. These *obiter dicta* consumed twenty of the twenty-seven pages! But as to the remedy, Marshall—an experienced political savant, here confronted with an utterly political situation—announced unmistakably that a writ of mandamus, issued by the Supreme Court under Section 13 of the Judiciary Act, was definitely *not* such a remedy, for it was *unconstitutional!*

It was unconstitutional, explained Marshall for himself and Associated Justices Paterson, Cushing, Chase, Washington, and Moore, who voted unanimously against it, because *by incorporating it into the Judiciary Act of 1789 the Congress had added to the original jurisdiction of the Supreme Court by law*—which Article III, the judicial article of the Constitution, does not sanction. And, continued Marshall in an unprecedented pithy, 1500-word display of a combination of judicial self-abnegation and judicial assumption of power—for there is no doubt that judicial review, "the ultimate conservative response to the 'evils of democracy,' "[72] was a goal of the democracy-distrusting Federalists—in Section 13 Congress had given to the Court a power which it could not legally receive. That section of the act had actually figured in earlier Supreme Court decisions, yet no one had chosen to raise the present constitutional issue. *"An act repugnant to the Constitution is void,"* explained Marshall, thus echoing Hamilton's *Fed-*

[71] A lecture at Princeton University, September 1950.
[72] Wallace Mendelson, *Capitalism, Democracy, and the Supreme Court* (New York: Appleton-Century-Crofts, 1960), p. 20.

eralist #78, and, in so stating the matter, he enunciated clearly the doctrine of judicial review.[73] He elaborated:

> It is emphatically the province and duty of the judicial department to say what the law is. Those who apply the rule to particular cases, must of necessity expound and interpret that rule. . . . A law repugnant to the Constitution is void; . . . courts as well as other departments are bound by that instrument.[74]

Significance and Summary. In brief, John Marshall—thus ingeniously having managed to have his cake and eat is as well in what Senator Albert J. Beveridge of Indiana, his most famous biographer, perhaps somewhat extravagantly described as "a coup as bold in design and as daring as that by which the Constitution had been framed"[75]—clearly, cogently, and quite emphatically enunciated and interpreted three principles of the utmost significance to the young nation: (1) that the courts have the power of judicial review; (2) that the Constitution of the United States is the supreme law of the land; (3) that the *original* jurisdiction of the Supreme Court cannot be changed by simple law of Congress, since that particular jurisdiction is specifically limited by the language of the Constitution—although the *appellate* jurisdiction can be changed by simple legislation plainly because the letter of the Constitution so permits. (This, of course, has been done since, with the most famous illustration being the intriguing post-Civil War case of *ex parte McCardle*.[76] Here the Supreme Court had under consideration an already argued appeal in a *habeas corpus* proceeding—having unanimously rejected the government's motion to dismiss it for want of jurisdiction—in which the constitutionality

[73] For a different view, though wholly "pro" judicial review, see Charles L. Black, Jr., *The People and the Court: Judicial Review in a Democracy* (New York: The Macmillan Co., 1960), pp. 25ff. Black contends that judicial review had already been firmly established by then, and he calls a "myth" the usual belief that it was Marshall who gave it authoritative expression.

[74] *Marbury v. Madison*, 1 Cranch 137 (1803).

[75] *The Life of John Marshall* (Boston: Houghton Mifflin Co., 1919), Vol. I, p. 223, and Vol. III, p. 142.

[76] 7 Wallace 506 (1869). Colonel William H. McCardle, editor of the *Vicksburg [Miss.] Times* in the Fourth Reconstruction District, whose paper had been vociferously critical of Reconstruction policies and forces under the command of General Edward O. C. Ord, had been charged with numerous offenses, court-martialed, and sentenced to be shot.

of one of the Reconstruction Acts was at issue. Fearful that the Court might declare the act at issue unconstitutional—and thus conceivably strike a mortal blow against the entire Reconstruction program—Congress, over President Andrew Johnson's courageous but fruitless veto, amended the statute defining the appellate jurisdiction of the Supreme Court in these cases. It did this by withdrawing from that jurisdiction direct appeals to the Court from the circuit courts in certain classes of *habeas corpus* proceedings, including the present one.[77] Incidentally, the majority of the Court, which had simply postponed action pending the legislative and executive moves, was far from displeased about the congressional victory—although Associate Justices Field and Grier issued a bitter public dissent against what they viewed as an evasion of constitutional responsibility and deliberate procrastination. But the Court was unanimous in upholding the action of Congress—and the Reconstruction Acts were never tested by it.)

The importance of Marshall's decision in *Marbury v. Madison* to American constitutional development can hardly be overestimated.[78] There is no question that judicial review is crucial to the governmental process in the United States under its federal character and its separation of powers principle. Yet it cannot be gainsaid that Marshall strained the judicial process in making *Marbury v. Madison* his vehicle for the announcement of the doctrine of the judicial veto. We have already noted that he should probably have disqualified himself from sitting in the case because of his direct and personal involvement with both its fundamental issue and its personnel—after all, the case in effect arose out of his own negligence or apathy—and that, in any event, he did not really have to accept the case for review. He could readily have dismissed it for want of jurisdiction and directed the petitioner to apply for remedies in a lower federal court. Moreover, based on available precedent, he could easily have interpreted Section 13 and its empowering provision—indeed, he probably should have—in such a manner

---

77 In a letter to his son, Battle, shortly before he died—he was never tried for his alleged crimes and lived to a ripe old age—McCardle wrote that the Supreme Court had actually agreed to decide the case in his favor before Congress acted, the vote being 6:3 to hold his arrest unconstitutional.

78 Marbury and his fellow litigants disappeared into the obscurity whence they had come, of course, at the conclusion of the case. Marbury became president of a Georgetown bank in 1814 and died in 1835.

as to raise no substantial questions regarding statutory additions to the original jurisdiction of the Court. For a good case could be made for the contention, based on the intent of its framers in Congress, headed by the then soon-to-be-Chief Justice of the Supreme Court, Oliver Ellsworth, that Section 13 signified nothing more than that the Court had power to grant writs of mandamus in all instances when such a remedy would be appropriate in the disposition of cases duly and properly brought before it either on its original or its appellate docket. Specifically, it stated that the Supreme Court could issue the writ to "persons holding office under the authority of the United States"—and the justices *had* issued that writ in earlier cases without questioning Section13 for a moment. By no means was Section 13 thus necessarily intended to enlarge the original jurisdiction of the Court—but Marshall now claimed that the Court could not issue a writ of mandamus *except* in cases that came to it on appeal from a lower court.

Yet none of the above suggested alternate courses of action would have suited Marshall's purposes—one of which also was to avoid the potential embarrassment that would have resulted from the almost certain defiance of complying with it by President Jefferson. Having said and recognized that, however, we should acknowledge the genius of that powerful figure in American history and of the great service he performed in expounding the doctrine of judicial review when he did. Far from being a usurpation, it has powerful claims to authenticity. That debate on the justification and wisdom of the doctrine ensued almost at once, and that it has never really ceased, merely serves to add stature to its progenitor.

VIII

JUDICIAL REVIEW:

II CONTROVERSY AND LIMITATIONS

JUDICIAL REVIEW IN A DEMOCRATIC STATE: SAINT OR SINNER?

That no other federal law, or section thereof, was declared unconstitional by the Supreme Court between *Marbury v. Madison*[1] in 1803 and the *Dred Scott case*,[2] which was decided fully fifty-four years later, did not lessen the debate on the doctrine of judicial review. That it has remained fresh, indeed, and has lost none of its controversial characteristics, is testified to by the widespread public, often emotion-charged, debate surrounding the unanimous decision for the Court by Mr. Chief Justice Warren in the 1954 *Segregation Cases*[3]—in a sense the grandchildren of the Taney Court's decision in *Dred Scott*. The charge against the Warren Court: in holding compulsory segregation on account of race in the public schools to be a violation of the "equal protection of the laws" clause of the Fourteenth Amendment to the United States Constitution, the Court had not *judged,* not *interpreted,* not *reviewed,* but *legislated.* The indictment of judicial legislation is directly related, of course, to the power and doctrine of judicial review—once characterized as "the people's institutionalized means of self-control."[4]

[1] Cranch 137.

[2] *Dred Scott v. Sandford*, 19 Howard 393 (1857).

[3] *Brown v. Board of Education*, 347 U. S. 483 (1954) and *Bolling v. Sharpe*, 347 U. S. 497 (1954).

[4] Charles L. Black, Jr., *The People and the Court: Judicial Review in a Democracy* (New York: The Macmillan Co., 1960), p. 20. For some other vital recent works on judicial review, with varying points of view, cf. Alexander M. Bickel, *The Least Dangerous Branch* (Indianapolis: The Bobbs-Merrill Co., Inc., 1962), Herbert Wechsler, *Principles, Politics and Fundamental Law* (Cambridge: Harvard University Press, 1961); and Charles S. Hyneman, *The Supreme Court on Trial* (New York: Atherton Press, 1963).

Unfortunately, all too few professional observers of the judicial process and quite naturally even fewer laymen, however informed they may be, are resolutely consistent in their attitude toward either judicial review or the institution that exercises the power. To abide by Paul A. Freund's exhortation that "criticism . . . be informed by perspective and informed by philosophy"[5] is difficult. More often than not it has been a case of ". . . it all depends whose ox is being gored," to employ the pungent phrase of Al Smith. Yet it is entirely feasible to determine both articulate and reasonable "con" and "pro" positions regarding the doctrine, without resorting to the more passionate partisans of the controversy. Although a great deal of literature on the subject is available, we may well permit two of America's most honored and most literate governmental personages to speak for the two sides. It is fair to say that, had they not lived and functioned considerably more than a century apart, they would have respected and admired one another and would have made a worthy set of opponents in any public debate on the issue—Thomas Jefferson against, and Benjamin Cardozo for! With due allowance for certain deviations, their points of view, even their verbiage, are today very much representative of the two divergent attitudes on the question.

Con: Although he was among the first to suggest judicial review as a means of harmonizing the federal system, and although evidence contained in at least two letters written from Paris to James Madison is persuasive that Thomas Jefferson had favored some type or degree of direct judicial control at the time of the framing of the Constitution in Philadelphia and even almost two years later,[6] the great Virginian certainly never accepted the notion of judicial review as it was subsequently expounded by his political opponent John Marshall. Some observers[7] trace the genesis of his hostility to the enforcement of the hated Alien and Sedition Act of 1789—prior thereto he was demonstrably not opposed to

[5] *The Supreme Court of the United States* (Cleveland and New York: The World Publishing Co., 1961), p. 77.
[6] Dec. 20, 1787, and March 15, 1789.
[7] E.g. Wallace Mendelson, "Jefferson on Judicial Review: Consistency through Change," 29 *University of Chicago Law Review* 327–37 (Winter 1962).

judicial review at least in theory. In any event, Jefferson's opposition was based upon two major concepts: first, that the doctrine of judicial review—as applied by Marshall, for he saw no one else do it—violates that of the constitutionally mandated theory of the separation of powers; and second, that it represents a patent denial of the veritable popular will, the majority will, as expressed by the sovereign people through their duly elected representatives "in Congress assembled" (and in any other properly constituted legislative body). That the second assertion did not, however, blind him to the potential excesses of these representatives, is indicated clearly in one of his letters to Madison, to whom he voiced the fear that ". . . the tyranny of the legislatures is the most formidable dread at present and will be for many years."[8]

Nonetheless, Jefferson vehemently rejected the contention that the Founding Fathers had intended to give to one of the three branches the right to prescribe rules for the government of the others, "and to that one, too, which is unelected by and independent of the nation." He insisted that each of the three branches, being independent, "has an equal right to decide for itself the meaning of the Constitution in the cases submitted to its action; where it is to act ultimately without appeal."[9] To Jefferson, the doctrine of judicial review, with its inherent possibilities of leading to judicial *supremacy,* was both elitist and *anti*democratic.

This position has been echoed frequently since, but by none better than by a contemporary of Jefferson, Mr. Justice John B. Gibson of the Supreme Court of Pennsylvania—probably the most able adversary of judicial review in his day. From that bench in 1825, in his now famous dissenting opinion in *Eakin v. Raub*,[10] in which his colleagues upheld the power of Pennsylvania's state courts to declare state statutes unconstitutional, Gibson challenged the Marshallian argument in *Marbury v. Madison* lucidly and forcefully along the lines of the Jeffersonian response. One of his key points was the classic concept of popular democracy—that it is a "postulate in the theory of our government . . . that the people are wise, virtuous, and competent to manage their own affairs."[11]

[8] Letter of March 15, 1789.

[9] From his letter to Judge Spencer Roane of the Virginia Supreme Court, September 6, 1819.

[10] 12 S. & R. (Pa. S. Ct.) 330.

[11] Ibid., at 355.

Yet Gibson had apparently modified his viewpoint twenty years later. When an attorney, pleading his case before the Pennsylvania Supreme Court, cited the Gibson dissent in *Eakin v. Raub,* that Justice replied from the bench that he had changed his opinion for two reasons: one, that the Pennsylvania Constitutional Convention of 1838, by remaining silent on judicial review, had "sanctioned the pretensions of the courts to deal freely with the acts of the legislature"; and two, "from experience of the necessity of the case."[12] This does not necessarily connote a change of mind, but it assuredly does indicate at least that Mr. Justice Gibson, true to his philosophy of the representative legislative function, had accepted the latter's "surrender" to the doctrine.

Pro: Although he greatly admired Jefferson both as a man and as a political philosopher, Benjamin N. Cardozo, who served for many years on the New York State Court of Appeals as well as an Associate Justice of the United States Supreme Court for the regrettably brief period from 1932 to 1938, disagreed strongly with Jefferson's approach to, and rejection of, judicial review. Cardozo anchored his belief in that doctrine upon the firm conviction that while it must be employed cautiously and sparingly, it serves nonetheless as a necessary and proper check on possible excesses by both the federal and state legislatures. But it would be utterly wrong to label him a "judicial activist." More than a decade prior to his universally hailed appointment to the Supreme Court, where he mounted the seat vacated by Mr. Justice Oliver Wendell Holmes, Jr., Mr. Justice Cardozo advanced his key contention that it is the *restraining influence of its presence* rather than the frequency of its application that renders judicial review so vital to the governmental process in the United States of America. His characteristically beautiful style and language must be quoted directly:

> By conscious or subconscious influence, the presence of this restraining power aloof in the background, but none the less always in reserve, *tends to stabilize and rationalize the legislative judgment,* to infuse it with the glow of principle, to hold the standard aloft and visible for those who must run the race and keep the faith. . . . The restraining power of the judiciary does not manifest

12 See *Norris v. Clymer,* 2 Pa. St. 277 (1845), at 281, as reported by Robert E. Cushman and Robert F. Cushman, *Cases in Constitutional Law* (New York: Appleton-Century-Crofts, 1958), pp. 22–3.

320

its chief worth in the few cases in which the legislature has gone beyond the lines that mark the limits of discretion. Rather shall we find *its chief worth in making vocal and audible the ideals that might otherwise be silenced, in giving them continuity of life and expression, in guiding and directing choice within the limits where choice ranges.* This function should preserve to the courts the power that now belongs to them; if only the power is exercised with insight into social values, and with suppleness of adaption to changing social needs.[13]

The man whom Cardozo had succeeded was familiar with the above passage, fully concurred in its sentiment and credo, and had practised it throughout his three decades on the highest bench of the land. However, although Holmes was willing to grant that the United States would not "come to an end if we lost our power to declare an Act of Congress void," he firmly insisted that ". . . the Union would be imperiled if we could not make that declaration as to the laws of the several states."[14] United States Circuit Court Judge Learned Hand, the great contemporary of Holmes and Cardozo, frequently echoed this Holmesian creed. But he went considerably further than Holmes when, writing several years after his retirement from the bench, he endeavored to set up a test which would provide another modification of the doctrine: While agreeing that the Supreme Court must have the power and authority to review *grants* of power to and by Congress, he believed that it should not possess these sanctions regarding "a review of how the power has been *exercised*."[15] It is difficult to see how such an amendment of the doctrine of judicial review would not wound it seriously, if not, in effect, fatally.

The Jefferson and Cardozo viewpoints—and their attempted modifications—have ardent and articulate adherents.[16] Yet there is no longer any doubt that judicial review is a permanent fixture in

13 *The Nature of the Judicial Process* (New Haven: Yale University Press, 1921), pp. 93–4. (Italics supplied.)
14 Oliver Wendell Holmes, Jr., "Law and the Court," in *Collected Legal Papers* (New York: Harcourt, Brace, 1920), p. 295.
15 Learned Hand, *The Bill of Rights* (Cambridge: Harvard University Press, 1958), p. 66, pp. 93–4. (Italics supplied.)
16 For a conveniently "tabularized" list of arguments in favor and against judicial review, see Alan F. Westin's "Introduction" to Prentice-Hall's 1962 paper edition of Charles A. Beard's classic, *The Supreme Court and the Constitution* (Englewood Cliffs, N.J.: Prentice-Hall, Inc.), pp. 6–7.

the American structure and operation of government, notwith-standing the repeated, and presumably continued, frontal and guerilla attacks from both public and private sources.[17] It is, after all, an essential adjunct of democracy, a normal fact of American governmental life.

DRAWING THE LINE— OR ATTEMPTING TO DO SO

Directly related to the controversy over the doctrine of judicial review, and inevitably associated with it intimately, is the frequently voiced charge that the Supreme Court of the United States —and to a somewhat lesser degree the lower rungs of the judiciary—is guilty of *judicial legislating;* in other words, that many of its decisions are tantamount to legislating rather than judging. More often than not, this indictment of the judiciary admits, and indeed grants, that the Court must have the power to *interpret* legislation and, if "absolutely necessary," hold unconstitutional a law that is *clearly* contrary to the Constitution—although no yardstick is provided on the connotation of the modifier "clearly." But this school of thought insists that a line must be drawn between the exercise of judicial *judgment* and the imposition of judicial *will.* Judicial will is accordingly equated with legislating, presumably reserved to Congress and the legislatures of the fifty states. Like all fine lines, the one between "interpreting" or "judging" and "legislating" is highly tenuous. How is it to be drawn? By whom? Where? Under what circumstances? Clearly there is no simple or single response to these questions, so crucial to line-drawing in general, and the line at issue in particular.

JUDICIAL LEGISLATING

The polar extremes in the controversy over the absence or presence of the concept of judicial legislating become readily apparent by

17 For summary analysis of attempted legislative checks on the power, see Sheldon D. Elliott, "Court-Curbing Proposals in Congress," 33 *Notre Dame Lawyer* 597–605 (August 1958). Two excellent books dealing with the problem are Walter F. Murphy, *Congress and the Court* (Chicago: University of Chicago Press, 1962) and C. Herman Pritchett, *Congress versus the Supreme Court* Minneapolis: University of Minnesota Press, 1961).

the following two quotes, taken from active and honorable participants on both sides of the aisle—institutionally as well as philosophically. Arising on the floor of the United States Senate, of which he constituted one of the finest and most purposeful members for many years, George W. Norris of Nebraska, the "gentle knight of progressive ideals," shouted:

> We have a legislative body, called the House of Representatives, of over 400 men. We have another legislative body, called the Senate, of less than 100 men. We have, in reality, another legislative body, called the Supreme Court, of nine men; and they are more powerful than all the others put together.[18]

The diametrically opposite point of view is represented in a passage from an address to the New York State Bar Association by Mr. Justice David Brewer of the United States Supreme Court:

> They [courts and judges] make no law, they establish no policy, they never enter into the domain of popular action. They do not govern. Their functions in relation to the state are limited to seeing that popular action does not trespass upon right and justice as it exists in written constitutions and natural law.[19]

Both expressions are equally extreme in their thesis as they represent gross oversimplifications, notwithstanding the sincerity and conviction of the two men involved.

Most justices of the highest tribunal do not claim to have a pat answer to the vexatious question presented by the controversy over *the line*. But they have often come to grips with the crux of the matter in recognizing the human element that is so inevitably involved in the judicial process. In the realistic words of Mr. Justice John H. Clarke:

> I have never known any judges, no difference how austere of manner, who discharged their judicial duties in an atmosphere of pure, unadulterated reason. Alas! we are all "the common growth of Mother Earth,"—even those of us who wear the long robe.[20]

The blunt-spoken Mr. Justice McReynolds insisted that a judge should not be "an amorphous dummy, unspotted by human emo-

[18] *Congressional Record,* 71 Cong. 2d Sess., Vol., 72, Part 4, p. 3566 (February 13, 1930).

[19] Address to the New York State Bar Association, *Proceedings* (1893).

[20] Hoyt L. Warner, *The Life of Mr. Justice Clarke* (Cleveland: Western Reserve University Press, 1959), p. 69.

tions." "Judges are men, not disembodied spirits," once remarked Mr. Justice Frankfurter; ". . . as men they respond to human situations. They do not reside in a vacuum." "Our judges are not monks or scientists," wrote Mr. Chief Justice Warren, "but participants in the living stream of our national life, steering the law between the dangers of rigidity on the one hand and formlessness on the other."[21]

In any event, the justices are agreed that they judge the cases and controversies that reach the Court in accordance with the Constitution and the laws of the land. There is no doubt that the nine justices—the judges on all levels of the judicial process—necessarily "legislate" in interpreting constitutional phraseology. The question is how much and how far they are justified in such judicial legislating. The often quoted jurist, however apocryphal the story may be, who responded to the question of whether judges make law replied, "Of course we do; made some myself," may sound somewhat extreme—but he is undoubtedly close to the truth of the situation. One of the wisest among the men ever to sit on the bench of the Supreme Court, the revered Mr. Justice Holmes, who has been so well described as the official judicial philosopher for the modern age,[22] also recognized "without hesitation" that judges *do and must* legislate"; but he added that they ". . . can do so only interstitially; they are confined from molar to molecular motions."[23]

Mr. Chief Justice Marshall, however, who was fully aware of the problem at issue, nevertheless insisted on commenting in one case that "judicial power, as contradistinguished from the power of the law, has no existence. Courts are the mere instruments of the law, and can will nothing."[24] Yet this man, who is generally recognized as the most competent and successful of all the Chief Justices to date, and ranked among the two or three most powerful and influential jurists ever to sit on the highest bench, was hardly one to be loath to interpret broadly the Constitution and legislation passed under its authority—and in accordance with what Mr.

21 "The Law and the Future," 52 *Fortune* 106 (November 1955).
22 Fred V. Cahill, Jr., *Judicial Legislation* (New York: The Ronald Press, 1952), p. 32.
23 *Southern Pacific Co. v. Jensen*, 244 U. S. 205 (1916), at 221. (Italics supplied.)
24 *Osborn v. United States Bank*, 9 Wheaton 738 (1824).

Justice Holmes later referred to as "the felt necessities of the time." After all, had not that same Marshall written, in the great *McCulloch v. Maryland* decision, that our laws were made under a Constitution that was "intended to endure for ages to come and, consequently, to be adapted to the various crises of human affairs"?[25] Probably not a single justice did more of this "adapting," and more incisively, than did Mr. Chief Justice Marshall, who often reminded his countrymen that "we must never forget that it is a *Constitution* we are expounding!" Did he *interpret* or did he *legislate?* Undoubtedly both; but who is to say, who to judge with finality?

More on the Line and on the Goring of Oxen. Marshall's long-term successor, Mr. Chief Justice Roger B. Taney, stared into the heart of the problem when, in rendering the majority opinion in the *Dred Scott* case, he held:

> The Constitution speaks not only in the same words, but with the same meaning and intent with which it spoke when it came from the hands of its framers, and was voted on and adopted by the people of the United States. Any other rule of construction would abrogate the judicial character of this Court and make it the mere reflex of the popular opinion or passion of the day.[26]

But the *Dred Scott* decision has been denounced more often as sheer "legislation" than any other decision of the Court, with the possible exception of the 1954 *Segregation Cases.*[27] When he was informed of the decision in *Dred Scott,* Senator Hale of New Hampshire introduced a resolution to *abolish* the Supreme Court. Yet again depending upon the point of view, those people who hailed the *Dred Scott* judgment as "statesmanlike interpretation" would have violently denounced the *Segregation Cases* as "blatant legislation," whereas the champions of the latter decisions would have roundly denounced the former on reverse grounds! Indeed some of the torrent of linguistic abuse poured upon the Court by *Segregation Cases* critics is almost identical in verbiage to that employed by the enemies of their Southern ancestors, the Radical Republicans of the North, in attacking *Dred Scott!* Could it be

[25] 4 Wheaton 316 (1819).
[26] *Dred Scott v. Sandford,* 19 Howard 393 (1857).
[27] *Brown v. Board of Education,* 347 U. S. 483 (1954) and *Bolling v. Sharpe,* 347 U. S. 497 (1954).

that the popular judgment does, indeed, depend upon whose ox is being gored?

Mr. Justice Owen J. Roberts, always searching for, if not inevitably contributing to, a modicum of consistency on the bench, attempted to draw the line once and for all in 1936—"the slot machine theory," commented Roscoe Pound acidly—when he spoke for a majority of six in the significant case of *United States v. Butler*, in which the Court struck down the Agricultural Adjustment Act of 1933:

> When an act of Congress is appropriately challenged in the Courts as not conforming to the constitutional mandate the judicial branch of the Government has only one duty—*to lay the article of the Constitution which is invoked beside the statute which is challenged and to decide whether the latter squares with the former.*[28]

"Bravo," applauded the *opponents* of the New Deal, "great judicial statesmanship, proper and precise interpretation of the Constitution!" "An unwarranted, outrageous assumption of legislative authority," countered the *proponents* of the New Deal, "arrogant disregard of constitutional limitations of judicial power." And President Roosevelt, scarcely one year after *Butler*, moved—unsuccessfully—to pack the Court by statutory provision, setting off one of the most interesting, most heated, and most sustained controversies in the entire history of Court and Nation.[29]

It was in the *Butler* case that the issue was perhaps most nearly faced by Mr. Justice Harlan Fiske Stone, not too many years hence to be the Chief Justice, when he dissented from the opinion of the majority and admonished the members on that side of the decision that

> . . . while unconstitutional exercise of power by the executive and legislative branches is subject to judicial restraint, *the only check on our own exercise of power is our own sense of self-restraint.* . . . Courts are not the only agency of government that must be assumed to have capacity to govern. . . . For the removal of unwise laws from the statute books appeal lies not to the courts, but to the ballot and to the processes of democratic government.[30]

28 297 U. S. 1 (1936), at 79. (Italics supplied.)

29 For a timely, engagingly written account, see Joseph Alsop and Turner Catledge, *The 168 Days* (New York: Doubleday, Doran, 1938).

30 *United States v. Butler*, 297 U. S. 1 (1936), at 94. (Italics supplied.)

This would seem to be as close to the facts of judicial life as is attainable. In a sense, and although he would very likely have disapproved of the comparison, the Stone comment was almost an echo of a famous statement made twenty years earlier by Charles Evans Hughes while he was the Republican Presidential nominee. He had just become an ex-Associate Justice of the United States Supreme Court; was an ex-Governor of New York; a future Secretary of State in the Administrations of Presidents Harding and Coolidge; and ultimately would ascend the Court for a second time as Chief Justice. While stumping during the campaign, a campaign which almost won him the Presidency, he publicly repeated a statement he had made some years earlier: *"We are under the Constitution, but the Constitution is what the judges say it is."*[31] That assertion represents both too drastic and too oversimplified an analysis of the complex position of the judiciary and the Court, and it is subject to considerable substantive modification. Surely, in the final analysis, the Constitution is or becomes what the people of the nation want it to be or to become—a fact of political life that is very much on the mind of judges—and it must be considered, as Holmes said, "in the light of our whole experience and not merely in that of what was said a hundred years ago." Moreover, while the Constitution, for the sake of argument, may well be what the judges say it is, that does by no means ascertain appropriate compliance, as has been repeatedly demonstrated. With these essential qualifications in mind, however, the Hughes campaign statement, coupled with the Stone dissent in the *Butler* case, could serve by and large as the definitive view of the Court's attitude. It has frequently been echoed by other articulate members of the highest bench, such as that philosophical devotee of British legislative supremacy and majority rule, Mr. Justice Frankfurter, who, in dissenting in the controversial expatriation case of *Trop v. Dulles,* lectured that:

All power is, in Madison's phrase, "of an encroaching nature." . . . Judicial power is not immune against this human weakness. It must also be on guard against encroaching beyond its proper bounds, and not the less so since *the only restraint upon it is self-restraint. . . .*[32]

31 Professor Hyneman claims—not entirely convincingly—that the Supreme Court specifically confirmed this notion in the "Little Rock Case," *Cooper v. Aaron,* 358 U. S. 1 (1958). (See his *The Supreme Court on Trial*, op. cit. pp. 78–80.)
32 356 U. S. 86 (1958), at 113. (Italics supplied.)

Vast differences about this aspect of the vexatious line exist now and have always existed among the justices themselves, but most, in fact probably all, would in candor subscribe to the essence of the suggested Stone-Hughes formula, however at variance their interpretation and application of it may be. One thing is clear above all: in the realistic words of Mr. Justice Cardozo—not only one of the most proficient and most beloved justices ever to sit on the Supreme Court, but also one of its finest and most haunting stylists: *"The great tides and currents which engulf the rest of men, do not turn aside in their course, and pass the judges idly by."*[33]

Mr. Justice George Sutherland, one of the six man majority in the *Butler* case, justified judicial activism—which he and his jurisprudent soulmates, Justices Van Devanter, McReynolds, and Butler applied chiefly in the economic *laisser faire* camp—as natural judicial involvement. As one student of Sutherland analyzed his posture, according to Sutherland the oath of office taken by each justice required him to decide cases in terms of his own best judgment. "Self-restraint, therefore, had no place among judicial duties. To surrender one's deliberate judgment, indeed, except as it might be modified by the persuasion of those holding different views, would constitute a violation of his oath of office."[34] To quote Sutherland directly from his dissenting opinion in the 1937 "switch-in-time-that-saved-nine" *West Coast Hotel* case:

> Self-restraint belongs in the domain of will and not of judgment. The check upon the judge is that imposed of his oath of office, by the Constitution, and by his own conscience and informed convictions.[35]

In any event, as Mr. Justice Frankfurter put the matter cogently, the Court cannot, in the long run, escape judging; it must adjudicate; it must decide. Not one to judge lightly or hastily—Professor Wallace Mendelson has aptly called him a "humilitarian" among jurists with respect to the legal process[36]—Frankfurter, while deeply dedicated to the concept of judicial self-restraint, neverthe-

---

[33] *The Nature of the Judicial Process*, op. cit. p. 168 (Italics supplied.)

[34] Carl Brent Swisher, *The Growth of Constitutional Power in the United States*, 2d ed. (Chicago: University of Chicago Press, 1963), p. 221.

[35] *West Coast Hotel Co. v. Parrish*, 300 U.S. 379, at 402.

[36] "Mr. Justice Frankfurter—Law and Choice," 10 *Vanderbilt Law Review* 333 (February 1957).

less clearly met the problem in his concurring opinion in the well-known *Sweezy* case:

> To be sure, this [opinion] is a conclusion based on a judicial judgment in balancing two contending principles—the right of a citizen to political privacy, as protected by the Fourteenth Amendment, and the right of the State to self-protection. And striking the balance implies the exercise of judgment. This is the inescapable judicial task in giving substantive content, legally enforced, to the Due Process Clause, and it is a task ultimately committed to this Court. It must not be an exercise of whim or will. *It must be an overriding judgment founded on something much deeper and more justifiable than personal preference. As far as it lies within human limitations, it must be impersonal judgment. It must rest on fundamental presuppositions rooted in history to which widespread acceptance may fairly be attributed.* Such a judgment must be arrived at in a spirit of humility when it counters the judgment of the State's highest court. *But, in the end, judgment cannot be escaped—the judgment of this Court.*[37]

That this awesome and even agonizing duty of finding and drawing the line between judicial will and judicial judgment in rendering a necessary decision conscientiously is not confined to the highest level of the federal judiciary, may be illustrated by a decision of the Supreme Court of Michigan. In a consortium case replete with human factors, a closely divided (4:3) Court not only reversed a lower court decision but negated precedent of long standing. Speaking for the majority, Mr. Justice Talbot Smith recognized that the decision represented a drastic departure from the past and would surely be viewed as judicial legislating. Yet having braved the expected storm, he admitted that the decision to permit the wife of a man seriously injured in an automobile accident to sue for loss of consortium—i.e. marital comfort, affection, and companionship—marked a stride away from the "outworn legal views" derived from old English and Roman law that a wife is merely a "vassal, chattel, and household drudge." He concluded:

> Were we to rule upon precedent alone, we would have no trouble with this case. We would simply tell this woman to be gone, and

[37] *Sweezy v. New Hampshire, by Wyman, Attorney-General,* 354 U.S. 234 (1957). (Italics supplied.)

take her shattered husband with her. . . . Legally today, the wife stands on a par with her husband. . . . *The obstacles to the wife's [court] action were judge-invented and they are herewith judge-destroyed.*[38]

The anticipated critical storm of charges of crass judicial legislating broke over the heads of author and Court at once. Yet, perhaps Mr. Justice Smith had simply been unusually frank in writing his opinion as he did—rather than disguising it in judicial semantics. Perhaps he had not been unaware of the famous statement of judicial philosophy expressed by Chancellor Kent of New York a century and a half earlier:

I saw where justice lay, and the moral issue decided the court [Kent] half the time; and I then sat down to search the authorities. . . . I might once in a while be embarrassed by a technical rule, but I almost always found principles suited to my views of the case. . . .[39]

In summary, depending, of course, upon the facts and posture of each individual case, both verbiage and line are very much matters of degree. But, as Mr. Justice Frankfurter took pain to admonish, to say that courts make law just as legislatures do is ". . . to deny essential features in the history of our democracy. It denies that legislation and adjudication have had different lines of growth, serve vitally different purposes, function under different conditions, and bear different responsibilities."[40]

JUDGES LIMITED:
THE TAUGHT TRADITION OF THE LAW

Moreover, it must be clearly understood that judges are not free agents in rendering their decisions, regardless of the impression given by some. Again in words by Mr. Justice Frankfurter: "We do not sit like kadi under a tree, dispensing justice according to considerations of individual expediency."[41] A deplorable tendency exists in the mind of the public to oversimplify the process of

38 *Montgomery v. Stephan,* 359 Mich. 33 (1960).
39 William Kent (ed.), *The Memoirs and Letters of James Kent* (Boston: Little Brown and Co., 1898), pp. 158–9.
40 "Reflections on Reading Statutes," 2 *The Record* 213 (June 1947).
41 *Terminiello v. Chicago,* 347 U.S. 1 (1949).

judicial decision-making, the area of government obviously least understood by the man on the street, however interested he may be. Although it may perhaps overstate the case somewhat, there is much merit in the contention of the very same Mr. Justice Talbot Smith just cited above in the Michigan case, that "we are rigidly bound within walls that are unseen" (by the layman).[42] These walls are built of the heritage of the law, the spirit of the Anglo-Saxon law, the impact of the cases as they come down through the years—in brief, *the taught tradition of the law*. No one expressed the heart of the matter better than Mr. Justice Cardozo when he said that

> a jurist is not to innovate at pleasure. He is not a knight-errant, roaming at will in pursuit of his own ideal of beauty or of goodness. He is to draw his inspiration from consecrated principles. He is not to yield to spasmodic sentiment, to vague and unregulated benevolence. He is to exercise a discretion informed by tradition, methodized by analogy, disciplined by system, and subordinated to the primordial necessity of order in the social life.[43]

Among the vital aspects of this taught tradition are: an abiding sense of judicial integrity; a close and necessary regard for the rules of procedure; considerations of equal treatment before the law; the deference shown to legislative enactments; judicial recognition of the realities of the cultural, ideological, and institutional setting which the judges share with their fellow citizens, not excluding the political realities; and there is *stare decisis,* the adherence to precedent.

STARE DECISIS

The desirability and, indeed, the need for certainty in planning our affairs, both in their internal (professional) and external aspects, render reliance on precedent an attractive and useful doctrine. "Imitation of the past," observed Mr. Justice Holmes, "until we have a clear reason for change, no more needs justification than appetite. It is a form of the inevitable to be accepted until we have a clear vision of what different things we want."[44]

---

[42] Statement to author, August 15, 1958 (Madison, Wisconsin).

[43] *The Nature of the Judicial Process,* op. cit. p. 141.

[44] "Holdsworth's English Law," in *Collected Legal Papers* (Boston: A. Harcourt, 1920), p. 290.

Yet, be it noted at once that *stare decisis* is a principle of policy and not a mechanical formula of adherence to the latest decision, "however recent and questionable, when such adherence involves collision with a prior doctrine more embracing in its scope, intrinsically sounder, and verified by experience."[45] *"Stare decisis,"* in the words of Mr. Justice Brandeis,

> is usually the wise policy, because in most matters it is more important that the applicable rule of law be settled than that it be settled right. . . . This is commonly true even where the error is a matter of serious concern, provided correction can be had by legislation. But in cases involving the Federal Constitution, where correction through legislative action is practically impossible, this Court has often overruled its earlier decisions. The Court bows to the lessons of experience and the force of better reasoning, recognizing that the process of trial and error, so fruitful in the physical sciences, is appropriate also in the judicial function."[46]

The doctrine of *stare decisis* requires a careful weighing in each doubtful case "of the advantages of adherence to precedent and the necessity for judicially planned social and economic progress."[47] The law, as Dean Pound has stated, must be stable and yet it cannot stand still. Or, as Viscount Kilmuir, then the Lord High Chancellor of Britain, told a distinguished audience of legal scholars in 1960: "Critics are apt to allege that we treat existing law with such reverence that every antique is replaced unaltered. I believe in an occasional spring cleaning."[48]

Reliance on precedent presents difficult problems to the judge, especially since the question to be resolved comes, normally speaking, to a *choice* of precedents. "Sometimes," commented Mr. Justice Jackson wistfully in his last book, "one is tempted to quote his former self, not only to pay his respects to the author, but to demonstrate the consistency of his views, if not their correctness."[49] Precedents abound and not all precedents are of equal

---

45 Mr. Justice Frankfurter, for the Court, in *Helvering v. Hallock,* 309 U.S. 106 (1940), at 110.

46 *Burnet v. Coronado Oil & Gas Co.,* 285 U.S. 293 (1932), at 406.

47 Robert A. Sprecher, "The Development of the Doctrine of Stare Decisis and the Extent to Which It Should Be Applied," 31 *American Bar Association Journal* 501–9 (1945).

48 Speech on the occasion of the dedication ceremony of the University of Chicago Law Center, April 30, 1960.

49 Robert H. Jackson, *The Supreme Court in the American System of Government* (Cambridge: Harvard University Press, 1955), p. 11.

rank; a good many judges generally seem to accord considerably more sanctity to very old and hallowed "precedents," such as most of Mr. Chief Justice John Marshall's decisions, than to those of relatively recent vintage. Progress, in any event, does not stand still, and a precedent may have to be overruled or reversed in time. "Our assurance that our children will live, as we have, under a constitutional democracy," commented the then U.S. Solicitor-General Stanley F. Reed, "rests upon the power of the form of government to adjust itself. . . . The position of the Supreme Court on *stare decisis* makes that adjustment possible."[50] In at least ninety decisions between 1810 and 1957 the Supreme Court of the United States *overruled* its own previous determinations.[51] Many additional cases are *distinguished* from precedent, which is somehow viewed as a less disrespectful device. "From age to age," commented Mr. Justice Douglas in an able treatment of the issue.

> the problem of constitutional adjudication is the same. It is to keep the power of government unrestrained by the social or economic theories that one set of judges may entertain. *It is to keep one age unfettered by the fears or limited vision of another.*[52]

Precedents, in Mr. Justice Talbot Smith's blunt words, being "judge-invented," may thus be "judge-destroyed." The judge must speak and through him society speaks. His function, as a leading student of constitutional law put it so lucidly, is "necessarily something more than to be a grammarian . . . [but] it is decidedly less than to be a zealot."[53] Lord Coke's practice to the contrary, few, if any, judges would today create a maxim out of whole cloth and then recite, "as the old maxim saith. . . ." (Yet it was the same Lord Coke who lauded *stare decisis* as "the known certaintie of the law which is the saftie of all."[54])

To sum up, the judge is assuredly not a free agent. On the

50 "Stare Decisis," 35 *Pennsylvania Bar Association Journal Quarterly* 150 (1938).
51 For a list of these 90 instances and a discussion of the entire "overruling" problem, see A. P. Blaustein and A. H. Field, "Overruling Opinions in the Supreme Court," 57 *Michigan Law Review* 2 (1957).
52 William O. Douglas, *Stare Decisis* (New York: The Association of the Bar of the City of New York, 1949), p. 31.
53 Paul A. Freund, *The Christian Science Monitor*, March 26, 1956.
54 Robert von Moschzisker, "Stare Decisis," 37 *Harvard Law Review* 409 (1924), at 429.

other hand no matter what it may be termed or how it may be styled, of necessity the judge "makes" the law—to some degree, at least. The delicate question will ever be how to aid its development without violating the confines of the constitutional structure. Let Mr. Justice Cardozo state the case:

> . . . [but] no doubt the limits for the judges are narrower. He legislates only between gaps. He fills the open spaces of the law. How far he may go without traveling beyond the walls of the interstices cannot be staked out for him upon a chart. He must learn it for himself as he gains the sense of fitness and proportion that comes with years of the practice of an art . . . None the less, within the confines of those open spaces and those of precedent and traditions, choice moves with a freedom which stamps its actions as creative. The law which is the resulting product is not found, but made. The process, being legislative, demands the legislator's wisdom.[55]

Surely, to echo a comment once made by Max Lerner, ". . . judicial decisions are not babies brought by constitutional storks." They are the carefully considered, more or less practical, judgments by the human beings who, sensitive to their calling, wield judicial authority—as judges, not as legislators.

OTHER LIMITATIONS
ON JUDICIAL POWER AND EFFECTIVENESS

Yet there remain several other qualifying considerations—checks may be a better term—upon judicial authority, even at the highest level of the federal courts. First, the Supreme Court's rulings may be effectively reversed by other participants in the process of government; second, they are almost inevitably responsive to overall policy formulations—sooner or later; third, for enforcement they must look to the executive branch of the government; and fourth, as we have seen in Chapter V, compliance with them is not necessarily automatic.

REVERSING THE COURT

In a variety of ways, although not without some toil and trouble, the Supreme Court of the United States may be reversed by direct

[55] *The Nature of the Judicial Process,* op. cit. pp. 113–15.

or indirect action of other institutions in the political process. Although its decisions unquestionably constitute the supreme law of the land—as they must if government under law is to have any meaning in American society—and are thus final and binding, even that high body "has the last say only for a time." This truth is readily documented by briefly examining the fate of the aforementioned ninety-four-odd cases in which the Court, as of its 1967–68 term—and unanimously in almost one-third of these instances—had struck down as unconstitutional one hundred and two provisions of federal laws.

No fewer than twenty-nine times has Congress passed legislation that has had the effect of reversing the Court either totally or in substantial measure—as it had in passing the Federal Employers' Liability Act of April 22, 1908, designed to replace that of 1906 which the Court had declared unconstitutional 5:4 as an illegal invasion of intrastate commerce in the *First Employers' Liability Cases*[56] earlier in 1908. Since Congress seemed to have corrected the alleged constitutional deficiency of the earlier statute, the Court found no difficulty in upholding it unanimously when the test came in the *Second Employers' Liability Cases*[57] in 1912. In other instances the circumstances or situation of the controversy had either changed or become moot, thus rendering insignificant or totally unimportant the erstwhile decision handed down by the Court—as, for example, the withdrawal of improperly delegated legislative power by action of the legislature or the revocation or amendment of a challenged administrative or executive order, both actions coming prior to the full effect of the Court's decision.[58] In some instances it simply *distinguished* cases from often very similar earlier decisions—as it did when it upheld the second New Deal Agricultural Act of 1938 in *Mulford v. Smith*[59] in 1939 even though it struck down the first A.A.A. in *U.S. v. Butler*[60] three years earlier. True, the statutes were not exactly alike, and the personnel of the Court had changed, but the essential features and purposes of the statutes were unchanged. In other cases, the Court itself questioned, reversed, modified, or even negated its

[56] 207 U. S. 463.
[57] 223 U. S. 1.
[58] E.g. *Lewis Publishing Co. v. Wyman,* 228 U. S. 610 (1913).
[59] 307 U. S. 38.
[60] 297 U. S. 1.

earlier judgments—by no means solely because of changes in its personnel—as it did so prominently in the four *Covert-Krueger Cases* between 1955 and 1960.[61] And in six to eight (depending upon one's point of view) instances—constitutional amendments were passed in order to reverse the Court: the *Eleventh* (1798), reversing the 1793 decision in *Chisholm v. Georgia*,[62] by amending the original jurisdiction of the Supreme Court to hear certain suits against the several states; the *Thirteenth, Fourteenth,* and *Fifteenth* (the Civil War Amendments, adopted in 1865, 1868, and 1870 respectively), reversing various Supreme Court decisions —including the *Dred Scott case*[63]—dealing with suffrage, slavery, and civil rights; and the *Sixteenth* (1913), the Income Tax Amendment, giving Congress power to tax incomes from whatever source derived, thereby effectively reversing the 1895 decisions in *Pollock v. Farmers' Loan and Trust Co.*[64] which had held various income tax *statutes,* designed to accomplish the same end, unconstitutional as a violation of Article 1, Section 9, Clause 4. Some would include the *Seventeenth* (direct election of U.S. Senators); *Nineteenth* (women suffrage, 1920); and the *Twenty-Fourth* (abolition of the poll tax in federal elections). The adoption of a constitutional amendment is the most authoritative and most certain method of reversing the Court, but it is also often the most difficult politically to attain, and almost always the most time-consuming.

Going beyond the one hundred and two provisions, the Court *overruled* thirty-two of its decisions between 1937 and 1946 alone —the immediate post-"switch-in-time-that-saved-nine" era. Prior thereto, the Court had overruled itself at least forty-six times. (These two figures cover not only overrulings of provisions previously held unconstitutional, but also those made on other than constitutional grounds.)[65] Unless it seems to be absolutely necessary, however, the Court is disinclined to resort to the strong

61 *Kinsella v. Krueger,* 357 U. S. 470 and *Reid v. Covert,* 351 U. S. 487 (June 11, 1956); 352 U. S. 901 (November 5, 1956); 354 U. S. 1 (June 10, 1957); and *Kinsella v. Singleton et al.,* 361 U. S. 234 (January 18, 1960).

62 2 Dallas 419.

63 *Dred Scott v. Sandford,* 19 Howard 393 (1857).

64 158 U. S. 601 and 157 U. S. 429.

65 For a complete chart of overrulings between 1790 and 1957, see S. Sidney Ulmer, "Lawmaking of the Supreme Court," 8 *Journal of Public Law* 418–23 (1957).

concept of *overruling*. Thus, in only eight instances among the aforementioned one hundred and two did the Court in subsequent decisions *specifically and literally* acknowledge an overruling—as it did, for example, in upholding the entire federal Fair Labor Standards Act of 1938 in the case of *United States v. Darby*[66] in 1941. There, among others, addressing itself to the child labor provisions of that statute, it *specifically* overruled its 1918 decision in *Hammer v. Dagenhart*,[67] where it had declared the federal Keating-Owen Child Labor Law of 1916 unconstitutional. Overruling differs from reversing as a matter of definition: technically speaking, a case may be *reversed* only on rehearing; thus, the original decision and the reversing decision are applicable to the *identical case*. An example of that procedure is the Court's decision in *Jones v. Opelika,* 316 U.S. 584, on June 8, 1942, upholding 5:4 an Opelika, Alabama, statute which required payment of the usual license tax or fee even by those groups (here the Jehovah Witnesses) that claimed exemption on grounds of freedom of religion —a decision which the Court *vacated* 5:4 on rehearing less than eleven months later, in *Jones v. Opelika,* 319 U.S. 103, on May 3, 1943, and then *reversed* on the same day in *Murdock v. Pennsylvania,* 319 U.S. 105.

The various statistics just cited do not take into account the many instances in which the Court overrules precedents *sub silentio*—i.e. when it overrules an earlier decision without saying so, but where the effect is clearly the same as an expressed overruling —as it did on several occasions in the last quarter of the past century and the first quarter of this century in the realm of commerce and taxation (and probably for sound policy reasons). Nor do the above figures account for those instances in which Congress, disagreeing with the Supreme Court's reading of a statute, simply rewrites or repeals it. For example, between 1944 and 1961 alone, Congress took fifty actions in economic matters which collectively overturned seventy-five Supreme Court rulings.

Thus, although many of the Supreme Court's decisions on questions of constitutionality last, quite a few are ultimately modified or neutralized by the Court itself or by valid action of other branches of the government, led by Congress. America's system of judicial

[66] 312 U. S. 100.
[67] 247 U. S. 251.

review, as Professor Freund has noted cogently, indeed produces frustrations, but it has a saving grace of resiliency.

POLICY FORMULATIONS AND CONSIDERATIONS

In any case, the policy views of the Court, the members of which, after all, are "children of their times,"[68] never remain for long out of line with the policy views of the lawmaking majority—with the probable, but not inevitable, exception of decisions involving the Bill of Rights, particularly those made between 1940–49 and 1954–57 when the Court on a good number of occasions stood as a veritable bastion against the popular majority viewpoint. On major public policy issues both the Chief Executive and Congress may be expected to succeed—speaking generally and *in the long run*,[69] although in the short run they may well have to bow. If the Court is to thrive, as Professor Wallace Mendelson has said so well, it "must respect the social forces that determine elections and other major political settlements. No court can long withstand the morals of its era."[70] It is the "child of its time." The Court, however, cannot be a mere register of public opinion; it must be a leader of it. As Francis Biddle said, its justices "must not get away too far from life and should continually touch earth for renewed vitality."[71]

This judicial alignment with the other two major branches on overriding policy matters may not always follow axiomatically, but it comes very close to reality. Some observers of the scene have even contended that far from representing a dependable means of preventing "legislative tyranny," judicial review of national policy seems to have but marginal value.[72] Whatever the actual merits of

68 Robert G. McCloskey, *The American Supreme Court* (Chicago: University of Chicago Press, 1961), p. 182.

69 ". . . and the run must not be too long either!," as Professor Edward S. Corwin once observed. (*Court Over Constitution*. Princeton: Princeton University Press, 1938, p. 127.)

70 *Justices Black and Frankfurter: Conflict in the Court*, 2d ed. (Chicago: University of Chicago Press, 1967), pp. 75–6. On this point see also the excellent article by Robert A. Dahl, "Decision-Making in a Democracy: The Supreme Court as a National Policy-Maker," 6 *Journal of Public Law* 279 (1957).

71 *Justice Holmes, Natural Law, and the Supreme Court* (New York: The Macmillan Co., 1961), p. 73.

72 E.g. S. Sidney Ulmer, "Judicial Review as Political Behavior: A Temporary Check on Congress," 4 *Administrative Science Quarterly* 426 (March 1960).

this judgment may be, the Court is well aware of the limitations upon its powers. Mr. Justice Frankfurter, the "conscience of the Court" during most of his lengthy tenure, thus addressed himself to the question of reversing the Supreme Court in his now well known separate concurring opinion in the unanimously decided Little Rock School Case, *Cooper v. Aaron*,[73] in which he quoted at length from his concurring opinion in the *United Mine Workers Case* of 1947:

> Even this court has the last say only for a time. Being composed of fallible men, it may err. But revision of its errors must be by orderly process of law. The court may be asked to reconsider its decisions, and this has been done successfully again and again throughout our history. Or, what this court has deemed its duty to decide may be changed by legislaiton, as it often has been, and, on occasion, by constitutional amendment.[74]

He might have added that one of the major catalysts in revision and reconsideration is the inevitably changing personnel composition of the Court—yet any recognition of that crucial element in judicial decision-making must carefully guard against a pat and oversimplified catch-all analysis of its significance. In any event, reversal of judicial action is possible, and it has frequently been effectuated. Decisions running counter to the broad concensus simply do not last in the long run. The toast offered in 1801 at a dinner honoring the justices, "To the Judiciary of the United States—independent of party, independent of power, independent of popularity!,"[75] merits skeptical analysis.

COMPLIANCE AND ENFORCEMENT

But there is more to be said. In Chapter V it was demonstrated at some length that the judgments of the Supreme Court of the United States are not necessarily accepted as automatically binding by those who ought to be bound. A decision may be simply ignored, as was proved by, for example, the continuation of the practice of "released time"[76] in numerous public secondary schools

[73] 358 U. S. 1 (1958).

[74] *United States v. United Mine Workers*, 330 U. S. 258.

[75] As quoted in *Connecticut Courant*, February 9 and 16, 1801.

[76] For an explanation and an analysis of "released time" see my *Freedom and the Court: Civil Rights and Liberties in the United States* (New York: Oxford University Press, 1967), Ch. VI.

in situations and settings identical to that struck down as an unconstitutional violation of the principle of separation of state and church in *McCollum v. Board of Education.*[77] In 1966, four years after the decisions in the *Prayer and Bible Reading Cases,*[78] some 60 per cent of the states reported continued violations of the Court's mandates.[79] Or a decision may be circumvented, and even opposed by force, to which the 1954 and 1955 *Segregation Cases* and their progeny bear ample witness. And there is the already described host of calculated, interminable delays in compliance.[80]

Moreover, with very few exceptions of the original jurisdiction docket cases, the Court formulates *general* policy. It is the lower federal and state courts, as the case may be, that *apply* it, presumably "not inconsistent with this opinion," as the Supreme Court's mandate normally reads. In so applying the opinion, the lower courts may, and often do, materially modify the Supreme Court's determination. These modifications, moreover, are not at all astonishing in view of the not infrequent habit of Supreme Court justices to mix dogma with dicta. On the other hand, some of the so-called "modifications" or "interpretations" clearly have been little short of outright defiance—especially by state courts.[81]

There is also the obvious fact that, lacking any source of physical power of its own, the Supreme Court depends on the political branches of the government for the enforcement of its mandates, in particular on the Chief Executive—who has the vital obligation to ascertain obedience to all court orders. If the Court fails to obtain that co-operation in those instances where it is vital for compliance, it necessarily stands helplessly on the sidelines. The most famous case in point is the, perhaps apocryphal, comment by President Andrew Jackson who, according to Mr. Chief Justice Marshall's biographer, once exploded, "John Marshall has made his decision:—*now let him enforce it!*"[82] The outburst reputedly

[77] 333 U.S. 203 (1948).

[78] *Engel v. Vitale,* 370 U.S. 421 (1962) and *Abington School District v. Schempp* and *Murray v. Curlett,* 374 U.S. 203 (1963).

[79] See the enlightening study by Ellis Katz, "Patterns of Compliance with the *Schempp* Decision," 14 *Journal of Public Law* 2 (1966).

[80] See Ch. V, pp. 225–31.

[81] On this general point see the informative article by Walter Murphy, "Lower Court in Supreme Court Power," 53 *American Political Science Review* 1017–31 (December 1959).

[82] Albert J. Beveridge, *The Life of John Marshall,* Vol. 4 (Boston: Houghton Mifflin Co., 1919), p. 551.

occurred as a result of Marshall's decision in *Worcester v. Georgia*,[83] in which his Court upheld the rights of the Cherokee Indians in a dispute with Georgia, and he strongly implied in his opinion that it was the President's duty to honor and back the Cherokee Nation's rights under federal law. Apocryphal or not, the Jackson comment illustrates the Court's dependence and its quandary when the necessary executive support is not forthcoming. Its effectiveness in the absence of the executive sword is as limited as its operations in general would be without the necessary appropriations from the legislative purse, and the legislative assent to its jurisdictional and procedural needs. In essence, as Mr. Justice Jackson stated this fact of judicial life starkly, ". . . [the Court] can perform but one function—that of deciding litigations—and can proceed in no manner except by the judicial process."[84] Thus he echoed an oft-quoted remark by Mr. Justice Samuel Miller that "in the division of the powers of government between the three great departments, executive, legislative, and judicial, the judicial is the weakest for purposes of self-protection and for the enforcement of the power which it exercises."[85] But not only do we often expect too much from the Court, we let it—or wish it would—settle *policy* matters that ought to be settled by one of the other two branches, notably the legislative, but which for a variety of reasons, chiefly political, are not.[86] Glaring illustrations of such policy matters are reapportionment/redistricting; segregation/desegregation; and criminal justice. And there are others where the proverbial buck has been passed to the judicial branch!

MACHTKAMPF: THE SUPREME COURT IN THE POLITICAL POWER STRUGGLE

Despite the implications of the preceding paragraphs, the Supreme Court has been a participant in what may be viewed as a continuous struggle by the three "separated branches" of the federal government to attain a position of dominance, if not ultimate con-

83 6 Peters 515 (1832). Worcester was a missionary preaching the gospel.

84 *The Supreme Court in the American System of Government* (Cambridge: Harvard University Press, 1955), p. 12.

85 *In re Neagle*, 135 U.S. 1 (1890), at 63.

86 On that point see the address by Mr. Justice Harlan at dedication ceremonies of the American Bar Center at Chicago, Illinois, August 13, 1963.

trol, in the American political system. Since it lacks the potent weapons of the other two branches, especially weapons that would aid its self-protection and its enforcement of the powers which it exercises, the Court has necessarily been less prominent in this *Machtkampf* (struggle for power); but its own important tool of judicial review has provided it with a genuine measure of authority. And, as just pointed out, it has often been propelled into action precisely because the other organs of government have failed to fulfill their own responsibilities.

Victory in the *Machtkampf* of the three branches has been in the form of supremacy which has alternated from branch to branch; although sometimes the struggle has been featured by a quasi-alliance of two branches against the third over a period of time. A pertinent example is the frustrated and frustrating protracted effort of the closely allied New Deal Legislature and New Deal Executive commencing in 1933, which, on many major issues, had to wait for victory over the Supreme Court until four years later when the "switch-in-time-that-saved-nine" took place.

In general, however, the *tone* of dominance has been set by the person and personality of the elected Chief Executive, who, after all, is the sole individual in the American federal governmental process to have a nation-wide constituency, and who, within limits, is in the position of interpreting his powers narrowly or broadly. In other words, whenever the President has been of the category commonly called "active" or "strong"—e.g. Washington, Jackson, Polk, Lincoln, Wilson, the two Roosevelts, and Lyndon Johnson—the Executive branch, *in the long run,* has been able to acquire supremacy. Where he has been "passive" or "weak" or simply lacked sufficient support in Congress or by the people—e.g. John Quincy Adams, Pierce, Buchanan, Andrew Johnson, Grant, McKinley, Harding, Coolidge, Hoover—supremacy was acquired by Congress or, on occasion, by the Supreme Court. In several instances no clear-cut supremacy can be pinpointed. This is true, for example, of the Presidencies of Madison and Monroe—perhaps even Jefferson, although historians and political scientists differ sharply in evaluating his role in office—Hayes, Cleveland, Taft, Truman, Eisenhower (near the end of his second term after the dismissal of Sherman Adams and the death of John Foster Dulles—there is no doubt about the presence of congressional supremacy

342

TABLE IX
PERIODS OF DISCERNIBLE TENDENCIES TOWARD
SUPREMACY OF BRANCHES OF THE GOVERNMENT

Years	President(s)	Chief Justice(s)	Commentary
A. *Tendencies Toward Legislative Supremacy*			
1809–1829	Madison Monroe J. Q. Adams	Marshall	Supremacy facilitated and advanced by powerful Court.
1837–1845	Van Buren W. H. Harrison Tyler	Taney	Aided by strong Court and passive Presidents.
1849–1861	Taylor Fillmore Pierce Buchanan	Taney	Nadir of Presidency. *Dred Scott* case.
1865–1885	Johnson Grant Hayes Garfield Arthur	S. P. Chase Waite	Partially effective opposition by Johnson and Hayes.
1919–1921	Wilson	White	Defeat of League. President ill.
1921–1933	Harding Coolidge Hoover	Taft Hughes	Co-operative Court. Weak, passive Presidents.
1957–1959	Eisenhower	Warren	Strong Court. Passive President.
B. *Tendencies Toward Executive Supremacy*			
1789–1797	Washington	Jay Rutledge Ellsworth	Co-operative Congress. Weak, docile Court.
1801–1809	Jefferson	Marshall	Some doubt about Executive Supremacy, but tendency.
1829–1837	Jackson	Marshall Taney	President in high form. Last years of Marshall Court.
1845–1849	Polk	Taney	Underrated President.
1861–1865	Lincoln	Taney S. P. Chase	High-water mark of Presidency. Civil War.
1901–1908	T. Roosevelt	Fuller	Assertive Court. Popular President.

Years	President(s)	Chief Justice(s)	Commentary
1913–1919	Wilson	White	President lost control to Republican Congressional majority in 1919.
1933–1945	F. D. Roosevelt	Hughes	Revolution on Court, 1937. "Packing."
		Stone	Powerful President.
1945–1947	Truman	Vinson	Truman "Honeymoon."
1963–	L. B. Johnson	Warren	Powerful President.

C. *Tendencies Toward Judicial Supremacy*

Years	President(s)	Chief Justice(s)	Commentary
1801–1829	Jefferson Madison Monroe J. Q. Adams	Marshall	The greatest Chief Justice at power's peak.
1857	Pierce Buchanan	Taney	The *Dred Scott* case.
1889–1910	B. Harrison Cleveland McKinley	Fuller	Some doubt re Cleveland term (his second).
1935–1936	F. D. Roosevelt	Hughes	13 New Deal Laws declared unconstitutional.
1954–1957	Eisenhower	Warren	Civil libertarian activism.

D. *Not Readily Discernible Supremacy Tendencies*

Years	President(s)	Chief Justice(s)	Commentary
1797–1801	John Adams	Ellsworth	President and Congress shared.
1885–1889	Cleveland	Waite	Probably President, but . . .
		Fuller	
1910–1913	Taft	White	Uncertainty.
1947–1953	Truman	Vinson	Divided foreign and domestic tendencies.
1959–1960	Eisenhower	Warren	Sudden assertion of power by President. Democratic Congressional majority.
1961–1963	Kennedy	Warren	Divided foreign and domestic tendencies. Strong Court.

during Eisenhower's first term in office), and Kennedy. Finally, it should be noted that during some Presidencies the Executive has tended to dominate in foreign affairs and the Congress in internal matters, e.g. Truman, Eisenhower, and Kennedy.

At the risk of some oversimplification and generalization— which inevitably attend categorization and classification—Table IX is designed to indicate periods of American history in which existed fairly discernible tendencies toward supremacy by one branch or two allied branches against a third. Some periods will be listed in more than one category, for example the first four years of the New Deal era, when Presidential supremacy was un- questioned—or, rather, when there was surrender by Congress to President Roosevelt, but during which time the Supreme Court proved to be a major roadblock to the New Deal program.

There is no doubt that the Supreme Court of the United States has repeatedly *challenged* the authority of both President and Congress. But in spite of the four or five indicated periods of tendencies toward judicial supremacy, the Court has never really actively *bid* for the role of dominant governmental agency of the land—although a good case could be made for there having been such a bid during the era of Mr. Chief Justice Marshall. During that period, as well as during the heyday of the Hughes Anti-New Deal Court, we may speak of periodic "government by judiciary" or "judicial supremacy," yet even then there was never any genuine likelihood that the Court would *in the final analysis* effectively *dominate* the Executive and/or the Legislative branches. When all is said and done, the Supreme Court of the United States does not possess the political power, the arsenal of potent weapons of gov- ernment, the tools of the publicity media, or the strategic position in the government or in the body politic generally enjoyed by the other two branches.

An Historical Note. If we take a closer look at the Supreme Court's role in the *Machtkampf* on the American political scene we see that the high tribunal began on a very inauspicious note. Its dozen or so pre-Marshall years, during which three Chief Jus- tices came and went—the second of whom, John Rutledge, was not confirmed by the Senate—were characterized by a lack of popular esteem and understanding, little work, and dissatisfied personnel. The first Chief Justice, John Jay, so thoroughly disliked his job and so loathed circuit-riding, that he not only spent one year during his tenure in England on a diplomatic mission, but twice ran for Governor of New York, succeeding on the second try, whereupon he happily resigned the Chief Justiceship! When President Adams offered to re-appoint him as Chief Justice in 1801, he refused categorically. And, as already pointed out, the third Chief Justice, Oliver Ellsworth, happily left his office for a diplomatic post. The Court did, however, soon make clear that it intended to act as an arbiter in legal disputes between the states and the federal government; and it became quickly apparent that its judicial sympathies lay with the latter.

The Marshall era, of course, brought about a drastic change. The Chief Justice completely dominated the Court—with dissents confined almost solely to Mr. Justice William Johnson. It is quite clear that Marshall, more than any other man in the history of the Court, determined the character of America's federal constitutional system. From its lowly, if not discredited, level John Marshall raised the United States Supreme Court to a position of equality with the Executive and the Legislature. He called his constitutional interpretations as he saw them, always adhering to his previously discussed, oft-expressed doctrine that ". . . it is a constitution we are expounding . . . intended to endure for ages to come and, consequently, to be adapted to the various crises of human affairs."[87] Yet, as we know, he hastened to insist that "judicial power, as contradistinguished from the power of law, has no existence. Courts are the mere instruments of the law, and can will nothing."[88] Thus, "willing nothing," Marshall handed down, among many others, four of the most momentous decisions in the history of Court and Country, without which it is doubtful that the nation would have grown and prospered as it has: (1) *Marbury v. Madison*[89] (judicial review, supremacy of the U.S. Constitution); (2) *McCulloch v. Maryland*[90] (implied powers of Congress, reaffirmation of the supremacy of the U.S. Constitution, federal immunity from involuntary state taxation, federal government held to have its powers directly from the people rather than by way of the states); (3) *Gibbons v. Ogden*[91] (plenary federal control over interstate commerce); and (4) *Dartmouth College v. Woodward*[92]

[87] *Osborn v. United States Bank*, 9 Wheaton 738 (1824), at 866.
[88] *McCulloch v. Maryland*, 4 Wheaton 316 (1819).
[89] 1 Cranch 137 (1803).
[90] Loc. cit.
[91] 9 Wheaton 1 (1824).
[92] 4 Wheaton 518 (1819).

(inviolability of contracts). Truly, the Court led and, leading, gave the federal government the means to develop and work.

Whereas the Marshall Court had by its decisions placed the emphasis upon the national commercial-creditor-propertied classes, its successor, the also powerful Taney Court, pursued a different emphasis. The sanctity of property remained a primary consideration of the tribunal, but it devolved upon a different segment of society and, incidentally, of the country. A Southerner from Maryland, the Jackson-appointed Roger B. Taney, a Democrat and a Catholic—the first of his religious persuasion to be on the bench— by his decisions favored "states rights" and *agrarian* property, that is, land and slaves. From a totally different milieu than the great constitutional nationalist who preceded him, Taney, and with him a majority of his Court, demonstrated a faithful attachment to the economic interests of the South and the rapidly developing frontier of the West. But disaster loomed on the horizon: after pursuing the aforementioned policies determinedly, and with little, if any, interference from the other two branches for twenty years, Taney, then in his eightieth year, lonely and frustrated, met his and the Court's judicial Waterloo in 1857 with his opinion in *Dred Scott v. Sandford*[93]—leaked in advance by Mr. Justice Catron, the sole known such breach of secrecy on record.

This decision—"more than a crime . . . a blunder"[94]—by his Southern-dominated Court, with but two Justices dissenting, John McLean[95] and Benjamin Curtis, Curtis's opinion having been circulated in advance in the Northern press, featured nine separate opinions, including Taney's. It stipulated among other things: no Negro could be a citizen; that the Negro was "a person of an inferior order"; that he was a slave and thus his master's permanent property no matter whether the latter took him to slave or free parts of the country; that the Missouri Compromise was unconstitutional; and that no individual of African descent was "a portion of this American people." *Dred Scott* permanently marred Taney's reputation, dragged the Supreme Court of the United States into its lowest depths, hastened the dawn of the Civil War and with it

[93] 19 Howard 393.

[94] Bickel, *The Least Dangerous Branch*, op. cit. p. 45.

[95] For a discussion of McLean's political motivations and aspirations see fn. 98, Ch. V *supra*. See also Bickel's commentary in his *Politics and the Warren Court* (New York: Harper & Row, 1965), p. 135.

the Emancipation Declaration and the Civil War Amendments (XIII, XIV, and XV). In the words of a Washington newspaperman, "If epithets and denunciations could sink a judicial body, the Supreme Court of the United States would never be heard of again."[96]

With *Dred Scott*—which has been widely viewed as the most disastrous opinion ever issued by it[97]—the Court invited a violent congressional reaction. While that took a while to take concrete form, the influence of the Court declined at once. The country as a whole was hardly willing to consider, let alone accept, Mr. Justice James M. Wayne's anxious explanation *cum plea* in his concurring opinion that

> . . . there had become such a difference of opinion that the peace and harmony of the country required the settlement of the slavery issues by judicial decision. . . . In our action we have only discharged our duty as a distinct and efficient department of the Government, as the framers of the Constitution meant the judiciary to be. . . .[98]

Far from alleviating the incipient sectional strife, the Court had promoted it. During and after the Civil War, with Taney's role reduced to one of bitterness and unhappiness, Congress demonstrated its utter contempt of the Supreme Court by *thrice* changing its size in six years; up from nine to ten in 1863; down from ten to seven in 1866; up again from seven to nine in 1869. Quite obviously, all this was done for policy purposes. And, as we have seen earlier in these pages, when in 1868–69 the post-Taney Court indicated a possible declaration of unconstitutionality of some of the military Reconstruction Acts, an angry Congress, acting under its powers derived from the Constitution to limit the Court's appellate jurisdiction, simply deprived it of the power to decide the case.[99] This was the beginning of the Chief Justiceship of the politically ambitious Salmon P. Chase (1864–74)[100] and

96 As quoted by Hyneman, op. cit. p. 31.

97 E.g. McCloskey, op. cit. p. 94.

98 *Dred Scott v. Sandford*, loc. cit., at 454–5.

99 *Ex parte McCardle*, 7 Wallace 506 (1869).

100 Prior to his assumption of the Chief Justiceship, Chase had been a candidate at the Republican Presidential conventions of 1856 and 1860. In 1868, while on the highest bench, he unsuccessfully sought the Presidential nomination on *both* tickets!

348

of Morrison R. Waite (1874–88), both Northern Republicans, during whose tenure the Court, predictably, was chiefly concerned, in addition to safeguarding property, with maintaining the status quo: state authority over individuals and federal authority over interstate commerce—which represented the two great post-Civil War problems. The former included the Waite Court's nullification of the attempted use of the due process of law clause of the Fourteenth Amendment by the federal government as a national arm to protect civil rights in the states in the historic *Civil Rights Cases*[101]—something the Chase Court had already done in connection with the Amendment's "privileges and immunities" clause when citizens of Louisiana attempted to invoke it.[102] Indeed, the Chase Court, in a burst of judicial activism, did declare ten acts of Congress unconstitutional; but, as explained above, in the final analysis it bowed before the power of the Radical Republicans in Congress, and it was effectively "packed" by President Grant in 1871, thus nullifying within fifteen months its briefly successful attempt to battle for what it had regarded as stable currency in the *Legal Tender Cases*.[103] One important contribution of the Waite Court to be noted, notwithstanding its generally proprietarian bent, was the highly significant development of the "affectation with the public interest" doctrine, announced by the Chief Justice himself in his opinion for a majority of seven in the leading *Granger* case of *Munn v. Illinois*.[104] There, while still clinging to the notion of due process laid down in *The Slaughterhouse Cases*,[105] Waite held that, under certain circumstances, the state police power could be employed to regulate private property in the public interest.

With the long Chief Justiceship of the Cleveland-appointed Melville W. Fuller of Illinois, however, the Court all but bid for policy leadership. It did this, above all, by striking out on a path designed to re-assure the sanctity of property, as the majority of the Court saw it. This majority was now composed of a group of highly conservative, property-conscious justices, who, when given the opportunity, began to strike down as unconstitiutional a fair

101 109 U.S. 3 (1883).
102 *The Slaughterhouse Cases*, 16 Wallace 36 (1873).
103 12 Wallace 457 (1871) and *Hepburn v. Griswold*, 8 Wallace 603 (1870).
104 94 U.S. 113 (1877).
105 16 Wallace 36 (1873).

number of federal and state laws in the economic and social sphere. *Laisser faire* seemed secure, indeed! Until roughly this time, state laws, for example, had been held unconstitutional largely because they were viewed as conflicting either with the interstate commerce or the obligation-of-contract clauses of the Constitution. Of 128 state laws invalidated by the federal courts *before* 1888, 50 involved the former clause, 50 the latter, and only one the taking of property "without due process of law." The Fuller Court, on the other had, ultimately struck down a large number of state laws on that last ground, holding that the several legislative "experimentations" at issue deprived "persons" of liberty and property without *substantive* due process of law. Substantive due process had truly come of age! And the concept of "persons" now also included *corporations,* thanks to a unanimous Court ruling in the *Santa Clara* case,[106] a decision invalidating assessments on portions of railroad property. It was featured by a casual *announcement* at the hearing stage by Mr. Chief Justice Waite, who did not even write the opinion: "The Court does not wish to hear argument on the question whether the provision in the Fourteenth Amendment to the Constitution, which forbids a State to deny to any person within its jurisdiction the equal protection of the laws, applies to these Corporations. We are all of the opinion that it does."[106] This was a rather cavalier manner of disposing of a highly significant constitutional issue—one that was neither before the Court nor had been argued in the case at bar!

The states, however, and—considerably later—the federal government insistently wished to pioneer in the realm of economic and social legislation, as they deemed that to be the desire of the majority of the voters. Yet in most areas—viz., maximum hours, minimum wages, working conditions, regulation of woman and child labor, compulsory arbitration, employer liability, and many others—the legislatures ran into the judicial vetoes not only of the Fuller Court, but also those of his successors, the White and Taft Courts and, until 1937, the Hughes Court—despite the Waite "affectation with the public interest doctrine." Throughout this period the Supreme Court demonstrated again and again a remarkable regard for the protection of *property* under its inter-

---

106 *Santa Clara County v. Southern Pacific Railroad Co.,* 118 U.S. 394 (1886), at 396.

pretations of the "liberty and property" phases of the "due process of law" clauses of the Fifth and Fourteenth Amendments to the United States Constitution. But, oddly enough, the Court found these clauses no barrier against legislative invasions of the *cultural and political* fields, often referred to as "civil rights" or "civil liberties."

From the turn of the century on, when the great Mr. Justice Oliver Wendell Holmes, Jr., was appointed to what was to be his thirty-year tenure on the Court by President Theodore Roosevelt, dissenting voices to the majority's policies were increasingly heard. As of 1916 Holmes was joined in dissents, although frequently for quite different reasons, by his colleague Louis D. Brandeis, and with the advent of Justices Harlan F. Stone in 1925 and Benjamin N. Cardozo in 1932, the dissenting voices in this area had swelled to just one short of a majority. The previously described switch by Mr. Chief Justice Hughes, and, to a lesser extent, Mr. Justice Owen D. Roberts's, ultimately brought on what the eminent American constitutionalist, Edward S. Corwin, aptly called "a Constitutional Revolution." Having lost the battle of "packing" the Court in February 1937, President F. D. Roosevelt won the "war" when fate, in the form of deaths and resignations, weeded out the remaining four ultra-conservative justices on the bench between 1937 and 1941—Associate Justices Willis Van Devanter, George Sutherland, James C. McReynolds, and Pierce Butler—ultimately allowing him to fill nine vacancies on the Court.[107]

By no means all of these Roosevelt appointees saw the law as he had hoped they would, but certainly the New Deal now had clear sailing, and there was no doubt that the new justices rejected outright the "thou-shalt-not-pass" doctrines of their predecessors relative to legislative experimentation in the economic-proprietarian sphere. As Mr. Justice Black was to comment later: "Whether the legislature takes for its textbook Adam Smith, Herbert Spencer, Lord Keynes, or some other is no concern of ours."[108] Judicial self-restraint on legislative policy-making in these areas of public life became the avowed policy of the Court—just as the "Old Court" had practised a similar restraint on legislative policies in

[107] Black, Reed, Frankfurter, Douglas, Murphy, Stone (promotion to Chief Justice), Byrnes, Jackson, and Rutledge.
[108] *Ferguson v. Skrupa*, 372 U.S. 726 (1963), at 732.

the cultural and political realms (e.g. the "separate but equal" concept and abridgement on speech, press, and assembly). Yet, interestingly enough, the "New Court" immediately commenced to complete the cycle of policy reversal by throwing up judicial vetoes in the face of a good many legislative encroachments, as the Court saw these, on civil liberties. Thus the nature and character of the Court's labors began to change dramatically. Of the 160 decisions in which it had written opinions in the 1935–36 term, a *mere two* dealt with civil rights and liberties. That ratio began to climb steadily so that a decade later 20 times as many opinions fell into that category, and 15 years later fully 54 cases dealt with that vital area of public life—a fact of judicial life that has continued, of course, to the present.[109]

When Justices Murphy and Wiley Rutledge joined Mr. Chief Justice Stone and Justices Black and Douglas in the early 1940's, these "libertarian activists" were generally in firm control—certainly until the death of the Chief Justice in April 1946. They briefly relinquished that control during the last four years of the Vinson Court upon the death of Justices Murphy and Rutledge in 1949 and their replacement by Justices Clark and Minton, when the Court tended, broadly speaking, to side with government rather than the individual in the general field of national security, that so difficult and emotion-charged "Cold War" problem. But they more or less regained it during the first four years of the Warren Court, from 1953 to 1957, Mr. Chief Justice Warren having replaced Mr. Chief Justice Vinson on Vinson's death. However, with the Court led by the consistently "nonactivist" Mr. Justice Frankfurter, the 1957–58 term saw a return to readily discernable judicial self-restraint even in *that* area of public and constitutional policy—some would contend largely as a result of the veritable barrage of congressional and public criticism against the Court following its spate of "pro-civil liberty" decisions in 1956–57. Yet with the retirement of Justices Whittaker and Frankfurter in 1962, and their replacement by Justices Byron White and Arthur Goldberg, the latter in turn yielding to Abe Fortas in 1965, plus the Thurgood Marshall replacement of Mr. Justice Clark, the libertarian

[109] Compiled from statistics provided annually by the Commission on Law and Social Action of the American Jewish Congress in its publication *The Civil Rights and Liberties Decisions of the United States Supreme Court.*

image of the Warren Court was restored. It has been continued and, indeed accentuated, ever since—and the Court is likely to pursue that judicial approach to *the* public issue of our times.

If we reflect on these several considerations in this analysis of the *Machtkampf,* the work of the Supreme Court and the force and implications of its decisions come into closer focus. At times the Court has clearly led the country (e.g. the Marshall era); at other times it has more or less held the line (e.g. the Chase-Waite era—with important qualifications); at times it has deliberately stimulated social and economic progress (e.g. the post-1937 Court); at others it has deliberately delayed it (e.g. the Fuller Court). At times it has looked to a majority sentiment, as it were, by following the election returns (e.g. the *Insular* decisions at the turn of the last century);[110] at others it has defied majority sentiment (e.g. some of the 1956–57 term "civil liberties" decisions).[111] At times its decisions have been seemingly motivated by "sectional" or "class" considerations (e.g. *Dred Scott,*[112] proclaiming corporations as "persons,"[113] and the 1954 *Segregation Cases*);[114] at others they have been truly "national" in spirit and effect (e.g. the first two major Marshall decisions, cited earlier). In a very real sense, the Court, through the years has thus been the conscience of the country. In a measure, it has represented the *volonté générale* of the land, in a qualitative rather than a quantitative sense. It has done this through its decisions, speaking through its justices, who—almost always of a rather high caliber—have interpreted the Constitution as they saw it, in line with the taught tradition of the law.

Of course, the Supreme Court of the United States is engaged in the political process—but, in Mr. Justice Frankfurter's admonitory prose, it is "the Nation's ultimate judicial tribunal, not a super-legal aid bureau."[115] Of course, the justices—who, in the words of E. V. Rostow, are "inevitably teachers in a vital national

---

110 *Downes v. Bidwell,* 182 U. S. 244 (1901) and *De Lima v. Bidwell,* 182 U. S. 1 (1901).

111 E.g. *Watkins v. United States,* 354 U. S. 178; *Jencks v. United States,* 353 U. S. 657; *Yates v. United States,* 354 U. S. 298.

112 *Dred Scott v. Sandford,* loc. cit.

113 *Santa Clara County v. Southern Pacific Railroad Co.,* loc. cit.

114 *Brown v. Board of Education,* 347 U. S. 483; *Bolling v. Sharpe,* 347 U. S. 497.

115 *Uveges v. Pennsylvania,* 335 U. S. 437, (1948) at 450.

seminar"[116]—consult their own policy preferences. But they do so in an institutional setting that forces responsibility upon them. They must meet and maintain high standards of integrity, intelligence, logic, reflectiveness, and consistency. They must ever demonstrate a sense of history complete with the realities and vagaries of public affairs, a task that Judge Joseph C. Hutcheson, Jr., of Texas once called "the hunch of intuition about the inner life of American democracy."[117] They have the exciting, yet delicate task of heeding the "felt necessities of the time"—to employ once again Mr. Justice Holmes's inspired phrase—while holding aloft the banner of constitutional fundamentals.

[116] "The Democratic Character of Judicial Review," 66 *Harvard Law Review* 195 (1952).

[117] As quoted by Rostow in his *The Sovereign Prerogative: The Supreme Court and the Quest for Law* (New Haven: Yale University Press, 1962), p. 110.

IX

CODA:

A REALISTIC BULWARK

If the foregoing analysis of the role of the Supreme Court of the United States in the political process has proved anything at all, it ought to be that there is a recognition of the overriding need for judicial self-restraint. Its acceptance plays an omnipresent and omnipotent part in the attitude of the nine members of the highest court in the United States. No matter how the judicial record of these nine individuals may appear on a chart or graph, no matter how predictable or unpredictable their position on certain issues may be—a factor that on balance is probably far more of a blessing than a curse—they are fully aware of their role in, and responsibility to, the democratic body politic which they serve with such dedication. They serve as a collective institution of government; but it is an institution that is characterized more than any other by individual absorption in the tasks at hand, an absorption that calls for more direct personal evaluation and more direct hard work than any other. (The one possible exception is the President of the United States at the instance of casting the die of a decision when he is, indeed, at once the most lonely and the most powerful individual in the free world.) As has been demonstrated throughout these pages, *each member of the Supreme Court* normally participates in every stage of the consideration of a case—from the review stage through the evaluation of briefs through oral argument through discussion and vote in Conference to the writing of or participation in the ultimate opinion of the Court. At every stage of the life of a case the justices are fully aware of their responsibilities as members of the governmental process, and thus practise much procedural as well as substantive judicial self-restraint—both in the type of cases they will hear *and* in the kind of decisions they will render. This emphasis on what Alexander Bickel wisely termed "passive virtues,"[1] is a simple, and yet immensely complicated, fact of judicial life—whatever the opinion of expert as well as laymen outsiders on judicial legislating may be. But there is little doubt that the justices believe with Johann Wolfgang von Goethe that "self-limitation is the first mark of the master."[2]

Throughout the almost two centuries of its existence, the Court has developed a host of unwritten laws, practices, precedents, and attitudes which we may well view as a code of behavior for the highest judicial body in the United States—a series of significant *maxims of judicial self-restraint*. In analyzing the most commonly accepted of these, the reader should be aware that any such enumeration will necessarily involve some generalization—and that maxims, like rules, are sometimes broken quite deliberately.

THE SIXTEEN GREAT
MAXIMS OF JUDICIAL SELF-RESTRAINT

There is nothing holy about either the number of these maxims or the order in which they will appear below. They are presented roughly in the order in which they would normally confront the justices as an issue reaches the Supreme Court in the form of a case or controversy—presumably when it has become "ripe" for adjudication.

ONE: Before the Court will even glance at a particular issue or dispute officially, a definite "case" or "controversy" at law or in equity between bona fide adversaries under the Constitution must exist, involving the protection or enforcement of valuable legal rights, or the punishment, prevention, or redress of wrongs directly concerning the party or parties bringing the justiciable suit. Mr. Justice Jackson viewed this maxim as "perhaps the most significant and least comprehended limitation upon the judicial power."[3] The judicial system of the United States is constructed upon specific cases with specific facts. Thus when a group of federal employees endeavored to join one George P. Poole in a suit testing the validity

---

1 *The Least Dangerous Branch: The Supreme Court at the Bar of Politics* (Indianapolis: The Bobbs-Merrill Co., 1963), title of Ch. IV.

2 From the sonnet "Was wir bringen," 1802. ("In der Beschränkung zeigt sich erst der Meister.")

3 Robert H. Jackson, *The Supreme Court in the American System of Government* (Cambridge: Harvard University Press, 1955), p. 11.

of that portion of the Hatch Act of 1939 which forbids members of the executive civil service to take an active part in "political management or in political campaigns," the Supreme Court disqualified them as appellants since they, unlike Poole, had not violated the provision in question.[4] Refusing to take jurisdiction, the Court thereby reiterated its oft-expressed stand against "every form of pronouncement on abstract, contingent, or hypothetical issues."[5] Except for Poole's claims, no case or controversy directly involving the interest of the appellants was involved here in the face of the Supreme Court's first maxim—regardless of what lower tribunals might have held. Probably the most famous illustration of the "case or controversy" problem is the Court's 1911 decision in *Muskrat v. United States*.[6] At issue was an act of Congress that had authorized Muskrat and others to bring suit in the Court of Claims, with an appeal to the Supreme Court *to determine the validity of certain acts of Congress* which altered the terms of specific prior allotments of Cherokee Indian lands. Speaking for a unanimous Court, Mr. Justice Day rejected the appeal as not meeting the "case or controversy" requirement. "If such actions as are here attempted, to determine the validity of legislation are sustained," lectured Day, "the result will be that this court, instead of keeping within the limits of judicial power and deciding cases or controversies arising between opposing parties, as the Constitution intended it should, will be required to give opinions in the nature of advice concerning legislative action, *a function never conferred upon it by the Constitution. . . .*[7]

TWO: Closely related to the need for the presence of a case or controversy is the logical demand that *the party or parties bringing suit must have "standing."* There are two major aspects to the difficult and intricate concept[8] of standing. The *first,* to raise a con-

[4] *United Public Workers of America v. Mitchell,* 330 U.S. 75 (1947).

[5] Jackson, loc. cit. p. 12.

[6] 219 U.S. 346.

[7] Ibid., at 362. (Italics supplied.)

[8] The doctrine of "standing" was dramatically invoked—some would contend "cowardly"—by the International Court of Justice at The Hague in 1966 when it narrowly ruled 8:7 that it could not accept a case concerning South Africa's racial practices brought by Ethiopia and Lybia because these two complainants lacked sufficient *legal* (as distinguished from emotional) interests in the subject of their complaint. (The decisive eighth vote was cast by Court President Sir Percy Spender, who, under the tribunal's rules, was empowered to cast a second vote to break the 7:7 tie—which, ironically, had been created by Sir Percy's initial vote *against* assuming jurisdiction!)

stitutional issue with proper standing, is a showing that the one who seeks to challenge the statute or action is personally and substantially injured by it, or is in substantial danger of such injury. A possible relaxation of that rule, at least in the so sensitive free speech area, is contained in the tenor of the Court's landmark 1965 ruling in *Dombrowski v. Pfister*, where it held 5:2 that federal district judges should have the power to enjoin the enforcement of unconstitutional laws—i.e. laws presumed unconstitutional "on their face"—if these laws as per Justice Brennan's majority opinion, pose a "chilling effect" upon freedom of expression by the mere "fact of prosecution, unaffected by the prospects of its success or failure . . . [Thus, courts may] avoid making vindication of freedom of expression await the outcome of protracted litigation."[9] The *second* is that a petitioner must not only have a personal and substantial interest infringed by the statute or action, but that he must also "bring himself, by proper averment and showing, within the class as to whom the act thus attacked is unconstitutional."[10] Once the dispute is properly before it, however, the Court must decide it in one way or another; it cannot refuse because the task may be difficult, vexatious, or controversial—as indeed almost all judgments of the Court necessarily are. The sole action that is not considered a *decision* by the Court is a *postponement*.

One of the most famous illustrations of a *lack of standing* on record is the case of Dr. Wilder Tileston, a Connecticut physician, who wanted to challenge the constitutionality of that state's statutory prohibitions—enforced but three times between the time of its birth in 1879 and its death at the bar of the United States Supreme Court in 1965[11]—of "the use of drugs or instruments to prevent conception, and the giving of assistance or counsel in their use." Having lost his appeal in the Connecticut Supreme Court of Errors below, he endeavored to get federal Supreme Court review. Because of their importance to the concept of standing, the pertinent sections of that court's *per curiam* decision are reproduced herewith:

> . . . Appellant [Dr. Tileston] alleged that the statute, if applicable to him, would prevent his giving professional advice concerning the use of contraceptives to three patients whose condition of health was such that their lives would be endangered by child-

9 380 U.S. 479, at 487.
10 *Southern Railroad Co. v. King*, 217 U.S. 524 (1910), at 534.
11 *Griswold v. Connecticut*, 381 U.S. 479 (1965).

bearing, and that appellees [Abraham S. Ullman and other law enforcement officers of the state], intend to prosecute any offense against the statute and "claim or may claim" that the proposed professional advice would constitute such an offense. The complaint set out in detail the danger to the lives of appellant's patients in the event that they should bear children, but *contained no allegation asserting any claim under the Fourteenth Amendment of infringement of appellant's liberty or his property rights.* The relief prayed was a declaratory judgment [to be explained in the next maxim] as to whether the statutes are applicable to appellant and if so whether they constitute a valid exercise of constitutional power "within the meaning and intent of Amendment XIV of the Constitution of the United States prohibiting a state from depriving any person *of life* without due process of law." . . .

We are of the opinion that the proceedings in the state courts *present no constitutional question which appellant has standing to assert. The sole constitutional attack upon the statutes under the Fourteenth Amendment is confined to their deprivation of life—obviously not appellant's but his patients'.* There is no allegation or proof that appellant's life is in danger. *His patients are not parties to this proceeding* and there is no basis on which we can say that he has standing to secure an adjudication of his patient's constitutional right to life, *which they do not assert in their own behalf.* . . . *No question is raised in the record with respect to the deprivation of appellant's liberty or property in contravention of the Fourteenth Amendment.* . . . Since the *appeal must be dismissed on the grounds that appellant has no standing to litigate the constitutional question which the record presents,* it is unnecessary to consider whether the record shows the existence of a genuine case or controversy essential to the exercise of jurisdiction of this Court. . . . Dismissed.[12]

In short, Dr. Tileston had no standing to sue: his patient might well have had such, but *they* did not bring suit; *he* might have had such, but he brought suit on nonjusticiable grounds. Of course, the Court was not about to get into the delicate matter of birth control if it could avoid doing so, and it had every judicial right to do just that—at least at this stage of the process.

Not to be outdone, opponents of the Connecticut statute tried again in 1961, and this time with patients *and* a physician as plaintiffs. The Supreme Court was hard pressed to reject the appeal for adjudication of the issue and thus to continue to refuse to get in-

[12] *Tileston v. Ullman,* 318 U. S. 44 (1943). (Italics supplied.)

volved in the sticky problem. But it managed: Led not surprisingly by Mr. Justice Frankfurter, and narrowly dividing 5:4, the majority held the controversy *not* to be "fit for adjudication"; that no one had in fact been injured, such as being jailed or fined, and that consequently, ". . . this Court cannot be umpire to debates concerning harmless, empty shadows."[13] Frankfurter pointed out that the law had rarely been the subject of a prosecution, that, perhaps it had died of disuse and would therefore not ever be enforced. Yet the statute's opponents were not mollified. More determined than ever to test its constitutionality, they continued to try to obtain standing to challenge it. They opened a birth-control clinic in New Haven, frankly advertising its existence—and, to their utter delight, the state decided to prosecute them! Best of all, Mrs. Estelle T. Griswold, the Executive Director of the Planned Parenthood League of Connecticut and Dr. C. Lee Buxton, a licensed physician, who served as medical director for the league's New Haven Center, found themselves convicted and fined $100 each. Now they had standing at last and, losing in the courts below, appealed to the Supreme Court on the grounds that the Connecticut statute, as applied to them, violated the Fourteenth Amendment. In 1965 the Court granted their appeal by pointing out that persons prosecuted must surely have standing to challenge the relevant statute. And by a vote of 7:2 in an opinion by Mr. Justice Douglas, plus three concurring and two dissenting opinions, it declared the law to be an unconstitutional infringement not only of Amendment Fourteen, but also of Amendments I, III, IV, V, and IX.[14] Whatever the merits of the Connecticut case may be—standing is assuredly essential to an orderly and efficacious judicial process; to adhere to its requirements is a small price to pay.[15]

13 *Poe v. Ullman and Buxton v. Ullman,* 367 U.S. 497 (1961).
14 *Griswold v. Connecticut,* 381 U.S. 479 (1965).
15 Another fascinating and contentious aspect of this problem is the precedent established by the Supreme Court ruling in *Frothingham v. Mellon,* 262 U.S. 447 (1923), which determined that an "ordinary tax payer" is generally precluded from contesting the constitutionality of *federal* expenditures—such as expenditures to sectarian schools and other institutions on the grounds that he does not possess "sufficient interest" to bring suit. In *Frothingham* (also known as *Massachusetts v. Mellon*) Mr. Justice Sutherland held for the unanimous Court that a taxpayer's interest in the moneys of the Treasury "is shared with millions of others; is comparatively minute and indeterminable; the effect upon future taxation . . . is so remote . . . that no basis is afforded for an appeal to the preventive power of the Court." As a consequence, a *federal* taxpayer (but not necessarily a *state* taxpayer in his capacity as a state

THREE: The Court does not render advisory opinions, i.e. judicial rulings upon the constitutionality of governmental action in the absence of a case or controversy requiring such a ruling for its disposition—nor do the lower federal constitutional courts. In effect, this was settled as early as 1793, when President Washington addressed the members of the Supreme Court, asking them to define for him the authority given him by the Constitution to decide certain questions involved in the United States policy of neutrality with respect to a war such as the one then in progress in Europe. Mr. Chief Justice Jay responded for the Court that it would not and could not tender legal advice—that its role was confined to the decision of cases that arose in the course of bona fide litigation. Legislative courts, however, give advisory opinions, and so do many of the courts of the fifty states—such as Colorado, Masaschusetts, and South Dakota. *All* courts, on the other hand, are empowered to render *declaratory judgments*—a device that enables courts generally to enter a final judgment between litigants *in an actual controversy,* defining their respective rights under a statute, contract, will, or other document, *without* attaching to the otherwise binding judgment any consequential or coercive relief. The crucial distinction between a declaratory judgment and an advisory opinion is the presence of an actual controversy in the case of a declaratory judgment, whereas an advisory opinion would deal with an abstract, hypothetical question insofar as the judicial process is concerned. Today, three-quarters of the states and the federal government under the Federal Declaratory Judgment Act of 1934, permit declaratory judgments. In the words of the federal statute,

---

citizen, for many states do allow such "taxpayer suits"), whose rights guaranteed by, for example, the First Amendment, are actually deemed violated, may be without a judicial remedy. This dilemma became particularly acute with the passage of the Federal Elementary and Secondary Aid to Education Act of 1965, with its attendant overtones of the Separation of Church and State controversy. Consequently, legislation to provide for judicial review of the constitutionality of grants and loans under seven specific federal statutes —including the aid-to-education measure just mentioned—plus any other statute administered by the Department of Health, Education, and Welfare was introduced in and passed by the Senate on four occasions—only to die in the House in each instance. But in a dramatic development the Court in October 1967 agreed to hear arguments of seven taxpayers (*Flast v. Gardner*), who contended that they have a right as citizens to challenge the constitutionality of federal aid to parochial schools, notwithstanding the *Frothingham* precedent. (No decision has been handed down as of early March 1968.)

such a judgment—which is reviewable above—answers the following question in an actual controversy: ". . . whether or not further relief is or could be prayed." It was for just such a declaratory judgment that Dr. Tileston had pleaded initially, and unsuccessfully, because he then lacked standing.

The Supreme Court itself has admitted the obvious: that the line between advisory opinions and declaratory judgments is a thin one, and that "it would be difficult, if it would be possible, to fashion a precise test for determining in every case whether there is such a controversy [as is demanded by a declaratory judgment]."[16] But it insisted in the *Ashwander* case[17] that the Federal Declaratory Judgment Act "does not attempt to change the essential requisites for the exercise of judicial power," and, on an earlier occasion, that it cannot be invoked to "obtain in advisory decree up on a hypothetical state of facts."[18]

FOUR: Not only must the complainant in federal court expressly declare that he is invoking the Constitution of the United States— "the ultimate touchstones of constitutionality," in Mr. Justice Frankfurter's phrase—*but a specific live rather than dead constitutional issue citing the particular provision on which he relies in that document must be raised by him; the Court will not entertain generalities.* Indeed, it has held specifically that an attack upon a statute as "violative of the Constitution of the United States" is insufficient on its face.[19] Nor will a simple contention that a statute is "in violation of the Fifth or Seventh Amendments to the Constitution" do.[20] Specific, careful, closely reasoned documentation is essential. Moreover, the issue must be raised *seasonably*; that is, timely assertion of the constitutional issue must be made before a tribunal having proper jurisdiction, and it must be reasserted at every opportunity in the course of the litigation. The Court is not, nor can it be, concerned with dead or moot and thus inappropriate problems—as, for example, one caused by the death of an essential party, here the defendant, in an appeal in a criminal action.[21]

16 *Maryland Casualty Co. v. Pacific Coal & Oil Co.,* 312 U. S. 270 (1941), at 273.
17 *Ashwander v. Tennessee Valley Authority,* 297 U. S. (1936), at 325.
18 *Electric Bond & Share Co. v. Securities & Exchange Commission, 303 U. S.* 419 (1938), at 443.
19 *Herndon v. Georgia,* 295 U. S. 441 (1935).
20 *Chapin v. Frye,* 179 U. S. 127 (1900).
21 *List v. Pennsylvania,* 131 U. S. 396 (1888).

FIVE: The Court looks askance at any attempt to have the judicial decision-cake and eat it, too. Thus, *it will not pass upon the constitutionality of a statute or of an official action at the instance of one who has availed himself of its benefits, but then decides to challenge its legality anyway.* An illustration is the case of a St. Louis, Missouri, casting company, in the role of owner of property within a special sewer district who connected his premises with a freshly constructed sewer and availed himself of its benefits. But then he challenged the validity of the statute that permitted a tax levy against him as a recipient of the services, as being an unconstitutional infringement of his property rights under the Fourteenth Amendment.[22] The Supreme Court held unanimously that by accepting and availing himself of the benefits of the construction and zoning involved, the owner was "estopped from maintaining a suit" on the grounds and under the circumstances here involved.

SIX: All remedies in the pertinent lower federal and/or state courts must have been exhausted, and prescribed lower court procedure duly followed, before making application to the United States Supreme Court for review. As Judge Augustus N. Hand of the Second Circuit Court of the United States once observed, "the rule of exhaustion is the only rule which is consistent with orderly government." Thus, the highest court of the land will not review a judgment of a state court unless on the face of the record it affirmatively appears that a *federal question constituting an appropriate ground* for such review was presented in, and expressly or necessarily decided by, such a state court. For example, in 1963 the Court ruled 6:3 that a New York state judgment had not been taken to the highest New York court empowered to consider it, as statutorily required for Supreme Court review. Hence it dismissed a writ it had granted earlier to hear the case as having been "improvidentially granted."[23] No matter how vital, inviting, timely, or attractive the issue involved may be, the Supreme Court will not accept a case unless the remedies below have been exhausted; nor does it matter that a lower tribunal might not be "friendly" to the substance of a suit—as has occurred frequently in connection with state court adjudication of such contentious problems as desegregation, criminal justice, and Bible-reading in the public schools.[24]

---

[22] *St. Louis v. Prendergast Co.*, 260 U. S. 459 (1923).
[23] *Gotthilf v. Sills*, 375 U.S. 79.
[24] See Ch. V, *supra*, for specific illustrations, esp. pp. 225–31.

Orderly procedure is of the very essence of the judicial process; judicial and administrative chaos is the alternative.

SEVEN: Assuming it has been properly raised, *the federal question at issue must be substantial rather than trivial; it must be the pivotal point of the case; and it must be part of the plaintiff's case rather than a part of his adversary's defense.* Whatever the subjective overtones of the term "substantial" may be, it is normally not an overwhelming job to distinguish between a "substantial" and a "trivial" federal question. For example, the controversies surrounding the extent of the federal government's authority in connection with the Tennessee Valley Authority projects, raised in sundry respects in the famous case of *Ashwander v. T.V.A.,*[25] and the attempt by the State of California to close its borders to a destitute noncitizen traveling in interstate commerce,[26] are pertinent instances of substantial federal questions. On the other hand, the endeavors of some Greek-letter fraternities on various campuses in New York and Colorado to have the Supreme Court review requirements by the Trustees of the State University of New York and those of the University of Colorado setting deadlines on removing restrictive racial and/or religious clauses from fraternity "constitutions" on pain of revocation of campus privileges, were summarily—and quite predictably—turned aside as not involving a substantial question.[27]

EIGHT: Although it would be an oversimplification, if not entirely incorrect, to state that the Supreme Court reviews only questions of law, it is nonetheless generally true that *questions of fact—as distinct from questions of law—are not normally accepted as proper bases for review.* This is especially true of the area of judicial review of administrative construction of statutes, where a *purely* factual question has no chance of a hearing at all, for Congress has statutorily provided for the finality of administrative finding of fact.

However, it is axiomatic that the problem of which questions are of "law," which of "fact," and which "mixtures" is a difficult one. Here again, any attempt to draw a rigid line poses a genuine problem because of the very nature of the two concepts. In the words of one seasoned student of the subject, ". . . matters of law grow

[25] 297 U.S. 288 (1936).
[26] *Edwards v. California,* 314 U.S. 160 (1941).
[27] *Webb v. State University of New York,* 348 U.S. 867 (1954), and *The New York Times,* September 21, 1966.

downward into roots of fact, and matters of fact reach upward, without a break, into matters of law."[28] In any event, to cite one example, the Court will not permit administrative procedures—which most frequently are at issue in this particular dichotomy—to fall below what it is prone to regard as a "constitutional minimum," a concept that is clearly a matter of law subject to judicial review.

NINE: While Britain's highest tribunal, the House of Lords, considered itself *bound* by its own prior decisions until it publicly and expressly renounced that doctrine in 1966,[29] *the Supreme Court of the United States has never held itself absolutely bound by its precedents.* It has often adhered to many of these, of course, and will presumably continue to do so, but it has not permitted itself to become enslaved by past decisions. Nor could it do so—the law does not stand still; Mr. Justice Holmes's "felt necessities of the times" are ever compelling facts of governmental life. We must not expect from the Court, in Mr. Chief Justice Hughes's trenchant warning, "the icy stratosphere of certainty." But a decision of the Supreme Court is utterly binding *in federal matters* on all courts below, state as well as federal—regardless of sporadic foot-dragging and aberrations.[30]

TEN: The Court has been inclined to defer to certain legislative or executive actions by classifying an issue otherwise quite properly before it as a political question—hence refusing to come to grips with it. Depending upon one's point of view—after all, is not every constitutional question or decision "political" to some extent?—this intriguing practice or formula is either a mere *device* for transferring the responsibility for a question or decision to another branch of the government, or it is in fact *required* by the constitutionally explicit or implicit realities and necessities of the presence of the separation of powers principle. What really *is* a "political question"? Giving short shrift to this inquiry, Mr. Justice Holmes, coming to the core of an issue briskly and pithily as always, once characterized it as ". . . little more than a play on

---

28 John Dickinson, *Administrative Justice and the Supremacy of Law* (Cambridge: Harvard University Press, 1927), p. 55.

29 See the Lord Chancellor's (Lord Gardiner's) announcement, in *House of Lords Official Reports*, Vol. 276, No. 43, col. 677, July 26, 1966. *Parliamentary Debate (Hansard Weekly).*

30 See pp. 200–204, 290–92, and 297–8, *supra.*

words."[31] He would have no part of the concept as a judicial mechanism—while nevertheless fully recognizing, of course, the realities of the political facts of life.

Professor Edward S. Corwin essayed the following, perhaps not entirely helpful, definition of the vexatious verbiage in his last monumental annotation of the Constitution:

> . . . a political question relates to the possession of political power, of sovereignty, of government, the determination of which is vested in Congress and the President, and whose decisions are binding on the courts.[32]

In a different vein, Jack W. Peltason, one of the students of the revered Princeton scholar, preferred to view political questions as "those which judges choose not to decide, and a question becomes political by the judges' refusal to decide it."[33] And Judge Learned Hand labeled it—insofar as its scope is undefined—as a "stench in the nostrils of strict constructionists,"[34] a description eminently applicable to the stance on the problem of his ardent admirer Frankfurter! A good many of the Supreme Court's decisions, while not necessarily invalidating Professor Corwin's analysis, would seem to support Professor Peltason's more realistic evaluation. However, judges can, and do, change their minds, depending upon the posture and setting of an issue, and what may be rejected or avoided as a political question today may quite conceivably be accepted for review on its merit at a later date—of which the legislative reapportionment-redistricting decisions are pertinent illustrations, indeed.

For years—to be precise until its precedent-shattering decision in what must be regarded as one of the two or at most three most significant Supreme Court decisions of the twentieth century, namely *Baker v. Carr* in 1962[35]—the Court simply would not get

31 *Nixon v. Herndon,* 273 U. S. 536 (1927), at 540.
32 Edward S. Corwin, *The Constitution of the United States,* revised and annotated (Washington, D. C.: United States Government Printing Office, 1953), p. 547.
33 Jack W. Peltason, *Federal Courts in the Political Process* (Garden City, N.Y.: Doubleday, 1955), p. 10.
34 *The Bill of Rights* (Cambridge: Harvard University Press, 1958) p. 15, n. 3.
35 369 U.S. 186. An earlier case was *Gomillion v. Lightfoot,* 364 U.S. 339 (1960). The latter was argued on October 9, 1961, and was decided in favor of plaintiff, 6:2, on March 26, 1962, as 369 U.S. 186 (1962).

involved in the question of the constitutionality or even the justiciability of the way in which legislatures and constitutions either did or did not apportion or district state and/or congressional districts—no matter how obvious, how outrageous, and yes, even how illegal the apportionment or districting or lack of it might have been! The Court, in the words of the main advocate of this Bastille-like stand, Mr. Justice Frankfurter, was not going to get itself involved in such a "patently political question," in such a "political thicket," which in his view was, after all, an area of the "exclusive authority" of legislatures.[36]

Thus, the constitutionality of the well-known county unit system of Georgia—a prime example of anti-urban, pro-rural legislative gerrymandering—had been before the Court on several occasions. Under that system, each of the various counties received a minimum of two and a maximum of six electoral votes for the eight most populous counties, including Fulton County (Atlanta), with each county's electoral vote going to the candidate receiving the highest popular vote therein. The net effect had been that the one million inhabitants of Fulton County—a considerable proportion of whom were registered Negroes—received but one-third more votes than the handful of residents in numerous small rural counties. In other words a vote in the small counties of Georgia had from 11 to 120 times as much weight as one in Fulton! Yet attempts to have the Supreme Court come to grips with the matter came to naught as recently as 1950, 1951, 1958, and 1959. The Court stood by its pronouncement in the first of these cases, *South v. Peters*[37] that "a state's geographical distribution of electoral strength among its political subdivision" is a political question. Thereby the Court continued to cling to the general philosophy and tactics it had enunciated in *Colegrove v. Green* in 1946,[38] a case concerning congressional districts in Illinois. Here, appellants had contended that the Illinois law apportioning congressional districts was unconstitutional because the various districts were characterized by rank inequalities. For example, a Chicago congressional district had 914,053 inhabitants, whereas one in southern Illinois comprised a mere 112,116. But in its decision the Supreme Court,

---

[36] See his opinion for the Court in *Colegrove v. Green*, 328 U.S. (1946), discussed below.

[37] 339 U.S. 276 (1950).

[38] 328 U.S. 549.

with only seven justices participating, and these split three ways, nevertheless held through Mr. Justice Frankfurter that it could not intervene in such a political question, one that it regarded as being up to the legistlature to determine and alleviate. If the Court did intervene, wrote Frankfurter, it would be entering into a "political thicket," and that, anyway, it is "hostile to a democratic system to involve the judiciary in the politics of the people."[39] Speaking also for Justices Douglas and Murphy, Mr. Justice Black dissented vigorously, contending that the State of Illinois's failure to redistrict was tantamount to "wilful legislative discrimination" and constituted a denial of the equal protection of the laws presumably guaranteed by the Fourteenth Amendment to the Constitution of the United States.

But the days of the "political question" doctrine in *this* sector of public law were clearly numbered when the Court, after twice having noted probate jurisdiction in its 1960–61 term, agreed to hear argument in 1961 in a Tennessee case involving that state's outright refusal to reapportion the General Assembly among its ninety-five counties, seats that had been arbitrarily and capriciously apportioned by a 1901 statute—and never touched since, despite an almost fivefold growth of eligible voters and major shifts of population to urban from rural areas generally. The case was the aforementioned, *Baker v. Carr*. Knowing its significance, the Supreme Court ordered three and a half hours of oral argument,[40] with United States Solicitor-General Cox arguing as *amicus curiae* on the side of the plaintiff on behalf of the United States Government. The mere willingness to accept *Baker v. Carr* for review served notice of the possibility, if not the probability, of a dramatic "political question" shift. And dramatic it was! There were six opinions, covering a total of 165 pages, with Mr. Justice Frankfurter's agitated and angry dissenting opinion for Mr. Justice Harlan and himself consuming 65 pages alone! Still, what Mr. Justice Brennan actually decided in his opinion for the Court, can be de-

39 Ibid., at 554. The decisive fourth vote in the case was provided by Mr. Justice Rutledge, who in effect agreed with the three dissenters that the issue per se was justiciable, but nonetheless chose to concur in the Frankfurter opinion for the Court in view of "the shortness of time remaining" before the next election and the difficulties of an election at large in a state with so many Congressional districts.

40 *Baker v. Carr*, 368 U.S. 804 (1961).

scribed quickly: (1) that the federal courts *do* have jurisdiction in apportionment-districting cases; (2) that the Baker complaint did present a *justiciable controversy*; and (3) that Baker and his co-appellants had *standing* to bring the suit. Notwithstanding Frankfurter's deeply felt warnings—in what was to prove his last opinion prior to his retirement for reasons of health later in that year of 1962—that the judiciary was damaging itself by getting into such "political matters," that it was immersing itself dangerously and wrongly in a "mathematical quagmire," the Court majority of six (Mr. Justice Whittaker had not participated in the case), without addressing itself to the specific merits of Baker's contentions, (a) regarded them as eminently justiciable in the courts, i.e. capable of adjudication and (b) remanded the case to the lower federal court whence it came for purposes of such adjudication. (Ultimately, Tennessee was ordered to redistrict. It complied, albeit haltingly.) In short, rejecting the Frankfurter admonition that ". . . in a democratic society like ours, relief [for political mischief] must come through an aroused popular conscience that sears the conscience of the people's representatives,"[41] the highest court in the land in effect reformulated the "political question" concept and doctrine. No longer would it apply to the matter at issue. In Brennan's words, the political question doctrine applies properly to "the relationship between the judiciary and the coordinate branches of the Federal Government, and not the federal judiciary's relationship to the states. . . ."[42] Over Frankfurter's specific disagreement on the point, Brennan thus confined "political questions," by way of the *Baker v. Carr* decision, to "a function of the separation of powers."[43]

And as a logical result of the decision, struck down as unconstitutional by the Supreme Court were the infamous, although by then somewhat revised, Georgia County Unit System for state legislative apportionment in *Gray v. Saunders* in 1963[44] plus state legislative mal-apportionment of congressional districts in 1964 in *Wesberry v. Saunders*;[45] and later in 1964, most far-reaching and most contentious of all of the myriad of post-*Baker v. Carr* deci-

[41] Ibid., 369 U.S. 186 (1962), at 270.
[42] Ibid., at 210.
[43] Ibid., at 217.
[44] 372 U.S. 368.
[45] 376 U.S. 1.

sions, came the Court's requirement that *both* houses of state legislatures be apportioned on the basis of *population*—announced in a six-case "package," known by its lead-case of *Reynolds v. Sims*.[46]

It should be clear, however, that the important contraction brought about by *Baker v. Carr* has by no means removed the concept of "political question" doctrine as such. A case like the well-known 1849 *Luther v. Borden*[47] would today assuredly continue to be treated—in line with the new Brennan formula announced in *Baker v. Carr*—as a political question. *Luther v. Borden* arose out of the Rhode Island Dorr Rebellion early in America's history. Very briefly, the facts of the case were such that the Supreme Court found itself confronted with the crucial decision as to *which one* of two governments battling for legal supremacy in Rhode Island in 1842 was *the* legal one. The Court concluded that this was clearly a "political question" since the President of the United States, in exercising the power conferred upon him by Congress to send federal troops to aid states in suppressing insurrection, had indicated that he regarded the original— the "charter"—government as the lawful one of the two, and that this judgment was binding upon the judiciary.

If one accepts the concept of the political question at all, the *Luther* example is obviously a much more clear-cut one than those involving legislative apportionment. Yet what is a political question remains difficult to determine. Generalization of the doctrine is still virtually impossible. Moreover, as Mr. Justice Brennan pointed out in *Baker v. Carr*, ". . . the mere fact that [a] suit seeks protection of a political right does not mean it presents a political question. Such an objection is little more than a play upon words."[48] And as his brother Clark put the matter in his concurring opinion in that case, ". . . national respect for the courts is more enhanced through the forthright enforcement of [basic national rights such as fair legislative apportionment] than by rendering them nugatory through the interposition of subterfuges."[49] However attractive in theory, the "political question" maxim is a treadmill; perhaps to a fatal degree its supporting logic is circular.

[46] 377 U.S. 533.
[47] 7 Howard 1.
[48] Opinion for the Court, 369 U.S. 186, at 209.
[49] Ibid., at 261–2.

ELEVEN: In the event of a validly challenged statute the presumption of its constitutionality is always in its favor. As early as 1827, Mr. Justice Bushrod Washington wrote:

> It is but a decent respect to the wisdom, integrity, and patriotism of the legislative body, by which any law is passed, to presume in favor of its validity, until its violation of the Constitution is proved beyond a reasonable doubt.[50]

Hence, as the history of the Court shows, if a legislative enactment can be construed to be in reasonable harmony with the Constitution, a majority of the Court will almost always do so. Obviously, the views of the justices have differed somewhat, often drastically, on the meaning of the word "reasonable." Thus, while there is today practically no judicial interference with legislation dealing with economic and social matters, the Court remains seriously divided on what constitutes "reasonable" legislative restrictions in certain areas of civil rights and liberties, such as the national security sector in the face of the specific guarantees under the First Amendment. On this point, generally speaking, a hard core of five members of the 1966–67 Warren bench—the Chief Justice himself and Justices Black, Douglas, Brennan, and Fortas—would brook little, if any, legislative encroachments, whereas a hard core of three—Justices Clark, Harlan, and White— would exercise more or less judicial self-restraint, with Mr. Justice Stewart more unpredictable here, given his great concern for freedom of expression.

In any event, the Court will not normally formulate a rule of constitutional law broader than is required by the precise facts to which it is to be applied. "The cardinal principle of statutory construction," wrote Mr. Chief Justice Hughes in a famous case,

> is to save and not to destroy. We have repeatedly held that as between two possible interpretations of a statute, by one of which it would be unconstitutional and the other valid, our plain duty is to adopt that which will save the act. Even to avoid a serious doubt the rule is the same.[51]

On the other hand, Mr. Justice Stone—normally a firm adherent to the philosophy of presumption of constitutionality—implied an important exception to the general rule in his footnote in the

[50] *Ogden v. Saunders,* 12 Wheaton 213 (1827).
[51] *N.L.R.B. v. Jones & Laughlin Steel Corporation,* 301 U. S. 1 (1937).

otherwise rather unimportant *Carolene Products* case,[52] which became one of the most famous footnotes of all time! It was there that he stated that perhaps there might be occasion for departing from the normal presumption of constitutionality for legislation in cases *where the legislative action in question involved a restriction or curtailment of the ordinary political processes which could generally be expected to be employed to bring about the negation of undesirable legislation*, or *where it appeared to be within "a specific prohibition of the Constitution, such as those of the first ten amendments*, which are deemed equally specific when held to be embraced within the Fourteenth."[53]

TWELVE: In the exercise of what some commentators have been fond of styling "judicial parsimony," *if a case or controversy can be decided upon any other than constitutional grounds—such as by statutory construction, which constitutes the greatest single area of the Court's work, or if it can rest on an independent state ground—the Court will be eager to do so.* For it will not decide questions of a constitutional nature unless absolutely necessary to the decision of the case, and even then it will draw such a decision as narrowly as possible, ever being loath to formulate a rule of constitutional law broader than is clearly required by the precise facts to which it is to be applied. Nor will it anticipate a question of constitutional law in advance of the necessity of deciding it. Mr. Justice Frankfurter succinctly underscored the latter point in an edifying exchange with Thurman Arnold, who was acting as counsel for Dr. J. P. Peters, petitioner in the loyalty-security case of *Peters v. Hobby*.[54] Mr. Arnold pleaded with the Court that he would not like to win the case on the narrow procedural, statutory ground to which a majority of the members of the bench was evidently inclining. Responded Mr. Justice Frankfurter: "The question is not whether you want to win the case on that ground or not. This Court reaches constitutional issues last, not first."[55] He might well have quoted Mr. Justice Brandeis's famous assertion that the ". . . most important thing we do is not doing."

[52] *United States v. Carolene Products Co.*, 304 U. S. 144 (1938), at 152–3, fn. 4.

[53] Ibid. (Italics supplied.) On the issue of what has been regarded as a judicial "double standard," see my *Freedom and the Court: Civil Rights and Liberties in the United States*, op. cit. Ch. II.

[54] 349 U. S. 311 (1955).

[55] As reported in 23 *U. S. Law Week* 265–6 (1955).

The loyalty-security field affords a host of pertinent illustrations of the Court's preference for a resort to its potent weapon of statutory construction rather than to constitutional grounds. This delicate and emotion-laden area of public policy is tailor-made for such an approach, which preserves the statute while sometimes smoothing certain ragged edges. Thus the Court effects a gain, however moderate it may be, for individual civil rights, while retaining the generally popular and politically desirable law. To cite just two instances, this is precisely what the Court did in narrowing executive authority to dismiss government employees under the Summary Suspension Act of 1950 by holding that the act did not authorize dismissal of employees holding "non-sensitive" positions;[56] and in limiting the power of the Secretary of State to withhold a passport from a citizen "for any substantive reason he may choose," holding that the Immigration and Nationality Act of 1952 did not authorize such sweeping discretionary powers.[57] In both instances, congressional reaction was to the effect that "we did *so* intend to authorize what you say we did not," but in the absence of the passage of any clarifying or amplifying amendments the two statutes stood as judicially construed. After all, statutory construction is an act of judgment and, as Mr. Justice Holmes once observed succinctly, applies to cases "in which there is a fair contest between two readings."

THIRTEEN: The Court will not ordinarily impute illegal motives to the lawmakers. "So long as Congress acts in pursuance of its constitutional power," explained Mr. Justice Harlan in a much-debated decision upholding certain aspects of the investigative authority of the House Committee on Un-American Activities,[58] "the judiciary lacks authority to intervene *on the basis of the motives* which spurred the exercise of that power." And as early as 1810 Mr. Chief Justice Marshall had written that it "may well be doubted how far the validity of a law depends upon the motives of its framers."[59] Indeed, the Court is not supposed to consider *motives* at all; but, as Max Radin once put it, that concept is indeed a "transparent and absurd fiction"[60]—to which the decision in the *Child Labor Tax Case* of 1922, for example, bears eloquent witness.

56 *Cole v. Young,* 351 U. S. 536 (1956).
57 *Kent and Briehl v. Dulles,* 357 U. S. 116 (1958).
58 *Barenblatt v. United States,* 360 U. S. 109 (1959). (Italics supplied.)
59 *Fletcher v. Peck,* 6 Cranch 87.
60 "Statutory Interpretation," 43 *Harvard Law Review* 863 (April 1930).

To compound the problem, the Supreme Court is, however, expected to, and very frequently does, take legislative *intent* or *purpose* into account—yet, it is no easy task to separate motives and intent, and Mr. Justice Frankfurter, for one, consistently refused to do so. "I only want to know what the words mean," wrote Mr. Justice Holmes. Still, ". . . words are not crystals," and he found *policy* in words.[61] Or, as Mr. Justice Cardozo wrote so appropriately, "a great principle of constitutional law is not susceptible of comprehensive statement in an adjective."[62] The *Steel Seizure Case*[63] of 1952, in which seven separate opinions were written, provided a basis for an opinion for the Court only because a sufficient number of justices was able to agree on the single point that Congress, in enacting the Taft-Hartley Act, had deliberately intended that it *not* provide for Presidential authority to seize struck plants. Here the intent of Congress proved to be the basis for the Court's judgment that the Chief Executive had usurped legislative power, with the justices, as is their custom, equating intent with legislative history.

This approach is sometimes styled "psychoanalyzing Congress" by some of the less reverent observers of the governmental scene, who have considerable—and perhaps well-grounded—doubt of the infallibility of the contention, frequently quoted by Mr. Justice Frankfurter, that ". . . a page of history is worth a volume of logic." Yet whatever their merits otherwise, for this purpose at least the *Congressional Record* and the reports of the various committees of Congress are a constant and evidently fertile source of reference for the members of the Supreme Court. Thus, in unanimously upholding the Voting Rights Act of 1965, the Court repeatedly referred to congressional intent to eradicate the "substantial voting discrimination" in *specific* sections of the country because it "knew" about these and wanted to remove them. Again and again Mr. Chief Justice Warren used the term "Congress knew," thus underscoring its intent or purpose.[64]

FOURTEEN: If the Court does find that it must hold a law unconstitutional, it will usually try hard to confine the holding to that

---

61 See Felix Frankfurter, "Some Reflections on the Readings of Statutes," Sixth Annual Benjamin N. Cardozo Lecture before the Association of the Bar of the City of New York, March 8, 1947. (Reprinted in 47 *Columbia Law Review* 527–46.)

62 *Carter v. Carter Coal Co.,* 298 U.S. 238 (1936), at 327.

63 *Youngstown Sheet and Tube Co. v. Sawyer,* 343 U.S. 579.

64 *South Carolina v. Katzenbach,* 383 U.S. 301 (1966), *passim.*

particular section of the statute which was successfully challenged on constitutional grounds—provided such a course of action is at all feasible. It would not be feasible, of course, if the section at issue constituted the veritable heart of the legislation, in which case the Court would follow a well-established rule of statutory construction: if the various parts of a statute are inextricably connected to such degrees as to warrant the assumption that the legislature intended the law to function as a whole, then if some portions of the statute are unconstitutional the law must be treated as unconstitutional in its entirety.[65] "Sectionalized" unconstitutionality is known as *separability*, for which Congress now customarily, and quite specifically, provides in its statutes. A typical separability clause—taken from the Taft-Hartley Act of 1947—reads:

> If any provision of this Act is declared unconstitutional or the applicability thereof to any person or circumstances is held invalid, the validity of the remainder of the Act and the applicability of such provisions to other persons and circumstances shall not be affected thereby.

This not only serves to save those sections not affected by the Court's particular decision, but it may also act to preserve the law's entire structure for a test involving different litigants.

The series of decisions declaring portions of the Uniform Code of Military Justice Act of 1950 unconstitutional are cases in point;[66] certain powers delegated to the armed services under it are no longer valid, but the balance of the act stands and is enforced. On the other hand, although initially it was merely the "hot oil" provisions of the National Industrial Recovery Act of 1933—standing apart from those provisions of the act dealing with codes of fair competition—that fell as an unconstitutional delegation of legislative power in January 1935,[67] four months later the codes, too, and with them the entire structure of the act, fell on similar grounds.[68]

FIFTEEN: A legislative enactment—or an executive action—may be unwise, unjust, unfair, undemocratic, injudicious, ". . . if you

[65] For example, see *Pollock v. Farmers' Loan and Trust Co.*, 158 U.S. 601 (1895).
[66] *United States ex rel Toth v. Quarles*, 350 U. S. 11 (1955) *Reid v. Covert* 354 U. S. 1 (1957), *Kinsella v. Singleton*, 361 U.S. 234 (1960), among others.
[67] *Panama Refining Co. v. Ryan*, 293 U. S. 388.
[68] *Schechter v. United States*, 295 U. S. 495.

like . . . even tyrannical,"[69] *or simply stupid, but still be consti-*
tutional in the eyes of the Court. Much deference is thus paid to
the legislature and justly so under the American system of separation of powers and division of powers. In the clipped language
of a Holmes opinion: "We fully understand . . . the powerful
argument that can be made against the wisdom of this legislation,
but on that point we have no concern."[70] Mr. Justice Holmes
once stated this constitutional and judicial philosophy in typically
colorful fashion to the then sixty-one-year-old Mr. Justice Stone:

> Young man, about 75 years ago I learned that I was not God.
> And so, when the people . . . want to do something I can't find
> anything in the Constitution expressly forbidding them to do, I
> say, whether I like it or not, "Goddamit, let 'em do it."[71]

Or, as he said to John W. Davis on another occasion: "Of course
I know, and every other sensible man knows, that the Sherman
law [the Sherman Anti-Trust Act of 1890] is damned nonsense,
but if my country wants to go to hell, I am here to help it."[72]
The man who was appointed to the Holmes seat on the Court after
Mr. Justice Cardozo's death in 1938, Mr. Justice Frankfurter, continued to champion that philosophy of judicial self-restraint eloquently, repeatedly, and consistently. Thus, he dissented vigorously
from the majority's declaration of unconstitutionality of a section
of the Immigration and Nationality Act of 1940 in *Trop v. Dulles:*

> It is not easy to stand aloof and allow want of wisdom to prevail,
> to disregard one's own strongly held view of what is wise in the
> conduct of affairs. But it is not the business of this Court to pro-
> nounce policy. It must observe a fastidious regard for limitations
> on its own power, and this precludes the Court's giving effect to
> its own notions of what is wise or politic. That self-restraint is of
> the essence in the observation of the judicial oath, for the Con-
> stitution has not authorized the justices to sit in judgment on the
> wisdom of what Congress and the Executive Branch do. . .[73]

[69] Mr. Justice Holmes, dissenting in *Lochner v. United States,* 198 U. S. 45
(1905).

[70] *Noble State Bank v. Haskell,* 219 U. S. 575 (1910).

[71] As quoted by Charles P. Curtis in his *Lions Under the Throne* (Boston:
Houghton Mifflin Co., 1947), p. 281.

[72] As told by Francis Biddle, *Justice Holmes, Natural Law and the Supreme
Court* (New York: The Macmillan Co., 1961), p. 9.

[73] 356 U. S. 86 (1958).

But once again much, if not all, depends upon how the justices see the line between self-restraint, which they indubitably all recognize as an essential element in the judicial process, and *ultra vires* legislative and executive actions. If, in drawing this line, some justices, on some issues, are prone to address themselves more to the judicial heart than the judicial mind, who is to say where and how the Founding Fathers of the Constitution of the United States would today distinguish between that document's heart and mind? They too were men, just as judges are men, "not disembodied spirits," in Mr. Justice Frankfurter's words; they are men who "respond to human situations . . . [who] do not reside in a vacuum." And his mentor, Holmes, believed that judges "should not be too rigidly bound to the tenets of judicial self-restraint in cases involving civil liberties."[74] Of course, even pedigreed champions of the latter may well disagree on the point in certain specific cases—as is intriguingly demonstrated by Justices Black and Douglas in the *Connecticut Birth Control Case* of 1965.[75] There, speaking for the seven-man majority that held the state's anti-birth control law unconstitutional on a host of grounds, Douglas insisted that ". . . we do not sit [in rendering this decision] as a super-legislature to determine the wisdom, need, and propriety of laws that touch economic problems, business affairs, or social conditions. This law, however, operates directly on an intimate relation of husband and wife, and their physician's role in one aspect of that relation."[76] Black, however, dissenting together with his colleague Stewart, regarded the Court's action as one "based on subjective considerations of 'natural justice' [a formula that] is no less dangerous when used to enforce this Court's views about personal rights than those about economic rights."[77] Judges are men. . . .

SIXTEEN: *The Supreme Court* has reiterated time and again that it *is not designed to serve as a check against inept, unwise, emotional, unrepresentative legislators.* Mr. Chief Justice Waite put it well when he wrote in 1876 that for *"protection against abuses by legislatures the people must resort to the polls not the courts."*[78]

---

[74] As quoted by Mr. Chief Justice Stone to Professor Clinton Rossiter, April 12, 1941, related by Alpheus T. Mason in *Harlan Fiske Stone: Pillar of the Law* (New York: The Viking Press, 1956), p. 516.

[75] *Griswold v. Connecticut*, 381 U.S. 479.

[76] Ibid., at 482.

[77] Ibid., at 522.

[78] *Munn v. Illinois*, 94 U.S. 113. (Italics supplied.)

Some eighty years later, Mr. Justice Douglas reiterated this point of view forcefully: "Congress acting within its constitutional powers, has the final say on policy issues. If it acts unwisely the electorate can make a change."[79] This fundamental truth lies at the very core of the democratic process—a process which enables the people and their representatives at once to rise to soaring heights of wisdom and magnanimity and to descend to the depths of folly and pettiness. Yet that process, under law, proscribes *unconstitutional* action.

THE BULWARK

The Supreme Court of the United States of America—which Woodrow Wilson reviewed as "the balance wheel of our whole constitutional system . . . a vehicle of the Nation's life . . ."[80]—may be steeped in controversy; it may not always have exercised all of its power, or exercised it wisely when it did; it may on occasion have gone beyond that presumed power; it may have deliberately avoided issues that might have proved to be potentially troublesome; it may not always have been able to make its decisions "stick"; and there may well be considerable room for improvement. No institution of government can be devised by human beings that will be satisfactory to all people at all times. Paraphrasing Professor Freund, the question is not whether the Court can do everything, but whether it can do something. It can escape neither controversy nor criticism—nor should it. In Mr. Justice Holmes's oft-quoted words: "We are very quiet there, but it is the quiet of a storm center, as we all know." As an institution at once legal, political, governmental, and human, the Courts possesses both the assets and the liabilities that attend these descriptive characteristics.

Yet, when all is said and done, the Court, at the head of the United State judiciary, is not only the most fascinating, the most influential, and the most powerful judicial body in the world, it is also the "living voice of [the] Constitution," as Lord Bryce, who knew America well indeed, once phrased it. As such it is both arbiter and educator and, in essence, represents the sole solution short of anarchy under the American system of government as we

[79] *Railway Employees' Department v. Hansen*, 351 U.S. 225 (1956).
[80] *Constitutional Government in the United States* (New York: Columbia University Press, 1907), p. 142.

know it. It acts, in the words of one commentator, "as the instrument of national moral values that have not been able to find other governmental expression."[81] As such, as U.S. Circuit Court of Appeals Judge J. Skelly Wright concluded, it acts "as the collective conscience of a sovereign people."[82] And, as Alexander Meiklejohn had observed, no other institution "is more deeply decisive in its effect upon our understanding of ourselves and our government"—it defines values and proclaims principles. It is a corrective force in our life.

Beyond that, moreover, the Supreme Court is the chief protector of the Constitution, of its great system of balances, and of the people's liberties. It is the greatest institutional safeguard we possess. It may have retreated, even yielded to pressures now and then, but without its vigilance our liberties would scarcely have survived. Few have sounded this call more eloquently than did Mr. Justice Black in his memorable opinion for the Court in *Chambers v. Florida:*

> Under our constitutional system, courts stand against any winds that blow as havens of refuge for those who might otherwise suffer because they are helpless, weak, outnumbered, or because they are non-conforming victims of prejudice and public excitement. No higher duty, no more solemn responsibility, rests upon this Court, than that of translating into living law and maintaining this constitutional shield deliberately planned and inscribed for the benefit of every human being subject to our Constitution—of whatever race, creed, or persuasion.[83]

Within the limits of procedure and deference to the presumption of constitutionality of legislation, the Court—our "sober second thought," as Charles Black speaks of it[84]—is the natural forum in our society for the individual and for the small group. Thus, it must be prepared to say "no" to the government—which Madison, the father of the Bill of Rights, hoped fervently it would always do. There are many citizens—indeed most citizens, once they have

81 Anthony Lewis, *The New York Times Magazine,* June 17, 1962, p. 28.
82 "The Role of the Courts: Conscience of a Sovereign People," 29 *The Reporter* 5 (September 29, 1963).
83 309 U.S. 227 (1940), at 241.
84 Charles L. Black, Jr., *The People and the Court: Judicial Review in a Democracy* (New York: The Macmillan Co., 1960), p. 12.

given the problem the careful thought it merits—who will feel far more secure in the knowledge that *that* guardianship by the Court is generally characterized by common sense and by a willingness to stand up and be counted, than if it were primarily exercised by the far more easily pressured, more impulsive, and more emotion-charged legislative or executive branches. Far too easily do these two yield to the politically expedient and the popular—for they are close, indeed, to what Judge Learned Hand once called "the pressure of public hysteria, public panic, and public greed." The Court, which often has had to act as a "moral goad" to public panic and public greed, is neither engaged nor interested in a popularity contest—its function is *not* one of counting constituents. Should the time ever arrive when that is the Court's function, the supreme judicial tribunal will have lost its meaning.

Even if a transfer of that guardianship to other institutions of government were theoretically desirable, which few thoughtful citizens believe, it would be politically impossible. "Do we desire constitutional questions," asked Charles Evans Hughes when off the bench, in his fine book on the Court, ". . . to be determined by political assemblies and partisan division?"[85] The response must be a ringing "no!" In the 1955 Godkins Lectures, which he was to deliver at Harvard University but death intervened, Mr. Justice Jackson expressed this conviction eloquently and ably:

> The people have seemed to feel that the Supreme Court, whatever its defects, is still the most detached, dispassionate, and trustworthy custodian that our system affords for the translation of abstract into concrete constitutional commands.[86]

And we may well agree with Thomas Reed Powell that the logic of American constitutional law is the common sense of the Supreme Court. As a commentary on the point, that distinguished observer of Court and Constitution reported a striking incident that took place after the turn of the century in a debate on the floor of the United States Senate between Senators Spooner of Wisconsin and Tillman of South Carolina. At one juncture of the proceedings, Tillman exclaimed: "I am tired of hearing what the

85 *The Supreme Court of the United States* (New York: Columbia University Press, 1928), p. 236.

86 Jackson, op. cit. p. 23.

Supreme Court says. What I want to get at is the common sense of the matter." Rejoined Senator Spooner: "I too am seeking the common sense of the matter. But, as for me, I prefer the common sense of the Supreme Court of the United States to that of the Senator from South Carolina."[87]

In the long run common sense has always served the Supreme Court of the United States well in its ceaseless striving to maintain the blend of change and continuity which is the *sine qua non* for a desirable stability in the governmental process of a democracy. In that role it will live in history.

[87] "The Logic and Rhetoric of Constitutional Law," 15 *Journal of Philosophy, Psychology, and Scientific Method*, 656 (1918).

FOUR SELECTED BIBLIOGRAPHIES

I CLASSIFIED GENERAL WORKS

A. ADMINISTRATIVE JUSTICE

(Administrative law and agencies in the United States; independent regulatory commissions.)

Association of American Law Schools, *Selected Essays on Constitutional Law* (Foundation Press, 1938).

Cushman, R. E., *The Independent Regulatory Commissions* (Oxford University Press, 1941).

Dickinson, J., *Administrative Justice and the Supremacy of Law* (Russell, 1959).

Fesler, J. W., *Area and Administration* (University of Alabama Press, 1949).

Frank, J. F., *If Men Were Angels* (Harper, 1942).

Friendly, H. J., *The Federal Administration Agencies: The Need for Definition of Standards* (Harvard University Press, 1962).

Gellhorn, W., *Federal Administrative Proceedings* (Johns Hopkins Press, 1941).

Jaffe, L. and N. Nathanson, *Administrative Law: Cases and Materials* (Little, Brown, 1961).

Landis, J. M., *The Administrative Process* (Yale University Press, 1938).

Langallatag, A., *The Department of Justice of the United States* (Johns Hopkins Press, 1927).

McFarland, C., *Judicial Control of the F.T.C. and the I.C.C.* (Harvard University Press, 1933).

Mayers, L., *The American Legal System*, rev. ed. (Harper, 1964).

Nichols, P., *Power of Eminent Domain* (Boston Book Company, 1909).

Paulson, M. C. (ed.), *Legal Institutions Today and Tomorrow* (Columbia University Press, 1959).

Pennock, J. R., *Administration and the Rule of Law* (Rinehart, 1941).

Pound, R., *Administrative Law: Its Growth, Procedure, Significance* (University of Pittsburgh Press, 1942).

Schwartz, B., *An Introduction to American Administrative Law*, 2d ed. (Oceana, 1962).

————, *The Professor and the Commissions* (Knopf, 1959).

B. APPORTIONMENT, GERRYMANDERING, AND
REDISTRICTING

Bain, C. W., *Annexation in Virginia: The Use of the Judicial Process for Readjusting City-County Boundaries* (University of Virginia Press, 1966).

Baker, G. E., *The Reapportionment Revolution: Representation, Political Power, and the Supreme Court* (Random House, 1966).

Boyd, W. J. D., *Patterns of Apportionment* (National Municipal League, 1962).

381

382

————, *State Constitutions: Reapportionment,* rev. ed. (National Municipal League, 1962).

————, *Rural Versus Urban Political Power* (Random House, 1955).

Commission on Intergovernmental Relations, *Apportionment of State Legislatures* (United States Government Printing Office, 1962).

Congressional Quarterly, Representation and Apportionment (Congressional Quarterly, 1966).

de Grazia, A., *Apportionment and Representative Government* (Praeger, 1963).

Dixon, R. G., Jr., *Democratic Representation: Reapportionment in Law and Politics* (Oxford University Press, 1968).

Hacker, A., *Congressional Districting: The Issue of Equal Representation* (Brookings, 1963).

Hamilton, H. (ed.), *Legislative Apportionment: Key to Power* (Harper & Row, 1964).

Hanson, R., *The Political Thicket: Reapportionment and Constitutional Democracy* (Prentice-Hall, 1963).

Havard, W. C. and L. C. Beth, *The Politics of Mis-Representation* (Atherton, 1962).

Jewel, M. E. (ed.), *The Politics of Reapportionment* (Atherton, 1962).

Larson, J. E., *Reapportionment and the Court* (University of Alabama Press, 1962).

Lee, C. B. T., *One Man, One Vote: WMCA and the Struggle for Equal Representation* (Scribner's, 1967).

McKay, R. B., *Reapportionment and the Federal Analogy* (National Municipal League, 1962).

————, *Reapportionment: The Law and Politics of Equal Representation* (Twentieth Century Fund, 1965).

National Municipal Review, *Court Decisions on Legislative Reapportionment* (National Municipal League, 1962).

Shubert, G. A. (ed.), *Reapportionment* (Scribner's, 1965).

Taper, B., *Gomillion v. Lightfoot: Apartheid in Alabama* (McGraw-Hill, 1963).

————, *Gomillion v. Lightfoot: The Tuskegee Gerrymander Case* (McGraw-Hill, 1962).

C. CASEBOOKS—AMERICAN CONSTITUTIONAL LAW

Aqueduct Books (eds.), *Decisions of the United States Supreme Court* (Aqueduct, 1965 ff).

Barrett, E. L., *et al., Constitutional Law: Cases and Materials* (Foundation Press, 1959).

Bartholomew, P. C., *Summaries of Leading Cases on the Constitution,* 5th ed. (Littlefeld, Adams, 1965).

Berns, W. F., *Constitutional Cases in American Government* (Cornell University Press, 1963).

Cahill, P. V. and R. J. Steamer, *The Constitution: Cases and Comments* (Ronald, 1959).

Cushman, R. E., *Leading Constitutional Decisions,* 13th ed. (Appleton-Century-Crofts, 1966).

———— and R. F. Cushman, *Cases in Constitutional Law* (Appleton-Century-Crofts, 1958).

Dodd, W. F., *Cases and Materials on Constitutional Law* (West, 1954).

Dowling, N. T., *Cases on Constitutional Law,* 6th ed. (Foundation Press, 1959).

——— and R. A. Edwards, *American Constitutional Law* (Foundation Press, 1954).

Evans, L. B., *Cases on American Constitutional Law*, 6th ed. (Callaghan, 1952).

Fairman, C., *American Constitutional Decisions* (Holt, 1950).

Fenwick, C. G., *Evans, Cases on Constitutional Law*, 7th ed. (Callaghan, 1957).

Frank, J. P., *Cases and Materials on Constitutional Law*, rev. ed. (McGraw-Hill, 1952).

Freund, P. A., *et al.*, *Constitutional Law* (Little, Brown, 1961).

Garrity, J. A. (ed.), *Quarrels That Have Shaped the Constitution* (Harper & Row, 1964).

Hall, J. P., *Cases on Constitutional Law* (West, 1913).

Hare, J. I. C., *American Constitutional Law* (Brown, 1889).

Heller, F. H., *Introduction to American Constitutional Law* (Harper, 1952).

Jones, R. W., *The Law of Journalism* (Washington Law Book Company, 1940).

Kauper, P. G., *Constitutional Law—Cases and Materials* (Little, Brown, 1961).

Lockhart, W. B., Y. Kamisar, and J. H. Chopper (eds.), *Cases and Materials on the American Constitution* (West, 1967 ff).

———, *Dodd's Cases on Constitutional Law* (West, 1962).

McKay, R. B. (ed.), *The American Constitutional Law Reader* (Oceana, 1958).

Mason, A. T. and W. B. Beaney, *American Constitutional Law: Introductory Essays and Selected Cases*, 3d ed. (Prentice-Hall, 1964).

Mendelson, W., *The Constitution and the Supreme Court*, 2d ed. (Dodd, Mead, 1965).

Mishkin, P. J. and C. Morris, *On Laws and Courts: An Introduction to Judicial Development of Case and Statute Study* (Foundation Press, 1966).

Polsky, S. (ed.), *Medico-Legal Reader* (Oceana, 1956).

Pritchett, C. H., *American Constitutional Issues* (McGraw-Hill, 1962).

——— and A. F. Westin (eds.), *The Third Branch of Government* (Harcourt, Brace & World, 1963).

Sayre, A. B., *Cases and Materials on Constitutional Law* (Callaghan, 1965).

Schmidhauser, J. R., *Constitutional Law in the Political Process* (Rand McNally, 1963).

Schwartz, B., *American Constitutional Law* (Cambridge University Press, 1955).

Scott, J. B., *Judicial Settlement of Controversies Between States of the American Union* (Clarendon Press, 1918).

Spaith, J. H., *The Warren Court: Cases and Commentary* (Chandler, 1966).

Swisher, C. B., *Historic Decisions of the Supreme Court* (University of Toronto Press, 1958).

Thayer, J. B., *Cases on Constitutional Law* (Macmillan, 1959).

Tresolini, R. J., *American Constitutional Law* (Macmillan, 1965).

———, *Constitutional Decisions in American Government* (Lippincott, 1965).

———, *Justice and the Supreme Court* (Lippincott, 1963).

Ziegler, B. M., *The Supreme Court and American Economic Life* (Row, Peterson, 1962).

D. COMPARATIVE ASPECTS

Abraham, H. J., *Courts and Judges: An Introduction to the Judicial Process* (Oxford University Press, 1959).

Andrews, W. G. (ed.), *Constitutions and Constitutionalism*, 2d ed. (Van Nostrand, 1963).

Borchard, E. M., *Declaratory Judgments*, 2d ed. (Banks-Baldwin, 1941).

Bowie, R. R. and C. J. Friedrich (eds.), *Studies in Federalism* (Little, Brown, 1954).

Burgess, J. W., *Political Science and Comparative Constitutional Law* (Ginn, 1890).

Dawson, J. P., *A History of Lay Judges* (Doubleday, 1956).

Friedrich, C. J., *Constitutional Government and Democracy*, 3d ed. (Ginn 1964).

Gray, C. M., *Copyhold, Equity, and the Common Law* (Harvard University Press, 1963).

Harding, A. L. (ed.), *The Administration of Justice in Retrospect* (Southern Methodist University Press, 1957).

Haynes, E., *The Selection and Tenure of Judges* (National Press Conference of Judicial Councils, 1944).

Karlen, D., *Appellate Courts in the United States and England* (New York University Press, 1963).

Kempin, F. G., Jr., *Legal History: Law and Social Change* (Prentice-Hall, 1963).

Macmahon, A. W. (ed.), *Federalism Mature and Emergent* (Doubleday, 1953).

McWhinney, E., *Judicial Review in the English-Speaking World*, 2d ed. (University of Toronto Press, 1961).

Newan, R. A., *Equity and Law: A Comparative Study* (Oceana, 1961).

Pollock, Sir F., *Essays in the Law* (Macmillan, 1922).

Read, C. (ed.), *The Constitution Reconsidered* (Columbia University Press, 1938).

Robson, W. A., *Justice and Administrative Law: A Study of the British Constitution* (Stevens, 1951).

Rossiter, C. L., *Constitutional Dictatorship: Crisis Government in the Modern Democracies* (Princeton University Press, 1948).

Schwartz, B., *The Code Napoleon and the Common Law World* (New York University Press, 1956).

Spiro, H., *Government by Constitution* (Random House, 1959).

Stannard, H., *The Two Constitutions: A Comparative Study of British and American Constitutional Systems* (Van Nostrand, 1959).

Sutherland, A. E. (ed.), *Government Under Law* (Harvard University Press, 1956).

Wagner, W. J., *Federal States and their Judiciary: Comparative Study in Constitutional Law and Organization of Courts in Federal States* (Mouton, 1959).

Wheare, K. C., *Federal Government*, 4th ed. (Oxford University Press, 1964).
———, *Modern Constitutions* (Oxford University Press, 1951).

Douglas, W. O., *We the Judges* (Doubleday, 1956).

E. THE CONGRESS

(The legislative organ—a branch of the separation of powers of our national government.)

Deantonio, E. and D. Talbot, *Point of Order! A Documentary of the Army-McCarthy Hearings* (Norton, 1964).

Egger, R. and J. P. Harris, *The President and Congress* (McGraw-Hill, 1963).

Ettrude, D. J. (ed.), *The Power of Congress To Nullify Supreme Court Decisions* (Wilson, 1924).

Goldfarb, R. L., *The Contempt Power* (Columbia University Press, 1963).

Harris, J. P., *The Advice and Consent of the Senate: A Study of the Confirmation of Appointments by the United States Senate* (University of California Press, 1953).

Hurst, J. W., *The Growth of American Law: The Lawmakers* (Little, Brown, 1950).

Lawson, J. F., *The General Welfare Clause* (J. F. Lawson, 1934).

Lowi, T. J. (ed.), *Legislative Politics, USA*, 2d ed. (Little, Brown, 1965).

Mason, A. T. and W. B. Beaney, *The Supreme Court in a Free Society* (Prentice-Hall, 1959).

Morgan, D. L., *Congress and the Constitution: A Study of Responsibility* (Harvard University Press, 1967).

Murphy, W. F., *Congress and the Court* (University of Chicago Press, 1962).

Nichols, E. R., *Congress or the Supreme Court: Which Shall Rule America?* (Noble, 1935).

Paulson, M. C. (ed.), *Legal Institutions Today and Tomorrow* (Columbia University Press, 1959).

Polsby, N. W., *Congress and the Presidency* (Prentice-Hall, 1963).

Pritchett, C. H., *Congress versus the Supreme Court* (University of Minnesota Press, 1961).

Wilson, W., *Congressional Government* (Houghton Mifflin, 1885).

F. THE COURTROOM

(Cases in court: administering justice. Also, the problem of the case load and time.)

Borchard, E. M., *Convicting the Innocent* (Yale University Press, 1932).

Cozzens, J. G., *The Just and the Unjust* (Harcourt, Brace, 1942).

Dangel, E. M., *Contempt* (National Lawyers' Manual Company, 1939).

Davenport, W. H. (ed.), *Voices in Court* (Macmillan, 1958).

Fox, J. C., *The History of Contempt of Court* (Oxford University Press, 1927).

Frank J. F., *Courts on Trial: Myth and Reality in American Justice* (Princeton University Press, 1959).

——— and B. Frank, *Not Guilty* (Doubleday, 1957).

Goldfarb, R. L., *The Contempt Power* (Columbia University Press, 1963).

Karlen, D., *Appellate Courts in the United States and England* (New York University Press, 1963).

Kunstler, W. M., *First Degree* (Oceana, 1960).

Laurent, F. W., *The Business of a Trial Court* (University of Wisconsin Press, 1959).

Munsterberg, H., *On the Witness Stand* (Boardman, 1925).

Nizer, L., *My Life in Court* (Doubleday, 1961).

Oswald, J. F., *Contempt of Court* (Butterworth, 1911).

Porter, E. S., *Conscience of the Court* (Prentice-Hall, 1962).

Stryker, L. P., *Courts and Doctors* (Macmillan, 1932).

Taylor, G. C., *Fifty Years in the Law* (Philosophical Library, 1963).

Thomas, C. H., *Problems of Contempt of Court* (Horn-Shafers, 1934).

Warren, G., *Traffic Courts* (Little, Brown, 1942).

Westin, A. F., *Anatomy of a Constitutional Law Case* (Macmillan, 1958).

Zeisel, H., H. Kalvern, Jr., and B. Bucholz, *Delay in the Court* (Little Brown, 1959).

386

G. FEDERALISM

1. General

Allen, R. S., Our Sovereign States (Vanguard, 1949).

Ames, H. V. (ed.), State Documents on Federal Relations, 1789–1861 (University of Pennsylvania Press, 1900).

Anderson, W., The Nation and the States, Rivals or Partners? (University of Minnesota Press, 1955).

Association of American Law Schools, Selected Essays on Constitutional Law (Foundation Press, 1938).

Benson, G. C. S., The New Centralization (Rinehart, 1941).

Bloch, C., States Rights: The Law of the Land (Harrison, 1958).

Bordon, M. (ed.), The Anti-Federalist Papers (Michigan State University Press, 1965).

Bowie, R. R. and C. J. Friedrich (eds.), Studies in Federalism (Little, Brown, 1954).

Brannon, H. A., Treaties on the Rights and Privileges Guaranteed by the Fourteenth Amendment to the Constitution of the U.S. (Anderson, 1901).

Clark, J. P., The Rise of a New Federalism (Columbia University Press, 1938).

Cooley, R. M., Constitutional Limitations, 17th ed. (Little, Brown, 1907).

Corwin, E. S., The Doctrine of Judicial Review (Princeton University Press, 1914).

————, National Supremacy: Treaty Power versus State Power (Holt, 1913).

Dietze, G., The Federalist: A Classic on Federalism and Free Government (Johns Hopkins Press, 1960).

Douglas, W. O., We the Judges (Doubleday, 1956).

Guthrie, W. D., Lectures on the 14th Article of Amendment to the Constitution of the United States (Little, Brown, 1898).

Hamilton, A., J. Jay, and J. Madison, The Fedaralist Papers (McLean, 1788).

Hart, H. M., Jr., and H. Wechsler, The Federal Court and the Federal System (Foundation Press, 1953).

Heins, A. J., Constitutional Restrictions Against State Debt (University of Wisconsin Press, 1963).

Hopkins, V. C., Dred Scott's Cases (Fordham University Press, 1951).

Hutchins, R. M., Two Faces of Federalism (Center for the Study of Democratic Institutions, 1962).

Kilpatrick, J. J., The Sovereign States (Regnery, 1957).

Lien, A. J., Concurring Opinion (St. Louis: Washington University Press, 1957).

Livingston, W. S., Federalism and Constitutional Change (Oxford University Press, 1956).

Macmahon, A. W. (ed.), Federalism Mature and Emergent (Doubleday, 1955).

Main, J. T., The Antifederalist Critics of the Constitution, 1781–1788 (Quadrangle, 1964).

Mason, A. T., Free Government in the Making, 3d ed. (Oxford University Press, 1965).

————, The States Rights Debate: Antifederalism and the Constitution (Prentice-Hall, 1964).

Merrian, C. E., The Written Constitution and the Unwritten Attitude (R. R. Smith, 1931).

Morley, F., Freedom and Federalism (Regnery, 1959).

Orfield, L. B., The Amending of the Federal Constitution (Calahan, 1942).

Peltason, J. W., *Fifty-Eight Lonely Men: Southern Federal Judges and School Desegregation* (Harcourt, Brace & World, 1961).

Pound, R., C. H. McIlwain, and R. F. Nichols, *Federalism as a Democratic Process* (Rutgers University Press, 1942).

Powell, T. R., *Vagaries and Varieties in Constitutional Interpretations* (Columbia University Press, 1956).

Ramaswamy, M., *The Creative Role of the Supreme Court of the United States* (Stanford University Press, 1956).

Roberts, O. J., *The Court and the Constitution* (Harvard University Press, 1951).

Rockefeller, N. A., *The Future of Federalism* (Harvard University Press, 1962, and Atheneum, 1963).

Schmidhauser, J. R., *The Supreme Court as Final Arbiter of Federal-State Relations* (Universtiy of North Carolina Press, 1958).

Ten-Broek, J., *Anti-Slavery Origins of the Fourteenth Amendment* (University of California Press, 1951).

Warren, C., *The Supreme Court and Sovereign States* (Princeton University Press, 1924).

Wheare, K., *Federal Government*, 4th ed. (Oxford University Press, 1964).

White, L. D., *The States and the Nation* (Louisiana State University Press, 1956).

Wilcox, T., *States Rights v. the Supreme Court* (Little, Brown, 1960).

2. The Commerce Clause

Baxter, M. G., *Daniel Webster and the Supreme Court* (University of Massachusetts Press, 1967).

Corwin, E. S., *The Commerce Power versus States Rights* (Princeton University Press, 1936).

Frankfurter, F., *The Commerce Clause Under Marshall, Taney, and Waite* (University of North Carolina Press, 1937).

Gavit, B. C., *The Commerce Clause of the United States Constitution* (Principia, 1956).

Hartman, J. P., *State Taxation of Interstate Commerce* (Dennis, 1953).

Kallenbach, J. E., *Federal Cooperation with the States under the Commerce Clause* (University of Michigan Press, 1942).

Lerner, M., *The Supreme Court and American Capitalism* (Yale Law Journal, 1933).

Mahany M. M., *Commerce Clause Tax Problems* (Wilkinson, 1940).

Melder, F. E., *State and Local Barriers to Interstate Commerce in the United States* (University of Maine Press, 1937).

Ramaswamy, M., *The Commerce Clause in the Constitution of the United States* (Longmans, Green, 1948).

Ribble, F. D. G., *State and National Power Over Commerce* (Columbia University Press, 1937).

Rottschaefer, H., *The Constitution and Socio-Economic Change* (University of Michigan Press, 1948).

Rutledge, W. B., *A Declaration of Legal Faith* (University of Kansas Press, 1947).

3. The Contract Clause

Magrath, P. B., *Yazoo: Law and Politics in the New Republic, The Case of Fletcher v. Peck* (Brown University Press, 1967).

Wright, B. F., *The Contract Clause of the Constitution* (Harvard University Press, 1938).

4. Full Faith and Credit

Jackson, R. H., *Full Faith and Credit: The Lawyer's Clause in the Constitution* (Columbia University Press, 1945).

5. Police Power

Roettinger, R., *The Supreme Court and the State Police Power: A Study in Federalism* (Public Affairs Press, 1957).

6. Relationship Among the States

Leach, R. H. and R. S. Sugg, Jr., *The Administration of Interstate Compacts* (Louisiana State University Press, 1959).

Scott, J. B., *Judicial Settlement of Controversies between States of the American Union* (Clarendon Press, 1918).

Thursby, V. B., *Interstate Cooperation: A Study of the Interstate Compact* (Public Affairs Press, 1953).

Zimmerman, F. L. and M. Wendell, *The Interstate Compact Since 1925* (Council of State Governments, 1951).

7. State Courts and Federal Relationships

Council of State Governments, *Courts of Last Resort of the States* (Council of State Governments, 1955).

Elliott, S. D., *Improving Our Courts* (Oceana, 1959).

Mitchel, W., *Relations between Federal and State Courts* (Columbia University Press, 1950).

Vanderbilt, A. T., *Minimum Standards of Judicial Administration* (New York University Press, 1949).

Wendell, M., *Relations Between the Federal and State Courts*, rev. ed. (Columbia University Press, 1953).

8. The Taxing Power and Other Monetary Problems

Dunne, G. T., *Monetary Decisions of the Supreme Court* (Rutgers University Press, 1960).

Hansen, A. and H. Perloff, *State and Local Finance in the National Economy* (Norton, 1944).

Heins, A. J., *Constitutional Restrictions Against State Debt* (University of Wisconsin Press, 1963).

Maxwell, J. A., *Fiscal Impact of Federalism in the United States* (Harvard University Press, 1946).

H. ASPECTS OF AMERICAN CONSTITUTIONAL DEMOCRACY

(Works dealing with many areas of our system, but not specifically with any one feature—many are cross-referenced in other categories.)

Association of American Law Schools, *Selected Essays on Constitutional Law* (Foundation Press, 1938).

Aumann, F. A., *The Instrumentalities of Justice: Their Forms, Functions, and Limitations* (Ohio State University Press, 1956).

Beard, C. A., *The Republic* (Viking, 1943).

Berman, H. J., *Talks on American Law* (Random House, 1961).

Black, C. L., Jr., *Perspectives in Constitutional Law* (Prentice-Hall, 1963).

Burdick, C. K., *The Law of the American Constitution: Its Origins and Development* (Putnam, 1922).

Burlingame, R., *The American Conscience* (Knopf, 1957).

Cardozo, B. N., *Law and Literature and Other Essays* (Harcourt, Brace, 1931).

Cohen, L. K. (ed.), *The Legal Conscience: Selected Papers of Felix S. Cohen* (Yale University Press, 1960).

Collyer, R. (Comp.), *In Defense of the Constitution: Excerpts from Addresses and Opinions of Chief Justices of the United States* (Yale University Press, 1960).

Commager, H. S., *The American Mind* (Yale University Press, 1950).

Corwin, E. S., *A Constitution of Powers in a Secular State* (University of Virginia Press, 1951).

———, *Our Expendable Constitution* (University of Illinois Press, 1955).

Curtis, C. P., *It's Your Law* (Harvard University Press, 1954).

Dahl, R. A., *A Preface to Democratic Theory* (University of Chicago Press, 1956).

Daniels, J., *Frontier on the Potomac* (Macmillan, 1946).

Denning, A., *The Road to Justice* (Stevens, 1955).

Dietze, G. (ed.), *Essays on the American Constitution* (Prentice-Hall, 1964).

Dilliard, I. (ed.), *The Spirit of Liberty: Papers and Addresses of Learned Hand* (Knopf, 1959).

Douglas, W. O., *Being an American* (Way, 1948).

———, *We the Judges* (Doubleday, 1956).

Edwards, N., *The Courts and the Public Schools* (University of Chicago Press, 1962).

Fainsod, M. and L. Gordon, *Government and the American Economy* (Norton, 1948).

Fesler, J. W., *Area and Administration* (University of Alabama Press, 1949).

Frankfurter, F., *Of Law and Men: Papers and Addresses,* ed. by Philip Elman (Harcourt, Brace, 1956).

———, *Law and Politics* (Harcourt, Brace, 1939).

———, *The Public and Its Government* (Oxford University Press, 1930).

Freedman, V., *Society on Trial: Current Court Decision and Social Change* (Thomas, 1965).

Garrison, L. K., J. W. Hurst, C. A. Auerbach, and S. Mermin, *The Legal Process,* rev. ed. (Chandler, 1961).

The Gaspar Bacon Lectures on the Constitution of the United States, 1940–1950 (Boston University Press, 1953).

Gordon, R. M., *Nine Men Against America* (Devin-Adair, 1958).

Hagrath, E. P. (ed.), *The Constitutional System* (Scott, Foresman, 1966).

Hare, J. I. C., *American Constitutional Law* (Brown, 1889).

Holcombe, A. N., *The Constitutional System,* rev. ed. (Scott, Foresman, 1965).

Kaplan, B. and L. Hall (eds.), *Judicial Administration and the Common Man* (Lippincott, 1953).

Kauper, P. G., *Frontiers of Constitutional Liberty* (University of Michigan Press, 1956).

Laski, H. J., *The American Democracy* (Viking, 1948).

Lasswell, H. D., *Power and Personality* (Norton, 1948).

McCloskey, R. G., *Essays in Constitutional Law* (Knopf, 1957).

390

McKay, R. B. (ed.), *The American Constitutional Law Reader* (Oceana, 1958).

McLaughlin, A. S., *The Courts, the Constitution, and Parties* (University of Chicago Press, 1912).

Mason, A. T. and W. M. Beaney, *The Supreme Court in a Free Society* (Prentice-Hall, 1959).

Matthews, J. M., *The American Constitutional System* (McGraw-Hill, 1940).

Mayers, L., *The American Legal System*, rev. ed. (Harper & Row, 1964).

Morlan, R. L., *Capital, Courthouse and City Hall*, 3d ed. (Houghton Mifflin, 1966).

Paulson, M. C. (ed.), *Legal Institutions Today and Tomorrow* (Columbia University Press, 1959).

Pekelis, A. H., *Law and Social Action* (Cornell University Press, 1950).

Pomeroy, J. N., *An Introduction to the Constitutional Law of the U.S.* (Hurd and Houghton, 1886).

Pritchett, C. H., *The American Constitutional System* (McGraw-Hill, 1963).

Read, C. (ed.), *The Constitution Reconsidered* (Columbia University Press, 1938).

Rickard, J. A. and J. H. McCroip, *Our National Constitution* (Stackpole, 1956).

Rottschaefer, H., *The Constitution and Socio-Economic Change* (University of Michigan Law School, 1949).

Schoulder, J., *Constitutional Studies* (Dodd, Mead, 1897).

Schwartz, B., *American Constitutional Law* (Harvard University Press, 1955).

———, *A Commentary on the Constitution of the United States* Part I, *The Powers of Government* (Macmillan, 1963).

———, *The Powers of Government* (Macmillan, 1965).

Shapiro, M. M. (ed.), *The Supreme Court* (Scott, Foresman, 1967).

———, *The Supreme Court and Constitutional Law* (Scott, Foresman, 1965).

Smith, H. R., *Democracy and the Public Interest* (University of Georgia Press, 1960).

Sutherland, A. E., *Constitutionalism in America* (Blaisdells, 1964).

———, *The Law and One Man Among Many* (University of Wisconsin Press, 1956).

——— (ed.), *Government Under Law* (Harvard University Press, 1956).

Taft, W. H., *Popular Government* (Yale University Press, 1913).

Tiffany, J., *A Treatise on Government and Constitutional Law* (Little, 1867).

Truman, D. B., *The Governmental Process* (Knopf, 1951).

Vanderbilt, A. T., *The Doctrine of Separation of Powers and Its Present Day Significance* (University of Nebraska Press, 1963).

Warren, E., *The Law in the Future* (*Fortune Magazine*, 1955).

Watson, D. K., *The Constitution of the United States: Its History, Application, and Construction* (Callaghan, 1910).

Weaver, S. P., *Constitutional Law and Its Administration* (Callaghan, 1946).

Wechsler, H., *Principles, Politics, and Fundamental Law: Selected Essays* (Harvard University Press, 1961).

Welch, J., *The Constitution* (Houghton Mifflin, 1956).

Westin, A. F., *The Uses of Power: 7 Cases in American Politics* (Harcourt, Brace & World, 1962).

Wilson, W., *Constitutional Government in the United States* (Columbia University Press, 1908).

Wright, B. F., *Growth of American Constitutional Law* (Reynal and Hitchcock, 1942, and Phoenix, 1967).

I. THE JUDICIAL PROCESS: GENERAL

(The federal judicial process and court system; especially the Supreme Court and its jurisprudence.)

Abraham, H. J., *Courts and Judges: An Introduction to the Judicial Process* (Oxford University Press, 1959).

——, *The Judiciary: The Supreme Court in the Governmental Process* (Allyn and Bacon, 1964).

Acheson, P. C., *The Supreme Court: America's Judicial Heritage* (Dodd, Mead, 1961).

Arneson, B. A., *Elements of Constitutional Law* (Harper, 1928).

Baade, H. W. (ed.), *Jurimetrics* (Duke University Press, 1963).

Baldwin, S. E., *The American Judiciary* (Century, 1905).

Bent, J. A., *The Independent Judiciary* (Morgantown, 1925).

Bickel, A., *The Least Dangerous Branch: The Supreme Court as the Bar of Politics* (Bobbs-Merrill, 1963).

Callison, I. P., *Courts of Injustice* (Twayne, 1956).

Clayton, J. E., *The Making of Justice: The Supreme Court in Action* (Dutton, 1964).

Cook, W. W. (ed.), *Fundamental Legal Concepts as Applied in Judicial Reasoning* (Yale University Press, 1964).

Cooley, R. M., *Constitutional Limitations* (Putnam's, 1868).

Cooley, T. M., *Principles of Constitutional Law*, 2d ed. (Little, Brown, 1891).

Coy, H., *The First Book of the Supreme Court* (Watts, 1958).

Curtis, C. P., *Lions Under the Throne* (Houghton Mifflin, 1947).

Douglas, E. O., *We, The Judges* (Doubleday, 1956).

Farnsworth, E. A., *An Introduction to the Legal System of the United States* (Oceana, 1963).

Felscher, H. and M. Rosen, *The Press in the Jury Box* (Macmillan, 1966).

Frank, J., *If Men Were Angels* (Harper, 1942).

Frank, J. P., *Marble Palace: The Supreme Court in American Life* (Knopf, 1958).

Freund, P. A., *The Supreme Court of the United States: Its Business, Purposes, and Performance* (Meridian, 1961).

——, *On Understanding the Supreme Court* (Little, Brown, 1949).

Hirschfield, R., *The Court and the Constitution* (Random House, 1960).

Horn, R. A., *Groups and the Constitution* (Stanford University Press, 1956).

Hughes, C. E., *The Supreme Court of the United States* (Columbia University Press, 1928).

Hyneman, C. S., *The Supreme Court on Trial* (Atherton, 1963).

Jackson, P. E. (ed.), *The Wisdom of the Supreme Court* (University of Oklahoma Press, 1962).

Jackson, R. H., *The Supreme Court in the American System of Government* (Harvard University Press, 1955).

Jacob, H., *Justice in America: Courts, Lawyers, and the Judicial Process* (Little, Brown, 1965).

Johnson, G. W., *The Supreme Court* (Morrow, 1962).

Journal of Public Law, Symposium, "Policy-Making in a Democracy: The Role of the United States Supreme Court" (1957).

Judson, R. N., *The Judiciary and the People* (Yale University Press, 1913).

Kirschheimer, O., *Political Justice: The Use of Legal Procedure for Political Ends* (Princeton University Press, 1961).

Krislov, S., *The Supreme Court in the Political Process* (Macmillan, 1965).

Kurland, P. (ed.), *The Supreme Court Review* (University of Chicago Press, 1960 ff).

Kutler, S. I. (ed.), *The Dred Scott Decision: Law or Politics* (Houghton Mifflin, 1967).

McRuer, J. C., *The Evolution of the Judicial Process* (Clarke, Irwin, 1957).

Mason, A. T., *The Supreme Court: Instrument of Power or of Revealed Truth?* (Boston University Press, 1953).

———, *The Supreme Court: Palladium of Freedom* (University of Michigan Press, 1962).

Mayers, L., *The Machinery of Justice: An Introduction to Legal Structure and Process* (Prentice-Hall, 1963).

Mendelson, W., *The Supreme Court: Law versus Discretion* (Bobbs-Merrill, 1967).

Moreland, C. C., *Equal Justice Under the Law* (Oceana, 1957).

Murphy, W. F., *A Case Study in the Judicial Process* (Random House, 1964).

——— and C. H. Pritchett (eds.), *Courts, Judges, and Politics* (Random House, 1961).

North, A. A., *The Supreme Court: Judicial Process and Judicial Politics* (Appleton-Century-Crofts, 1966).

Norton, T. J., *Losing Liberty Judicially* (Macmillan, 1928).

———, *Undermining the Constitution* (Devin-Adair, 1950).

Peltason, J. W., *Federal Courts in the Political Process* (Doubleday, 1955).

Ramaswamy, M., *The Creative Role of the Supreme Court of the United States* (Stanford University Press, 1956).

Roche, J. P. and L. W. Levy (eds.), *The Judiciary: Documents in American Government* (Harcourt, Brace & World, 1964).

Solomon, L. I. (ed.), *The Supreme Court* (Wilson, 1961).

Schmidhauser, J. R., *The Supreme Court: Its Politics, Personalities, and Procedures* (Holt Rinehart and Winston, 1960).

Schubert, G. A., *Constitutional Politics* (Holt, Rinehart and Winston, 1960).

———, *Judicial Policy Making* (Scott, Foresman, 1965).

Schwartz, B., *A Commentary on the Constitution of the United States* Part I, *The Powers of Government* (Macmillan, 1963).

———, *The Supreme Court: Constitutional Revolution in Retrospect* (Ronald, 1954).

Scigliano, R. G., *The Courts: A Reader in the Judicial Process* (Little, Brown, 1962).

Shapiro, M., *Law and Politics in the Supreme Court: New Approaches to Political Jurisprudence* (Stamford University Press, 1964).

Spaeth, H. J., *An Introduction to Supreme Court Decision Making* (Chandler, 1965).

Starr, I., *The Federal Judiciary* (Oxford Book Company, 1957).

Swisher, C. B., *The Growth of Constitutional Power in the United States*, 2d ed. (University of Chicago Press, 1963).

———, *The Supreme Court in Modern Role* (New York University Press, 1958).

Tully, A., *Supreme Court* (Simon and Schuster, 1963).

Vines, K. N. and H. Jacob, *Studies in Judicial Politics* (Tulane University Press, 1962).

Westin, A. F., *The Supreme Court: Views from Inside* (Norton, 1961).

Willoughby, W. F., *Principles of Judicial Administration* (Brookings Institute, 1929).

393

1. General

(Sweeping surveys as well as specific eras and institutions.)

Alfange, D., *The Supreme Court and the National Will* (Doubleday, 1937).

Alloway, C. C., *United States Constitutional Law, 1850–1875* (Oceana, 1958).

Angell, E., *Supreme Court Primer* (Reynal and Hitchcock, 1937).

Bates, E. S., *The Story of the Supreme Court* (Bobbs-Merrill, 1936, and Cornerstone, 1963).

Bauer, E. K., *Commentaries on the Constitution 1790–1860* (Columbia University Press, 1952).

Beck, J. M., *The Constitution of the United States* (Doran, 1922).

Boudin, L. B., *Government by Judiciary* (Godwin, 1932).

Burdick, C. K., *The Law of the American Constitution: Its Origins and Development* (Putnam, 1922).

Carson, H. L., *The History of the Supreme Court of the United States* (Keller, 1891).

Commager, H. S. (ed.), *Documents of American History*, 6th ed. (Appleton-Century-Crofts, 1958).

Cooley, T. M., *Constitutional History of the United States* (Putnam's 1889).

Crosskey, W. W., *Politics and the Constitution in the History of the United States* (University of Chicago Press, 1953).

Cummings, H. S. and C. McFarland, *Federal Justice* (Macmillan, 1937).

Donald, P., *The Politics of Reconstitution* (Louisiana State University Press, 1966).

Edmunds, P. D., *Law and Civilization* (Public Affairs Press, 1959).

Ernst, M. L., *The Ultimate Power* (Doubleday, 1937).

Fairman, C., *The Bacon Lectures on the Constitution of the United States, 1940–1950* (Boston University Press, 1953).

Fenn, P. T., *The Development of the Constitution* (Appleton-Century-Crofts, 1948).

Flack, H. B., *The Adoption of the Fourteenth Amendment* (Johns Hopkins Press, 1908).

Fox, J. C., *The History of Contempt of Court* (Oxford University Press, 1927).

Frankfurter, F., *The Commerce Clause Under Marshall, Taney, and Waite* (University of North Carolina Press, 1937).

Fribourd, M. G., *The Supreme Court in American History* (Macrae Smith, 1965).

Friedrich, C. J. and R. G. McCloskey, *From the Declaration of Independence to the Constitution* (Bobbs-Merrill, 1964).

Fuess, C. M., *Daniel Webster* (Little, Brown, 1930).

Haines, C. G., *The Role of the Supreme Court in American Government and Politics 1789–1835* (University of California Press, 1944).

—— and F. H. Sherwood, *The Role of the Supreme Court in American Government and Politics, 1835–1864* (University of California Press, 1957).

Hamilton, W. H. and D. Adair, *The Power To Govern: The Constitution Then and Now* (Norton, 1937).

Hartz, L., *Economic Policy and Democratic Thought* (Harvard University Press, 1948).

Hendrick, B. J., *Bulwark of the Republic* (Little, Brown, 1939).

Hockett, C. H., *The Constitutional History of the United States, 1826–1876* (Macmillan 1939).

394

Jackson, R. H., *The Struggle for Judicial Supremacy* (Knopf, 1941).

Jacobs, C. E., *Law Writers and the Courts* (University of California Press, 1954).

James, J. B., *The Framing of the Fourteenth Amendment* (University of Illinois Press, 1956, and 1965).

Jensen, M. D., *The Articles of Confederation* (University of Wisconsin Press, 1940).

Kelly, A. H. and W. Harbison, *The American Constitution—Its Origin and Development*, 3d ed. (Norton, 1963).

Kempin, F. G., Jr., *Legal History: Law and Social Change* (Prentice-Hall, 1963).

Kendrick, B. J., *Journal of the Joint Committee of Fifteen on Reconstruction* (Scribner's, 1914).

Lacy, D., *The Meaning of the American Revolution* (New American Library, 1960).

Lasson, N. B., *The History of the Development of the Fourteenth Amendment* (Johns Hopkins Press, 1937).

Leedham, C., *Our Changing Constitution* (Dodd, Mead, 1964).

McCloskey, R. G., *The American Supreme Court* (University of Chicago Press, 1960).

McCune, W., *The Nine Young Men* (Harper, 1947).

McIlwain, C. H., *Constitutionalism, Ancient and Modern*, rev. ed. (Cornell University Press, 1947).

McLaughlin, A. C., *The Constitutional History of the United States* (Appleton-Century, 1935).

Mason, A. T., *The Supreme Court from Taft to Warren* (Louisiana State University Press, 1958).

Maverick, M., *In Blood and Ink* (Modern Age, 1939).

Mendelson, W., *Capitalism, Democracy, and the Supreme Court* (Appleton-Century, 1960).

Miller, P. (ed.), *The Legal Mind in America: From Independence to the Civil War* (Doubleday, 1962).

Morgan, E. S., *The Birth of the Republic* (University of Chicago Press, 1956).

Munro, W. B., *The Makers of the Unwritten Constitution* (Macmillan, 1930).

Murray, W. H., *The Supreme Court, The President, and Seven Senators* (Meador, 1959).

Myers, G., *History of the Supreme Court of the United States* (Kerr, 1912).

Padover, S. K., *The Living United States Constitution* (New American Library, 1953).

Paul, A. M., *Conservative Crisis and the Rule of Law Attitudes of Bar and Bench, 1887–1895* (Cornell University Press, 1960).

Pollak, L. H. (ed.), *The Constitution and the Supreme Court: A Documentary History* (World, 1966).

Pritchett, C. H., *The American Constitution* (McGraw-Hill, 1959).

Rachlis, F., *They Came To Kill* (Random House, 1961).

Randall, J. G., *The Civil War and Reconstruction* (Heath, 1937).

———, *Constitutional Problems Under Lincoln*, rev. ed. (University of Delaware Press, 1956).

Read, C. (ed.), *The Constitution Reconsidered* (Columbia University Press, 1938).

Ribble, F. D. G., *State and National Power Over Commerce* (Columbia University Press, 1937).

Rodell, F., *Nine Men: A Political History of the Supreme Court from 1790–1955* (Random House, 1955).

Rodick, B. C., *American Constitutional Custom: A Forgotten Factor in the Founding* (Philosophical Library, 1953).

Rogers, H. S. (ed.), *Constitutional History of the U.S. as Seen in the Development of American Law* (Bender, 1890).

Schovler, J., *Constitutional Studies* (Dodd, Mead, 1897).

Schwartz, B., *The Reins of Power: A Constitutional History of the United States* (Hill & Wang, 1963).

Silver, D. M., *Lincoln's Supreme Court* (University of Illinois Press, 1956).

Smith, J. M. and P. L. Murphy, *Liberty and Justice* (Knopf, 1958).

Story, J., *A Familiar Exposition on the Constitution of the United States: Containing a Brief Commentary* (Petersburgh, 1840).

Swisher, C. B., *American Constitutional Development*, 2d ed. (Houghton Mifflin, 1954).

Tocqueville, A. de, *Democracy in America* (Langley, 1841).

Towle, N., *A History and Analysis of the Constitution of the U.S.* (Little, Brown, 1860).

Twiss, B. R., *Lawyers and the Constitution: How Laissez Faire Came to the Supreme Court* (Princeton University Press, 1942).

Wallace, H. A., *Whose Constitution?* (Reynal and Hitchcock, 1936).

Warren, C., *The Supreme Court in United States History*, rev. ed. (Little Brown, 1937).

Wright, B. F., *The Contract Clause of the Constitution* (Harvard University Press, 1938).

2. Specific

a. The Franklin D. Roosevelt Era

Alsop, J. and T. Catledge, *The 168* (Doubleday, 1938).

Baker, L., *Back to Back: The Duel Between FDR and the Supreme Court* (Macmillan, 1967).

Barnes, W. R. and A. W. Littlefield, *The Supreme Court Issue and the Constitution* (Barnes & Noble, 1937).

Brant, I., *Storm Over the Constitution* (Bobbs-Merrill, 1936).

Burns, J. M., *The Lion and the Fox* (Harcourt, Brace, 1956).

Cope, A. H. and F. Krinsky, *Franklin D. Roosevelt and the Supreme Court* (Heath, 1952).

Corwin, E. S., *Constitutional Revolution, Ltd.* (Claremont College Press, 1941).

Ericksson, E. M., *The Supreme Court and the New Deal* (University of California Press, 1940).

Goldberg, L. and E. Levenson, *Lawless Judges* (Rand School Press, 1935).

Jackson, R. H., *The Struggle for Judicial Supremacy* (Knopf, 1941).

Johnson, J. E., *Reorganization of the Supreme Court* (Wilson, 1937).

Lippmann, W., *The Supreme Court: Independent or Controlled?* (Harper, 1937).

Mason, A. T., *The Supreme Court: Vehicle of Revealed Truth or Power Group, 1930–1937* (Boston University Press, 1953).

Pearson, D. and R. S. Allen, *The Nine Old Men* (Doubleday, 1936).

Pritchett, C. H., *The Roosevelt Court: A Study in Judicial Politics and Values, 1937–1947* (Macmillan, 1947).

Pusey, T. R., *The Supreme Court Crisis* (Macmillan, 1937).

Sommer, F. H., *Reforming the Supreme Court* (New York University Press, 1951).

b. Origin, Formation, and Ratification of the Constitution

Baldwin, H., *A General View of the Origin and Nature of the Constitution and Government of the United States* (Clark, 1837).

Bancroft, G., *History of the Formation of the Constitution of the United States of America* (Appleton, 1882).

Beard, C. A., *An Economic Interpretation of the Constitution of the United States* (Macmillan, 1913).

Bowen, C. D., *Miracle at Philadelphia: The Story of the Constitutional Convention May to September 1787* (Little, Brown, 1966).

Brant, I., *The Bill of Rights* (Bobbs-Merrill, 1965).

———, *James Madison: Father of the Constitution, 1787–1800* (Bobbs-Merrill, 1950).

Brown, R. E., *Charles Beard and the Constitution: A Critical Analysis of an Economic Interpretation of the Constitution* (Princeton University Press, 1956).

Buchanan, J. M. and G. Tullock, *The Calculus of Consent: Logical Foundations of Constitutional Democracy* (University of Michigan Press, 1960).

Corwin, E. S., *American Constitutional History*, essays ed. by A. J. Mason and G. Harvey (Harper & Row, 1963).

Dietze, G., *The Federalist: A Classic on Federalism and Free Government* (Johns Hopkins Press, 1960).

Elliot, J. (ed.), *The Debates in the Several State Conventions on the Adoption of the Federal Constitution*, 2d ed. (Lippincott, 1854).

Farrand, M., *The Framing of the Constitution of the U.S.* (Yale University Press, 1913).

———, *The Records of the Federal Convention of 1787* (Yale University Press, 1911).

Hamilton A., J. Jay, and J. Madison, *The Federalist Papers* (McLean, 1788).

Hunt, C. and J. B. Scott (eds.), *The Debates in the Federal Convention of 1787* (Oxford University Press, 1920).

Hyneman, C. S. and G. W. Davy, *A Second Federalist, Congress Creates a Government* (Appleton-Century-Crofts, 1966).

Jaffa, H. V., *Equality and Liberty: Theory and Practice in American Society* (Oxford University Press, 1965).

Jameson, J. F., *Essays in the Constitutional History of the U.S. in the Formative Period, 1775–1789* (Houghton Mifflin, 1889).

Jensen, M. O., *The Making of the American Constitution* (Anvil, 1964).

Konefsky, S. S., *John Marshall and Alexander Hamilton: Architects of the American Constitution* (Macmillan, 1965).

Latham, E. (ed.), *The Declaration of Independence and the Constitution* (Heath, 1956).

Long, B., *Genesis of the Constitution of the United States of America* (Macmillan, 1926).

McCloskey, P. N., Jr., *The United States Constitution* (Addison-Wesley, 1964).

McDonald, F., *We the People: The Economic Origins of the Constitution* (University of Chicago Press, 1958).

McLaughlin, A. C., *The Confederation and the Constitution, 1783–1789* (Harper, 1905).

Madison, J., *Journal of the Federal Convention* (Laugtree and O'Sullivan, 1840).

Mason, A. T., *The States Rights Debate: Antifederalism and the Constitution* (Prentice-Hall, 1964).

Miller, J. C., *Origins of the American Revolution* (Little, Brown, 1943).

Morrison, S. F., *Sources and Documents Illustrating the American Revolution, 1764–1788 and the Formation of the Federal Constitution* 2d ed. (Oxford University Press, 1929).

Prescott, A. T. (Comp.), *Drafting the Federal Constitution* (Louisiana State University Press, 1941).

Rossiter, C., *Seedtime of the Republic* (Harcourt, Brace, 1953).

———, *1787: The Grand Convention* (Macmillan, 1966).

Schachner, N., *The Founding Fathers* (Putnam's, 1954).

Schuyler, R. N., *The Constitution of the U.S.: An Historical Survey of its Formation* (Macmillan, 1923).

Scott, J. B., *The Declaration of Independence, the Articles of Confederation, the Constitution of the U.S.* (Oxford University Press, 1917).

Shapiro, M. (ed.), *The Constitution of the U.S. and Related Documents* (Appleton-Century-Crofts, 1966).

Solberg, W. N., *The Federal Convention and the Formation of the Union of American States* (Liberal Arts, 1958).

Stevens, C. E., *Sources of the Constitution of the United States* (Macmillan, 1894).

Story, J., *Commentaries on the Constitution of the United States* (Little, 1833).

Van Doren, C. C., *The Great Rehearsal: The Story of the Making and Ratifying of the Constitution of the United States* (Viking, 1948).

Warren, C., *The Making of the Constitution* (Little, Brown, 1937).

Wright, B. F., *Consensus and Continuity, 1776–1787* Boston University Press, 1958).

K. INTERNATIONAL RELATIONS

(Treaties, executive agreements, international law.)

Bishop, W., *International Law*, 2d ed. (Little, Brown, 1961).

Blix, H., *Treaty-Making Power* (Praeger, 1960).

Byrd, E. M., Jr., *Treaties and Executive Agreements in the United States: Their Separate Roles and Limitations* (Nijhoff, 1960).

Corwin, E. S., *The Constitution and World Organization* (Princeton University Press, 1944).

———, *The Doctrine of Judicial Review* (Princeton University Press, 1914).

———, *National Supremacy: Treaty Power versus State Power* (Holt, 1913).

Greenspan, M., *The Modern Law and Land Warfare* (University of California Press, 1959).

McClure, W., *International Executive Agreements* (Columbia University Press, 1941).

Stone, J., *Quest for Survival: The Role of Law and Foreign Policy* (Harvard University Press, 1961).

Whitaker, U. G., Jr., *Politics and Power: A Text in International Law* (Harper & Row, 1964).

Wilson, R. R., *U. S. Commercial Treaties and International Law* (Hauser, 1959).

L. INTERPRETATIONS OF THE CONSTITUTION

(Analyses and interpretations of the written Constitution, clause by clause. Also aspects of the "unwritten" Constitution: practices which modify the written document.)

Antieau, C. J., *Commentaries on the Constitution of the United States* (University of Buffalo Press, 1960).

Brannon, H., *A Treatise on the Rights and Privileges Guaranteed by the Fourteenth Amendment to the Constitution of the United States* (Anderson, 1961).

Corwin, E. S., *The Constitution and What It Means Today*, 12th rev. ed. (Princeton University Press, 1958).

—— (ed.), *Constitution of the United States: Analysis and Interpretation* (United States Government Printing Office, 1953).

—— and J. Peltason, *Understanding the Constitution*, 4th ed. (Holt, 1967).

Dumbauld, E., *The Constitution of the United States* (University of Oklahoma Press, 1964).

Guthrie, W. D., *Lectures on the 14th Amendment to the Constitution of the United States* (Little, Brown, 1898).

Hamilton A., J. Jay, and J. Madison, *The Federalist Papers* (McLean, 1788).

Heathcock, C. L., *The United States Constitution in Perspective* (Allyn and Bacon, 1963).

Horwill, H. W., *The Usages of the American Constitution* (Oxford University Press, 1925).

Jones, P. F. (ed.), *The Constitution of the United States, 1787–1962* (University of Pittsburgh Press, 1963).

Leedham, C., *Our Changing Constitution* (Dodd, Mead, 1964).

Lieberman, J. K., *Understanding the Constitution* (Walker, 1967).

McBain, H. L., *The Living Constitution* (Macmillan, 1927).

Merrian, C. C., *The Written Constitution and the Unwritten Attitude* (R. R. Smith, 1931).

Mitchell, B. and L. P. Mitchell, *A Biography of the Constitution of the United States* (Oxford University Press, 1964).

Orfield, L. B., *The Amending of the Federal Constitution* (Callaghan, 1942).

Pritchett, C. H., *The American Constitution* (McGraw-Hill, 1959).

Schouler, J., *Constitutional Studies* (Dodd, Mead, 1897).

Schwartz, B., *A Commentary on the Constitution of the United States* Part I, *The Powers of Government* (Macmillan, 1963).

Small, N. J. (ed.), *Constitution of the United States of America*, rev. & ann. ed. (United States Government Printing Office, 1964).

Smith, O. G., *The Convention and the Constitution: The Political Ideas of the Founding Fathers* (St. Martin's, 1965).

Story, J., *Commentaries on the Constitution of the United States* (Little, 1833).

——, *A Familiar Exposition on the Constitution of the United States: Containing a Brief Commentary* (Petersburg, 1840).

Ten-Broek, J., *Anti-Slavery Origins of the Fourteenth Amendment* (University of California Press, 1951).

Tiffany, J., *A Treatise on Government and Constitutional Law* (Little, 1867).

Towle, N., *A History and Analysis of the Constitution of the U.S.* (Little, Brown, 1860).

Willoughby, W. W., *The Constitutional Law of the United States* (Baker, 1929).

M. JUDGES AND JUSTICES

(The men and their behavior in their decision-making function.)

Baxter, M. G., *Daniel Webster and the Supreme Court* (University of Massachusetts Press, 1967).

Becker, T., *Political Behavioralism and Modern Jurisprudence* (Rand McNally, 1965).

Bickel, A. M., *Politics and the Warren Court* (Harper & Row, 1966).

Borkin, J., *The Corrupt Judge* (Potter, 1962).

Botein, B., *Trial Judge* (Simon and Schuster, 1952, and Cornerstone, 1963).

Bruce, A. A., *The American Judge* (Macmillan, 1924).

Cardozo, B. N., *The Nature of the Judicial Process* (Yale University Press, 1921).

Danelski, D. J., "The Chief Justices of the Supreme Court." Unpublished Ph.D. dissertation, University of Illinois, 1961.

———, *A Supreme Court Justice is Appointed* (Random House, 1964).

Davenport, W. H. (ed.), *Voices in Court* (Macmillan, 1958).

Douglas, E. O., *We, The Judges* (Doubleday, 1956).

Frankfurter, F., *Of Law and Men: Papers and Addresses of Felix Frankfurter*, ed. by Philip Elman (Harcourt, Brace, 1956).

Friendly, H. J., *Benchmarks* (University of Chicago Press, 1967).

Goldberg, L. and L. Levenson, *Lawless Judges* (Rand School Press, 1935).

Hurst, J. W., *The Growth of Americal Law: The Lawmakers* (Little, Brown, 1950).

Kirchheimer, O., *Political Justice: The Use of Legal Procedure for Political Ends* (Princeton University Press, 1961).

Knox, J. C., *A Judge Comes of Age* (Scribner's, 1940).

Kristein, B. F. (ed.), *A Man's Reach: The Philosophy of Judge Jerome Frank* (Macmillan, 1965).

Levy, L. W., *The Law of the Commonwealth and Chief Justice Shaw* (Harvard University Press, 1957).

Lummus, H. T., *The Trial Judge* (Foundation Press, 1937).

Nagel, S., "Judicial Characteristics and Judicial Decision-Making." Unpublished Ph.D. dissertation, Northwestern University, 1961.

Peltason, J. W., *Fifty-Eight Lonely Men: Southern Federal Judges and School Desegregation* (Harcourt, Brace & World, 1961).

Porter, E. S., *Conscience of the Court* (Prentice-Hall, 1962).

Pritchett, C. H., *The Roosevelt Court: A Study in Judicial Politics and Values, 1937–1947* (Macmillan, 1947).

Roe, G. E. *Our Judicial Oligarchy* (Huebsch, 1912).

Rosenblum, V. G., *Law as a Political Instrument* (Doubleday, 1955).

Schubert, G. A., *Constitutional Politics* (Holt, Rinehart and Winston, 1960).

———, *Judicial Behavior: A Reader in Theory and Research* (Rand McNally, 1964).

———, *The Judicial Mind: The Attitudes and Ideologies of the Supreme Court, 1943–1963* (Northwestern University Press, 1965).

———, *Quantitative Analysis of Judicial Behavior* (Free Press, 1959).

——— (ed.), *Judicial Decision-Making* (Free Press, 1959).

Shientag, B. L., *Moulders of Legal Thought* (Viking, 1943).

Stansbury, A. J., *Report of the Trial of James H. Peck* (Hilliard, Gray, 1833).

Todd, A. L., *Justice on Trial: The Case of Louis D. Brandeis* (McGraw-Hill, 1964).

Tompkins, D. C., *The Supreme Court of the United States: A Bibliography* (University of California Press, 1959).

Tresolini, R. J., *Justice and the Supreme Court* (Lippincott, 1963).

Ulman, J. N., *A Judge Takes the Stand* (Knopf, 1933).

Vanderbilt, A. T., *Judges and Jurors: Their Functions, Qualifications, and Selection* (Boston University Press, 1956).

Westin, A. F., *The Supreme Court: Views from Inside* (Norton, 1961).

Wyzanski, C. E., Jr., *Whereas—A Judge's Premise: Essays in Judgment, Ethics, and the Law* (Atlantic, Little, Brown, 1965).

N. JUDICIAL REVIEW

Association of American Law Schools, *Selected Essays on Constitutional Law* (Foundation Press, 1938).

Beard, C. A., *The Supreme Court and the Constitution*, rev. ed. with a new introduction by Alan F. Westin (Prentice-Hall, 1962).

Beck, J. M., *The Changed Conception of the Constitution* (University of Rochester Press, 1925).

Black, C. L., Jr., *Old and New Ways in Judicial Review* (Bowdoin College Press, 1957).

———, *The People and the Court: Judicial Review in a Democracy* (Macmillan, 1960).

Boudin, L. B., *Government by Judiciary* (Godwin, 1932).

Cahn, E., *Supreme Court and Supreme Law* (Indiana University Press, 1954).

Carr, R. K., *Democracy and the Supreme Court* (University of Oklahoma Press, 1936).

———, *The Supreme Court and Judicial Review* (Farrar and Rinehart, 1942).

Cooley, T. M., *Constitutional Limitations* (Putnam's, 1868).

Corwin, E. S., *Court Over Constitution: A Study of Judicial Review as an Instrument of Popular Government* (Princeton University Press, 1938).

———, *The Doctrine of Judicial Review* (Princeton University Press, 1914).

———, *The Establishment of Judicial Review* (Princeton University Press, 1930).

———, *Our Constitutional Revolution and How To Round it Out* (Philadelphia Brandeis Lawyer Society, 1951).

Coxe, B., *Judicial Power and Unconstitutional Legislation* (Kay, 1893).

Crosskey, W. W., *Politics and the Constitution in the History of the United States* (University of Chicago Press, 1953).

Cushman, R. E., *The Role of the Supreme Court in a Democratic Nation* (Public Affairs Committee, 1938).

———, *The Supreme Court and the Constitution* (Public Affairs Committee, 1940).

———, *What's Happening to Our Constitution* (Public Affairs Committee, 1942).

Davis, H. A., *The Judicial Veto* (Houghton Mifflin, 1914).

Dean, H., *Judicial Review and Democracy* (Random House, 1966).

Dougherty, J. H., *The Power of the Federal Judiciary over Legislation* (Putnam, 1912).

Fennell, W. G., *The "Reconstructed Court"* (New York University Press, 1942).

Freedman, M., W. M. Beaney, and E. V. Rostow, *Perspectives on the Court* (Northwestern University Press, 1967).

Gilbert, W. C. (Comp.), *Provisions of Federal Law Held Unconstitutional by the Supreme Court of the United States* (United States Government Printing Office, 1936).

Haines, C. G., *The American Doctrine of Judicial Supremacy*, 2d ed. rev. and enl. (University of California Press, 1959).

——, *A Government of Laws or a Government of Men* (University of California Press, 1929).

Hand, L., *The Bill of Rights* (Harvard University Press, 1958, and Atheneum, 1964).

Henry, J. M., *Nine Above the Law: Our Supreme Court* (Lewis, 1936).

Hyneman, C. S., *The Supreme Court on Trial* (Atherton, 1963).

Johnson, J. E. (ed.), *Limitation of the Power of the Supreme Court to Declare Acts of Congress Unconstitutional* (Wilson, 1935).

Levy, B. H., *Our Constitution: Toll or Testament* (Knopf, 1941).

Levy, L. W. (ed.), *Judicial Review and the Supreme Court: Selected Essays* (Harper & Row, 1967).

Lewinson, J. L., *Limiting Judicial Review* (Parker, Stone and Braid, 1937).

Loewenstein, K., *Political Power and the Governmental Process*, Ch. VIII (University of Chicago Press, 1956).

Long, H. A., *Usurpers, Foes of Free Men* (Post, 1957).

McCloskey, R. G., *American Conservatism in the Age of Enterprise* (Harvard University Press, 1957).

——, *The American Supreme Court* (University of Chicago Press, 1960).

McKay, R. B. (ed.), *The American Constitutional Law Reader* (Oceana, 1958).

McLaughlin, A. C., *The Courts, Constitution and Parties* (University of Chicago Press, 1912).

McWhinney, E., *Judicial Review in the English-Speaking World*, 2d ed. (University of Toronto Press, 1961).

Mason, A. T., *The Supreme Court: Palladium of Freedom* (University of Michigan Press, 1962).

Meigs, W. M., *The Relation of the Judiciary to the Constitution* (Neale, 1919).

Moore, B. F., *The Supreme Court and Unconstitutional Legislation* (Columbia University Press, 1913).

Nichols, E. R., *Congress or the Supreme Court: Which Shall Rule America?* (Noble, 1935).

Powell, T. R., *Vagaries and Varieties in Constitutional Interpretations* (Columbia University Press, 1956).

Roe, G. E., *Our Judicial Oligarchy* (Huebsch, 1912).

Rostow, E. V., *The Sovereign Prerogative: The Supreme Court and the Quest for Law* (Yale University Press, 1962).

Senior, M. R., *The Supreme Court: Its Power of Judicial Review with Respect to Congressional Legislation* (George Washington University Press, 1937).

Smith, F. A., *Judicial Review of Legislation in New York, 1906–1938* (Columbia University Press, 1952).

Syracuse Law Review, Symposium, "Controversy over the Supreme Court" (Spring, 1959).

Tompkins, D. C., *The Supreme Court of the United States: A Bibliography* (University of California Press, 1959).

Von Moschzisker, R., *Judicial Review of Legislation* (National Association for Constitutional Government, 1923).

Warren, C., *Congress, the Constitution, and the Supreme Court* (Little, Brown, 1935).

Wechsler, H., *Principles, Politics and Fundamental Law* (Harvard University Press, 1961).

Wright, B. F., *The Growth of American Constitutional Law* (Reynal and Hitchcock, 1942).

O. JURIES

Bentham, J., *The Elements of the Art of Packing as Applied to Special Juries*
(Effingham-Wilson, 1821).
Busch, F. X., *Law and Tactics in Jury Trial* (Bobbs-Merrill, 1949).
Clementson, G. B., *Special Verdicts and Special Findings by Juries* (West, 1905).
Dawson, J. P., *A History of Lay Judges* (Harvard University Press, 1960).
Devlin, Sir P., *Trial by Jury* (Stevens, 1956).
Forsyth, W., *History of Trial by Jury,* new ed. (Cockcroft, 1875).
Francis, P., *How To Serve on a Jury* (Oceana, 1953).
Frank, J., *Courts on Trial: Myth and Reality in American Justice* (Princeton
University Press, 1949).
Green, L., *Judge and Jury* (Vernon, 1930).
Joiner, C. W., *Civil Justice and the Jury* (Prentice-Hall, 1962).
Kalvin, H., Jr., and H. Zeisel, *The American Jury* (University of Chicago Press,
1966).
Keeney, B. C., *Judgment by Peers* (Harvard University Press, 1949).
McCart, S., *Trial by Jury* (Chelton, 1964).
Osborn, A. S., *The Mind of the Juror* (Boyd, 1937).
Scigliano, R. G., *The Michigan One-Man Grand Jury* (Michigan State University
Press, 1957).
Vanderbilt, A. T., *Judges and Jurors: Their Functions, Qualifications, and Selec-
tion* (Boston University Press, 1956).
Wellman, F. L., *Gentlemen of the Jury* (Macmillan, 1936).
Younger, R. D., *The People's Panel: The Grand Jury in the United States, 1634–
1941* (Brown University Press, 1963).

P. JURISDICTION AND ORGANIZATION OF COURTS

Annual Reports of the Director of the Administrative Office of the U.S. Courts
(Department of Justice).
Brennan, W. J., *Modernizing the Courts* (Institute of Judicial Administration,
1957).
Bunn, C. W., *A Brief Survey of the Jurisdiction and Practice of the Courts of
the United States,* 5th ed. (West, 1949).
Callender, C. N., *American Courts: Their Organization and Procedure* (McGraw-
Hill, 1927).
Coner, J. P., *The Forging of the Federal Indigent Code* (Principia, 1966).
Countryman, E., *The Supreme Court of the United States* (Bender, 1913).
Dobie, A. N., *Handbook of Federal Jurisdiction and Procedure* (West, 1928).
Ferguson, J. H. and D. L. Cowells, *Minor Courts in Pennsylvania: A Study of
the Justices of the Peace and Alderman* (Pennsylvania State University
Press, 1962).
Fins, H. G., *Federal Jurisdiction and Procedure* (Bobbs-Merrill 1960).
Gressman, E., *Supreme Court Practice* (Bureau of National Affairs, 1950).
Harding, A. L. (ed.), *The Administration of Justice in Retrospect* (Southern
Methodist University Press, 1957).

Harris, R. J., *The Judicial Power of the United States* (Louisiana State University Press, 1940).

Hart, H. M., Jr., and H. Wechsler, *The Judicial Code and Rules of Procedure in the Federal Courts* (Foundation Press, 1954).

Institution of Public Administration, *The Minor Courts in Pennsylvania* (Pennsylvania State University Press, 1962).

Lepawsky, A., *The Judicial System of Metropolitan Chicago* (University of Chicago Press, 1932).

Moley R., *Our Criminal Courts* (Minton, Balch, 1930).

Post, C. G., Jr., *The Supreme Court and Political Questions* (Johns Hopkins Press, 1936).

Pound, R., *Organization of Courts* (Little, Brown, 1940).

Robertson, R., *Jurisdiction of the Supreme Court on the United States* (Bender, 1951).

Rose, J. C., *Jurisdiction and Procedure of Federal Courts* (Bender, 1938).

Rosenheim, M. K., *Justice for the Child: The Juvenile Court in Transition* (Macmillan, 1962).

Stern, R. L. and E. Gressman, *Supreme Court Practice*, 3d ed. (Bureau of National Affairs, 1962).

Sunderland, E. R., *Judicial Administration* (Callaghan, 1939).

United States Senate, Committee on the Judiciary, *Composition and Jurisdiction of the United States Supreme Court* (United States Government Printing Office, 1954).

Vines, K. N. and R. J. Richardson, *The Politics of the Federal Courts* (Little, Brown, 1966).

Wolfson, R. F. and P. Kurland, *Jurisdiction of the Supreme Court of the United States*, rev. ed. (Bender, 1951).

Wright, B. F., *Federal Courts* (West, 1963).

Q. LABOR LAW AND LEGISLATION

Frankfurter, F. with N. Greene, *The Labor Injunction* (Macmillan, 1930).

Groat, G. C., *Attitude of American Courts in Labor Cases* (Longmans, Green, 1911).

Mueller, S. J. and A. H. Myers, *Labor Law and Legislation*, 3d ed. (Southwestern Publishing Company, 1962).

Parker, R. A., *A Guide to Labor Law* (Praeger, 1961).

Raushenbush, C. and E. Stein, *Labor Cases and Materials* (Crofts, 1941).

Taylor, A. G., *Labor and the Supreme Court*, 2d ed. (University of Michigan Press, 1960).

R. THE LAW

(Principles of law, what the law is, development of the law.)

Allen, C. K., *Law in the Making*, 7th ed. (Oxford University Press, 1964).

Arens, R. and H. D. Lasswell, *In Defense of Public Order: The Emerging Field of Sanction Law* (Columbia University Press, 1961).

Arneson, B. A., *Elements of Constitutional Law* (Harper, 1928).

Aumann, F. R., *The Changing American Legal System* (Ohio State University Press, 1940).

Belli, M. M., *Ready for the Plaintiff* (Holt, 1956).

Berman, H. J., *The Nature and Function of Law* (Foundation Press, 1958).

—— (ed.), *Talk on America's Law* (Random House, 1961).

Black, C. L., Jr., *The Occasions of Justice: Essays Mostly in Law* (Macmillan, 1964).

Bodenheimer, E., *Jurisprudence* (McGraw-Hill, 1947).

Borchard, E. M., *Declaratory Judgments*, 2d ed. (Banks-Baldwin, 1941).

Brownell, E. A., *Legal Aid in the United States*, with Supplement (Lawyers' Cooperative Publishing Company, 1961).

Buckland, W. W. and A. D. McNair, *Roman Law and the Common Law*, rev. ed. (Cambridge University Press, 1952).

Carpenter, W. S., *Foundations of Modern Jurisprudence* (Appleton-Century, 1958).

Cataldo, B. F., *et al.*, *Introduction to Law and the Legal Process* (Wiley, 1965).

Cooley, T. M., *Constitutional Limitations* (Putnam's, 1868).

Cooper, F. E., *Living the Law* (Bobbs-Merrill, 1958).

Davenport, W. H. (ed.), *Voices in Court* (Macmillan, 1958).

Davis, F. J., *et al.*, *Society and the Law: New Meaning for an Old Profession* (Free Press, 1962).

Desmond, C. S., *Through the Courtroom Window* (West, 1959).

Donnelly, R. C., J. Goldstein, and R. D. Schwartz, *Criminal Law* (Free Press, 1962).

Edmunds, P. D., *Law and Civilization* (Public Affairs Press, 1959).

Edwards, N., *The Courts and the Public Schools* (University of Chicago Press, 1962).

Evan, W. M. (ed.), *Law and Sociology* (Free Press, 1962).

Field, O. P., *The Effect of an Unconstitutional Statute* (University of Minnesota Press, 1935).

Fordham, J. B., *Local Government Law* (Foundation Press, 1949).

Freund, E., *The Police Power, Public Policy, and Constitutional Rights* (Callaghan, 1904).

Fuller, L. L., *The Morality of Law* (Yale University Press, 1964).

Gavong, C. K. and R. W. Pearce, *Law and Society* (Irwin, 1965).

Gray, C. M., *Copyhold, Equity, and the Common Law* (Harvard University Press, 1963).

Gray, J. C., *The Nature and Sources of the Law*, 2d ed. (Macmillan, 1948, and Beacon, 1963).

Green, L., *Judge and Jury* (Vernon Law Book Company, 1930).

Griswold, E. N., *Law and Lawyers in the United States: The Common Law under Stress* (Harvard University Press, 1964).

Hare, J. I. C., *American Constitutional Law* (Brown, 1889).

Henderson, G. C., *The Position of Foreign Corporations in American Constitutional Law* (Harvard University Press, 1960).

Henson, R. D. (ed.), *Landmarks of Law: Highlights of Legal Opinion from 1890 to the Present* (Harper, 1960, and Beacon, 1963).

Hoebel, E. A., *The Law of Privitive Man* (Harvard University Press, 1954).

Hogue, A. R., *Origins of the Common Law* (University of Indiana Press, 1966).

Hohfeld, W. N., *Fundamental Legal Conceptions* (Yale University Press, 1964).

Holdsworth, Sir W., *A History of English Law* (Goodhart and Hanbury, 1956).

Holmes, O. W., *The Common Law* (Little, Brown, 1881; new ed., ed. by Mark De Wolfe Howe, Harvard University Press, 1963).

Honnold, J., *The Life of the Law: Readings on the Growth of Legal Institutions* (Free Press, 1964).

Jackson, P. E., *Justice and the Law* (Michie, 1964).

Jahr, A. D., *The Law of Eminent Domain—Valuation and Procedure* (Boardman, 1953).

Keeton, R. E., *Legal Cause in the Law of Torts* (Ohio State University Press, 1963).

Kent, J., *Commentaries on American Law*, 5th ed. (Little, Brown, 1830).

Kirchheimer, O., *Political Justice: The Use of Legal Procedure for Political Ends* (Princeton University Press, 1961).

Lee, L. T., *Consular Law and Practice* (Praeger, 1961).

London, E., *The World of Law* (Simon and Schuster, 1960).

Lunt, D. C., *The Road to Law* (Norton, 1962).

McCormick, C. T., *Handbook of the Law of Evidence* (West, 1954).

McKean, D., *The Integrated Bar* (Houghton Mifflin, 1963).

Macmillan, H. P., *Law and Other Things* (Cambridge University Press, 1937).

Maine, Sir H., *Ancient Law* (Murray, 1917).

Manning, B., *Federal Conflict of Interest Law* (Harvard University Press, 1964).

Marshall, J., *Law and Psychology in Conflict* (Bobbs-Merrill, 1966).

Mellinkoff, D., *The Language of the Law* (Little, Brown, 1963).

Morris, R. B., *Studies in the History of American Law* (Lippincott, 1959).

Newan, R. A., *Equity and Law: A Comparative Study* (Oceana, 1961).

Oceana Publications, Inc. (eds.), *Annual Survey of American Law* (Oceana, 1960 ff.).

———, *The Legal Almanac Series* (Oceana, 1955 ff.).

Palmer, E. E. (ed.), *Current Law and Social Problems* (University of Toronto Press, 1963).

Paton, G. W., *A Textbook of Jurisprudence* (Claredon, 1951).

Perkins, R. M., *Cases on Criminal Law and Procedure* (Foundation Press, 1959).

Phelps, C. E., *Elements of Judicial Equity* (King, 1890).

Plucknett, F. T. A., *A Concise History of the Common Law*, 3d ed. (Butterworth, 1940).

Nice, R. W. (ed.), *Treasury of Law* (Philosophical Library, 1964).

Pollock, Sir F., *Essays in the Law* (Macmillan, 1922).

———, *The Expansion of the Common Law* (Macmillan, 1904).

———, *A First Book in Jurisprudence*, 4th ed. (Macmillan, 1918).

———, *Jurisprudence and Legal Essays* (St. Martin's, 1962).

Post, C. G., *An Introduction to the Law* (Prentice-Hall, 1963).

Pound, R., *The Formative Era of American Law* (Little, Brown, 1938).

Radin, M., *The Law and Mr. Smith* (Bobbs-Merrill, 1938).

———, *The Law and You* (Mentor, 1948).

Rodell, F., *Woe Unto You Lawyers*, rev. ed. (Pageant, 1956).

Rogers, H. S., *Constitutional History of the U.S. as Seen in the Development of American Law* (Bender, 1890).

Ross, M. J., *Handbook of Everyday Law*, rev. enl. ed. (Harper & Row, 1967).

Rottschaefer, H., *Handbook of American Constitutional Law* (West, 1939).

Schnapper, M. B., *Constraint by Copyright* (Public Affairs Press, 1962).

Seagle, W., *Law, the Science of Inefficiency* (Macmillan, 1952).

———, *The Quest for Law* (Knopf, 1941).

406

Shartel, B., *Our Legal System and How It Operates* (University of Michigan Law School, 1950).

Simon, T. R., *The Tradition of Natural Law* (Fordham University Press, 1965).

Simpson, S. P. and J. Stone, *Law and Society* (West, 1948–49).

Steigleman, W. A., *The Newspaperman and the Law* (Brown, 1950).

Surrency, E., B. Field, and J. Crea, *A Practical Guide to Legal Research*, 2d ed. (Oceana, 1959).

Sutherland, A. E., *An Introduction to Law* (Harvard University Press, 1957).

———, *Statutes and Statutory Construction* 3d ed. (Horack, 1943).

Thayer, J. B., *Legal Essays* (Boston Book Company, 1908).

United States Code, Title 28 (comprising the *Federal Judicial Code*).

University of Michigan Law School 1955 Conference, *Aims and Methods of Legal Research* (University of Michigan Press, 1958).

Vanderbilt, A. T., *Studying Law*, 2d ed. (New York University Press, 1955).

Vinogradoff, P., *Common Sense in Law*, 3d ed. rev. by H. G. Hanbury (Oxford University Press, 1949).

———, *Outlines of Historical Jurisprudence* (Oxford University Press, 1920).

Weaver, S. P., *Constitutional Law and Its Administration* (Callaghan, 1946).

Weissman, J., *Law in a Business Society* (Prentice-Hall, 1963).

Wigmore, J. H., *Wigmore on Evidence*, 3d ed. (Little, Brown, 1940).

Willoughby, W. W., *The Constitutional Law of the United States* (Baker, 1929).

Wormser, R. A., *The Story of Law* (Simon and Schuster, 1962).

Wortley, B. A., *Jurisprudence* (Oceana, 1966).

S. THE LEGAL PROFESSION

(The men, their work, their education.)

Arnold, T., *Fair Fights and Foul: A Dissenting Lawyer's Life* (Harcourt, Brace & World, 1965).

Blaustein, A. D. and C. O. Porter, *The American Lawyer* (University of Chicago Press, 1954).

Botein, B., *The Prosecutor* (Simon and Schuster, 1956).

Bowen, C. D., *The Lion and the Throne: The Life and Times of Sir Edward Coke, 1552–1634* (Little, Brown, 1957).

Brown, C. G., *You May Take the Witness* (University of Texas Press, 1955).

Brown, E. L., *Lawyers, Law Schools and the Public Service* (Russell Sage Foundation, 1948).

Butler, C. H., *A Century at the Bar of the Supreme Court* (Putnam's, 1942).

Carlin, J. E., *Lawyer's Ethics: A Survey of the New York City Bar* (Russell Sage Foundation, 1966).

———, *Lawyers on their Own: A Study of Individual Practitioners in Chicago* (Rutgers University Press, 1964).

Chambers, M. M., *Colleges and the Courts* (Columbia University Press, 1952).

Choust, A. H., *The Rise of the Legal Profession in America* (University of Oklahoma Press, 1965).

Curtis, C. P., *It's Your Law* (Harvard University Press, 1954).

Davenport, W. H. (ed.), *Voices in Court* (Macmillan, 1958).

Donovan, J. W., *Modern Jury Trials* (Jennings, 1929).

Drinker, H. S., *Legal Ethics* (Columbia University Press, 1953).

Eulau, A. and T. D. S. Prague, *Lawyers in Politics: A Study in Professional Convergence* (Bobbs-Merrill, 1964).

Fordham, E. W., *Notable Cross-Examinations* (Macmillan, 1957).

Frank, J. P., *Lincoln as a Lawyer* (University of Illinois Press, 1961).

Frank, M. M., *The Diary of a D. A.* (Holt, Rinehart and Winston, 1960).

Garland, A. H., *Experience in the United States Supreme Court* (Philadelphia: Johnson, n.d.).

Goodhart, A. L., *Five Jewish Lawyers of the Common Law* (Oxford University Press, 1959).

Grossman, J., *Lawyers and Judges* (Wiley, 1965).

Hine, R. L., *Confessions of an Un-Common Attorney* (Macmillan, 1945).

Horton, J. T., *James Kent: A Study in Conservatism* (Appleton-Century, 1939).

Hurst, J. W., *The Growth of American Law: The Lawmakers* (Little, Brown, 1950).

Knox, J. C., *A Judge Comes of Age* (Scribner's, 1940).

Kutner, L., *The Lawyer* (Dodd, Mead, 1966).

Lewis, W. D. (ed.), *Great American Lawyers* (Winston, 1907).

Llewellyn, K. N., *The Bramble Bush: On Our Law and Its Study* (Oceana, 1957).

McKean, D., *The Integrated Bar* (Houghton Mifflin, 1963).

Morris, C., *How Lawyers Think* (Swallow, 1962).

Musmanno, M. M., *Verdict* (Doubleday, 1958).

Nizer, L., *My Life in Court* (Doubleday, 1961).

Paulson, M. C. (ed.), *Legal Institutions Today and Tomorrow* (Columbia University Press, 1959).

Pike, J. A., *Beyond the Law: The Religious and Ethical Meaning of the Lawyer's Vocation* (Doubleday, 1963).

Pound, R., *The Lawyer from Antiquity to Modern Times* (West, 1953).

Rossman, G., *Advocacy and the King's English* (Bobbs-Merrill, 1960).

Rutherford, M. L. S., "The Influence of the American Bar Association on Public Opinion and Legislation." Unpublished Ph.D. dissertation, University of Pennsylvania, 1937.

St. John, A. R., *Final Verdict* (Doubleday, 1962).

Schientag, B. L., *Moulders of Legal Thought* (Viking, 1943).

Schmidhauser, J. R., *The Supreme Court: Its Politics, Personalities, and Procedures* (Holt, 1960).

Smigel, E. O., *The Wall Street Lawyer* (Free Press, 1964).

Smith, T., *Lawyer: Opportunities for Careers in the Legal Profession* (Macmillan, 1961).

Stryker, L. P., *The Art of Advocacy* (Simon and Schuster, 1954, and Cornerstone, 1963).

Sunderland, E. R., *Judicial Administration* (Callaghan, 1939).

Taylor, G. C., *Fifty Years in the Law* (Philosophical Library, 1963).

Vanderbilt, A. T., *Men and Measures in the Law* (Knopf, 1949).

——, *Studying Law*, 2d ed. (New York University Press, 1955).

Warren, C., *A History of the American Bar* (Little, Brown, 1911).

Weinberg, A. and I. Weinberg (eds.), *Clarence Darrow's Verdicts Out of Court* (Quadrangle, 1963).

Wellman, F. L., *The Art of Cross-Examination*, 4th ed. (Macmillan, 1936).

——, *Day in Court* (Macmillan, 1910).

Weyrauch, W. O., *The Personality of Lawyers* (Yale University Press, 1964).

Whitney, H. C., *Life on the Circuit with Lincoln* (Estes-Lauriat, 1892).

Williston, S., *Life and Law* (Little, Brown, 1940).

Winters, G. R., *Bar Association Organization and Other Activities* (American Judicature Society, 1954).

408

T. THE MILITARY

(Law, courts, control.)

Aycock, W. B. and B. W. Wurfel, *Military Law Under the Uniform Code of Military Justice* (University of North Carolina Press, 1955).

Corwin, E. S., *Total War and the Constitution* (Knopf, 1947).

Edwards, M. O. and C. L. Decker, *The Serviceman and the Law* (Stackpole, 1951).

Everett, R. O., *Military Justice in the Armed Forces of the United States* (Military Service Publication Company, 1956).

Feld, B. A., *A Manual of Courts-Martial Practice and Appeal* (Oceana, 1957).

Huntington, S. P., *The Soldier and the State* (Vintage, 1963).

McNair, L. and A. D. Watts, *The Legal Effects of War*, 4th ed. (Cambridge University Press, 1966).

Millis, W., *The Constitution and the Common Defense* (Fund for the Republic, 1959).

Smith, L., *American Democracy and Military Power: A Study of Civil Control of the Military Power in the United States* (University of Chicago Press, 1951).

Spanier, J. W., *The Truman-MacArthur Controversy and the Korean War* (Harvard University Press, 1959).

Wiener, F. B., *The Uniform Code of Military Justice* (Combat Forces Press, 1950).

U. PHILOSOPHICAL AND THEORETICAL ASPECTS OF LAW

Anderson, W. R. (ed.), *Studies in Legal Philosophy* (Vanderbilt Law School, 1961).

Arnold, T. W., *The Symbols of Government* (Yale University Press, 1935).

Association of the Bar of the City of New York, *Conflict of Interest and Federal Service* (Harvard University Press, 1960).

Berman, H. J., *Talks on American Law* (Random House, 1961).

Blackstone, W., *Commentaries* (Beacon, 1962).

———, *Of Public Wrongs* (Beacon, 1963).

Bodenheimer, E., *Jurisprudence* (McGraw-Hill, 1947).

———, *Jurisprudence: The Philosophy and Method of the Law* (Harvard University Press, 1962).

Boorstin, D. J., *The Mysterious Science of the Law* (Beacon, 1963).

Braden, G. D., "The Search for Objectivity in Constitutional Law," *Yale Law Journal,* February 1948.

Brandt, R. B. (ed.), *The Concept of Social Justice* (Prentice-Hall, 1962).

Brown, B. F. (ed.), *The Natural Law Reader* (Oceana, 1960).

Burgess, J. W., *Political Science and Comparative Constitutional Law* (Ginn, 1890).

———, *Recent Changes in American Constitutional Theory* (Columbia University Press, 1923).

Cahill, F. V., *Judicial Legislation: A Study in American Legal Theory* (Ronald, 1952).

Cahn, E., *The Moral Decision: Right and Wrong in the Light of American Law* 2d ed. (Indiana University Press, 1959).

———, *The Sense of Injustice* (New York University Press, 1951).

—— (ed.), *The Predicament of Democratic Man* (Macmillan, 1961).

Cahn, L. (ed.), *Confronting Justice: The Edward Cahn Reader* (Little, Brown, 1966).

Calhoun, J. C., *A Disquisition on Government* (Political Science Classics, 1947).

Cardozo, B. N., *The Growth of the Law* (Yale University Press, 1924).

——, *Law and Literature and Other Essays* (Harcourt, Brace, 1931).

——, *The Nature of the Judicial Process* (Yale University Press, 1921).

——, *The Paradoxes of Legal Science* (Columbia University Press, 1928).

Carpenter, W. S., *Foundations of Modern Jurisprudence* (Appleton-Century-Crofts, 1958).

Cohen, L. K. (ed.), *The Legal Conscience: Selected Papers of Felix S. Cohen* (Yale University Press, 1960).

Cohen, M. R., *Law and Social Order* (Harcourt, Brace, 1933).

——, *My Philosophy of Law* (West, 1941).

——, *Reason and Law* (Collier, 1961).

——, *Reason and Nature* (Harcourt, Brace, 1931).

Corwin, E. S., *Constitutional Revolution, Ltd.* (Claremont College Press, 1941).

——, *The Higher Law Background of American Constitutional Law* (Cornell University Press, 1929).

——, *The Twilight of the Supreme Court: A History of Our Constitutional Theory* (Yale University Press, 1934).

Cowan, T. (ed.), *The American Jurisprudence Reader* (Oceana, 1955).

Currie, B., *Selected Essays on the Conflict of Laws* (Drake, 1963).

Curtis, C. P., *Law as Large as Life* (Simon and Schuster, 1959).

Dalzell, G. W., *Benefit of Clergy in American and Related Matters* (Blair, 1955).

Dias, R. M. W. and G. B. J. Hughes, *Jurisprudence* (Butterworth, 1957).

Dilliard, I. (ed.), *The Spirit of Liberty: Papers and Addresses of Learned Hand* (Knopf, 1959).

Ehrlich, E., *Fundamental Principles of the Sociology of Law* (Harvard University Press, 1936).

Einaudi, M., *The Physiocratic Doctrine of Judicial Control* (Harvard University Press, 1938).

Evan, W. M. (ed.), *Law and Sociology* (Free Press, 1962).

Frank, J. F., *Law and the Modern Mind* (Brentano's, 1949).

Friedmann, W., *Law in a Changing Society* (University of California Press, 1959).

——, *Legal Theory*, 4th ed. (Stevens, 1960).

Friedrich, C. J., *The Philosophy of Law in Historical Perspective*, 2d ed. (University of Chicago Press, 1962).

——, *Transcendent Justice: The Religious Dimensions of Constitutionalism* (Duke University Press, 1963).

—— and J. W. Chapman (eds.), *Justice* (Atherton, 1963).

Gerhart, E. C., *American Liberty and National Law* (Beacon, 1953).

Gierke, O. von, *Natural Law and the Theory of Society*, trans. by E. Barker (Cambridge University Press, 1934, and Beacon, 1963).

Ginsberg, M., *On Justice in Society* (Penguin, 1965).

Haines, C. G., *The Revival of Natural Law Concepts* (Harvard University Press, 1930).

Hall, J., *Readings in Jurisprudence* (Bobbs-Merrill, 1938).

Harding, A. L. (ed.), *The Administration of Justice in Retrospect* (Southern Methodist University Press, 1957).

Hare, J. I. C., *American Constitutional Law* (Brown, 1889).

Hart, H. L. A., *The Concept of Law* (Oxford University Press, 1961).

Henson, R. D. (ed.), *Landmarks of Law: Highlights of Legal Opinion from 1890 to the Present* (Harper, 1960).

Holcombe, A. N., *Our More Perfect Union: From 18th Century Principles to 20th Century Practice* (Harvard University Press, 1950).

Holmes, O. W., *The Common Law* (Little, Brown, 1881; new ed., ed. by Mark DeWolfe Howe, Harvard University Press, 1963).

Hook, S. (ed.), *Law and Philosophy: A Symposium* (New York University Press, 1964).

Jackson, P. E. (Comp.), *Justice and the Law* (Michie, 1964).

Kelsen, H., *General Theory of Law and State* (Harvard University Press, 1945).

———, *What Is Justice?* (University of California Press, 1957).

Levi, E. H., *An Introduction to Legal Reasoning* (University of Chicago Press, 1949).

Llewellyn, K. N., *Jurisprudence: Realism in Theory and Practice* (University of Chicago Press, 1962).

Lloyd, D. (ed.), *Introduction to Jurisprudence* (Praeger, 1960).

McCloskey, R. G., *American Conservatism in the Age of Enterprise* (Harvard University Press, 1957).

McIlwain, C. H., *The American Revolution: A Constitutional Interpretation* (Macmillan, 1928).

———, *Constitutionalism, Ancient and Modern*, rev. ed. (Cornell University Press, 1947).

———, *Constitutionalism and the Changing World* (Macmillan, 1939).

Maine, Sir H., *Ancient Law* (Murray, 1917, and Beacon, 1963).

Mason, A. T. and R. H. Leach, *In Quest of Freedom: American Political Thought and Practice* (Prentice-Hall, 1959).

Moore, R. F., *Stare Decisis* (Simmons-Broadman, 1958).

Morris, C. (ed.), *The Great Legal Philosophers: Selected Readings in Jurisprudence* (University of Pennsylvania Press, 1959).

Mullin, C., *In Quest of Justice* (U. Murray, 1931).

Nice, R. W. (ed.), *Treasury of Law* (Philosophical Library, 1965).

Northrup, F. C. S., *Complexity of Legal and Ethical Experience* (Little, Brown, 1959).

Olafson, F. A., *Society, Law, and Morality* (Prentice-Hall, 1961).

——— (ed.), *Justice and Social Policy* (Prentice-Hall, 1961).

Paton, G. W., *A Textbook of Jurisprudence* (Claredon, 1951).

Patterson, C. P., *Constitutional Principles of Thomas Jefferson* (University of Texas Press, 1953).

Paul, J., *The Legal Realism of Jerome N. Frank: A Study of Fact-Scepticism and the Judicial Process* (Nijhoff, 1959).

Petrazycki, L. J., *Law and Morality* (Harvard University Press, 1955).

Pollock, Sir F., *Essays in the Law* (Macmillan, 1922).

———, *Jurisprudence and Legal Essays* (St. Martin's, 1962).

Pound, R., *Contemporary Juristic Theory* (Claremont College Press, 1940).

———, *The Future of the Common Law* (Harvard University Press, 1937).

———, *Interpretations of Legal History* (Harvard University Press, 1946).

———, *An Introduction to the Philosophy of Law*, rev. ed. (Yale University Press, 1959).

————, *Justice According to Law* (Yale University Press, 1951).

————, *Law Finding Through Experience and Reason* (University of Georgia Press, 1960).

————, *Law and Morals* (University of North Carolina Press, 1924).

————, *New Paths of the Law* (University of Nebraska Press, 1950).

————, *Social Control Through Law* (Yale University Press, 1942).

————, *The Spirit of the Common Law* (Marshall, Jones, 1931, and Beacon, 1963).

————, *The Task of Law* (Franklin and Marshall, 1944).

Radin, M., *The Law as Logic and Experience* (Yale University Press, 1940).

Robson, W. A., *Civilization and the Growth of Law* (Macmillan, 1935).

Ross, A., *On Law and Justice* (Stevens, 1959).

————, *Towards a Realistic Jurisprudence* (Munksgaard, 1946).

Rossiter, C. A., *Seedtime of the Republic* (Harcourt, Brace, 1953).

Rostow, E. V., *The Sovereign Prerogative: The Supreme Court and the Quest for Law* (Yale University Press, 1962).

Shklar, J. N., *Legalism* (Harvard University Press, 1964).

Shuman, S. I., *Legal Positivism: Its Scope and Limitations* (Wayne State University Press, 1963).

Simpson, S. P. and J. Stone, *Law and Society* (West, 1948–49).

Smith, J. A., *The Spirit of American Government* (Macmillan, 1907).

Stone, J., *Human Law and Human Justice* (Stanford University Press, 1965).

————, *Legal System and Lawyers' Reasonings* (Stanford University Press, 1964).

————, *The Province and Function of Law* (Harvard University Press, 1950).

Sutherland, A. E. (ed.), *Government Under Law* (Harvard University Press, 1956).

————, *The Law and One Man Among Many* (University of Wisconsin Press, 1956).

Tiedeman, C. G., *The Unwritten Constitution of the United States* (Putnam's, 1890).

Timasheff, N. S., *An Introduction to the Sociology of Law* (Harvard University Press, 1938).

Tocqueville, A. de, *Democracy in America* (Langley, 1841).

Toulmin, S., *The Place of Reason in Ethics* (Cambridge University Press, 1953).

Vinogradoff, P., *Common Sense in Law,* 3d ed. rev. by H. G. Hanbury (Oxford University Press, 1949).

————, *Outlines of Historical Jurisprudence* (Oxford University Press, 1920).

Von Moschzisker, R., *Stare Decisis, Res Judicata, and Other Essays* (Cyrus-Dixon, 1929).

Wasserstrom, R. A., *The Judicial Decision: Toward a Theory of Legal Justification* (Stanford University Press, 1961).

Whitehead, A. N., *Symbolism* (Macmillan, 1927).

Wormuth, F. D., *The Origins of Modern Constitutionalism* (Harper, 1949).

Wright, B. F., *American Interpretations of Natural Law* (Harvard University Press, 1931).

Wu, J. C. H., *Foundation of Justice* (Sheed and Ward, 1959).

Zelermyer, W., *The Process of Legal Reasoning* (Prentice-Hall, 1963).

V. THE PRESIDENCY

(The executive organ of the United States government—a branch of the separation of powers of our national government.)

Binkley, W. E., *President and Congress,* 3d. rev. ed. (Knopf, 1962).

Corwin, E. S., *The President: Office and Powers,* 4th ed. (New York University Press, 1957).

————, *Total War and the Constitution* (Knopf, 1947).

Cotter, C. P. and J. M. Smith, *Powers of the President During National Crises* (Public Affairs Press, 1959).

Egger, R. and J. P. Harris, *The President and Congress* (McGraw-Hill, 1963).

Grundstein, N. D., *Presidential Delegation of Authority in Wartime* (University of Pittsburgh Press, 1961).

Haight, D. and L. Johnston (eds.), *The Presidency: Roles and Powers* (Rand McNally, 1965).

Koenig, L. W., *The President and the Crisis: Powers of the Office from the Invasion of Poland to Pearl Harbor* (King Crown, 1944).

Learned, H. B., *The President's Cabinet* (Yale University Press, 1912).

McConnell, G., *The Presidency* (St. Martin's, 1967).

————, *The President Seizes the Steel Mills* (University of Alabama Press, 1960).

————, *Steel and the Presidency, 1962* (Norton, 1963).

McKay, R. B. (ed.), *The American Constitutional Law Reader* (Oceana, 1958).

Mason, A. T. and W. B. Beaney, *The Supreme Court in a Free Society* (Prentice-Hall, 1959).

May, E. R., *The Ultimate Decision: The President as Commander in Chief* (Braziller, 1960).

The New York Times, The Assassination of a President (Viking, 1964).

Polsby, N. W., *Congress and the Presidency* (Prentice-Hall, 1963).

Randall, J. G., *Constitutional Problems Under Lincoln,* rev. ed. (University of Delaware Press, 1956, and University of Illinois Press, 1964).

Rankin, R. S. and W. R. Dallmayr, *Freedom and Emergency Powers in the Cold War* (Appleton-Century-Crofts, 1964).

Rich, B. N., *The President and Civil Disorder* (Brookings, 1941).

Rossiter, C., *The Supreme Court and the Commander-in-Chief* (Cornell University Press, 1951).

Schubert, G. A., *The Presidency in the Courts* (University of Minnesota Press, 1957).

Smith, M. J. and C. P. Cotter, *Powers of the President During Crises* (Public Affairs Press, 1960).

Taft, W. H., *Our Chief Magistrate and His Powers* (Columbia University Press, 1916).

Westin, A. F., *Anatomy of a Constitutional Law Case* (Macmillan, 1958).

W. PROCEDURES IN THE COURTS

Annual Reports of the Director of the Administrative Office of the U.S. Courts.

American Bar Association, Section of Judicial Administration, *The Improvement of the Administration of Justice: A Handbook,* 4th ed. (1961).

Barron, W. W. and A. Holtzoff, *Federal Practice and Procedure* (Thompson, 1950–58).

Bureau of Municipal Research, *The Magistrate Courts of Philadelphia*, rev. ed. (Pennsylvania Economy League, 1958).

Callendar, C. N., *American Courts: Their Organization and Procedure* (McGraw-Hill, 1927).

Dangel, E. M., *Contempt* (National Lawyers Manual Company, 1939).

Doble, A. M., *Handbook of Federal Jurisdiction and Procedure* (West, 1928).

Douglas, W. O., *Stare Decisis* (Association of the Bar of City of New York, 1949).

Fins, H. G., *Federal Jurisdiction and Procedure* (Bobbs-Merrill, 1960).

Fox, J. C., *The History of Contempt of Court,* (Oxford University Press, 1927).

Gavit, B. C., *Procedure in State Courts* (Practicing Law Institute, 1946).

Goldfarb, R. L., *The Contempt Power* (Columbia University Press, 1963).

Harding, A. L. (ed.), *The Administration of Justice in Retrospect* (Southern Methodist University Press, 1957).

Hart, H. M., Jr., and H. Wechsler, *The Judicial Code and Rules of Procedure in the Federal Courts* (Foundation Press, 1954).

Karlen, D., *The Citizen in Court: Litigant, Witness, Juror, Judge* (Holt, Rinehart and Winston, 1964).

————, *Primer of Procedure* (Campus Publishing Co., 1950).

Llewellyn, K. N., *The Common Law Tradition: Deciding Appeals* (Little, Brown, 1960).

McCarty, D. G., *Psychology for the Lawyer* (Prentice-Hall, 1929).

MacDougal, C. D., *Covering the Courts* (Prentice-Hall, 1946).

Matthews, P., *How To Try a Criminal Case* (Dennis, 1960).

Moore, R. F., *Stare Decisis* (Simmons-Boardman, 1958).

Peck, D. A., *Decision at Law* (Dodd, Mead, 1961, and Cornerstone, 1963).

Perkins, R. M., *Cases on Criminal Law and Procedure* (Foundation Press, 1959).

Pound, R., *Appellate Procedure in Civil Cases* (Little, Brown, 1941).

Rose, J. C., *Jurisdiction and Procedure of Federal Courts* (Bender, 1938).

Rosenberg, M., *The Pretrial Conference and Effective Justice* (Columbia University Press, 1965).

St. John, A. R., *Final Verdict* (Doubleday, 1962).

Stern, R. L. and E. Gressman, *Supreme Court Practice,* 3d ed. (Bureau of National Affairs, 1962).

Taylor, G. C., *Fifty Years in the Law* (Philosophical Library, 1963).

Thomas, C. H., *Problems of Contempt of Court* (Horn-Shafer, 1943).

Vanderbilt, A. T., *Men and Measures in the Law* (Knopf, 1949).

Von Moschzisker, R., *Stare Decisis, Res Judicata, and Other Essays* (Cyrus-Dixon, 1929).

Wright, B. F., *Federal Courts* (West, 1963).

X. REFORMS

(Discussions of change in the Constitution and the courts.)

Association of the Bar of the City of New York, *Conflict of Interest and Federal Service* (Harvard University Press, 1960).

Bureau of Municipal Research, *The Magistrates Courts of Philadelphia*, rev. ed. (Pennsylvania Economy League, 1958).

Elliott, W. Y., *The Need for Constitutional Reform* (Whittlesey, 1935).

Goodnow, F. J., *Social Reform and the Constitution* (Macmillan, 1911).

Hazlitt, H., *A New Constitution Now* (McGraw-Hill, 1942).

Hehmeyer, A., *Time for a Change: A Proposal for a Second Constitutional Convention* (Rinehart, 1943).

Vanderbilt, A. T., *The Challenge of Law Reform* (Princeton University Press, 1955).

Wheeler, J. P. (ed.), *Salient Issues of Constitutional Revision* (National Municipal League, 1960).

Y. STAFFING THE COURTS

(Selection and tenure.)

Carpenter, W. S., *Judicial Tenure in the United States* (Yale University Press, 1918).

Davis, J. W., *Selecting Judges* (Andrews, 1933).

Harris, J. P., *The Advice and Consent of the Senate: A Study of the Confirmation of Appointments by the United States Senate* (University of California Press, 1953).

Haynes, E., *The Selection and Tenure of Judges* (National Press Conference of Judicial Councils, 1944).

McHargue, D., "Appointments to the Supreme Court." Unpublished Ph.D. dissertation, University of California, Los Angeles, 1949).

Schmidhauser, J. R., *The Supreme Court: Its Politics, Personalities, and Procedures* (Holt, 1960).

Scigliano, R. G., *The Courts: A Reader in the Judicial Process* (Little, Brown, 1962).

Vanderbilt, A. T., *Judges and Jurors: Their Functions, Qualifications, and Selection* (Boston University Press, 1956).

Winters, G. R., *Selection of Judges in New York and in Other States* (Lawyer's Committee, 1913).

II BIOGRAPHIES, AUTOBIOGRAPHIES, AND RELATED WORKS OF AND BY JUSTICES OF THE SUPREME COURT OF THE UNITED STATES

Adams, J. S. (ed.), *An Autobiographical Sketch by John Marshall* (University of Michigan Press, 1937).

Barbar, J., *The Honorable Eighty-Eight* (Vanguard, 1957).

Barry, R., *Mr. Rutledge of South Carolina* (Duell, Sloan, & Pierce, 1942).

Bates, E. S., *The Story of the Supreme Court* (Bobbs-Merrill, 1936).

Bent, S., *Justice Oliver Wendell Holmes* (Vanguard, 1932).

Beveridge, A. J., *The Life of John Marshall* (Houghton, 1916).

Bickel, A. M., *The Unpublished Opinions of Mr. Justice Brandeis: The Supreme Court at Work* (Harvard University Press, 1957, and Phoenix, 1967).

Biddle, F., *Justice Holmes, Natural Law, and the Supreme Court* (Macmillan, 1961).

———, *Mr. Justice Holmes* (Scribner's, 1942).

Binney, H., *Bushrod Washington* (Sherman, 1858).

Blaisdell, D., "Mr. Justice James Clark McReynolds." Unpublished Ph.D. dissertation, University of Wisconsin, 1948.

415

Bolner, J., "Chief Justice Vinson: A Study of His Politics and His Constitutional Law." Unpublished Ph.D. dissertation, University of Virginia, 1962.

Bowen, C. D., *A Yankee from Olympus* (Little, Brown, 1944).

Bradley, C. (ed.), *Miscellaneous Writings of Joseph P. Bradley* (Harham, 1901).

Brown, F. J., *The Social and Economic Philosophy of Pierce Butler* (Catholic University of America Press, 1945).

Brown, J. M., *Through These Men* (Harper, 1956).

Brown, W. G., *The Life of Oliver Ellsworth* (Macmillan, 1905).

Bynes, J. F., *All in One Lifetime* (Harper, 1958).

Cahn, E. (ed.), *The Great Rights* (Macmillan, 1963).

Campbell, T. W., *Four-Score Forgotten Men* (Pioneer, 1950).

Cate, W. A., *Lucius Q. C. Lamar* (University of North Carolina Press, 1935).

Christman, H. M. (ed.), *The Public Papers of Chief Justice Earl Warren* (Simon and Schuster, 1959).

Clark, F. B., *The Constitutional Doctrines of Justice Harlan* (Johns Hopkins Press, 1915).

Clifford, P. G., *Nathan Clifford, Democrat* (Putnam's, 1922).

Commager, H. S., *The Writings of Justice Joseph Story* (Bobbs-Merrill, 1966).

Connor, H. G., *John A. Campbell, Associate Justice of the United States Supreme Court, 1853–1861* (Houghton, 1920).

Corwin, E. S., *John Marshall and the Constitution: A Chronicle of the Supreme Court,* (Yale University Press, 1921).

Cotton, J. P., Jr., (ed.), *The Constitutional Decisions of John Marshall* (Putnam's, 1905).

Countryman, V. (ed.), *Douglas of the Supreme Court: A Selection of His Opinions* (Doubleday, 1959).

Curtis, B. R., *A Memoir of Benjamin Curtis, L.L.D.* (Little, Brown, 1879).

Danelski, D. J., *A Supreme Court Justice Is Appointed* (Random House, 1964).

DeHaas, J., *Louis D. Brandeis* (Block, 1929).

Delaplaine, E. S., *The Life of Thomas Johnson* (Hitchcock, 1927).

Dilliard, I., *One Man's Freedom: Mr. Justice Black and the Bill of Rights* (Knopf, 1963).

—— (ed.), *Mr. Justice Brandeis: Great American* (Modern View Press, 1941).

Dillon, J. M. (ed.), *John Marshall: Complete Constitutional Decisions* (Callaghan, 1903).

Douglas, W. O., *We the Judges* (Doubleday, 1956).

Dunham, A. and P. B. Kurland (eds.), *Mr. Justice,* rev. enl. ed. (Phoenix, 1964).

Early, S. T., Jr., "James Clark McReynolds and the Judicial Process." Unpublished Ph.D. dissertation, University of Virginia, 1954.

Ewing, C. A. M., *Judges of the Supreme Court, 1789–1938* (University of Minnesota Press, 1938).

Fairman, C., *Mr. Justice Miller and the Supreme Court, 1862–1890* (Harvard University Press, 1939).

Fitzgerald, M. J., "Justice Reed: A Study of a Center Judge." Unpublished Ph.D. dissertation, University of Chicago, 1950.

Flanders, H., *The Lives of the Chief Justices of the U.S. Supreme Court* (Lippincott, 1858).

Frank, J. P., "The Appointment of Supreme Court Justices: Prestige Principles and Politics," *Wisconsin Law Review,* 172, 343, 461 (1941).

————, *Justice Daniel Dissenting: A Biography of Peter V. Daniel, 1784–1860* (Harvard University Press, 1964).

————, *Mr. Justice Black: The Man and His Opinions* (Knopf, 1949).

———— and Y. Karsh, *The Warren Court* (Macmillan, 1964).

Fraenkel, O. K. (ed.), *The Curse of Bigness: Miscellaneous Papers of Louis D. Brandeis* (Viking, 1934).

Frankfurter, F., *Of Law and Men* (Harcourt, Brace, 1956).

————, *Mr. Justice Brandeis* (Yale University Press, 1932).

————, *Mr. Justice Holmes and the Constitution* (Harvard University Press, 1938).

————, *Mr. Justice Holmes and the Supreme Court*, 2d ed. (Atheneum, 1965).

————, *The Public and its Government* (Beacon, 1964).

————, *et. al, Mr. Justice Holmes* (Coward-McCann, 1931).

Freund, P., *The Writings of Louis D. Brandeis* (Bobbs-Merrill, 1966).

Gerhart, E. C., *America's Advocate: Robert H. Jackson* (Bobbs-Merrill, 1958).

Goldman, S. (ed.), *The Words of Mr. Justice Brandeis* (Schuman, 1953).

Gregory, C. N., *Samuel Freeman Miller* (State Historical Society of Iowa, 1907).

Hall, M. E. (ed.), *Selected Writings of Benjamin N. Cardozo* (Fallon, 1947).

Harper, F. W., *Justice Rutledge and the Bright Constellation* (Bobbs-Merrill, 1965).

Hart, A. B., *Salmon P. Chase* (Houghton, 1899).

Hellman, G. S., *Benjamin N. Cardozo—American Judge* (Whittlesey, 1940).

Hendel, S., *Charles Evans Hughes and the Supreme Court* (Columbia University Press, 1951).

Hendricks, B. M., *Bulwark of the Republic: A Biography of the Constitution* (re. P. V. Daniel). (Little, Brown, 1957).

Hill, A. B., "The Constitutional Doctrine of Chief Justice White." Unpublished Ph.D. dissertation, University of California, 1922.

Holmes, O. W., *Collected Legal Papers* (Harcourt, 1920).

————, *Speeches*, (Little, Brown, 1913).

Howard, J. W., Jr., "Frank Murphy: A Liberal's Creed." Unpublished Ph.D. dissertation, Princeton University 1959.

Howe, M. de W., *Justice Oliver Wendell Holmes: The Proving Years, 1870–1882* (Harvard University Press, 1963).

————, *Justice Oliver Wendell Holmes: The Shaping Years, 1841–1870* (Harvard University Press, 1957).

———— (ed.), *The Holmes-Laski Letters, 1916–1935* (Harvard University Press, 1953, and Atheneum, 1963).

———— (ed.), *The Holmes-Pollock Letters, 1874–1932* rev. ed., (Harvard University Press, 1963, and Atheneum, 1963).

———— (ed.), *The Occasional Speeches of Justice Oliver Wendell Holmes* (Harvard University Press, 1963).

Hughes, C. E., *Addresses* (Harper, 1908).

Hurst, W. J., *Justice Holmes on Legal History* (Macmillan, 1964).

Iowa Law Review, Symposium, "Wiley B. Rutledge" (Summer, 1950).

Jacobs, C. E., *Justice Frankfurter and Civil Liberties* (University of California Press, 1961).

Jay, W., *The Life of John Jay* (Harper, 1833).

Johnston, H. P. (ed.), *Correspondence of John Jay* (Putnam's 1890).

Jones, W. M. (ed.), *Chief Justice John Marshall: A Reappraisal* (Cornell University Press, 1956).

Katcher, L., *Earl Warren: A Political Biography* (McGraw-Hill, 1967).

Kent, C. A., *Memoir of Henry Billings Brown* (Dunfield, 1915).

Kentucky Law Journal, Symposium, "John Marshall Harlan, 1833–1911" (Spring, 1958).

King, W. L., *Lincoln's Manager: David Davis* (Harvard University Press, 1960).

———, *Melville Weston Fuller: Chief Justice of the United States, 1888–1910* (Macmillan, 1950, and Phoenix, 1967).

Klinkhamer, Sister Marie Carolyn, Edward Douglas White, Chief Justice of the United States. Unpublished Ph.D. dissertation, Catholic University of America, 1943.

Konefsky, S. J., *Chief Justice Stone and the Supreme Court* (Macmillan, 1946).

———, *John Marshall and Alexander Hamilton: Architects of the American Constitution* (Macmillan, 1965).

———, *The Legacy of Holmes and Brandeis: A Study in the Influence of Ideas* (Macmillan, 1956).

——— (ed.), *The Constitutional World of Mr. Justice Frankfurter* (Macmillan, 1949).

Kurland, P. B., *Felix Frankfurter, the Judge* (Harvard University Press, 1955).

——— (ed.), *Of Law and Life and Other Things That Matter: Papers and Addresses of Felix Frankfurter, 1956–1963* (Harvard University Press, 1965).

Lamar, C. P., *The Life of Joseph Rucker Lamar, 1857–1916* (Putnam's, 1926).

Lawrence, A. A., *James More Wayne: Southern Unionist* (University of North Carolina Press, 1943).

Lerner, M. (ed.), *The Mind and Faith of Justice Holmes* (Little, Brown, 1943).

Levy, B. H., *Cardozo and Legal Thinking* (Oxford University Press, 1938).

Lewis, W., *Without Fear or Favor: A Biography of Chief Justice Roger Brooke Taney* (Houghton Mifflin, 1965).

Lewis, W. D., *Great American Lawyers* (Winston, 1908).

Lief, A., *Brandeis: The Personal History of an American Ideal* (Stackpole, 1936).

——— (ed.), *The Dissenting Opinions of Mr. Justice Holmes* (Vanguard, 1943).

Livingston, E. B., *The Livingstons of Livingston Manor* (Knickerbocker, 1910).

Loth, D., *Chief Justice: John Marshall and the Growth of the Republic* (Norton, 1949).

Lunt, R. D., *The High Ministry of Government: The Political Career of Frank Murphy* (Wayne State University Press, 1965).

Macleish, A., and E. F. Richard (eds.), *Law and Politics: Occasional Papers of Mr. Justice Frankfurter* (Harcourt, Brace, 1939).

McCune, W., *The Nine Young Men* (Harper, 1947).

McDevitt, M., *Joseph McKenna* (Catholic University of America Press, 1946).

Magrath, C. P., *Morrison R. Waite: The Triumph of Character* (Macmillan, 1963).

McHale, F., *President and Chief Justice: The Life and Public Services of William Howard Taft* (Dorrance, 1931).

McLean, J. E., *William Rufus Day, Supreme Court Justice from Ohio* (Johns Hopkins Press, 1947).

McRee, G. F. (ed.), *The Life and Correspondence of James Iredell* (Peter Smith, 1949).

Marke, J. (ed.), *The Holmes Reader,* 2d ed. (Oceana, 1964).

Mason, A. T., *Brandeis—A Free Man's Life* (Viking, 1946).

———, *Brandeis: Lawyer and Judge in the Modern State* (Princeton University Press, 1933).

———, *The Brandeis Way* (Princeton University Press, 1933).

———, *Harlan Fiske Stone: Pillar of the Law* (Viking, 1956).

———, *William Howard Taft: Chief Justice* (Simon and Schuster, 1965).

Mayes, E., *Lucius Q. C. Lamar* (Barbee, 1895).

Mendelson, W., *Justices Black and Frankfurter*, 2d ed. (University of Chicago Press, 1966).

——— (ed.), *Felix Frankfurter: The Judge* (Reynal, 1965).

———, *Felix Frankfurter: A Tribute* (Reynal, 1964).

Merrill, H. S., *Bourbon Leader* (re: L. Q. J. Lamar) (Little, Brown, 1957).

Michigan Law Review, Symposium, "Mr. Justice Frank Murphy" (April, 1950).

Mitchell, S. R., "Mr. Justice Horace Gray." Unpublished Ph.D. dissertation, University of Wisconsin, 1961.

Monoghan, F., *John Jay* (Bobbs-Merrill, 1935).

Morgan, D. G., *Justice William Johnson: The First Dissenter* (University of South Carolina Press, 1954).

Moynihan, D. P. (ed.), *The Defenses of Freedom: The Public Papers of Arthur J. Goldberg* (Harper & Row, 1966).

Norris, H., *Mr. Justice Murphy and the Bill of Rights* (Oceana, 1965).

O'Brien, F. W., *Justice Reed and the First Amendment: The Religion Clauses* (Georgetown University Press, 1958).

Palmer, B. W., *Marshall and Taney: Statesmen of the Law* (University of Minnesota Press, 1939).

Paschal, J. F., *Mr. Justice Sutherland: A Man Against the State* (Princeton University Press, 1951).

Perkins, D., *Charles Evans Hughes and American Democratic Statesmanship* (Little, Brown, 1956).

Phillips, H. B. (ed.), *Felix Frankfurter Reminisces* (Reynal, 1960).

Pollack, E. H. (ed.), *The Brandeis Reader* (Oceana, 1956).

Pollard, J. P., *Mr. Justice Cardozo: A Liberal Mind in Action* (Yorktown, 1940).

Pringle, H., *The Life and Times of William Howard Taft* (Farrar & Rinehart, 1939).

Pusey, M. J., *Charles Evans Hughes* (Macmillan, 1951).

Ransom, W. L., *Charles Evans Hughes: The Statesmen as Shown in the Opinions of the Jurist.* (Dutton, 1916).

Roberts, O. J., "In Memoriam," *University of Pennsylvania Law Review* (December, 1955).

Roche, J. P., *The Writings of John Marshall* (Bobbs-Merrill, 1966).

Schuckers, J. W., *The Life and Public Services of Salmon Portland Chase* (Appleton, 1874).

Schwartz, M. D. and J. C. Hogan, *Joseph Story: A Collection of Writings by an Eminent American Jurist* (Oceana, 1959).

Scott, W. W., *History of Orange County* (re: P. P. Barbour (Waddey, 1907).

Seagle, W., *Men of Law: From Hammurabi to Holmes* (Macmillan, 1947).

Servies, J. A., *A Bibliography of John Marshall* (United States Commission for Celebration of 200th Anniversary of Birth of John Marshall, 1956).

Shiras, G., III, (ed.), *Justice George Shiras, Jr., of Pittsburgh* (University of Pittsburgh Press, 1953).

Smith, C. H., *James Wilson, Founding Father* (University of North Carolina Press, 1956).

Smith, C. W., *Roger B. Taney: Jacksonian Jurist* (University of North Carolina Press, 1936).

Stanford Law Review, Symposium, "Mr. Justice Jackson" (December, 1955).

Steamer, R. J., "The Constitutional Doctrine of Mr. Justice Robert H. Jackson." Unpublished Ph.D. dissertation, Cornell University, 1954.

Steiner, B. C., *The Life of Roger Brooke Taney* (Williams & Wilkins, 1922).

Stone, I., *Earl Warren* (Prentice-Hall, 1948).

Story, W. W. (ed.), *Life and Letters of Joseph Story* (Little, 1851).

Strickland, S. P. (ed.), *Hugo Black and the Supreme Court* (Bobbs-Merrill, 1967).

Surrency, E. (ed.), *The Marshall Reader* (Oceana, 1955).

Swayne, N. W. (Comp.), *The Descendants of Francis Swayne and Others* (Lippincott, 1921).

Swisher, C. B., *Roger B. Taney* (Macmillan, 1935).

———, *Stephen J. Field: Craftsman of the Law* (Brookings, 1930).

Thayer, J. B., *John Marshall* (Phoenix, 1967).

Thomas, H. S., *Felix Frankfurter: Scholar on the Bench* (Johns Hopkins Press, 1960).

Todd, A. L., *Justice on Trial: The Case of Louis D. Brandeis* (McGraw-Hill, 1964).

Tresolini, R. J., *Justice and the Supreme Court* (Lippincott, 1962).

Trimble, B. R., *Chief Justice Waite: Defender of the Public Interest* (Princeton University Press, 1938).

Tyler, S., *Memoir of Roger Brooke Taney* (Murphy, 1872).

Umbreit, K. B., *Our Eleven Chief Justices: A History of the Supreme Court in Terms of Their Personalities* (Harper, 1938).

University of Chicago Review "Justices Frankfurter and Douglas," (Autumn, 1958).

Vanderbilt Law Review, Symposium, "Studies in Judicial Biography," Vol. X, No. 2, 1957.

Van Santvoord, G., *Sketches of the Lives and Judicial Services of the Chief Justices of the Supreme Court of the U.S.* (Scribner's, 1854).

Warner, H. L., *The Life of Mr. Justice Clarke: A Testimony to the Power of Liberal Dissent in America* (Western Reserve University Press, 1959).

Weaver, J. D., *Warren: The Man, The Court, The Era* (Little, Brown, 1967).

Weiner, F. B., *The Life and Judicial Career of William Henry Moody* (Harvard University Press, 1937).

Weisenburger, F. P., *The Life of John McLean: A Politician on the United States Supreme Court* (Ohio State University Press, 1937).

Westin, A. F. (ed.), *An Autobiography of the Supreme Court* (Macmillan, 1963).

Williams, C., *Hugo L. Black: A Study in the Judicial Process* (Johns Hopkins Press, 1950).

Wilson, J., *The Works of the Hon. James Wilson* (Bronson & Chaunch, 1804).

Wood, G. S., *William Paterson of New Jersey, 1745–1806* (Fair Lawn Press, 1933).

Woodbury, C. L. (ed.), *Writings of Levi Woodbury* (Little, Brown, 1852).

Wyman, T. B., *Geneology of the Name and Family of Hunt* (Wilson, 1962).

Yale Law Journal, Symposium, "Mr. Justice Felix Frankfurter," (December, 1957).

———, Symposium, "Mr. Justice Black," (February, 1956).

Yale Law Library, *Louis Dembitz Brandeis, 1856–1914: A Bibliography* (Yale University Press, 1958).

420

III. COMPARATIVE LAW

Abel-Smith, B. and R. Stevens, *Lawyers and the Courts: A Sociological Study of the English Legal System* (Heinemann, 1966).

Alexandrowicz, C. H., *Constitutional Developments in India* (Oxford University Press, 1957).

Allen, Sir C. K., *Administrative Jurisdiction* (Stevens, 1956).

———, *Law in the Making*, 6th ed. (Oxford University Press, 1958).

———, *Law and Orders: An Inquiry into the Nature and Scope of Delegated Legislative and Executive Powers in England*, 3d ed. (Stevens, 1965).

———, *The Queens Peace* (Stevens, 1953).

Almond, G. and J. L. Coleman (eds.), *The Politics of the Developing Areas* (Princeton University Press, 1960).

Amery, L. S., *Thoughts on the Constitution*, 2d ed. (Oxford University Press, 1953).

Amos, Sir M., *British Criminal Justice*, rev. ed. (Longmans, 1957).

Amos, Sir M. S., and F. P. Walton, *Introduction to French Law* (Oxford University Press, 1935).

Anderson, J. N. D. (ed.), *Changing Law in Developing Countries* (Praeger, 1963).

——— (ed.), *Islamic Law in the Modern World*, (New York University Press, 1959).

Anson, Sir W. R., *Law and Custom of the Constitution* (Oxford University Press, 1922–35).

Appleman, J. A., *Military Tribunals and International Crimes* (Bobbs-Merrill, 1954).

Archer, P., *The Queen's Courts* (Penguin, 1956).

Arendt, H., *Eichmann in Jerusalem* (Viking, 1963 and 1966).

Bagehot, W., *The English Constitution*, 2d ed. (World's Classics, 1928).

Banerjee, D. N., *Our Fundamental Rights: Their Nature and Extent (As Judicially Determined)* (World Press, 1960).

Barlow, R. B., *Citizenship and Conscience: A Study in the Theory and Practice of Religious Toleration in England During the Eighteenth Century* (University of Pennsylvania Press, 1963).

Bar-Yaacov, N., *Dual Nationality* (Praeger, 1961).

Bataille, A., *Inside the French Courts* (Hutchinson, 1941).

Bayley, D. H., *Public Liberties in the New States* (Rand McNally, 1964).

Bebr, G., *Judicial Control of the European Communities* (Praeger, 1962).

Bedford, S., *The Faces of Justice: A Traveller's Report* (Simon and Schuster, 1961).

Bentham, J., *Rationale of Judicial Evidence* (Hunt and Clarke, 1827).

Benton, W. E. and G. Grimm, (eds.), *Nuremburg: German Views of the War Trials* (Southern Methodist University Press, 1955).

Berman, H. J., *Justice in Russia: An Interpretation of Soviet Law*, rev. enl. ed. (Vintage, 1963).

——— and J. W. Spindler, *Soviet Criminal Law and Procedure: The RSFSR Codes* (Harvard University Press, 1966).

Berry, B., *Race and Ethnic Relations*, 3d ed. (Houghton Mifflin, 1965).

Birch, A. H., *Federalism, Finance and Social Legislation in Canada, Australia, and the United States* (Oxford University Press, 1955).

Bishop, W., *International Law: Cases and Materials*, 2d ed. (Dennis, 1962).

Blackstone, Sir W., *Commentaries on the Laws of England: of Public Wrongs* (Harper, 1854, and Beacon, 1962).

Bloomfield, L. P., *International Military Forces* (Little, Brown, 1964).

Boutmy, E. G., *Studies in Constitutional Law: France, England, United States*, 2d ed. (Macmillan, 1891).

Bowett, D. W., *The Law of International Institutions* (Praeger, 1963).

Brierly, J. L., *The Law of Nations*, 6th ed. (Oxford University Press, 1963).

Brohi, A. K., *Fundamental Law of Pakistan* (Din Muhammadi Press, 1958).

Brookes, E. H. and J. B. Macaulay, *Civil Liberty in South Africa* (Oxford University Press, 1958).

Brown, E. G., *British Statutes in American Law, 1776–1836* (University of Michigan Press, 1965).

Bunn, R. and W. G. Andrews (eds.), *Civil Liberties in Europe* (Van Nostrand, 1967).

Cam, H. M., *Law-Finders and Law-Makers in Medieval England* (Barnes & Noble, 1963).

Carlston, K. S., *Law and Organization in World Society* (University of Illinois Press, 1962).

Carr, Sir T., *Concerning English Administrative Law* (Columbia University Press, 1941).

Casteberg, F., *Freedom of Speech in the West* (Oceana, 1960).

———, *Problems of Legal Philosophy* (Allen and Unwin, 1958).

Central Office of Information, *The English Legal System* (Her Majesty's Stationary Office, 1964).

Chapman, B., *The Profession of Government* (Allen and Unwin, 1959).

Charles, R., *La Justice en France* (Presses Universitaires, 1958).

Christoph, J. P., *Capital Punishment and British Politics* (University of Chicago Press, 1962).

Claglett, H., *Administration of Justice in Latin America* (Oceana, 1952).

Clyde, W. M., *The Struggle of the Freedom of the Press from Caxton to Cromwell* (Oxford University Press, 1934).

Cohen, M. (ed.), *Law and Politics in Space* (McGill, 1964).

Conrad, J. P., *Crime and its Correction: An International Survey of Attitudes and Practices* (University of California Press, 1965).

Cowen, Z., *Federal Jurisdiction in Australia* (Oxford University Press, 1959).

Cross, R., *Precedent in English Law* (Oxford University Press, 1961).

David R. and H. P. de Vries, *The French Legal System: An Introduction to Civil Law Systems* (Oceana, 1958).

Davidson, E. *The Trial of the Germans: Nuremberg 1945–1946* (Macmillan, 1967).

Davis, H. E., *Government and Politics in Latin America* (Ronald, 1958).

Dawson, F. P., *A History of Lay Judges* (Harvard University Press, 1960).

Dawson, R. McG., *The Government of Canada*, 3d. ed. (University of Toronto Press, 1957).

Delolme, *The Rise and Progress of the English Constitution* (Parker, 1838).

Denning, Sir A., *The Changing Law* (Stevens, 1953).

Devlin, Sir P., *The Criminal Prosecution in England* (Yale University Press, 1958).

———, *The Enforcement of Morals* (Oxford University Press, 1965).

———, *Trial by Jury* (Stevens, 1956).

422

Dicey, A. V., *Introduction to the Study of the Law on the Constitution*, 10th ed. (St. Martin's, 1959, and Macmillan, 1961).

——, *Law and Public Opinion in England During the 19th Century* (Torch, 1958).

Duguit, L., *Law in the Modern State* (Huebsch, 1919).

Eaves, J., Jr., *Emergency Powers and the Parliamentary Watchdog* (Hansard Society, 1957).

Eder, P. J., *A Comparative Survey of Anglo-American and Latin-American Law* (New York University Press, 1950).

Emden, C. S., *The People and the Constitution*, 2d ed. (Oxford University Press, 1956).

Engel, S. with R. A. Metall (eds.), *Law, State, and International Legal Order: Essays in Honor of Hans Kelsen* (University of Tennessee Press, 1964).

Ensor, R. C. K., *Courts and Judges in France, Germany, and England* (Oxford University Press, 1933).

Erades, L. and W. L. Gould, *The Relations between International Law and Municipal Law in the Netherlands and in the United States* (Oceana, 1960).

Falk, R. A., *The Role of Domestic Courts in the International Legal Order* (Syracuse University Press, 1964).

——, *et. al, Essays on International Jurisdiction* (Ohio State University Press, 1961).

Feifer, G., *Justice in Moscow* (Simon and Schuster, 1964).

Fellman, D., *The Defendant's Rights Under English Law* (University of Wisconsin Press, 1966).

Fitzgibbon, R. H. (ed.), *The Constitution of the Americas* (University of Chicago Press, 1951).

Flecher, J. K., *The British Courts: Traditions and Ceremonial* (Cassell, 1953).

Flender, H., *Rescue in Denmark* (Macfadden-Bartell, 1964).

Fliess, P. J., *Freedom of the Press in the German Republic, 1918–1933* (Louisiana State University Press, 1955).

Foreign Languages Publishing House, *Fundamentals of Soviet Criminal Legislation, The Judicial System, and Criminal Court Procedure* (Foreign Languages Publishing House, 1960).

Fouilee, A., *et. al., Modern French Legal Philosophy* (Macmillan, 1921).

Freedeman, C. E., *The Conseil D'Etat in Modern France* (Columbia University Press, 1961).

Friedmann, W., *The Changing Structure of International Law* (Columbia University Press, 1964).

——, *Law and Social Change in Contemporary Britain* (Stevens, 1951).

——, *Law in a Changing Society* (University of California Press, 1959).

Geldart, W. M., *Elements of English Law*, 6th ed. (Holt, 1959).

Gilbert, G. M., *Nuremberg Diary* (New American Library, 1960).

Giles, F. T., *The Criminal Law* (Penguin, 1955).

——, *The Juvenile Courts: Their Work and Problems* (Allen & Unwin, 1946).

——, *The Magistrates' Courts*, rev. ed. (Stevens, 1963).

Ginsberg, M. (ed.), *Law and Opinion in England in the Twentieth Century* (University of California Press, 1959).

Gledhill, A., *The Republic of India: The Development of Its Laws and Constitution* (Stevens, 1951).

Golay, O. F., *The Founding of the Federal Republic of Germany* (University of Chicago Press, 1958).

Golyakov, I. T., *The Role of the Soviet Court* (Public Affairs Press, 1948).

Goodhart, A. H., *English Law and the Moral Law* (Stevens, 1953).

——, *Precedent in English and Continental Law* (Stevens, 1934).

Gough, J. W., *Fundamental Law in English Constitutional History* (Oxford University Press, 1955).

Graveson, R. H., *The Conflict of Laws* (Sweet & Maxwell, 1965).

Griffith, J. H. G. and J. Street, *Principles of Administrative Law*, 2d ed. (Pitman, 1958).

Groves, H. E., *Comparative Constitutional Law* (Oceana, 1963).

Grzybowski, K., *The Socialist Commonwealth of Nations, Organizations and Institutions* (Yale University Press, 1964).

——, *Soviet Legal Institutions* (University of Michigan Press, 1962).

Gsovsky, V. and K. Grzybowski (eds.), *Government, Law, and the Courts in the Soviet Union and Eastern Europe* (Praeger, 1960).

Guins, G. C., *Soviet Law and Soviet Society* (Nijhoff, 1954).

Haley, A. G., *Space Law and Government* (Appleton-Century-Crofts, 1963).

Hall, J., *Comparative Law and Social Theory* (Louisiana State University Press, 1963).

Hamson, C. J., *Executive Discretion and Judicial Control: An Aspect of the French Conseil d'Etat* (Stevens, 1954).

Hanbury, H. G., *English Courts of Law*, 3d ed. (Oxford University Press, 1960).

Harding, A., *A Social History of English Law* (Penguin, 1966).

Harris, W. R., *Tyranny On Trial: The Evidence at Nürnberg* (Southern Methodist University Press, 1954).

Harrison, W., *The Government of Britain*, 6th ed. (Hutchinson, 1960).

Hart, J. M. *The British Police* (Allen & Unwin, 1951).

Hauriou A., *Droit Constitutionnel et Institutions Politiques* (Monchrestien, 1966).

Hausher, G., *Justice in Jerusalem* (Harper & Row, 1966).

Hawgood, J. A., *Modern Constitutions Since 1787* (Macmillan, 1939).

Hay, P., *Federalism and Supranational Organizations: Patterns for New Legal Structures* (University of Illinois Press, 1966).

Hazard, J. N., *Law and Social Change in Soviet Society* (University of Toronto Press, 1953).

——, *Settling Disputes in Soviet Society: The Formative Years in Legal Institutions*, rev. ed. (Columbia University Press, 1960).

—— and I. Shapiro, *The Soviet Legal System: Post-Stalin Documentation and Historical Commentary* (Oceana, 1962).

Henderson, E. G., *Foundations of English Administrative Law: Certiorari and Mandamus in the Seventeenth Century* (Harvard University Press, 1963).

Heuss, T., *Verfassungsrecht und Verfassungspolitik* (Scherpe-Verlag, 1950).

Heuston, R. F. V., *Essays in Constitutional Law* (Stevens, 1961).

Holdsworth, Sir W., *A History of English Law*, 7th ed., (Goodhart & Hanbury, 1956).

Hyde, H. M., Lord Justice, *The Life and Times of Lord Birkett of Ulverston* (Random House, 1965).

Ioffe, O. S., *Soviet Civil Law* (International Arts and Sciences Press, 1961).

—— and M. D. Shargorodskii, *Problems of Legal Theory* (International Arts and Sciences Press, 1961).

Jackson, R. H., *The Nuremberg Case* (Knopf, 1947).

Jackson, R. M., *The Machinery of Justice in England*, 4th ed. (Cambridge University Press, 1964).

James, P. S., *Introduction to English Law*, 4th ed. (Butterworth, 1959).

Jenks, C. W., *The Common Law of Mankind* (Praeger, 1959).

———, *Space Law* (Praeger, 1965).

Jennings, Sir W. I., *The British Constitution*, 3d ed. (Cambridge University Press, 1950).

———, *Constitutional Law and the Commonwealth* (Oxford University Press, 1957).

———, *The Law and the Constitution*, 4th ed. (University of London Press, 1958).

Jones, A. H. M., *Studies in Roman Government and Law* (Praeger, 1960).

Kahin, G. McT., *Major Government of Asia* (Cornell University Press, 1958).

Karlen, D., *Appellate Courts in the United States and England* (New York University Press, 1963).

———, G. Sawer, and E. M. Wise, *Anglo-American Criminal Justice* (Oxford University Press, 1968).

Keeton, G. W., *The Passing of Parliament*, 2d ed. (Benn, 1954).

———, D. Lloyd, T. B. Smith, and L. A. Sheridan, *The United Kingdom, The Development of Its Laws and Constitution: England, Wales, Northern Ireland, The Isle of Man; Scotland; The Channel Islands* (Stevens, 1955).

Keir, Sir D. L., *The Constitutional History of Modern Britain Since 1485*, 6th ed. (Black, 1960).

——— and F. H. Lawson (eds.), *Cases in Constitutional Law*, 4th ed. (Oxford University Press, 1954).

Kelsen, H., *The Communist Theory of Law* (Praeger, 1960).

———, *Principles of International Law*, 2d ed. (Holt, Rinehart and Winston, 1966).

Kempin, F. G., Jr., *Legal History: Law and Social Change* (Prentice-Hall, 1963).

Kidd, R., *British Liberty in Danger* (Lawrence & Wishart, 1942).

Kinnane, C. H., *Anglo-American Law*, 2d ed. (Bobbs-Merrill, 1952).

Kiralfy, A. K., *The English Legal System*, 3d ed. (Sweet & Maxwell, 1960).

Kirchheimer, O., *Political Justice* (Princeton University Press, 1961).

Konstantinovsky, B. A., *Soviet Law in Action: The Recollected Cases of a Soviet Lawyer* (Harvard University Press, 1953).

Kucherov, S., *Courts, Lawyers, and Trials Under the Last Three Tsars* (Praeger, 1953).

Kutner, L., *World Habeas Corpus* (Oceana, 1962).

La Fave, W. R., *Law in the Soviet Society* (University of Illinois Press, 1966).

La Forest, G. V., *Extradition to and from Canada* (Hauser, 1962).

Lapenna, I., *State and Law: Soviet and Yugoslav Theory* (Yale University Press, 1964).

Lasky, H. J., *Studies in Law and Politics* (Allen & Unwin, 1932).

Lauterpacht, Sir H., *The Development of International Law in the International Court* (Praeger, 1958).

———, *The Function of Law in the International Community* (Oxford University Press, 1933).

Lawson, F. H., *A Common Lawyer Looks at the Civil Law* (Oxford University Press, 1955).

————, *The Rational Strength of English Law* (Stevens, 1951).

————, *et. al., Amos and Walton's Introduction to French Law*, 2d ed. (Oxford University Press, 1963).

Lewy, C., *et. al., Essays on French Law* (Washington Law Society, 1958).

Lloyd, D. (ed.), *Introduction to Jurisprudence*, rev. ed. (Praeger, 1966).

MacDonald, R. St. J. (ed.), *Changing Legal Objectives* (University of Toronto Press, 1963).

Mac Guigan, M. R., *Jurisprudence: Readings and Cases*, 2d ed. (University of Toronto Press, 1966).

MacMillan, W. M., *The Road to Self-Rule: A Study in Colonial Evolution* (Faber, 1959).

Maitland, F. W., *The Constitutional History of England* (Cambridge University Press, 1961).

————, *Selected Historical Essays* (Beacon, 1963).

Maki, J. M., *Court and Constitution in Japan: Selected Supreme Court Decisions, 1948–60* (University of Washington Press, 1964).

Mangione, G. J., *The Elements of International Law: A Casebook* (Dorsey, 1962).

Mann, A., *Judgment at Nuremberg* (New American Library, 1960).

Marshall, G. and G. C. Moodie, *Some Problems of the Constitution* (Hutchinson, 1959).

McDougal, M. S. and F. P. Feliciano, *Law and Minimum World Public Order* (Yale University Press, 1962).

————, H. D. Lasswell, and I. A. Vlasic (Yale University Press, 1963).

McIlwain, C. H., *The High Court of Parliament* (Yale University Press, 1910).

McWhinney, E., *Comparative Federalism: States' Rights and National Power* (University of Toronto Press, 1963).

————, *Constitutionalism in Germany and the Federal Constitutional Court* (Sythoff, 1962).

———— (ed.), *Canadian Jurisprudence: The Civil Law and the Common Law in Canada* (University of Toronto Press, 1958).

————, *Judicial Review in the English-Speaking World*, 2d ed. (University of Toronto Press, 1961).

Megarry, Q. C., *Lawyer and Litigant in England* (Stevens, 1962).

Milner, J. B. (ed.), *Community Planning: A Casebook on Law and Administration* (University of Toronto Press, 1963).

Morgan, G. G., *Soviet Administrative Legality: The Role of the Attorney General's Office* (Stanford University Press, 1962).

Morris, N. and C. Howard, *Studies in Criminal Law* (Oxford University Press, 1964).

Moskowitz, M., *Human Rights and World Order* (Oceana, 1960).

Mueller, G. O. W. (ed.), *The French Penal Code* (Rothman, 1960).

Muhammad, V. A. S., *The Legal Framework of World Trade* (Praeger, 1958).

Newman, K. J., *Essays on the Constitution of Pakistan* (Dacca, 1956).

Newman, R. A., *Equity and the Law: A Comparative Study* (Oceana, 1960).

Ogilvie, Sir C., *The King's Government and the Common Law, 1471–1641* (Oxford University Press, 1958).

O'Sullivan, R., *The Inheritance of the Common Law* (Stevens, 1950).

Papadatos, P., *The Eichmann Trial* (Praeger, 1965).

Parker, J., *Some Aspects of French Law* (Scribner's, 1929).

Parry, C., *Nationality and Citizenship Laws of the Commonwealth* (Stevens, 1960).

Peaslee, A. J., *Constitutions of Nations*, 2d ed. (Nijhoff, 1956).

Phillips, O. H., *The Constitutional Law of Great Britain and the Commonwealth*, 2d ed. (Sweet & Maxwell, 1957).

Plischke, E., *Contemporary Government of Germany* (Houghton Mifflin, 1961).

Plucknett, T. F. T., *Early English Legal Literature* (Cambridge University Press, 1958).

Pollard, R. S. W. (ed.), *Administrative Tribunals at Work: A Symposium* (Stevens 1950).

Pompe, C. A., *Aggressive War an International Crime* (Nijhoff, 1953).

Potter, H., *An Historical Introduction to English Law and Its Institutions*, 3d ed. (Sweet & Maxwell, 1948).

Pratt, O. C., *Tort Liability of the State* (University of Illinois Press, 1947).

Proehl, P. O. (ed.), *Legal Problems of International Trade* (University of Illinois Press, 1959).

Radcliffe, G. R. Y. and G. Cross, *The English Legal System*, 3d ed. (Butterworth, 1954).

Report of the (Franks) Committee on Administrative Tribunals and Enquiries (Her Majesty's Stationery Office, Cmd. 218 of 1957).

Rice, W. G., *Law Among States in Federacy: A Survey of Decisions of the Swiss Federal Tribunal in Intercantonal Controversies* (Nelson, 1959).

Roberts, G. D., *Law and Life* (W. H. Allen, 1964).

Robertson, A. H., *European Institutions* (Praeger, 1959).

———, *Human Rights in Europe* (Manchester University Press, 1963).

Robinson, J., *And the Crooked Shall Be Made Straight: The Eichmann Trial, the Jewish Catastrophe, and Hannah Arendt's Narrative* (Macmillan, 1965).

Robson, W. A., *Justice and Administrative Law: A Study of the English Constitution*, 3d ed. (Stevens, 1951).

Rogger, H. and E. Weber, *The European Right: A Historical Profile* (University of California Press, 1966).

Romashkin, P. S. (ed.), *Fundamentals of Soviet Law* (Foreign Language Publishing House, 1961).

Ronning, C. N., *Law and Politics in Outer-American Diplomacy* (Wiley, 1963).

Runes, D. D., *The Disinherited and the Law* (Philosophical Library, 1964).

Sandifer, D. V. and L. R. Scheman, *The Foundations of Freedom* (Praeger, 1966).

Schact, J., *An Introduction to Islamic Law* (Oxford University Press, 1964).

Schlesinger, R., *Comparative Law*, 2d ed. (Foundation Press, 1960).

———, *Soviet Legal Theory* (Regan Paul, 1964).

———, *Soviet Legal Theory: Its Social Background and Development* (Humanities, 1951).

Schmeiser, D. A., *Civil Liberties in Canada* (Oxford University Press, 1964).

Schuyler, R. L., *British Constitutional History Since 1832* (Van Nostrand, 1962).

Schwelb, E., *Human Rights and the International Community* (Quadrangle, 1964).

Schwartz, B. (ed.), *The Code Napoleon and the Common Law World* (New York University Press, 1956).

———, *French Administrative Law and the Common Law World* (New York University Press, 1954).

———, *Law and the Executive in Britain* (New York University Press, 1949).

Scofield, C. L., *A Study of the Court of Star Chamber* (University of Chicago Press, 1960).

427

Scott, F. R., *Civil Liberties and Canadian Federalism* (University of Toronto Press, 1959).

Sharswood, G., *Blackstone's Commentaries on the Laws of England* (Lippincott, 1891).

Siebert, F. S., *Freedom of the Press in England: 1476–1776* (University of Illinois Press, 1952, and 1965).

Sieghart, M. A., *Government by Decree* (Stevens, 1950).

Simpson, J. L. and H. Fox, *International Arbitration: Law and Practice* (Praeger, 1959).

Siyar, S., *The Islamic Law of Nations* (Johns Hopkins Press, 1966).

de Smith, S. A., *Judicial Review of Administrative Action* (Stevens, 1960).

Smith, D. E. (ed.), *South Asian Politics and Religion* (Princeton University Press, 1966).

Smith, G., *A Constitutional and Legal History of England* (Scribner's, 1955).

Smith, M., *The Developments of European Law* (Columbia University Press, 1928).

Sommerich, O. C. and B. Busch, *Foreign Law—A Guide to its Pleading and Proof* (Oceana, 1959).

St. John-Stevas, N., *Life, Death, and the Law: Law and Christian Morals in England and the United States* (Indiana University Press, 1961).

Stanger, R. J. (ed.), *Essays on Espionage and International Law* (Ohio State University Press, 1962).

Stannard, H., *The Two Constitutions: A Comparative Study of British and American Constitutional Systems* (Van Nostrand, 1949).

Stephenson, C. and F. G. Marcham (eds.), *Sources of English Constitutional History* (Harper, 1937).

Starke, J. G., *Introduction to International Law*, 5th ed. (Butterworth, 1963).

Stevens, R. B., *Questions and Answers on Constitutional Law and Legal History*, 7th ed. (Sweet & Maxwell, 1959).

Stewart, Z. (ed.), *The Ancient World: Justice, Heroism, and Responsibility* (Prentice-Hall, 1966).

Stone, J., *Human Law and Human Justice* (Stevens, 1965).

———, *The International Court and World Crisis* (Carnegie Endowment, 1962).

———, *Legal System and Lawyers' Reasonings* (Stevens, 1964).

———, *Social Dimensions of Law and Justice* (Stanford University Press, 1965).

Street, H., *Freedom, The Individual and the Law* (Penguin, 1963).

———, *Governmental Liability: A Comparative Study* (Cambridge University Press, 1953).

Strong, C. F., *Modern Political Constitutions: An Introduction to their Comparative Study and Existing Form*, 5th ed. (Sidgwich & Jackson, 1958).

Stumpf, S. E., *Morality and the Law* (Vanderbilt University Press, 1966).

Szirmai, Z. (ed.), *Law in Eastern Europe* (Hillary, 1959).

Szladits, C., *Bibliography of Foreign and Comparative Law Books and Articles in English* Vol. I (Oceana, 1955), and Vol. 2 (Oceana, 1961).

———, *A Guide to Foreign Legal Materials-French, German, Swiss* (Oceana, 1959).

Taswell-Langmead, T. P., *English Constitutional History*, 11th ed., rev. by T. F. T. Plucknett (Houghton Mifflin, 1960).

The Inns of Court, *Rule of Law: A Study by the Inns of Court* (Conservative and Unionist Central Office, 1955).

Triska, J. F. and R. M. Slusser, *The Theory, Law, and Policy of Soviet Treaties* (Stanford University Press, 1962).

Tuttle, E. O., *The Struggle Against Capital Punishment in Great Britain* (Stevens, 1961).

Vile, M. J. C., *Constitutionalism and the Separation of Power* (Oxford University Press, 1967).

Vinogradoff, Sir P., *Common Sense in Law*, 3d ed. (Oxford University Press, 1959).

Von Glahn, G., *Law Among Nations* (Macmillan, 1964).

Von Knieriem, A., *The Nuremberg Trials* (Regnery, 1959).

Von Mehren, A. T., *The Civil Law Systems: Cases and Materials for the Comparative Study of Law* (Little, Brown, 1957).

———— (ed.), *Law in Japan: The Legal Order in a Changing Society* (Harvard University Press, 1963).

Vyshinsky, A. Y., *Law of the Soviet State* (Macmillan, 1948).

Wade, E. C. S., *Administrative Law* (Oxford University Press, 1961).

————, *Dicey's Introduction to the Study of the Law of the Constitution*, 10th ed. (Macmillan, 1960).

———— and G. G. Phillips (eds.), *Constitutional Law*, 6th ed. (Longmans, 1960).

Wade, H. W. R., *Towards Administrative Justice* (University of Michigan Press, 1963).

Wagner, W. J., *Federal States and their Judiciary: Comparative Study* (Mouton, 1959).

Walker, D. M., *The Scottish Legal System* (Green, 1959).

Walker, N., *Crime and Punishment in Britain* (University of Edinburgh Press, 1965).

Watkins, R. D., *The State as a Party Litigant* (Johns Hopkins Press, 1927).

Watson, J. S. and W. C. Costin, *The Law and Working of the Constitution: Documents, 1660–1914* (London: Adam and Charles Black, 1952).

Weil, G., *The European Convention on Human Rights* (Sythoff, 1963).

Weyrauch, W. O., *The Personality of Lawyers* (Yale University Press, 1964).

Wheare, K. G., *The Constitutional Structure of the Commonwealth* (Oxford University Press, 1961).

————, *Modern Constitutions*, 2d ed. (Oxford University Press, 1966).

Whitaker, H. G., *Politics and Power: A Text in International Law* (Harper & Row, 1964).

White, G. M., *The Use of Experts by International Tribunals* (Syracuse University Press, 1965).

Wilson, H. H. and H. Glickmann, *The Problem of Internal Security in Great Britain, 1948–1953* (Random House, 1954).

Wiseman, H. V., *The Cabinet in the Commonwealth* (Stevens, 1958).

Woetzel, R., *The Nuremberg Trials in International Law*, rev. ed. (Praeger, 1962).

Woodhouse, A. S. P., *Puritanism and Liberty*, 2d ed. (University of Chicago Press, 1951).

Wright, G. and A. Mejia, Jr., *An Age of Controversy* (Dodd, Mead, 1963).

Zaitsev, Y. and O. Poltorak, *The Soviet Bar* (Foreign Languages Publishing House, 1959).

Zurcher, A. J., *Constitutions and Constitutional Trends since World War II* 2d ed. (New York University Press, 1955).

IV. CLASSIFIED WORKS ON CIVIL RIGHTS AND LIBERTIES

A. GENERAL AND BACKGROUND

1. Historical

Abernathy, M. G., *Civil Liberties Under the Constitution* (Dodd, Mead, 1968).

Avins, A. (ed.), *The Reconstruction Amendments' Debates: The Legislative History and Contemporary Debates in Congress on the 13th, 14th, and 15th Amendments* (National Committee on Constitutional Government, 1967).

Barrington, B. C., *Magna Charta*, 2d ed. (Campbell, 1900).

Becker, C. L., *The Declaration of Independence* (Harcourt, Brace, 1922).

Brant, I., *The Bill of Rights: Its Origin and Meaning* (Bobbs-Merrill, 1965).

Brown, S. G., *The First Republicans: Political Philosophy and Public Policy in the Party of Jefferson and Madison* (Syracuse University Press, 1954).

Carter, H., *The Angry Scar: The Story of Reconstruction* (Doubleday, 1959).

Castberg, F., *Freedom of Speech in the West* (Oceana, 1960).

Chafee, Z., *How Human Rights Got Into the Constitution* (Boston University Press, 1952).

Chicago, University of, *The People Shall Judge*, 2 vols. (University of Chicago Press, 1949).

Commager, H. S. and L. W. Levy, *The Bill of Rights* (Bobbs-Merrill, 1966).

Cranston, M., *Freedom: A New Analysis* (Longmans, Green, 1953).

Dietze, G., *Magna Carta and Property* (University of Virginia Press, 1965).

Dollard, J., *Mr. Lincoln and the Negroes: The Long Road to Equality* (Atheneum, 1963).

Dumbauld, E., *The Bill of Rights and What It Means Today* (University of Oklahoma Press, 1957).

Eaton, C., *Freedom of Thought in the Old South* (Duke University Press, 1940).

Ekirch, A. A., *The Decline of American Liberalism* (Longmans, Green, 1955).

Flack, H. B., *The Adoption of the Fourteenth Amendment* (Johns Hopkins Press, 1908).

Harlan, L. B., *Separate and Unequal* (University of North Carolina Press, 1958).

Harris, R. J., *The Quest for Equality: The Constitution, Congress, and the Supreme Court* (Louisiana State University Press, 1960).

Holt, J. C., *The Making of Magna Carta* (University of Virginia Press, 1965).

Hurst, J. W., *Law and the Conditions of Freedom in the Nineteenth Century United States* (University of Wisconsin Press, 1956).

Hyman, H. H., *To Try Men's Souls: Loyalty Tests in American History* (University of California Press, 1959).

Hyman, H. M., *Era of the Oath: Northern Loyalty Tests During the Civil War and Reconstruction* (University of Pennsylvania Press, 1954).

James, J. B., *The Framing of the Fourteenth Amendment* (University of Illinois Press, 1956).

Jensen, M., *The Articles of Confederation* (University of Wisconsin Press, 1960).

Johnson, D., *The Challenge to American Freedoms* (University of Kentucky Press, 1963).

Kelley, A. H., *Where Constitutional Liberty Came From* (Catt Memorial Fund, 1954).

430

Kemper, D. J., *Decade of Fear: Senator Hennings and Civil Liberties* (University of Missouri Press, 1965).

Knight, H., *With Liberty and Justice For All* (Oceana, 1966).

Konvitz, M. R., *A Century of Civil Rights* (Columbia University Press, 1961).

Lasson, N. B., *The History of the Development of the Fourteenth Amendment* (Johns Hopkins Press, 1937).

Levy, L. W., *Legacy of Suppression: Freedom of Speech and Press in Early American History* (Harvard University Press, 1960).

Lewis, A. and The New York Times, *Portrait of a Decade* (Random House, 1965).

MacIver, R. M. (ed.), *Great Expressions of Human Rights* (Harper, 1950).

Markmann, C. L., *The Noblest Cry: A History of the American Civil Liberties Union* (St. Martin's, 1965).

McPherson, J. M., *The Struggle for Equality: Abolitionists and the Negro in the Civil War and Reconstruction* (Princeton University Press, 1965).

Meador, D. J., *Habeas Corpus and Magna Carta: Dualism of Power and Liberty* (University of Virginia Press, 1966).

Mennix, D. P. and M. Cowley, *Black Cargoes: A History of the Atlantic Slave Trade, 1581–1865* (Viking, 1962).

Metz, H. W. and C. A. H. Thomson, *Authoritarianism and the Individual* (Brookings Institution, 1950).

Muller, H. J., *Freedom in the Ancient World* (Harper, 1961).

———, *Freedom in the Western World* (Harper, 1964).

Myers, H. A., *Are Men Equal?* (Cornell University Press, 1955).

Nye, R. B., *Fettered Freedom: Civil Liberties and the Slavery Controversy, 1830–1860* (Michigan State College Press, 1949).

Pound, R., *The Development of Constitutional Guarantees of Liberty* (Yale University Press, 1957).

Preston, W., Jr., *Aliens and Dissentus: Federal Suppression of Radicals, 1903–1933* (Harvard University Press, 1963).

Quarles, B., *Lincoln and the Negro* (Oxford University Press, 1961).

Randall, J. G., *The Civil War and Reconstruction* (Heath, 1937).

———, *Constitutional Problems under Lincoln*, rev. ed. (University of Illinois Press, 1951).

Roche, J. P., *The Quest for the Dream: the Development of Civil Rights and Human Relations in Modern America* (Macmillan, 1963).

Rossiter, C., *Seedtime of the Republic: The Origin of American Tradition of Political Liberty* (Harcourt, Brace, 1953).

Rutland, R. A., *The Birth of the Bill of Rights, 1776–1791* (Collier, 1962).

Scheiber, H. N., *The Wilson Administration and Civil Liberties* (Cornell University Press, 1960).

Shotwell, J. T., *The Long Way to Freedom* (Bobbs-Merrill, 1960).

Silver, D. M., *Lincoln's Supreme Court* (University of Illinois Press, 1956).

Smith, J. M., *Freedom's Fetters: The Alien and Sedition Laws and American Civil Liberties* (Cornell University Press, 1956).

Stenton, D. M., *After Runnymede: Magna Carta in the Middle Ages* (University of Virginia Press, 1965).

Stevens, W. O., *Footsteps to Freedom* (Dodd, Mead, 1954).

Swindler, W. F., *Magna Carta: Legend and Legacy* (Bobbs-Merrill, 1965).

Tenbroek, J., *Equal Under Law* (Collier, 1965).

————, E. N. Barnhart, and F. W. Matson, *The Anti-Slavery Origins of the Fourteenth Amendment* (University of California Press, 1951).

Weyl, N., *Treason: The Story of Disloyalty and Betrayal in American History* (Public Affairs Press, 1950).

Whipple, L., *The Story of Civil Liberty in the United States* (Vanguard, 1927).

White, W., *How Far the Promised Land?* (Viking, 1955).

Woodward, C. V., *The Strange Career of Jim Crow*, rev. ed. (Oxford University Press, 1957).

Wright, Esmond, *Fabric of Freedom, 1963–1800* (Hill & Wang, 1961).

Wynes, C. E., *Race Relations in Virginia, 1870–1902* (University of Virginia Press, 1961).

Zabel, O. H., *God and Caesar in Nebraska: A Study of the Legal Relationship of Church and State, 1854–1954* (University of Nebraska Press, 1955).

2. Documents and Reports

American Civil Liberties Union, *Annual Report(s)* (American Civil Liberties Union).

Angle, P., *By These Words,* (Rand McNally, 1954).

Becker, C. L., *The Declaration of Independence* (Harcourt, Brace, 1922).

Berman, D. M., *A Bill Becomes a Law: The Civil Rights Act of 1960* (Macmillan, 1962).

Boyd, J. P., *The Declaration of Independence* (Princeton University Press, 1945).

Brooks, A. D. (ed.), *Civil Rights and Liberties in the United States* (Civil Liberties Educational Foundation, 1962).

Brown, S. G. (ed.), *We Hold These Truths,* (Harper, 1948).

Chafee, Z., *Documents on Fundamental Human Rights: The Anglo-American Tradition* (Harvard University Press, 1952, and Atheneum, 1963).

————, *Three Human Rights in the Constitution of 1787* (University of Kansas Press, 1956).

Commager, H. S., *Living Ideas in America* (Harper, 1951).

———— (ed.), *Documents of American History,* 4th ed. (Appleton-Century-Crofts, 1949).

Davis, J. P. (ed.), *The American Negro Reference Book* (Prentice-Hall, 1966).

Dixon, R. G. and E. Plischke (eds.), *American Government: Basic Documents and Materials,* (Van Nostrand, 1950).

Hamilton, A., J. Madison, and J. Jay, *The Federalist,* ed. by B. F. Wright, Harvard University Press, 1961).

Hanson, H. A., *et al., Fighting for Freedom,* (Winston, 1947).

Monaghan, F., *Heritage of Freedom,* (Princeton University Press, 1947).

Murray, P., *Human Rights U.S.A.: 1948–1966* (Board of Missions, the Methodist Church, 1967).

————, *State Laws on Race and Color* (Christian Service, 1950).

Perry, R. L. (ed.), *Sources of Our Liberties: Documentary Origins of Individual Liberties in the U.S. Constitution and Bill of Rights* (American Bar Foundation, 1959).

————, *Sources of Our Liberties: English and American Documents From Magna Charta to the Bill of Rights* (McGraw-Hill, 1964).

Rankin, R. S., *State Constitutions: The Bill of Rights* (National Municipal League, 1960).

Smith, J. M. and P. L. Murphy, *Liberty and Justice—An Historical Record of American Constitutional Development,* (A. Knopf, 1958).

3. Casebooks

General

Amaker, N. C., *Civil Liberty and Civil Rights,* 4th ed. (Oceana, 1966).

Catterell, H. H. (ed.), *Judicial Cases Concerning American Slavery and the Negro* (Carnegie Institute, 1926–37).

Cushman, R. E. and R. F. Cushman, *Leading Constitutional Decisions,* 13th ed. (Appleton-Century-Crofts, 1966).

Emerson, T. I. and D. Haber, *Political and Civil Rights in the United States,* 3d ed. (Little, Brown, 1967).

Fairman, C., *American Constitutional Decisions,* 2d ed. (Holt, 1950).

Freedman, W., *Society on Trial: Current Court Decisions and Social Change* (Thomas, 1965).

Gweck, S., *Cases on Criminal Law and Its Enforcement* (West, 1951).

Haiman, F. S., *Freedom of Speech: Issues and Cases* (Random House, 1965).

Hays, A. C., *Let Freedom Ring* (Boni & Liverright, 1937).

Inbau, F. E. and C. Sowle, *Cases and Comments on Criminal Justice* (Foundation Press, 1960).

Knight, H. V., *With Liberty and Justice for All* (Oceana, 1967).

Konvitz, M. R., *Bill of Rights Reader: Leading Constitutional Cases,* 3d ed. (Cornell University Press, 1965).

Lockhart, W. B., Y. Kamisar, and J. H. Choper, *Cases and Materials on Constitutional Rights and Liberties,* 2d ed. (West, 1967).

Mason, A. T. and W. M. Beaney, *American Constitutional Law: Introductory Essays and Selected Cases,* 3d ed. (Prentice-Hall, 1964).

Michaell J. and H. Wechsler (eds.), *Criminal Law and Its Administration: Cases, Statutes, and Commentaries* (Foundation Press, 1940).

Parker, D., R. M. O'Neil, and N. Econopouly, *Civil Liberties: Case Studies and the Law* (Houghton Mifflin, 1965).

Paulsen, M. G. and S. H. Kadish, *Criminal Law and Its Processes* (Little, Brown, 1962).

Pritchett, C. H., *American Constitutional Issues* (McGraw-Hill, 1962).

Reimel, T., *Handbook on Criminal Law in Pennsylvania* (Bisel, 1958).

Spaeth, H. J., *The Warren Court: Cases and Commentary* (Chandler, 1966).

Sweet, E. C., *Civil Liberties in America: A Casebook* (Van Nostrand, 1966).

Weinberger, A. D., *Freedom and Protection: The Bill of Rights* (Chandler, 1962).

4. General Outlines

(See also B., 2., Theories and Aspects of Freedom, Rights, and Liberties; also see specific rights D., 2–14).

Association of the Bar of the City of New York, *Freedom To Travel: Report of the Special Committee To Study Passport Procedures,* (Dodd, Mead, 1958).

Barker, L. J. and T. W. Marker, Jr., *Freedom, Courts, Politics: Studies in Civil Liberties* (Prentice-Hall, 1965).

Bishop, H. M. and S. Hendel, *Basic Issues of American Democracy* (Appleton-Century-Crofts, 1961).

Bontecou, E. (ed.), *Freedom in the Balance: Opinions of Judge Henry W. Edgeton Relating to Civil Liberties* (Cornell University Press, 1953).

Brannon, H. A., *Treaties on the Rights and Privileges Guaranteed by the Fourteenth Amendment to the Constitution of the U.S.* (Anderson, 1901).

Brennan, W. J., Jr., *The Bill of Rights and the States* (Center for Study of Democratic Institutes, 1961).

Brookes, E. H. and J. B. Maculay, *Civil Liberty in South Africa* (Oxford University Press, 1959).

Brooks, A. D., *Civil Rights and Liberties in the United States: An Annotated Bibliography* (Civil Liberties Education Foundation, 1962).

Cahn, E., *Can the Supreme Court Defend Civil Liberties?* (Sidney Hillman Foundation, 1956).

———, (ed.), *The Great Rights* (Macmillan, 1963).

Columbia University, Teachers College, Citizenship Education Project, *When Men Are Free; Premises of American Liberty* (Houghton Mifflin, 1955).

Commager, H. S., R. K. Carr, Z. Chafee, W. Gellhorn, C. Bok, and J. P. Baxter, *Civil Liberties Under Attack* (University of Virginia Press, 1943).

Cushman, R. E., *Civil Liberties in the United States: A Guide to Current Problems and Experience* (Cornell University Press, 1956).

Davis, E., *But We Were Born Free* (Bobbs-Merrill, 1954).

Douglas, W. O., *The Anatomy of Liberty* (Trident, 1963).

———, *A Living Bill of Rights* (Doubleday, 1961).

———, *The Right of the People* (Doubleday, 1958).

Edman, I., *Fountainhead of Freedom* (Reynal and Hitchcock, 1941).

Edwards, R. A., *The Fourteenth Amendment and Civil Liberty* (Catt Memorial Fund, 1955).

Fleishman, H., *Let's Be Human* (Oceana, 1960).

Frankel, O. K., *Our Civil Liberties* (Viking, 1944).

Gellhorn, W., *American Rights: The Constitution in Action* (Macmillan, 1960).

Hanely, T. O. B., *Their Rights and Liberties* (Newman Press, 1959).

Hutchins, R. M., *Freedom, Education and the Fund: Essays and Addresses, 1946–1956* (Meridian Books, 1956).

Jacobs, C. E., *Justice Frankfurter and Civil Liberties* (Berkeley: University of California Press, 1961).

Kauper, P. G., *Civil Liberties and the Constution* (University of Michigan Press, 1962).

———, *Frontiers of Constitutional Liberty* (University of Michigan Press, 1956).

Kemper, D. J., *Decade of Fear: Senator Hennings and Civil Liberties* (University of Missouri Press, 1956).

Konvitz, M. R., *First Amendment Freedom: Selected Cases on Freedom of Religion, Speech, Press, Assembly* (Cornell University Press, 1963).

——— and C. Rossiter (eds.), *Aspects of Liberty: Essays Presented to Robert E. Cushman* (Cornell University Press, 1958).

Kunstler, W. M., *. . . and Justice for All* (Oceana, 1962).

Lamont, C., *The Right To Travel* (Basic Pamphlet, 1957).

Murphy, The Rev. T. J., *Censorship: Government and Obscenity* (Helicon, 1963).

Newman, E. S., *The Law of Civil Rights and Civil Liberties* (Oceana, 1958).

——— (ed.), *The Freedom Reader* (Oceana, 1955).

———, *Civil Liberty and Civil Rights* (Oceana, 1965).

Penrose, W. O., *Freedom is Ourselves* (University of Delaware Press, 1952).

Reppy, A., *Civil Rights in the United States* (Central Books, 1951).

Roche, J. P., *Courts and Rights: The American Judiciary in Action*, 2d ed. (Random House, 1966).

Schwartzman, R. and J. Stein, *Law of Personal Liberties* (Oceana, 1955).

434

Senser, R., *Primer on Interracial Justice* (Helicon, 1962).

Shapiro, M., *The Court and Civil Rights* (Scott, Foresman, 1966).

Smith, T. V., *The Bill of Rights and Our Individual Liberties* (Catt Memorial Fund, 1954).

Spicer, G. W., *The Supreme Court and Fundamental Freedom* rev. ed. (Appleton-Century-Crofts, 1967).

Starr, I., *Human Rights in the United States*, rev. ed. (Oxford University Press, 1964).

Starzinger, V., *Civil Rights* (St. Martin's 1965).

Superintendent of Documents, *The Report of the United States Commission on Civil Rights* (United States Government Printing Office, 1959ff).

Thomas, N. C., *Politics, Administration and Civil Rights* (Random House, 1966).

Wattenberg, W. W. (ed.), *All Men Are Created Equal* (Wayne State University Press, 1966).

Way, H. F., *Liberty in the Balance: Current Issues in Civil Liberties* (McGraw-Hill, 1964).

Wilcox, C. (ed.), *Civil Liberties Under Attack* (University of Pennsylvania Press, 1952).

Yeager, F. B. and J. R. Stark, *Your Inalienable· Rights* (Public Affairs Press, 1960).

B. PHILOSOPHY OF CIVIL RIGHTS AND LIBERTIES

1. General

   a. Due Process

(See also D., I., Procedural Due Process: General.)

Cunningham, M., *et al.*, *Free Man Versus His Government* (Southern Methodist University Press, 1958).

Francis, P., *Protection Through the Law* (Oceana, 1965).

Newman, E. S., *Police, the Law and Personal Freedom* (Oceana, 1965).

Williams, E. B., *One Man's Freedom* (Athenium, 1962).

Wood, V., *Due Process of Law 1932–1949* (Louisiana State University Press, 1951).

   b. Equal Protection

(See also D., Criminal Law and Procedure.)

Association of the Bar of the City of New York, *Equal Justice for the Accused* (Dodd, Mead, 1959).

Berger, M., *Equality by Statute: The Revolution in Civil Rights*, rev. ed. (Doubleday, 1967).

Foundation of Federal Bar Association, *Equal Justice Under the Law* (Grosset, 1965).

Harris, R. J., *The Quest for Equality: The Constitution, Congress and the Supreme Court* (Louisiana State University Press, 1960).

Hentoff N., *The New Equality* (Viking, 1964).

2. Theories and Aspects of Freedom, Rights, and Liberties

Abraham, H. J., *Freedom and the Court: Civil Rights and Liberties in the United States* (Oxford University Press, 1967).

Adler, M., *The Idea of Freedom*, Vols. I and II (Doubleday, 1958 and 1961).

Angle, P. M. (ed), *Created Equal—The Complete Lincoln-Douglas Debates of 1858* (University of Chicago Press, 1958).

Anshen, R. N., *Freedom: Its Meaning* (Harcourt, Brace, 1940).

Bachrach, P., *Problems in Freedom* (Stackpole, 1953).

Barth, A., *Law Enforcement Versus the Law* (Collier, 1963).

Bay, C., *The Structure of Freedom* (Stanford University Press, 1958).

Bayley, D. H., *Public Liberties in the New States* (Rand McNally, 1964).

Chafee, Z., *The Blessings of Liberty* (Lippincott, 1956).

Chagla, M. C., *The Individual and the State* (Asia Publication House, 1961).

Coffin, W. S., Jr., and C. E. Whitaker, *Law, Order, and Civil Disobedience* (American Enterprise Institute, 1967).

Cohen, M. P., *The Faith of a Liberal* (Holt, 1946).

Collins, C. W., *The Fourteenth Amendment and the States* (Little, Brown, 1912).

Commager, H. S., *Freedom and Order: A Commentary on the American Political Science* (Braziller, 1966).

Corwin, E. S., *Liberty Against Government: The Rise, Flowering and Decline of a Famous Juridical Concept* (Louisiana State University Press, 1948).

Cowling, M., *Mill and Liberalism* (Cambridge University Press, 1963).

Cranston, M., *Freedom: A New Analysis* (Longmans, Green, 1953).

Dahl, R. A., *A Preface to Democratic Theory* (University of Chicago Press, 1956).

Douglas, W. O., *An Almanac of Liberty* (Doubleday, 1954).

———, *The Anatomy of Liberty* (Trident, 1963).

Dowden, W. S. and T. N. March (eds.), *The Heritage of Freedom: Essays on the Rights of Free Man* (Harper & Row, 1962).

Ekirch, A. A., Jr., *The Decline of American Liberalism* (Longmans, Green, 1955).

——— (ed), *Voices in Dissent: An Anthology of Individualist Thought in the United States* (Citadel, 1964).

English, R. (ed.), *The Essentials of Freedom* (Kenyon, 1960).

Feller, L. (ed.), *Wendell Phillips on Civil Rights and Freedom* (Hill & Wong, 1965).

Fosdick, D., *What Is Liberty* (Harper, 1939).

Foster, A., *A Measure of Freedom* (Doubleday, 1950).

Friedrich, C. J. (ed.), *Authority* (Harvard University Press, 1958).

Gerhart, E. C., *American Liberty and "Natural Law"* (Beacon, 1953).

Green, J. F., *The United Nations and Human Rights* (Brookings Institute, 1956).

Hand, L., *The Bill of Rights* (Harvard University Press, 1958).

———, *The Spirit of Liberty: Papers and Addresses of Learned Hand*, 3d ed. (Knopf, 1960).

Handlin, O. and M. Handlin, *The Dimensions of Liberties* (Harvard University Press, 1961).

Hartz, L., *The Liberal Tradition in America* (Harcourt, Brace, 1955).

Horn, R. A., *Groups and the Constitution* (Stanford University Press, 1956).

Johnson, G. W., *This American People* (Harper, 1951).

Kallen, H. M., *A Study of Liberty* (Antioch, 1959).

Kennedy, R. E., *The Pursuit of Justice* (Harper & Row, 1965).

Laski, R., *Liberty in the Modern State* (Viking, 1930).

Levy, L. W., *Jefferson and Civil Liberties: The Darker Side* (Harvard University Press, 1963).

Lisber, F., *Civil Liberty and Self-Government*, 3d ed., (Lippincott, 1875).

MacIver, R. M., *Conflice of Loyalties* (Harper, 1952).

MacLeish, A., *Freedom Is the Right To Choose* (Beacon, 1951).

Maritain, J., *Man and the State* (University of Chicago Press, 1951).

Markman, C. L., *The Noblest Cry* (St. Martin's, 1965).

Mayer, M. (ed.), *The Tradition of Freedom* (Oceana, 1960).

Meiklejohn, A., *Political Freedom: The Constitutional Powers of the People* (Oxford University Press, 1965).

Meiklejohn, D., *Freedom and the Public: Public and Private Morality in America* (Syracuse University Press, 1965).

Medina, H. R., *The Anatomy of Freedom* (Holt, 1959).

Mill, J. S., *Prefaces to Liberty: Selected Writings of John Stuart Mill,* ed. by B. Wishy (Beacon Press, 1959).

————, *On Liberty* (Appleton-Century-Crofts, 1851).

Miller, H. H., *The Case for Liberty* (University of North Carolina Press, 1965).

Milton, J., *Areopagitica* (Dent, 1925).

Mims, E., Jr., *The Majority of the People* (Modern Age Books, 1941).

Morgan, C., *Liberties of the Mind* (Macmillan, 1952).

————, *A Time To Speak* (Harper & Row, 1964).

Muller, H. J., *Issues of Freedom: Paradoxes and Promises* '(Harper, 1960).

————, *The Individual in a Revolutionary World* (Ryerson, 1964).

Newman, E. S., *Civil Liberty and Civil Rights* (Oceana, 1965).

Nock, A. J., *Our Enemy the State* (Capton, 1946).

Oppenheim, F. E., *Dimensions of Freedom* (St. Martin's, 1961).

Orton, W. A., *The Liberal Tradition: Social and Spiritual Conditions of Freedom* (Oxford University Press, 1945).

Patterson, B. B., *The Forgotten Ninth Amendment* (Bobbs-Merrill, 1955).

Pennock, J. R., *Liberal Democracy* (Rinehart, 1950).

Pfeffer, L., *The Liberties of an American: The Supreme Court Speaks* (Beacon, 1956, and 1963).

Rogge, O. J., *The First and the Fifth* (Nelson, 1959).

Russell, B., *Authority and the Individual* (Simon and Schuster, 1949).

Smith, B., *The Democratic Spirit* (Knopf, 1941).

Spencer, H., *Man Versus the State* (Appleton, 1884).

Spitz, D., *Essays in the Liberal Idea of Freedom* (University of Arizona Press, 1964).

Stouffer, S. A., *Communism, Conformity and Civil Liberties: A Cross-Section of the Nation Speaks Its Mind* (Doubleday, 1955).

Tawney, R. H., *Equality* (Barnes & Noble, 1965).

Thomas, N., *Great Dissenters* (Norton, 1954).

Thoreau, H. D., *On the Duty of Civil Disobedience* (Yale University Press, 1849).

Trueblood, D. E., *Declaration of Freedom,* (Harper, 1955).

Truman, H. S, *Freedom and Equality* (University of Missouri Press, 1960).

Tussman, J., *Obligation and the Body Politic* (Oxford University Press, 1960).

United Nations, *Yearbook on Human Rights* (annual).

Walker, P. G., *Restatement of Liberty,* (Hutchinson, 1951).

Whipple, L., *Our Ancient Liberties* (Wilson, 1927).

Wild, J., *Human Freedom and Social Order* (Duke University Press, 1961).

Woodhouse, A. S. P., *Puritanism and Liberty,* 2d ed. (University of Chicago Press, 1951).

3. The Role of the Supreme Court

(See also B., 4., "Line Drawing.")

Abraham, H. J., *The Judiciary: The Supreme Court in the Governmental Process* (Allyn & Bacon, 1965).

Acheson, P. C., *The Supreme Court: America's Judicial Heritage* (Dodd, Mead, 1961).

Becker, C. L., *et al.*, *Safeguarding Civil Liberty Today* (Cornell University Press, 1945).

Bickel, A. M., *Politics and the Warren Court* (Harper & Row, 1965).

Cahn, E., *Can the Supreme Court Defend Civil Liberties?* (Sidney Hillman Foundation, 1956).

Carr, R. K., *Federal Protection of Civil Rights: Quest for a Sword* (Cornell University Press, 1945).

Cushman, R. E. (ed.), *Safeguarding Civil Liberty Today* (Cornell University Press, 1945).

Frankel, O. K., *The Supreme Court and Civil Liberties*, 2d ed. (Oceana, 1963).

Freedman, M., W. H. Beaney, and E. V. Rostow, *Perspectives on the Court* (Northwestern University Press, 1967).

Gordon, R., *Nine Men Against America: The Supreme Court and Its Attack on American Liberties* (Devin-Adair, 1958).

Johnson, D., *The Challenge to American Freedoms* (University of Kentucky Press, 1963).

Konvitz, M. R., *Expanding Liberties: The Emergence of New Civil Liberties and Rights in Postwar America* (Viking, 1967).

Laponce, J. A., *The Protection of Minorities* (Los Angeles: University of California Press, 1960).

Lee, F. F., *Negro and White in Connecticut Town* (Bookman, 1961).

McCloskey, R. G. (ed.), *The American Supreme Court* (University of Chicago Press, 1960).

Mason, A. T. and W. M. Beaney, *The Supreme Court in a Free Society* (Prentice-Hall, 1959). .

Pritchett, C. H., *Congress Versus the Supreme Court, 1957–1960* (University of Minnesota Press, 1961).

———, *The Political Offender and the Warren Court* (Boston University Press, 1958).

Roche, J. P., *Courts and Rights* (Random House, 1961).

Shapiro, H. H., *Federal Enforcement of the Criminal Civil Rights Statutes* (Rutgers University Press, 1960).

Shapiro, M. (ed.), *The Court and Civil Rights* (Scott, Foresman, 1966).

Tussman, J., *The Supreme Court on Racial Discrimination* (Oxford University Press, 1963).

Ziegler, B. M., *Desegregation and the Supreme Court* (Heath, 1958).

4. "Line Drawing"

(See also B., 3., The Role of the Supreme Court.)

Abraham, H. J., *Freedom and the Court: Civil Rights and Liberties in the United States* (Oxford University Press, 1967).

Buckley, W. F., Jr., *God and Man at Yale* (Regnery, 1951).

438

Commager, H. S., *Majority Rule and Minority Rights* (University of Virginia Press, 1943).

Cook, T. I., *Democratic Rights versus Communist Activity* (Doubleday, 1954).

Hand, L., *The Bill of Rights* (Harvard University Press, 1958).

Hook, S., *Heresy, Yes—Conspiracy, No!* (Day, 1953).

———, *The Paradoxes of Freedom* (University of California Press, 1962).

Kariel, H., *The Decline of American Pluralism* (Stanford University Press, 1961).

King, D. B. and C. W. Quick (eds.), *Legal Aspects of the Civil Rights Movement* (Wayne State University Press, 1964).

Mendelson, W., *Justices Black and Frankfurter: Conflict in the Court*, 2d ed. (University of Chicago Press, 1966).

Sowle, C. R. (ed.), *Police, Power and Individual Freedom: The Quest for Balance* (Aldine, 1962).

Street, H., *Freedom, the Individual, and the Law* (Penguin, 1964).

5. States' Rights

(See also C., 4., The South and Its Viewpoint.)

Bloch, C. J., *States Rights: The Law of the Land* (Harrison, 1958).

Brady, T. P., *Black Monday* (Mississippi Association of Citizens Councils, 1955).

Kilpatrick, J. J., *The Sovereign States: Notes of a Citizen of Virginia* (Regnery, 1957).

Marshall, B., *Federalism and Civil Rights* (Columbia, 1963).

Pittman, R. C., *The Supreme Court, the Broken Constitution, and the Shattered Bill of Rights* (Dalton, 1956).

Putnam, C., *Race and Reason* (Public Affairs Press, 1961).

6. The Economic Sphere

Baldwin, R. N., *Civil Liberties and Industrial Conflict* (Harvard University Press, 1938).

Becker, C. L., *Freedom and Responsibility in the American Way of Life* (Knopf, 1945).

Berle, A. A., Jr., *Economic Power and the Free Society* (Fund for the Republic, 1957).

Gellhorn, W., *Individual Freedom and Governmental Restraints* (Louisiana State University Press, 1956).

Gregory, C. O., *Labor and Law* (Norton, 1958).

Hale, R. L., *Freedom through Law* (Columbia University Press, 1952).

Hayek, F. V., *The Constitution of Liberty* (University of Chicago Press, 1960).

Lieberman, E., *Unions Before the Bar* (Harper, 1950).

Lien, A. J., *Concurring Opinion: The Privileges of Immunities Clause of the Fourteenth Amendment* (Washington University Press, 1957).

Mason, A. T., *Security Through Freedom: American Political Thought and Practice* (Cornell University Press, 1955).

Mason, L., *The Language of Dissent* (World, 1959).

Millis, H. A. and E. C. Brown, *From the Wagner Act to Taft-Hartley* (University of Chicago Press, 1950).

Morison, S. E., *Freedom in Contemporary Society* (Little, Brown, 1956).

Parker, R., *A Guide to Labor Law* (Praeger, 1961).

Polsky, S. (ed.), *The Medico-Legal Reader* (Oceana, 1956).

Rostow, E. V., *Planning for Freedom* (Yale University Press, 1963).

Schnapper, M. B., *Constraint by Copyright* (Public Affairs Press, 1962).

Tawney, R. H., *Equality*, 5th ed. (Putnam's, 1961).

Thomas, N. C., *Politics, Administration, and Civil Rights* (University of Michigan Press, 1966).

C. PHILOSOPHY OF PREJUDICE, MINORITY GROUPS, AND RACE RELATIONS

1. General

Allport, G. W., *The Nature of Prejudice* (Doubleday, 1960).

———, *Personality and Social Encounter: Selected Essays* (Beacon, 1960).

Barron, M. L. (ed.), *Minorities in a Changing World* (Knopf, 1967).

Baruch, D. W., *Glass House of Prejudice* (Morrow, 1946).

Barzun, J., *Race: A Study in Modern Superstition* (Harcourt, Brace, 1937).

Benedict, R., *Race: Science and Politics* (Viking, 1947).

Berger, M., *Equality by Statute: Legal Controls over Group Discrimination* (Columbia University Press, 1952).

Bibby, C., *Race, Prejudice, and Education* (Praeger, 1961).

Brink, W. and L. Harris, *Black and White: A Study of U.S. Racial Habits Today* (Simon and Schuster, 1967).

Burlingame, R., *The Sixth Column* (Lippincott, 1962).

Clark, K. B., *Prejudice and Your Child* (Beacon Press, 1955).

Cox, O. C., *Caste, Class and Race: A Study in Social Dynamics* (Doubleday, 1948).

Davis, A., B. B. Gardner, and M. R. Gardner, *Deep South: A Social Anthropological Study of Caste and Class* (University of Chicago Press, 1954).

Dexter, H. H., *What's Right with Race Relations* (Harper, 1959).

Dollard, J., *Caste and Class in a Southern Town*, 3d ed. (Doubleday, 1957).

Dykeman, W. and J. Stokely, *Neither Black Nor White* (Rinehart, 1957).

———, *Seeds of Southern Change: The Life of Will Alexander* (University of Chicago Press, 1962).

Fineberg, S. A., *Punishment Without Crime: What You Can Do About Prejudice* (Doubleday, 1949).

Gittler, J. P., *Understanding Minority Groups* (Wiley, 1956).

Glazer, N. and D. P. Moynihan, *Beyond the Melting Pot* (Massachusetts Institute of Technology Press, 1965).

Goodman, M. E., *Race Awareness in Young Children* (Addison-Wesley, 1952).

Gordon, M. M., *Assimilation in American Life: The Role of Race, Religion, and National Origin* (Oxford University Press, 1964).

Greenberg, J., *Race Relations and American Law* (Columbia University Press, 1959).

Grimes, A. P., *Equality in America: Religion, Race and the Urban Majority* (Oxford University Press, 1964).

Handlin, O., *Race and Nationality in American Life* (Little, Brown, 1957).

———, *The Uprooted* (Little, Brown, 1951).

Hansen, M. L., *The Immigrant in American History* (Harvard University Press, 1940).

Hirsh, G., *The Fears Men Live By* (Harper, 1955).

Jahoda, M., *Race Relations and Mental Health* (Columbia University Press, 1960).

Katz, S. (ed.), *Negro and Jew: An Encounter in America* (Macmillan, 1967).

Laponee, J. A., *The Protection of Minorities* (University of California Press, 1960).

440

Lee, F. F., *Negro and White in Connecticut Town* (Bookman, 1961).

Lubell, S., *White and Black: Test of a Nation* (Harper & Row, 1964).

Marcus, L., *The Treatment of Minorities in Secondary School Textbooks* (Anti-Defamation League of B'nai Brith, 1961).

Mason, P., *Common Sense About Race* (Macmillan, 1961).

Masuoka, J. and P. Valien, *Race Relations: Problems and Theory* (University of North Carolina Press, 1961).

Myers, G. A., *History of Bigotry in the United States* (Random House, 1943).

Raab, E., *American Race Relations Today* (Anchor, 1962).

Rose, A. M., *Race Prejudice and Discrimination: Readings in Intergroup Relations in the United States* (Knopf, 1951).

Rose, P. I., *They and We: Racial and Ethnic Relations in the United States* (Random House, 1964).

Roy, R. L., *Apostles of Discord* (Beacon, 1953).

Saenger, G., *The Social Psychology of Prejudice* (Harper, 1953).

Simpson, G. E. and J. M. Yinger, *Racial and Cultural Minorities* (Harper, 1958).

Snyder, L. L., *The Idea of Racialism: Its Meaning and History* (Van Nostrand, 1962).

Thompson, E. T. and E. C. Hughes, *Race: Individual and Collective Behavior* (Free Press, 1958).

———, *Race Relations and the Race Problem* (Duke University Press, 1939).

Trager, H. G. and M. R. Yarrow, *They Learn What They Live: Prejudice in Young Children* (Harper, 1952).

Tumin, M. M. (ed.), *Race and Intelligence* (Anti-Defamation League of B'nai Brith, 1963).

UNESCO, *The Race Question in Modern Science* (Morrow, 1956).

———, *Race and Science: The Race Question in Modern Science* (Columbia University Press, 1961).

United States Commission on Civil Rights, *Justice* (United States Government Printing Office, 1961).

Vanderbilt University School of Law, *The Race Relations Law Reporter*, 1956 ff.

Vander Zanden, J. W., *American Minority Relations: The Sociology of Peace and Ethnic Groups*, 2d ed. (Ronald, 1966).

Westin, A. F. (ed.), *Freedom Now! The Civil Rights Struggle in America* (Basic Books, 1964).

Young, W. M., Jr., *To Be Equal* (McGraw-Hill, 1964).

2. The Negroes

(See also F., Segregation)

Aptheker, H., *Soul of the Republic: The Negro Today* (Marzani & Munsell, 1964).

Bardolph, R., *The Negro Vanguard* (Rinehart, 1961).

Bontemps, A., *100 Years of Negro Freedom* (Dodd, Mead, 1961).

Booker, S., *Black Man's America* (Prentice-Hall, 1964).

Brink, W. and L. Harris, *The Negro Revolution in America* (Simon and Schuster, 1964).

Brown, I. C., *The Story of the American Negro* (Friendship Press, 1957).

Burns, W. H., *The Voices of Negro Protest in America* (Oxford University Press, 1963).

Conrad, E., *Jim Crow America* (Duell, Sloan, & Pearce, 1947).

Davie, M. R., *Negroes in American History,* (McGraw-Hill, 1949).

441

Davis, J., *Character Assassination* (Philosophical Library, 1951).

Essien-Udom, E. U., *Black Nationalism: A Search for Identity in America* (University of Chicago Press, 1962).

Farmer, J., *Freedom—When?* (Random House, 1966).

Franklin, J. H., *From Slavery to Freedom: A History of American Negroes,* rev. ed. (Knopf, 1967).

Frazier, E. F., *Black Bourgeoisie* (Free Press, 1957).

Ginzberg, E. and A. S. Eichner, *The Troublesome Presence: American Democracy and the Negro* (Free Press, 1964).

Goldwin, R. A., *100 Years of Emancipation* (Rand McNally, 1964).

Greger, R. and E. McDonald, *A Look Down the Lonesome Road* (Doubleday, 1964).

Griffin, J. H., *Black Like Me* (Houghton Mifflin, 1960).

Handlin, O., *The Dimensions of Liberties* (Harvard University Press, 1958).

Hansberry, L., *The Movement: Documentary of a Struggle for Equality* (Simon and Schuster, 1965).

Hentoff, N., *The New Equality* (Viking, 1964).

Issacs, H. R., *The New World of Negro Americans* (Day, 1963).

Javits, J. K., *Discrimination—U.S.A.* (Harcourt, Brace, 1960).

Kalven, H., Jr., *The Negro and the First Amendment* (Ohio State University Press, 1965).

Kardiner, A. and L. Ovesey, *The Mark of Oppression* (Meridian, 1962).

Kephart, W. M., *Racial Factors and Urban Law Enforcement* (University of Pennsylvania Press, 1958).

Killian, L. and C. Grigg, *Racial Crisis in America: Leadership in Conflict* (Prentice-Hall, 1964).

Ladd, E., *Negro Political Leadership in the South* (Cornell University Press, 1966).

Lincoln, E. R., *The Black Muslims in America* (Beacon, 1961).

Litwack, L. F., *North of Slavery: The Negro in the Free States, 1790–1860* (University of Chicago Press, 1961).

Logan, R. W., *The Negro in the United States* (Van Nostrand, 1957).

Lomax, L. E., *The Negro Revolt* (Harper & Row, 1962).

Mangum, C. S., *The Legal Status of the Negro* (University of North Carolina Press, 1940).

Mannix, D. P. and M. Cowley, *Black Cargoes: A History of the Atlantic Slave Trade, 1581–1865* (Viking, 1962).

Matthews, D. R. and J. W. Prothro, *Negroes and the New Southern Politics* (Harcourt, Brace & World, 1966).

Mitchell, G. E. and W. H. Peace, III, *The Angry Black South: Southern Negroes Tell Their Own Story* (Citadel, 1962).

Myrdahl, G., *An American Dilemma: The Negro Problem and Modern Democracy* (Harper & Row, 1962).

Nolan, V. A., *Communism versus the Negro* (Regnery, 1951).

Nordholt, J. W., *The People that Walk in Darkness: A History of the Negro People in America* (Ballantine, 1960).

Parsons T. and K. B. Clark (eds.), *The Negro American* (Beacon, 1967).

Putnam, C., *Race and Reason* (Public Affairs Press, 1961).

Redding, J. S., *On Being Negro in America* (Bobbs-Merrill, 1951).

Rose, A., *The Negro in America* (Beacon, 1956).

Rowan, C., *Go South to Sorrow* (Random House, 1957).

————, *South of Freedom* (Knopf, 1952).

Silberman, C. E., *Crisis in Black and White* (Random House, 1965).

Warren, R. P., *Who Speaks for the Negro?* (Random House, 1965).

Welsch, E. K., *The Negro in the United States: A Research Guide* (Indiana University Press, 1965).

Weyl, N., *The Negro in American Civilization* (Public Affairs Press, 1960).

Yinger, J. M., *A Minority Group in American Society* (McGraw-Hill, 1965).

3. Other Minority Groups: The Japanese, Anti-Semitism, etc.

Belth, N. C. (ed.), *Barriers: Patterns of Discrimination Against Jews* (Friendly House, 1958).

Bloom, L. and R. Riemer, *Removal and Return* (University of California Press, 1949).

Bosworth, A. R., *America's Concentration Camps* (Norton, 1967).

Daniels, R., *The Politics of Prejudice: The Anti-Japanese Movement in California and the Struggle for Exclusion* (University of California Press, 1962).

Davis, E., *But We Were Born Free* (Bobbs-Merrill, 1954).

Epstein, B. R. and A. Forster, *"Some of My Best Friends . . . "* (Farrar, Strauss, 1962).

Forster, A. and B. H. Epstein, *Cross-Currents* (Doubleday, 1957).

————, *The Trouble-Makers* (Doubleday, 1952).

Glock, C. Y. and R. Stark, *Christian Beliefs and Anti-Semitism* (Anti-Defamation League of B'nai Brith, 1966).

Grodzins, M., *Americans Betrayed: Politics and the Japanese Evacuations* (University of Chicago Press, 1949).

Handlin, O., *The Dimensions of Liberties* (Harvard University Press, 1961).

Higham, J., *Strangers in the Land: Patterns of American Nativism, 1869–1929* (Rutgers University Press, 1955).

Javits, J. K., *Discrimination—U.S.A.* (Harcourt, Brace, 1960).

Konvitz, M. R., *The Alien and Asiatics in American Law* (Cornell University Press, 1946).

Kramer, J. R. and S. Leventman, *Children of the Gilded Ghetto* (Yale University Press, 1961).

Mack, R. W. and T. S. Duster, *Patterns of Minority Relations* (Anti-Defamation League of B'nai Brith, 1965).

McWilliams, C., *A Mask for Privilege* (Little, Brown, 1948).

————, *North from Mexico* (Lippincott, 1949).

————, *Prejudice—Japanese-American—Symbols of Racial Intolerance* (Little, Brown, 1944).

Mears, E. G., *Resident Orientals of the American Pacific Coast* (University of Chicago Press, 1928).

Reel, A. F., *The Case of General Yamashita* (University of Chicago Press, 1949).

Rosenstock, M., *Louis Marshall: Defender of Jewish Rights* (Wayne State University Press, 1966).

Seldes, G., *"We hold these Truths . . . "* (League of American Writers, 1939).

Sindler, A. P., *Change in the Contemporary South* (Duke University Press, 1964).

Smith, B., *Americans from Japan* (Lippincott, 1948).

Tenbroek, J., *et al.*, *Japanese-American Evacuation and Resettlement* (University of California Press, 1944).

————, *Prejudice, War, and the Constitution* (University of California Press, 1954).

Thomas, D. S., *The Salvage* (University of California Press, 1952).

—— and R. S. Nishimito, *The Spoilage* (University of California Press, 1946).

Tumin, M. M., *An Inventory & Appraisal of Research on American Anti-Semitism* (Anti-Defamation League of B'nai Brith, 1961).

Van Every, D., *Disinherited: The Lost Birthright of the American Indian* (Morrow, 1966).

Weintraub, R. G., *How Secure These Rights* (Doubleday, 1949).

Yinger, J. M., *Anti-Semitism: A Case Study in Prejudice and Discrimination* (Anti-Defamation League of B'nai Brith, 1964).

4. The South and Its Viewpoint

(See also B., 5., States' Rights.)

Carter, H., *The South Strikes Back* (Doubleday, 1959).

——, *Southern Legacy* (Louisiana State University Press, 1950).

Cash, W. J., *The Mind of the South* (Knopf, 1956).

Chaze, E., *Tiger in the Honeysuckle* (Scribner's, 1965).

Clark, T. D., *The Emerging South* (Oxford University Press, 1961).

Cousins, R. E., *et al.*, *South Carolinians Speak: A Moderate Approach to Race Relations* (University of North Carolina Press, 1957).

Dabbs, J. M., *The Southern Heritage* (Knopf, 1958).

Eaton, C., *The Mind of the Old South* (Louisiana State University Press, 1964).

Gates, R. L., *The Making of Massive Resistance* (University of North Carolina Press, 1965).

Hays, B. A., *A Southern Moderate Speaks* (University of North Carolina Press, 1959).

Highsaw, R. B. (ed.), *The Deep South in Transformation* (University of Alabama Press, 1964).

Leiserson, A. (ed.), *The American South in the 1960's* (Praeger, 1965).

McGill, R., *The South and the Southerner* (Little, Brown, 1963).

McKean, K. F., *Cross Currents in the South* (Swallow, 1963).

Morris, W., *The South Today: 100 Years After Appomadox* (Harper & Row, 1965).

Newby, I. A., *Jim Crow's Defenses: Anti-Negro Thought in America, 1900–1930* (Louisiana University Press, 1965).

Nicholls, W. A., *Southern Tradition and Regional Progress* (University of North Carolina Press, 1960).

Norris, H. (ed.), *We Dissent* (St. Martin's, 1962).

Rubin, L. D. and J. J. Kilpatrick, *The Lasting South* (Regnery, 1957).

Savage, H., Jr., *The Seeds of Time: The Background of Southern Thinking* (Holt, 1959).

Silver, J. W., *Mississippi: The Closed Society*, enl. ed. (Harcourt, Brace & World, 1966).

Sindler, A. P. (ed.), *Change in the Contemporary South* (Duke University Press, 1964).

Thorp, W., *A Southern Reader* (Knopf, 1955).

Tisdale, J. W., *A Southerner's Reflections about the 1954 Supreme Court Decision Concerning Racial Segregation in the Public Schools* (Jarrett's Press, 1956).

Warren, R. P., *Who Speaks for the Negro?* (Random House, 1965).

Workman, W. D., Jr., *The Case for the South* (Devin-Adair, 1960).

Zinn, H., *The Southern Mystique* (Knopf, 1964).

444

D. CRIMINAL LAW AND PROCEDURE

1. Procedural Due Process: General
(See also specific aspects 2.-14. below.)
Alexander, F., *The Criminal, The Judge and the Public* (Free Press, 1961).
Barth, A., *The Price of Liberty* (Viking, 1962).
Chute, C. L. and M. Bell, *Crime, Courts, and Probation* (Macmillan, 1956).
Cray, E., *The Big Blue Line* (Coward-McCann, 1967).
Dienstein, W., *Are You Guilty?* (Thomas, 1954).
Eldridge, W. B., *Narcotics and the Law* (New York University Press, 1962).
Fellman, D., *The Defendant's Rights* (Rinehart, 1958).
Felsher, H. and M. Rosen, *The Press in the Jury Box* (Macmillan, 1966).
Francis, P., *Protection Through the Law* (Oceana, 1965).
George, B. J., Jr., *Constitutional Limitations on Evidence in Criminal Cases* (University of Michigan Press, 1966).
Goldfarb, R. L., *The Contempt Power* (Columbia University Press, 1963).
Grant, J. A., *Our Common Law Constitution* (Boston University Press, 1960).
Griswald, E. N., *The Fifth Amendment Today* (Harvard University Press, 1955).
Harding, A. L. (ed.), *Fundamental Law in Criminal Prosecutions* (Southern Methodist University Press, 1959).
Harris, W. R., *Tyranny on Trial: The Evidence at Nuremberg* (Southern Methodist University Press, 1954).
Kamisar, Y., F. E. Inbau, and T. Arnold, *Criminal Justice in Our Time* (University of Virginia Press, 1965).
Kirchheimer, O., *Political Justice: The Use of Legal Procedure for Political Ends* (Princeton University Press, 1961).
Moreland, C. C., *Equal Justice Under Law* (Oceana, 1965).
Mott, R. L., *Due Process of Law* (Bobbs, 1926).
Newman, E. S., *Police, the Law and Personal Freedom* (Oceana, 1965).
Orton, W. A., *The Liberal Tradition: Social and Spiritual Conditions of Freedom* (Oxford University Press, 1945).
Paulsen, M. G., *Equal Justice for the Poor Man* (Public Affairs Pamphlets, 1965).
Peterson, V. W., *Barbarians in Our Midst* (Little, Brown, 1952).
Ploscowe, M., *The Truth About Divorce* (Hawthorne, 1955).
Pound, R., *Criminal Justice in America* (Holt, 1945).
Putkammer, E. W., *Administration of Criminal Law* (University of Chicago Press, 1953).
Seagle, W., *Acquitted of Murder* (Regnery, 1958).
Silverstein, L., *Defense of the Poor* (American Bar Association, 1965).
Trebach, A. S., *The Rationing of Justice: Constitutional Rights and the Criminal Process* (Rutgers University Press, 1964).

2. Fair Trial

Heller, F. H., *The Sixth Amendment to the Constitution of the United States: A Study in Constitutional Development* (University of Kansas Press, 1951).
Morris, R. B., *Fair Trial: Fourteen Who Stood Accused from Anne Hutchinson to Alger Hiss* (Knopf, 1952).
Orfield, L. B., *Criminal Procedure from Arrest to Appeal* (New York University Press, 1947).
Sullivan, Harold W., *Trial by Newspaper* (Patriot Press, 1961).

Wigmore, Sir J. H., *A Treatise on the Anglo-American System of Evidence in Trials at Common Law*, 3d ed. (Little, Brown, 1940).

Williams, E. B., *One Man's Freedom* (Athenium, 1962).

3. Self-Incrimination

Griswold, E. N., *The Fifth Amendment Today* (Harvard University Press, 1955).

Hook, S., *Common Sense and the Fifth Amendment* (Criterion, 1959).

Inbau, F. E., *Self-Incrimination* (Thomas, 1950).

Maguire, J. N., *Evidence of Guilt: Restrictions upon Its Discovery or Compulsory Disclosure* (Little, Brown, 1959).

Mayers, L., *Shall We Amend the Fifth Amendment?* (Harper, 1959).

Rogge, O. J., *When Men Confess* (Nelson, 1959).

Schwartzman, R. and J. Stein, *The Law of Personal Liberties* (Oceana, 1955).

4. Confessions

Beisel, A. R., *Control Over Illegal Enforcement of the Criminal Law: Role of the Supreme Court* (Boston University Press, 1955).

George, J. B. (ed.), *A New Look at Confessions: Escobedo—The Second Round* (University of Michigan Press, 1966).

Inbau, F. and J. E. Reid, *Criminal Interrogation and Confessions* (Williams & Wilkins, 1962).

Reid, J. E. and F. E. Inbau, *Truth and Deception: The Polygraph ("Lie Detector") Technique* (Williams & Wilkins, 1966).

Reik, T., *The Compulsion To Confess* (Farrar, Straus & Cudhay, 1959).

Rogge, O. J., *Why Men Confess* (Nelson, 1959).

United States Commission on Civil Rights, *Justice* (United States Government Printing Office, 1961).

5. Searches and Seizures

Beisel, A. R., *Control Over Illegal Enforcement of the Criminal Law: Role of the Supreme Court* (Boston University Press, 1955).

Brenton, M., *The Privacy Invaders* (Coward-McCann, 1964).

Cantey, R. C., *The Law of Search and Seizure* (University of Georgia Press, 1957).

Cogan, J. J., *Law of Search and Seizure* (Oceana, 1950).

Donovan, J. B., *Strangers on a Bridge: The Case of Colonel Abel* (Atheneum, 1964).

Gross, H., *Privacy—Its Legal Protection* (Oceana, 1965).

Hofstadter, S. H. and G. Horowitz, *The Right of Privacy* (Central Book Company, 1964).

Landynski, J. W., *Search and Seizure and the Supreme Court* (Johns Hopkins Press, 1966).

Maguire, J. M., *Evidence of Guilt: Restrictions upon its Discovery or Compulsory Disclosure* (Little, Brown, 1959).

Packard, V., *The Naked Society* (McKay, 1964).

Ringel, W. E., *Lawyers Guide to Legal and Illegal Searches* (Gould, 1965).

Schwartzman, R. and J. Stein, *The Law of Personal Liberties* (Oceana, 1955).

Varon, J. A., *Searches, Seizures and Immunities* (Bobbs-Merrill, 1961).

Zelermeyer, W., *Invasion of Privacy* (Syracuse University Press, 1959).

6. Wiretapping and Eavesdropping

(See also D., 5., Searches and Seizures.)

Beisel, A. R., *Control Over Illegal Enforcement of the Criminal Law: Role of the Supreme Court* (Boston University Press, 1955).

Dash, S., R. Schwartz, and R. E. Knowlton, *The Eavesdroppers* (Rutgers University Press, 1959).

Ernst, M. L. and A. V. Schwartz, *Privacy: The Right To Be Let Alone* (Macmillan, 1962).

Long, E. V., *The Intruders: The Invasion of Privacy by Government and Industry* (Praeger, 1967).

Murphy, W. F., *Wiretapping on Trial: A Case Study in the Judicial Process* (Random House, 1965).

Westin, A. F., *Privacy and Freedom* (Atheneum, 1967).

7. Counsel

Beaney, W. M., *The Right to Counsel in American Courts* (University of Michigan Press, 1955).

Heller, F. H., *The Sixth Amendment to the Constitution of the United States A Study in Constitutional Development* (University of Kansas Press, 1951).

Lewis, A., *Gideon's Trumpet* (Random House, 1964).

8. Juries

Heller, F. H., *The Sixth Amendment to the Constitution of the United States: A Study in Constitutional Development* (University of Kansas Press, 1951).

Orfield, L. B., *Criminal Procedure from Arrest to Appeal* (New York University Press, 1947).

9. Bail

Beeley, A. L., *The Bail System in Chicago* (University of Chicago Press, 1927, and 1966).

De Hass, E., *Antiquities of Bail: Origin and Historical Development in Criminal Cases to the Year 1275* (Columbia University Press, 1940).

Goldfarb, R., *Ransom: A Critique of the American Bail System* (Harper & Row, 1965).

Thompkins, D. C. (ed.), *Bail in the United States: A Bibliography* (University of California Press, 1964).

10. Cruel and Unusual Punishment

Barnes, H. E., *The Story of Punishment* (Stratford, 1930).

Beccaria, C., *On Crime and Punishment* (Indianapolis, 1963).

Prettyman, B. E., Jr., *Death and the Supreme Court* (Harcourt, Brace, 1961).

11. Police Agencies and Enforcement

Collins, F. L., *The F.B.I. in Peace and War*, rev. enl. ed. by L. Dember (Ace Books, 1962).

Cook, F. J., *The F.B.I. Nobody Knows* (Macmillan, 1964).

Cray, E., *The Big Blue Line* (Coward-McCann, 1967).

Deutsch, A., *The Trouble with Cops* (Crown, 1955).

Hopkins, E., *Our Lawless Police* (Viking, 1931).

Inbau, F. E. and J. R. Thompson (eds.), "The Supreme Court and the Police," *The Journal of Criminal Law, Criminology, and Police Science*, (September and December, 1966).

Lowenthal, M., *The Federal Bureau of Investigation* (Sloane, 1950).

Millspaugh, A. C., *Crime Control by the National Government* (Brookings Institution, 1937).

447

Niederhoffer, A., *Behind the Shield: The Police in Urban Society* (Doubleday, 1967).

Skolnick, J., *Justice Without Trial* (Wiley, 1966).

Smith, B., *Police Systems in the United States*, rev. ed. (Harper, 1945).

Sowle, C. R. (ed.), *Police Power and Individual Freedom: The Quest for Balance* (Aldine, 1965).

United States Commission on Civil Rights, *Justice* (United States Government Printing Office, 1961).

Whitehead, D., *The F.B.I. Story: A Report to the People* (Random House, 1956).

12. Arrest and Preliminaries

Lafave, W., *Arrest: The Decision To Take a Person Into Custody* (Little, Brown, 1965).

Orfield, L. B., *Criminal Procedure from Arrest to Appeal* (New York University Press, 1947).

Schwartzman, R. and J. Stein, *The Law of Personal Liberties* (Oceana, 1955).

Smith, H. M., *Arrest, Search and Seizure* (Thomas, 1959).

13. Capital Punishment

Bedau, H. M. (ed.), *The Death Penalty in America*, rev. ed. (Anchor, 1967).

Bok, C., *Star Wormwood* (Knopf, 1959).

Chessman, C., *Cell 2455 Death Row* (Prentice-Hall, 1954).

Christoph, J. B., *Capital Punishment and British Politics* (University of Chicago Press, 1962).

DiSalle, M. V., *The Power of Life or Death* (Random House, 1965).

Duffy, H. S., and A. Hirshberg, *88 Men and 2 Women* (Doubleday, 1962).

Joyce, J. A., *Capital Punishment* (Nelson, 1961).

Karpman, B., *The Sexual Offender and His Offenses: Etiology, Pathology, Psychodynamics and Treatment* (Julian, 1954).

Koestler, A., *Reflections on Hanging* (Macmillan, 1957).

Laurence, J., *A History of Capital Punishment* (Citadel, 1960).

Prettyman, E. B., Jr., *Death and the Supreme Court* (Harcourt, Brace & World, 1961).

St. John-Stevas, N., *Life, Death, and the Law* (Secker & Warburg, 1956).

Williams, B., *Due Process* (Morrow, 1960).

14. Principles of Crime and Criminology

Allen, F. A., *The Borderland of Criminal Justice* (University of Chicago Press, 1964).

Alexander, F. and H. Staub, *The Criminal, The Judge, and the Public: A Psychological Analysis* (Macmillan, 1963).

Bakal, C., *The Right to Bear Arms* (McGraw-Hill, 1966).

Barnes, H. E. and N. K. Teeters, *New Horizons in Criminology* (Prentice-Hall, 1944).

Blumberg, A., *Criminal Justice* (Quadrangle, 1967).

Caughey, J. W., *Their Majesties the Mob* (University of Chicago Press, 1960).

Glaser, D., *The Effectiveness of a Prison and Parole System* (Bobbs-Merrill, 1964).

Glueck, S., *Law and Psychiatry: Cold War or Entente Cordiale* (John Hopkins Press, 1962).

Goldstein A. S., *The Insanity Defense* (Viking, 1967).

Kefauver, E., *Crime in America* (Doubleday, 1951).

Mannheim, H., *Criminal Justice and Social Reconstruction* (Paul, French, Tuebner, 1946).

Robitscher, J. B., *Pursuit of Agreement: Psychiatry and the Law* (Lippincott, 1966).

Rubin, S., *Crime and Juvenile Delinquency*, 2d ed. (Oceana, 1961).

————, *Illusion, Fiction and Myths* (Oceana, 1965).

Skolnick, J., *Justice on Trial* (Wiley, 1966).

Sutherland, E. M. and D. R. Creesey, *Principles of Criminology* (Lippincott, 1960).

Szasz, T. S., *Law, Liberty and Psychiatry* (Macmillan, 1964).

————, *Psychiatric Justice* (Macmillan, 1965).

Tappan, R. W., *Crime, Justice and Correction* (McGraw-Hill, 1960).

E. MILITARY JUSTICE IN PEACE AND WAR

1. General

Anthony, J. G., *Hawaii Under Army Rule* (Stanford University Press, 1955).

Coffin, T., *The Passion of the Hawks* (Macmillan, 1964).

Corwin, E. S., *Total War and the Constitution* (Knopf, 1947).

Fairman, C., *The Law of Martial Rule* (Callaghan, 1943).

Herring, P., *The Impact of War* (Farrar & Rinehart, 1941).

Huntington, S. P., *The Soldier and the State: The Theory and Politics of Civil Military-Relations* (Belknap of Harvard, 1957).

Millis, W., *Individual Freedom and the Common Defense* (Fund for the Republic, 1957).

————, *et al, Arms and the State: Civil-Military Elements in National Policy* (Twentieth Century Fund, 1958).

Paxon, F. C., *America at War, 1917–1918* (Houghton Mifflin, 1939).

Peterson, H. C. and G. C. Fita, *Opponents of War, 1917-1918* (University of Wisconsin Press, 1957).

Rankin, R. S., *When Civil Law Fails: Martial Law and its Legal Basis in the U. S.* (Duke University Press, 1939).

Reel, A. F., *The Case of General Yamashita* (University of Chicago Press, 1949).

Rossiter, C., *The Supreme Court and the Commander-in-Chief* (Cornell University Press, 1951).

Scheiber, H. N., *The Wilson Administration and Civil Liberties* (Cornell University Press, 1960).

Sibley, M. Q. and P. E. Jacob, *Conscription of Conscience: The American State and the Conscientious Objector, 1940–1947* (Cornell University Press, 1952).

Smith, L., *American Democracy and Military Power* (University of Chicago Press, 1951).

Snow, C. P., *Science and Government* (Harvard University Press, 1961).

Summers, R. E., *Wartime Censorship of Press and Radio* (Wilson, 1942).

Stein, H. (ed.), *American Civil-Military Decisions* (University of Alabama Press, 1963).

Swomley, J. M., Jr., *The Military Establishment* (Beacon, 1964).

2. Civilians

Bloom, L. and R. Riemer, *Removal and Return* (University of California Press, 1949).

449

Cable, J. L., *Loss of Citizenship: Denaturalization—the Alien in Wartime* (National Law Book Company, 1943).

Grodzins, M., *The Loyal and the Disloyal: Social Boundaries of Patriotism and Treason* (University of Chicago Press, 1956).

McWilliams, C., *Prejudice-Japanese-American-Symbols of Racial Intolerance* (Little, Brown, 1944).

Sibley, M. Q. and P. E. Jacob, *Conscription of Conscience: The American State and the Conscience Objector* (Cornell University Press, 1952).

Tenbroeck, J., *et al.*, *Japanese-American Evacuation and Resettlement* (University of California Press, 1944).

———, *Prejudice, War, and the Constitution* (University of California Press, 1954).

Thomas, D. S., *The Salvage* (University of California Press, 1952).

——— and R. S. Nishimito, *The Spoilage* (University of California Press, 1946).

Willoughby, G., *Handbook for Conscientious Objectors* (Larchwood, 1964).

3. Military Personnel

Avins, A., *The Law of AWOL* (Oceana, 1957).

Aycock, W. B. and S. W. Wurfel, *Military Law under the Uniform Code of Military Justice* (University of North Carolina Press, 1962).

Edwards, M. O. and C. L. Decker, *The Serviceman and the Law* (Stockpole, 1951).

Everett, R. O., *Military Justice in the Armed Forces of the United States* (Military Service Publishing Company, 1956).

Walker, D. (ed.), *Military Law* (Prentice-Hall, 1954).

F. SEGREGATION

1. General

Ashmore, H. S., *Epitaph for Dixie* (Norton, 1957).

———, *The Other Side of Jordan: Negroes Outside the South* (Norton, 1960).

Barnett, R. and J. Garal, *Where the States Stand in Civil Rights* (Bold Face, 1962).

Bennett, L., Jr., *Confrontation: Black and White* (Penguin, 1966).

Brink, W. and L. Harris, *Black and White: A Study of Racial Attitudes Today* (Simon and Schuster, 1967).

Cable, G. W., *The Negro Question: A Selection of Writings on Civil Rights in the South* (Doubleday, 1890).

Carmichael, P. A., *The South and Segregation* (Public Affairs Press, 1965).

———, *The South and Segregation* (Public Affairs Press, 1966).

Clark, K. B., *Dark Ghetto: Dilemmas of Social Power* (Harper & Row, 1965).

Coles, R., *The Desegregation of Southern Schools: A Psychiatric Study* (Southern Regional Council and Anti-Defamation League of B'nai Brith, 1963).

Countryman, J. (ed.), *Discrimination and the Law* (University of Chicago Press, 1965).

Dabbs, J. M., *Who Speaks for the South?* (Funk & Wagnalls, 1965).

Freedman, L. (ed.), *Southern Justice* (Pantheon, 1965).

Graham, E. D., *Crisis in Print: Desegregation and the Press in Tennessee* (Vanderbilt University Press, 1967).

Handlin, O., *Fire-Bell in the Night: The Crisis in Civil Rights* (Little, Brown, 1964).

450

Hill, H. and J. Greenberg, *Citizen's Guide to De-Segregation* (Beacon, 1955).

Hoffman, N. J., *Mississippi Notebook* (White, 1965).

Huie, W. B., *Three Lives for Mississippi* (W.C.C., 1965).

Johnson, C. S., *Patterns of Negro Segregation* (Harper, 1943).

Kutler, S. I. (ed.), *The Dred Scott Decision: Law and Politics* (Houghton Mifflin, 1967).

Leiserson, A. (ed.), *The American South in the 1960's* (Praeger, 1964).

Loth, D. and H. Flemming, *Integration North and South* (Fund for the Republic, 1956).

Lubell, S., *White and Black: Test of a Nation* (Harper & Row, 1964).

MacIver, R. M. (ed.), *Discrimination & National Welfare* (Harper, 1949).

Mendelson, W., *Discrimination* (Prentice-Hall, 1963).

Michael, W. E., *The Age of Error* (Vantage, 1957).

Mitchell, G. E. and W. H. Peace, III, *The Angry Black South: Southern Negroes Tell Their Own Story* (Citadel, 1962).

Morgan, C., Jr., *A Time to Speak* (Harper & Row, 1964).

Muse, B., *Ten Years of Prelude* (Viking, 1964).

Nichols, L., *Breakthrough on the Color Front* (Random House, 1954).

O'Neill, J. E. (ed.), *The Breaking of the Wall: Aspects of Segregation* (Macmillan, 1961).

—— (ed.), *A Catholic Case Against Segregation* (Macmillan, 1961).

Peters, W., *The Southern Temper* (Doubleday, 1959).

Pettigrew, T. F., *Epitaph for Jim Crow* (Anti-Defamation League of B'nai Brith, 1964).

Reid, I. (ed.), *Racial Desegregation and Integration* (American Academy, 1956).

Silberman, C. E., *Crisis in Black and White* (Random House, 1964).

Silver, J. W., *Mississippi: The Closed Society*, enl. ed. (Harcourt, Brace & World, 1966).

Simkins, F. B., *The Everlasting South* (Louisiana State University Press, 1963).

Sindler, A. P. (ed.), *Change in the Contemporary South* (Duke University Press, 1964).

Southern Regional Council, *Intimidation, Reprisal and Violence in the South's Racial Crisis* (Southern Regional Council, 1959).

Stahl, D., F. B. Sussman, and N. J. Bloomfield, *The Community and Racial Crisis* (Practicing Law Institute, 1966).

Stampp, K., *The Peculiar Institution* (Knopf, 1963).

Stoff, S., *The Two-Way Street: Guideposts to Peaceful School Desegregation* (David Stewart, 1967).

Suchman, E. A., J. P. Dean, and R. M. Williams, Jr., *Desegregation* (Anti-Defamation League of B'nai Brith, 1963).

Talmadge, H. E., *You and Segregation* (Dulcan, 1955).

Tucker, S., *Mississippi from Within* (Arco, 1965).

Tumin, N. M., *Desegregation: Readiness and Resistance* (Princeton University Press, 1958).

Tussman, J., *The Supreme Court on Racial Discrimination* (Oxford University Press, 1963).

United States Commission on Civil Rights, *Enforcement: A Report on Equal Protection in the South* (United States Government Printing Office, 1965).

——, *With Liberty and Justice for All* (United States Government Printing Office, 1959).

Vander Zanden, J. W., *Race Relations in Transition: The Segregation Crisis in The South* (Random House, 1965).

451

Warren, R. P., *Segregation: The Inner Conflict in the South* (Random House, 1956).

Woodward, C. V., *The Strange Career of Jim Crow*, 2d rev. ed. (Oxford University Press, 1966).

Woofter, T. J., *Southern Race Progress: the Wavering Color Line* (Public Affairs Press, 1957).

Young, W. M., *To Be Equal* (McGraw-Hill, 1964).

Ziegler, B. M., *Desegregation and the Supreme Court* (Heath, 1953).

Zinn, H., *The Southern Mystique* (Knopf, 1965).

2. Education

Anderson, M., *The Children of the South* (Farrar, Straus & Giroux, 1966).

Ashmore, H. S., *The Negro and the Schools*, rev. ed. (University of North Carolina Press, 1954).

Barrett, R. H., *Integration at Ole Miss.* (Quadrangle, 1965).

Bates, D., *The Long Shadow of Little Rock: A Memoir* (McKay, 1963).

Berman, D. M., *It Is So Ordered* (Norton, 1966).

Blaustein, A. P. and C. C. Ferguson, Jr., *Desegregation and the Law* (Vintage, 1962).

Blossom, V., *It Has Happened Here* (Harper, 1959).

Boyle, S. P., *The Desegregated Heart* (Morrow, 1962).

Brady, T. P., *Black Monday* (Mississippi Association of Citizens Councils, 1955).

Brickman, W. W. and S. Lehrer, *The Countdown on Segregated Education*, (Society for the Advancement of Education, 1960).

Brown, R. R., *Bigger than Little Rock* (Seabury, 1958).

Campbell, E. A., *When a City Closes Its Schools* (University of North Carolina Press, 1960).

Campbell, E. A. and T. F. Pettigrew, *Christiana in Racial Crisis: A Study of Little Rock's Ministry* (Public Affairs Press, 1959).

Carmichael, O. and W. James, *The Louisville Story* (Simon and Schuster, 1957).

Caughey, J. and L. Caughey, *School Segregation on Our Doorstep: The Los Angeles Story* (Quail, 1966).

Coles, R., *The Desegregation of Southern Schools: A Psychiatric Study* (Southern Regional Council and Anti-Defamation League of B'nai Brith, 1963).

Dean, J. P. and A. Rosen, *A Manual of Intergroup Relations* (University of Chicago Press, 1955).

Dobbs, J. M., *The Southern Heritage* (Knopf, 1958).

Faulkner, W., B. Mays, and C. Sims, *The Segregation Decisions: Three Views* (Southern Regional Council, 1956).

Fellman, D. (ed.), *The Supreme Court and Education* (Columbia University Press, 1960).

Fleming, H. C. and J. Constable, *What's Happening in School Integration* (Public Affairs Press, 1956).

Fletcher, J. L., Jr., *The Segregation Case and the Supreme Court* (Boston University Press, 1958).

Fuchs, E., *Pickets at the Gates: The Challenge of Civil Rights in Urban Schools* (Free Press, 1966).

Gates, R. L., *The Making of Massive Resistance: Virginia; Politics of Public School Desegregation, 1954–1956* (University of North Carolina Press, 1964).

Giles, H. H., *The Integrated Classroom* (Basic Books, 1959).

Ginzberg, E., *The Negro Potential* (Columbia University Press, 1956).

452

Green, D. R. and W. E. Gauerke, *If the Schools are Closed* (Southern Regional Council, 1959).

Gwaltney, F. I., *The Numbers of Our Days* (Random House, 1959).

Harlan, L. R., *Separate and Unequal* (University of North Carolina Press, 1958).

Holley J. W., *Education and the Segregation Issue* (Frederick, 1955).

Humphrey, H. H. (ed.), *Schools Segregation: Documents and Commentaries* (Crowell, 1964).

Ivey, H. and J. Corey, *Action Patterns in School Desegregation: A Guidebook* (Phi Delta Kappa, Inc., 1959).

Jones, L. G. E., *Negro Schools in the Southern States* (Oxford University Press, 1928).

Kilpatrick, J. J., *The Southern Case for School Segregation* (Crowell, Collier, 1962).

Lord, W., *The Past that Would Not Die* (Harper & Row, 1965).

Martin, J. B., *The Deep South Says Never* (Ballantine, 1957).

Maston, T. B., *Segregation and Desegregation: A Christian Approach* (Macmillan, 1959).

McCauley, P. and E. D. Bell (eds.), *Southern Schools: Progress and Problems* (Southern Educational Reporting Service, 1959).

Miller, A. S., *Racial Discrimination and Private Education* (University of North Carolina Press, 1957).

Miller, L., *The Petitioners: The Story of the Supreme Court of the United States and the Negro* (Pantheon, 1966).

Muse, B., *Virginia's Massive Resistance* (Indiana University Press, 1961).

Peltason, J. W., *Fifty-Eight Lonely Men* (Harcourt, Brace, 1961).

Pierce, T. M., *et al, White and Negro Schools in the South* (Prentice-Hall, 1955).

Quint, H. H., *Profile of Black and White: A Frank Portrait of South Carolina* (Public Affairs Press, 1958).

Record, W., *Little Rock, U.S.A.* (Chandler, 1960).

Reutter, E. E., *Schools and the Law* (Oceana, 1965).

Scott, J. I. E., *Negro Students and their Colleges* (Meador, 1949).

Shoemaker, D. (ed.), *With All Deliberate Speed* (Harper, 1957).

Silverman, C., *The Little Rock Story* (University of Alabama Press, 1959).

Smith, L., *Now is the Time* (Viking, 1955).

Spurlock, C., *Education and the Supreme Court* (University of Illinois Press, 1955).

Sterling, D. and D. Gross, *Tender Warriors* (Hill & Wang, 1958).

Sullivan, N. V., *et al, Bound for Freedom: An Educator; Adventures in Prince Edward County* (Little, Brown, 1965).

Swanson, E. W. and J. A. Griffin, *Public Education in the South Today and Tomorrow* (University of North Carolina Press, 1955).

Tipton, J. H., *Community in Crisis: The Elimination of Segregation from a Public School System* (Columbia University Press, 1953).

Trillin, C., *An Education in Georgia* (Viking, 1964).

United States Commission on Civil Rights, *Education: Book 2 of 1961 Report* (United States Government Printing Office, 1961).

———, *Equal Protection of the Laws in Public Higher Education* (United States Government Printing Office, 1960).

University of North Carolina Press, *When a City Closes its Schools* (University of North Carolina Press, 1960).

Williams, R. J. and M. W. Ryan (eds.), *Schools in Transition: Community Experience in Desegregation* (University of North Carolina Press, 1954).

453

3. Housing

Abrams, C., *Forbidden Neighbors: A Study of Prejudice in Housing* (Harper, 1955).

Black, A., *Who's My Neighbor?* (Public Affairs Committee, 1956).

Braden, A., *The Wall Between* (Monthly Review Press, 1958).

Clark, K. B., *Dark Ghetto* (Harper & Row, 1965).

——, *Prejudice and Your Child* (Beacon, 1955).

Commission on Race and Housing, *Where Shall We Live? Report of the Commission on Race and Housing* (University of California Press, 1958).

Deutsch, M., *Interracial Housing* (University of Minnesota Press, 1951).

Glazer, N. and D. McEntire (ed.), *Studies in Housing and Minority Groups* (University of California Press, 1961).

Grier, E. and G. Grier, *Privately Developed Interracial Housing: An Analysis of Experience* (University of California Press, 1961).

Laurenti, L., *Property Values and Race: Studies in Seven Cities* (University of California Press, 1960).

Long, H. H. and C. S. Johnson, *People v. Property: Race Restrictive Covenants in Housing* (Fisk University Press, 1947).

McIntire, Davis, *Residence and Race: Final and Comprehensive Report to the Commission on Race and Housing* (University of California Press, 1961).

Northwood, L. K. and E. A. E. Barth, *Urban Desegregations: Negro Pioneers and Their White Neighbors* (University of Washington Press, 1965).

Rapkin, C. and G. Grigsby, *The Demand for Housing in Racially Mixed Areas: A Study of Neighborhood Change* (University of California Press, 1961).

Schroeder, O., Jr., and D. T. Smith (eds.), *De Facto Segregation and Civil Rights* (Hem, 1963).

Vose, C. E., *Caucasians Only: The Supreme Court, the NAACP and the Restrictive Covenant Cases* (University of California Press, 1959).

Weaver, R. P., *The Negro Ghetto* (Harcourt, Brace, 1948).

Wheeler, K., *Peaceable Lane* (Simon and Schuster, 1960).

Williams, R. J. and W. W. Ryan (eds.), *Schools in Transition: Community Experiences in Desegregation* (University of North Carolina Press, 1954).

4. Employment

Becker, G. S., *The Economics of Discrimination* (University of Chicago Press, 1957).

Bullock, P., *Merit Employment: Non-Discrimination in Industry* (Institute of Industrial Relations, University of California, Los Angeles, 1960).

Edwards, G. F., *The Negro Professional Class* (Free Press, 1959).

Ginzberg, E., *The Negro Potential* (Columbia University Press, 1956).

Graves, W. B., *Fair Employment Practice Legislation in the United States: Federal-State-Municipal* (Library of Congress, 1951).

Greer, S., *Last Man in: Racial Access to Union Power* (Free Press, 1959).

Hope, J., II, *Equality of Opportunity: A Union Approach to Fair Employment* (Public Affairs Press, 1956).

Kesselman, L. C., *The Social Politics of the FEPC: A Study in Reform Pressure Movement* (University of North Carolina Press, 1948).

Mandelbaum, D. G., *Soldier Groups and Negro Soldiers* (University of California Press, 1952).

Moon, B., *The High Cost of Prejudice* (Messner, 1947).

Nelson, D. D., *The Integration of the Negro into the U.S. Navy* (Farrar, Strauss, 1951).

454

Norgren, P. H., *Employing the Negro in American Industry: A Study of Management Practices* (Industrial Relations Counselors, 1959).

Reitzes, D. C., *Negroes and Medicine* (Harvard University Press, 1958).

Ross, M., *All Manner of Men* (Reynal and Hitchcock, 1948).

Ruchames, L., *Race, Jobs and Politics: The Story of F.E.P.C.* (Columbia University Press, 1953).

Smith, H. S., *Freedom to Work* (Vantage Press, 1955).

Southall, S. E., *Industry's Unfinished Business: Achieving Sound Industrial Relations and Fair Employment* (Harper, 1950).

Sovern, M. I., *Legal Restraints on Racial Discrimination in Employment* (Twentieth Century Fund, 1966).

5. Techniques of the Negro Civil Rights Movement

(The NAACP, sit-ins, the leaders of the general "civil rights" activities.)

Belfrage, S., *Freedom Summer* (Viking, 1965).

Burns, W. H., *The Voices of Negro Protest in America* (Oxford University Press, 1963).

Clark, K. B. (ed.), *The Negro Protest* (Beacon, 1963).

Clarke, C. J., *These Rights They Seek* (Public Affairs Press, 1962).

Coffin, W. S. and C. E. Whitaker, *Law, Order, and Civil Disobedience* (American Enterprises Institute, 1967).

Cohen, J. and W. S. Murphy, *Burn, Baby, Burn! The Los Angeles Race Riot August, 1965* (Dutton, 1966).

Ehle, N., *The Free Men* (Harper & Row, 1965).

Garfinkel, H., *When Negroes March* (Free Press, 1959).

Guerin, D., *Negroes on the March* (Weissman, 1956).

Hamilton, C. V., *The Politics of Civil Rights* (Random House, 1967).

Hayden, T., *Rebellion in Newark: Official Violence and Ghetto Response* (Random House, 1967).

Hughes, L., *Fight for Freedom: The Story of the NAACP* (Norton, 1963).

King, M. L., *Stride Toward Freedom: The Montgomery Story* (Harper, 1958).

———, *Where Do We Go From Here? Chaos or Community?* (Harper & Row, 1967).

Ladd, E. C. Jr., *Negro Political Leadership in the South* (Cornell University Press, 1961).

Lincoln, E. R., *The Black Muslims in America* (Beacon, 1961).

Lomax, L. E., *The Negro Revolt* (Harper & Row, 1962).

Matthews D. R. and J. W. Prothro, *Negroes and the New Southern Politics* (Harcourt, Brace, 1964).

Meler, A. and F. L. Broderick, *Negro Protest Thought in the Twentieth Century* (Bobbs-Merrill, 1966).

Peck, J., *Freedom Ride* (Simon and Schuster, 1962).

Powledge, F., *Black Power—White Resistance: Notes on the New Civil War* (World, 1967).

Proudfoot, M., *Diary of a Sit-In* (University of North Carolina Press, 1962).

Record, W., *The NAACP and the Communist Party in Conflict* (Cornell University Press, 1964).

Reddick, L. D., *Crusader Without Violence* (Harper, 1959).

Sutherland, E. (ed.), *Letters from Mississippi* (McGraw-Hill, 1965).

Von Hoffman, N., *Mississippi Notebook* (Daniel White, 1965).

Wakefield, D., *Revolt in the South* (Grove, 1960).

Waskow, I., *From Race-Riot to Sit-In: 1919 and the 1960's* (Doubleday, 1966).

Zinn, H., *SNCC: The New Abolitionists* (Beacon, 1965).

G. VOTING: RACIAL DISCRIMINATION

(See also F., 1., Segregation, General.)

Aikin, C., *The Negro Votes* (Chandler, 1962).

Gillette, W. M., *The Right to Vote Politics and the Passage of the Fifteenth Amendment* (Johns Hopkins Press, 1965).

Grimes, A. D., *The Puritan Ethnic and Woman Suffrage* (Oxford University Press, 1967).

Key, V. O., Jr., *Southern Politics in State and Nation* (Knopf, 1949).

Lewinson, P., *Race, Class, and Party: A History of Negro Suffrage and White Politics in the South* (Grosset and Dunlap, 1964).

Ogden, A. R., *The Poll Tax in the South* (Catholic University of America Press, 1958).

President's Committee on Civil Rights, *To Secure These Rights* (United States Government Printing Office, 1947).

Price, H. D., *The Negro in Southern Politics* (New York University Press, 1957).

Smith, C. E., *Voting and Election Laws* (Oceana, 1960).

Taper, B., *Gomillion Versus Lightfoot: The Tuskegee Gerrymander Case* (McGraw-Hill, 1962).

United States Commission on Civil Rights, *Voting* (United States Government Printing Office, 1961).

H. EXPRESSION: SPEECH, PRESS, AND PETITION

(The Press, radio, television, motion pictures, books, libel, petition.) (See also K., Academic Freedom and L., Morals, Obscenity, and Censorship.)

Alexander, J., *A Brief Narrative of the Case and Trial of John Peter Zenger*, ed. by S. N. Katz (Belknap, 1963).

Angoff, C., *The Book of Libel*, 2d ed. (Barnes & Noble, 1966).

Arthur, W. A. and R. L. Crossman, *The Law of Newspapers* (McGraw-Hill, 1940).

Becker, C. L., *Freedom and Responsibility in the American Way of Life* (Knopf, 1945).

Berns, W., *Freedom, Virtue, and the First Amendment* (Louisiana State University Press, 1957).

Blumer, H. and P. Hauser, *Movies, Delinquency and Crime* (Macmillan, 1933).

Brucker, H., *Freedom of Information* (Macmillan, 1949).

Buranelli, V. (ed.), *The Trial of Peter Zenger* (New York University Press, 1957).

Casey, R. D. (ed.), *The Press in Perspective* (Louisiana University Press, 1963).

Castberg, F., *Freedom of Speech in the West* (Oceana, 1960).

Caughey, J. W., *In Clear and Present Danger: The Critical State of Our Freedoms* (University of Chicago Press, 1958).

Chafee, Z., *Free Speech in the United States* (Harvard University Press, 1954).

———, *Freedom of Speech* (Harcourt, 1920).

———, *Freedom of Speech and Press* (Harvard University Press, 1955).

———, *Government and Mass Communication: A Report From the Commission on Freedom-of-the-Press*, rev. ed. (Anchor, 1965).

456

———, *Thirty-five Years with Freedom of Speech* (Harvard University Press, 1952).

Chenery, W. L., *Freedom of the Press* (Harcourt, Brace, 1955).

Clyde, W., *The Struggle for Freedom of the Press from Caxton to Cromwell* (Oxford University Press, 1934).

Cogley, J., *Report on Blacklisting* Vol. I; *Movies* Vol II; *Radio-TV* (Fund for the Republic, 1956).

Commager, H. S., *Freedom, Loyalty, Dissent* (Oxford University Press, 1954).

Commission on Freedom of the Press, *American Radio: A Report on the Broadcasting in the United States* (University of Chicago Press, 1947).

———, *A Free and Responsible Press: A General Report on Mass Communication* (University of Chicago Press, 1947).

———, *Freedom of the Movies: A Report of Self-Regulation from the Commission on Freedom of the Press by Ruth A. Inglis* (University of Chicago Press, 1947).

———, *Freedom of the Press: A Framework of Principle* (University of Chicago Press, 1947).

———, *People Speaking to People: A Report on International Mass Communication* (University of Chicago Press, 1948).

Gill, J., *Tide Without Turning: Elijah P. Lovejoy and Freedom of the Press* (Starr King, 1958).

Cooper, K., *The Right To Know: An Exposition of the Evils of News Suppression and Propaganda* (Farrar, Straus & Cudahy, 1956).

Craig, A., *The Bannet Books of England and Other Countries* (George Allen, 1962).

Cross, H. L., *The People's Right To Know* (Columbia University Press, 1953).

Daniels, W. M. (ed.), *The Censorship of Books* (Wilson, 1954).

Dawson, S. A., *Freedom of the Press* (Columbia University Press, 1924).

Dean, J., *Hatred, Ridicule, or Contempt: A Book of Libel Cases* (Constable, 1953).

Downs, R. B. (ed.), *The First Freedom: Liberty and Justice in the World of Books and Reading* (American Library Association, 1960).

Drinker, H. S., *Some Observations of the Freedoms of the First Amendment* (Boston University Press, 1957).

Emerson, T. I., *Toward a General Theory of the First Amendment* (Random House, 1966).

Ernst, M. L., *The First Freedom* (Macmillan, 1946).

Faulk, J. H., *Fear on Trial* (Simon and Schuster, 1964).

Fellman, D., *The Limits of Freedom* (Rutgers University Press, 1959).

Felsher, H. and M. Rosen, *The Press in the Jury Box* (Macmillan, 1966).

Fliess, Peter J., *Freedom of the Press in the German Republic 1918–1933* (Louisiana State University Press, 1955).

Friendly A. and R. L. Goldfarb, *Crime and Publicity: The Impact of News in the Administration of Justice* (Twentieth Century Fund, 1967).

Gerald, J. E., *The Press and the Constitution, 1931–1947* (University of Minnesota Press, 1948).

Gillett, C. R., *Banned Books*, 2 Vols. (Columbia University Press, 1932).

Gillmor, D. M., *Free Press and Fair Trial* (Public Affairs Press, 1966).

Hachten, W. A., *The Supreme Court and the Press* (Public Affairs Press, 1965).

Haight, A. L., *Banned Books* (Bowker, 1956).

Haiman, F. S., *Freedom of Speech: Issues and Cases* (Random House, 1965).

Haney, R. W., *Comstockery in America* (Houghton-Mifflin, 1956).

Hocking, W. E., *Freedom of the Press: A Framework of Principle* (University of Chicago Press, 1945).

Hudon, E. G., *Freedom of Speech and Press in America* (Public Affairs Press, 1963).

Hughes, Frank, *Prejudice and the Press,* (Devin-Adair, 1950).

Hyde, H. M., *Privacy and the Press* (Butterworth, 1947).

Ickes, H. L., *Freedom of the Press Today* (Vanguard, 1941).

Inglis, R. A., *Freedom of the Movies* (University of Chicago Press, 1947).

Jackson, H., *The Fear of Books* (London, 1932).

Jennison, P., *Freedom to Read* (Public Affairs Pamphlets, 1965).

Johnson, G. W., *Peril and Promise: An Inquiry into Freedom of the Press* (Harper, 1958).

Kahn, G., *Hollywood on Trial* (Boni and Gear, 1948).

Kalven, H., Jr., *The Negro and the First Amendment* (University of Chicago Press, 1965).

Konvitz, M. R., *First Amendment Freedoms: Selected Cases on Freedom of Religion, Speech, Press, Assembly* (Cornell University Press, 1963).

———, *Fundamental Liberties of a Free People: Religion, Speech, Press, Assembly* (Cornell University Press, 1957).

Lacy, D., *Freedom and Communication* (Illinois University Press, 1961).

Levy, L. W., *Freedom of the Press from Zenger to Jefferson* (Bobbs-Merrill, 1966).

———, *Legacy of Suppression: Freedom of Speech and Press in Early American History* (Harvard University Press, 1960).

Lofton, J., *Justice and the Press* (Beacon, 1967).

Meiklejohn, A., *Free Speech and Its Relation to Self-Government* (Harper, 1948).

———, *Political Freedom: The Constitutional Powers of the People* (Oxford University Press, 1960 and 1965).

Miller, J. O., *Crisis in Freedom: The Alien and Sedition Acts* (Little, Brown, 1951).

Miller, M., *The Judges and the Judged* (Doubleday, 1952).

Nelson, H. L., *Libel in News of Congressional Investigating Committees* (University of Minnesota Press, 1961).

——— (ed.), *Freedom of the Press from Hamilton to the Warren Court 1800–1965* (Bobbs-Merrill, 1966).

Nizer, L., *The Jury Returns* (Doubleday, 1966).

Patterson, G., *Free Speech and a Free Press* (Little, Brown, 1939).

Phelps, R. E. and E. D. Hamilton, *Libel* (Macmillan, 1967).

Raymond, A., *The People's Right To Know: A Report on Government News Suppression* (American Civil Liberties Union, 1955).

Royal Commission on the Press, *Report of the Royal Commission on the Press, 1947–1949* (Her Majesty's Government Post Office, 1949).

Seldes, G., *Freedom of the Press* (Bobbs-Merrill, 1935).

———, *The People Don't Know* (Gaer Association, 1949).

Shapiro, M., *Freedom of Speech: The Supreme Court and Judicial Review* (Prentice-Hall, 1966).

Siebert, F. S., *Freedom of the Press in England, 1476–1776* (University of Illinois Press, 1952).

———, *The Rights and Privileges of the Press* (Appleton-Century, 1934).

Smead, E. E., *Freedom of Speech by Radio and Television* (Public Affairs Press, 1958).

Smith, H. L., *Behind the Press in South Africa* (Stewart, 1947).

Smith, J. M., *Freedom of Speech by Radio and Television* (Public Affairs Press, 1958).

Special Committee on Radio and Television of the Association of the Bar of the City of New York, *Radio Television and the Administration of Justice* (Columbia University Press, 1967).

Spring, S., *Risks and Rights in Publishing, Television, Radio, Motion Pictures, Advertising, and the Theatre* (Allen & Unwin, 1952).

Sullivan, H., *Trial by Newspaper* (Patriot, 1961).

Swayze, H., *Political Control of Literature in the U.S.S.R.:1946–1959* (Howard, 1962).

Thayer, F., *Legal Control of the Press* (Foundation Press, 1944).

Thomas, E. C., *Libel and Slander* (Oceana, 1949).

Wasserstrom, W., *Civil Liberties and the Arts* (Syracuse University Press, 1964).

White, L., *The American Radio* (University of Chicago Press, 1947).

Wiggins, J. R., *Freedom or Secrecy?* (Oxford University Press, 1956).

Williams, F., *Press, Parliament, and People* (Heinemann 1946).

Wittenberg, P. (ed.), *Dangerous Words: A Guide to the Law of Libel* (Columbia University Press, 1960).

Yankewich, L. R., *It's Libel or Contempt If You Print It* (Parker, 1950).

I. ASSEMBLY AND ASSOCIATION

Abernathy, G., *The Right of Assembly and Association* (American Jewish Committee, 1957).

American Jewish Committee, *Assault Upon Freedom of Association* (American Jewish Committee, 1957).

Blau, J. L. (ed.), *Cornerstones of Religious Freedom in America* (Beacon, 1955).

Fellman, D., *The Constitutional Right of Association* (University of Chicago Press, 1963).

Kauper, P. G., *Civil Liberties and the Constitution* (University of Michigan Press, 1962).

Kalven, H., Jr., *The Negro and the First Amendment* (Ohio State University Press 1965).

Mintz, B. with R. Spenser and J. R. Robinson, *Assault Upon Freedom of Association* (American Jewish Committee, 1959).

Rice, C. E., *Freedom of Association* (New York University Press, 1962).

Robertson, D. B. (ed.), *Voluntary Association: A Study of Groups in Free Societies* (Knox, 1966).

J. RELIGION

(See also E., Military Justice in Peace and War, H., Speech, Press, and Petition, and L., Morals and Censorship.)

1. Free Exercise

Allport, G. W., *The Individual and His Religion* (Macmillan, 1954).

Bates, M. S., *Religious Liberty: An Inquiry* (Harper, 1954).

Blackhan, H. J., *Religion in a Modern State* (Ungar, 1966).

Blakely, W. A., *American State Papers and Related Documents on Freedom in Religion* (Religious Liberty Association, 1949).

Blau, J. L. (ed.), *Cornerstones of Religious Freedom in America* (Beacon, 1949).

459

Brady, Joseph H., *Confusion Twice Confounded: The First Amendment and the Supreme Court* (Seton Hall University Press, 1954).

Burstein, A., *Law Concerning Religion in the United States* (Oceana, 1950).

Cogley, J. (ed.), *Religion in America* (Meridian, 1958).

Cohen, R., *Sunday in the Sixties* (Public Affairs Pamphlets, 1965).

Drinker, H. S., *Some Observations on the Freedoms of the First Amendment* (Boston University Press, 1957).

Dunn, W. K., *What Happened to Religious Education: The Decline of Religious Teaching in the Public Elementary School, 1776–1861* (Johns Hopkins Press, 1958).

Educational Policies Commission, *Moral and Spiritual Values in the Public Schools* (National Education Association, 1951).

Fellman, D., *The Limits of Freedom* (Rutgers University Press, 1959).

Fenton, J. H., *The Catholic Vote* (Hauser, 1960).

Hartford, E. F., *Moral Values in Public Education: Lessons from the Kentucky Experience* (Harper, 1958).

Henry, V., *The Place of Religion in Public Schools: A Handbook To Guide Communities* (Harper, 1950).

Herberg, W., *Protestant-Catholic-Jew*, rev. ed. (Doubleday, 1960).

Jacobs, C. E. and J. F. Gallagher, *The Selective Service Act* (Dodd, Mead, 1967).

Manwaring, D. R., *Render Unto Caesar: The Flag Salute Controversy* (University of Chicago Press, 1962).

Marnell, W. H., *The First Amendment: The History of Religious Freedom in America* (Doubleday, 1964).

———, *The First Amendment: Religious Freedom in America from Colonial Days to the School Prayer Controversy* (Anchor, 1966).

McCollum, V., *One Woman's Fight*, rev. ed. (Beacon, 1961).

McGrath, J. J. (ed.), *Church and State in American Law* (Bruce, 1962).

Miller, W. L., *Religion and the Free Society* (Fund for the Republic, 1958).

O'Brien, F. W., *Justice Reed and the First Amendment: The Religion Clauses* (Georgetown University Press, 1958).

Pike, E. R., *Jehovah's Witnesses* (Philosophical Library, 1954).

Porter, E. S., *Conscience and the Court* (Prentice-Hall, 1962).

Raab, E. (ed.), *Religious Conflict in America: Studies of the Problem Beyond Bigotry* (Doubleday, 1964).

Rutherford, J. F., *Enemies* (Watchtower Society, 1937).

Stroup, H., *The Jehovah's Witnesses* (Columbia University Press, 1945).

Torpey, W. G., *Judicial Doctrines of Religious Rights in America* (University of North Carolina Press, 1948).

2. Separation of Church and State

Acton, Baron J., *Essays on Church and State* (Viking, 1953).

American Association of School Administrators, *Religion in the Public Schools* (American Association of School Administrators, 1964).

Barker, Sir E., *Church, State and Education* (University of Michigan Press, 1957).

Barnes, R. P., *Under Orders: The Churches and Public Affairs* (Doubleday, 1961).

Beth, L. P., *The American Theory of Church and State* (University of Florida Press, 1958).

Blanshard, P., *American Freedom and Catholic Power* (Beacon, 1958).

——, *Communism, Democracy, and Catholic Power* (Beacon, 1951).

——, *God and Man in Washington* (Beacon, 1960).

——, *Religion and the Schools: The Great Controversy* (Beacon, 1963).

Boles, D. E., *The Bible, Religion and the Public Schools* (Iowa State University Press, 1961).

Brickman, W. W. and S. Lehrer, *Religion, Government, and Education* (Society for the Advancement of Education, 1961).

Brown, N. C. (ed.), *The Study of Religion in the Public Schools: An Appraisal* (American Council on Education, 1958).

Butts, R. F., *The American Tradition in Religion and Education* (Beacon, 1950).

Cogley, J. (ed.), *Religion in America* (Meridian, 1958).

Costanzo, J. S. J., *This Nation Under God: Church, State, and Schools in America* (Herder and Herder, 1964).

Dawson, J. M., *America's Way in Church, State and Society* (Macmillan, 1953).

——, *Separate Church and State Now* (R. R. Smith, 1948).

Douglas, W. O., *The Bible and the Schools* (Little, Brown, 1966).

Drinan, R. F., *Religion, the Courts, and Public Policy* (McGraw-Hill, 1963).

Drinker, H. S., *Some Observations on the Freedoms of the First Amendment* (Boston University Press, 1957).

Drovin, E. G., *The School Question: A Bibliography and Church-State Relationship in American Education 1940–1960* (Catholic University of America Press, 1963).

Dulce, B. and E. J. Richter, *Religion and the Presidency* (Macmillan, 1962).

Ebersole, L., *Church Lobbying in the Nation's Capitol* (Macmillan, 1951).

Edwards, N., *The Courts and the Public Schools* (University of Chicago Press, 1933).

Ehler, S. E. and J. B. Morral, *Church and State through the Centuries* (Newman, 1954).

Fellman, D., *Religion in American Public Law* (Boston University Press, 1965).

Fellman, D. (ed.), *The Supreme Court and Education* (Columbia University Press, 1960).

Freund, P. A. and R. Ulich, *Religion and the Public Schools* (Harvard University Press, 1965).

Frommer, A. (ed.), *The Bible and the Public Schools* (Liberal Press, 1963).

Gabel, R. J., *Public Funds for Church and Private Schools* (Catholic University of America Press, 1937).

Georgetown University Institute for Church State Law, *Freedom from Federal Establishment* (Bruce, 1964).

Gianella, D. A. (ed.), *Religion and the Public Order* (University of Chicago Press, 1964, 1965, 1966, 1967).

Gordis, R., *Religion and the Schools* (Fund for the Republic, 1959).

Greene, E. B., *Religion and the State: The Making and Testing of an American Tradition* (Cornell University Press, 1959).

Heeley, A. V., *Why the Private School?* (Harper, 1951).

Hook, S., *Religion in a Free Society* (University of Nebraska Press, 1967).

Howe, M. de W., *Cases on Church and State in the United States* (Harvard University Press, 1952).

——, *The Garden and the Wilderness: Religion and Government in American Constitutional History* (University of Chicago Press, 1965).

461

Johnson, A. W. and F. Yost, *Separation of Church and State in the United States* (University of Minnesota Press, 1948).

Johnson, F. E. (ed.), *American Education and Religion: The Problem of Religion in the Schools* (Harper, 1952).

Kallen, H. M., *Secularism Is the Will of God: An Essay in the Social Philosophy of Democracy and Religion* (Twayne, 1954).

Katz, W. G., *Religion and American Constitutions* (Northwestern University Press, 1964).

Kauper, P. G., *Civil Liberties and the Constitution* (University of Michigan Press, 1962).

——, *Religion and the Constitution* (Louisiana State University Press, 1964).

Kerwin, J. G., *Catholic Viewpoint on Church and State* (Hanover House, 1960).

Kik, J. M., *The Supreme Court and Prayer in the Public Schools* (Presbyterian, 1963).

Kilpatrick, J. J., *The Southern Case for School Segregation* (Crowell Collier, 1962).

Kurland, P. B., *Religion and the Law: of Church and State and the Supreme Court* (Aldir ، 1962).

Lekachman, R., *et al.*, *The Churches and the Public* (Center for the Study of Democratic Institutions, 1960).

Lenski, G., *The Religion Factor* (Doubleday, 1961).

McCluskey, N. G., *Catholic Viewpoint on Education* (Hanover House, 1959).

McGill, R., *A Church, A School* (Abington, 1959).

Madden, W., *Religious Values in Education* (Harper, 1951).

Mason, R. E., *Moral Values and Secular Education* (Columbia University Press, 1950).

Masters, N. A., R. H. Salisbury, and T. H. Eliot, *State Politics and the Public Schools* (Knopf, 1964).

Moehlman, C., *Wall of Separation Between Church and State* (Beacon, 1951).

Nichols, R. F., *Religion and American Democracy* (Louisiana State University Press, 1959).

Oaks, D. H. (ed.), *The Wall Between Church and State* (University of Chicago Press, 1963).

Odegard, P. H., *Religion and Politics* (Oceana, 1960).

O'Neill, J. M., *Catholicism and American Freedom* (Harper, 1952).

——, *Religion and Education Under the Constitution* (Harper, 1949).

Parsons, W. P., S. J., *The First Freedom: Considerations on Church and State in the United States* (McMullen, 1948).

Pfeffer, L., *Church, State and Freedom*, rev. enl. ed. (Beacon, 1967).

——, *Creeds in Competition* (Harper, 1959).

Pike, J. A., *A Roman Catholic in the White House* (Doubleday, 1960).

Powell, T., *The School Bus Law: A Case Study in Education, Religion, and Politics* (Wesleyan University Press, 1960).

Reutter, E. E., Jr., *Schools and the Law* (Oceana, 1965).

Rice, C. E., *The Supreme Court and Public Prayer: The Need for Restraint* (Fordham University Press, 1964).

Rock, J., *The Time Has Come* (Knopf, 1963).

Schultz, H. E., *Religious Education and the Public Schools* (University of California Press, 1955).

Shaver, E. L., *The Weekday Church School* (Pilgrim, 1956).

Shields, C., *Democracy and Catholicism in America* (McGraw-Hill, 1958).

462

St. John-Stevas, N., *Birth Control and Public Policy* (Center for the Study of Democratic Institutions, 1960).

Stedman, M. S., Jr., *Religion and Politics in America* (Harcourt, Brace and World, 1964).

Stokes, A. P., *Church and State in the United States*, 3 vols. (Harper, 1950).

—— and L. Pfeffer, *Church and State in the United States*, 1 vol. rev. ed. (Harper & Row, 1964).

Sturzo, L., *Courts and Doctors* (Macmillan, 1932).

Thayer, V. T., *The Attack Upon the American Secular School* (Beacon, 1951).

——, *The Role of the School in American Society*, 2d ed. (Dodd, Mead, 1966).

Tussman, J., *The Supreme Court on Church and State* (Oxford University Press, 1962).

Umbrey, L., *Render unto the People* (Abingdon, 1946).

Walter, E. A. (ed.), *Religion and the State University* (University of Michigan Press, 1958).

Ward, H. H., *Space-Age Sunday* (Macmillan, 1960).

Ward, L. R., *Federal Aid to Private Schools* (Newman, 1964).

——, *Religion in All the Schools* (Fides, 1960).

Wilson, J. F. (ed.), *Church and State in American History* (Heath, 1965).

Zabel, O. H., *God and Caesar in Nebraska: A Study of the Legal Relationship of Church and State, 1854–1954* (University of Nebraska Press, 1955).

K. ACADEMIC FREEDOM

(See also H., Expression: Speech, Press, and Petition and L., Morals, Obscenity, and Censorship.)

Baade, H. W. and R. O. Everett, *Academic Freedom: The Scholar's Place in Modern Society* (Oceana, 1964).

Barth, A., *The Loyalty of Free Men*, new ed. (Anchor, 1965).

Beale, H. K., *Are American Teachers Free?* (Scribner's, 1936).

Byse, C. and L. Joughin, *Tenure in American Higher Education* (Cornell University Press, 1959).

Caughey, J. W., *In Clear and Present Danger: The Critical State of Our Freedoms* (University of Chicago Press, 1960).

Chambers, M. M., *The Colleges and the Courts, 1946–50: Judicial Decisions Regarding Higher Education in the United States* (Columbia University Press, 1952).

Countryman, V., *Un-American Activities in the State of Washington* (Cornell University Press, 1951).

Ehlers, H. and C. L. Gordon (ed.), *Crucial Issues in Education* (Holt, 1959).

Fellman, D. (ed.), *The Supreme Court and Education* (Columbia University Press, 1960).

Gardner, D. P., *The California Oath Controversy* (University of California Press, 1967).

Hardin, C. M., *Freedom in Agricultural Education* (University of Chicago Press, 1955).

Hofstadter, R. and W. P. Metzger, *The Development of Academic Freedom in the United States* (Columbia University Press, 1955).

Hook, S., *Heresy, Yes—Conspiracy, No!* (Day, 1953).

Hurlburd, D., *This Happened in Pasadena* (Macmillan, 1951).

Iversen, R. W., *The Communists and the Schools* (Harcourt, Brace, 1959).

Jones, H. M. (ed.), *Primer of Intellectual Freedom* (Harvard University Press, 1949).

Kahn, J., *The Threat to Academic Freedom* (Horizon, 1956).

Kirk, R., *Academic Freedom: An Essay in Definition* (Regnery, 1955).

Lamont, C., *Freedom Is As Freedom Does: Civil Liberties Today* (Horizon, 1956).

MacIver, R. M., *Academic Freedom in Our Time* (Columbia University Press, 1955).

Melby, E. O. and M. Puner, *Freedom and Public Education* (Praeger, 1953).

Metzger, W. P. and R. Hofstadter, *Academic Freedom in the United States* (Columbia University Press, 1955).

Moos, M. and F. Rourke, *The Campus and the State* (Johns Hopkins Press, 1959).

Morison, S. E., *Freedom in Contemporary Society* (Little, Brown, 1956).

National Council of Teachers of English, *The Student's Right to Read* (National Council of Teachers of English, 1963).

Nelson, J. and G. Roberts, Jr., *The Censor and the Schools* (Little, Brown, 1963).

Reutter, E. E., Jr., *The School Administrator and Subversive Activities* (Columbia University Press, 1951).

Stewart, G. R., *The Year of the Oath: The Fight for Academic Freedom at the University of California* (Doubleday, 1950).

Summers, R. E. (ed.), *Freedom and Loyalty in Our Colleges* (Wilson, 1954).

Taylor, H., *On Education and Freedom* (Abelard-Schuman, 1954).

Van Doren, M., *Man's Right to Knowledge, and the Free Use Thereof* (Columbia University Press, 1954).

Walter, E. A. (ed.), *Religion and the State University* (University of Michigan Press, 1958).

L. MORALS, OBSCENITY, AND CENSORSHIP

(See also H., Expression: Speech, Press, and Petition; J., Religion, and K., Academic Freedom.)

Beman, L., *Selected Articles on Censorship of the Theatre and Moving Pictures* (Wilson, 1961).

Blanshard, P., *The Right to Read: The Battle Against Censorship* (Beacon, 1955).

Brickman, W. W. and S. Lehrer, *Religion, Government, and Education* (Society for Advancement of Education, 1961).

Broun, H. and M. Leech, *Anthony Comstock Roundsman of the Lord* (Boni, 1927).

Brucker, H., *Freedom of Information* (Macmillan, 1945).

Carmen, I. H., *Movies, Censorship and the Law* (University of Michigan Press, 1966).

Caughney, J. W., *In Clear and Present Danger: The Critical State of Our Freedoms* (University of Chicago Press, 1958).

Chafee, Z., *Government and Mass Communication* (University of Chicago Press, 1947).

Chandos, J. (ed.), *To Deprave and Corrupt* (Association Press, 1963).

Cogley, J., *Report on Blacklisting* Vol. I: *Movies;* Vol. II: *Radio-TV* (Fund for the Republic, 1956).

Commission on Freedom of the Press, *Mass Communication: A Report from the Commission of Freedom of the Press* (University of Chicago Press, 1947).

——, *People Speaking to People: A Report on International Mass Communication* (University of Chicago Press, 1948).

Craig, A., *Suppressed Books: A History of the Conception of Literary Obscenity* (World, 1963).

Crowther, B., *Movies and Censorship* (Public Affairs Pamphlets, 1965).

Daniels, W. M. (ed.), *The Censorship of Books* (Wilson, 1954).

Dennett, M. W., *Birth Control Laws: Shall We Keep Them, Change Them or Abolish Them?* (Hitchcock, 1926).

Devlin, Sir P., *The Enforcement of Morals* (Oxford University Press, 1965).

Ernst, M. L. and A. Lindley, *The Censor Marches On* (Doubleday, Doran, 1940).

—— and A. U. Schwartz, *Censorship: The Search for the Obscene* (Macmillan, 1964).

—— and W. Seagle, *To the Pure: A Study of Obscenity and the Censor* (Viking, 1928).

Fellman, D., *The Censorship of Books* (Hauser, 1957).

Fiske, M., *Book Selection and Censorship* (University of California Press, 1959).

Ford, J., *Criminal Obscenity: A Plea for its Suppression* (Revell, 1926).

Gardiner, R. C., *Catholic Viewpoints on Censorship* (Hanover House, 1957).

Gerber, A. B., *Sex, Pornography and Justice* (Lyle Steward, 1966).

Haight, A. L., *Banned Books* (Bowker, 1956).

Haney, R. W., *Comstockery in America* (Beacon, 1960).

Hart, H. L. A., *Law, Liberty and Morality* (Stanford University Press, 1963).

Hyde, H. M., *A History of Pornography* (Farrar, Strauss, & Giroux 1965).

Inglis, R. A., *Freedom of the Movies* (University of Chicago Press, 1947).

Kahn, J., *The Threat to Academic Freedom* (Horizon, 1956).

Kauper, P. G., *Civil Liberties and the Constitution* (University of Michigan Press, 1962).

Kerr, W., *Criticism and Censorship* (Bruce, 1954).

Kilpatrick, J. J., *The Smut Peddlers* (Doubleday, 1960).

Kronhausen, E. and P. Kronhausen, *Pornography and the Law,* rev. ed. (Ballantine, 1965).

Kyle-Keith, R., *The High Price of Pornography* (Public Affairs Press, 1961).

Lindesmith, A. R., *The Addict and the Law* (Indiana University Press, 1965).

McCormick, J. and M. Macinnes (eds.), *Versions of Censorship* (Doubleday, 1962).

McKeown, R., R. D. Merton, and W. Gellhorn, *The Freedom to Read: Perspective and Program* (Bowker, 1957).

Marcuse, L., *Obscene* (Macgibbon and Key, 1965).

Meiklejohn, D., *Freedom and the Public: Public and Private Morality in America* (Syracuse University Press, 1965).

Mueller, G., *Legal Regulation of Sexual Conduct* (Oceana, 1960).

Mumford, H. (ed.), *Primer of Intellectual Freedom* (Harvard University Press, 1949).

Murphy, The Rev. T. J., *Censorship: Government and Obscenity* (Helicon, 1963).

Nelson, J. and G. Roberts, Jr., *The Censor and the Schools* (Little, Brown, 1963).

Okudaira, Y. *Political Censorship in Japan: 1931–1945* (Institute of Legal Research, University of Pennsylvania Press, 1962).

Paul, J. C. N. and M. L. Schwartz, *Federal Censorship: Obscenity in the Mail* (Free Press, 1961).

Putnam, G. H., *The Censorship of the Church of Rome* (Putnam's, 1906).

St. John-Stevas, N., *Obscenity and the Law* (Secker & Warburg, 1956).

Sanger, M., *An Autobiography* (Norton, 1938).

Schumach, M., *The Face on the Cutting Room Floor: The Story of Movie and Television Censorship* (Morrow, 1964).

Smead, E. E., *Freedom of Speech by Radio and Television* (Public Affairs Press, 1958).

Spring, S., *Risks and Rights in Publishing, Television, Radio, Motion Pictures, Advertising, and the Theatre* (Allen & Unwin, 1952).

Stumpf, S. E., *Morality and the Law* (Vanderbilt, 1966).

Summers, R. E., *Wartime Censorship of Press and Radio* (Wilson, 1942).

Thomas, J. L., *Lotteries, Frauds, and Obscenity in the Mails* (Stephens, 1900).

Vidal, G., *The City and the Pillar*, rev. ed. (Dutton, 1965).

Wertham, F., *Seduction of the Innocent* (Rinehart, 1954).

M. IMMIGRATION, CITIZENSHIP, AND ALIENAGE

Alexander, N., *The Rights of Aliens Under the Federal Constitution* (Capitol, 1931).

The Annals (E. B. Hutchinson, spec. ed.), "The New Immigration" (American Academy of Political and Social Science, September 1966).

Averbach, F. L., *Immigration Laws of the United States* (Bobbs-Merrill, 1961).

————, *The Immigration and Nationality Act* (Common Council for American Unity, 1952).

Bennett, M. T., *American Immigration Policies* (Public Affairs Press, 1964).

Bernard, W. S. (ed.), *American Immigration Policy: A Reappraisal* (Harper, 1950).

Bouscaren, A. T., *The Security Aspects of Immigration Work* (Marquette University Press, 1959).

Bruce, J. C., *The Irony of Our Immigration Policy* (Random House, 1954).

Cable, J. L., *Loss of Citizenship: Denaturalization—the Alien in Wartime* (National Law Book Company, 1943).

Clark, J. P., *The Deportation of Aliens from the U.S. to Europe* (Columbia University Press, 1931).

Divine, R. A., *American Immigration Policy, 1924–52* (Yale University Press, 1957).

Gettys, C. L., *The Law of Citizenship in the United States* (University of Chicago Press, 1934).

Gordon, C. and H. Rosenfield, *Immigration Law and Procedure* (Banks, 1959).

Gordon, M. M., *Assimilations in American Life: The Role of Race, Religion and National Origin* (Oxford University Press, 1964).

Handlin, O., *Immigration as a Factor in American History* (Prentice-Hall, 1959).

————, *The Uprooted* (Little, Brown, 1951).

Hansen, M. L., *The Immigrant in American History* (Harvard University Press, 1940).

Hicks, J. D., *The American Nation* (Houghton Mifflin, 1959).

Higham, J., *Strangers in the Land: Patterns of American Nativism, 1860–1929* (Rutgers University Press, 1955).

Hutchinson, E. P., *Immigrants and Their Children, 1850–1950* (Wiley, 1956).

Jones, M. A., *American Immigration* (University of Chicago Press, 1960).

Kansas, S., *U. S. Immigration, Exclusion, Deportation, and Citizenship of the United States of America*, 2d ed. (Bender, 1940).

Kent, D. P., *The Refugee Intellectual: The Americanization of the Immigrants of 1933–1941* (Columbia University Press, 1953).

Knauff, E. R., *The Ellen Knauff Story* (Norton, 1952).

Konvitz, M. R., *The Alien and Asiatics in American Law* (Cornell University Press, 1946).

———, *Civil Rights in Immigration* (Cornell University Press, 1953).

Kraus, M., *Immigration, the American Maxims from Pilgrims to Modern Refugees* (Van Nostrand, 1966).

Lowenstein, E. (ed.), *The Alien and the Immigration Law* (Oceana, 1958).

Post, L. F., *The Deportation Delirium of Nineteen-Twenty* (Kerr, 1923).

President's Commission on Immigration and Naturalization, *Whom We Shall Welcome* (United States Government Printing Office, 1953).

Schrieke, B., *Alien Americans* (Viking, 1936).

Sellin, H. (ed.), *Practice and Procedure under the Immigration and Nationality Act* (New York University Press, 1954).

Solomon, B. M., *Ancestors and Immigrants: A Changing New England Tradition* (Harvard University Press, 1956).

Silving, H., *Immigration Laws of the U. S.* (Oceana, 1949).

Taiang, I. M., *The Question of Expatriation in America Prior to 1907* (Johns Hopkins Press, 1942).

Tyler, P., *Immigration and the United States* (Wilson, 1956).

Ziegler, B. M. (ed.), *Immigration: An American Dilemma* (Heath, 1953).

N. INTERNAL SECURITY: LOYALTY, SECURITY, THOUGHT CONTROL, CLASSIFIED DATA

1. General

Association of the Bar of the City of New York, *Equal Justice for the Accused* (Dodd, Mead, 1959).

Biddle, F., *The Fear of Freedom* (Doubleday, 1951).

Bontecou, E. (ed.), *The Federal Loyalty-Security Program* (Cornell University Press, 1953).

Brookings Institution, *Suggested Standards for Determining Un-American Activities* (Brookings Institution, 1945).

Chafee, Z., *Watchman, What of the Night?* (University, 1942).

Chapin, B., *The American Law of Treason: Revolutionary and Early National Origin* (University of Washington Press, 1964).

Chase, H. W., *Security and Liberty: The Problem of Native Communists, 1947–1955* (Doubleday, 1955).

Commager, H. S., *Freedom, Loyalty, Dissent* (Oxford University Press, 1954).

Cook, T. I., *Democratic Rights Versus Communist Activity* (Doubleday, 1954).

Curtil, M., *The Roots of American Loyalty* (Columbia University Press, 1946).

Davis, J., *Character Assassination* (Philosophical Library, 1951).

Dowell, S. F., *A History of Criminal Syndicalism Legislation in the United States* (Johns Hopkins Press, 1939).

Gellhorn, W., *Security, Loyalty and Science* (Cornell University Press, 1950).

Ginzburg, B., *Rededication to Freedom* (Simon and Schuster, 1959).

Goldbloom, M., *American Security and Freedom* (American Jewish Committee, 1955).

Grodzins, M., *The Loyal and the Disloyal: Social Boundaries of Patriotism and Treason* (University of Chicago Press, 1956).

Guttman, A. and B. M. Ziegler, *Communism, The Courts and the Constitution* (Heath, 1964).

Laswell, H. D., *National Security and Individual Freedom* (McGraw-Hill, 1950).

Miller, J. C., *Crisis in Freedom* (Little, Brown, 1951).

Murphy, The Rev. T. J., *Censorship: Government and Obscenity* (Helicon, 1963).

Murray, R. K., *Red Scare: A Study in National Hysteria 1919–1920* (University of Minnesota Press, 1955).

Peltason, J., *Constitutional Liberty and Seditious Activity* (Catt Memorial Fund, 1954).

Rankin, R. S. and W. R. Dallmayr, *Freedom and Emerging Powers in the Cold War* (Appleton-Century-Crofts, 1963).

Rourke, R. E., *Secrecy and Publicity: Dilemmas of Democracy* (Johns Hopkins Press, 1961).

Schaar, J. H., *Loyalty to America: The Background and Consequences* (University of California Press, 1957).

Shils, E. A., *The Torment of Secrecy: American Security Policies* (Free Press, 1956).

Summers, R. E., *Federal Information Controls in Peacetime* (Wilson, 1949).

Wahlke, J. C., *Loyalty in a Democratic State* (Heath, 1952).

Weyl, N., *The Battle Against Disloyalty* (Crowell, 1951).

——, *Treason: The Story of Disloyalty and Betrayal in American History* (Public Affairs Press, 1950).

Wilson, H. H. and H. Glickman, *The Problem of International Security in Great Britain, 1948–1953* (Doubleday, 1954).

2. Federal and State Statutes

Gellhorn, W. (ed.), *The States and Subversion* (Cornell University Press, 1952).

Preston, W., Jr., *Aliens and Dissenters: Federal Suppression of Radicals, 1903–1933* (Harvard University Press, 1963).

Weinstein, S. and H. S. Brown Jr., *Personnel Security Programs of the Federal Government* (Fund for the Republic, 1954).

3. Government Employment

Andrews, B. and P. Andrews, *A Tragedy of History: A Journalist's Confidential Role in the Hiss-Chambers Case* (McKay, 1962).

Brown, R. S., Jr., *Loyalty and Security: Employment Tests in the United States* (Yale University Press, 1958).

Chambers, W., *Witness* (Random House, 1956).

Hiss, A., *In the Court of Public Opinion* (Knopf, 1957).

Hook, S., *The Paradoxes of Freedom* (University of California Press, 1962).

Lamont, C., *Freedom is as Freedom Does: Civil Liberties Today* (Horizon, 1956).

Westin, A., *The Constitution and Loyalty Programs* (Catt Memorial Fund, 1954).

Yarmolinsky, A., *Case Studies in Personal Security* (Bureau of National Affairs, 1955).

4. Legislative Investigations

(McCarthyism, HUAC, Alger Hiss)

Alsop, J. W., Jr., and Stewart, *We Accuse: The Story of the Miscarriage of American Justice in the Case of J. Robert Oppenheimer* (Simon and Schuster, 1954).

468

Anderson, J. and R. W. May, *McCarthy: The Man, The Senator, The "Ism,"* (Beacon, 1952).

Andrews, B. and P. Andrews, *A Tragedy of History: A Journalist's Confidential Role in the Hiss-Chambers Case* (McKay, 1962).

———, *Washington Witch Hunt* (Random House, 1948).

DeAntonio, E. and D. Talbot, *Point of Order! Documentary of the Army-Mc-Carthy Hearings* (Norton, 1964).

Dimock, M. E., *Congressional Investigating Committees* (Johns Hopkins Press, 1929).

Barrett, E. L., Jr., *The Tenney Committee: Legislative Investigation of Subversive Activities in California* (Cornell University Press, 1951).

Barth, A., *Government by Investigation* (Viking, 1955).

———, *When Congress Investigates Loyalty and Security in a Democracy* (Public Affairs Committee, 1956).

———, *The Loyalty of Free Men*, new ed. (Archon, 1965).

Beck, C., *Contempt of Congress* (Hauser, 1959).

Bessie, A., *Inquisition in Eden* (Macmillan, 1965).

Buckley, W. F., Jr., and the Editors of the *National Review, The Committee and its Critics* (Putnam, 1962).

Buckley, W. F., Jr., and L. B. Bozell, *McCarthy and His Enemies* (Regnery, 1953).

Carr, R. K., *The Constitution and Congressional Investigating Committees* (Cornell University Press, 1954).

———, *The House Committee on Un-American Activities, 1945-50* (Cornell University Press, 1952).

Chamberlain, L. H., *Loyalty and Legislative Action: A Survey of Activity by the New York State Legislature, 1919-1949* (Cornell University Press, 1952).

Chambers, W., *Witness* (Random House, 1956).

Cook, F. J., *The Unfinished Story of Alger Hiss* (Morrow, 1958).

Cooke, A., *A Generation on Trial* (Knopf, 1950).

Cornell University Study, *The Tenney Committee: Study of Legislative Investigations of Subversive Activities in California* (Cornell University Press, 1962).

Donner, F. J., *The Un-Americans* (Ballantine, 1961).

Eberling, E. J., *Congressional Investigation* (Columbia University Press, 1928).

Gellerman, W., *Martin Dies,* (John Day, 1944).

Gillmor, D., *Fear the Accusor* (Abelard-Schuman, 1954).

Goldfarb, R. L., *The Contempt Power* (Columbia University Press, 1963).

Gore, L., *Joe Must Go* (Messner, 1954).

Hiss, A., *In the Court of Public Opinion* (Knopf, 1957).

Hook, S., *Political Power and Personal Freedom: Critical Studies in Democracy, Communism, and Civil Rights* (Criterion, 1959).

Johnson, J. E., *Investigating Powers of Congress* (Wilson, 1951).

Jowitt, The Earl, *The Strange Case of Alger Hiss* (Doubleday, 1953).

Kallen, H. M., *The Lamont Case: History of a Congressional Investigation* (Horizon, 1957).

Kemper, D. J., *Decade of Fear* (University of Missouri Press, 1965).

Lamb, E., *Trial by Battle* (Center for Study of Democratic Institutions, 1964).

Lamont, C., *Freedom Is as Freedom Does: Civil Liberties Today* (Horizon, 1956).

Lattimore, O., *Ordeal by Slander* (Little, Brown, 1950).

McGeary, M. N., *The Development of Congressional Investigative Power* (Columbia University Press, 1940).

McWilliams, C., *Witch Hunt: The Revival of Heresy* (Little, Brown, 1950).

Matusow, H., *False Witness* (Cameron & Kahn, 1955).

Merson, M., *The Private Diary of a Public Servant* (Macmillan, 1955).

Nelson, H. L., *Libel in News of Congressional Investigating Committees* (University of Minnesota Press, 1961).

Ogden, A. R., *The Dies Committee*, 2d ed. (Catholic University of America Press, 1946).

Oxnam, G. B., *I Protest: My Experience with the House Committee on Un-Activities* (Harper, 1954).

Packer, H. L., *Ex-Communist Witnesses: Four Studies in Fact Finding* (Stanford University Press, 1962).

Potter, C. E., *Days of Shame* (Coward-McCann, 1965).

Rorty, J. and M. Decter, *McCarthy and the Communists* (Beacon, 1954).

Rovere, R., *Senator Joe McCarthy* (Harcourt, Brace, 1959).

Seldes, G., *Witch Hunt* (Modern Age Books, 1940).

Sommerville, J., *The Communist Trials and the American Tradition: Expert Testimony on Force and Violence* (Cameron, 1956).

Straight, M., *Trial by Television: The Army-McCarthy Hearings* (Beacon, 1954).

Taylor, T., *Grand Inquest: The Story of Congressional Investigations* (Simon and Schuster, 1955).

Thomas, N., *The Test of Freedom* (Norton, 1954).

Uphaus, W., *Commitment* (McGraw-Hill, 1964).

Warren, F. A., *Liberals and Communism: The "Red Decade" Revisited* (Indiana University Press, 1966).

Wittenberg, P., *The Lamont Case: History of a Congressional Investigation* (Horizon, 1957).

5. The Communists

Almond, G. A., *The Appeals of Communism* (Princeton University Press, 1954).

Blanshard, P., *Communism, Democracy, and Catholic Power* (Beacon, 1951).

Bochenski, J. M. and G. Niemeyer, *Handbook on Communism* (Praeger, 1963).

Decter, M. (ed.), *The Profile of Communism: A Fact-by-Fact Primer* (Collier, 1962).

Dennis, E., *Ideas They Cannot Jail* (International Publications, 1950).

Draper, T., *The Roots of American Communism* (Viking, 1957).

Eberling, E. J., *Congressional Investigations* (Columbia University Press, 1928).

Ernst, M. L. and D. Loth, *Report on the American Communist* (Holt, 1952).

Fund for the Republic, *Bibliography on the Communist Problem in the United States*, (Fund for the Republic, 1955).

Gates, J., *The Story of an American Communist* (Nelson, 1958).

Hoover, J. E., *A Study of Communism* (Holt, Rinehart and Winston, 1962).

———, *Masters of Deceit* (Holt, 1958).

Howe, I. and L. Coser, *The American Communist Party: A Critical History 1919–1960*, rev. ed. (Praeger, 1962).

Hunit, R. N. G. (ed.), *Books on Communism* (Amperstand, 1959).

Iversen, R. W., *The Communists and the Schools* (Harcourt, Brace, 1959).

Johnsen, J. E., *Should the Communist Party Be Outlawed?* (Wilson, 1949).

Latham, E., *The Communist Controversy in Washington: From the New Deal to McCarthy* (Harvard University Press, 1966).

Miller, W. J., H. L. Roberts, and M. D. Shulman, *The Meaning of Communism* (Simon and Schuster, 1963).

Monnerot, J., *Sociology and Psychology of Communism* (Beacon, 1953).

Overstreet, H. and B. Overstreet, *What We Must Know About Communism* (Norton, 1958).

Palmer, E. E. (ed.), *The Communist Problems in America* (Crowell, 1951).

Record, W., *Race and Radicalism: The NAACP and the Communist Party in Conflict* (Cornell University Press, 1964).

Roy, R. L., *Communism and the Churches* (Harcourt, Brace, 1960).

Shannon, D. A., *The Decline of American Communism: A History of the Communist Party of the United States Since 1945* (Harcourt, Brace, 1959).

Sutherland, A. E., *Two Reference Volumes on Communism in the United States* (Harvard University Press, 1956).

Wechsler, J. A., *The Age of Suspicion* (Random House, 1953).

6. The Right Wing

Alexander, C. C., *The Ku Klux Klan in the Southwest* (University of Kentucky Press, 1965).

Bell, D. (ed.), *The Radical Right* (Doubleday, 1963).

Broyles, J. A., *The John Birch Society* (Beacon, 1964).

Chalmer, D. M., *Hooded Americanism: The First Century of the Ku Klux Klan*, (Doubleday 1965).

Ellsworth, R. E. and S. M. Harris, *American Right Wing* (University of Illinois Press, 1960).

Epstein, B. R. and A. Forster, *Report on the John Birch Society 1966* (Random House, 1966).

——, *The Radical Right: Report on the John Birch Society and its Allies* (Random House, 1967).

Forster, A. and B. R. Epstein, *Danger on the Right* (Random House, 1964).

Hapgood, N. (ed.), *Professional Patriots* (Boni, 1927).

Hofstadter, R., *The Paranoid Style: American Politics and Other Essays* (Knopf, 1965).

Janson, D. and B. Eisman, *The Far Right* (McGraw-Hill, 1963).

Overstreet, H. and B. Overstreet, *The Strange Tactics of Extremism* (Norton, 1964).

Randel, W. P., *The Ku Klux Klan: A Century of Infamy* (Chilton, 1965).

Rice, A. S., *The Ku Klux Klan in American Politics* (Public Affairs, Press, 1962).

Rogger, H. and E. Weber, *The European Right: A Historical Profile* (University of California Press, 1966).

Roy, R. L., *Apostles of Discord* (Beacon, 1953).

Sheinberg, M. and A. Kraditor, *Peddlers of Fear* (Public Affairs Press, 1966).

Sherwin, M., *The Extremists* (St. Martin's, 1963).

Welch, R., *Blue Book of the John Birch Society* (John Birch Society, 1958).

O. FAMOUS CASES INVOLVING CIVIL RIGHTS AND LIBERTIES

1. Sacco-Vanzetti

Burlingham, C. C. and B. Flexner (eds.), *The Sacco-Vanzetti Case: Transcript of the Trial of Nicola Sacco and Bartolomeo Vanzetti in the Courts of Mass. and Subsequent Proceedings 1920–1927* (Holt, 1928).

Ehrmann, H. B., *The Untried Case: The Sacco-Vanzetti Case and the Morelli Gang*, rev. ed. (Vanguard, 1960).

Felix, D., *Protest: Sacco-Vanzetti and the Intellectuals* (Indiana University Press, 1965).

Frankel, O. K., *The Sacco-Vanzetti Case* (Knopf, 1931).

Frankfurter, F., *The Case of Sacco and Vanzetti: A Critical Analysis for Lawyers and Laymen* (Little, Brown, 1927, 1961, and 1962).

Frankfurter, M. D. and G. Jackson, *The Letters of Sacco and Vanzetti* (Viking, 1928).

Joughin, L. and E. M. Morgan, *The Legacy of Sacco and Vanzetti* (Quadrangle, 1964).

Lyons, E., *The Life and Death of Sacco and Vanzetti* (Never, 1927).

Montgomery, R. H., *Sacco-Vanzetti: The Murder and the Myth* (Devin-Adair, 1960).

Musmanno, M. S., *After Twelve Years: The Sacco-Vanzetti Case* (Knopf, 1939).

Russell, F., *Tragedy in Dedham—The Story of the Sacco-Vanzetti Case* (McGraw-Hill, 1962).

Stark, L., *We Saw It Happen* (Simon and Schuster, 1939).

2. Loeb-Leopold

Darrow, C. S., *The Story of My Life* (Scribner's, 1958).

Leopold, N. F., *Life Plus 99 Years* (Doubleday, 1958).

McKernan, M., *The Amazing Crime and Trial of Leopold and Loeb* (New American Library, 1958).

Weinberg, A., *Attorney for the Damned* (Simon and Schuster, 1957).

3. Peter Zenger

Alexander, J., *A Brief Narrative of the Case and Trial of John Peter Zenger*, ed. by S. N. Katz (Belknap, 1963).

Buranelli, V. (ed.), *The Trial of Peter Zenger* (New York University Press, 1957).

Galt, T., *Peter Zenger, Fighter for Freedom* (Crowell, 1951).

James, A., *A Brief Narrative of the Case and Trial of Peter Zenger, Printer of the New York Weekly Journal* (Harvard University Press, 1963).

Levy, L. W. (ed.), *Freedom of the Press from Zenger to Jefferson* (Bobbs-Merrill, 1967).

Rutherford, L., *John Peter Zenger* (Peter Smith, 1904).

4. John Scopes—"The Monkey Trial"

Darrow, C. S., *The Story of My Life* (Scribner's, 1958).

de Camp, L. S., *The Great Monkey Trial* (Doubleday, 1968).

Ginger, R., *Six Days of Forever: Tennessee v. John Thomas Scopes* (Signet, 1960).

Grebstein, S. H. (ed.), *Monkey Trial: The State of Tennessee vs. John Thomas Scopes* (Houghton Mifflin, 1960).

Scopes, J. T. and J. Presley, *Center of the Storm: Memoirs of John T. Scopes* (Holt, Rinehart and Winston, 1967).

Tompkins, J. R. (ed.), *John Scopes and Others: D-Days at Dayton—Reflections on the Scopes Trial* (Louisiana State University Press, 1965).

Weinberg, A., *Attorney for the Dammed* (Simon and Schuster, 1957).

5. Jack Ruby, Lee Harvey Oswald, and the Warren Commission

Belli, M. M., *Dallas Justice: The Real Story of Jack Ruby and his Trial* (McKay, 1964).

Epstein, E. J., *Inquest: The Warren Commission and the Establishment of Truth* (Viking, 1966).

Kaplan, J. and J. R. Walz, *The Trial of Jack Ruby* (Macmillan, 1965).

Lane, M., *Rush to Judgement: A Critique at the Warren Commission Inquiry* (Holt, Rinehart and Winston, 1966).

Sauvage, L., *The Oswald Affair: An Examination of the Contradictions and Omissions of the Warren Report* (World, 1966).

Warren Commission, *The Official Warren Commission Report on the Assassination of President John F. Kennedy* (Doubleday, 1964).

6. Others

Chalmers, A. K., *They Shall be Free* (Doubleday, 1951).

Chessman, C., *Cell 2455 Death Row* (Prentice-Hall, 1954).

Corwell, Julien, *The Trial of Ezra Pound* (Day, 1966).

Davidson, I. D. and R. Gehman, *The Jury Is Still Out* (Harper, 1959).

Donovan, J. B., *Strangers on a Bridge: The Case of Colonel Abel* (Athenum, 1964).

Dickler, G., *Man on Trial* (Delta, 1964).

Fineberg, S. A., *The Rosenberg Case: Fact and Fiction* (Oceana, 1953).

Flynn, E. G., *The Alderson Story: My Life as a Political Prisoner* (International Publishers, 1963).

Foner, P. S., *The Case of Joe Hill* (International Publishers, 1965).

Franklin, C., *World-Famous Trials* (Taplinger, 1966).

Furneaux, R., *Courtroom USA: 1* (Penguin, 1964).

————, *Courtroom USA: 2* (Penguin, 1964).

Gentry, K., *Frame-Up* (Norton, 1967).

Golden, H., *A Little Girl Is Dead* (World, 1965).

Grover, D. H., *Debaters and Dynamiters: The Story of the Haywood Trial* (Oregon State University Press, 1964).

Hopkins, V. C., *Dred Scott's Case* (Fordham University Press, 1951).

Huie, W. B., *Three Lives for Mississippi* (W.C.C. Books, 1965).

Kunstler, W. M., *The Minister and the Choir Singer: The Hall-Mills Murder Case* (Morrow, 1964).

Lustgarten, E., *The Murder and the Trial* (Scribner's, 1958).

Marke, J. J., *Vignettes of Legal History* (Rothman, 1965).

Nizer, L., *The Jury Returns* (Doubleday, 1966).

Patterson, H. and E. Conrad, *Scottsboro Boy* (Doubleday, 1950).

Prettyman, E. B., Jr., *Death and the Supreme Court* (Avon, 1964).

Reynolds, Q., *Courtroom* (Farrar, Straus 1950).

Ruben W. A., *The Mark Fein Case* (Dial, 1966).

Sharp, M. P., *Was Justice Done?: The Rosenberg-Sobell Case* (Monthly Review, 1956).

I: GENERAL SUBJECT INDEX

II: NAME INDEX